Marketing is an organizational function and a set of processes for creating, capturing*, communicating and delivering value to customers and for managing customer relationships in ways that benefit the organization and its stakeholders.

The definition of *marketing*, established by the American Marketing Association, 2004.
*Added by authors.

Marketing

Marketing

Dhruv Grewal, PhD
Babson College

Michael Levy, PhD
Babson College

McGraw-Hill
Irwin

Boston   Burr Ridge, IL   Dubuque, IA   New York   San Francisco   St. Louis
Bangkok   Bogotá   Caracas   Kuala Lumpur   Lisbon   London   Madrid   Mexico City
Milan   Montreal   New Delhi   Santiago   Seoul   Singapore   Sydney   Taipei   Toronto

MARKETING

Published by McGraw-Hill, a business unit of The McGraw-Hill Companies, Inc., 1221 Avenue of the Americas, New York, NY 10020.

Some ancillaries, including electronic and print components, may not be available to customers outside the United States.

This book is printed on acid-free paper.

1 2 3 4 5 6 7 8 9 0 WCK/WCK 0 9 8 7

ISBN   978-0-07-304902-1
MHID   0-07-304902-6

Editorial director: *John E. Biernat*
Publisher: *Andy Winston*
Developmental editor: *Sarah Crago*
Marketing manager: *Trent Whatcott*
Media producer: *Benjamin Curless*
Lead project manager: *Christine A. Vaughan*
Lead production supervisor: *Michael McCormick*
Senior designer: *Kami Carter*
Senior photo research coordinator: *Jeremy Cheshareck*
Photo researcher: *Mike Hruby*
Media project manager: *Lynn M. Bluhm*
Typeface: *10/12 Palatino*
Compositor: *Precision Graphics*
Printer: *Quebecor World Versailles*
Cover image: *© Jess Dixon Photography*

Library of Congress Cataloging-in-Publication Data
Grewal, Dhruv.
    Marketing / Dhruv Grewal, Michael Levy.
       p. cm.
    Includes index.
      ISBN-13: 978-0-07-304902-1 (alk. paper)
      ISBN-10: 0-07-304902-6 (alk. paper)
      1. Marketing. I. Levy, Michael. II. Title.
HF5415.G675 2008
658.8—dc22
                              2006100298

www.mhhe.com

To those who had a strong positive influence
on the early years of our careers:

James Littlefield, Professor of Marketing, Virginia Tech
Kent B. Monroe, John M. Jones Professor of Marketing,
University of Illinois
A. Coskun Samli, Professor of Marketing,
University of North Florida
Dianna L. Stone, Professor of Management,
University of Central Florida

—*Dhruv Grewal*

James L. Ginter, Professor Emeritus,
The Ohio State University
Roger A. Kerin, Harold C. Simmons Distinguished Professor
of Marketing, Southern Methodist University
Mike Harvey, Hearin Professor of Global Business,
The University of Mississippi
Bernard J. LaLonde, Professor Emeritus,
The Ohio State University
Barton A. Weitz, JCPenney Eminent Scholar,
The University of Florida

—*Michael Levy*

about the authors

Authors Michael Levy (left) and Dhruv Grewal (right).

Dhruv Grewal

Dhruv Grewal, PhD (Virginia Tech), is the Toyota Chair in Commerce and Electronic Business and a professor of marketing at Babson College. His research and teaching interests focus on marketing foundations, marketing research, retailing, pricing, and value-based strategies. He was awarded the 2005 Lifetime Achievement in Behavioral Pricing Award by Fordham University. He is a "Distinguished Fellow" of the Academy of Marketing Science. He has also coauthored *Marketing Research* (2004, 2007).

Professor Grewal has published over 70 articles in journals such as *Journal of Marketing, Journal of Consumer Research, Journal of Marketing Research, Journal of Retailing,* and *Journal of the Academy of Marketing Science.* He currently serves on numerous editorial review boards, including *Journal of Retailing, Journal of the Academy of Marketing Science, Journal of Interactive Marketing,* and *Journal of Public Policy & Marketing.* He served as co-editor of *Journal of Retailing* from 2001–2007.

Professor Grewal has won many awards for his teaching including, 2005 Sherwin-Williams Distinguished Teaching Award, SMA; 2003 AMA Award for Innovative Excellence in Marketing Education; 1999 AMS Great Teachers in Marketing Award; Executive MBA Teaching Excellence Award (1998); School of Business Teaching Excellence Awards (1993, 1999); and Virginia Tech Certificate of Recognition for Outstanding Teaching (1989). He co-chaired: 1993 AMS Conference, 1998 Winter AMA Conference, a 1998 Marketing Science Institute Conference, 2001 AMA doctoral consortium, and 2006 Summer AMA Conference.

Professor Grewal has taught executive seminars and courses and/or worked on research projects with numerous firms, such as IRI, TJX, Radio Shack, Monsanto, McKinsey, Motorola, and numerous law firms. He has taught seminars in the U.S., Europe, and Asia.

Michael Levy

Michael Levy, PhD, is the Charles Clarke Reynolds Professor of Marketing and Director of the Retail Supply Chain Institute at Babson College. He received his PhD in business administration from The Ohio State University and his undergraduate and MS degrees in business administration from the University of Colorado at Boulder. He taught at Southern Methodist University before joining the faculty as professor and chair of the marketing department at the University of Miami.

Professor Levy has developed a strong stream of research in retailing, business logistics, financial retailing strategy, pricing, and sales management. He has published over 50 articles in leading marketing and logistics journals, including the *Journal of Retailing, Journal of Marketing, Journal of the Academy of Marketing Science,* and *Journal of Marketing Research.* He currently serves on the editorial review board of the *Journal of Retailing, Journal of the Academy of Marketing Science, International Journal of Logistics Management, International Journal of Logistics and Materials Management, ECR Journal,* and *European Business Review.* He is coauthor of *Retailing Management,* 6e (2007), the best-selling college-level retailing text in the world. Professor Levy was co-editor of *Journal of Retailing* from 2001–2007.

Professor Levy has worked in retailing and related disciplines throughout his professional life. Prior to his academic career, he worked for several retailers and a housewares distributor in Colorado. He has performed research projects with many retailers and retail technology firms, including Accenture, Federated Department Stores, Khimetrics, Mervyn's, Neiman Marcus, ProfitLogic (Oracle), Zale Corporation, and numerous law firms. He co-chaired the 1993 Academy of Marketing Science conference and the 2006 Summer AMA conference.

Welcome to the first edition of *Marketing*!

We are proud to say that our book is the first new, comprehensive textbook in marketing in over two decades. In the summer of 2004, the American Marketing Association revised its nearly 20 year old definition of marketing, redefining marketing as "an organizational function and a set of processes for creating, communicating, and delivering value to customers and for managing customer relationships in ways that benefit the organization and its stakeholders." Our book, *Marketing*, is the first marketing principles textbook to fully integrate this new definition, emphasizing the value and the role of the customer in marketing organizations and activities.

When we, the authors, sat down to write this book, it seemed imperative that the evolution of the field and practice of marketing be at the forefront. We wanted to be sure that we were fully educating today's student about current marketing trends and practices, so we integrated newer concepts such as value creation, globalization, technology, entrepreneurship, ethics, and services marketing into the traditional marketing instruction. In this book, we will examine how firms assess, analyze, create, deliver, communicate, and capture value. We will explore both the fundamentals in marketing and new influencers, such as value-based pricing and the Internet that are shaping the way businesses communicate with their customers in today's marketing environment.

It is not often that textbook authors get the opportunity to design, plan, and write a book that is totally up to date and reflects not only the current trends in the marketplace, but also the needs of instructors and students. During the writing and revising of this book, over the course of three years, we've sought the advice and expertise of hundreds of marketing and educational professionals, and we've taken all of their guidance to heart. We are grateful to the hundreds of individuals who participated in the focus groups, surveys, and personal conversations that helped mold this book, and we hope that you, the reader, will learn from and enjoy the results.

what is *marketing*?

Regardless of your age, your gender, or the city in which you live, you already know something about marketing. You have been an involved consumer in the marketing process since childhood when, for example, you accompanied your mother or father to the supermarket and asked to buy a particular brand of cereal because you saw a friend eating it or heard about it on television. The prize inside the box of cereal was of value to you as a child; the nutritional information offered on the box panel was of value to your mother or father. Once you begin to explore the many ways in which companies and brands create value for their customers through marketing, you will also begin to appreciate the complex set of decisions and activities that are necessary to provide you with the products and services you use every day.

The function of marketing is multi-faceted, but its fundamental purpose is to create value. Consider these examples:

Not too long ago water was simply one of the most basic natural elements. It came out of a faucet in your home and was consumed for the purposes of drinking, washing, etc. Taking a cue from European firms like Perrier in France and San Pellegrino in Italy, US-based firms such as Poland Springs, Arrowhead, and Aquafina created new products that customers find valuable by bottling water in attractive and easy to carry packages. Today bottled water is a $35 billion worldwide industry with US sales in excess of $6 billion.

Why do people buy roughed-up jeans for well over a hundred dollars when they could buy Wrangler jeans at Wal-Mart for under twenty? The answer lies in marketing brand value: because brands like Diesel and Seven for All Mankind have created a cache for their brands with edgy advertising and innovative washes and styles. When trendsetters start to wear these brands, others follow.

The prevalence and power of the Internet have created a marketplace of better informed and savvy customers than ever before. Those who teach the marketers of the future need to account for the consumer's ability to assess the marketplace at their fingertips and discern good value from poor value. This textbook, **Marketing 1e,** is all about the core concepts and tools that help marketers create value for customers. Throughout this book you will find many other examples that define how companies create value for customers through branding, packaging, pricing, retailing, service, and advertising. We introduce the concept of value in Chapter 1 and carry it through the entire text:

• **The first section** of the text contains four chapters, and the central theme of the section is "Assessing the Marketplace." Following an introduction to marketing in Chapter 1, Chapter 2 then focuses on how a firm develops a marketing plan. A central theme of the chapter is how firms can effectively create, capture, deliver and communicate value to their customers. Chapter 3 focuses attention on Marketing Ethics. An ethical decision framework is developed and presented. The key ethical concepts are linked back to the marketing plan introduced in Chapter 2. Finally, Chapter 4 (Analyzing the Marketing Environment) focuses on how marketers can systematically uncover and evaluate opportunities. Key elements of scenario planning are introduced and presented to demonstrate how to analyze and capitalize on opportunities presented.

• **The second section** of the book deals with "Understanding the Marketplace" and is composed of three chapters. Chapter 5, Consumer Behavior, focuses on all aspects of understanding why consumers purchase products and services. The consumer decision process is highlighted. Chapter 6, Business-to-Business Marketing, focuses on all aspects pertaining to why and how business-to-business buying takes place. Finally, Chapter 7 focuses on global markets. Thus, the three chapters move from creating value for the individual/consumer to the firm/business to the global level.

• **The third section** of the book deals with "Targeting the Marketplace." Two chapters compose this section. Chapter 8 focuses on Segmentation, Targeting, and Positioning. In this chapter, we focus on how firms segment the marketplace, then pick a target market and finally position their good/service in line with their customers' needs and wants. Chapter 9 on Marketing Research identifies the various tools and techniques that marketers use to uncover these needs and ensure that they create goods and services that provide value to their target markets.

- *Marketing* devotes three chapters to **Value Creation**. The first two, Chapter 10, "Product, Branding, and Packaging Decisions," and Chapter 11, "Developing New Products" cover the development and management of products and brands. While many of the concepts involved in developing and managing services are similar to those of physical brands, Chapter 12, "Services: The Intangible Product" addresses the unique challenges of the marketing of services.

- Pricing is the activity within a firm responsible for **Value Capture** by bringing in money and affecting revenues. *Marketing* devotes two chapters to pricing capturing values for the firm. Chapter 13 examines the importance of setting the right price, the relationship between price and quantity sold, break-even analysis, the impact of price wars, and how the Internet has changed the way people shop. Chapter 14 looks specifically at how to set prices.

- One important reason why Wal-Mart has become the world's largest retailer is their **Value Delivery** system. They time the delivery of merchandise to get to stores just

in time to meet customer demand. To achieve this, they have initiated many innovative programs with their vendors and developed sophisticated transportation and warehousing systems. *Marketing* devotes two chapters to value delivery. Chapter 15 takes a look at the entire supply chain, while Chapter 16 concentrates on retailing.

- Today's methods of **Value Communication** are more complex because of new technologies that add e-mail, Blogs, Internet, and Pod casts to the advertising mix that once only utilized radio and television to relay messages to consumers. *Marketing* devotes three chapters to value communication. Chapter 17 introduces the breadth of integrated marketing communications. Chapter 18 is devoted specifically to advertising, while Chapter 19 covers personal selling.

- You will also find the value theme integrated throughout the text in the **Adding Value** boxes that occur in each chapter. These features illustrate how firms find ultimate success by adding value to their products and services.

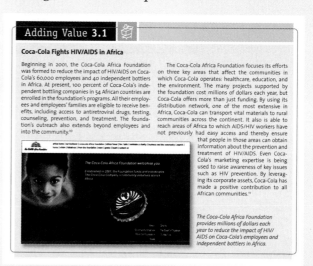

Adding Value 3.1

Coca-Cola Fights HIV/AIDS in Africa

Beginning in 2001, the Coca-Cola Africa Foundation was formed to reduce the impact of HIV/AIDS on Coca-Cola's 60,000 employees and 40 independent bottlers in Africa. At present, 100 percent of Coca-Cola's independent bottling companies in 54 African countries are enrolled in the foundation's programs. All their employees and employees' families are eligible to receive benefits, including access to antiretroviral drugs, testing, counseling, prevention, and treatment. The foundation's outreach also extends beyond employees and into the community.[10]

The Coca-Cola Africa Foundation focuses its efforts on three key areas that affect the communities in which Coca-Cola operates: healthcare, education, and the environment. The many projects supported by the foundation cost millions of dollars each year, but Coca-Cola offers more than just funding. By using its distribution network, one of the most extensive in Africa, Coca-Cola can transport vital materials to rural communities across the continent. It also is able to reach areas of Africa to which AIDS/HIV workers have not previously had easy access and thereby ensure that people in those areas can obtain information about the prevention and treatment of HIV/AIDS. Even Coca-Cola's marketing expertise is being used to raise awareness of key issues such as HIV prevention. By leveraging its corporate assets, Coca-Cola has made a positive contribution to all African communities.[11]

The Coca-Cola Africa Foundation provides millions of dollars each year to reduce the impact of HIV/AIDS on Coca-Cola's employees and independent bottlers in Africa.

In addition to our emphasis on value in *Marketing*, you will also find integrated and highlighted coverage of ethics, entrepreneurship, services, and globalization within the framework of the marketing discipline:

• *Marketing* contains an entire chapter on **Marketing Ethics**. Placed early in the text (Chapter 3), it provides rich illustrations of corporate responsibility, and introduces an ethical decision-making framework that is useful for assessing potentially ethically troubling situations that are posed throughout the rest of the book. It therefore sets the tone for ethical material in each subsequent chapter. In addition, each chapter contains an Ethical Dilemma box with a compelling ethical discussion and end-of-chapter discussion questions that force students to consider and evaluate each situation.

Ethical Dilemma 7.2   Protesting the War with the Wallet

Is "Made in the U.S.A" more a hindrance than a help in U.S. firms' efforts to penetrate the global marketplace?²² According to the results of a recent survey of 8,000 consumers in five countries (Canada, China, France, Germany, Russia, and the United Kingdom), being an American firm may increasingly become a hindrance. The survey found that 20 percent of respondents from Europe and Canada stated that they were consciously avoiding purchasing U.S. products as a form of protest against U.S. foreign policy, especially its actions in Iraq.

The survey also asked the respondents if they were intentionally avoiding purchasing products from 40 U.S. corporations. Corporations viewed as being "more American" fared the worst. Sixty percent of respondents said that they would not buy Marlboro, and 48 percent claimed they would "definitely avoid" using American Express. The other brands that respondents stated they were "most avoiding" were Exxon-Mobile, AOL, Chevron, Texaco, United Airlines, Budweiser, Chrysler, Barbie Dolls, Starbucks, and General Motors. Adding to the bad news for U.S. corporations, 50 percent of the survey respondents stated they distrusted U.S. firms because of their perceived involvement in foreign policy.

The dilemma U.S. firms face is how to counter this negativity abroad but retain their patriotic reputation within the United States. Most of these quintessentially American firms operate through local partners and purchase from local suppliers in their global operations. So should these U.S. companies distance themselves from their U.S. identity? Should they highlight that boycotts harm local economies perhaps even more than they do the U.S. economy?

Protesters in Manila boycott McDonald's and other U.S.-based firms to protest the U.S.-led war on Iraq.

• **Entrepreneurship**. An entrepreneurial spirit pervades most marketing innovations and is necessary to keep firms growing and healthy. *Marketing* nurtures that entrepreneurial spirit by providing examples of young entrepreneurial firms and successful entrepreneurs wherever possible. Each chapter also contains an Entrepreneurial Marketing box that depicts recognizable and interesting young entrepreneurial firms.

• *Marketing* defines **Services** as the intangible product and devotes Chapter 12 to the topic. A balanced approach to presenting products and services is used throughout. Examples of great service businesses and how product-oriented businesses provide great service abound.

• Most firms are involved in **Global Marketing** at some level. Giant firms such as Procter & Gamble, Starbucks, and United Airlines have global operations. But small entrepreneurial firms are also involved because they get their materials, products, or services from firms located in other countries. Global examples are woven throughout each chapter of *Marketing*. In addition, Chapter 7 is devoted exclusively to the topic.

Entrepreneurial Marketing 11.1

Geox, the Holy Shoe⁵³

Mario Moretti Polegato was attending a wine convention in Reno, Nevada, in the early 1990s when, due to the heat and his allergies, he found he needed to poke holes in the soles of his shoes to let air circulate around his feet. When he went back to Italy, Polegato decided to work further on this idea for staying cool and soon left his family wine business to manufacture his innovation: Geox shoes. The name Geox is derived from "Geo," Greek for Earth, and "x," to suggest a technological feel.

Polegato took his innovative idea for "breathable" or "ventilated" shoes to leading manufacturers such as Fila, Nike, Adidas, and Timberland. None was interested. But when Polegato introduced Geox shoes himself in Europe, despite an otherwise saturated shoe market, the brand was a big hit. Now sold in the firm's own chain of stores and in the United States through upscale retail chains, Geox sells approximately 10 million pairs of shoes annually and plans to expand to 150 stores in Italy and 100 overseas.

Mario Moretti Polegato created Geox ventilated shoes to keep his feet cool in hot weather.

why will **instructors** enjoy using this book?

- **Tradition.** *Marketing* draws from a history of outstanding marketing texts. As such, users of other books will feel confident and comfortable with the material in this new text. We honor all the traditional marketing concepts, but make them current, relevant and fun for your students to learn.

- **Assessment.** Business schools and accrediting organizations are demanding that students be accountable for specific material that is essential for any marketing practitioner. Of course, *Marketing* provides students with the knowledge of the language of marketing. In addition, students will come away with a set of tools that is essential to be successful in marketing careers. But the material goes beyond the printed page. The Online Learning Center contains an **Interactive Student Tool Kit**. The **Tool Kit** is a set of interactive exercises that are working models of the concepts presented in the text. Sophisticated, fun, and instructive, this Interactive Tool Kit contains up to 3 gradable assignments on each of the following concepts:

- SWOT Analysis (Chapter 2)
- Compensatory versus Non-compensatory Consumer Decision Making (Chapter 5)
- Vendor Evaluation Analysis (Chapter 6)

- Market Positioning Map (Chapter 8)
- Service Quality (Chapter 12)
- Break-even Analysis (Chapter 13)
- Developing an Advertisement (Chapter 18)

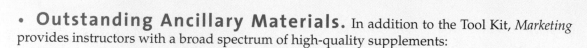

- **Outstanding Ancillary Materials.** In addition to the Tool Kit, *Marketing* provides instructors with a broad spectrum of high-quality supplements:

- Two sets of state-of-the-art PowerPoint presentations for each chapter. One set contains pictures, screen grabs, key terms, interactive exhibits, and embedded videos. The other is a frills-free version, ideal for customizing.

- A user-friendly, yet comprehensive Instructors' Manual. In addition to the lecture notes and end of chapter solutions, you will also find additional assignments, examples, and in-class activities that you can use to enhance your classroom lectures. This IM is available on the Instructor's side of the Online Learning Center and in hard copy.

- A video program on DVD consisting of more than 15 segments in a variety of lengths to provide flexibility for your classroom. Some of the firms featured in these videos are Newman's Own Organics, Taco Bell, and Netflix. The bottled water industry is covered in one long segment that integrates several of the key concepts discussed in this book.

- One of the most important aspects of the teaching package is the Test bank. The model for this test bank is unique, and was designed by a focus group of instructors. The test bank provides approximately 130 questions per chapter. Each question is keyed to chapter learning objectives and linked to the current AACSB standards. In this test bank you will find a balanced mixture of true/false, multiple-choice, short answer, and essay questions that are labeled as definition, conception, or application driven.

why will **students** enjoy using this book?

- ## A Compelling Read.
  Marketing was written with the student in mind. The examples are current and appealing, and feature a wide range of products and services that will be recognizable to a diverse group of readers.

- ## Unique End-of-Chapter Applications and Exercises
  - **Marketing Applications.** Each chapter concludes with eight to eleven Marketing Applications. These questions ask students to apply what they have learned to marketing scenarios that are relevant to their lives.

  - **Ethical Dilemma.** At least one of the Marketing Applications in each chapter poses an ethical dilemma based on material covered in the chapter. For instance, in Chapter 7 on global marketing, we pose the issue of offshore tax preparation work being done at a local accounting firm that communicates a personal commitment to each customer. Students can apply the ethical decision-making framework introduced in Chapter 3 to these marketing situations.

  - **Net Savvy.** Each chapter contains two exercises that force students to the Internet to apply material covered in the text. For example, in Chapter 18 on advertising we direct students to the Childrens's Advertising Review Unit, one of the major self-regulatory bodies for childrens's advertising at www.caru. org. We ask students to choose a press release and discuss what action CARU took against the identified company or group and the legal and ethical issues addressed in the case.

  - **End-of-Chapter Cases.** Each chapter ends with a 2-3 page case covering a current marketing idea, concept, or company.

- ## Web Site for Students (www.mhhe.com/grewal-levy)
  The Online Learning Center will help students and instructors use *Marketing* effectively. Some of the features on the Web site are:
  - The Interactive Student Tool Kit
  - Multiple-choice questions on the student site
  - Marketer's Showdown and other selections from the book's video program

We've created this book and support package to give both instructors and students the best possible learning experience. We truly hope that you and your students fully enjoy this book and the tools that accompany it.

acknowledgments

Throughout the development of this text, several outstanding individuals were integrally involved and made substantial contributions. In particular, we'd like to thank Larry D. Compeau (Clarkson University), Rajesh Chandrashekaran (Fairleigh Dickinson University), Rajiv Dant (University of Southern Florida), Nancy Dlott (Babson College), Gopal Iyer (Florida International University), Jeanne S. Munger (University of Southern Maine), Julie H. Rusch, and Morgan Walters (Babson College) for their contributions to several chapters.

We also acknowledge the contributions of our colleagues at Babson College, particularly, Danna Greenberg, Kate McKone-Sweet and Lydia Moland, for conceptualizing the ethical decision-making framework in Chapter 3. We also wish to thank Ross Petty at Babson College for his insights on legal issues discussed in the text, and to Abdul Ali, Britt Hackmann, Kathy Harris, Robb Kopp, Joan Lindsey-Mullikin, Anne Roggeveen, David Snavely, and Zhen Zhu for sharing teaching materials, reviewing manuscript, and being sounding boards for ideas.

We wish to express our sincere appreciation to Cathy Curran-Kelly (University of Massachusetts, Dartmouth), for preparing the Instructor's Manual, Caroline Juszczak for the Powerpoint slides, David Folson for the test bank, and Kelly Luchtman and Jennifer Locke with the video production. We also appreciate the feedback provided by Elisabeth Nevins Caswell and Elisa Adams.

The support, expertise, and occasional coercion from our publisher, Andy Winston, sponsoring editor, Barrett Koger and development editor, Sarah Crago, are greatly appreciated. The book would also never have come together without the editorial and production staff at McGraw-Hill/Irwin: Trent Whatcott, marketing manager; Christine Vaughan, lead project manager; Kami Carter, senior designer; Jeremy Cheshareck, senior photo research coordinator; Mike Hruby, photo researcher; Cathy Tepper, lead media project manager; Ben Curless and Aliya Haque, media technology producers; and Michael McCormick, lead production supervisor.

Our colleagues in industry have been invaluable in providing us with case, video, advertising, and photo materials. They include: Jacquelyn A. Ottman (J. Ottman Consulting); Andrea Gallagher (IRI); Marty Ordman and Betta Gallego (Dole); Michael Buckley, Mark Bauer, and Max Ward (Staples); Peter Meehan and Nell Newman (Newman's Own Organics); Steve Swasey (NetFlicks); Will Bortz (Taco-Bell); Dan Sullivan (New Balance), Jenny Dervin, (JetBlue); Susan Heaney (Avon Foundation); Nancy Hirshberg (Stonyfield Farms); Zoe Jackson (MOMA); and Douglas Riggan (Burger King).

Over the years, we have had the opportunity to work with many talented and insightful colleagues. We have benefited from our research and discussions with them. Some of these colleagues are: Arun Sharma, A. Parasuraman, R. Krishnan, Howard Marmorstein, Anuj Mehrotra and Michael Tsiros and Maria Giordano (all from University of Miami); Glenn Voss and Mitzi Montoya-Weiss (North Carolina. State University); Kathleen Seiders (Boston College); Rob Palmatier (University of Cincinnati); Praveen Kopalle, Scott Neslin and Kusum Ailawadi (Dartmouth); Robert Peterson and Andrea Godfrey (University of Texas at Austin); Don Lehmann (Columbia); Ruth Bolton, Steve Brown and Terry Bristol (Arizona State University), Julie Baker and William Cron (Texas Christian University); Venkatesh Shankar, Len Berry and Manjit Yadav (Texas A&M); Jerry Gotlieb (University of Western Kentucky); Hooman Estelami (Fordham University); Ken Evans (University of Oklahoma); Monika Kukar Kinney (University of Richmond); Ronnie Goodstein (Georgetown); James Hess (University of Houston); Anthony Miyazaki and Walfried Lassar (Florida International University); Tamara Mangleburg (Florida Atlantic University); David Hardesty (University of Kentucky); Greg Marshall (Rollins College); M. Joseph Sirgy, Julie Ozanne, Ed Fern (Virginia Tech); Merrie Brucks, Ajith Kumar (University of Arizona); Valerie Folkes (University of Southern California); Carolyn Costley (University of Waikato); William Dodds (Ft. Lewis College); Ramon Avila (Ball State University); Douglas M. Lambert, Walter Zinn (The Ohio State University); Eugene Stone-Romeo (University of Central Florida); Norm Borin (Cal Poly San Luis Obispo); Abhijit Biswas and Sujay Dutta (Wayne State University); Wagner Kamakura (Duke); Raj Srivastava (Emory); Cheryl Nikata (University of Illinois, Chicago); K. Sivakumar (Lehigh University); Namwoon Kim (Hong Kong Polytechnic University); Raj Suri (Drexel); Jean-Charles Chebat (HEC Montreal); Thomas Rudolph (St. Gallen University); Alan Dubinsky (Purdue University); Michael M. Van Breda, Daniel J. Howard, Jack Webster; (Southern Methodist University); Charles A. Ingene (University of Mississippi); and Dwight Grant (University of New Mexico).

Marketing has benefited from the reviews, focus groups, and individual discussions with several leading scholars and teachers of marketing. Together, these reviewers spent hundreds of hours reading, discussing, and critiquing the manuscript.

We gratefully acknowledge

Dennis Arnett
Texas Tech University

Ainsworth Bailey
University of Toledo

Joyce Banjac
Myers University

Harvey Bauman
Lees McRae College

Sandy Becker
Rutgers Business School

Ellen Benowitz
Mercer County Community College

Gary Benton
Western Kentucky University

Joseph Ben-Ur
University of Houston at Victoria

Patricia Bernson
County College of Morris

Jan Bingen
Little Priest Tribal College

Karen Bowman
University of California

Tom Boyd
California State University Fullerton

Nancy Boykin
Tarleton State University

Cathy Brenan
Northland Community and Technical College

Martin Bressler
Houston Baptist University

Claudia Bridges
California State University

Greg Broekemier
University of Nebraska Kearney

Rae Caloura
Johnson & Wales University

Michaelle Cameron
St. Edwards University

Lindell Chew
Linn University of Missouri

Dorene Ciletti
Duquesne University

Joyce Claterbos
University of Kansas

Gloria Cockerell
Collin County College

Mark E Collins
University of Tennessee

Sherry Cook
Southwest Missouri State University

Joseph DeFilippe
Suffolk County Community College

Kimberly Donahue
Indiana University Purdue University at Indianapolis

Michael Drafke
College of DuPage

Leon Dube
Texas A & M University

Nancy Evans
New River Community College

Joyce Fairchild
Northern Virginia Community College

David J. Faulds
University of Louisville

Larry Feick
University of Pittsburg

Leisa Flynn
Florida State University

William Foxx
Auburn University

Douglas Friedman
Penn State University

Stanley Garfunkel
Queensborough Community College

S J Garner
Eastern Kentucky University

David Gerth
Nashville State Community College

Kelly Gillerlain
Tidewater Community College

Jana Goodrich
Penn State Behrend

Robin Grambling
University of Texas at El Paso

Kimberly D. Grantham
University of Georgia

James I. Gray
Florida Atlantic University

Reetika Gupta
Lehigh University

Clark Hallpike
Elgin Community College

James E. Hansen
University of Akron

Lynn Harris
Shippensburg University

Linda Hefferin
Elgin Community College

Lewis Hershey
Fayetteville State University

Adrienne Hinds
Northern Virginia Community College at Annandale

Ronald Hoverstad
University of the Pacific

James Hunt
University of North Carolina Wilmington

Julie Huntley
Oral Roberts University

Doug Johansen
University of North Florida

Janice Karlen
CUNY – LaGuardia Community College

Eric J. Karson
Villanova University

Dennis Lee Kovach
Community College of Allegheny County

John Kuzma
Minnesota State University at Mankato

Sandie Lakin
Hesser College

Timothy Landry
University of Oklahoma

Don Larson
Ohio State University

Felicia Lassk
Northeastern University

J Ford Laumer
Auburn University

Kenneth Lawrence
New Jersey IT

Paul Londrigan
Mott Community College

Terry Lowe
Heartland Community College

Renee Pfeifer-Luckett
University of Wisconsin at Whitewater

Alicia Lupinacci
Tarrant Community College

Stanley Madden
Baylor University

Lynda Maddox
George Washington University

Cesar Maloles
California State University, East Bay

Karl Mann
Tennessee Tech University

Cathy Martin
University of Akron

Tamara Masters
Brigham Young University

Erika Matulich
University of Tampa

Nancy McClure
University of Central Oklahoma

Ivor Mitchell
University of Nevada Reno

Mark Mitchell
University of South Carolina

Rex Moody
Central Washington University at Ellensburg

James E. Murrow
Drury University

Noreen Nackenson
Nassau Community College

Sandra Blake Neis
Borough of Manhattan Community College

John Newbold
Sam Houston State University

Martin Nunlee
Syracuse University

Karen Overton
Houston Community College

Deborah L. Owens
University of Akron

Richard Pascarelli
Adelphi University

Glenn Perser
Houston Community College

Diane Persky
Yeshiva University

Susan Peters
California State Polytechnic University at Pomona

Gary Pieske
Minnesota State Community and Technical College

Jeff Podoshen
Temple University

Carmen Powers
Monroe Community College

Rosemary Ramsey
Wright State University

Srikumar Rao
Long Island University

Kristen Regine
Johnston & Wales University

Joseph Reihing
Nassau Community College

Janet Robinson
Mount St. Mary's College

Heidi Rottier
Bradley University

Juanita Roxas
California State Polytechnic University

Shikhar Sarin
Boise State University

Carl Saxby
University of Southern Indiana

Laura Shallow
St. Xavier University

Erin Sims
Devry University at Pomona

Lois J. Smith
University of Wisconsin

Brent Sorenson
University of Minnesota-Crookston

Randy Stuart
Kennesaw State University

James Swanson
Kishwaukee College

Robert R. Tangsrud, Jr.
Univeristy of North Dakota

Frank Tobolski
Lake in the Hills

Louis A. Tucci
College of New Jersey

Ven Venkatesan
University of Rhode Island at Kingston

Steve Vitucci
Tarleton University Central Texas

Keith Wade
Webber International University

Bryan Watkins
Dominican University, Priory Campus

Ludmilla Wells
Florida Gulf Coast University

Thomas Whipple
Cleveland State University

Tom Whitman
Mary Washington College

Kathleen Williamson
University of Houston-Clear Lake

Phillip Wilson
Midwestern State University

Doug Witt
Brigham Young University

Kim Wong
Albuquerque Tech Institute

Esther Page-Wood
Western Michigan University

Finally, we'd like to thank our families: Diana, Lauren and Alex Grewal, and Marcia and Eva Levy for their support and encouragement in this endeavor.

brief contents

table of contents

SECTION FOUR   Value Creation   268

SECTION FIVE   Value Capture   354

Marketing

1

QUESTIONS

- What is the role of marketing in organizations?

- How do marketers create value for a product or service?

- Why is marketing important both within and outside the firm?

SECTION ONE
Assessing the Marketplace

Overview of Marketing

What do Google, AOL Instant Messenger, and eBay have in common, other than being Internet-based firms?[1] In its own way, each has found a place in the lives of its customers by providing a great *value*—each firm gives more to its customers than those customers spend in terms of their time and money.

Google

Remarkable for its rapid technology development, Google is the world's number one Internet search engine, consistently outpacing competition like Yahoo!, MSN, AOL, Netscape, and Ask.com. But great technology means little unless customers believe that it gives them a more valuable experience than its competition does. And so Google delivers. Its PageRank enables users to retrieve valuable search results without the clutter of irrelevant Web pages. Froogle, one of Google's offshoots, was developed to facilitate searches for customers who wanted Internet retailers only. Google's AdSense provides value not to consumers but to the businesses that advertise on Google by delivering customized ads matched precisely to the content of the page the customer is viewing. Thus, Google provides a lot of value to users and advertisers alike.

AOL Instant Messenger (AIM)

Almost 50 percent of American homes with access to the Internet use instant messaging, and half of these choose AOL Instant Messenger (AIM) as their means of text communication. With this product, AIM users can listen to free music stations—a great value because free music exchanges have become illegal, and most online music services charge a monthly or per-song fee. In addition, the AIM Remote service gives Web designers from other companies the ability to connect directly with visitors to their sites, make comments, or ask questions. In yet another extension, AIM Developer, a Macromedia and AOL partnership, enables Web developers to create online discussion forums and person-to-person interactions that extend beyond simple text and include video messaging. So, why does AIM beat out Yahoo! Messenger and MSN? Because even though all instant messaging services are free, AIM offers more value.

eBay

Want to buy an old cowboy belt for $1 or a vintage Rolls Royce for $30,000? eBay, a virtual community of buyers and sellers, is just the place. By opening geographical boundaries that normally make it difficult for buyers and sellers to find one another, eBay provides value to its users. Sellers can dispose of unwanted items or build a business through eBay, while buyers can purchase items they may never be able to find in the stores they normally frequent. Direct buyer–seller contact builds a sense of community, and the eBay rating systems provide participants with a sense of trust and support unparalleled in online shopping venues. eBay is not only a good place to find a good deal; it is a good place to find good value!

So what do Google, AIM, and eBay have in common? Each of these innovative marketing companies succeeds because it provides a good value to its customers.

■ ■ ■

What Is Marketing?

Unlike other subjects you may have studied, marketing already is very familiar to you. You start your day by agreeing to do the dishes in exchange for a freshly made cup of coffee. Then you fill up your car with gas. You attend a class that you have chosen and paid for. After class, you pick up lunch at the cafeteria, have your hair cut, buy a few tunes from Apple's iTunes, and take in a movie. In each case, you have acted as the buyer and made a decision about whether you should part with your time and/or money to receive a particular service or merchandise. If, after you return home from the movie, you decide to post a CD on eBay, you have become a seller. And in each of these transactions, you were engaged in marketing.

The American Marketing Association states that "**Marketing** is an organizational function and a set of processes for creating, *capturing*, communicating, and delivering value to customers and for managing customer relationships in ways that benefit the organization and its stakeholders."[2] What does this definition really mean? Good marketing is not a random activity; it requires thoughtful planning with an emphasis on the ethical implications of any of those decisions on society in general. Firms develop a **marketing plan** (Chapter 2) that specifies the marketing activities for a specific period of time. The marketing plan also is broken down into various components—how the product or service will be conceived or

When you buy a song on iTunes, you are engaging in marketing.

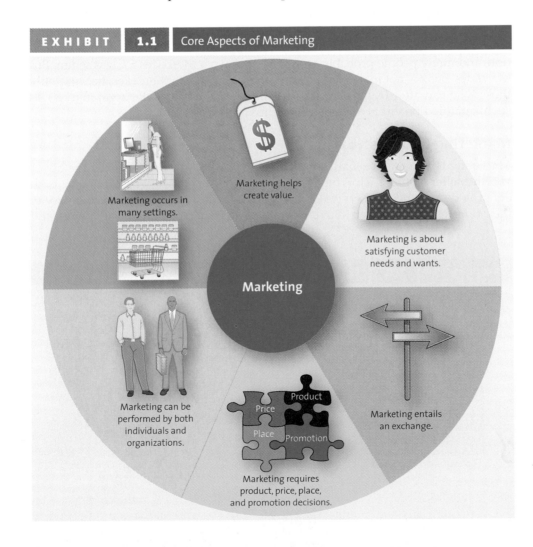

EXHIBIT 1.1 Core Aspects of Marketing

Marketing occurs in many settings.

Marketing helps create value.

Marketing is about satisfying customer needs and wants.

Marketing

Marketing can be performed by both individuals and organizations.

Marketing entails an exchange.

Price, Product, Place, Promotion

Marketing requires product, price, place, and promotion decisions.

designed, how much it should cost, where and how it will be promoted, and how it will get to the consumer. In any exchange, the parties to the transaction should be satisfied. In our previous example, you should be satisfied or even delighted with the iTune you downloaded, and Apple should be satisfied with the amount of money it received from you. Thus, the core aspects of marketing are found in Exhibit 1.1. Let's see how these core aspects look in practice.

Marketing Is about Satisfying Customer Needs and Wants

Understanding the marketplace, and especially consumer needs and wants, is fundamental to marketing success. In the broadest terms, the marketplace refers to the world of trade. More narrowly, however, the marketplace can be segmented or divided into groups of people who are pertinent to an organization for particular reasons. For example, even though the marketplace for toothpaste users may include most of the people in the world, the makers of Crest could divide them into adolescent, adult, and senior users or perhaps into smokers, coffee drinkers, and wine drinkers. If you manufacture a toothpaste that removes tar and nicotine stains, you want to know for which marketplace segments your product is most relevant and then make sure that you build a marketing strategy that targets those groups.

Although marketers would prefer to sell their products and services to everyone, it is not practical to do so. Because marketing costs money, good marketers carefully seek potential customers who have both an interest in the product and an ability to buy. For example, everyone has a need for some form of transportation, and many people probably would like to own a Mercedes S Class sedan. But Mercedes-Benz is not interested in everyone who wants a Mercedes, because only those who can afford such a product are included in the viable target market. As such, qualified potential buyers are of primary interest to marketers.

Marketing Entails an Exchange

Marketing is about an **exchange**—the trade of things of value between the buyer and the seller so that each is better off as a result. As depicted in Exhibit 1.2, sellers provide products or services, then communicate and facilitate the delivery of their offering to consumers. Buyers complete the exchange by giving money and

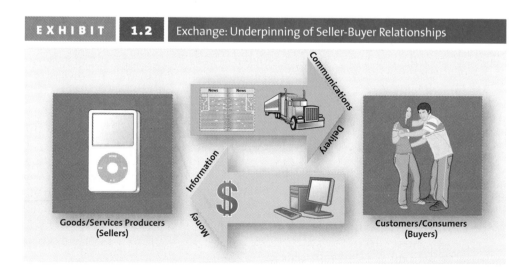

EXHIBIT **1.2** Exchange: Underpinning of Seller-Buyer Relationships

Goods/Services Producers (Sellers)

Communications

Delivery

Information

Money

Customers/Consumers (Buyers)

When you purchase a new Coldplay CD, you are engaging in a marketing exchange. You get the CD, and the exchange partners get money and information about you.

information to the seller. Suppose you learn about a new Coldplay CD by reading *Rolling Stone,* which published a review of the CD and included an ad noting that the CD was available at Barnes & Noble and online (bn.com). You go online and purchase the CD. Along with gathering your necessary billing and shipping information, Barnes & Noble creates a record of your purchase, information that may be used in the coming months to inform you of the introduction of Coldplay's next CD. Thus, in addition to making money on this particular transaction, Barnes & Noble can use the valuable information it has obtained to facilitate an exchange in the future and solidify a relationship with you.

Marketing Requires Product, Price, Place and Promotion Decisions

Marketing traditionally has been divided into a set of four interrelated decisions known as the **marketing mix,** or **four Ps:** product, price, place, and promotion as defined in Exhibit 1.3.[3] Together, the four Ps comprise the marketing mix, which is the controllable set of activities that the firm uses to respond to the wants of its target markets. But what does each of them mean?

Product: Creating Value   Although marketing is a multifaceted function, its fundamental purpose is to create value by developing a variety of offerings, including goods, services, and ideas, to satisfy customer needs. Take, for example, water. Not too long ago, consumers perceived this basic commodity as simply water. It came out of a faucet and was consumed for drinking and washing. But taking a cue from European firms like Perrier (France) and San Pellegrino (Italy), several U.S.-based firms such as Poland Springs, Arrowhead, and Pepsi's Aquafina have created a product with benefits that consumers find valuable. In addition to easy access to water, an essential part of this created value is the products' brand image, which lets users say to the world, "I'm healthy," "I'm smart," and "I'm chic."[4]

EXHIBIT 1.3	The Marketing Mix	
Marketing Mix	**Value**	
Product	Creating	
Price	Capturing	
Place	Delivering	
Promotion	Communicating	

Goods are items that you can physically touch. Reebok shoes, Coca-Cola, Budweiser, Kraft cheese, Tide, and countless other products are examples of goods. Reebok primarily makes shoes but also adds value to its products by, for example, designing them under its Rbk label to have high fashion appeal. (See Entrepreneurial Marketing 1.1.)

Unlike goods, services are intangible customer benefits that are produced by people or machines and cannot be separated from the producer. Air travel, banking, insurance, beauty treatments, and entertainment all are services. If you attend a concert by Click-Five or Fall Out Boy, you are consuming a service. Getting money from your bank using an ATM or teller is another example of using a service. In this case, cash machines usually add value to your banking experience by being conveniently located, fast, and easy to use.

Many offerings represent a combination of goods and services. When you go to an optical center, you get your eyes examined (service) and purchase new contact lenses (good). If you enjoy Norah Jones's music, you can attend a concert that, similar to other services like surgery or a football game, can be provided only at a particular time and place. At the concert, you can purchase a Norah Jones concert CD, the tangible good that has provided you with a combination of a good and a service.

Ideas include thoughts, opinions, and philosophies, and intellectual concepts such as these also can be marketed. Groups promoting bicycle safety go to schools, give talks, and sponsor bike helmet poster contests for the members of their primary market—children. Then their secondary target market segment, parents and siblings, gets involved through their interactions with the young contest participants. The exchange of value occurs when the children listen to the sponsors' presentation and wear their helmets while bicycling, which means they have adopted, or become "purchasers," of the safety idea that the group marketed.

Entrepreneurial Marketing **1.1**

Rbk Goes Hollywood[5]

Paul Fireman, entrepreneur, founder and former CEO of Reebok built his company from a small athletic shoe company to one of the biggest global apparel and footwear companies. After taking on Nike in the athletic apparel and shoe markets, Reebok has now decided to go after the fashion sneaker market with its Rbk brand. The company hopes to increase its sales substantially by attracting television and movie stars instead of athletes to adopt its products.

Reebok's Los Angeles store is not the average "choose, try, buy" store. In the corner of a VIP room rests a chilled supply of Dom Perignon and Cristal champagne. On the second floor, retractable movie screens can convert the space to allow for exclusive screenings and parties. Reebok hopes the glitz and glamour will appeal to movie stars because when a celebrity wears a brand,

that brand has hit gold. For example, the sale of Ugg boots soared after Pamela Anderson was photographed wearing them. Reebok wants to create the same effect for its sneakers. To promote its products to celebrities, Reebok also created a new position in the company, the manager of entertainment, whose role is to generate friendships and relationships with Hollywood influencers and offer them free Reebok merchandise.

Although Reebok may be the first shoe company to turn to entertainment and fashion as an outlet for sneakers, the idea of selling on style is nothing new. Fewer than one-third of the people who buy basketball shoes use them on the court, and fewer than one-quarter of the people who purchase running shoes actually run in them. To Reebok, it simply makes sense to pursue fashion.

Paul Fireman, former chairman and CEO, Reebok International LTD (center), Philadelphia 76ers Allen Iverson (right), and children hold 10 new-style Rbk shoes that symbolize Rbk's celebration of ten years of Allen Iverson.

Many offerings are a combination of goods and services. At a Norah Jones concert you can enjoy the concert (a service) and buy her CD (a good).

Price: Capturing Value   Everything has a price, though it doesn't always have to be monetary. **Price,** therefore, is everything the buyer gives up—money, time, energy—in exchange for the product. Marketers must determine the price of a product carefully on the basis of the potential buyer's belief about its value. For example, United Airlines can take you from New York to Denver. The price you pay for that product depends on how far in advance you book the ticket, the time of year, and whether you want to fly coach or business class. If you value the convenience of buying your ticket at the last minute for a ski trip between Christmas and New Year's Day and you want to fly business class, you can expect to pay four or five times as much as you would for the cheapest available ticket. That is, you have traded off a lower price for convenience. For marketers, the key to determining prices is figuring out how much customers are willing to pay so that they are satisfied with the purchase and the seller achieves a reasonable profit.

Pepsi's Aquafina has created a product with benefits that consumers find valuable.

Place: Delivering the Value Proposition   The third P, place or supply chain management, describes all the activities necessary to get the product to the right customer when that customer wants it.

H&H sells millions of bagels every year, partly because people are able to place orders from the firm's Internet site (www. hhbagels.com) and have them delivered to any location in the continental United States by the end of the next business day.

Specifically, *supply chain management* refers to a set of approaches and techniques that firms employ to efficiently and effectively integrate their suppliers, manufacturers, warehouses, stores, and other firms involved in the transaction, such as transportation companies, into a seamless value chain in which merchandise is produced and distributed in the right quantities, to the right locations, and at the right time, as well as to minimize systemwide costs while satisfying the service levels required by their customers.[6] Many marketing students initially overlook the importance of supply chain management because a lot of the activities are behind the scenes. But without a strong and efficient supply chain system, merchandise isn't available when customers want it. They are disappointed, and sales and profits suffer.

To illustrate how supply chain management delivers the value proposition, consider the experience of H&H Bagels. H&H has two New York City locations. You therefore might think that customers come from just a few blocks away, yet the company sells millions of bagels every year, partly because people are able to place orders from its Internet site (www.hhbagels.com) and have them delivered to any location in the continental United States by the end of the next business day. This service adds so much value over and above what other bagel stores offer that H&H Bagels can command a whopping $25 per dozen bagels.

Promotion: Communicating the Value Proposition   Even the best products and services will go unsold if marketers cannot communicate their value to customers. Countless Internet companies sank in the late 1990s, at least partly because they did not communicate successfully with their customers. Some such firms had great products at very fair prices, but when customers could not find them on the Internet, the companies simply failed. Promotion thus is communication by a marketer that informs, persuades, and reminds potential buyers about a product

Calvin Klein is known for selling youth, fun, and sex appeal in its fragrance promotions. In this photo CK One models dance to the sounds of DJ Ruckus as they live in a billboard shaped like a giant CK One bottle overlooking the streets of Times Square in New York City.

or service to influence their opinions or elicit a response. Promotion generally can enhance a product or service's value, as happened for Calvin Klein fragrances. The company's provocative advertising has helped create an image that says more than "Use this product and you will smell good." Rather, the promotion sells youth, style, and sex appeal.

Marketing Can Be Performed by Both Individuals and Organizations

Imagine how complicated the world would be if you had to buy everything you consumed directly from producers or manufacturers. You would have to go from farm to farm buying your food and then from manufacturer to manufacturer to purchase the table, plates, and utensils you need to eat that food. Fortunately, marketing intermediaries, such as retailers, accumulate merchandise from producers in large amounts and then sell it to you in smaller amounts. The process in which businesses sell to consumers is known as **B2C (business-to-consumer) marketing,** whereas the process of selling merchandise or services from one business to another is called **B2B (business-to-business) marketing.** However, with the advent of various auction sites, such as eBay, consumers have started marketing their products and services to other consumers, which requires a third category in which consumers sell to other consumers: **C2C marketing.** These marketing transactions are illustrated in Exhibit 1.4.

Individuals can also undertake activities to market themselves. When you apply for a job, for instance, the research you do about the firm, the resumé and cover letter you submit with your application, and the way you dress for an interview and conduct yourself during it are all forms of marketing activities. Accountants, lawyers, financial planners, physicians, and other professional service providers also constantly take part in marketing their services.

EXHIBIT	1.4	Marketing Can Be Performed by Both Individuals and Organizations

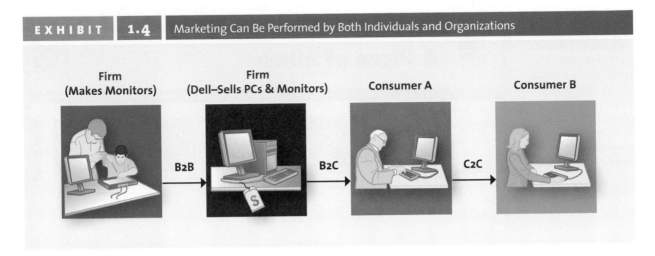

Marketing Occurs in Many Settings

Most people think of marketing as a way for a firm to make profits. But marketing works equally well in the not-for-profit sector. Think about what influenced your selection of your college or university, other than family, friends, and convenience. It's likely that your college has a sophisticated marketing program to attract and retain students. Hospitals, theaters, charities, museums, religious institutions, politicians, and even governments rely on marketing to communicate their message to their constituents.

In addition, marketing isn't useful only in big countries with well-developed economies. It can also jump-start the economies of less developed countries by actually creating markets, that is, putting buyers and sellers together. A Piece of Africa, for example, buys art from African artists and, through its Web site, makes that art available to customers all over the world, thereby creating a market that otherwise would not exist. Customers become exposed to an array of products from various countries that previously would have been available exclusively through expensive galleries, and the tribal artists can spend their earnings locally, which stimulates the local economy. Finally, the firm donates 3 percent of the online sales to goodwill projects in Africa, which solidifies its socially responsible appeal.

Marketing often is designed to benefit an entire industry, which can help many firms simultaneously. The dairy industry has used a very successful, award-winning campaign with its slogan "Got Milk," aimed at different target

The dairy industry's "Got Milk" ad campaign has created high levels of awareness about the benefit of drinking milk and has increased milk consumption by using celebrities like Hilary Duff in its ads.

A Piece of Africa buys art from African artists and, through its Web site (www.bizinsa.com/apieceofafrica), makes that art available to customers all over the world, thereby creating a market that otherwise would not exist.

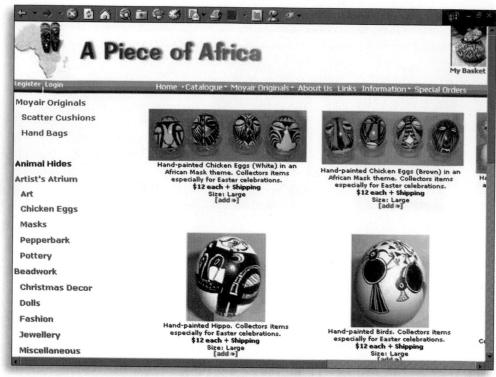

segments. This campaign has not only created high levels of awareness about the benefits of drinking milk but also increased milk consumption in various target segments,[7] possibly through the use of actors such as Angelina Jolie and athletes such as boxer Oscar de la Hoya. Overall, this campaign benefits the entire dairy industry, not just one dairy.

Marketing Helps Create Value

Marketing didn't get to its current prominence among individuals, corporations, and society at large overnight. To understand how marketing has evolved into its present-day, integral business function of creating value, let's look for a moment at some of the milestones in marketing's short history (Exhibit 1.5).

Production-Oriented Era   Around the turn of the 20th century, most firms were production oriented and believed that a good product would sell itself. Henry Ford, the founder of Ford Motor Co., once famously remarked, "Customers can have any color they want so long as it's black." Manufacturers were concerned with product innovation, not with satisfying the needs of individual consumers, and retail stores typically were considered places to hold the merchandise until a consumer wanted it.

Sales-Oriented Era   Between 1920 and 1950, production and distribution techniques became more sophisticated, and the Great Depression and World War II conditioned customers to consume less. As a result, manufacturers had the capacity to produce more than customers really wanted to buy. Firms found an answer to their overproduction in becoming sales oriented; they depended on heavy doses of personal selling and advertising.

Market-Oriented Era   After World War II, soldiers returned home, got new jobs, and started families. At the same time, manufacturers turned from focusing on the war effort and toward consumer products. Suburban communities sprouted up around the country, and the new suburban fixture, the shopping center, began to replace cities' central business districts as the hub of retail activity and a place to just hang out. Some products, once in limited supply because of World War II, became plentiful. And the United States entered a buyers' market—the customer became king! When consumers again had choices, they were able to make purchasing decisions on the basis of factors such as quality, convenience, and price. Manufacturers and retailers thus began to focus on what consumers wanted and needed before they designed, made, or attempted to sell their products and services. It was during this period that firms discovered marketing.

Value-Based Marketing Era   Most successful firms today are market oriented.[8] That means they generally have transcended a production or selling orientation and attempt to discover and satisfy their customers' needs and wants. Before the turn of the 21st century, better marketing firms recognized that there was more to good marketing than simply discovering and providing what consumers wanted and needed; to compete successfully, they would have to give their customers greater value than their competitors did.

Value reflects the relationship of benefits to costs, or what you *get* for what you *give*.[9] In a marketing context, customers seek a fair return in goods and/or services for their hard-earned money and scarce time. They want products or services that meet their specific needs or wants and that are offered at competitive prices. The challenge for firms is to find out what consumers are looking for and attempt to provide those goods and services but still make a profit.

Every value-based marketing firm must implement its strategy according to what its customers value. Sometimes providing greater value means providing a lot of merchandise for relatively little money, such as a Whopper for 99¢ at Burger King or a diamond for 40 percent off the suggested retail price at Costco. But value is in the eye of the beholder and doesn't always come cheap. Satisfied BMW buyers probably believe their car is a good value because they have gotten a lot of benefits for a reasonable price. Similarly, teenagers may be willing to pay a premium for Apple's iPod because of its extraordinary design and packaging, even though cheaper substitutes are available. This is the power of marketing in general

EXHIBIT   1.5   Marketing Evolution: Production, Sales, Marketing, and Value

Turn of the Century   1920   1950   1990

Production   Sales   Marketing   Value-Based Marketing

and branding in particular. London's Harrods department store adds value to its customers' various loyalty programs. (See Adding Value 1.1.)

In the next section, we explore the notion of value-based marketing further. Specifically, we look at various options for attracting customers by providing them with better value than the competition does. Then we discuss how firms compete on the basis of value. Finally, we examine how firms transform the value concept into their value-driven activities.

What Is Value-Based Marketing?

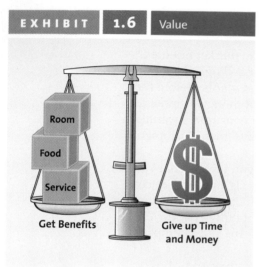

EXHIBIT **1.6** Value

Room
Food
Service

Get Benefits

$

Give up Time and Money

Consumers make explicit and/or implicit trade-offs between the perceived benefits of a product or service and their costs. Customers naturally seek options that provide the greatest benefits at the lowest costs. Marketing firms attempt to find the most desirable balance between providing benefits to customers and keeping their costs down, as illustrated in Exhibit 1.6.

To better understand value and to develop a value-based marketing orientation, a business must also understand what customers view as the key benefits of a given product or service and how to improve on them. For example, some benefits of staying at a Sheraton hotel might include the high level of service quality provided by the personnel, the convenience of booking the room at Sheraton.com, and the overall quality of the room and meals offered. In broader terms, some critical benefits may be service quality, convenience, and merchandise quality.

The other side of the value equation entails the firm's ability to provide either a better product/service mix at the same cost or the same level of quality and convenience for a lower cost. The customer's potential cost elements, in terms of value-based marketing strategies, for the Sheraton hotel in our example would include the price of the room and meals, the time it takes to book a room or check in at the hotel, and the risk of arriving at the hotel and finding it overbooked.

How Firms Compete on the Basis of Value

With such a simple formula, marketers should be able to deliver value consistently, right? Well, not exactly. In today's quickly changing world, consistently creating and delivering value is quite difficult. Consumer perceptions change quickly, competitors constantly enter markets, and global pressures continually reshape opportunities. Thus, marketers must keep a vigilant eye on the marketplace so they can adjust their offerings to meet customer needs and keep ahead of their competition.

Value-based marketing, however, isn't just about creating strong products and services; it should be at the core of every firm's functions. For example, Wal-Mart does not serve those customers who are looking to impress their friends with conspicuous consumption. Rather, it is for those who want convenient one-stop shopping and low prices—and on those values, it consistently delivers. But good value is not limited just to low prices. Although Wal-Mart carries low-priced pots, pans, and coffee pots, cooking enthusiasts may prefer the product selection, quality, and expert sales assistance at Williams-Sonoma. The prices there aren't as low as at Wal-Mart, but Williams-Sonoma customers believe they are receiving a good value—because of the selection, quality, and service they receive—when they shop there.

Adding Value 1.1

Harrods by Invitation

Creating value isn't always about the relationship between benefits and monetary costs. With its value proposition, London's Harrods Department Store offers its customers top-quality merchandise and impeccable service that are unavailable at most other retailers. Harrods is extremely conscious of its luxury image so when management initiated a loyalty program, maintaining a feel of luxury was imperative. The goal was to create a loyalty program that had significant "Wow" factor for the most valuable customers.

Through careful screening, Harrods identified 47,000 customers out of its 700,000 customer database, then sent a mailing inviting these customers to join the "By Invitation" program. The mailer was carefully constructed to reflect the luxury brand image of Harrods. It also included a personal invitation from the Harrods chairman.

As in most loyalty programs, consumers in the "By Invitation" program accumulate points according to how much they spend and then redeem those points for special incentives.[10] What is unique are the incentives Harrods is offering. They include a day trip to Florence with a Harrods bed linen buyer, a chauffeur-driven trip to visit a jeweler to design a custom piece, or a day at Harrods' owner's estate. To begin collecting the points necessary to choose one of these incentives, consumers must spend a minimum of $4,000. Harrods is awarding those who spend over $88,000 with membership in the Chairman's Club, which offers additional benefits and incentives.

Harrods works extremely hard to ensure that all members of By Invitation are treated as individuals and that their unique needs and preferences, including how

London's Harrods Department Store maintains a loyalty program that offers its best customers perks like a day trip to Florence with Harrods bed linen buyer, a chauffeur-driven trip to visit a jeweler to design a custom piece, or a day at Harrods owner's estate.

they wish to pay for transactions, is known and communicated to the staff. In this manner Harrods keeps its best customers extremely happy. Happy customers tend to come back again and again.[11]

How Do Firms Become Value Driven?

Firms become value driven by focusing on three activities. (See Exhibit 1.7.) First, they share information about their customers and competitors across their own organization and with other firms that might be involved in getting the product or service to the marketplace, such as manufacturers and transportation companies. Second, they strive to balance their customers' benefits and costs. Third, they concentrate on building relationships with customers.

Sharing Information In a value-based, marketing-oriented firm, marketers share information about customers and competitors, which has been collected through customer relationship management, and integrate it across the firm's various departments. The fashion designers for Zara, the Spain-based fashion retailer, for

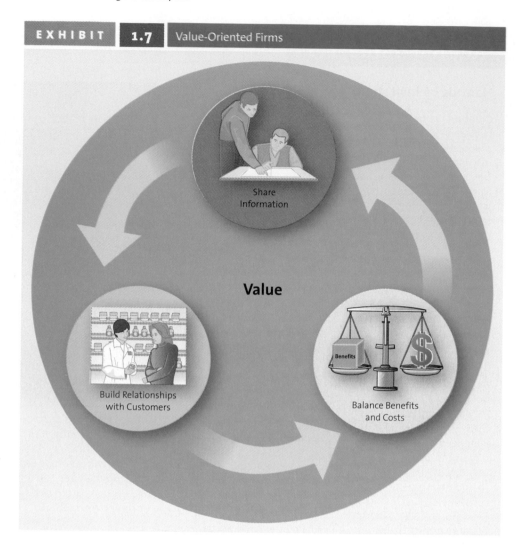

| EXHIBIT | 1.7 | Value-Oriented Firms |

Value

Share Information

Build Relationships with Customers

Balance Benefits and Costs

Benefits $

instance, collect purchase information and research customer trends to determine what their customers will want to wear in the next few weeks; simultaneously, the logisticians—those persons in charge of getting the merchandise to the stores—use the same purchase history to forecast sales and allocate appropriate merchandise to individual stores. Sharing and coordinating such information represents a critical success factor for any firm. Imagine what might happen if Zara's advertising department were to plan a special promotion but not share its sales projections with those people in charge of creating the merchandise or getting it to stores.

Balancing Benefits with Costs   Value-oriented marketers constantly measure the benefits that customers perceive against the cost of their offering. In this task, they use available customer data to find opportunities in which they can better satisfy their customers' needs and in turn develop long-term loyalties. Such a value-based orientation has helped Target and Wal-Mart outperform the Standard & Poor's retail index, Kohl's to outperform other department stores, Ryanair and Southwest Airlines to outperform mainstream carriers, and Dell to outperform its personal computing rivals.[12]

Fashion designers for Zara, the Spain-based fashion retailer, collect purchase information and research customer trends to determine what their customers will want to wear in the next few weeks. They share this information with other departments to forecast sales and coordinate deliveries.

Until recently, it sometimes cost more to fly within Europe than to fly from the United States to Europe. But low-frills, low-cost carriers such as Ryanair and EasyJet,[13] modeled on Southwest Airlines and Jet Blue, now offer customers what they want: cheap intra-Europe airfares. Like their American counterparts, Ryanair and EasyJet offer no food service and generally fly to and from out-of-the-way airports like Stansted, about 34 miles northeast of London. But many customers find value despite such minor inconveniences. Consider, for example, the London to Salzburg, Austria, route for $65 or London to Sweden for $70. Values such as these are also what have given low-cost carriers in the United States approximately 25 percent of the market share. They are so popular that conventional airlines have started their own low frills/low cost airlines: United Airlines has introduced "Ted," Singapore Airlines provides Tiger, and Australia's Quantas offers Jetstar.

To provide a great value, U.K.-based EasyJet offers no food service and generally flies to and from out-of-the-way airports.

Building Relationships with Customers During the past decade or so, marketers have begun to realize that they need to think about their customer orientation in terms of relationships rather than transactions.[14] A **transactional orientation** regards the buyer–seller relationship as a series of individual transactions, so anything that happened before or after the transaction is of little importance. For example, used car sales typically are based on a transactional approach; the seller wants to get the highest price for the car, the buyer wants to get the lowest, and neither expects to do business with the other again.

A **relational orientation**, in contrast, is based on the philosophy that buyers and sellers should develop a long-term relationship. According to this idea, the lifetime profitability of the relationship matters, not how much money is made during each transaction. For example, UPS works with its shippers to develop efficient transportation solutions. Over time, UPS becomes part of the fabric of the shippers' organizations, and their operations become intertwined. In this scenario, they have developed a long-term relationship.

Firms that practice value-based marketing also use a process known as **customer relationship management (CRM)**, a business philosophy and set of strategies, programs, and systems that focus on identifying and building loyalty among the firm's most valued customers.[15] Firms that employ CRM systematically collect information about their customers' needs and then use that information to target their best customers with the products, services, and special promotions that appear most important to those customers.

Now that we've examined what marketing is and how it creates value, let's consider how it fits into the world of commerce, as well as into society in general.

Why Is Marketing Important?

Marketing once was only an afterthought to production. Early marketing philosophy went something like this: "We've made it; now how do we get rid of it?" However, marketing not only has shifted its focus dramatically, it also has evolved into a major business function that crosses all areas of a firm or organization, as illustrated in Exhibit 1.8. Marketing advises production about how much of the company's product to make and then tells logistics when to ship it. It creates long-lasting, mutually valuable relationships between the company and the firms from which it buys. It identifies those elements that local customers value and makes it possible for the firm to expand globally. Marketing has had a significant impact on consumers as well. Without marketing, it would be difficult for any of us to learn about new products and services. Understanding marketing can even help you find a job after you finish school.

Marketing Expands Firms' Global Presence

A generation ago, Coca-Cola was available in many nations, but Levi's and most other U.S. brands weren't. Blue jeans were primarily an American product—made in the United States for the U.S. market. But today most jeans, including Levi Strauss & Co., are made in places other than the United States and available nearly everywhere. Thanks to MTV and other global entertainment venues, cheap foreign travel, and the Internet, you share many of your consumption behaviors with college students in countries all over the globe. The best fashions, music, and even food trends disseminate rapidly around the world.

Take a look at your next shopping bag. Whether it contains groceries, apparel, or furniture, you will find goods from many countries—produce from Mexico,

These brands can be found in many countries.

EXHIBIT **1.8** Importance of Marketing

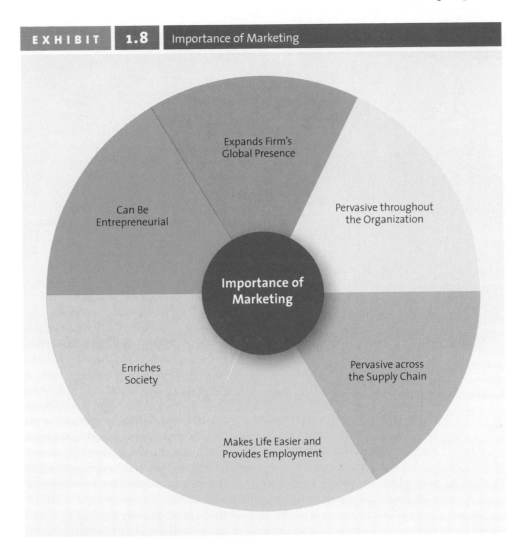

jeans from Italy, chairs from Vietnam. Global manufacturers and retailers continue to make inroads into the U.S. market as well. Companies such as Honda, Swatch, Sony, Heineken, and Nestlé sell as well in the United States as they do in their home countries. Sweden's fashion retailer H & M operates in 22 countries;[16] its upscale competitor, Spain's Zara, operates in 62.[17] The Dutch grocery store giant Ahold is among the top five grocery store chains in the United States, though you may never have heard of it because it operates under names such as Stop & Shop, Giant-Landover, and Bruno's in the United States.[18]

How does marketing contribute to a company's successful global expansion? Understanding customers is critical. Without the knowledge that can be gained by analyzing new customers' needs and wants on a segment-by-segment, region-by-region basis—one of marketing's main tasks—it would be difficult for a firm to expand globally. Starbucks, for instance, has adjusted its U.S. menu to meet customer wants in the Japanese market more effectively. In some Japanese outlets, it sells drinks with alcohol—a first for Starbucks. It also is experimenting with other items, like the "DoubleShot," a cold, creamy coffee drink vigorously mixed in a cocktail shaker, and green-tea Frappuccinos. In Japan, Starbucks even serves hot food from ovens: pork and pastrami sandwiches and tuna-and-basil pizzas.[19]

Starbucks has adjusted its U.S. menu to meet customer wants in the Japanese market more effectively.

Marketing Is Pervasive across the Organization

In value-based marketing firms, the marketing department works seamlessly with other functional areas of the company to design, promote, price, and distribute products. Consider the Scion, designed for the less affluent youth market, which sometimes has been referred to as "Generation Y."[20] Scion's marketing department worked closely with engineers to ensure that the new car exceeded customers' expectations in terms of design but remained affordable. The company also coordinated the product offering with an innovative communications strategy. Because Generation Y is famous for its resistance to conventional advertising, Scion introduced a virtual road race in which participants receive mileage points for sending Scion e-cards. The more "places" they visited, the more mileage points they received. At the end of the competition, each driver's points were totaled and compared with other racers' scores. The driver with the most points won an onboard navigation system worth more than $2,000. In addition, because Scion is a new car, the marketing department must work closely with the distribution department to ensure that advertising and promotions reach all distributors' territories and that distribution exists where those promotions occur. Marketing thus is responsible for coordinating all these aspects of supply and demand.

Marketing Is Pervasive across the Supply Chain

Firms typically do not work in isolation. Manufacturers buy raw materials and components from suppliers, which they sell to retailers or other businesses after they have turned the materials into their products (see Exhibit 1.9). Every time materials or products are bought or sold, they are transported to a different location, which sometimes requires that they be stored in a warehouse operated by yet another organization. The group of firms that make and deliver a given set of goods and services is known as a **supply chain**.

Scion introduced a virtual road race in which participants received mileage points for sending Scion e-cards. At the end of the competition the driver with the most points won an onboard navigation system worth more than $2,000.

As we discussed earlier, some supply chain participants take a transactional orientation in which the participating parties don't care much about their trading partners as the merchandise passes among them. Each link in the chain is out for its own best interest. Manufacturers, for example, want the highest price, whereas retailers want to buy the product at the lowest cost. Supply chain members do not enjoy any cooperation or coordination. But for the supply chain to provide significant value to the ultimate customer, the parties must establish long-term relationships with one another and cooperate to share data, make joint forecasts, and coordinate shipments. Effectively managing supply chain relationships often has a marked impact on a firm's ability to satisfy the consumer, which results in increased profitability for all parties.

EXHIBIT	1.9	Supply Chain

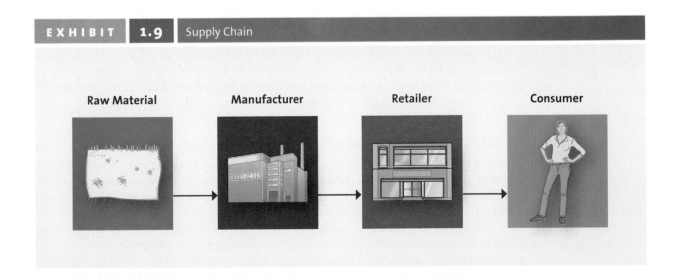

Raw Material → **Manufacturer** → **Retailer** → **Consumer**

Consider Levi Strauss & Co. and its close relationship with its major retailers. Not too many years ago, only about 40 percent of orders from the jeans manufacturer to its retailers arrived on time, which made it very difficult for retailers to keep all sizes in stock and therefore keep customers, who are generally not satisfied with anything less than the correct size, happy. Today however, Levi's uses an automatic inventory replenishment system through which it manages the retailers' inventory itself. When a customer buys a pair of jeans, the information is transferred directly from the retailer to Levi's, which then determines which items the retailer needs to reorder and automatically ships the merchandise. The relationship benefits all parties: Retailers don't have to worry about keeping their stores stocked in jeans and save money because they don't have to invest as much money in inventory. Because Levi's has control of the jeans inventory, it can be assured that it won't lose sales because its retailers have let their inventory run down. Finally, customers benefit by having the merchandise when they want it—a good value.

A supply chain comprises more than buyers and sellers however. Firms build strategic alliances with consulting firms, marketing research firms, computer firms, and transportation firms, just to name a few. For example, UPS provides much more than a package delivery service; it also offers insurance services, supply chain management, and e-commerce support to small and medium-sized customers. Through UPS Capital, firms even can obtain funds to finance their inventory or ease their cash flow.[21]

Marketing Makes Life Easier and Provides Employment Opportunities

Marketers provide you, as a consumer, with product and service choices, as well as information about those choices, to ensure that your needs are being met. They balance the product or service offering with a price that makes you comfortable with your purchase, and after the sale, they provide reasonable guarantees and return policies. Marketing's responsibility also includes offering pleasant and convenient places for you to shop. In essence, marketers make your life easier, and in that way, they add value.

Marketing also offers a host of employment opportunities that require a variety of skills. On the creative side, positions such as artists, graphic designers, voice talent, animators, music composers, and writers represent just a few of the opportunities available to talented individuals. On the analytical side, marketing requires database analysts, market researchers, and inventory managers who can quickly digest information, cross-reference data, and spot trends that might make or break a company. In the business arena, marketing requires strategists, project/product managers, sales associates, and analysts who are capable of designing and implementing complex marketing strategies that positively affect the bottom line.

Marketing Enriches Society

Should marketing focus on factors other than financial profitability, like good corporate citizenry? Many of America's best known corporations seem to think so, because they encourage their employees to participate in activities that benefit their communities and invest heavily in socially responsible actions and charities. As Kellogg's CEO Carlos M. Gutierrez explains, Kellogg's has always had a strong commitment to the welfare of its many stakeholders—customers, employees, and the community at large.[22] The firm's commitment to civic responsibility, wherever it does business, is driven by its corporate mission statement, which promises

EXHIBIT	**1.10**	Ben & Jerry's Mission

■ **Product Mission**

To make, distribute and sell the finest quality all natural ice cream and euphoric concoctions with a continued commitment to incorporating wholesome, natural ingredients and promoting business practices that respect the Earth and the Environment.

■ **Economic Mission**

To operate the company on a sustainable financial basis of profitable growth, increasing value for our stockholders and expanding opportunities for development and career growth for our employees.

■ **Social Mission**

To operate the company in a way that actively recognizes the central role that business plays in society by initiating innovative ways to improve the quality of life locally, nationally and internationally.

"commitment to provide and maintain environmentally responsible practices for the communities in which we are located." These practices include recycling campaigns and water management systems in communities in Australia, Germany, India, Korea, and the United States. Thus, customers can feel better knowing that almost all Kellogg's cartons are made of 100 percent recycled fiber and that products with minor quality defects (such as too many yellow Froot Loops in a box) are donated to charitable organizations.

Similar sentiments are echoed by Colgate-Palmolive, which clearly states that "Our three fundamental values—Caring, Global Teamwork and Continuous Improvement—are part of everything we do."[23] Executives at Ben & Jerry's, the Vermont-based ice cream producer, actively embrace social responsibility by focusing their company around three key types of missions: product, economic, and social (see Exhibit 1.10).[24]

These firms, and hundreds more like them, recognize that including a strong social orientation in their business is a sound strategy that is in both their and their customers' best interest. It shows the consumer marketplace that the firm will be around for the long run and can be trusted with their business. In a volatile market, investors view firms that operate with high levels of corporate responsibility and ethics as safe investments. Similarly, firms have come to realize that good corporate citizenship through socially responsible actions should be a priority because it will help their bottom line in the long run.[25]

Marketing Can Be Entrepreneurial

Whereas marketing plays a major role in the success of large corporations, it also is at the center of the successes of numerous new ventures initiated by entrepreneurs, or people who organize, operate, and assume the risk of a business venture.[26] Key to the success of many such entrepreneurs is that they launch ventures that aim to satisfy unfilled needs. Some examples of successful ventures (and their founders) that understood their customers and added value include

■ Ben & Jerry's (Ben Cohen and Jerry Greenfield).

■ The Body Shop (Anita Roddick).

■ Bose Corporation (Ambar Bose).

■ Kinko's (Paul Orfalae).

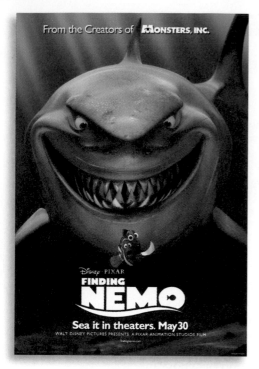

Entrepreneur Steve Jobs, founder of Apple Computer, also cofounded Pixar Studios along with Ed Catmull. Their computer-animated films, like Finding Nemo, *have won several Academy Awards.*

■ Apple Computers and Pixar Studios (Steve Jobs).

■ *The Oprah Winfrey Show* and other ventures (Oprah Winfrey).

Steve Jobs probably is best known for founding Apple Computers and helping usher in the age of personal computing, but though Apple continues its record of innovation with the phenomenally successful iPod and iTunes Music Store, it is not his only entrepreneurial success. Jobs is the cofounder, along with Ed Catmull, of Pixar Studios, an Academy Award–winning studio that has seen its five computer-animated films (*Toy Story, Toy Story 2, A Bug's Life, Monsters, Inc.,* and *Finding Nemo*) earn more than $2 billion worldwide.[27] Disney recently acquired Pixar for $7.4 billion,[28] and the joint Disney–Pixar release, *Cars,* promises to be another success.

Another extraordinary entrepreneur and marketer is Oprah Winfrey. A self-made billionaire before she turned 50, Oprah went from being the youngest person and first African-American woman to anchor news station WTVF-TV in Nashville, Tennessee, to being only the third woman in history to head her own production studio. Under the Oprah Winfrey banner, you can find Harpo Productions, Inc.; *O, The Oprah Magazine; O at Home* magazine; Harpo Films; and the Oxygen television network. In addition, Oprah's philanthropic contributions are vast and varied. Through the Oprah Winfrey Foundation, women around the world enjoy a champion supporting their rights to education and empowerment. Her humanitarian efforts in Africa have helped thousands of children get a better start in life, and her efforts in the United States resulted in President Bill Clinton signing into law the national "Oprah Bill" to establish a national database of convicted child abusers.[29]

Each of these distinguished entrepreneurs had a vision about how certain combinations of products and services could satisfy unfilled needs. Each understood the marketing opportunity (i.e., the unfilled need), conducted a thorough examination of the marketplace, and developed and communicated the value of their product and services to potential consumers.

When you think of Oprah Winfrey, think big: Harpo Productions, Inc.; O, The Oprah Magazine; O at Home *magazine; Harpo Films; the Oxygen television network, not to mention her philanthropic work with the Oprah Winfrey Foundation.*

Summing Up

1. What is the role of marketing in organizations?

In definition form, "Marketing is an organizational function and a set of processes for creating, communicating, and delivering value to customers and for managing customer relationships in ways that benefit the organization and its stakeholders." Marketing strives to *create value* in many ways. If marketers are to succeed, their customers must believe that the firm's products and services are valuable; that is, they are worth more to the customers than they cost.

Marketers also enhance the value of products and services through various forms of *communication*, such as advertising and personal selling. Through communications, marketers educate and inform customers about the benefits of their products and services and thereby increase their perceived value.

Marketers facilitate the *delivery of value* by making sure the right products and services are available when, where, and in the quantities their customers want. Better marketers are not concerned about just one transaction with their customers; they recognize the value of loyal customers and strive to develop *long-term relationships* with them.

2. How do marketers create value for a product or service?

Value represents the relationship of benefits to costs. Firms can improve their value by increasing benefits, reducing costs, or both. The best firms integrate a value orientation into everything they do. If a move doesn't increase benefits or reduce costs, it probably shouldn't occur. Marketers also have found that providing good value is one of the best ways to maintain a sustainable advantage over their competitors.

Firms become value driven by finding out as much as they can about their customers and those customers' needs and wants. They share this information with their partners, both up and down the supply chain, so the entire chain collectively can focus on the customer. The key to true value-based marketing is the ability to design products and services that achieve the right balance between benefits and costs—not too little, not too much.

Finally, value-based marketers aren't necessarily worried about how much money they will make on the next sale. Instead, they are concerned with developing a lasting relationship with their customers so those customers return again and again.

3. Why is marketing important both within and outside the firm?

The marketing function is important both within and outside the firm. Many brands and stores now appear in multiple countries, which complicates the challenge for marketers. Successful firms integrate marketing throughout their organizations so that marketing activities coordinate with other functional areas such as product design, production, logistics, and human resources.

Marketing also helps facilitate the smooth flow of goods through the supply chain, all the way from raw materials to the consumer. From a personal perspective, the marketing function facilitates your buying process, and knowledge of marketing will help you in virtually any career you may decide to pursue.

Marketing also can be important for society through its embrace of solid, ethical business practices. For instance, a firm clearly has "done the right thing" when it sponsors charitable events, but that effort also helps endear customers to the firm. Finally, marketing is a core cornerstone of entrepreneurialism. Not only have many great companies been founded by outstanding marketers, but an entrepreneurial spirit pervades the marketing decisions of firms of all sizes.

Key Terms

- B2C (business-to-consumers) 12
- B2B (business-to-business) 12
- C2C (consumer-to-consumer) 12
- customer relationship management (CRM) 20
- exchange 6
- goods 8
- ideas 8
- marketing 5
- marketing mix (four Ps) 7
- marketing plan 5
- price 10
- relational orientation 20
- services 8
- supply chain 22
- transactional orientation 19
- value 15

Marketing Applications

1. When apparel manufacturers develop their marketing strategies, do they concentrate on satisfying their customers' needs or wants? What about a utilities company or a cellular phone company?

2. Choose a product that you use every day. Describe its 4Ps.

3. Provide examples of three firms that are involved in both B2C and B2B marketing.

4. Pick a firm that you believe provides its customers with a good value. Justify your answer by explaining how the firm competes on value.

5. Assume you have been hired into the marketing department of a major consumer products manufacturer such as Colgate-Palmolive. You are having lunch with some new colleagues in other departments—finance, manufacturing, and logistics. They are arguing that the company could save millions of dollars if they just got rid of the marketing department. Develop an argument that would persuade them otherwise.

6. Why do marketers find it important to embrace societal needs and ethical business practices? Provide an example of a societal need or ethical business practice that a specific marketer is addressing.

Net Savvy

1. Whole Foods (www.wholefoods.com/) touts itself as the world's largest retailer of natural and organic foods. Visit its Web site and describe how it delivers value above and beyond that provided by traditional grocery retailers. Describe the ways in which the company communicates this value through its Web site.

2. Lands' End (www.landsend.com) has successfully built its market share by providing a great value to consumers. Visit its Web site and describe the ways in which it creates value for consumers and how it differs from a traditional apparel store. Although it is common for Lands' End to underprice its competition, consumers also can accrue nonmonetary benefits. Identify some of these.

Chapter Case Study

eBAY: CREATING VALUE IN THE MARKETPLACE[30]

With 180.6 million registered users and net revenues of $4.55 billion, eBay has become the most popular shopping site for goods and services for a diverse community of consumers and businesses.[31] Founder Pierre Omidyar attributes much of its success to its trust among that community of users.

Originally introduced to create an efficient forum for people to trade with one another, eBay pioneered online trading by developing a Web-based community of browsers, buyers, and sellers. Initially, eBay capitalized on increases in consumer-to-consumer (C2C) transactions through traditional channels such as classified advertisements, collectibles shows, garage sales, flea markets, and auction houses. But the company has grown beyond individual consumers with extra Beanie Babies to include merchants, small to medium-sized businesses, global corporations, and government agencies that sell office supplies, raw materials, and furniture in bulk. In addition to facilitating trading, eBay provides a place for socialization and discussion. Trading activities in individual categories often evolve into unique communities of buyers and sellers who maintain category-specific bulletin boards and chat rooms. To make trading easier, eBay also sponsors payment services, insurance, shipping, authentication, appraisal, vehicle inspection, and escrow services.

Online buyers typically enter the site through eBay's home page, which contains a listing of major product categories and featured items. (A sample page is presented in Exhibit C1.1.) Users can search for specific items by browsing within a category, and then they "click through" to a detailed description of a particular item. Users also can perform a keyword search for specific items, in response to which the site's search engine generates lists of relevant items with links to the detailed descriptions. Furthermore, users can search for a

EXHIBIT C1.1 eBay's Home Page

particular bidder or seller by name to review that person's listings and feedback history or for products by a specific region or other attributes.

A registered user who has found a desired item can enter a bid for the maximum amount he or she is willing to pay at that time. For those listings that offer the "Buy-It-Now" feature, the user may purchase the item by accepting the Buy-It-Now price established by the seller. In the event of competitive bids, the eBay service automatically increases bidding in increments from the current high bid up to the bidder's maximum price.

eBay views its market as comprised of both sellers and buyers and has developed services to satisfy both in a vibrant trading environment. Various dimensions distinguish the two; for example, sellers range from individuals selling a few personal items to large companies liquidating excess stock. However, both buyers and sellers can benefit from eBay's rating systems, which gather aggregated ratings from buyers after each transaction. The overall score then is available to browsers when they want to gather information about a seller.

To maintain a strong sense of community, trust, and safety, eBay has fostered an honest and open marketplace in which individual users are treated with respect. The site also commits to several trust and safety initiatives designed to bolster its reputation as a safe place to trade, such as user verification, a requirement that new sellers have a credit card on file, insurance, vehicle inspections, escrow, authentication, and appraisal, as well as a well-articulated privacy statement. As a founding member of the Online Privacy Association, it also has built a reputation for leading the way to protect consumer privacy on the Internet.

Questions

1. According to the breakdown presented in Exhibit 1.5, which of the four orientations best describes eBay? Justify your answer.

2. Does eBay create greater value for buyers of collectables, beyond that provided by traditional channels? For sellers? Explain your answers in terms of greater benefits, reduced costs, or a combination.

3. Visit the eBay Web site to explore some of its features. How well does eBay facilitate the exchanges of goods? Does it have the same potential for exchanges that involve services? Explain your answer.

2

QUESTIONS

- How does a firm set up a marketing plan?

- How are SWOT analyses used to analyze the marketing situation?

- How does a firm choose what group(s) of people to pursue with its marketing efforts?

- How does the implementation of the marketing mix increase customer value?

- How can firms grow their businesses?

Developing Marketing Strategies

Disney: Daringly Digital

M anagers at Disney noticed that attendance at their theme parks was declining.[1] Visitors cited long lines and high ticket prices as the major deterrents to visiting the theme park. Disney thus was challenged to adjust its strategy to create a better in-park experience and deliver more value for the $63-a-day ticket price.

Their answer: A strategy heavy on technology that makes the park experience more personal and relevant to each visitor. To reinvent the customer experience, influence visitor behavior, and ease crowding throughout the parks, it combined global positioning satellites, smart sensors, wireless technology, and mobile devices.

Consider Pal Mickey. The 10.5-inch doll, available for rent or purchase, is equipped

Disney is investing in technologies like Pal Mickey to provide a better in-park experience and deliver more value to its customers.

with a central processing unit, an internal clock, small speakers, and an infrared sensor. As patrons move through the park, the sensor acquires wireless data uploads from beacons concealed in lampposts, rooftops, and bushes. When the doll receives information, it giggles and vibrates, which means "It's time to tell a secret" about shorter lines for rides in the area, the time of the upcoming parade, or trivia about the area in which the patron is walking. Pal Mickey also contains 700 prerecorded messages to keep kids entertained with jokes and games while they wait in line. And Pal Mickey speaks Spanish too!

The concept of working with data to create a more individual experience has migrated to other applications as well. For example, Disney plans to send text messages about dinner reservations, fireworks displays, and tee times via a visitor's cell phone or PDA. If a visitor spends a long time in the Dinosaur Exhibit at Animal Kingdom and purchases dinosaur merchandise, Disney figures that he or she might like to receive a special e-mail notification about an upcoming DVD release about dinosaurs. With Disney's digital-imaging services, park visitors can even view pictures taken throughout the day on their hotel television sets and purchase them with the touch of a button.

■ ■ ■

The Strategic Marketing Planning Process

Effective marketing doesn't just happen. Firms like Disney carefully plan their marketing strategies to react to changes in the environment, the competition, and their customers. The **strategic marketing planning process** (see Exhibit 2.1) represents a set of steps a marketer goes through to develop a strategic marketing plan.[2] A **marketing plan** is a written document composed of an analysis of the current marketing situation, opportunities and threats for the firm, marketing objectives and strategy specified in terms of the 4 Ps, action programs, and projected or pro-forma income (and other financial) statements.[3] The three major phases of the strategic planning process are planning, implemenation, and control.

In Step 1 of the **planning phase**, marketing executives, in conjunction with other top managers, define the mission and/or vision of the business. For the second step, they evaluate the situation by assessing how various players, both in and outside the organization, affect the firm's potential for success (Step 2). In the **implementation phase**, marketing managers identify and evaluate different opportunities by engaging in a process known as segmentation, targeting, and positioning (STP) (Step 3). They then are responsible for implementing the marketing mix using the four Ps (Step 4). Finally, the **control phase** is for evaluating the performance of the marketing strategy and taking any necessary corrective actions (Step 5).

As indicated in Exhibit 2.1, it is not always necessary to go through the entire process for every evaluation (Step 5). For instance, a firm could evaluate its performance in Step 5, then go directly to Step 2 to conduct a situation audit without redefining its overall mission.

In the first part of this chapter, we will discuss each of the steps involved in the strategic marketing planning process. Then we will consider ways of analyzing a

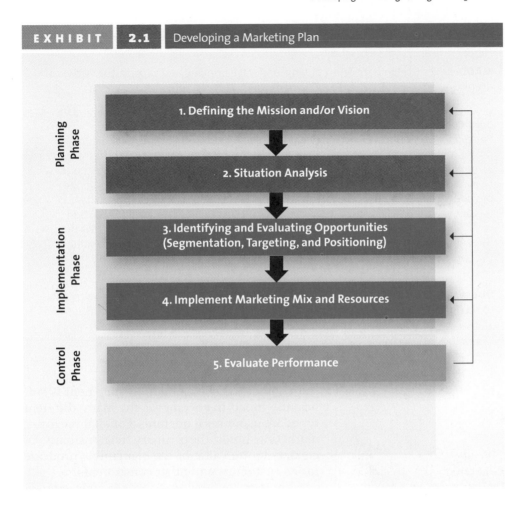

EXHIBIT | 2.1 | Developing a Marketing Plan

Planning Phase

1. Defining the Mission and/or Vision

2. Situation Analysis

Implementation Phase

3. Identifying and Evaluating Opportunities (Segmentation, Targeting, and Positioning)

4. Implement Marketing Mix and Resources

Control Phase

5. Evaluate Performance

marketing situation, as well as identifying and evaluating marketing opportunities. We also will examine some specific strategies marketers use to grow a business. Finally, we consider how the implementation of the marketing mix increases customer value.

Step 1: Define the Business Mission

The **mission statement,** a broad description of a firm's objectives and the scope of activities it plans to undertake,[4] attempts to answer two main questions: What type of business are we? What do we need to do to accomplish our goals and objectives? These fundamental business issues must be answered at the highest corporate levels before marketing executives can get involved. Most firms want to maximize stockholders' wealth by increasing the value of the firms' stock and paying dividends.[5] However, owners of small, privately held firms frequently have other objectives, such as achieving a specific level of income and avoiding risks. (See Exhibit 2.2 for several mission statement examples.)

Nonprofit organizations, such as Mothers Against Drunk Driving (MADD) have nonmonetary objectives like eliminating drunk driving and underage drinking. Coca-Cola's mission statement recognizes that it must bring value to all the parties with which it interacts—customers, suppliers, employees, and

EXHIBIT	2.2	Mission Statements

MADD strives to eliminate drunk driving, underage drinking and support the victims of drunk driving.

Coca-Cola states its mission this way:
The Coca-Cola Company exists to benefit and refresh everyone it touches. The basic proposition of our business is simple, solid and timeless. When we bring refreshment, value, joy and fun to our stakeholders, then we successfully nurture and protect our brands, particularly Coca-Cola. That is the key to fulfilling our ultimate obligation to provide consistently attractive returns to the owners of our business. Thus, in its mission statement, Coca-Cola recognizes that it must bring value to all the parties with which it interacts—customers, suppliers, employees, and shareholders. Within this framework, marketing holds the primary responsibility of enhancing the value of the company's products for its customers.

Disney, with its many business units, broadly describes its mission as its commitment to producing creative entertainment experiences based on story telling.

[6]*Sources:* "About Us" www.MADD.org; http://www2.coca-cola.com/ourcompany/ourpromise.html; and "Company Overview" www.corporate.disney.go.com.

If 17,000 people died tomorrow, would you notice?

Of course you would. There would be 24-hour news coverage. Dramatic headlines. And a devastating effect on our country forever. But last year, drinking and driving did kill about 17,000 people. It injured half a million more. But because it happened over a year rather than in a single day, most of us hardly noticed. It's a growing problem, with a simple answer. If you drink, find a safe way home. And help remove the marks that drunk driving leaves on our country.

Activism : Victim Services : Education
www.madd.org

Pin placements do not represent actual crash sites.

What is the mission for a non-profit organization like Mothers Against Drunk Driving (MADD)?

shareholders. Disney's mission statement is sufficiently broad to encompass the many different types of businesses it operates. For all three firms, marketing holds the primary responsibility of enhancing the value of the company's products for its customers and other constituents.

Another key goal or objective often embedded in a mission statement is building a **sustainable competitive advantage,** namely, something the firm can persistently do better than its competitors. Although any business activity that a firm engages in can be the basis for a competitive advantage, some advantages are sustainable over a longer period of time, whereas others, like low prices, can be duplicated by competitors almost immediately.[7] For example, since artificial sweetener Splenda entered the market in 2000 it has grown to $187 million in sales, surpassing Equal and Sweet'N Low combined. Equal and Sweet'N Low could cut their prices to steal market share back from Splenda, but it would be hard for them to obtain a long-term advantage by doing so because Splenda could easily match any price reduction. Splenda has successfully attracted consumers because it has positioned itself as a healthy alternative to sugar that can be used for baking and not just a substitute for sugar. However, if it were easy for Sweet'N Low and Equal to copy Splenda's successful formula and marketing, they would do so. Attributes like formula and image thus can provide firms with a long-term (i.e., sustainable) competitive advantage.

A competitive advantage acts like a wall that the firm has built around its position in a market. This wall makes it hard for outside competitors to contact customers inside—otherwise known as the marketer's target market. Of course, if the marketer has built a wall around an attractive market, competitors will attempt to break down the wall. Over time, advantages will erode because of these competitive forces, but by building high, thick walls, marketers can sustain their advantage, minimize competitive pressure, and boost profits for a longer time. Thus, establishing a sustainable competitive advantage is key to long-term financial performance.

Splenda has been successful because it is perceived as a healthy and sugar-free alternative to sugar and can be used for baking, unlike Equal and Sweet 'N Low.

Step 2: Conduct a Situation Analysis Using SWOT

After developing its mission, a firm next must perform a **situation analysis,** using a SWOT analysis that assesses both the internal environment with regard to its **S**trengths and **W**eaknesses and the external environment in terms of its **O**pportunities and **T**hreats.

Let's look at how a corporation like The Walt Disney Company (Disney) might conduct the SWOT analysis pictured in Exhibit 2.3. The strengths (Exhibit 2.3, upper left) are positive and internal attributes of the firm. In addition to Disney being known as one of the world's best known brands, another strength is its many diverse businesses. They operate in four very distinct businesses: media networks, studio entertainment, parks and resorts, and consumer products. These diverse businesses provide opportunities for growth and reduce the firm's overall risk. Its cable stations appeal to a broad range of interests and age groups with channels such as ABC, Lifetime Television, A&E, Toon Disney, SoapNet, and ESPN. Disney owns and operates Disneyland in California, Walt Disney World Resort, and Disney Cruise Line, both in Florida, while earning royalties from Tokyo Disneyland Resort. It also has a 41 percent equity stake in Euro Disney. Under the names of Walt Disney Pictures, Touchstone, Miramax, and Dimension, Disney produces and distributes movies worldwide. Its consumer products segment licenses the Walt Disney name and uses Disney Stores and catalogs in direct retail distribution.

EXHIBIT 2.3	SWOT Analysis for Disney	
Environment	**Evaluation**	
	Positive	**Negative**
Internal	**Strengths** ■ Diverse businesses ■ Well-known brand	**Weaknesses** ■ Over-reliance on relationships ■ Seasonal fluctuations ■ Risky foreign operations
External	**Opportunities** ■ Building the current brand and businesses both in the U.S. and abroad	**Threats** ■ Increasing competitive pressures

Home release of some Disney videos such as Pirates of the Caribbean *and* Finding Nemo *are demonstrating consistently strong sales.*

The opportunities (Exhibit 2.3, lower left) are positive aspects of the external environment. Like Disney's strengths, it has many opportunities, not the least of which is its ability to build its current brand and businesses both in the U.S. and globally. For instance, release of some videos such as *Pirates of the Caribbean* and *Finding Nemo* are demonstrating consistently strong sales. The acquisition of Pixar Animation Studios is expected to restrengthen its position as the leader in animated films. As this book went to press, ABC had three of the strongest series on television and ESPN was proving to be one of Disney's strongest media assets. Walt Disney World Resort is seeing record numbers of visitors during the holidays, and Disney Princess Cruise Lines is also posting record numbers. The Disney name is a recognized brand, and when people see it on any of its products they know they will be entertained.

Every firm has its weaknesses, and Disney is no different. The weaknesses (Exhibit 2.3, upper right) are negative attributes of the firm. For instance, it relies heavily on its relationships with cable operators to expand its distribution. Without them, their continued growth would be in jeopardy. Also, the natural seasonal fluctuations inherent in the tourism industry affect its theme park and resort operations. The linked nature of Disney's businesses can have a domino effect. If a movie is not successful, then its merchandise will not sell either. Finally, foreign operations are fraught with risk. Euro Disney, for instance, was not successful when it first opened.

Threats (Exhibit 2.3, lower right) are negative aspects of the external environment. For Disney, stiff competition in all markets can have a negative impact on their businesses.

Step 3: Identifying and Evaluating Opportunities Using STP (Segmentation, Targeting, and Positioning)

After completing the situation audit, the next step is to identify and evaluate opportunities for increasing sales and profits using STP (segmentation, targeting, and positioning). With STP, the firm first divides the marketplace into subgroups or segments, determines which of those segments it should pursue or target, and finally decides how it should position its products and services to best meet the needs of those chosen targets.

Segmentation   Many types of customers appear in any market, and most firms cannot satisfy everyone's needs. For instance, among Internet users, some do research online, some shop, some look for entertainment, and many may do all three. Each of these groups might be a market segment consisting of consumers who respond similarly to a firm's marketing efforts. The process of dividing the market into groups of customers with different needs, wants, or characteristics—who therefore might appreciate products or services geared especially for them—is called market segmentation. For example, as illustrated in Exhibit 2.4, Disney targets its Pleasure Island to singles and couples, Epcot to families with older children and adults, and the Magic Kingdom to families with younger children. Firms identify segments in various ways. For instance, Disney may use demographics like gender, age, and income to identify the young families it is pursuing for the Magic Kingdom; but use psychological or behavioral factors, like those who like to party or go dancing, to identify the singles and couples it is pursuing for Pleasure Island.

EXHIBIT **2.4** Segmentation, Targeting, and Positioning

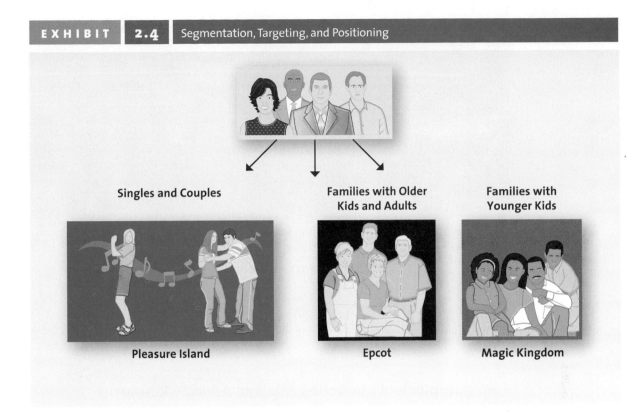

Singles and Couples

Families with Older
Kids and Adults

Families with
Younger Kids

Pleasure Island

Epcot

Magic Kingdom

Targeting   After a firm has identified the various market segments it might pursue, it evaluates each segment's attractiveness and decides which to pursue using a process known as **target marketing** or **targeting.** From our previous example, Disney realizes that its primary appeal for the Magic Kingdom is to young families, so the bulk of its marketing efforts for this business is directed toward that group. Soft drink manufacturers have divided the market into many submarkets or segments. Coca-Cola, for instance, makes several different types of Coke, including regular, Coke II, Cherry Coke, Diet Coke, and caffeine free—and then it adds in various combinations of these types. It also markets Sprite for those who don't like dark colas, Fruitopia and Minute Maid for more health-conscious consumers, and Dasani bottled water for purists.

Positioning   Finally, when the firm decides which segments to pursue, it must determine how it wants to be positioned within those segments. **Market positioning** involves the process of defining the marketing mix variables so that target customers have a clear, distinctive, desirable understanding of what the product does or represents in comparison with competing products. Disney, for instance, defines itself as an entertainer. Its Florida Walt Disney World Resort owns and operates four theme parks, golf courses, 17 hotels and resorts, water parks, a sports complex, and a retail and dining complex.

After identifying its target segments, a firm must evaluate each of its strategic opportunities. Firms typically are most successful when they focus on those opportunities that build on their strengths relative to those of their competition. In Step 4 of the strategic marketing planning process, the firm implements its marketing mix and allocates resources to different products and services.

Coca-Cola targets several markets with many different products.

Step 4: Implement Marketing Mix and Allocate Resources

When the firm has identified and evaluated different growth opportunities by performing an STP analysis, the real action begins. It has decided what to do, how to do it, and how many resources should be allocated to it. In the fourth step of the planning process, marketers implement the actual marketing mix—product, price, promotion, and place—for each product and service on the basis of what they believe their target markets will value (Exhibit 2.5). At the same time, they make important decisions about how they will allocate their scarce resources to their various products and services.

Product and Value Creation   Products, which include services, constitute the first of the four Ps. Because the key to the success of any marketing program is the creation of value, firms attempt to develop products and services that customers perceive as valuable enough to buy. Sirius, for instance, understood that the radio marketplace was full of opportunities. Sirius is one of two existing satellite radio companies. Satellite radio is a service that customers pay for through a subscription plan. Customers can choose the radio that suits their needs best. They can choose table top, car, or portable units. These radios display the singer and song title on the screen. Sirius also offers a *sportster* unit, which allows the user to choose the type of sport updates they would like to see scroll live across the screen.

Sirius and satellite radio have over 120 stations of music and talk radio stations with a deep music catalog. Unlike terrestrial radio, Sirius can offer shows such as *The Bob Dylan Hour* that would normally have too small an audience to support it. Sirius radio has added value to generic radio through a pay service, specialized receivers, and a broad range of stations that allow Sirius consumers to customize their own radio.

Price and Value Capture   Recall that the second element of the marketing mix is price. As part of the exchange process, a firm provides a product or a service,

EXHIBIT   **2.5**   Developing the Marketing Mix

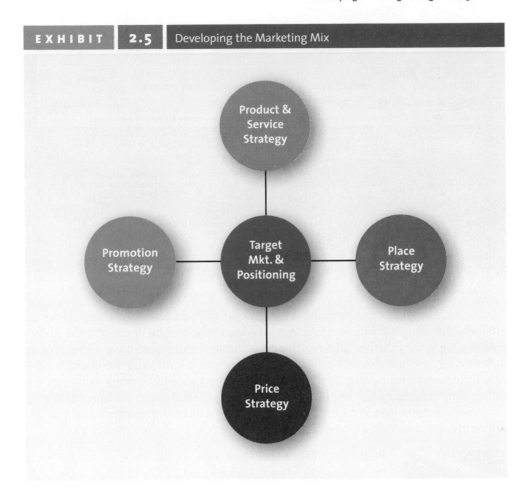

or some combination thereof, and in return, it gets money. Value-based marketing requires that firms charge a price that customers perceive as giving them a good value for the product they receive. Firms practice three types of pricing strategies. The first pricing strategy, **cost-based pricing,** is when a firm determines the costs of producing or providing its product and then adds a fixed amount above that total to arrive at the selling price. For example, a bookstore might purchase a book at the publisher's wholesale price and then mark it up a standard 35 percent. The second type, the **competitor-based pricing** strategy, is when a firm prices below, at, or above its competitors' offerings. For example, the same bookstore might decide to take the top 10 books on *The New York Times* bestseller list and price them $2 less than its primary competitors' prices.

Although relatively simple to implement, neither of these methods alone ensures that customers will perceive they are getting a good value for the products or services. That perception requires the third approach, termed **value-based pricing,** in which the firm first determines the perceived value of the product from the customer's point of view and then prices accordingly. For example, the bookstore might determine from its prior experience that students have various attitudes toward textbooks and their prices: Some students want a new book, whereas others accept a used one for a lesser price. Giving them a choice of both options provides value to both groups.

Sirius created value for a product and a market that didn't previously exist.

However, value-based pricing remains one of the least understood areas of business decision making, even though it is one of the few business activities with a direct impact on profits. Clearly, it is important for a firm to have a clear focus in terms of what products to sell, where to buy them, and what methods to use in selling them. But pricing is the only activity that actually brings in money by influencing revenues. If a price is set too high, it will not generate much volume. If a price is set too low, it may result in lower-than-necessary margins and profits. Therefore, price should be based on the value that the customer perceives.

Using a kiosk at a Staples store, customers connect and order from staples.com.

Place and Value Delivery   For the third P, place, the firm must be able, after it has created value through a product and/or service, to make the product or service readily accessible when and where the customer wants it. Consider how Staples has integrated its stores with its Internet operations. Staples' overall goal has been to become the leading office product and service provider by combining its existing experience, extensive distribution infrastructure, and customer service expertise with Web-based information technology. In learning that its sales increased when customers used more than one channel of distribution (store and Internet), Staples turned the integration of its different channels into a seamless customer experience, a key value driver for the company.[8] A consumer now can connect and order from staples.com either from home or via a kiosk in the store. Therefore, even if a particular item is not readily available in the store, Staples is less likely to lose the customer's business. At the same time, the alternative channels have enabled Staples to discontinue slow-moving or expensive items from its in-store inventory, which reduces its costs. Instead, the company keeps some inventory of those slow-moving items at central warehouses and ships them directly to the customer. In this way, it has effectively integrated its stores with its Internet operation and used place to create value in its delivery process.

Promotion and Value Communication The fourth and last P of the marketing mix is promotion. Marketers communicate the value of their offering, or the value proposition, to their customers through a variety of media including television, radio, magazines, the sales force, and the Internet, the last boon for specialty retailers across the globe. It is now possible for firms in out-of-the-way locations to expand their market area to the whole world. Need earplugs? Go to http://store. yahoo.com/earplugstore/ or stop by the Earplug Store in Hulbert, Oklahoma, to find every type of earplug you could imagine—and then some. Want a new watchband? Contact http://www.stores.ebay.com/rustwatch in New York City, and it will ship one out to you. These retailers and thousands like them have added value to their offerings through their efficient and effective communications strategies.

Marketers therefore must consider which are the most efficient and effective methods to communicate with their customers, which goes back to understanding customers, the value created, and the message being communicated. Recently, e-mail has become more valuable to marketers since the federal "Do Not Call" registry limited the potential impact of telemarketing. Cox Communications, for example, developed a campaign to sign up new customers for its cable and Internet service in which it advertised a sweepstakes to give away a 50-inch television, which drew people to its Web site. Once there, visitors found a link to a $20 money-back offer if they would sign up for Cox's service. The highly successful campaign also was much less expensive than a similar mailed promotional campaign would have been.[9]

As cases like Cox's show, marketers must balance the effectiveness of their value communication activities with their costs. For example, Google offers a service called AdWord Select that charges advertisers on the basis of the number of actual clicks on their advertisements, not when, where, or how often it was placed, which is a more common strategy among traditional media outlets.[10]

Allocating Resources The second part of Step 4 involves allocating resources, for which marketers have several tools. In portfolio analysis, for example, management evaluates the firm's various products and businesses—its "portfolio"— and allocates resources according to which products are expected to be the most profitable for the firm in the future. A popular tool for portfolio analysis was developed by the Boston Consulting Group and is described in this chapter's appendix. Portfolio analysis is typically performed at the strategic business unit (SBU) or product line level of the firm, though managers also can use it to analyze brands or even individual items. An SBU is a division of the firm itself that can be managed and operated somewhat independently from other divisions and may have a different mission or objectives. For example, within DaimlerChrysler the Mercedes Car Group consists of Mercedes-Benz, Maybach, and Smart, and the Chrysler Group consists of Chrysler, Dodge, and Jeep.[11] Each of these brands is an SBU. A product line, in contrast, is a group of products that consumers may use together or perceive as similar in some way. There are several product lines within the Mercedes-Benz SBU: sedans, coupes, convertibles, roadsters, wagons, SUVs, and high performance vehicles.

Within Daimler-Chrysler there is the Mercedes Car Group consisting of three SBUs: Mercedes-Benz, Maybach, and smart, and the Chrysler Group, also with three SBUs: Chrysler, Dodge, and Jeep.

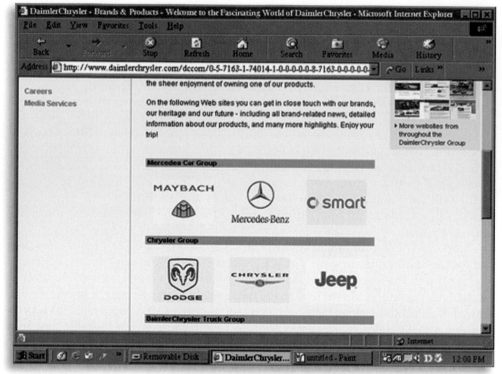

Step 5: Evaluate Performance and Make Adjustments

The final step in the planning process includes evaluating the results of the strategy and implementation program. The firm must determine why it achieved or did not achieve its performance goals. Was the success or failure due to factors that were within the firm's control? For instance, did it spend too much to buy its parts or ingredients? Were the results due to economic or competitive factors such as a new product in the marketplace? Understanding the causes of the performance, regardless of whether that performance exceeded, met, or fell below the firm's goals, enables firms to make appropriate adjustments.

Typically, managers begin by reviewing the implementation programs, and their analysis may indicate that the strategy (or even the mission statement) needs to be reconsidered. Problems can arise both when firms successfully implement poor strategies and when they poorly implement good strategies.

To evaluate a brand, a manager could measure brand awareness (i.e., how aware customers are of the brand name), the number of people who bought the product, or what the repeat purchase rate is. To evaluate the performance of a specific item, the manager would consider sales, profitability, and turnover.[12]

As an illustration of how a firm evaluates its performance and makes appropriate adjustments, consider the case of a beverage company. The firm, in conjunction with a leading marketing research provider, IRI, sought to determine why one of its beverages was not performing as well as expected. Using sophisticated Web graphics that examine sales data by product and geography, managers were able to pinpoint the root causes of the problem: competition from other beverage companies and underperforming displays. They also found that the largest sales declines occurred in the west and south. Armed with this new information, the company made appropriate adjustments by establishing an immediate turnaround plan with the particular regional marketing managers that improved the features supporting the product and redesigned its displays. Sales improved significantly within two weeks.

Strategic Planning Is Not Sequential

The planning process in Exhibit 2.1 suggests that managers follow a set sequence when they make strategic decisions. Namely, after they've defined the business mission, they perform the situation audit, identify strategic opportunities, evaluate alternatives, set objectives, allocate resources, develop the implementation plan, and, finally, evaluate their performance and make adjustments. But actual planning processes can move back and forth among these steps. For example, a situation audit may uncover a logical alternative, even though this alternative might not be included in the mission statement, which would mean that the mission statement would need to be revised. The development of the implementation plan also might reveal that insufficient resources have been allocated to a particular product for it to achieve its objective. In that case, the firm would need to either change the objective or increase the resources; alternatively, the marketer might consider not investing in the product at all.

Now that we have gone through the steps of the strategic marketing planning process, let's look at some strategies that have been responsible for making many marketing firms successful.

Growth Strategies

Firms consider pursuing various market segments as part of their overall growth strategies, which may include the four major strategies shown in Exhibit 2.6.[13] The rows distinguish those opportunities a firm possesses in its current markets from those it has in new markets, whereas the columns distinguish between the firm's current marketing offering and that of a new opportunity. Let's consider each of them in detail.

Market Penetration

A **market penetration strategy** employs the existing marketing mix and focuses the firm's efforts on existing customers. Such a growth strategy might be achieved by attracting new consumers to the firm's current target market or encouraging current customers to patronize the firm more often or buy more merchandise on each visit.

EXHIBIT 2.6	Market/Product and Services Strategies	
Markets	**Products and Services**	
	Current	**New**
Current	Market Penetration	Product Development
New	Market Development	Diversification

A market penetration strategy generally requires greater marketing efforts, such as increased advertising, additional sales and promotions, or intensified distribution efforts in geographic areas in which the product or service already is sold.

For example, to persuade existing customers to buy more merchandise, the Home Shopping Network (HSN) has redesigned its Web site HSN.com to interact better with its television network.[14] The Web interface provides live television broadcasts and reinforces the benefits of multichannel shopping by offering new promotions. HSN has also implemented a sales promotion in which its 1,500 telephone representatives offer additional merchandise when callers placed an order. After refining the program to ensure the most relevant items were offered and to provide better monetary incentives to the sales force, HSN has significantly increased its revenue.[15]

Market Development and the Case for Global Expansion

A **market development strategy** employs the existing marketing offering to reach new market segments, whether domestic or international. International expansion generally is riskier than domestic expansion because firms must deal with differences in government regulations, cultural traditions, supply chain considerations, and language. However, many U.S. firms enjoy a competitive advantage in global markets—such as Mexico, Latin America, Europe, China, and Japan—because, especially among young people, American culture is widely emulated for consumer products.

For example, due to rising prosperity worldwide and rapidly increasing access to cable television that offers U.S. programming, fashion trends from the United States have spread to young people in emerging countries. The global MTV generation prefers soft drinks to tea, athletic shoes to sandals, French fries to rice, and credit cards to cash.

McDonald's is practicing a market development strategy by opening restaurants in China, like this one in Beijing.

In the past few years, China's major cities have sprouted plenty of American stores and restaurants, including KFC, Pizza Hut, and McDonald's. Before Starbucks came to town, coffee simply was not the drink of choice in China, but Shanghai and Beijing each have more than two dozen Starbucks currently, and Chinese urban dwellers go there to impress friends or because it symbolizes a new kind of lifestyle. Although Western products and stores have generally gained a reputation for high quality and good service, in some ways, it is more the specifically American culture that Chinese consumers want.[16]

Product Development

The third growth strategy option, a **product development strategy,** offers a new product or service to a firm's current target market. Consider Time Inc., the world's leading magazine publisher of more than 130 magazines. To stay in the forefront, Time must continually reevaluate its readers and their needs; therefore, its market development strategy consists of carefully defining its target markets and expanding its offerings to meet their needs. Time's women's magazines (e.g.,

People, In Style, Real Simple, Parenting, Health) collectively reach more than 45 million women in the United States. To develop this market further, the publisher recently added *All You* to target value-conscious American women specifically.[17]

The pursuit of market penetration and product development strategies is not always simple. Ethical Dilemma 2.1 examines how Microsoft has had to come to grips with numerous ethical issues and has faced legal challenges in its strategies.

Diversification

A **diversification strategy,** the last of the growth strategies from Exhibit 2.6, introduces a new product or service to a market segment that currently is not served. Diversification opportunities may be either related or unrelated. In a related diversification opportunity, the current target market

Time Inc. pursues a product development strategy by carefully segmenting the women's magazine market based on needs and producing different magazines to reach each segment.

and/or marketing mix shares something in common with the new opportunity. In other words, the firm might be able to purchase from existing vendors, use the same distribution and/or management information system, or advertise in the

---

| Ethical Dilemma **2.1** | | Microsoft's Market Penetration and Product Development Strategies |

Microsoft (MS) has faced litigation in both the United States and the European Union for pursuing marketing strategies that the respective governments believe violate their antitrust laws.[18] The central question in these cases is, when is a firm too big and too powerful? Antitrust laws, intended to preserve and promote competition, attempt to prevent a monopolist firm from dominating a particular market. Did Microsoft's size and power in the marketplace create an unfair advantage over smaller providers?

When it had achieved a high penetration of the market by entering into contracts with PC manufacturers like IBM to load its DOS operating system onto PCs, MS turned its attention to developing new products and including additional software with its operating system, Windows. However, when it added Internet Explorer and Media Player to the Windows operating system, competitors complained to antitrust authorities that they could no longer sell their products competitively because consumers received the MS versions "for free" when they bought Windows, and consumers had little choice but to buy Windows.

Microsoft defended itself first in the United States and then in the European Union. In the United States, it narrowly avoided a court order to split the company in half. In the eventual settlement, Microsoft agreed to stop certain practices but was allowed to continue including Internet Explorer with Windows.

Things went differently for MS in the European Union. The EU Court ordered MS to pay the largest antitrust fine in its history (more than $600 million) and sell a version of Windows that did not include Media Player. In addition, MS had designed Windows to work better with MS servers than with other brands. The European Union challenged this tactic as well and ordered MS to release its Windows server communications protocols so any server could be made to work well with Windows. Both these orders are currently under appeal before the European Court of Justice.

Entrepreneurial Marketing **2.1**

FedEx Acquires Kinko's: Diversification or What?

When you've conquered express shipping and supply chain services, where do you look to increase earnings, cash flow, and returns?[19] For FedEx, the answer lay in diversification. In 1970, Paul Orfalea started the first Kinko's close to the University of California at Santa Barbara to provide appropriate products and services to college students at a reasonable price. From this single location in 1970, Kinko's had grown to more than 1,100 locations worldwide when FedEx recently acquired it.[20]

The benefits to both firms are significant. FedEx's global expertise and strong financial position can help Kinko's expand globally. Likewise, by using Kinko's as a storefront, FedEx can tap into a broader mix of small-, medium-, and large-scale businesses that use Kinko's printing and other services at its physical locations.

This acquisition looks at first like a simple case of diversification: new service/new market. But couldn't it also be perceived as market penetration: current service/current market? FedEx will earn more business among its current customers who like the lower cost and convenience of taking their packages to Kinko's. Likewise, current Kinko's customers might use Kinko's other services more often when they visit the store to send a FedEx package.

Furthermore, this growth strategy also could be interpreted as product development: new service/current market. After all, the current customers of both Kinko's and FedEx will have greater exposure to some

Paul Orfalea founded Kinko's in 1970.

new service. But what about market penetration: current service/new market? By combining, both Kinko's and FedEx will reach new markets—namely, the other firm's current customer base. So, depending on how we define both the market and the service, FedEx's acquisition of Kinko's might be interpreted as any of the four growth strategies that have been described.

same newspapers to target markets that are similar to their current consumers. In contrast, in an unrelated diversification, the new business lacks any common elements with the present business. Entrepreneurial Marketing 2.1 describes FedEx's acquisition of Kinko's, which may appear at first to be an unrelated diversification strategy. But is it?

Macro Strategies

Growth strategies are not the only way a firm might improve its business. For example, macro, or overarching, strategies focus on elements of excellence to create and deliver value and to develop sustainable competitive advantages. As we depict in Exhibit 2.7 , many marketing firms have turned to three such strategies to give them a sustainable long-term advantage over their competition:[21]

■ **Customer excellence,** which focuses on retaining loyal customers and excellent customer service.

■ **Operational excellence** through efficient operations and excellent supply chain management.

■ **Product excellence,** or achieving high-quality products; effective branding and positioning are key.

Customer Excellence

Customer excellence is achieved when a firm develops value-based strategies for retaining loyal customers and provides outstanding customer service.

Retaining Loyal Customers   Customer loyalty means that customers are committed to buying from a particular firm. Sometimes, the methods a firm uses to maintain a sustainable competitive advantage help attract and maintain loyal customers. For instance, having a strong brand, unique merchandise, and superior customer service all help solidify a loyal customer base. But in addition, having loyal customers is, in and of itself, an important method of sustaining an advantage over competitors. Loyalty is more than simply preferring to purchase from one firm instead of another;[22] it means that customers are reluctant to patronize competitive firms. For example, loyal customers continue to buy Nike running shoes even if Reebok shoes are available at more convenient locations or provide a slightly superior assortment or slightly lower prices.

More and more firms realize the value of achieving customer excellence through focusing their strategy on retaining their loyal customers. For instance, a good dry cleaners doesn't think in terms of washing and pressing a single shirt for $2. Instead, it is concerned with satisfying the customer who spends $25 per week, 50 weeks a year, for 10 years or more. This customer isn't a $2 customer; he's a $12,500 customer. Viewing customers with a life-time value perspective, rather than on a transaction-by-transaction basis, is key to modern customer retention programs.[23]

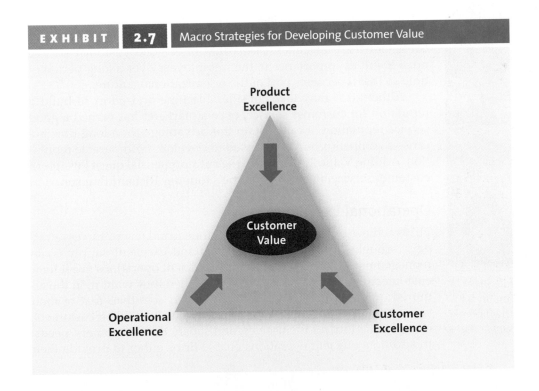

EXHIBIT 2.7 Macro Strategies for Developing Customer Value

Product Excellence

Customer Value

Operational Excellence

Customer Excellence

The world's largest independent credit card issuer, MBNA, recognizes the significant value of serving and retaining loyal customers.[24] According to the company's estimates, a 5 percent decrease in defection rates—that is, decreasing the number of customers who move to another bank—increases its average customer value by more than 125 percent. In turn, MBNA believes that by decreasing its defection rate by 10 percent, it could double the average amount of time customers remain with the company and increase its profits sixteenfold. In general, experts suggest that companies can boost profits by almost 100 percent if they can retain an additional 5 percent of their customers.[25]

Marketers use several methods to build customer loyalty. One such way involves developing a clear and precise positioning strategy. For instance, loyal Coke drinkers have such a strong attachment to the product that they would rather go without than drink Pepsi.

Another method of achieving customer loyalty creates an emotional attachment through loyalty programs.[26] Loyalty programs, which constitute part of an overall customer relationship management (CRM) program as we described in Chapter 1, prevail in many industries from airlines to hotels to movies theatres to retail stores. With such programs, firms can identify members through the loyalty card or membership information the consumer provides when he or she makes a purchase. Using that purchase information, analysts determine which types of merchandise certain groups of customers are buying and thereby can tailor their offering to better meet the needs of their loyal customers. For instance, by analyzing their databases, financial institutions such as Bank of Montreal develop profiles of customers who have defected in the past and use that information to identify customers who may defect in the future. Once it identifies these customers, the firm can implement special retention programs to keep them.

Some firms develop a sustainable competitive advantage through operational excellence with efficient operations and excellent supply chain management.

Customer Service Marketers also may build sustainable competitive advantage by offering excellent customer service,[27] though consistently offering excellent service can prove difficult. Customer service is provided by employees, and invariably, humans are less consistent than machines. Firms that offer good customer service must instill its importance in their employees over a long period of time so that it becomes part of the organizational culture.

Although it may take considerable time and effort to build a reputaton for customer service, once a marketer has earned a good service reputation, it can sustain this advantage for a long time because a competitor is hard pressed to develop a comparable reputation. Adding Value 2.1 describes the entrepreneurial quest for superb customer service by Virgin Atlantic's founder Richard Branson.

Operational Excellence

Firms achieve operational excellence, the second macro success strategy, through their efficient operations and excellent supply chain management. All marketers strive for efficient operations to get their customers the merchandise they want, when they want it, in the required quantities, and at a lower delivered cost than that of their competitors. By so doing, they ensure good value to their customers, earn profitability for themselves, and satisfy their customers' needs. In addition, efficient operations enable firms either to provide their

Adding Value 2.1

Customer Service at Virgin Atlantic

Virgin Atlantic, the second largest long-haul international airline, operates services out of London's Heathrow and Gatwick airports to 22 destinations across the world—Shanghai, the Caribbean, and, of course, the United States.[28] Virgin's customer service orientation is heralded in its mission statement: "to grow a profitable airline that people love to fly and where people love to work."

In an age of dwindling airline services and disgruntled passengers, Virgin Atlantic set out to distinguish itself by providing the best possible service at the best possible price for all classes of tickets. Moreover, it set out to do so differently than anyone else. The result is a loyal group of travelers, agents, and employees who know the value of excellent customer service.

Virgin Atlantic retains loyal customers through great customer service.

What does Virgin do that makes it so special? Consider the offerings in the box below. While economy service is good, there are lots of extras for premium economy. Upper service is just out of sight!

Service Class	Distinctive Features
Upper	■ In-flight massages and manicures ■ Airport lounges with putting greens ■ Full-service spas and beauty salons ■ Onboard stand-up bars ■ Full reclining seats ■ Free limousine transfer ■ Drive-through check-in service standard with fare
Premium Economy	■ Dedicated check-in ■ Fast Track processing line ■ Priority baggage handling ■ Eight inches more leg room than standard in the industry
Economy	■ Full in-flight meals ■ Free individual entertainment for each seat (28 channels with movies, television shows, and games) ■ Free drinks ■ Amenity kits with stylishly fun socks, eye shades, tooth brushes, combs, rejuvenating toiletries, and seat-back stickers with slogans like "Do Not Disturb," "Wake Me For Meals," and "Wake Me For Duty Free."

consumers with lower priced merchandise or, even if their prices are not lower than those of the competition, to use the additional margin they earn to attract customers away from competitors by offering even better service, merchandise assortments, or visual presentations.

Firms achieve these efficiencies by developing sophisticated distribution and information systems as well as strong relationships with vendors. Similar to customer relationships, vendor relations must be developed over the long term and generally cannot be easily offset by a competitor.[29] Furthermore, firms with strong relationships may gain exclusive rights to (1) sell merchandise in a particular region, (2) obtain special terms of purchase that are not available to competitors, or (3) receive popular merchandise that may be in short supply.

In one such relationship, Levi Strauss & Co. has partnered with the world's largest retailer, Wal-Mart, even though for years it resisted selling to the retail giant because it believed such a partnership would tarnish its image and anger those of its customers willing to pay higher prices. But times have changed. Wal-Mart offers too much business to pass up, and Levi's market share has eroded. Its relationship with Wal-Mart even goes beyond an agreement to sell some jeans. Levi's has introduced a less expensive Signature line just for Wal-Mart and, to ensure the timely delivery of the line, has beefed up its distribution system accordingly.

Product Excellence

Product excellence, the third macro success strategy, occurs through branding and positioning. Some firms have difficulty developing a competitive advantage through their merchandise and service offerings, especially if competitors can deliver similar products or services easily. However, others have been able to maintain their sustainable competitive advantage by investing in their brand itself; positioning their product or service using a clear, distinctive brand image; and constantly reinforcing that image through their merchandise, service, and promotion. For instance, *BusinessWeek*'s top global brands—Coca-Cola, Microsoft, IBM, GE, Intel, Nokia, Disney, McDonald's, and Mercedes—are all leaders in their respective industries, at least in part because they have strong brands and a clear position in the marketplace.[30]

One of the world's top known brands, Lexus was conceived in 1983 when Toyota Chairman Eiji Toyoda determined that the "time is right to create a luxury vehicle to challenge the best in the world." The Lexus 400 and ES250 were introduced in 1989; by 1990, the LS 400 was acclaimed by the trade press and industry experts as one of the best vehicles in the world.[31] Today, the Lexus brand is synonymous with luxury and quality. How did Toyota take the Lexus concept from obscurity to a tangible vehicle that rivals such long-standing brands as Mercedes, BMW, and Porsche? Lexus developed its brand by focusing on the most important variables that predict whether a person will purchase a new luxury

Lexus achieves customer value by creating a luxurious, high quality automobile.

car: income, current car ownership, age of current vehicle, and distance from a dealership.

Armed with this information, the company created integrated marketing campaigns to cater to specific market profiles. For example, an early campaign sent a safety kit or picnic basket to those potential customers who test drove a Lexus. Although these promotional items were expensive, the company found that the offer was necessary to get the busy luxury car buyers to visit its dealerships.[32]

In most cases, however, a single strategy, such as low prices or excellent service, is not sufficient to build a sustainable competitive advantage.[33] Firms require multiple approaches to build a "wall" around their position that stands as high as possible. For example, Southwest Airlines has achieved success by providing customers with a good value that meets

Southwest Airlines provides good service at a good price—a good value—and they have fun doing it!

their expectations, offering good customer service, maintaining good customer relations, and offering great prices. By fulfilling all these strategies, Southwest Airlines has developed a huge cadre of loyal customers.

Southwest consistently has positioned itself as a carrier that provides good service at a good value—customers get to their destination on time for a reasonable price. At the same time, its customers know not to have extraordinary expectations. They don't expect food service, seat assignments, or flights out of the top airports (e.g., flights are out of Midway as opposed to O'Hare in the Chicago area and out of Ft. Lauderdale as opposed to Miami International Airport). But they do expect—and even more important, get—on-time flights that are reasonably priced. By developing its unique capabilities in several areas, Southwest has built a very high wall around its position as the value player in the airline industry.

In this chapter we have considered how a firm develops its marketing strategy by completing a marketing plan. In particular, we have described how firms analyze their marketing situation, evaluate it, and then develop a segmentation, targeting, and positioning strategy in response. Then we studied how the marketing mix can be used to increase customer value. Finally, we detailed several generic strategies for growing a business and three overarching macro strategies that many firms have implemented successfully.

Summing Up

1. **How does a firm set up a marketing plan?**

A marketing plan is composed of an analysis of the current marketing situation, its objectives, the strategy for the four Ps, and appropriate financial statements. A marketing plan represents the output of a three-phase process: planning, implementation, and control. The planning phase requires that managers define the firm's mission and vision and assess the firm's current situation. It helps answer the questions, "What business are we in now, and what do we intend to be in in the future?" In the second phase, implementation, the firm specifies, in more operational terms, how it plans to implement its mission and vision. Specifically, to which customer groups does it wish to direct its marketing efforts, and how does it use its marketing mix to provide good value? Finally, in the control phase, the firm must evaluate its performance to determine what worked, what didn't, and how performance can be improved in the future.

2. How are SWOT analyses used to analyze the marketing situation?

Recall that SWOT stands for strengths, weaknesses, opportunities, and threats. A SWOT analysis occurs during the second step in the strategic planning process, the situation analysis. By analyzing what the firm is good at (its strengths), where it could improve (its weaknesses), where in the marketplace it might excel (its opportunities), and what is happening in the marketplace that could harm the firm (its threats), managers can assess their firm's situation accurately and plan its strategy accordingly.

3. How does a firm choose what group(s) of people to pursue with its marketing efforts?

Once a firm identifies different marketing opportunities, it must determine which are the best to pursue. To accomplish this task, marketers go through a segmentation, targeting, and positioning (STP) process. Firms segment various markets by dividing the total market into those groups of customers with different needs, wants, or characteristics who therefore might appreciate products or services geared especially toward them. After identifying the different segments, the firm goes after, or targets, certain groups on the basis of the firm's perceived ability to satisfy the needs of those groups better than competitors and profitably. To complete the STP process, firms position their products or services according to the marketing mix variables so that target customers have a clear, distinctive, and desirable understanding of what the product or service does or represents relative to competing products or services.

4. How does the implementation of the marketing mix increase customer value?

The marketing mix consists of the four Ps—product, price, promotion, and place—and each P contributes to customer value. To provide value, the firm must offer a mix of products and services at prices their target markets will view as indicating good value. Thus, firms make trade-offs between the first two Ps, product and price, to give customers the best value. The third P, promotion, informs customers and helps them form a positive image about the firm and its products and services. The last P, place, adds value by getting the appropriate products and services to customers when they want them and in the quantities they need.

5. How can firms grow their businesses?

Firms use four basic growth strategies: market penetration, market development, product development, and diversification. A market penetration strategy directs the firm's efforts toward existing customers and uses the present marketing mix. In other words, it attempts to get current customers to buy more. In a market development strategy, the firm uses its current marketing mix to appeal to new market segments, as might occur in international expansion. A product development growth strategy involves offering a new product or service to the firm's current target market. Finally, a diversification strategy takes place when a firm introduces a new product or service to a new customer segment. Sometimes a diversification strategy relates to the firm's current business, such as when a women's clothing manufacturer starts making and selling men's clothes, but a more risky strategy is when a firm diversifies into a completely unrelated business. Great marketing firms also employ three macro strategies to achieve their sustainable competitive advantage: customer excellence through retaining loyal customers and providing excellent customer service, operational excellence through efficient supply chain management and operations, and product excellence through branding and positioning.

Key Terms

- competitor-based pricing, 39
- control phase, 32
- cost-based pricing, 39
- customer excellence, 46
- diversification strategy, 45
- implementation phase, 32
- market development strategy, 44
- market growth rate, 56
- market penetration strategy, 43
- market positioning, 37

- market segment, 36
- market segmentation, 36
- marketing plan, 32
- mission statement, 33
- operational excellence, 47
- planning phase, 32
- product development strategy, 44
- product excellence, 47
- product line, 41

- relative market share, 56
- situation analysis, 35
- STP, 36
- strategic business unit (SBU), 41
- strategic marketing planning process, 32
- sustainable competitive advantage, 34
- target marketing/targeting, 37
- value-based pricing, 39

Marketing Applications

1. How has Southwest Airlines created a sustainable competitive advantage?

2. Perform a SWOT analysis for your college or university.

3. Describe the primary target markets for the New York Yankees, Victoria's Secret, and Gatorade. How do these three firms position their products and services so that they appeal to their respective target markets?

4. Pick your favorite product, service provider, or retailer. How do they add value through the implementation of the four Ps?

5. Of the four growth strategies described in the chapter, which is the most risky? Which is the easiest to implement? Why?

6. Choose three retailers. You believe the first builds customer value through product excellence, the second through operational excellence, and the third through customer excellence. Justify your answer.

 ## Toolkit

SWOT ANALYSIS

Assume you are a marketing analyst for a major company and are trying to conduct a situation analysis using SWOT analysis. Use the toolkit provided at www.mhhe .com/grewal-levy, and complete the SWOT grids for each company using the appropriate items.

Net Savvy

1. Ben and Jerry's Ice Cream is considered a progressive company in terms of its values and the mission statement that drives its business. Visit its Web site (www.benjerry.com) and review the portion that discusses the company, its mission, and its values. Discuss aspects of its mission and values that might be considered progressive. (The company usually posts a social and environmental audit on its Web site identified as a student research link, which also provides insights into its values and mission.) Do you believe its progressive attitude creates a special position in the market that contributes to a sustainable competitive advantage?

2. More and more firms seem to be entering the dating service industry. Visit www.eharmony.com and tour its Web site to find the types of activities and methods such companies use to help match compatible couples. Now, analyze the environment that might affect Internet dating services using a SWOT analysis.

Chapter Case Study

SEGWAY: STRATEGIC PLANNING FROM CONCEPT TO MARKET[34]

On March 28, 2002, the first three Segways designed for the consumer market were auctioned off on Amazon.com for a total of over $350,000, drawing more than 500 bids. In line with creator Dean Kamen's desire to improve the world by inspiring an appreciation of science and technology in young people, the proceeds went to his charitable organization FIRST (For Inspiration and Recognition of Science and Technology) rather than to the company's coffers.[35]

The Segway—whose name stems from the word "segue," meaning to move seamlessly from one mode to another—was designed as the first self-balancing, electric-powered machine for

Do you believe that Segway will be a successful product in the long run?

human transport. Approximately 4 feet tall and weighing between 65 and 85 pounds, the upright, two-wheeled machine seems to predict the movements of the rider. When first introduced in 2001, the Segway generated a lot of fanfare, was marketed as "a set of magic sneakers,"[36] and was positioned as a short-distance travel machine for urban areas. Kamen envisioned a world where cars would be banished from metropolitan centers populated instead by his revolutionary product.[37]

To meet the anticipated onslaught of demand, a 77,000 square foot factory capable of producing 40,000 Segways a month was built near Manchester, New Hampshire. Kamen acknowledged some potential hurdles: ensuring product safety, setting a high selling price particularly during a recession, and launching a new product when the country was at war. But Kamen insisted these potential problems would fade into the background as consumers scrambled to buy the Segway once it was available.[38]

To avoid the perception of the Segway as a high-end toy rather than a practical, useful product, Kamen introduced it first in the commercial market after presenting it to the Postmaster General and the head of the National Parks. In April 2002, the first units were sold in the commercial market, but the $8,000 price tag minimized business purchases.

The company has been criticized for failing to recognize immediately that its innovative product would require governmental approval. Instead, it delayed public sales while it lobbied across the country for new laws that would allow the product on the sidewalks. Eventually, the company was able to persuade the Consumer Product Safety Commission (CPSC) that the Segway should be classified as a "consumer product" rather than a "motor vehicle," which led 46 states and the District of Columbia to allow Segways on sidewalks.[39]

In August 2002, a community of Segway enthusiasts and prospective owners launched www.segwaychat.com to share information and stories. In November of that year, Segway models went public, and in February 2003, they were shipped at selling prices of $3,995 to $4,495, depending on the model. Although the consumer version is now available from Amazon.com, Brookstone, and Segway-certified representatives, it experienced some resistance. Only 6,000 units had been sold by October 2003, when the entire inventory was recalled to repair a problem that caused people to fall off when the batteries ran low. Granted, the recall required only a 15-minute fix and the company was able to locate its customers relatively quickly, but the entire affair created some bad press.

After introduction, the company's strategy for long-term business success followed a three-step plan:[40]

1. Demonstrate the commercial productivity Segway can deliver to large enterprises and government workers such as police, emergency medical technicians, and letter carriers.

2. Demonstrate the Segway HT's pedestrian-friendly operation and earn regulatory approval and social acceptance on sidewalks.

3. Launch consumer sales, beginning with pilot tests in selected cities.

Prior to the launch, the company garnered tremendous media attention, including features on major networks, CNN, MSNBC, *60 Minutes*, and *Good Morning America*. Production capacity did not pan out as initially anticipated, and Segway has been forced to evaluate its spotty performance and take corrective action by looking for new markets. For instance, in December 2003, Segway sold 15 scooters to university researchers working on a project to develop robots that could be used on the battlefield. Segways are now used in the "Around the World at Epcot" tour in addition to a one-hour Simply Segway ride offered there since May 2005. Segway enthusiasts founded the National Segway Enthusiasts Group that organizes local glides and Segway polo matches. Members can log in to segamerica.org for benefits and upcoming event listings such as Segway Fests held several times a year around the United States. Electric Tour Company (www.electrictourcompany.com) offers tours of San Francisco and Sausalito California. But will Kamen ever achieve his lofty goals—which have little to do with profit—of revolutionizing how the world travels?[41]

Questions

1. Assess how the company progressed through the three phases of the strategic marketing planning process. Did it function well or poorly?

2. What do you think the company's mission is? Comment on the appropriateness of its mission.

3. Conduct a situation analysis for Segway using SWOT. To what extent are the company's segmentation, targeting, and positioning approaches appropriate for long-term success?

4. What do you perceive as Segway's competitive advantage? To what extent is this competitive advantage sustainable over time?

Chapter 2   Appendix

BOSTON CONSULTING GROUP'S PORTFOLIO ANALYSIS

One of the most popular portfolio analysis methods, developed by the Boston Consulting Group (BCG), requires that firms classify all their products into a two-by-two matrix, as depicted in Exhibit A2-1.[42] The circles represent brands, and their sizes are in direct proportion to the brands' annual sales. The horizontal axis represents the relative market share, a measure of the product's strength in a particular market, which we define as the sales of the focal product divided by the sales achieved by the largest firm in the industry. The vertical axis is the market growth rate, or the annual rate of growth of the specific market in which the product competes. Market growth rate thus measures how attractive a particular market is. Each quadrant has been named on the basis of the amount of resources it generates for and requires from the firm.

Stars. Stars (upper left quadrant) occur in high growth markets and are high market share products. That is, stars often require a heavy resource investment in such things as promotions and new production facilities to fuel their rapid growth. As their market growth slows, stars will migrate from heavy users of resources to heavy generators of resources and become cash cows.

EXHIBIT A2.1   BCG Growth-Share Matrix

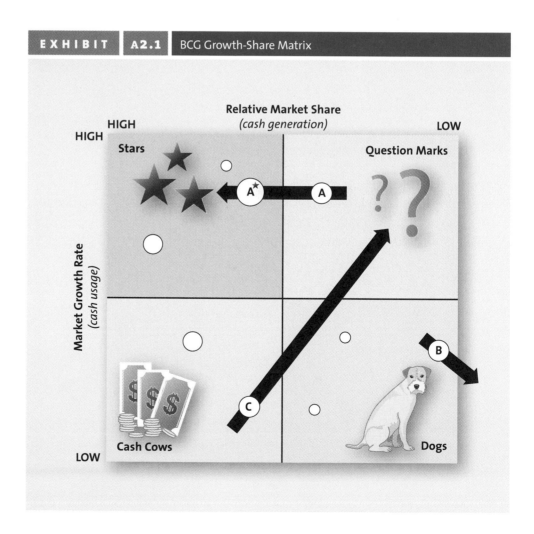

Cash cows. Cash cows (lower left quadrant) are in low growth markets but are high market share products. Because these products have already received heavy investments to develop their high market share, they have excess resources that can be spun off to those products that need it. For example, in Exhibit A2.1, Brand C uses its excess resources to fund products in the question mark quadrant.

Question marks. Question marks (upper right quadrant) appear in high growth markets but have relatively low market shares; thus, they are often the most managerially intensive products in that they require significant resources to maintain and potentially increase their market share. Managers must decide whether to infuse question marks with resources generated by the cash cows, so that they can become stars, or withdraw resources and eventually phase out the products. Brand A, for instance, is currently a question mark, but by infusing it with resources, the firm hopes to turn it into a star.

Dogs. Dogs (lower right quadrant) are in low growth markets and have relatively low market shares. Although they may generate enough resources to sustain themselves, dogs are not destined for stardom and should be phased out unless they are needed to complement or boost the sales of another product or for competitive purposes. In this case, the company has decided to stop making Brand B.

Although quite useful for conceptualizing the resource allocation task, the BCG approach, and others like it, is often difficult to implement in practice. In particular, it is difficult to measure both relative market share and industry growth. Furthermore, other measures easily could serve as substitutes to represent a product's competitive position and the market's relative attractiveness. Another issue for marketers is the potential self-fulfilling prophecy of placing a product into a quadrant. That is, suppose a product is classified as a dog though it has the potential of being a question mark. The firm might reduce support for the product and lose sales to the point that it abandons the product, which might have become profitable if provided with sufficient resources.

Because of these limitations, many firms have tempered their use of matrix approaches to achieve a more balanced approach to allocating their resources. Instead of assigning allocation decisions to the top levels of the organization, many firms start at lower management levels and employ checks and balances to force managers at each level of the organizational hierarchy to negotiate with those above and below them to reach their final decisions.

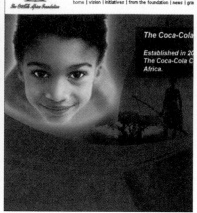

3

QUESTIONS

■ Why do marketers have to worry about ethics?

■ What does it take for a firm to be considered socially responsible?

■ How should a firm make ethically responsible decisions?

■ How can ethics and social responsibility be integrated into a firm's marketing strategy?

Marketing Ethics

n 1943, General Robert Wood Johnson wrote and published the first "Credo" for Johnson & Johnson (J&J),[1] a one-page document outlining the firm's commitments and responsibilities to its various stakeholders. Johnson's Credo received a lot of media attention because it contained a radical business philosophy: Put customers' needs first and shareholders' last. Johnson believed this ordering of company priorities just made good business sense, and history has shown how right he was.

The J&J Credo can be summarized as follows: We believe our first responsibility is to doctors, nurses, patients, mothers, fathers, and all others who use our products and services. We are responsible to our employees. We must respect their dignity and recognize their merit. Compensation must be fair and adequate and working conditions clean, orderly, and safe. We are responsible to the communities in which we live and work and to the world community as well. Our final responsibility is to our stockholders. When we operate according to these principles, the stockholders should realize a fair return.

The Credo was more than just a clever public relations ploy. Over the years, it has served as the guiding force for decision making at J&J. Perhaps at no other time was the company's commitment to the Credo more evident than during the Tylenol poisonings in the 1980s, when seven deaths were attributed to Tylenol that had been tampered with and poisoned with cyanide. It was unclear when the poison was put in the product—during production or as it sat on retailers' shelves. But because J&J's top priority is its customers, it refused to spend time worrying about where to attribute the blame and instead voluntarily withdrew all Tylenol from the market until it could ensure its products' safety. In a recent campaign, media reports about consumers' misuse of Tylenol

J&J's Tylenol wants to make sure that parents know how to use its products for their children.

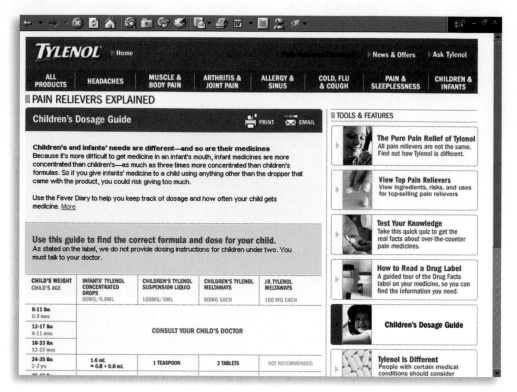

led to a series of advertisements reminding consumers to read the dosage directions and use Tylenol only according to those directions. If consumers were not going to use Tylenol according to those directions, the ad stated that they would rather consumers not use Tylenol at all.

In June 2005, J&J once again voluntarily removed one of its products from the market: all forms of Children's Tylenol packaged in blister packs[2] because consumers were confused about the proper dosages to be given to children of various ages. The company's primary concern was the risk that parents or caregivers would overdose children, which might cause liver damage in those young consumers.

When faced with ethical dilemmas, the choice for J&J is always clear: Refer to the Credo for guidance and assurance that J&J always does the right thing.

■ ■ ■

Which is a more important corporate objective: making a profit, or obtaining and keeping customers?[3] Although firms cannot stay in business without earning a profit, using profit as the sole guiding light for corporate action can lead to short-term decisions that may in fact cause the firm to lose customers in the long run. As we saw in the opening vignette, J&J chose to maintain a strong relationship with its customers by removing Tylenol from the market in cases of danger, temporarily giving up profit instead of looking toward a short-term, bottom-line result.

When customers believe that they can no longer trust a company or that the company is not acting responsibly, they will no longer support that company by purchasing its products or services or investing in its stock. For marketers, the firm's ability to build and maintain consumer trust by conducting ethical transactions must be of paramount importance.

In this chapter, we start by examining what marketing ethics is and why behaving ethically is so important to successful marketing. We then discuss how firms can create an ethical climate among employees and how individual behavior can affect the ability of the firm to act ethically. To help you make ethical marketing decisions, we also provide a framework for ethical decision making and then examine some ethical issues within the context of the strategic marketing planning process (from Chapter 2). Finally, we present some scenarios that highlight typical ethical challenges marketing managers often must face.

The Scope of Marketing Ethics

Business ethics refers to a branch of ethical study that examines ethical rules and principles within a commercial context, the various moral or ethical problems that might arise in a business setting, and any special duties or obligations that apply to persons engaged in commerce.[4] The cartoon below illustrates the importance of making good ethical decisions. **Marketing ethics,** in contrast, examines those ethical problems that are specific to the domain of marketing. Because the marketing profession often is singled out among business disciplines as the root cause of a host of ethical concerns (for example, unethical advertising or the promotion of shoddy products), anyone involved in marketing activities must recognize the ethical implications of their actions. These can include societal issues, such as the sale of products or services that may damage the environment; global issues, such as the use of sweatshops; and individual consumer issues, such as deceptive advertising and the marketing of dangerous products.[5]

Ethical Issues Associated with Marketing Decisions

Unlike other business functions like accounting or finance, people in marketing interact directly with the public. Because they are so much in the public's eye, it should not be surprising that marketing and sales professionals sometimes

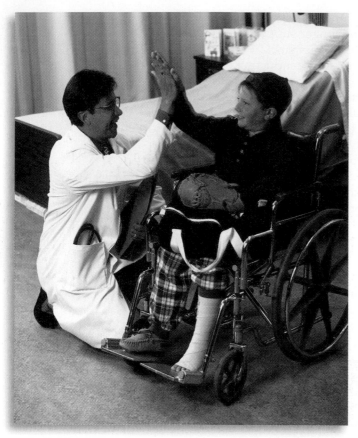

Nurses and doctors are among the most trusted professionals.

rank poorly in ratings of the most trusted professions. In a recent Gallup survey, most professions were rated much higher than marketing—car salespeople came in last and advertising practitioners fared only slightly better but not as well as lawyers![6] (See Exhibit 3.1.) For marketers, who depend on the long-term trust of their customers, this low ranking is very disappointing.

Yet there is some good news. In another survey, employees across the United States thought that the ethical climate in their firms had improved, with 83 percent of respondents stating that "top management keeps [its] promises and commitments."[7] Many consumers remain highly skeptical of business, however, and especially of marketing. But because the marketing function interacts with so many entities outside the firm on a regular basis, it has a tremendous opportunity to build the public's trust. As General Johnson correctly believed, creating an ethical climate that establishes the health and well-being of consumers as the firm's number one priority just makes good business sense.

Creating an Ethical Climate in the Workplace

The process of creating a strong **ethical climate** within a marketing firm (or in the marketing division of any firm) includes having a set of values that guides decision making and behavior, like Johnson & Johnson's Credo. Everyone within the firm must share the same understanding of these values and how they translate into the business activities of the firm, and they must share a consistent language to discuss them.

Once the values are understood, the firm must develop a set of explicit rules and implicit understandings that govern all the firm's transactions. Top management must commit to establishing an ethical climate, but employees throughout the firm also must be dedicated because the roots of ethical conflict often are the competing values of individuals. Each individual holds his or her own set of values, and sometimes those values result in conflicts between employees or even within them. For instance, a salesperson may believe that it is important to make a sale because her family depends on her for support, but at the same time she may feel that the product she is selling is not appropriate for a particular customer. Once the rules are in place, there must be a system of controls that rewards appropriate behavior—that is, behavior consistent with the firm's values—and punishes inconsistent behavior.

Many professions, including marketing, have their own codes of ethics that firms and individuals in the profession agree to abide by. The generally accepted code in marketing, developed by the American Marketing Association (see Exhibit 3.2), flows from general norms of conduct to specific values to which marketers should aspire. Each subarea within marketing, such as marketing research, adver-

EXHIBIT | **3.1** | Attitudes about the Ethical Standards of Various Professions

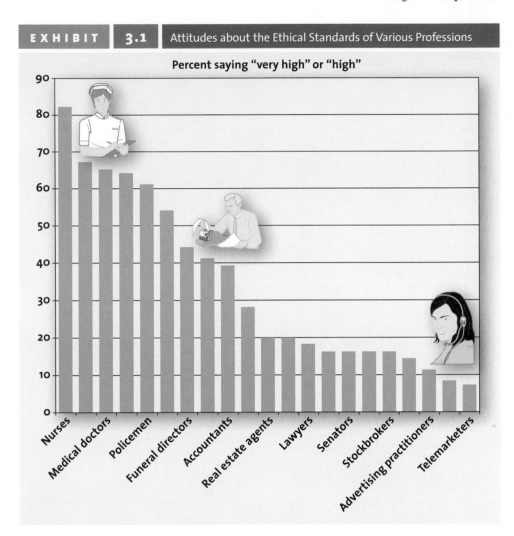

Percent saying "very high" or "high"

Nurses, Medical doctors, Policemen, Funeral directors, Accountants, Real estate agents, Lawyers, Senators, Stockbrokers, Advertising practitioners, Telemarketers

tising, pricing, and so forth, has its own code of ethics that deals with the specific issues that arise when conducting business in those areas.

Now we examine the role of the individuals within the firm and how they contribute to the firm's ethical climate.

The Influence of Personal Ethics

Every firm is made up of individuals, each with his or her own needs and desires. Let's look at why people may make unethical decisions and how firms can establish a process for decision making that ensures individuals choose ethical alternatives more often.

Why People Act Unethically   Every individual is a product of his or her culture, upbringing, genes, and various other influences. In spite of

It is not always clear why people act unethically and sometimes illegally, but when they do act in this manner, many people may be harmed. Here cartloads of file boxes are hauled to the federal courthouse for the fraud and conspiracy trial of former Enron executives.

EXHIBIT	3.2	American Marketing Association's Code of Ethics

ETHICAL NORMS AND VALUES FOR MARKETERS

Preamble

The American Marketing Association commits itself to promoting the highest standard of professional ethical norms and values for its members. Norms are established standards of conduct that are expected and maintained by society and/or professional organizations. Values represent the collective conception of what people find desirable, important and morally proper. Values serve as the criteria for evaluating the actions of others. Marketing practitioners must recognize that they not only serve their enterprises but also act as stewards of society in creating, facilitating and executing the efficient and effective transactions that are part of the greater economy. In this role, marketers should embrace the highest ethical norms of practicing professionals and the ethical values implied by their responsibility toward stakeholders (e.g., customers, employees, investors, channel members, regulators and the host community).

General Norms

1. Marketers must do no harm. This means doing work for which they are appropriately trained or experienced so that they can actively add value to their organizations and customers. It also means adhering to all applicable laws and regulations and embodying high ethical standards in the choices they make.
2. Marketers must foster trust in the marketing system. This means that products are appropriate for their intended and promoted uses. It requires that marketing communications about goods and services are not intentionally deceptive or misleading. It suggests building relationships that provide for the equitable adjustment and/or redress of customer grievances. It implies striving for good faith and fair dealing so as to contribute toward the efficacy of the exchange process.
3. Marketers must embrace, communicate and practice the fundamental ethical values that will improve consumer confidence in the integrity of the marketing exchange system. These basic values are intentionally aspirational and include honesty, responsibility, fairness, respect, openness and citizenship.

Ethical Values

Honesty—to be truthful and forthright in our dealings with customers and stakeholders.
- We will tell the truth in all situations and at all times.
- We will offer products of value that do what we claim in our communications.
- We will stand behind our products if they fail to deliver their claimed benefits.
- We will honor our explicit and implicit commitments and promises.

Responsibility—to accept the consequences of our marketing decisions and strategies.
- We will make strenuous efforts to serve the needs of our customers.
- We will avoid using coercion with all stakeholders.
- We will acknowledge the social obligations to stakeholders that come with increased marketing and economic power.
- We will recognize our special commitments to economically vulnerable segments of the market such as children, the elderly and others who may be substantially disadvantaged.

these factors, however, people do continue to grow emotionally in their understanding of what is and is not ethical behavior. For example, as a six-year-old child, you might have thought nothing of bonking your brother on the head with a toy; as an adult, you recognize that violence is an unethical means to interact with others. All of us vary in the way we view various situations, depending on our own level of understanding about ethical dilemmas.

Recent corporate scandals at companies such as Enron and WorldCom have many people asking two simple questions: What makes people take actions that create so much harm? Are all the individuals who engaged in that behavior just plain immoral or unethical? These questions have very complex answers.

In many cases, people must choose between conflicting outcomes. For example, a brand manager for a car company discovers, from conversations with a member of the development team, that a potentially dangerous design flaw resides in the hot new energy-efficient hybrid model that is set to go into full production shortly. There are two options for the brand manager: delay production and remedy the design flaw, which pushes production off schedule, delays revenue, and may re-

EXHIBIT   **3.2**   (continued)

Fairness—to try to balance justly the needs of the buyer with the interests of the seller.
- We will represent our products in a clear way in selling, advertising and other forms of communication; this includes the avoidance of false, misleading and deceptive promotion.
- We will reject manipulations and sales tactics that harm customer trust.
- We will not engage in price fixing, predatory pricing, price gouging or "bait-and-switch" tactics.
- We will not knowingly participate in material conflicts of interest.

Respect—to acknowledge the basic human dignity of all stakeholders.
- We will value individual differences even as we avoid stereotyping customers or depicting demographic groups (e.g., gender, race, sexual orientation) in a negative or dehumanizing way in our promotions.
- We will listen to the needs of our customers and make all reasonable efforts to monitor and improve their satisfaction on an ongoing basis.
- We will make a special effort to understand suppliers, intermediaries and distributors from other cultures.
- We will appropriately acknowledge the contributions of others, such as consultants, employees and coworkers, to our marketing endeavors.

Openness—to create transparency in our marketing operations.
- We will strive to communicate clearly with all our constituencies.
- We will accept constructive criticism from our customers and other stakeholders.
- We will explain significant product or service risks, component substitutions or other foreseeable eventualities that could affect customers or their perception of the purchase decision.
- We will fully disclose list prices and terms of financing as well as available price deals and adjustments.

Citizenship—to fulfill the economic, legal, philanthropic and societal responsibilities that serve stakeholders in a strategic manner.
- We will strive to protect the natural environment in the execution of marketing campaigns.
- We will give back to the community through volunteerism and charitable donations.
- We will work to contribute to the overall betterment of marketing and its reputation.
- We will encourage supply chain members to ensure that trade is fair for all participants, including producers in developing countries.

Implementation

Finally, we recognize that every industry sector and marketing subdiscipline (e.g., marketing research, e-commerce, direct selling, direct marketing, advertising) has its own specific ethical issues that require policies and commentary. An array of such codes can be accessed through links on the AMA Web site (marketingpower.com).

Source: http://www.Marketingpower.com.

---

sult in layoffs and loss of a bonus, or stay on schedule, put the flawed design into production, and hope it does not result in injuries to consumers and loss of revenue for the firm. This type of dilemma with its competing outcomes occurs nearly every day in thousands of different business environments.

When asked in a survey whether they had seen any unethical behavior among their colleagues, chief marketing officers responded that they had observed employees participating in high pressure, misleading, or deceptive sales tactics (45 percent); misrepresenting company earnings, sales, and/or revenues (35 percent); withholding or destroying information that could hurt company sales or image (32 percent); and conducting false or misleading advertising (31 percent).[8] Did all the marketers in these situations view their actions as unethical? In making marketing decisions, managers are often faced with the dilemma between doing what is beneficial for them and possibly the firm in the short run, and doing what is right and beneficial for the firm and society in the long run.

What is the "real" price? Did the manager bring the T-shirts in at an artificially high level and then immediately mark them down?

For instance, a manager might feel confident that earnings will increase in the next few months and therefore believe it benefits himself, his branch, and his employees to exaggerate current earnings just a little. Another manager might feel considerable pressure to increase sales in a retail store, so she brings in some new merchandise, marks it at an artificially high price, and then immediately puts it on sale. Consumers are deceived into thinking they are getting a good deal because they view the initial price as the "real" price. Each decision may have been justifiable at the time for the individual but also had potentially serious ethical consequences for the company.

To avoid these ethical consequences, the long-term goals of the firm must be aligned with the short-term goals of each individual within the firm. In our hybrid car example, the brand manager's short-term drive to receive a bonus conflicted with the firm's long-term aim of providing consumers with safe, reliable cars. As discussed in the previous section, to align personal and corporate goals, firms need to have a strong ethical climate, explicit rules for governing a firm's transactions including a code of ethics, and a system for rewarding and punishing behavior. In the next section, we discuss this link between ethics and social responsibility by businesses.

The Link between Ethics and Corporate Social Responsibility

Corporate social responsibility describes the voluntary actions taken by a company to address the ethical, social, and environmental impacts of its business operations and the concerns of its stakeholders.[9] For a company to act in a socially responsible manner, the employees within the company must also maintain high ethical standards and recognize how their individual decisions lead to the collective actions of the firm. Firms with strong ethical climates tend to be more socially responsible.

Ideally, firms should implement programs that are socially responsible, AND its employees should act in an ethically responsible manner. (See Exhibit 3.3, upper left quadrant.) But being socially responsible is generally considered beyond the norms of corporate ethical behavior. For example, a firm's employees may conduct their activities in an ethically acceptable manner but still not be considered socially responsible because their activities have little or no impact on anyone other than their closest stakeholders: their customers, employees, and stockholders (Exhibit 3.3, upper right quadrant). In this case, employees would not, for instance, be involved in volunteer activities to clean up a local park or coach the community's youth baseball league—socially responsible activities that improve the communities in which the company operates.

Likewise, some firms that are perceived as socially responsible can still take actions that are viewed as unethical (Exhibit 3.3, lower left quadrant). For instance, a

EXHIBIT 3.3	Ethics versus Social Responsibility	
	Socially Responsible	**Socially Irresponsible**
Ethical	Both ethical and socially responsible	Ethical firm not involved with the larger community
Unethical	Questionable firm practices, yet donates a lot to the community	Neither ethical nor socially responsible

firm might be considered socially responsible because it makes generous donations to charities but is simultaneously involved in questionable sales practices. Ethically, how do we characterize a firm that obtains its profits through illicit actions but then donates a large percentage of those profits to charity? The worst situation, of course, is when firms behave both unethically AND in a socially unacceptable manner (Exhibit 3.3, lower right quadrant).

Consumers and investors increasingly appear to want to purchase products and services from and invest in companies that act in socially responsible ways. Large global corporations, such as Coca-Cola, have recognized that they must be perceived as socially responsible by their stakeholders to earn their business. As a bonus, these companies earn both tangible and intangible benefits for acting in a socially desirable manner (see Adding Value 3.1); it just makes good business sense to take actions that benefit society.

An employee is acting in a socially responsible manner if he coaches the community's youth baseball team.

Adding Value 3.1

Coca-Cola Fights HIV/AIDS in Africa

Beginning in 2001, the Coca-Cola Africa Foundation was formed to reduce the impact of HIV/AIDS on Coca-Cola's 60,000 employees and 40 independent bottlers in Africa. At present, 100 percent of Coca-Cola's independent bottling companies in 54 African countries are enrolled in the foundation's programs. All their employees and employees' families are eligible to receive benefits, including access to antiretroviral drugs, testing, counseling, prevention, and treatment. The foundation's outreach also extends beyond employees and into the community.[10]

The Coca-Cola Africa Foundation focuses its efforts on three key areas that affect the communities in which Coca-Cola operates: healthcare, education, and the environment. The many projects supported by the foundation cost millions of dollars each year, but Coca-Cola offers more than just funding. By using its distribution network, one of the most extensive in Africa, Coca-Cola can transport vital materials to rural communities across the continent. It also is able to reach areas of Africa to which AIDS/HIV workers have not previously had easy access and thereby ensure that people in those areas can obtain information about the prevention and treatment of HIV/AIDS. Even Coca-Cola's marketing expertise is being used to raise awareness of key issues such as HIV prevention. By leveraging its corporate assets, Coca-Cola has made a positive contribution to all African communities.[11]

The Coca-Cola Africa Foundation welcomes you.

Established in 2001, the Foundation funds and coordinates The Coca-Cola Company's community initiatives across Africa.

The Coca-Cola Africa Foundation provides millions of dollars each year to reduce the impact of HIV/AIDS on Coca-Cola's employees and independent bottlers in Africa.

Whole Foods Market acts in socially responsible ways by, for instance, using solar energy to generate 25 percent of its power.

Consider, for example, companies such as Horizon Organic, which donates 10 percent of its net profits to charity, and Whole Foods Market, which uses solar energy to generate 25 percent of its power.[12] Such corporations, when planning and defining their strategic initiatives, increasingly include socially responsible programs. But unfortunately, being a socially responsible corporation does not ensure that all members of the firm or all subunits within it will act ethically; rather, it means only that the firm is committing time and resources to projects in the community that may not directly relate to generating profit.

We cannot expect every member of a firm to always act ethically. However, a framework for ethical decision making can help move people to work toward common ethical goals.

A Framework for Ethical Decision Making

Exhibit 3.4 outlines a simple framework for ethical decision making. Let's consider each of the steps.

Step 1: Identify Issues

The first step is to identify the issue. For illustrative purposes, we'll investigate the use (or misuse) of data collected from consumers by a marketing research firm. One of the issues that might arise is the way the data are collected. For instance, are the respondents told about the real purpose of the study? Another issue questions whether the results are going to be used in a way that might mislead or even harm the public.

Step 2: Gather Information and Identify Stakeholders

In this step, the firm focuses on gathering facts that are important to the ethical issue, including all relevant legal information. To get a complete picture, the firm must also identify and discuss with the individuals and groups that have a stake in how the issue is resolved.

Stakeholders typically include the firm's employees and retired employees, the natural environment, suppliers, the government, customer groups, stockholders, and members of the community in which the firm operates. Beyond these,

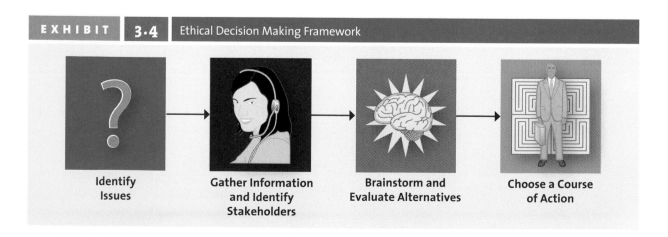

EXHIBIT   3.4   Ethical Decision Making Framework

Identify Issues → Gather Information and Identify Stakeholders → Brainstorm and Evaluate Alternatives → Choose a Course of Action

many firms now also analyze the needs of the industry and the global community, as well as "one off" stakeholders, such as future generations.

Exhibit 3.5 illustrates a stakeholder analysis matrix for our example.[13] Notice that each stakeholder has responsibilities to the others; in this case, the marketing researcher has ethical responsibilities to the public, the research subjects, and the client company, while the client has ethical responsibilities to the researcher, the subjects, and the public. Acknowledging the interdependence of responsibilities ensures that everyone's perspective is considered in the firm's decision making.

Step 3: Brainstorm Alternatives

After the marketing firm has identified the stakeholders and their issues and gathered the available data, all parties relevant to the decision should come together to brainstorm any alternative courses of action. In our example, these might include halting the market research project, making responses anonymous, instituting training on the AMA Code of Ethics for all researchers, and so forth. Management then reviews and refines these alternatives, leading to the final step.

Step 4: Choose a Course of Action

The objective of this last step is to weigh the various alternatives and choose a course of action that generates the best solution for the stakeholders using ethical practices. Management will rank the alternatives in order of preference, clearly establishing the advantages and disadvantages of each. It is also crucial

EXHIBIT 3.5	Stakeholder Analysis Matrix for a Marketing Research Firm		
Stakeholder	**Stakeholders' Concerns**	**Result or Impact on the Stakeholder**	**Potential Strategies for Obtaining Support and Diminishing Impact**
The Public	■ Get inaccurate and biased results. ■ Publish false, misleading or out of context results.	■ Lose trust in marketing research professionals. ■ Lose trust in the marketing research process.	■ Report accurate results. ■ Report study context and methodology. ■ Comply with American Marketing Association's (AMA) Code of Ethics.[14]
The Subjects/ Respondents	■ Invade privacy. Privacy will be compromised if they answer the survey. ■ Use marketing research as a guise to sell consumers goods or services.	■ Lose trust in the marketing research process. ■ Refuse to participate in future marketing research projects. ■ Provide incorrect information.	■ Comply with American Marketing Association's (AMA) Code of Ethics. ■ Protect respondent's confidential data. ■ Report aggregate, rather than individuals' results.
The Client	■ Conduct research that was not needed. ■ Use an inadequate sample to generalize to their target market. ■ Disclose sensitive data to others.	■ Reduce their spending and reliance on marketing research. ■ Make marketing decisions without doing research or doing inadequate research.	■ Ensure that the marketing research vendor signs a confidentiality agreement. ■ Comply with American Marketing Association's (AMA) Code of Ethics.

to investigate any potential legal issues associated with each alternative. Of course, any illegal activity should immediately be rejected.

To choose the appropriate course of action, marketing managers will evaluate each alternative using a process something like the sample ethical decision-making evaluation questionnaire in Exhibit 3.6. The marketer's task here is to ensure that he or she has applied all relevant decision-making criteria and to assess his or her level of confidence that the decision being made meets those stated criteria. If the marketer isn't confident about the decision, he or she should reexamine the other alternatives.

By using this ethical framework, decision makers will include the relevant ethical issues, evaluate the alternatives, and choose a course of action that will help them avoid serious ethical lapses. To see how the criteria in Exhibit 3.6 might be used, consider Ethical Dilemma 3.1, in which we show how ethical issues can arise at each stage of the strategic marketing planning process (for strategic planning process, see Chapter 2).

Integrating Ethics into Marketing Strategy

Ethical decision making is not a simple process, though it can get easier as decision makers within the firm become accustomed to thinking about the ethical implications of their actions from a strategic perspective. In this section, we examine how ethical decision making can be integrated into the strategic marketing planning process introduced in Chapter 2. Exhibit 3.7 summarizes the process, with an emphasis on identifying potential ethical pitfalls during each stage.

The questions vary at each stage of the strategic marketing planning process. For instance, in the planning stage the firm will decide what level of commitment to its ethical policies and standards it is willing to declare publicly. In the implementation stage, the tone of the questions switches from "can we?" serve the market

EXHIBIT 3.6 Ethical Decision-Making Evaluation Questionnaire					
	Confidence in Decision				
	Not Very Confident				Confident
Criteria	**1**	**2**	**3**	**4**	**5**
1. Have I/we thought broadly about any ethical issues associated with the decision that must be made?					
2. Have I/we involved as many possible people who have a right to offer input into or have actual involvement in making this decision and action plan?					
3. Does this decision respect the rights and dignity of the stakeholders?					
4. Does this decision produce the most good and the least harm to the relevant stakeholders?					
5. Does this decision uphold relevant conventional moral rules?					
6. Can I/we live with this decision alternative?					

Source: Adapted from Kate McKone-Sweet, Danna Greenberg, and Lydia Moland, "Approaches to Ethical Decision Making," Babson College Case Development Center, 2003.

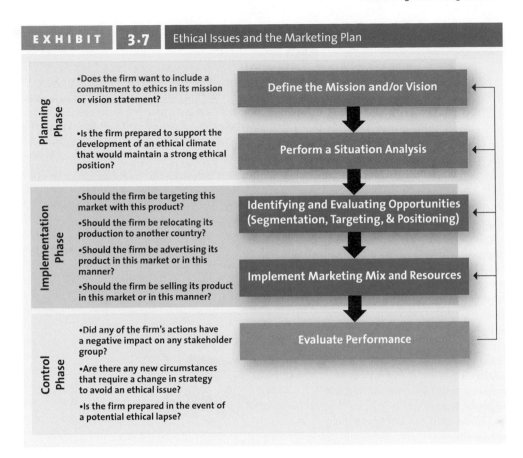

EXHIBIT **3.7** Ethical Issues and the Marketing Plan

Planning Phase

•Does the firm want to include a commitment to ethics in its mission or vision statement?

•Is the firm prepared to support the development of an ethical climate that would maintain a strong ethical position?

Implementation Phase

•Should the firm be targeting this market with this product?

•Should the firm be relocating its production to another country?

•Should the firm be advertising its product in this market or in this manner?

•Should the firm be selling its product in this market or in this manner?

Control Phase

•Did any of the firm's actions have a negative impact on any stakeholder group?

•Are there any new circumstances that require a change in strategy to avoid an ethical issue?

•Is the firm prepared in the event of a potential ethical lapse?

→ Define the Mission and/or Vision

→ Perform a Situation Analysis

→ Identifying and Evaluating Opportunities (Segmentation, Targeting, & Positioning)

→ Implement Marketing Mix and Resources

→ Evaluate Performance

with the firm's products or services in an ethically responsible manner to "should we?" be engaging in particular marketing practices. The key task in the control phase is to ensure that all potential ethical issues raised during the planning process have been addressed and that all employees of the firm have acted ethically. Let's take a closer look at how ethics can be integrated at each stage of the strategic marketing planning process.

Planning Phase

Marketers can introduce ethics at the beginning of the planning process simply by including ethical statements in the firm's mission or vision statements. Johnson & Johnson has its Credo; other firms use mission statements that include ethical precepts for shaping the organization. The mission statements from organizations such as The Body Shop and Ben and Jerry's Ice Cream are known for reflecting strong ethical climates. Even large firms such as General Mills provide a statement of "Values" that defines the priorities of the organization and its commitment to implanting those values in all that the firm does. Every year, General Mills issues a report discussing how the firm has performed against its own standards of ethical conduct.[15]

For example, General Mills recently announced it would be switching to whole grains in all its breakfast cereal lines—making it

Ben and Jerry's Ice Cream's mission statement is known for reflecting its strong ethical climate.

Ethical Dilemma **3.1**   A Questionable Promotion

Steve Jansen, the marketing manager for a retail store in a small town in the Midwest, received a notice about an upcoming promotion from the national chain to which his store belongs. The promotion is for a diet product called LeanBlast, which targets women between the ages of 20 and 30. Jenna Jones, the celebrity who will be featured in the promotion, is a young actress who recently lost weight and transitioned from child star to adult actor. Jenna is very popular with younger girls, who still watch her early television series in reruns. The

promotion is expected to generate a 30–40 percent increase in sales, and because LeanBlast has a high margin, the company looks for a sharp increase in revenue for this category. On the financial side, the promotion looks like a great opportunity for the store.

Recently, however, a local girl died from complications associated with an eating disorder. Her death at the age of 16 triggered a wide range of responses in the community to address eating disorders, as well as efforts to establish a healthier environment for young women.

Not only is Steve extremely nervous about the community's response to this campaign, he also is personally disturbed by the campaign because he knew the family of the girl who died. In addition, he has been thinking about his own adolescent daughters, who idolize Jenna, the celebrity endorsing the product. He wonders what his daughters' response will be to this campaign.

Using his training in ethical decision making, Steve recently sat down to evaluate his alternatives, beginning with identifying the various stakeholders that might be impacted by his decision. He came up with the following list: the employees, the shareholders, the customers, and the broader community. Each set of stakeholders has a different interest in the campaign and its outcome.

Steve then arrived at three possible alternatives:

1. Run the campaign as instructed.

2. Modify the campaign by stressing that products such as LeanBlast are to be used only by adult women who are overweight and only with the supervision of a medical professional.

3. Refuse to run this promotion in the local area.

Steve's next step was to evaluate each alternative through a series of questions similar to those in Exhibit 3.6:

Question 1: Have I thought about the ethical issues involved in his decision?

Steve feels confident that he has identified all the relevant ethical issues associated with this decision.

Question 2: Do I need to include anyone else in the decision process?

Because this decision ultimately belongs to him, Steve feels the responsibility to make it, and he believes he has an adequate understanding of all affected parties' positions on the issue. He does not believe that additional input would assist his decision making.

Question 3: Which of my alternatives respects the rights and dignity of the stakeholders and can be universally applied?[16]

In this case, Steve already has identified the relevant stakeholders as the local community, the customers, the employees, and the stockholders. The first alternative seems to violate the tenant of respect for persons, because many in the community will find the promotion offensive and contrary to the community's stated goals. The second alternative is an improvement over the first but still potentially offensive. Steve believes the third alternative—not running the promotion—is the right choice according to this criterion.

Question 4: Which alternative will produce the most good and the least harm?[17]

Using this criterion, the first alternative benefits those adult women who need and want LeanBlast. If the promotion achieves its projected revenues, it also benefits the employees and Steve, in that they will post above-average revenues in the category. The promotion also will draw traffic into the store and thereby increase storewide sales figures. However, the promotion harms those who have been affected by the recent tragedy, as well as those teenagers and young girls who would be drawn to the products in an attempt to emulate Jenna Jones's lean body image.

The second alternative requires that Steve supplement the promotion by spending extra funds to stress the proper use of products like LeanBlast, though it is not clear how effective the extra spending will be.

The third alternative costs the store the sales revenue it will lose by not participating in the promotion, and the national chain may assess Steve's store a penalty for failing to participate. The benefits of the third alternative are harder to quantify because most of them are social benefits. The costs, however, are very real in terms of lost revenue.

Question 5: Do any of the alternatives violate a conventional moral rule?[18]

Here Steve has an even more difficult time. None of the alternatives violates a conventional moral rule; all fall within legitimate business practices.

Question 6: Which alternatives can I personally live with?[19]

The first alternative is not one that Steve feels he can accept. He finds the choice of a young celebrity somewhat disturbing because her appeal is to a younger audience than the stated target market. Steve is forced to wonder whether the firm is trying to get younger women interested in its products.

The second alternative is more acceptable to Steve, but he is still concerned about the impact of the promotion, regardless of any modifications he might make.

Steve can most easily live with the third alternative of choosing not to run the promotion. This alternative is the one he can most easily justify and discuss with his family and friends.

On the basis of this exercise, Steve decides to call the national office to inform the parent company of his decision not to run the promotion in his store. Although Steve is extremely nervous while making this call, he is pleasantly surprised to hear that the national office also has been having some reservations about LeanBlast's choice of celebrity. Management clearly understands Steve's concerns about his community and in fact even offers to help Steve finance an educational session about eating disorders for his employees and the community. Steve decides that doing the right thing feels pretty good.

General Mills is switching to whole grains in all of its breakfast cereal lines, which should improve the dietary benefits.

the first of the mass-marketed cereal manufacturers to do so. This switch has been applauded by nutritionists who claim it dramatically improves the dietary benefits of the cereals. General Mills made the switch not necessarily to increase consumer demand; rather, in keeping with its stated values, it improved its cereal products to improve the health of its consumers.[20]

During planning, ethical mission statements can take on another role as a means to guide a firm's SWOT analysis. Fetzer Vineyards (see Entrepreneurial Marketing 3.1), for example, has what most of us would consider an ambitious mission statement.

Implementation Phase

An important element of Fetzer's continued commitment to its mission statement is that the values stated in it remain consistent with the values of the company's primary target market. Sometimes, however, a firm's choice of target market for its products can lead to charges of unethical behavior. In segmenting a market, the marketer determines what aspects of the product, service, and overall marketing effort are important to particular groups of consumers. Groups may be responsive to the firm's efforts and still not represent an appropriate target market; thus, the firm can serve this market but should not.

Procter & Gamble (P&G) teamed up with "tween" retailer Limited Too on a promotion featuring P&G's Secret Sparkle Body Spray. The promotion offered a contest open only to girls aged 7 to 14 years. But even as this group was being targeted, the Sparkle Body Spray product carried a warning label on its own packaging stating that it was to be kept out of children's reach. The spray also was being advertised in teen and tween magazines that attracted audiences under the age of 12 years.[21] Clearly, this promotion to young girls was inappropriate according to P&G's own labeling and was terminated when the Children's Advertising Review Unit of the Better Business Bureau stepped in and requested that P&G stop promoting the product to children. Had P&G considered all the potential ethical dilemmas at the implementation stage in its strategic marketing planning process, it might have avoided the issue of promoting spray to the same children it warned not to use the product.

The question of resource allocation in the implementation phase can also be an ethical minefield, and perhaps no business is more susceptible to charges of unethical resource allocation than the pharmaceutical industry. For example, AIDS activists claim that pharmaceutical companies are not doing enough to develop affordable drugs for underdeveloped countries to treat AIDS among their poor citizens. Some public health officials also have sounded alarm bells about the lack of research into the next generation of antibiotics, at a time when bacteria continue to become increasingly resistant to existing drugs. Critics of the pharmaceutical industry can also point to the increasing number of "lifestyle" drugs, such as those for erectile dysfunction, obesity, male-pattern baldness, nail fungus, and such, as possible causes for the lack of new treatments for serious diseases, even though the pharmaceutical companies vehemently deny that they have been transferring assets from research on treatments for life-threatening illnesses to fund lifestyle drugs.

Entrepreneurial Marketing 3.1

Fetzer Vineyards' Mission Is Win–Win

The Fetzer Vineyards' mission statement begins like this:

We Make Our Wines Responsibly. Please Drink Them Responsibly.

In 1958, Barney and Kathleen Fetzer purchased a rundown ranch in Mendocino, California, converted it into a vineyard, and created Fetzer Vineyards. Over time, the Fetzers have added other vineyards and are now the sixth-largest producer of premium wines in the United States. Fetzer Vineyards is unique in that its mission, in addition to providing the highest quality wine, is to protect the environment and benefit society.

The mission statement continues:

- ■ We are an environmentally and socially conscious grower, producer, and marketer of wines of the highest quality and value.

- ■ Working in harmony and with respect for the human spirit, we are committed to sharing information about the enjoyment of food and wine in a lifestyle of moderation and responsibility.

- ■ We are dedicated to the continuous growth and development of our people and business.[22]

While seeking to live up to this ambitious mission statement, Fetzer has been able to identify opportunities that others without a similar focus probably would have missed. For example, Fetzer is committed to using only organic grapes in its Bonterra line, which means it contains no pesticides, no fungicides, and no fertilizers.

Fetzer Vineyards produces organic wines.

This decision has actually translated into a cost savings for the firm because it no longer needs to purchase chemicals or supervise the level at which they are used on the grape fields.[23] Fetzer also has initiated innovative educational programs for its employees, including a very successful English as a Second Language program. Already consistent with the mission statement, these initiatives also provide win–win situations for the firm, its employees, and the community at large. Fetzer is a successful firm whose customers get healthier products, whose employees have greater access to education, and whose immediate community enjoys a healthier environment.

Sourcing decisions are another problem area for some firms. Charges that they use sweatshop labor to produce their goods have been made against many well-known companies. Locating production in an underdeveloped country can make economic sense, because it allows the company to take advantage of the lower production costs offered in poorer nations, but it also opens a Pandora's Box of ethical issues, the most prominent of which deals with responsibility. Who is responsible for ensuring that the workers in the factories that produce the goods are treated fairly and paid a living wage? Many firms, including Nike and Kmart, have had to face tough questioning from international labor rights organizations about the working conditions of employees making their products. Even the public faces of firms, such as Mary-Kate and Ashley Olsen and Kathy Lee Gifford, have been faulted for failing to take responsibility for the conditions in factories that produce products bearing their names. Environmental organizations have also joined the attack recently, noting that many overseas factories do not maintain the highest environmental standards.

Once the strategy is implemented, controls must be in place to be certain that the firm has actually done what it has set out to do. These activities take place in the next phase of the strategic marketing planning process.

Control Phase

Like any activity in the control phase of the strategic marketing planning process, managers must be evaluated on their actions from an ethical perspective. Systems must be in place to check whether each potentially ethical issue raised in the planning process was actually successfully implemented. Systems used in the control phase must also react to change. The emergence of new technologies and new markets ensures that new ethical issues continually arise. Many firms have emergency response plans in place just in case they ever encounter a situation similar to the Tylenol tampering emergency or an industrial accident at a manufacturing plant. These plans are designed to ensure the public, the employees, and all other stakeholders that the firm is aware of the potential for problems

---

Adding Value 3.2

Tragedy Hits Six Flags[24]

A day at an amusement park usually brings to mind fun: thrills, excitement, and entertainment. But what happens when it turns tragic? Amusement park operators in the United States, such as Disney and Six Flags Theme Parks, have excellent safety records, but injuries and even deaths sometimes happen. How a park responds to such a tragedy is key to its success; in the decision to attend a park only weather is more important to consumers than their perception of safety.

When a death occurred at a Six Flags park, the park responded immediately. A woman was standing inside the ride zone when a spinning ride started, causing one of the rotating cars to hit and kill her. In the days following the tragedy, Six Flags issued repeated statements and continually expressed sympathy for the victim's family and friends. The park responded not just with words but also with actions. It installed mirrors so that ride operators could verify that all observers were clear of the ride, as well as a public announcement system that notes when the ride begins moving. Industry crisis management experts lauded Six Flags for its response to this tragedy.

The key to handling situations like this, according to crisis management experts, is honest, open, and continual communication. It is crucial for theme parks to inform the public whether the accident was a result of human error or mechanical failure. Mechanical failure often indicates that there may be broad safety

Although theme parks like Six Flags are usually places for wholesome family fun, sometimes accidents happen. When they do, firms must respond honestly, quickly, decisively, and compassionately.

concerns; whereas human error is a chance occurrence for which the public probably does not hold the park responsible. However, informing the public about the circumstances of a death while respecting the rights of the family can be tricky. By balancing its message, Six Flags communicated the necessary information while showing appropriate respect for the family. As a result, park attendance after the tragedy did not suffer.

and equipped to deal with it appropriately. Firms that respond in the first few hours of a crisis with an organized plan and with compassion for those affected suffer fewer long-term negative effects on their reputation, credibility, and level of trust among consumers.[25]

Ethics thus remains a crucial component of the strategic marketing planning process and should be incorporated into all the firm's decision making. Adding Value 3.2 illustrates a case in which the theme park giant Six Flags had to handle a tragic accident.

Firms around the world are recognizing their responsibility to the people who make their products, even if they aren't their employees.

Understanding Ethics Using Scenarios

In the final section of this chapter, we present a series of ethical scenarios designed to assist you in developing your skills at identifying ethical issues. There is no one right answer to the dilemmas below, just as there will be no correct answers to many of the ethical situations you will face throughout your career. Instead, these scenarios can help you develop your sensitivity toward ethical issues, as well as your ethical reasoning skills.

Exhibit 3.8 provides simple tests to assist you in evaluating these scenarios. By asking yourself these simple questions, you can gauge your own ethical response.

EXHIBIT | **3.8** | The Six Tests of Ethical Action

The Publicity Test
- Would I want to see this action that I'm about to take described on the front page of the local paper or in a national magazine?
- How would I feel about having done this if everyone were to find out all about it, including the people I love and care about the most?

The Moral Mentor Test
- What would the person I admire the most do in this situation?

The Admired Observer Test
- Would I want the person I admire most to see me doing this?
- Would I be proud of this action in the presence of a person whose life and character I really admire?
- What would make the person I admire most proud of me in this situation?

The Transparency Test
- Could I give a clear explanation for the action I'm contemplating, including an honest and transparent account of all my motives, that would satisfy a fair and dispassionate moral judge?

The Person in the Mirror Test
- Will I be able to look at myself in the mirror and respect the person I see there?

The Golden Rule Test
- Would I like to be on the receiving end of this action and all its potential consequences?
- Am I treating others the way I'd want to be treated?

Source: Tom Morris, The Art of Achievement: Success in Business and in Life, Fine Communications, 2003.[26]

Scenario 1: Who Is on the Line?

A California company, Star38, has invented a computer program that allows certain telephone users to avoid caller ID systems. For $19.99 per month and $.07 per minute, a caller can log on to the company's Web site, type in the number he or she wants to call, and the number he or she wants to appear on the caller ID screen of the receiving phone. For an additional fee, the caller can create a name to appear along with the phony phone number. Star38 intends to sell its service to collection agencies, private detectives, and law enforcement agencies.

Is this an ethical business plan? Would your answer be the same if Star38 sold its services to any individual who signed up?

Marvin Smith, who runs a collection agency in Austin, Texas, is considering signing up for Star38. Should he?[27]

Scenario 2: West Virginia T-Shirts

A popular teen clothing retailer is selling a t-shirt for $22.50 picturing a map of West Virginia and the slogan: "It's All Relative in West Virginia." The governor of West Virginia has requested that the retailer remove the shirt from its stores and destroy all remaining inventory. In a letter to the president of the retail chain, the governor stated that this slogan is extremely offensive and perpetuates a negative stereotype of his state that undermines the state's efforts to portray the true spirit and values of its citizens.

The communications director for the retailer, in response to the governor's request, stated that the retailer had no plans to remove the shirt, a very popular item. He also stated that the retailer means no disrespect and in fact loves West Virginia. The retailer offers shirts depicting most of the 50 states, which it regards as a way of celebrating the states. By means of example, the communications director pointed to another t-shirt currently on sale: "New Hampshire: 40 Million Squirrels Can't Be Wrong."

Do you think the retailer's response to the governor was appropriate? Was the governor's request appropriate? What would you have done if you had been the retailer? Would your response be different if you knew that this retailer had previously been accused of using pornography in the marketing of its clothing?[28]

Scenario 3: Giving Credit Where Credit Isn't Due

A catalog retailer that carries home and children's items, such as children's furniture, clothing, and toys, was seeking a way to reach a new audience and stop the declining sales and revenue trends it was suffering. A market research firm hired by the cataloger identified a new but potentially risky market: lower-income single parents. The new market seems attractive because of the large number of single parents, but most of these homes are severely constrained in terms of their monetary resources.

The research firm proposed that the cataloger offer a generous credit policy that would allow consumers to purchase up to $500 worth of merchandise on credit without a credit check, provided they sign up for direct payment of their credit account from a checking account. Because these are high-risk consumers, the credit accounts would carry extremely high interest rates. The research firm believes that even with losses, enough accounts will be paid off to make the venture extremely profitable for the catalog retailer.

Should the cataloger pursue this new strategy?

Scenario 4: The Jeweler's Tarnished Image

Sparkle Gem Jewelers, a family-owned and operated costume jewelry manufacturing business, traditionally sold its products only to wholesalers. Recently however, Sparkle Gem was approached by the charismatic Barb Stephens, who convinced the owners to begin selling through a network of distributors she had organized. The distributors recruited individuals to host "jewelry parties" in their homes. Sparkle Gem's owners, the Billing family, has been thrilled with the revenue generated by these home parties and started making plans for the expansion of the distributor network.

However, Mrs. Billing just received a letter from a jewelry party customer, who expressed sympathy for her loss. Mrs. Billing was concerned and contacted the letter writer, who told her that Barb Stephens had come to the jewelry party at her church and told the story of Sparkle Gem. According to Barb's story, Mrs. Billing was a young widow struggling to keep her business together after her husband died on a missionary trip. The writer had purchased $200 worth of jewelry at the party and told Mrs. Billing that she hoped it helped. Mrs. Billing was stunned. She and her very much alive husband had just celebrated their 50th wedding anniversary.

What should Mrs. Billing do now?

Scenario 5: No Wonder It's So Good

Enjoy Cola is a new product produced by ABC Beverage and marketed with the slogan "Relax with Enjoy." Unlike other colas on the market, Enjoy does not contain caffeine and therefore is positioned as the perfect beverage to end the day or for a slow-paced weekend, and as a means to help consumers relax and unwind. The market response has been tremendous, and sales of Enjoy have been growing rapidly, especially among women.

ABC Beverage decided not to list on the ingredients label that Enjoy contains a small amount of alcohol because it is not required to do so by the government unless the alcohol content is more than 1 percent.

Mia Rodriquez, the marketing director for Enjoy, only recently learned that Enjoy contains small amounts of alcohol and is troubled about ABC's failure to disclose this information on the ingredients list. If the alcohol content is less than one percent, the beverage is not an alcoholic beverage. Currently there is not a requirement to list alcohol on the label if it is under that one percent. She worries about the impact of this omission on consumers who have alcohol sensitivities or those who shouldn't be consuming alcohol, such as pregnant women and recovering alcoholics.

What should Mia do? What would you do in Mia's place?

Scenario 6: Bright Baby's Bright Idea

Bartok Manufacturing produces a line of infant toys under the "Bright Baby" brand label. The Consumer Product Safety Commission (CPSC) recently issued a recall order for the Bright Baby car seat gym, a very popular product. According to the CPSC, the gym contains small parts that present a choking hazard. The CEO of Bartok Manufacturing, Bill Bartok, called an executive meeting to determine the firm's strategy in response to the recall.

Mike Henderson, Bartok's CFO, stated that the recall could cost as much as $1 million in lost revenue from the Bright Baby line. Noting that there had been no deaths or injuries from the product, just the *potential* for injury, Mike proposed that the remaining inventory of car seat gyms be sold in Mexico, where there are no rules such as the CPSC's. Sue Tyler, the marketing director for Bartok, recommended that the product be repackaged and sold in Mexico under a different brand name so that the Bright Baby name would not be associated with the product. Bill, though a bit leery of the plan, agreed to go along with it to avoid the monetary losses.

What would you have recommended to the CEO?

Summing Up

1. Why do marketers have to worry about ethics?

The most important reason to worry about making ethically correct decisions is that it is simply the right thing to do! Being a part of an ethically responsible firm should be important to every employee, but it is particularly important to marketers because they interact most directly with customers and suppliers, which offers them a multitude of opportunities to get involved in ethically challenged issues. It is often challenging to make ethically correct decisions because they can conflict with other personal or corporate objectives.

2. What does it take for a firm to be considered socially responsible?

Individuals and firms can (and should) act ethically, but the outcome of their acts may not affect anyone other than the firm's immediate stakeholders, such as its employees, customers, and suppliers. To be socially responsible, a firm also must take actions that benefit the community in a larger sense, such as helping people who have been affected by a natural disaster like a hurricane.

3. **How should a firm make ethically responsible decisions?**

First, firms can include ethics and social responsibility in their corporate mission. Second, they should institute policies and procedures to ensure that everyone working for the firm is acting in an ethically responsible manner. Third, firms can model their ethical policies after a well-established code of ethics like the one provided by the American Marketing Association. Fourth, when making ethically sensitive decisions, firms can utilize an ethical decision-making evaluation questionnaire, such as that described in Exhibit 3.6.

4. **How can ethics and social responsibility be integrated into a firm's marketing strategy?**

Firms can ensure that ethics and social responsibility issues are an integral part of their planning processes. These considerations even could be integrated into the firm's mission statement, as long as top management commits to supporting a strong ethical climate within the organization. When considering their marketing strategy, firms should ask not only "can we implement a certain policy?" but also "should we do it?" Finally, in the control phase, marketers must determine whether they truly have acted in an ethical and socially responsible manner. If not, they should quickly rectify the situation.

Key Terms

- business ethics, 61
- corporate social responsibility, 66
- ethical climate, 62
- marketing ethics, 61

Marketing Applications

1. Why are marketers likely to be faced with more ethical dilemmas than members of other functional areas of the firm, like finance, accounting, or real estate?

2. Develop an argument for why a pharmaceutical firm should build and maintain an ethical climate.

3. An insurance company gives generously to charities and sponsors cancer awareness programs. It also makes it difficult for elderly consumers to make claims on policies that they have owned for years. Evaluate this company from an ethical and social responsibility perspective.

4. A large U.S.-based shoe manufacturer is negotiating with a company in Brazil to make a new line of sneakers. The manufacturer wants a high quality shoe at a reasonable cost but is concerned that the Brazilian workers will be underpaid and asked to work long hours in unpleasant conditions. Develop a stakeholder analysis matrix similar to that in Exhibit 3.5 to assess the impact of this decision on the relevant stakeholders.

5. Based on the shoe manufacturing scenario you developed for Question 4, provide responses to the ethical decision-making evaluation questionnaire from Exhibit 3.6. Provide a rationale for your confidence score for each question.

6. A company that makes granola and other "healthy" snacks has the following mission statement: "Our goal is to profitably sell good-tasting, healthy products and to better society." Although its products are organic, they also are relatively high in calories. The company gives a small portion of its profits to the United Way. Evaluate the mission statement.

7. The granola company described in the last question is thinking about starting an advertising campaign directed at children that would air on Saturday morning television. Explain why you think it should or should not do so.

8. A health inspector found some rodent droppings in one batch of granola made by this same company. What should the company do?

Net Savvy

1. Perhaps no subdiscipline of marketing receives more scrutiny regarding ethical compliance than direct marketing, a form of nonstore retailing in which customers are exposed to and purchase merchandise or services through an impersonal medium such as telephone, mail, or the Internet.[29] Ethical issues in direct marketing cover a broad spectrum because this means of selling is conducted through all forms of communication. The Direct Marketing Association (DMA) takes ethics very seriously and has numerous programs to ensure that its member organizations comply with its Code of Ethics. Go to the Web site for the Direct Marketing Association (http://www.the-dma.org/) and type the word *ethics* in the search box. Discuss the results of your search. How many different ways did you find that the DMA was involved in assisting consumers and the industry to create a more ethical marketplace?

2. An increasing number of firms are stating their strong commitment to corporate social responsibility initiatives. The Corporate Social Responsibility Newswire Service keeps track of these various initiatives and posts stories on its Web site about what various corporations are doing. Go to http://www.csrwire.com/ and choose one story. Write a description of the corporation and the initiative.

Chapter Case Study

WHOSE SIDE ARE YOU ON?[30]

Britt Smith was recently hired by a large architecture and engineering firm as an assistant account manager in the government contracts division. The firm specializes in building hospitals, schools and other large-scale projects. Britt is excited to learn that she will be part of the marketing team that presents the firm's proposals to the clients. In this case the clients are primarily federal and state governmental agencies. The presentations are elaborate, often costing $50,000 or more to prepare. But the projects can be worth millions to the firm, so the investment is worth it. The firm has a solid record for building quality projects, on time, and the majority of the time within budget. The firm also has an impressive track record, being awarded government contracts an incredible 85 percent of the time. No other firm in the industry comes close to this record.

The first project Britt is assigned to is an enormous project to design a new military hospital complex. The team leader, Brian Jenkins, has stressed how crucial it is for the firm to land this contract. He hints that if the team is successful the members will be well compensated. In fact, Britt heard that the members of the winning team for the last contract this size each received a $10,000 bonus.

Not long after the project commences, Brian invites Britt to have lunch so they can get to know each other better. During lunch, a man approaches Brian and asks if he has received the information. The man says that he knows that with this information the firm is a sure winner. He also reminds Brian that he is due a bonus for getting such crucial information. Brian comes back and explains that the man was George Miller who was the former head of the division awarding the hospital contract. George had been helping Brian by talking to the decision team and getting information that was relevant to the bid. Brian explained that the information George gathered about the internal discussions among the buying team would be what made their proposal a clear winner. This was obviously good news for the team since a winning bid meant bonuses were almost assured.

After lunch Britt looked at the firm's ethics manual that she had been given just last week at a new employee orientation. Lobbying without disclosure and paying for insider information were clearly discussed as unethical practices. Yet Brian seemed perfectly comfortable discussing George's role with Britt.

Britt decides she should check with another team member about the use of insider information, so she asks Sue Garcia. Sue tells Britt that this kind of thing happens all the time. She jokes that most of the people in the division had at one time or another worked for the government. They all still knew people in the various agencies. As far as Sue was concerned, friends will talk and that is not illegal, so there was no problem. It was a win–win situation: the government got their building, the firm got their funding, and the employees got their bonuses.

Britt realizes that with her overdue credit card bill and her needed car repairs, the bonus money would really help out. Besides she is the most junior member of the team. If all the others are comfortable with this practice, why should she be concerned? After, all it is just friends talking, isn't it?

Should Britt go to the company's ethics officer and report what she knows about the use of insider information?

Questions

1. Using the framework for ethical decision making presented in the chapter (Exhibit 3.6), analyze Britt's dilemma. Should she go to the company's ethics officer and report what she knows about the use of insider information?

2. As the most junior member of the team, do you feel that Britt has less of an ethical duty to report the actions of the team than more senior members of the team do? Why or why not?

3. If you were the ethics officer for this firm would you address the belief among employees that it is acceptable to discuss a pending proposal with members of the decision team? If so, how? If you would not discuss this belief, why not?

4

QUESTIONS

- How do customers, the company, competitors, and corporate partners affect marketing strategy?

- Why do marketers have to think about their macroenvionment when they make decisions?

- How do marketers use scenario planning to determine which courses of action to take?

Analyzing the Marketing Environment

From cabbage soup to hypnosis to metabolic pills, the diet industry has reshaped not only physiques but also entire markets.[1] With more than 190 million overweight Americans awash in a culture that values youthful thinness, it is not surprising that the diet industry represents a $40 billion operation.

The push to find a miracle weight-loss cure has invaded bookstores, gymnasiums, grocery stores, and restaurants. Walk through any bookstore and find among the bestsellers books such as *Dr. Phil's Ultimate Weight Solution* and *The South Beach Diet*. Then take a trip through your local drug, grocery, or discount store and note the shakes, bars, and packaged foods bearing the exact same names.

The nation's fastest growing health club franchise, Curves, also is benefiting from the dietary boom. The female-only, 30-minute workout fitness center has grown from one location in 1995 to more than 9,500 in the United States, Canada, and abroad.

Perhaps the greatest indication of the power of the weight-loss movement appears in the restaurant industry. In February 2003, Darden Restaurants, Inc., the nation's largest casual dining restaurateur, opened Seasons 52, which features seasonally fresh entrees that contain fewer than 475 calories and appetizers and desserts with fewer than 250 calories.

National chains are following suit. Chili's menu now includes a section entitled "Guiltless Grill" with options including a black bean burger and grilled salmon. Likewise, Ruby Tuesdays' "Smart Eating" insignia can be found in all sections of its menu, including appetizers and desserts.

Curves is for women only. It's not a fast-food franchise. It's a fast-exercise franchise.

A Marketing Environment Analysis Framework

As the opening vignette of this chapter suggests, marketers have become more aware of recent changes in what their customers want with regard to weight-loss programs and products and have adapted their product and service offerings accordingly to meet those needs. By paying close attention to customer needs and continuously monitoring the environment in which it operates, a good marketer can identify potential opportunities.

Exhibit 4.1 illustrates the factors that affect the marketing environment, whose centerpiece, as always, is consumers. Consumers may be influenced directly by the immediate actions of the focal company, the company's competitors, and the corporate partners that work with the firm to make and supply products and services to consumers. The firm, and therefore consumers indirectly, is influenced by the macroenvironment, which includes various influences from culture and demographics, as well as social, technological, economic, and political/legal factors. We'll discuss each of these components in detail in this chapter and suggest how they might interrelate.

As illustrated in Exhibit 4.1, the consumer is the center of all marketing efforts. One of the goals of value-based marketing is to provide greater value to consumers than competitors offer. This provision requires that the marketing firm look at the entire business process from a consumer's point of view.[2] Consumers' needs and wants, as well as their ability to purchase, are affected by a host of factors that change and evolve over time. Firms use a variety of tools to keep track of their competitors' activities and communicate with their corporate partners. Furthermore, they monitor their macroenvironment to determine how such factors influence consumers and how they should respond to them. Sometimes, a firm can even anticipate trends.

For example, pharmaceutical companies have done an excellent job of monitoring consumers and responding to their needs and market trends. On the basis

| **EXHIBIT** | **4.1** | Understanding the Marketing Environment |

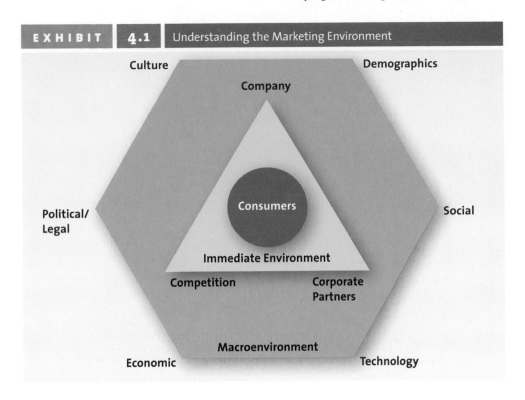

of observing and monitoring the aging Baby Boomer generation of consumers, they have made and marketed drugs to lower cholesterol, improve sexual performance, and retard hair loss. What's next on the list? Imagine the needs and wants of these consumers, and the answer—a new array of "lifestyle drugs, including those that improve intelligence, with the first step being memory enhancers"[3]—may appear obvious.

The Immediate Environment

Exhibit 4.2 illustrates the factors affecting the immediate environment: the company's capabilities, competitors and competitive intelligence, and the company's corporate partners.

Successfully Leveraging Company Capabilities

In the immediate environment, the first factor that affects the consumer is the firm itself. Successful marketing firms focus their efforts on satisfying customer needs that match their core competencies. The primary strength of Pepsi, for instance, rests in the manufacture, distribution, and promotion of carbonated beverages, but it has successfully leveraged its core competency in the bottled water arena with its Aquafina brand after recognizing the marketplace trend toward and consumer desire for bottled water. Marketers can use an analysis of the external environment, like the SWOT analysis described in Chapter 2, to categorize an opportunity as either attractive or unattractive and, if it appears attractive, to assess it relative to the firm's existing competencies.

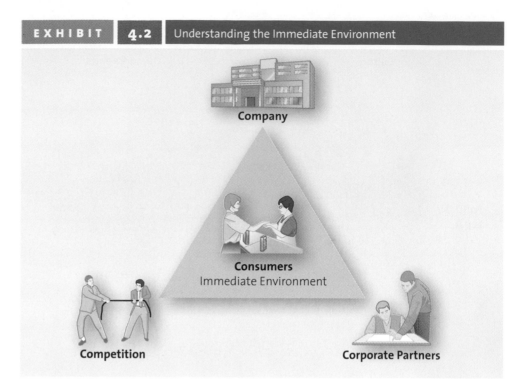

| EXHIBIT | 4.2 | Understanding the Immediate Environment |

Competitors and Competitive Intelligence

Competition also significantly affects consumers in the immediate environment. It is critical that marketers understand their firm's competitors, including their strengths, weaknesses, and likely reactions to marketing activities their own firm undertakes. Firms use **competitive intelligence (CI)** to collect and synthesize information about their position with respect to their rivals. In this way, CI enables companies to anticipate market developments rather than merely react to them.[4] In the United States, the Society of Competitive Intelligence Professionals reports that "the market for business intelligence amounts to about $2 billion annually" and that "a 1997 survey found that 82% of companies with revenues over $10 billion had some kind of intelligence."[5]

The strategies to gather CI can range from simply sending a retail employee to a competitive store to check merchandise, prices, and foot traffic to more involved methods, such as

■   Reviewing public materials including Web sites, press releases, industry journals, annual reports, subscription databases, permit applications, patent applications, and tradeshows.

■   Interviewing customers, suppliers, partners, or former employees.

■   Analyzing a rival's marketing tactics, distribution practices, pricing, and hiring needs.

These more sophisticated CI strategies are implicitly obvious in the modern razor market. Although men and women have been shaving for thousands of years, it wasn't until 1901 that anyone tried to sell a disposable, thin piece of metal sharp enough to shave hair. In its first year of production, the Gillette Safety Razor Company, as it was known then, sold 50 razor sets. The following year it sold

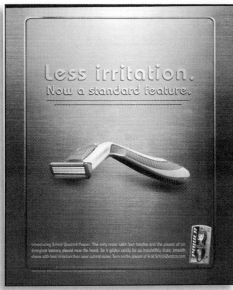

Who copied whom? Gillette and Schick introduced similar razors almost simultaneously.

12 million—obviously, the company anticipated a need well. Today, American men spend almost $2 billion annually on razors and blades. In 1998, Gillette, the U.S. market leader with 70 percent market share, changed the landscape again by launching the enormously successful Mach3, a three-blade razor.[6] Not to be outdone, Energizer Holding, the owner of Schick, introduced the Quattro razor, the world's first four-blade razor in 2003. The resulting battle for the title of "best razor" and for market share has resulted in a costly promotional and pricing battle. Razors that normally retail for up to $10 are being given away for free, and coupons for the corresponding razor blades appear everywhere.[7] In situations such as this, it becomes critical for firms like Gillette and Schick to keep close tabs on each other's activities using CI techniques. If Schick hadn't paid attention to the release of the Mach3, it may never have introduced the Quattro.

Although CI is widely regarded as a necessary function in today's world, certain methods of obtaining information have come under ethical and legal scrutiny. Take for example Gillette's case against Schick. Within hours of the press release introducing the Quattro in August 2003, Gillette had filed a patent infringement lawsuit claiming that the Quattro violates its Mach3 system's technology patent.[8] To file the suit so quickly, Gillette must have known about the impending launch well before Schick announced it, but how the company found out forms the core of the ethical question. According to the court papers that Gillette filed two weeks later, "a company engineer shared the results of scientific tests conducted on 10 Quattro cartridges obtained by the company." Schick quickly questioned how Gillette obtained the cartridges prior to their commercial release in an ethically appropriate manner. But Schick's ethical argument apparently held little sway, as the U.S. Appeals Court ruled on April 29, 2005, that Gillette's patent could extend to four or even five blades and was not limited to the number of blades currently installed in the Mach3.[9] Armed with this ruling, Gillette and Schick continue to compete head-to-head. Gillette released the manual and battery operated Fusion, one-upping the Quattro with five blades. Schick, in anticipation of the Fusion, created three stylized versions of the Quattro, the Schick Quattro Chrome, Midnight, and Power to appeal to shavers on a more aesthetic level.[10]

Adding Value 4.1

Toyota and a Little Help from Its Friends

Early one morning, a factory that supplied brake fluid proportioning valves to Toyota's 20 automobile plants in Japan was engulfed in flames.[11] Scheduled to produce 14,000 cars per day with JIT inventories that used a window of about four hours, Toyota faced a crippling dilemma that could have shut down its production for weeks. Acting quickly, Toyota acquired the blueprints for the valve, improvised tooling systems, and set up make-shift production lines within hours of the fire. The key to success was intense, rapid coordination across a diverse group of suppliers and other supply chain partners.

As a testament to Toyota's strong relationships with its suppliers and partners, four days later, 36 of Toyota's suppliers, aided by more than 150 other subcontractors, had created nearly 50 separate lines producing small batches of the brake valves. Thanks to their corporate partners, Toyota's production lines started up again and a disaster was averted.

At this Toyota plant in Georgetown, Kentucky, parts and materials arrive just in time for production.

Corporate Partners

The third factor that affects the consumer in the immediate environment is the firm's corporate partners. Few firms operate in isolation. For example, automobile manufacturers collaborate with suppliers of sheet metal, tire manufacturers, component part makers, unions, transport companies, and dealerships to produce and market their automobiles successfully. Even firms like Dell, which makes its own computers and sells them directly to customers, must purchase components, consulting services, advertising, and transportation from others. Those parties that work along with the focal firm can be viewed as its corporate partners.

Let's consider the role these partners play and how they work together with the firm to create one efficient manufacturing system. Companies such as Toyota, Dell, General Motors, and Ford have long realized the importance of their various corporate partners. Toyota, like many automobile companies, engages in a **just-in-time (JIT) inventory system** that keeps inventories of automobile components to a minimum because the company only orders them from suppliers to arrive just in time to be used. But even the best JIT systems face unforeseen situations, as Adding Value 4.1 illustrates.

Macroenvironmental Factors

In addition to understanding their customers, the company itself, their competition, and their corporate partners in their immediate environment, marketers must also understand the **macroenvironmental factors** that operate in the external environment, namely, the **c**ulture, **d**emographics, **s**ocial issues, **t**echnological advances, **e**conomic situation, and **p**olitical/regulatory environment, or CDSTEP, as shown in Exhibit 4.3.

EXHIBIT | **4.3** | The Macroenvironment

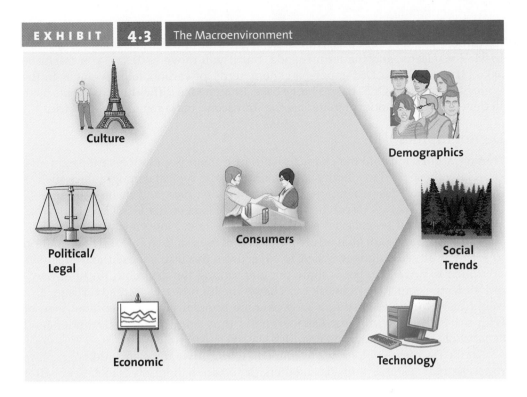

Culture

We broadly define **culture** as the shared meanings, beliefs, morals, values, and customs of a group of people.[12] Transmitted by words, literature, and institutions, culture gets passed down from generation to generation and learned over time. You participate in many cultures: Your family has a cultural heritage; your school or workplace also shares its own common culture. In a broader sense, you also participate in the cultural aspects of the town and country in which you live. The challenge for marketers is to determine whether their culture can serve as a relevant identifier for a particular group of people who would be interested in purchasing the firms' products and services. Our various cultures influence what, why, how, where, and when we buy. Two dimensions of culture that marketers must take into account as they develop their marketing strategies are the culture of the country and that of a region within a country.

Country Culture   The visible nuances of a country's culture, such as artifacts, behavior, dress, symbols, physical settings, ceremonies, language differences, colors and tastes, and food preferences, are easy to spot. But the subtle aspects of culture generally are trickier to identify and navigate. Volkswagen has successfully marketed its Jetta in the United States to a young, slightly offbeat subsegment of the population by providing subtle cultural cues in its promotions with its "Drivers Wanted" and "It's all grown up. Sort of" campaigns.

Regional Culture   The region in which people live in a particular country affects the way they refer to a particular product category. For instance, 38 percent of Americans refer to carbonated beverages as "soda," whereas another 38 percent call it "pop," and an additional 19 percent call any such beverage a "Coke," even when it is Pepsi. Eat lunch in Indiana, and you'll have the best luck ordering a pop from the Midwesterner who owns the restaurant, but if you then head to Atlanta for dinner, you'd better order your Coke, regardless of the brand you prefer. Head to Massachusetts, and the term is soda, but if you move to Texas, you might be asked if you'd like a Dr Pepper—a generic term for carbonated beverages in the Lone Star state and Dr Pepper's home base. Imagine the difficulty these firms have in developing promotional materials that transcend these regional boundaries.[13]

Demographics

Demographics indicate the characteristics of human populations and segments, especially those used to identify consumer markets. Typical demographics such as age—which includes generational cohorts—gender, race, and income are readily available from market research firms like ACNeilsen or the U.S. Census Bureau. For instance, Neilsen collects information about television viewership and sells it to networks and potential advertisers. The networks then use this information to set their advertising fees, whereas advertisers use it to choose the best shows on which to advertise. For a show popular among the desirable 18- to 35-year-old viewing segment, a network can charge the highest fees. But advertisers also might want to know whether a show is more popular with women than men or with urban or rural viewers. Demographics thus provide an easily understood "snapshot" of the typical consumer in a specific target market.

In the next few sections, we examine how firms use some such demographics to assess their customers' needs and therefore position themselves to deliver better value for those customers' desired merchandise and services.

Marketers position their products and services differently depending on which generational cohort they are targeting.

Generational Cohorts Consumers in a generational cohort—a group of people of the same generation—have similar purchase behaviors because they have shared experiences and are in the same stage of life. For instance, Baby Boomers (people born after World War II, 1946–1964) and Generation Xers (people born between 1965 and 1976) both gravitate toward products and services that foster a casual lifestyle; however, they tend to do so for different reasons.[14] The aging Baby Boomers, who grew up with jeans and khakis and brought casual dressing into the business arena, are often trying to maintain their youth. Xers, in contrast, typically wear jeans and khakis because they are less impressed with the symbols of conspicuous consumption that their parents seem to have embraced. Although there are many ways to cut the generational pie, we discuss five major groups, as listed in Exhibit 4.4.

Seniors Seniors make up America's fastest-growing group.[15] Between 1996 and 2010, the number of people aged 55 to 64 years will grow 65.2 percent. But just because they are a large segment, are they necessarily an important market segment for marketers to pursue? They're more likely to complain, need special attention, and take time browsing before making a purchase compared with younger groups. However, they generally have time to shop and money to spend.

In the past, seniors were very conservative with their savings because they wanted something to pass on to their children. But that attitude appears to be changing. Perhaps you have seen the bumper sticker: "I am spending my chil-

EXHIBIT	4.4	Generational Cohorts				
Generational Cohort	Tweens	Gen Y	Gen X	Baby Boomers	Seniors
Range of Birth Years	1996-2000	1977-1995	1965-1976	1946-1964	Before 1946
Age in 2008	8-12	13-31	32-43	44-62	63 and older

dren's inheritance"?[16] Older people seem to be buying goods and services at the same pace as younger generations. What do they spend their money on? Travel, second homes, luxury cars, electronic equipment, investments, home furnishings, and clothing are frequent purchases.

Specifically, seniors tend to like "made in the USA" items, natural fibers, recognizable brand names (but generally not designer labels), value, quality, and classic styles. They're typically loyal and willing to spend but are extremely quality conscious and demand hassle-free shopping, particularly in terms of convenient locations. Because most mature customers don't need the basics, they would prefer to buy a few high-quality items rather than a larger number of low-quality items.[17]

However many seniors who live alone and on fixed incomes often fall prey to unscrupulous marketing practices. Marketers who offer promises of high yield returns, "safe" investments, and even wonder cures find a vulnerable market in seniors. Other marketers prey on seniors' isolation and loneliness by "befriending" them and using that relationship to encourage the purchase of unnecessary products and services. Many states now have offices within the State's Attorney General's office designed to protect seniors from these abusive marketing practices. (See Ethical Dilemma 4.1.)

Baby Boomers   After World War II, the birth rate in the United States rose sharply, resulting in a group known as the Baby Boomers, the 78 million Americans born between 1946 and 1964. Although the Baby Boomer generation spans 18 years, experts agree that its members share several traits that set them apart from those born before World War II. First, they are individualistic. Second, leisure time represents a high priority for them. Third, they believe that they will always be able to take care of themselves, partly evinced by their feeling of economic security, even though they are a little careless about the way they spend their money. Fourth, they have an obsession with maintaining their youth. Fifth and finally, they will always love rock 'n roll.

The Baby Boomers' quest for youth, in both attitude and appearance, provides a constantly growing market. For instance, Boomers spend $30 billion per year on antiaging products and therefore have reenergized businesses ranging from food and cosmetics to pharmaceuticals and biotechnology.[18] Salon services used to be a purely feminine domain, but with Boomers turning 50 at the rate of seven per minute, providers are recognizing the potential of positioning themselves as

being in the rejuvenation business. In ways that previous generations would have considered unthinkable, men have begun pampering themselves with salon services such as manicures, facials, and pedicures. Taking advantage of this trend, male spas have begun popping up in areas such as Washington, DC, and Tucson, Arizona.[20]

Generation X   The next group, **Generation X** (Xers), includes those born between 1965 and 1976 and represents some 41 million Americans.[21] Vastly unlike their Baby Boomer parents, Xers are the first generation of latchkey children (those who grew up in homes in which both parents worked), and 50 percent of them have divorced parents.

Although fewer in number than **Generation Y** or Baby Boomers, Gen Xers possess considerable spending power because they tend to wait to get married and buy houses later in life. They're much less interested in shopping than their parents but far more cynical, which tends to make them astute consumers. They demand convenience and tend to be less likely to believe advertising claims or what salespeople tell them. Because of their experience as children of working parents, who had little time to shop, Xers developed shopping savvy at an early age and knew how to make shopping decisions by the time they were teenagers.

No matter how old they get, Baby Boomers will always love rock n' roll.

As a result, they grew more knowledgeable about products and more risk averse than other generational cohorts. Finally, Xers are much less interested in status products than older generations, not because they can't afford luxury brands but because they just don't see the point. They ask, "Why shop at Neiman Marcus when Kohl's and Target are just as good, cheaper, and more convenient?"

Generation Y   With 60 million in the United States alone, **Generation Y** is more than three times the size of Generation X and the biggest cohort since the original postwar baby boom. This group also varies the most in age, ranging from teenagers to young adults who have their own families.[22] Like Xers, Gen Y also is skeptical about what they hear in the media, which makes marketing to this group even more challenging. If a Gen Y member believes the sell is "too hard," he won't buy. Regardless of where they live, they watch an hour less of television than an average household, accept the use of personal Internet time at work, and expect a healthy option at fast-food restaurants.[23] Most experts believe the reason for the similarities among this broad group is, quite simply, the Web. To appeal to the first generation tied together by a worldwide media web, market-savvy firms can spot trends in one country and market them in others.

Multitasking is no big deal for Gen Y.

Exhibit 4.5 provides some interesting comparisons between Baby Boomers and their children—Generation X and Generation Y.

Tweens   Tweens—not quite teenagers, but not young children either—sit in beTWEEN. The importance of Tweens to marketers stems from their immense buying power, estimated at $260 billion annually in the United States alone.[24] In

EXHIBIT 4.5	Generational Cohort Comparisons	
Baby Boomers	**Generation X**	**Generation Y**
Diversity as a cause	Accept diversity	Celebrate diversity
Idealistic	Pragmatic/cynical	Optimistic/realistic
Mass movement	Self-reliant/individualistic	Self-inventive/individualistic
Conform to the rules	Reject rules	Rewrite the rules
Killer job	Killer life	Killer lifestyle
Became institutions	Mistrust institutions	Irrelevance of institutions
TV	PC	Internet
Have technology	Use technology	Assume tech
Task-technology	Multitask	Multitask fast
Ozzie and Harriet	Latch-key kids	Nurtured
Other boomers	Friend-not family	Friends-family

Source: "Gen Y and the future of mall retailing," *American Demographics*, December 2002 24. (11) p. J1.

Watch out for Tweens. They are fast, multitasking, technology-savvy, and easily bored.

China, this trend appears even more significant; as a result of China's 1979 one-child policy for families, parents and grandparents are intensely focused on the needs of their only child and spend nearly 40 percent of their household income on their "little emperor or empress."[25] These kids may look and act like children, but they sometimes surprise their parents and marketers by consuming like teenagers. Like their big brothers and sisters in Generation Y, much of their market power comes from Tweens' strong influence on family purchases.

Tweens are also known as Speeders, because they do everything at lightning speed.[26] The first generation born after the emergence of the Internet, technology has no novelty for them. They communicate with friends via instant messaging, talk on a cell telephone, and watch television simultaneously. Marketers reach this group primarily through television and the Internet, but because many parents limit television viewing times, the Internet provides a huge media opportunity. Marketers must be careful with this cohort though; once they get bored, Tweens are gone, off doing something else. So firms need to engage them quickly and with sincerity.

And what do Tweens like? In the food industry, they lean toward products like Heinz's green ketchup and Yoplait's GoGURT. For toys and clothing, they have made Build-A-Bear Workshop, Claire's, and Limited Too immensely popular. However, because they have little of their own money, Tweens tend to be value conscious, which makes them key targets for retailers such as Wal-Mart, Target, and Kohl's.

Income Income distribution in the United States has grown more polarized—the highest-income groups are growing, whereas many middle- and lower-income groups' real purchasing power keeps declining. According to the 2000 Census, the richest 20 percent of the households in the United States received 49.7 percent of all household income, whereas the bottom 20 percent accounted for merely 3.6 percent.[27] The increase in wealthy families may be due to the maturing of the general population, the increase in dual-income households, and the higher overall level of education. This broad range in incomes creates marketing opportunities at both the high and low ends of the market.

Although some marketers choose to target only affluent population segments, others have had great success delivering value to middle- and low-income earners. Consider, for example, the toys presented by the specialty retailer Hammacher Schlemmer versus the mass appeal of Wal-Mart's everyday low prices (EDLP), which has made it the world's largest toy retailer. Toy buyers at Wal-Mart are looking for inexpensive products; those at Hammacher Schlemmer go to great lengths to find exclusive, one-of-a-kind products, like a radio-controlled paraglider for $329.[28]

This water cannon electric boat from Hammacher Schlemmer is a rechargeable electric watercraft powerful enough for riders to navigate lakes and ponds for up to six hours per charge, and it has a built-in motorized water canon that can continuously spray a stream of water up to 35'. It can be yours for only $1995.95.

Another aspect of the income demographic relates to the concept of value. Why are customers searching for this value more today than in recent decades? During the first three decades after World War II, most American families experienced real income growth, but in the late 1970s through early 2000s, that growth began to stagnate. Family incomes have stayed slightly ahead of inflation (the general rate of price increases), but their health care costs, property taxes, and tuition bills have risen much faster than inflation.

Education   Studies show that higher levels of education lead to better jobs and higher incomes.[29] (See Exhibit 4.6.) According the U.S. Bureau of Labor, employment that requires a college or secondary degree will account for 42 percent of projected job growth between 2000 and 2010. Moreover, average annual earnings are higher for those with degrees than for those without. Those who did not graduate from high school have an average annual salary of $18,083; high school grads earn $26,104; those with a bachelor's degree earn $42,087.[30]

For some products, marketers can combine education level with other data like occupation and income and obtain pretty accurate predictions of purchase behavior. For instance, a full-time college student with a part-time job may have relatively little personal income but will spend his or her disposable dollars differently than would a high school graduate who works in a factory and earns a similar income. College students tend to be engaged in playing sports and going to clubs, whereas the high school graduate more likely watches sports and goes to bars. Marketers are therefore quite cognizant of the interaction among education, income, and occupation.

Since women are such an important segment of their customers, Lowe's, the giant home improvement chain, has designed their stores with women in mind.

Gender   Years ago, gender roles appeared clear, but those male/female roles have been blurred. This shift in attitude and behavior affects the way many firms design and promote their products and services. For example, more firms are careful about gender neutrality in positioning their products and, furthermore, attempt to transcend gender boundaries whenever they can.

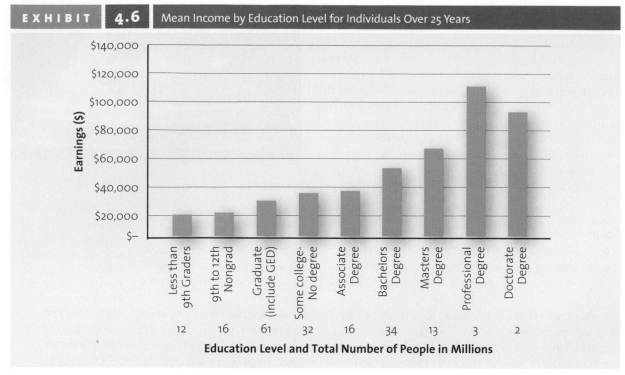

EXHIBIT 4.6 Mean Income by Education Level for Individuals Over 25 Years

Education Level and Total Number of People in Millions

Education Level	Number in Millions
Less than 9th Graders	12
9th to 12th Nongrad	16
Graduate (include GED)	61
Some college-No degree	32
Associate Degree	16
Bachelors Degree	34
Masters Degree	13
Professional Degree	3
Doctorate Degree	2

Source: www.census.gov

Women are no longer the only family member doing the grocery shopping.

From cars to copiers, sweaters to sweeteners, women make the majority of purchasing decisions and then influence most of the remainder. For instance, despite the traditional view that hardware stores appeal mostly to men, women shoppers are so important to Lowe's, the giant home improvement chain, that the stores have been designed with women in mind.[31] Furthermore, women now head almost 30 percent of American households.[32] Clearly, the working women's segment is a large, complex, lucrative market.

But that doesn't mean marketers have forgotten about men. The days of commercials that show Mom alone with the kids are over. To reflect changing family roles, commercials for most children's gear now include Dad interacting with the kids and being involved in purchase decisions. Men still earn more money than women, as indicated in Exhibit 4.7. As the income distribution shows, there are more women earning lower incomes, and more men earning higher incomes.

Ethnicity Due to immigration and increasing birth rates among various ethnic and racial groups, the United States continues to grow more diverse.[33] Approximately 80 percent of all population growth in the next 20 years is expected to come from Black, Hispanic, and Asian communities. Minorities now represent approximately one-quarter of the population; by 2050, they will represent about 50 percent. Most of the foreign-born American population and recent immigrants tend to concentrate in a handful of metropolitan areas, such as New York, Los Angeles, San Francisco, and Chicago.[34] (See Exhibit 4.8.)

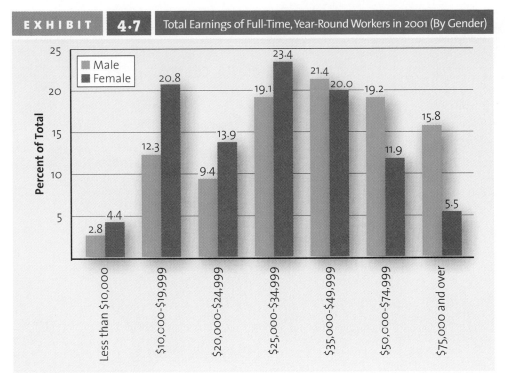

EXHIBIT **4.7** Total Earnings of Full-Time, Year-Round Workers in 2001 (By Gender)

Legend:
- Male
- Female

Y-axis: Percent of Total

Income Range	Male	Female
Less than $10,000	2.8	4.4
$10,000–$19,999	12.3	20.8
$20,000–$24,999	9.4	13.9
$25,000–$34,999	19.1	23.4
$35,000–$49,999	21.4	20.0
$50,000–$74,999	19.2	11.9
$75,000 and over	15.8	5.5

Source: www.census.gov

In 2002, the discretionary income of Blacks, Hispanics, and Asians was $646 billion, $581 billion, and $296 billion, respectively.[35] In response to this growing purchasing power, some firms—both retailers and manufacturers—are focusing on the large and growing middle and affluent classes among these minorities. In addition, minorities make up a bigger share of the retail workforce than in the past, particularly in arenas such as food stores, restaurants, and service retailers like dry cleaners and gas stations. Through these roles many immigrant entrepreneurs have revitalized neighborhoods and small towns.

Although African American households at large remain less affluent than other groups, they also represent some retailers' best customers. For instance, African Americans spend proportionally more on women's dress shoes, clothing for teenagers, jewelry, women's athletic wear, and children's shoes than do other ethnic groups. Retailers that provide products and services that enhance personal appearance should take special note of this market. In general, African Americans spend more than their white counterparts on big-ticket items such as cars, clothing, and home furnishings. Many also have an affinity for brand-name products because they equate them with quality.

Many retailers also pay particular attention to the Hispanic market.[36] About 350,000 Hispanic immigrants come to the United States every year, and they and their U.S.-born children should increase the number of Hispanic Americans from just under 17 million in 1995 to more than 52.7 million in 2020.[37] Hispanic households tend to be larger than those of other groups and represent a $171 billion annual market.

The United States is like a salad bowl, made up of people from every corner of the world.

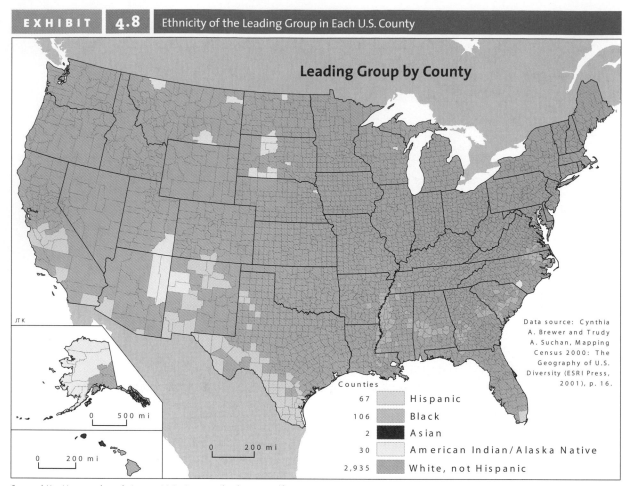

EXHIBIT 4.8 Ethnicity of the Leading Group in Each U.S. County

Leading Group by County

JT K

Data source: Cynthia
A. Brewer and Trudy
A. Suchan, Mapping
Census 2000: The
Geography of U.S.
Diversity (ESRI Press,
2001), p. 16.

0   500 mi

0   200 mi

0   200 mi

Counties		
67		Hispanic
106		Black
2		Asian
30		American Indian/Alaska Native
2,935		White, not Hispanic

Source: http://www.valpo.edu/geomet/pics/geo2oo/lead_group.pdf

The Hispanic market is so large in some areas that marketers develop entire marketing programs just to meet its needs.

Forty-one percent have annual incomes of at least $25,000, though Cubans have a much higher income than either Mexican or Puerto Rican consumers. There's little difference in education, employment, or income between whites and Hispanics who were born in the United States or have lived here at least five years. The Hispanic market is particularly large in certain states and cities, such as California, Arizona, New Mexico, Texas, Miami, New York City, and Chicago. To attract and communicate with Hispanic consumers, marketers have invaded channels such as Telemundo, CNNenEspanol.com, and Vanidades with commercials for their products.

Although Asian Americans comprise only about 3 percent of the U.S. population, they also represent the fastest growing minority population. They tend to earn more, have more schooling, and be more likely to be professionally employed or own a business than whites. As is also true for Hispanic consumers, marketers should not assume that they can target all Asians with one strategy. The Chinese, Japanese, Indian, Korean, and southeast Asian subgroups, such as the Vietnamese and Cambodian, all speak different languages and come from different regional and country cultures.

Social Trends

Various social trends appear to be shaping consumer values in the United States and around the world, including greener consumers, privacy concerns, and time-poor society. (See Exhibit 4.9.)

Greener Consumers[38]　Green marketing involves a strategic effort by firms to supply customers with environmentally friendly merchandise. Although this "green" trend is not new, it is growing. Many consumers, concerned about everything from the purity of air and water to the safety of beef and salmon, believe that each person can make a difference in the environment. For example, nearly half of U.S. adults now recycle their soda bottles and newspapers, and European consumers are even more green. Germans are required by law to recycle bottles, and the European Union does not allow beef raised on artificial growth hormones to be imported.

　　The demand for green-oriented products has been a boon to the firms that supply them. For instance, marketers encourage consumers to replace their older versions of washing machines and dishwashers with water- and energy-saving models and to invest in phosphate-free laundry powder

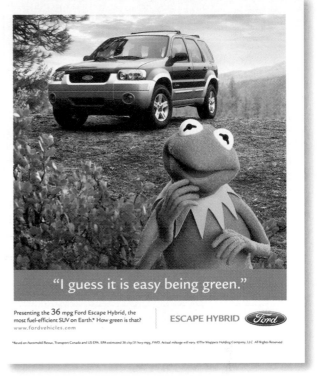

"I guess it is easy being green."

Presenting the **36** mpg Ford Escape Hybrid, the most fuel-efficient SUV on Earth.* How green is that?　　ESCAPE HYBRID　*Ford*
www.fordvehicles.com

*Based on Automobil Revue, Transport Canada and US EPA. EPA-estimated 36 city/31 hwy mpg, FWD. Actual mileage will vary. ©The Muppets Holding Company, LLC. All Rights Reserved.

Spawned by environmental concerns and rising gas prices, consumers are demanding more fuel-efficient hybrid cars.

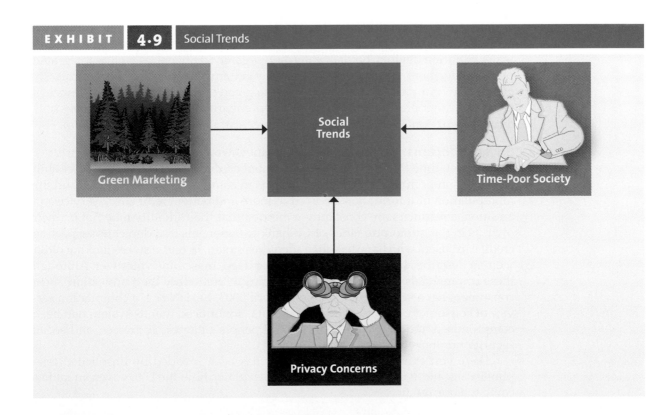

EXHIBIT　4.9　Social Trends

Green Marketing → Social Trends ← Time-Poor Society

Privacy Concerns

Entrepreneurial Marketing 4.1

Anita Roddick: An Environmental Entrepreneur and Founder of The Body Shop[39]

Begun by Anita Roddick in 1976 as a small shop in Brighton, England, The Body Shop has grown into a force capable of creating a niche market for natural hair and body products. Whereas once it sold approximately 25 products in its single store, it now sells over 600 products in more than 1,900 outlets that span 12 time zones. Due to its dedicated franchisees who share Roddick's values, The Body Shop has expanded its reach worldwide. The company and its founder have a strong commitment to protect the environment, animals, and human rights. Some of their core values include the following:

- Protesting the testing of products on animals.
- Supporting small producers around the world.
- Treating the customer as an individual.
- Supporting human rights.
- Embracing business's responsibility of protecting the environment.
- Promoting community volunteering.

Perhaps because of these core values, The Body Shop has enjoyed strong growth in operating profits and earnings over the last three years, to the point that, in 2005, earnings per share were up 22 percent.

and mercury-free and rechargeable batteries. America's love affair with recycling also has created markets for recycled building products, packaging, paper goods, and even sweaters and sneakers. This raised energy consciousness similarly has spurred the growth of more efficient appliances, lighting, and heating and cooling systems in homes and offices. Health-conscious consumers continue to fuel the markets for organic foods, natural cleaning and personal care products, air- and water-filtration devices, bottled water, and organic fertilizers, as well as integrated pest management systems that do not rely on any manufactured chemicals. By offering environmental responsibility, these green products add an extra ounce of value that other products don't have. Entrepreneurial Marketing 4.1 describes how entrepreneur Anita Roddick employed a green strategy with The Body Shop.

Privacy Concerns   More and more consumers worldwide sense a loss of privacy. At the same time that the Internet has created an exploding volcano of accessibility to consumer information, improvements in computer storage facilities and the manipulation of information have led to more and better credit check services. In addition, consumers are constantly reminded that their identity may not be their own, as in the humorous series of Citibank commercials that depict unsuspecting credit card users who have had their identities stolen. In one, a sweet-looking older woman describes her new pickup truck in a deep, masculine voiceover. Although these commercials promote a new credit card with identity theft protection, most consumers have no such protection. In April 2005, LexisNexis, a compilation service of consumer personal and financial data, announced that its system had been compromised and that more than 300,000 people's names, addresses, and social security numbers had been stolen.[40]

Have you ever felt that your privacy has been invaded by unsolicited telephone calls and e-mails? Adding Value 4.2 explains how the U.S. government has come to your rescue.

Adding Value 4.2

Do Not Call and Do Not E-Mail[41]

The U.S. government, responding to consumer outcries regarding unwanted telephone and e-mail solicitations, has undertaken one of the largest government initiatives of the decade, in response to which more than 55 million people have registered their telephone numbers with the Federal Trade Commission's (FTC) National Do Not Call Registry. In fact, 730,000 of those consumers registered the first day. Similarly, the House of Representatives has passed a bill that allows the FTC to create a "Do Not Email" list to stop SPAM, or unsolicited junk e-mail.

On February 18, 2004, the Tenth Circuit Court of Appeals in Denver ruled that the National Do Not Call Registry does not violate the First Amendment rights of telemarketers but rather allows consumers to prevent unwanted intrusions in their home. According to the ruling, "The national do-not-call registry offers consumers a tool with which they can protect their homes against intrusions that Congress has determined to be particularly invasive. Just as a consumer can avoid door-to-door peddlers by placing a 'No solicitations' sign in his or her front yard, the do-not-call registry lets consumers avoid unwanted sales pitches that invade the home via telephone, if they choose to do so. We are convinced the First Amendment does not prevent the government from giving consumers this option."[42]

These policy changes have had considerable impact on some firms' marketing strategy. For instance, AT&T ended all marketing operations to home consumers in August of 2003 just months after paying a fine of $490,000 to the Federal Communications Commission (FCC). Also impacted was *USA Today*, which historically generated 40 percent of its subscriptions through cold calling. Unfortunately, the Do Not Call Registry may have eliminated many honest telemarketers, leaving the wires open for the more crooked groups who often use nontraceable recordings to reach potential customers at home. In the end, most companies are moving resources away from telephone campaigns and refocusing them elsewhere.

The Time-Poor Society   Reaching a target market has always been a major challenge, but it is made even more complicated by several trends that increase the difficulty of grabbing those markets' attention. First, in the majority of families, both parents work, and the kids are busier than ever. Since 1973, the median number of hours that people say they work has jumped from 41 to 49 a week. During that same period, reported leisure time has dropped from 26 to 19 hours a week.[43]

When Leave It To Beaver *was on TV in the 1950s, viewers had only three or four channels from which to choose.*

Second, consumers have many more choices about the ways they might spend their dwindling leisure hours. When *Leave It to Beaver* ruled television, most viewers could choose from only three or four channels, plus a handful of AM radio stations. Today, they have hundreds of each. Competing with television and radio are DVDs, MP3 players, cell telephones, pagers, personal computers, and the Internet. Third, many consumers attempt to cope with their lack of leisure time by multitasking—watching television or listening to music while talking on the telephone or doing homework. Their divided attention simply cannot focus as well on advertisements that appear in those media.

Marketers must respond to the challenge of getting consumers' attention by adjusting, such as by moving their advertising expenditures from traditional venues like print media to movie screens, fortune cookies, baggage claim conveyor belts, billboards, and ads in airports

Self-checkout lanes speed the shopping process, but do they improve customer service?

and on taxis, buses, and mass transport vehicles.[44] Retailers are doing their part by making their products available to customers whenever and wherever they want. For instance, retailers like Target and Talbots are becoming full-fledged multichannel retailers that offer stores, catalogs, and Internet shopping options. Others, like Office Depot and Walgreens, have extended their hours of operation so that their customers can shop during hours that they aren't working. In addition, automated processes like self-checkout lanes and electronic kiosks speed the shopping process and provide customers with product and ordering information.

To find and develop such methods to make life easier for consumers in the time-poor society, marketers often rely on technology, another macroenvironmental factor and the topic of the next section.

Technological Advances

Technological advances have accelerated greatly during the past few decades, improving the value of both products and services. Since the birth of the first Generation Y baby in 1977, the world has realized the commercial successes of cellular telephones, MP3 players, Internet access, personal digital assistants (PDSs), WiFi, and digital cameras. Flat-screen and high-definition televisions, as well as video on demand, have begun to change the way we view television, and their impact is only expected to increase in the next few years. On the retail side, firms are able to track an item from the moment it was manufactured, through the distribution system, to the retail store, and into the hands of the final consumer using little radio frequency identification device (RFID) chips that are affixed to the merchandise. Because they are able to determine exactly how much of each product is at a point in the supply chain, retailers also can communicate with their suppliers—probably over the Internet—and collaboratively plan to meet their inventory needs. Exhibit 4.10 shows when some of these technological advances were introduced and their annual sales.

EXHIBIT 4.10	Advances in Technology			
	Cell Phone	**LCD Televisions**	**MP3 Player**	**Internet Access**
Year Introduced	1984	1988	1991	1993
2005 Sales	$13.5 Billion	$4 Billion	$3 Billion	$1.018 Billion

Source: Dan Nystedt, "U.S. Marks new cell phone record in 2005," *InfoWorld* April 07, 2006, www.infoworld.com (accessed August 25, 2006); "World Fact Book," www.cia.gov, (accessed August 25, 2006); Ilse Jurrien, "Consumer electronic sales record in 2006," www.letsgodigital.org January 5, 2006 (accessed August 25, 2006).

Economic Situation

Marketers monitor the general **economic situation**, both in their home country and abroad, because it affects the way consumers buy merchandise and spend money. Some major factors that influence the state of an economy include the rate of inflation, foreign currency exchange rates, and interest rates.

Inflation refers to the persistent increase in the prices of goods and services.[45] Increasing prices cause the purchasing power of the dollar to decline; in other words, the dollar buys less than it used to.

In a similar fashion, **foreign currency fluctuations** can influence consumer spending. For instance, in the summer of 2002, the Euro was valued at slightly less than U.S. $1. By the beginning of 2007, it cost approximately $1.27 in American currency. As the Euro becomes more expensive compared with the dollar, merchandise made in Europe and other countries tied to the Euro become more costly to Americans, whereas products made in the United States cost less for European consumers.

Tourists from other countries flock to the U.S. to shop because the value of the dollar is low compared to their own currency.

Finally, **interest rates** represent the cost of borrowing money. For example, when customers borrow money from a bank, they agree to pay back the loan, plus the interest that accrues. The interest, in effect, is the cost to the customers or the fee the bank charges those customers for borrowing the money. Likewise, if a customer opens a savings account at a bank, he or she will earn interest on the amount saved, which means the interest becomes the fee the consumer gets for "loaning" the money to the bank. If the interest rate goes up, consumers have an incentive to save more, because they earn more for loaning the bank their money; when interest rates go down, however, consumers generally borrow more.

How do these three important economic factors—inflation, foreign currency fluctuations, and interest rates—affect firms' ability to market goods and services? Shifts in the three economic factors make marketing easier for some and harder for others. For instance, when inflation increases, consumers probably don't buy less food, but they may shift their expenditures from expensive steaks to less expensive hamburgers. Grocery stores and inexpensive restaurants win, but expensive restaurants lose. Consumers also buy less discretionary merchandise. For instance, the sale of expensive jewelry, fancy cars, and extravagant vacations will decrease, but curiously, the sale of low-cost luxuries, such as personal care products and home entertainment, tends to increase. It appears that, instead of rewarding themselves with a new Lexus or a health spa vacation, consumers buy a few cosmetics and rent a movie.

Another, perhaps unexpected, result of the devaluation of the U.S. dollar compared with the Euro might allow U.S. manufacturers to win and European makers to lose. During such inflationary times, "made in America" claims become more important, which means that European manufacturers and U.S. retailers that specialize in European merchandise must decide whether they should attempt to maintain their profit margins or accept a lower price to protect their U.S. customer base. Finally, when interest rates go up, consumers tend to save more, which makes it easier for financial institutions to sell products like mutual funds. But at the same time, people have less incentive to buy discretionary products and services because they are enticed by the higher interest rates to save. Therefore, though a financial institution's mutual fund division might benefit, its mortgage department might suffer because people don't buy houses when they feel they are not getting a good value for the money they must spend and borrow.

Political/Regulatory Environment

The **political/regulatory environment** comprises political parties, government organizations, and legislation and laws. Organizations must fully understand and comply with any legislation regarding fair competition, consumer protection, or industry-specific regulation. Since the turn of the century, the government has enacted laws that promote both fair trade and competition by prohibiting the formation of monopolies or alliances that would damage a competitive marketplace, fostering fair pricing practices for all suppliers and consumers, and promoting free trade agreements among foreign nations.

Legislation also has been enacted to protect consumers in a variety of ways. First, regulations require manufactures to abstain from false or misleading advertising practices that might mislead consumers, such as claims that a medication can cure a disease when in fact it causes other health risks. Second, manufacturers are required to identify and remove any harmful or hazardous materials (e.g., asbestos) that might place a consumer at risk. Third, organizations must adhere to fair and reasonable business practices when they communicate with consumers. For example, they must employ reasonable debt collection methods and disclose any finance charges; as we noted in Adding Value 4.2, they also are limited with regard to their telemarketing and e-mail solicitation activities.

Last but not least, the government enacts laws focused on specific industries. These laws may be geared toward increasing competition, such as the deregulation of the telephone and energy industries, in which massive conglomerates like Ma Bell were broken into smaller, competing companies. Or they may be in response to current events, such as the laws passed following the terrorist attacks of September 11, 2001, when the government ushered through the Air Transportation Safety and System Stabilization Act to ensure that airlines could remain in business. A summary of the most significant legislation affecting marketing interests appears in Exhibits 4.11 and 4.12.

EXHIBIT 4.11		Competitive Practice and Trade Legislation
Year	**Law**	**Description**
1890	Sherman Antitrust Act	Prohibits monopolies and other activities that would restrain trade or competition. Makes fair trade within a free market a national goal.
1914	Clayton Act	Supports the Sherman Act by prohibiting the combination of two or more competing corporations through pooling ownership of stock and restricting pricing policies such as price discrimination, exclusive dealing, and tying clauses to different buyers.
1914	Federal Trade Commission	Established the Federal Trade Commission (FTC) to regulate antitrust claims and outlaw unfair competitive practices.
1936	Robinson-Patman Act	Outlaws price discrimination toward wholesalers, retailers, or other producers. Requires sellers to make ancillary services or allowances available to all buyers on proportionately equal terms.
1938	Wheeler-Lea Act	Makes unfair and deceptive advertising practices illegal and gives FTC jurisdiction over food and drug promotion.
1993	North American Free Trade Agreement (NAFTA)	International trade agreement among Canada, Mexico, and the United States removing tariffs and trade barriers to facilitate trade among the three nations.

EXHIBIT	4.12	Consumer Protection Legislation

Year	Law	Description
1906	Federal Food and Drug Act	Created the Food and Drug Administration. Prohibited the manufacture or sale of adulterated or fraudulently labeled food and drug products.
1938	Food, Drug and Cosmetics Act	Strengthens the 1906 Federal Food and Drug Act by requiring that food be safe to eat and be produced under sanitary conditions; drugs and devices are safe and effective for their intended use; and cosmetics are safe and made from appropriate ingredients.
1966	Fair Packaging and Labeling Act	Regulates packaging and labeling of consumer goods; requires manufacturers to state the contents of the package, who made it, and the amount contained within.
1966	Child Protection Act	Prohibits the sale of harmful toys and components to children. Sets the standard for child-resistant packaging.
1967	Federal Cigarette Labeling and Advertising Act	Requires cigarette packages to display this warning: "Warning: The Surgeon General Has Determined That Cigarette Smoking Is Dangerous To Your Health."
1972	Consumer Product Safety Act	Created the Consumer Product Safety Commission, which has the authority to regulate safety standards for consumer products.
1990	Children's Television Act	Limits the number of commercials shown during children's programming.
1990	Nutrition Labeling and Education Act	Requires food manufacturers to display nutritional contents on product labels.
1995	Telemarketing Sales Rule	Regulates fraudulent activities conducted over the telephone. Violators are subject to fines and actions enforced by the FTC.
2003	Controlling the Assault of Non-Solicited Pornography and Marketing Act of 2003 (CAN-SPAM Act)	Allows the FTC to regulate unsolicited e-mail and enforce penalties associated with "junk" e-mail.
2003	Amendment to the Telemarketing Sales Rule	Establishes a National Do Not Call Registry, requiring telemarketers to abstain from calling consumers who opt to be placed on the list.

Scenario Planning

Now that we have examined how the macroenvironment impacts a company, its competition, its corporate partners, and, most important, the way these entities market to customers, let's look at a process called **scenario planning** that integrates this information as a means to understand the potential outcomes of different applications of a firm's marketing mix.[46] By using the strategy elements that we discussed in Chapter 2, scenario planning enables a firm to predict, monitor, and adapt to the ever-changing future. All firms face strategic challenges in dealing with the opportunities and uncertainties of the marketplace due to the changes in cultural, demographic, social, technological, economic, and political forces. Thus, anticipating and interpreting change, and leveraging resources to address those changes, are key to developing winning value-based strategies.[47]

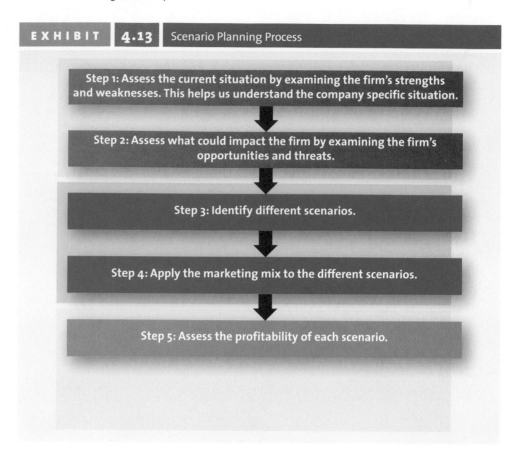

EXHIBIT 4.13 Scenario Planning Process

Step 1: Assess the current situation by examining the firm's strengths and weaknesses. This helps us understand the company specific situation.

Step 2: Assess what could impact the firm by examining the firm's opportunities and threats.

Step 3: Identify different scenarios.

Step 4: Apply the marketing mix to the different scenarios.

Step 5: Assess the profitability of each scenario.

As an outcome, a scenario planning exercise like the one outlined in Exhibit 4.13, develops a set of possible conclusions based on the plausible alternatives that a firm might pursue. By looking at alternative courses of action and imagining what might happen if they were taken, managers can better prepare for the future. To demonstrate how scenario planning works, we investigate a scenario plan for Wal-Mart to determine which strategic directions the giant retailer might pursue in coming years.

Step 1: Assess Strengths and Weaknesses

Step 1 includes the first half of a SWOT analysis: Assess the firm's strengths and weaknesses.

Strengths   Wal-Mart has many strengths, not the least of which is its sheer size—it is the largest company in the world. Just how big is it?[48]

- Wal-Mart is the world's largest retailer.
- Its sales equal 2.5 percent of the U.S. gross domestic product.
- Its workforce of 1.6 million people can employ the population of 31 countries.
- Over 138 million customers per week visit Wal-Mart worldwide.

However, being big isn't always strength; a huge company sometimes suffers from its sluggish reactions to change and cumbersome hierarchical decision making. But size has generally been one of Wal-Mart's key strengths, perhaps because it has been able to develop inventory and information systems rapidly, expand into

EXHIBIT | **4.14** | Wal-Mart Growth

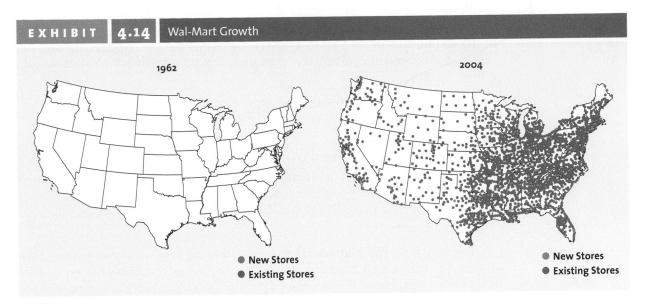

Source: Thomas J. Holmes, "Movie of Wal-Mart Store Openings," http://www.econ.umn.edu/~holmes/research.html; Jonathan J. Miller, *Organic Big Box Growth and Downtown Development,* http://matrix.millersamuel.com/?p=622.

new retail businesses, and negotiate with vendors better than most of its rivals. Wal-Mart's growth has been staggering. See Exhibit 4.14.

Another strength is Wal-Mart's unrelenting drive to provide the lowest price in every market in which it competes. How does Wal-Mart do it? Its suppliers know they can only offer the retailer the lowest price, and forget about price increases. If they don't, they simply won't retain Wal-Mart as a customer, and for most suppliers, losing a customer of this size isn't an option. It also operates a bare-bones, no-frills operation.

Some experts believe that Wal-Mart's biggest strength rests in its supply chain. The originator of the hub-and-spoke distribution center system, Wal-Mart locates all its stores at the end of a "spoke" with a distribution center at the "hub." Using this system, each store easily can access distribution center deliveries. Furthermore, the distribution centers are among the most advanced in the world, with miles and miles of conveyor belts moving merchandise in and out at lightning speed.

Wal-Mart's low prices are due, in part, to its advanced supply chain.

Weaknesses   Although Wal-Mart's weaknesses are few, they are potentially serious. No matter how hard it tries to be a good corporate citizen, it still manages to become the villain in many communities. Cities and towns of all sizes fear the demise of the small businesses that cannot compete with Wal-Mart's low prices. As a result of these demises, people lose their jobs and end up either unemployed or working for Wal-Mart at the substantially reduced wages that critics often deride Wal-Mart for imposing. Being the world's largest corporation also attracts substantial litigation, which leads to poor public relations.

Step 2: Assess Opportunities and Threats

In the second half of the SWOT analysis, we assess the firm's opportunities and threats. Consider some potential opportunities, many of which Wal-Mart already is investigating:

- Expand aggressively into fashion apparel to compete more effectively with other lower-priced fashion retailers, like Target and H&M.
- Enter India.
- Expand their neighborhood grocery store concept.
- Expand its computer, office equipment, and consumer electronics presence to compete aggressively with Staples, Office Depot, and Best Buy.
- Expand in-store financial services to make Wal-Mart even more of a one-stop shopping experience.

Like any firm, Wal-Mart also faces several threats, but unlike many firms, these threats appear relatively mild in comparison with its opportunities. First, on a global scale, several retail powerhouses like Carrefour (France) and Metro (Germany) have impeded its global expansion. Second, small but nimble local retailers eat into its market in certain categories. Some such retailers can beat Wal-Mart on assortment and service but usually not on price. Third, given Wal-Mart's size, it exists under constant governmental surveillance for possible legal infringements as it expands into new categories, expands within a category, or enters new markets.

Step 3: Identify Different Scenarios

On the basis of the analysis performed in Steps 1 and 2, executives can identify some alternative scenarios that might happen in the next five years. Two of the scenarios could be as follows:

- Wal-Mart expands its apparel category.
- Wal-Mart enters India.

Each of these alternative scenarios requires careful consideration and reflection to assess the risks, benefits, and costs of that move. To determine which are the best opportunities, it is useful to try to match the firm's competencies with the opportunity's attractiveness. Clearly, if the firm has a high competency to engage in an opportunity and the opportunity is attractive, it represents a likely opportunity to pursue.

Wal-Mart could examine the attractiveness of changing its apparel assortment. This would allow head-on competition in the apparel area with Target. An expansion into India would allow it to go after a certain percentage of the over 1 billion consumers. Wal-Mart already buys over $1.5 billion worth of merchandise from India.[49] However, to attract the Indian consumer would require Wal-Mart to carefully examine the Indian market.

Step 4: Apply the Marketing Mix to the Different Scenarios

In this step, the firm develops a potential strategy for each of the different scenarios created in Step 3. For simplicity, let's just consider the option of Wal-Mart entering India. It provides an intriguing yet straightforward option for several reasons. Because Wal-Mart is already buying over $1.5 billion worth of merchandise from India, the Indian government is not likely to throw roadblocks into its expansion efforts. The biggest potential problem is that Wal-Mart does not have a well-established supply chain as it has in other markets. Wal-Mart is used to doing things in a big way. It will probably need different types of trucks, equipment, and warehouses to operate in the Indian environment. Another difficult challenge the company would face in India would be to find great urban locations that have the square footage that Wal-Mart typically requires. Wal-Mart would also need to change the product assortment to conform to the Indian consumers' tastes and preferences. Wal-Mart may also adjust its communication mix to take advantage of outdoor advertising opportunities (e.g., billboards, banners, buses) that are so popular in India. Finally, the prices of the merchandise would have to be in line with price expectation of the Indian middle-class.

Firms like Wal-Mart may have to adjust their communications mix to add more billboards as they expand in India.

Step 5: Assess the Profitability of Each Scenario

After developing strategies for several options, as in Step 3, and applying the marketing mix as in Step 4, managers must finally assess the profitability of each option. In so doing, they weigh the expected revenues against the expected costs. The projects with the highest expected profit are the best to pursue. Therefore, if Wal-Mart finds that the expected revenues from an expansion into India exceed its expected costs, then the scenario is a viable option.

Summing Up

1. How do customers, the company, competitors, and corporate partners affect marketing strategy?

Everything a firm does should revolve around the customer; without the customer, nothing gets sold. Firms must discover their customers' wants and needs and then be able to provide a valuable product or service that will satisfy those needs. If there were only one firm and many customers, a marketer's life would be a piece of cake. But because this setup rarely occurs, firms must monitor their competitors to discover how they might be appealing to their customers. Without active competitive vigilance, a firm's customers might soon belong to its competitors. However, though marketing life certainly would be easier without competitors, it would be difficult, if not impossible, without corporate partners. Good marketing firms work closely with their suppliers, marketing research firms, consultants, and transportation firms to coordinate the extensive process of discovering what customers want and getting it to them when and where they want it. Each of these activities—discovering customer needs, studying competitive actions, and working with corporate sponsors—helps add value to firms' products and services.

2. Why do marketers have to think about their macroenvironment when they make decisions?

To be successful, marketers must understand fully what is going on outside their firm. For instance, what are the chances that a fast-food hamburger restaurant would be successful in a predominantly Hindu neighborhood? Right—not very good. Marketers must be sensitive to such cultural issues to be successful, and then they must also consider customer demographics—age, income, market size, education, gender, and ethnicity—to identify specific customer groups. In any society, major social trends influence the way people live. Understanding these trends—such as green marketing, privacy issues, and the time-poor society—can help marketers serve their customers better. Furthermore, in no other time in history has technology moved so rapidly and had such a pervasive influence on the way we live. Not only do marketers help develop technologies for practical, everyday uses, but technological advances also help marketers provide consumers with more products and services more quickly and efficiently. In addition, the general state of the economy influences how people spend their disposable income. When the economy is healthy, marketing grows relatively easy. But when the economy gets bumpy, only well-honed marketing skill can yield long-term successes. Naturally, all firms must abide by the law, but many legal issues also affect marketing directly. These laws can be broken into those that pertain to competitive practices, such as antitrust legislation, and those designed to protect consumers from unfair or dangerous practices, such as warning labels on cigarette packages.

3. How do marketers use scenario planning to determine which courses of action to take?

Scenario planning integrates information on how the macroenvironment impacts a company, its competition, its corporate partners, and its customers as a means to understand the potential outcomes of different applications of a firm's marketing mix. Scenario planning is performed in five steps. In the first two steps, it assesses its strengths, weaknesses, opportunities and threats (SWOT) in light of its macroenvironment in relation to its competition, corporate partners, and customers. Third, it identifies different scenarios. Fourth, it applies the marketing mix to the different scenarios. Finally, it assesses the profitability of each scenario. The scenario(s) with the highest potential are considered for implementation.

Key Terms

- Baby Boomers   92
- competitive intelligence (CI)   88
- country culture   91
- culture   91
- demographics   92
- economic situation   105
- foreign currency fluctuations   105
- Generation X   94
- Generation Y   95
- generational cohort   92
- green marketing   101
- inflation   105
- interest rates   105
- just-in-time (JIT) inventory system   90
- macroenvironmental factors   90
- political/regulatory environment   106
- regional culture   91
- scenario planning   107
- Seniors   92
- technological advances   104
- Tweens   95

Marketing Applications

1. Assume you are going to open a new store. Describe it. Who are your competitors? What would you do to monitor your competitors' actions?

2. In which generational cohort do you belong? What about your parents? How do you approach buying a car differently than your parents would? What about buying an outfit to wear to a party? How can firms use their knowledge of generational cohorts to market their products and services better?

3. How can firms use customer demographics like income, market size, education, and ethnicity to market to their customers better?

4. Identify some of the changes in the gender landscape. Describe how they might affect the marketing practices of (a) men's apparel retailers, (b) do-it-yourself home improvement retailers, and (c) upscale salon services.

5. Identify some recent technological innovations in the marketplace and describe how they have affected consumers' everyday activities.

6. Do you feel as if firms are invading or could invade your privacy? Why or why not?

7. Why should a shoe retailer in the United States care about the value of the Hong Kong dollar?

8. Time-poor consumers have adopted various approaches to "buy" themselves more time, such as (a) voluntarily simplifying their complex lives, (b) using new technologies for greater empowerment and control, (c) using their time productively when traveling or commuting, and (d) multitasking. Identify and describe some products and services that consumers use to implement each of these strategies.

9. Identify a company that you believe does a particularly good job of marketing to different cultural groups. Justify your answer.

10. You have recently been hired by a major department store in its marketing department. Your boss informs you that you are going to supervise a field research study. You arrive at the selected store in the chain and find out that the study consists of shadowing customers as they move around the store. The store has set up a "private" shopping event for store credit card holders. All who attend must swipe their card to receive the special discount coupon book. The shadow shoppers (who were hired by the store manager) are given handheld devices loaded with a specific customer's information and past purchase behavior. Thus each shadow shopper knows the name, address, income, family size, and spending patterns for the customer she or he is observing. You begin to feel uncomfortable about this study since the consumers have no idea that they are being tracked or the level of confidential information about them that a stranger has access to. You are also concerned that the shadow customers are not regular employees or employees of an established marketing research provider. What if anything would or should you do about your concerns?

Net Savvy

1. Seventh Generation is the leading brand of nontoxic, environmentally safe household products in the United States. Visit its Web site (www.seventhgeneration.com) and review the philosophy behind the business. Next, review the site to identify the products the company offers. Briefly summarize some of the consumer trends you note, and describe the ways in which its products address the wants and needs of its customers.

2. The Internet has been a double-edged sword for consumers. On the one hand, it provides easy access to many businesses and sources for information. On the other hand, consumers must give up some of their privacy to access this information. The Privacy Rights Clearinghouse provides information to consumers about privacy and opt-out strategies. Visit its Web site (www.privacyrights.org) and review the privacy survival guide. From that document, select and describe three actions you might take to protect your own privacy.

Chapter Case Study

STONYFIELD FARM:[50] CHANGING THE ENVIRONMENT OF BUSINESS

Overview

In 2001, Gary Hirshberg entered into a partnership with the multinational French corporation Groupe Danone after he had already built his organic Stonyfield Farm yogurt business from a small farm intended to fund his nonprofit ventures to a vast company with annual sales of $83 million. Three years later, with sales approaching $100 million, Groupe Danone increased its holding from 40 percent to 85 percent while maintaining Hirshberg as President and CEO.

A major reason for the company's rapid growth and popularity was its responsiveness to consumer demands for organic, natural food products. Stonyfield's popular yogurt and other products represented healthy alternatives to other brands, giving it a differential advantage in a marketplace in which more and more consumers had become choosier about the food products they bought. The company also supports various socially and environmentally beneficial causes. Because it provides superior value to consumers, Stonyfield Farm enjoys the number one market position for organic yogurt and is the number three branded yogurt in the industry.

Company History

In 1983, founders Gary Hirshberg and Samuel Kaymen started Stonyfield as an organic farming school to help revitalize New England agriculture and educate people about the environmental practices of local dairy farmers and the issues they face. Hirshberg and Kaymen began making high-quality yogurt as a way to raise money for their nonprofit school. Building on this tradition of environmental education, the company made pioneering social and environmental business practices central to their business, values, and growth. Essential to this goal is helping consumers realize the impact of their various purchases on the environment.

The Product

The company produces all natural and certified organic yogurts, smoothies, soy yogurt, frozen yogurt, ice cream and milk. Their products contain no gelatins, artificial colors, artificial flavors, or other chemical additives used in many other brands. Stonyfield Farm yogurts contain inulin, a natural dietary fiber that helps boost calcium absorption, and six live active cultures that together enhance digestion, fortify the body's natural defenses, improve the absorption of nutrients and decrease the presence of harmful bacteria. The result: A healthier, better tasting product appreciated by health-conscious consumers.

Walking the Talk

Stonyfield's environmental initiatives center on two major themes: consumer education and modeling successful approaches of socially and environmentally responsible business practices. Ongoing consumer efforts include an educational campaign that presents the company's support for organic products, endorsement of humane animal treatment, and support of health and environmental initiatives. It models its principles of environmental sustainability through its efforts to use environmental packaging and extensive recycling practices, and its award winning efforts around climate change. Furthermore, it addresses both themes by donating 10 percent of its profits to organizations that protect and restore the planet.

| EXHIBIT | C4.1 | Stonyfield Farm Ad Combining Advertising and Activism |

In September 2000, the company launched its first national print advertising campaign (Exhibit C4.1), featuring celebrities perceived as positive role models. In the ads, these high-profile individuals spotlighted both environmental and social causes, in addition to endorsing Stonyfield Farm's products. Beginning in 2002, the company rolled out more traditional ads that featured its major selling point: organic products. The company launched its first national campaign in 2003, using a combination of television, radio, and print ads that communicate that the products are organic and good for the consumer and that the company has a sense of humor and a mission[51] (Exhibit C4.2).

Engaging Consumers

Stonyfield considers getting consumers involved a major key to its success. Although consumers appreciate the company's healthful approach to its products, they also like becoming empowered via the company's programs. One such program was "Vote for the Future," in which customers were asked to sign the back of a yogurt lid in support of sustainable energy policies. The lids were delivered to Washington, DC, and customers who signed lids were entered into a "Flip your Lid" contest that featured energy-efficient products and kits as prizes.

Stonyfield's social and environmental focus draws both positive recognition and the according financial benefits. Sales of Stonyfield products experienced double-digit, compound annual growth from $3 million in 1990 to $211 million in 2005. These positive results, in

EXHIBIT C4.2 Stonyfield Farm Ad Stressing Their Vision

combination with the fulfillment of its company objectives, enable Stonyfield to present itself as both an environmentally responsible and profitable company.

Questions

1. Many of Stonyfield Farm's green initiatives are costly and time consuming. Do you think they are worth it?

2. Is Stonyfield Farms reacting to what its customers want, or is it helping customers define what they want?

5

QUESTIONS

■ When purchasing a product or a service, do you spend a lot of time considering your decision?

■ What steps do you go through when you decide to buy a product or service?

■ What determines how much time consumers will search for information before buying a product or a service?

■ How can understanding consumers' behavior help marketers sell products or services?

SECTION TWO

Understanding the Marketplace

Consumer Behavior

Netflix, an online provider of DVD rentals via postal mail, could have gone the way of other "dot bombs."[1] Instead, the company focused on changing consumer behavior and serving its customers, and as a result, its subscriber base has grown to a profitable 1.5 million households.

A subscription-based service, Netflix creates value by allowing its customers to select and rent a set number of DVDs for as long as they want without any additional costs. By maintaining a list of their desired titles, customers automatically receive new DVDs as they return ones they have already watched. Netflix even provides postage-paid return envelopes. The more than 18,000 titles and 25 strategically located distribution centers allow 60 percent of subscribers to receive their DVDs within one day.

In an industry built through brick-and-mortar video stores, Netflix understood the need to change the prevailing mindset so that DVD-renting consumers would think of subscriptions and mail instead of parking lots and aisles. Thus, every marketing dollar is spent educating consumers about its process and maintaining top-notch service. One productive strategy to develop interest and gain new customers has been the offer of a 10-day or two-week free trial. Of these free-trial customers, approximately 90 percent subsequently become paying customers.

Netflix also affiliates itself with partners that can spread the word in a cost-effective manner. For example, Best Buy, with its more than 1,900 outlets, allows customers to sign up for Netflix at their cash registers. Moreover, deals with DVD manufacturers such as Toshiba, Sony, and Panasonic enable Netflix to reach 84 percent of new DVD purchasers through inserts in the packaging. These strategies, along with word of mouth, have helped Netflix capture over 90 percent of the online rental market.

Netflix has changed the way Americans rent and watch movies.

Who has ever bought or received something from others? All of us have, of course; we are all consumers at one time or another. But we are also complex and irrational creatures who cannot always explain our own actions. This trait makes the vitally important job of marketing managers even more difficult, as they are tasked with explaining consumers' behavior so that marketers have as good an understanding of their customers as is possible. Using principles and theories from sociology and psychology, marketers have been able to decipher many consumer actions and develop basic strategies for dealing with their behavior.

To understand consumer behavior, we must ascertain why people buy products or services. Generally, people buy one product or service instead of another because they perceive it to be the better value for them; that is, the ratio of benefits to costs is higher for that product or service than for any other.[2] Consider Eva Carlyn, movie aficionada. She has just started college and is missing the premium cable channels that she used to watch at home. She has a great TV/DVD in her apartment and is considering whether to go to Blockbuster, subscribe to premium cable stations, or subscribe to Netflix. In making the decision about where she is going to get her movies, Eva asks herself

- Which alternative gives me the best overall value—the best selection and convenience at the lowest price?

- Which alternative is more likely to attract friends over to watch movies?

Because Eva might have several different reasons for subscribing to these items, it is critical for Netflix to key in on those specific benefits that are most important to her. Only then can it create a marketing mix that will satisfy Eva.

In this chapter, we explore the process that consumers go through when buying products and services. Then we discuss the psychological, social, and situational factors that influence this consumer decision process. Throughout the chapter, we emphasize what firms can do to influence consumers to purchase their products and services.

■ ■ ■

The Consumer Decision Process

Exhibit 5.1 illustrates the three types of buying decisions consumers go through. The buying process begins when consumers recognize that they have an unsatisfied need. Eva Carlyn recognized her need to have access to in-home movies when she went away to college. She sought information by asking around among her friends, then evaluated her different options and started searching online for options. After Eva's boyfriend started spending more time at her apartment watching movies, she recognized that her decision to subscribe to Netflix was worth the time and money she spent on it and touted the service to her friends. This process is an example of **limited problem solving,** which occurs during a purchase decision

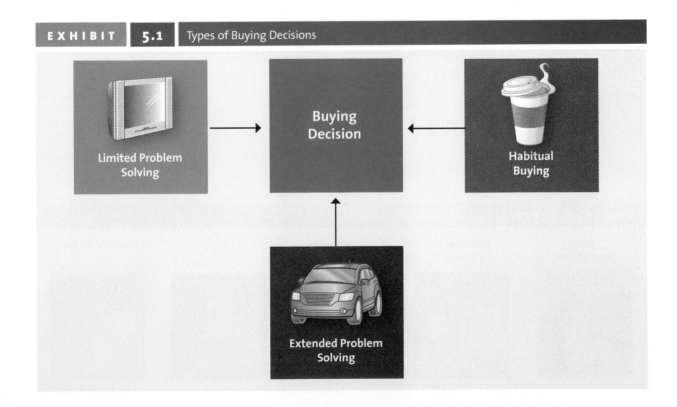

EXHIBIT **5.1** Types of Buying Decisions

Limited Problem Solving → Buying Decision ← Habitual Buying

Extended Problem Solving

that calls for, at most, a moderate amount of effort and time. Customers engage in this type of buying process when they have had some prior experience with the product or service and the perceived risk is moderate. Limited problem solving usually relies on past experience more than on external information.

A common type of limited problem solving is **impulse buying,** a buying decision made by customers on the spot when they see the merchandise.[3] When Eva went to the grocery store to do her weekly shopping, she also saw a display case full of popcorn and Dr Pepper at the checkout counter. Knowing that some of her friends were coming over to watch *Casablanca,* she stocked up. The popcorn and soda were an impulse purchase. Eva didn't go through the entire decision process; instead, she recognized her need and jumped directly to purchase without spending any time searching for additional information or evaluating alternatives. The grocery store facilitated this impulse purchase by offering the popcorn and soda in a prominent display, at a great location in the store, and at a reasonable price.

Some purchases require even less thought. **Habitual decision making** describes a purchase decision process in which consumers engage with little conscious effort. On her way home from Champs, for example, Eva walked into a Starbucks and purchased a tall nonfat latte. Eva always buys lattes from Starbucks when she craves caffeine. She doesn't ponder the potential benefits of going to Dunkin' Donuts for coffee; she engages in habitual decision making. Marketers strive to attract and maintain habitual purchasers by creating strong brands and store loyalty (see Chapters 10 and 11) because these customers don't even consider alternative brands or stores.

Now what would happen if Eva were buying a car or a house? It is highly likely that she would devote considerable time and effort to analyzing her alternatives. This **extended problem solving** is common when the customer perceives that the purchase decision entails a lot of risk. The potential risks associated with Eva's decision regarding buying her car include financial (did I pay too much?), physical (will it keep me safe in an accident?), and social (will my friends think I look cool?) risks. To reduce her perceived risk, Eva spent a lot of effort searching for information about cars before she actually made her purchase.

Regardless of their characteristics, however, these types of decision-making situations all embrace the consumer decision process to greater or lesser degrees. The consumer decision process model represents the steps that consumers go through before, during, and after making purchases. Because marketers often find it difficult to determine how consumers make their purchasing decisions, it is useful for us to break down the process into a series of steps and examine each individually, as in Exhibit 5.2.

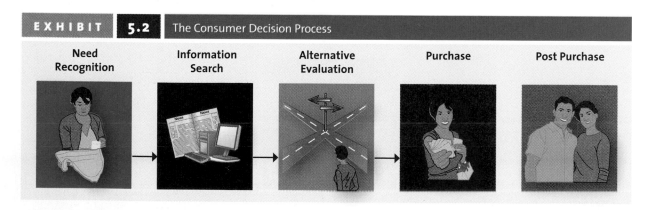

EXHIBIT 5.2 The Consumer Decision Process

| Need Recognition | Information Search | Alternative Evaluation | Purchase | Post Purchase |

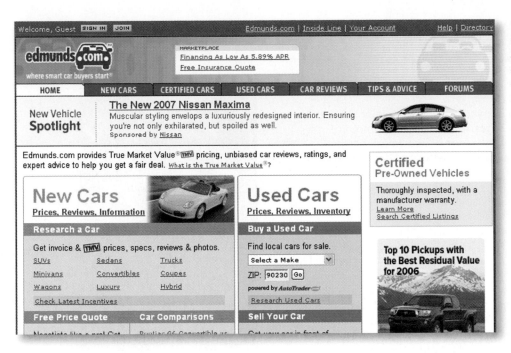

When involved in extended problem solving buying decisions like buying a car, consumers seek additional information at sites like Edmunds.com.

Need Recognition

The consumer decision process begins when consumers recognize they have an unsatisfied need and want to go from their actual, needy state to a different, desired state. The greater the discrepancy between these two states, the greater the **need recognition** will be. For example, your stomach tells you that you are hungry, and you would rather not have that particular feeling. If you are only a little hungry, you may pass it off and decide to eat later. But if your stomach is growling and you cannot concentrate, the need—the difference between your actual (hungry) state and your desired (not hungry) state—is greater, and you'll want to eat immediately to get to your desired state. Consumer needs like these can be classified as functional, psychological, or both.[4]

Sarah Jessica Parker's character, Carrie, on HBO's Sex in the City *made Manolo Blahnik's brand of expensive shoes a "must have" in some circles.*

Functional Needs **Functional needs** pertain to the performance of a product or service. For years, materials like GORE-TEX, Polartec, and Thinsulate have been viewed as functionally superior to others that might be used in rugged, high-performance outerwear. Knowing that consumers seek out these materials, high-end outdoor manufacturers such as North Face prominently display the material content on each piece of clothing and equipment they offer. Even mass merchandisers have jumped on this bandwagon.

Psychological Needs **Psychological needs** pertain to the personal gratification consumers associate with a product and/or service. Shoes, for instance, provide a functional need—to keep feet clean and protect them from the elements. So why would anyone pay $500 to $2,000 for shoes that may do neither? Because they are seeking a way to satisfy psychological needs. Sarah Jessica Parker's character Carrie on HBO's *Sex in the City* continually confessed her undying love for Manolo Blahnik's brand of exquisite shoes. Episode after episode, fans not only heard the stylish cast discuss his creations but

Adding Value 5.1

H.O.G. Heaven[6]

It seems as though everybody wants a piece of H.O.G. Heaven these days. For years, Harley-Davidson motorcycles have been the premier form of two-wheeled transportation for motorcycle enthusiasts, and demand has exceeded supply. Even though other manufacturers, such as BMW, Yamaha, Suzuki, Honda, and Kawasaki, offer functional, dependable, fast motorcycles, they cannot compete with the Harley mystique.

A rich history, rider support, and its protected brand have contributed to Harley's cultlike following. Ten short years after William S. Harley and Arthur Davidson assembled their first motorcycles in a wooden shed in 1903, the company had opened a Milwaukee factory, won several racing awards, incorporated and introduced its first V-twin–powered motorcycle, and patented the classic "Bar and Shield" logo. It then went on to supply the U.S. military with motorcycles during World War I. Since 1916, Harley's magazine, *Enthusiast,* has featured such notables as Elvis Presley atop Harleys during its run as the longest continually published motorcycle magazine

Perhaps the single most important event in Harley-Davidson's history came in 1983 when the company formed the Harley Owner's Group (H.O.G.)—the largest factory-sponsored motorcycle club in the world, whose more than 800,000 members' sole mission is "to ride and have fun." Not only do H.O.G. members receive copies of the *Enthusiast* and *Hog Tales,* H.O.G.'s official publication, but they also can take part in the Fly & Ride program, through which members get to fly to nearly 40 locations in the United States, Canada, Europe, and Australia, pick up a Harley at the local dealership, and tour the countryside. The best part about H.O.G. membership, though, is the camaraderie with like-minded devotees. In their local chapters, supported by their local dealers, and during special events throughout the world, H.O.G. members have been able to share their love of Harleys as a community.

Everyone wants to own a Harley, even Jay Leno.

In addition to remarkable rider support, Harley-Davidson has taken great care to create and protect its global brand. Ranked among the top 50 most recognized global brands, Harley offers a full range of branded parts, accessories, and apparel through various outlets, including retail stores, dealerships, and online. The look, feel, and sound of a Harley are unmistakable—the company even tried to patent the "distinctive" exhaust sound made by its V-twin engines in 1994.

Although Harley-Davidson encourages the idea that its riders are "rugged individualists" who can customize their Hogs to reflect their individual tastes, the company actually has created a band of brand loyalists who believe function is more than two wheels and a motor. It's art, it's history, and it's community.

---

also were treated to glimpses of his masterpieces. As a result, Blahniks have become a household word in some circles, and demand far surpasses the 15,000 pairs per month that four factories outside Milan can manufacture.[5]

Both these examples highlight that the vast majority of products and services are likely to satisfy both functional and psychological needs. Whereas the functional characteristics of GORE-TEX are its main selling point, it also maintains a fashionable appeal for mountain climber wannabes. In contrast, Manolo Blahnik shoes satisfy psychological needs that overshadow the functional needs they serve. For instance, you can get a $15 haircut at SuperCuts or spend $50 or more to get basically the same thing at an upscale salon. Are the two haircuts objectively different? The answer might vary depending on which you believe represents a good haircut and a good value. One person might value getting a really good deal; another might enjoy the extra attention and amenities associated with a fancy salon. A key to successful marketing is determining the correct balance of functional and psychological needs that best appeals to the firm's target markets. Harley-Davidson, for instance, produces motorcycles that do much more than get their riders to the mall and back. Harleys are a way of life, as we discuss in Adding Value 5.1.

Search for Information

The second step, after a consumer recognizes a need, is to search for information about the various options that exist to satisfy that need. The length and intensity of the search are based on the degree of perceived risk associated with purchasing the product or service. If the way your hair is cut is important to your appearance and self-image, you may engage in an involved search for the right salon and stylist. Alternatively, an athlete looking for a short "buzz" cut might go to the closest, most convenient, and cheapest barber shop. Regardless of the required search level, there are two key types of information search: internal and external, as depicted in Exhibit 5.3.

Internal Search for Information　　In an **internal search for information,** the buyer examines his or her own memory and knowledge about the product or service, gathered through past experiences. For example, every time Eva the movie fan wants to watch a movie, she orders it on Netflix. She relies on her memory of past experiences when making this purchase decision.

External Search for Information.　　In an **external search for information,** the buyer seeks information outside his or her personal knowledge base to help make the buying decision. Consumers might fill in their personal knowledge gaps by talking with friends, family, or a salesperson. They can also scour commercial media for unsponsored and (it is hoped) unbiased information, such as that available through *Consumer Reports,* or peruse sponsored media such as magazines, television, or radio. Sometimes consumers get commercial exposures to products or services without really knowing it. For instance, if Jessica Simpson appears in concert wearing Adriano Goldschmied jeans, her fans are being subtly influenced to follow her example. Likewise, when Stephen King appears on the *Oprah Winfrey Show* to talk about his new book, viewers get commercially prepared material that has been disguised as entertainment.

EXHIBIT | 5.3 Types of Information Search

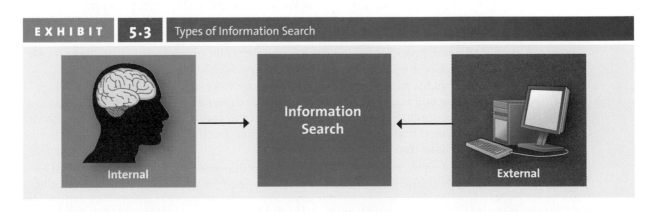

Internal　　Information Search　　External

Consumers also can search for information on the Internet using a shopping bot such as Bizrate.com or a search engine like Google. The term *googol* was coined by Milton Sirotta, nephew of American mathematician Edward Kasner, to describe the number 1 followed by 100 zeros. There is not a googol of anything in the universe. And yet the founders of the Internet search engine Google adapted the term to reflect their mission of "organizing the immense, seemingly infinite amount of information available on the Web."[7] Today Google is the number one search engine, organizing more than 2 billion Web pages[8] and addressing more than 200 million inquiries per day.[9]

Factors Affecting Consumers' Search Processes   It is important for marketers to understand the many factors that affect consumers' search processes. Among them are the following:

- *The perceived benefits versus perceived costs of search.* Is it worth the time and effort to search for information about a product or service? For instance, most families spend a lot of time researching the automobile market before they make a purchase because cars are a relatively expensive and important purchase with significant safety implications, whereas they likely spend little time researching which inexpensive plastic toy car to buy for the youngest member of the family.

- *The locus of control.* People who have an **internal locus of control** believe they have some control over the outcomes of their actions, in which case they generally engage in more search activities. With an **external locus of control,** consumers believe that fate or other external factors control all outcomes. In that case, they believe it doesn't matter how much information they gather; if they make a wise decision, it isn't to their credit, and if they make a poor one, it isn't their fault. People who do a lot of research before purchasing individual stocks have an internal locus of control; those who purchase mutual funds are more likely to believe that they can't predict the market and probably have an external locus of control.

- *Actual or perceived risk.* Three types of risk associated with purchase decisions can delay or discourage a purchase: performance, financial, and psychological. The higher the risk, the more likely the consumer is to engage in an extended search.

  Performance risk involves the perceived danger inherent in a poorly performing product or service. An example of performance risk might be the possibility that your cell phone battery would go bad when you were waiting for a call to set up a job interview.

  Financial risk is risk associated with a monetary outlay and includes the initial cost of the purchase, as well as the costs of using the item or service. Car manufacturers, for instance, recognize that extended warranties help alleviate financial risk because consumers fear extensive postpurchase repair costs. Great warranties reduce the financial risk of buying a car.

  Finally, **psychological risks** are those risks associated with the way people will feel if the product or service does not convey the right image. For example, Eva looked up reviews of the various movie rental alternatives and asked her friends because she wanted people to perceive her as the "ultimate" movie expert.

- *Type of product or service.* Another factor that affects the depth and type of search a consumer undertakes is the type of product or service—specifically,

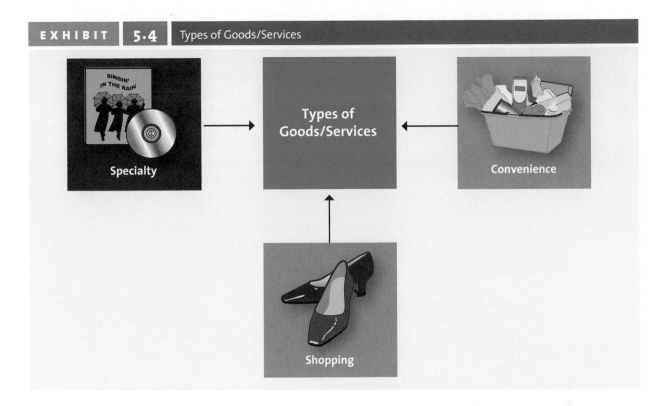

EXHIBIT | **5.4** | Types of Goods/Services

Specialty → Types of Goods/Services ← Convenience

Shopping

whether it is a specialty, shopping, or convenience product. (See Exhibit 5.4.)

Specialty goods/services are products or services toward which the customer shows a strong preference and for which he or she will expend considerable effort to search for the best suppliers. Because Eva wants the best selection of new as well as classic movies, she searches carefully on the Internet for reviews before she starts shopping.

Shopping goods/services are products or services for which consumers will spend time comparing alternatives, such as apparel, fragrances, and appliances. When Eva decides to buy some new sneakers for herself, she will go from store to store shopping—trying shoes on, comparing alternatives, and chatting with salespeople.

Convenience goods/services are those products or services that the consumer is not willing to spend any effort to evaluate prior to purchase. They are frequently purchased, usually with very little thought. Items such as soda, bread, and soap typically fall into this category.

Soda and bread are generally considered convenience goods (left). Shoes and t-shirts are shopping goods (middle). Products made by designers like Polo/Ralph Lauren are specialty goods (right).

Consumers can spend considerable time searching for both specialty and shopping goods or services; the difference lies in the kind of search. In some cases, the consumer's specific perceptions and needs help define the kind of search—and the type of product. For Eva, getting a haircut is a convenience purchase, so she visits the fastest, most convenient location. One of her friends, however, has tried

When you get your hair cut, do you consider it to be a convenience, shopping, or specialty purchase?

various salons, each time comparing the haircut she received with her previous experiences. For her, a haircut is a shopping service. Finally, another of Eva's friends patronizes the hairstylist he perceives to be the best in town. He often waits weeks for an appointment and pays dearly for the experience. For him, getting a haircut is a specialty service.

Evaluation of Alternatives

Once a consumer has recognized a problem and explored the possible options, he or she must sift through the choices available and evaluate the alternatives. Alternative evaluation often occurs while the consumer is engaged in the process of information search. For example, a vegetarian consumer might learn about a new brand of yogurt that he or she can immediately rule out as a viable alternative because it contains some animal byproducts. Consumers forgo alternative evaluations altogether when buying habitual products; you'll rarely catch a loyal Pepsi drinker buying Coca-Cola.

Attribute Sets   Research has shown that a consumer's mind organizes and categorizes alternatives to aid his or her decision process. **Universal sets** include all possible choices for a product category, but because it would be unwieldy for a person to recall all possible alternatives for every purchase decision, marketers tend to focus on only a subset of choices. One important subset is **retrieval sets,** which are those brands or stores that can be readily brought forth from memory. Another is a consumer's **evoked set,** which comprises the alternative brands or stores that the consumer states he or she would consider when making a purchase decision. If a firm can get its brand or store into a consumer's evoked set, it has increased the likelihood of purchase and therefore reduced search time because the consumer will think specifically of that brand when considering choices. Eva, for example, knows that not every movie rental store in her town (universal set) carries the movies she likes. She also recalls that the local Blockbuster store (retrieval set) sometimes carries her favorites, but the assortment is spotty. So, typically Eva rents her movies at Netflix. This is the only store in her evoked set, and she will begin her search there.

When consumers begin to evaluate different alternatives, they often base their evaluations on a set of important attributes or evaluative criteria. **Evaluative criteria** consist of a set of salient, or important, attributes about a particular product. For example, a consumer looking to buy a new automobile might take into consideration things like selling price, gas mileage, safety features, and the reputation of the dealership's service department. At times, however, it becomes difficult to evaluate different brands or stores because there are so many choices.

Would you consider these shampoos to be part of your universal set, retrieval set, or evoked set of products?

Consumers utilize several shortcuts to simplify the potentially complicated decision process: determinant attributes and consumer decision rules. **Determinant attributes** are product or service features that are *important* to the buyer and on which competing brands or stores are perceived to *differ*.[10] Because many important and desirable criteria are equal among the various choices, consumers look for something special—a determinant attribute—to differentiate one brand or store from another. Determinant attributes may appear perfectly rational, such as a low price for milk, or they may be more subtle and psychologically based, such as the insignia or stitching on the back pockets of jeans.

EXHIBIT 5.5	Compensatory versus Noncompensatory Choices for Buying a Car				
	Mileage	**Style**	**Price**	**Accessories**	**Overall Score**
Importance Weight	0.4	0.1	0.3	0.2	
Toyota	10	8	6	8	8.2
Honda	8	9	8	3	7.1
Saturn	6	8	10	5	7.2

Evaluations are based on a 1 (Very Poor) to 10 (Very Good) scale.

Compensatory: Toyota has the highest score.

Non-Compensatory (Based on Price): Saturn has best evaluation of Price.

Consumer decision rules are the set of criteria that consumers use consciously or subconsciously to quickly and efficiently select from among several alternatives. These rules take several different forms: compensatory, noncompensatory, or decision heuristics.

Compensatory   A **compensatory decision rule** assumes that the consumer, when evaluating alternatives, trades off one characteristic against another, such that good characteristics compensate for bad characteristics.[11] For instance, Morgan is looking to buy a new car and is considering several factors such as mileage, style, price, and accessories. Even if the car is priced a little higher than Morgan was planning to spend, the superb mileage offsets, or compensates for, the higher price.

Although Morgan probably would not go through the formal process of making the purchasing decision based on the model described in Exhibit 5.5, it illustrates how a compensatory model would work. Morgan assigns weights to the importance of each factor. These weights must add up to 1.0. So, for instance, mileage is the most important with a weight of .4 and style is least important with a weight of .1. Then she assigns weights to how well each of the cars might perform, with 1 being very poor, and 10 being very good. For instance, she thinks Toyota has the best mileage, so she assigns it a 10. Morgan multiplies each performance rating by its importance rating to get an overall score for each car. The rating for Toyota in this example is the highest of the three cars $((.4 \times 10) + (.1 \times 8) + (.3 \times 6) + (.2 \times 8) = 8.2)$.

Noncompensatory   Sometimes, however, consumers use a **noncompensatory decision rule,** in which they choose a product or service on the basis of a subset of its characteristics, regardless of the values of its other attributes.[12] Thus, Morgan might find a car with a lot of accessories with great mileage that costs considerably more then she is willing to spend. Morgan rejects the car simply on the basis of price. She rated the price of a Toyota as 6 on the 10 point scale. That is, the strength of the good points does not compensate for its biggest weakness—a high ticket price.

Decision Heuristics   Not everyone uses compensatory or noncompensatory decision rules. Some use **decision heuristics,** which are mental shortcuts that help a consumer narrow down his or her choices. Some examples of these heuristics include these:

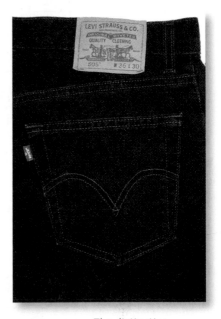

The distinctive stitching and label on these Levi's jeans are a determinant attribute that distinguishes the product from other brands.

- *Price.* Consumers can choose the more expensive option, thinking they are getting better quality along with the higher price ("You get what you pay for"), or they might buy the one priced in the middle of the alternatives, neither the most expensive nor the cheapest, thinking that it is a good compromise between the two extremes.[13]

- *Brand.* Always buying brand name goods allows some consumers to feel safe with their choices. Purchasing a national brand, even if it is more expensive, gives many consumers the sense that they are buying a higher quality item.[14]

- *Product presentation.* Many times, the manner in which a product is presented can influence the decision process. For example, two comparable homes that are comparably priced will be perceived quite differently if one is presented in perfectly clean and uncluttered condition, with fresh flowers and the smell of chocolate chip cookies wafting about, whereas the other appears messy, has too much furniture for the rooms, and emits an unappealing smell. Consumers want to see that some effort has been put into the selling process, and just the way the product is presented can make or break a sale.[15]

Once a consumer has considered the possible alternatives and evaluated the pros and cons of each, he or she can move toward a purchase decision. Adding Value 5.2 illustrates how Expedia has created value for consumers by making travel alternatives readily available, as well as how consumers evaluate different travel options.

Purchase and Consumption

Value is a strong driver of consumers' purchase decisions. Customers seek out and purchase the products and services that they believe provide them with the best value. Then, after consumers have access to the product or service, they usually consume it.

A special type of consumption is called **ritual consumption**, which refers to a pattern of behaviors tied to life events that affect what and how we consume. These behaviors tend to have symbolic meanings and vary greatly by culture. For instance, they might take the form of everyday rituals such as going to Starbucks for a cappuccino or brushing your teeth, or they can be reserved for special occasions, such as rites of passage or holiday rituals. Many firms try to tie their products and services to ritual consumption; just imagine, where would Hallmark be without holidays?

Postpurchase

The final step of the consumer decision process is postpurchase behavior. Marketers are particularly interested in postpurchase behavior because it entails actual rather than potential customers. Satisfied customers, whom marketers hope to create, become loyal, purchase again, and spread positive word of mouth, so they are quite important. There are three possible positive postpurchase outcomes as illustrated in Exhibit 5.6: increased customer satisfaction, decreased postpurchase dissonance, and increased customer loyalty.

Customer Satisfaction   Setting unrealistically high consumer expectations of the product through advertising, personal selling, or other types of promotion may lead to higher initial sales, but it eventually will result in dissatisfaction when the product fails to achieve the high performance expectations. This failure can lead to dissatisfied customers and the potential for negative word of mouth. For

Adding Value 5.2

Evaluating Travel Alternatives with Expedia[16]

To illustrate how we evaluate alternatives in a buying decision, consider Expedia, the world's leading online travel service and the fourth-largest travel agency in the United States, a company that knows customers have high expectations in the competitive world of travel. Expedia's Web site (www.expedia.com) makes alternative evaluation easy through a variety of innovations. It allows customers to plan their travel by date, by price, by interest, or by activity. Travelers can book flights, hotel accommodations, car rentals, cruises, and vacation packages with the click of a mouse. The site also offers travel tools, such as travel alerts, flight status checks, seat selectors, airport information, currency converters, driving directions, weather reports, and passport information.

Consumers can use Expedia to narrow their search from a universal set—all airlines—to their evoked set—say, only United, Delta, and American. They can also search according to determinant attributes, such as the lowest price or shortest flight. Some flyers use a non-compensatory decision rule; they will only fly United to Denver, no matter what the alternatives are, because they are members of the airline's frequent flyer program. Others will use a compensatory decision rule, so they will fly United or Frontier to Denver, depending on which airline has the best combination of the lowest price, shortest flight, and minimum number of stops. Finally, some travelers choose an airline on the basis of key product signals, such as legroom, number of in-flight movie options, or quality of the food.

Expedia makes every travel customer their own travel agent.

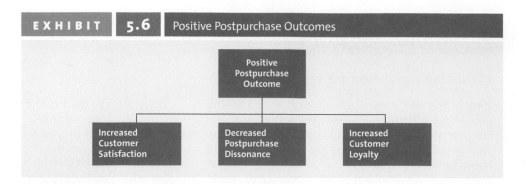

EXHIBIT 5.6 | Positive Postpurchase Outcomes

example, Starbucks recognized that it should worry when its market research suggested that it was not meeting customer expectations in terms of speed of service. With higher-than-average coffee cup prices, customers expect fast and precise service.[17]

But setting customer expectations too low is an equally dangerous strategy. Many retailers, for instance, don't "put their best foot forward"; no matter how good their merchandise and service may be, if their store is not clean and appealing from the entrance, customers are not likely to enter.

Marketers can take several steps to ensure postpurchase satisfaction, such as these:

- Build realistic expectations, not too high and not too low.
- Demonstrate correct product use—improper usage can cause dissatisfaction.
- Stand behind the product or service by providing money-back guarantees and warranties.
- Encourage customer feedback, which cuts down on negative word of mouth.
- Periodically make contact with customers and thank them for their support. This contact reminds customers that the marketer cares about their business and wants them to be satisfied. It also provides an opportunity to correct any problems. Customers appreciate human contact, though it is more expensive for marketers than e-mail or postal mail contacts.

Postpurchase Dissonance   Sometimes, if expectation levels are not met and customers are in some way dissatisfied with the product or service, postpurchase dissonance results. Postpurchase dissonance, also known as buyers' remorse, is the psychologically uncomfortable state produced by an inconsistency between beliefs and behaviors that in turn evokes a motivation to reduce the dissonance. Postpurchase dissonance generally occurs when a consumer questions the appropriateness of a purchase after his or her decision has been made.

Postpurchase dissonance is especially likely for products that are expensive, infrequently purchased, and are associated with high levels of risk. Aware of the negativity involved with postpurchase dissonance, some marketers even direct efforts at consumers after the purchase is made to address the issue. For example, General Electric sends a letter to purchasers of its appliances, positively reinforcing the message that the customer made a wise decision by mentioning the high quality that went into the product's design and production. Some clothing manufacturers include a tag on their garments to offer the reassurance that because of their special manufacturing process, perhaps designed to provide a soft, vintage appearance, there may be variations in color that have no effect on the quality of the item.

Eva rented the movie classic, *Casablanca*. Her belief is, "I'm going to end up watching this movie all alone and cry all the way through it." Her behavior says, "I love to watch Humphrey Bogart and Ingrid Bergman, so I rented it anyway." Dissonance results and manifests itself as that uncomfortable, unsettled feeling Eva has as a result of the inconsistency between what she believes and her behavior. To reduce the dissonance, Eva can take several actions:

- Cancel her order.
- Pay attention to positive information about the rental, such as looking up old reviews of *Casablanca* or articles about Bogart and Bergman.
- Get positive feedback from friends, as when Eva's friends commented positively about the movie.
- Seek negative information about products not selected. For example, Eva could go onto Netflix.com and read all the mediocre reviews of all the new movies out this month. Reading these reviews makes her feel more comfortable about renting the movie.

Consumers often feel dissonance when purchasing products or services. It is that uncomfortable feeling of mixed emotions—the movie makes me sad, but I love Bogart and Bergman.

Loyalty In the postpurchase stage of the decision-making process, marketers attempt to solidify a loyal relationship with their customers. They want customers to be satisfied with their purchase and buy from the same company again. Loyal customers will only buy certain brands and shop at certain stores, and they include no other firms in their evoked set. As we explained in Chapter 2, such customers are therefore very valuable to firms, and marketers have designed customer relationship management (CRM) programs specifically to retain them.

Undesirable Consumer Behavior Although firms want satisfied, loyal customers, sometimes they fail to attain them. Passive consumers are those that don't repeat purchase or recommend the product to others. More serious and potentially damaging, however, is negative consumer behavior, such as negative word of mouth and rumors.

Negative word of mouth occurs when consumers spread negative information about a product, service, or store to others. When customers' expectations are met or even exceeded, they often don't tell anyone about it. But when consumers believe that they have been treated unfairly in some way, they usually want to complain, often to many people. To lessen the impact of negative word of mouth, firms provide customer service representatives—whether online, on the phone, or in stores—to handle and respond to complaints. If the customer believes that positive action will be taken as a result of the complaint, he or she is less likely to complain to family and friends or through the Internet and certain Web sites, which are a great source of negative word of mouth (see Ethical Dilemma 5.1).

Ethical Dilemma 5.1 Dissatisfied Customers Use Ihate[company].com[18]

Dissatisfied consumers are taking to the Internet for vindication, and it's working. From rude customer service associates to misrepresented agreements, complaints proliferate online. *Forbes* has even ranked the best corporate complaint sites, including Allstate, PayPal, and American Express. According to some experts, Internet hate sites such as **Ihate[insert company name].com** have helped resolve more consumer complaints than any other method.

Some companies have tried to fight hate sites but with little success. Legal recourse is available only if the hate site uses the offending firm's trademarks, brand names, or other intellectual property in a way that might confuse the public. For the most part though, consumers who set up these sites are protected under freedom of speech and expression laws and have argued that no reasonable person would confuse **Ihate[company].com** with the company's actual site, as in **<your company>.com.**

For consumers, the question is why they have to resort to posting a complaint to a Web site? The answer is simple: there is a breakdown in customer service or in the business's communication with customers. For firms the question is how to protect themselves from these sites. The solution is once again simple: provide better more timely customer service and complaint resolution. The best strategy for marketers in dealing with hate sites is to stay on top of them and address their complaints immediately. If a company addresses a problem quickly, the originator may remove the site once his or her need to vent frustration has been satisfied. This disappearance, in turn, discourages new postings by other disgruntled customers. Companies can post their resolution on the site to show customers they are concerned and want to rectify a negative situation.

One thing's for sure—even though companies have attempted to curb this phenomenon by buying domain names such as **Ihate[their company name].com,** consumers will find a way to share their thoughts online. In addition to the numerous communities and Web sites, aggregators like TheComplaintStation.com offer a central repository for consumer complaints, with pages dedicated to specific companies. Similarly, TheVault.com creates a forum for current and previous employees to share their insider views of a company.

Factors Influencing the Consumer Decision Process

The consumer decision process can be influenced by several factors, as illustrated in Exhibit 5.7. First are the elements of the marketing mix, which we discuss throughout this book. Second are psychological factors, which are influences internal to the customer, such as motives, attitudes, perception, and learning. Third, social factors, such as family, reference groups, and culture, also influence the decision process. Fourth, there are situational factors, such as the specific purchase, a particular shopping situation, or the time of day, that affect the decision process.

Every decision people make as consumers will take them through some form of the consumer decision process. But, like life itself, this process does not exist in a vacuum.

Psychological Factors

Although marketers themselves can influence purchase decisions, a host of psychological factors affects the way people receive marketers' messages. Among

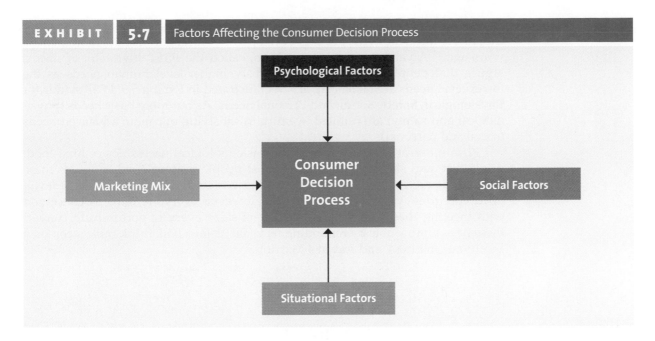

EXHIBIT | **5.7** | Factors Affecting the Consumer Decision Process

them are motives, attitudes, perception, and learning (see Exhibit 5.8). In this section, we examine how such psychological factors can influence the consumer decision process.

Motives In Chapter 1, we argued that marketing is all about satisfying customer needs and wants. When a need, such as thirst, or a want, such as a Diet Coke, is not satisfied, it motivates us, or drives us, to get satisfaction. So, a **motive** is a need or want that is strong enough to cause the person to seek satisfaction.

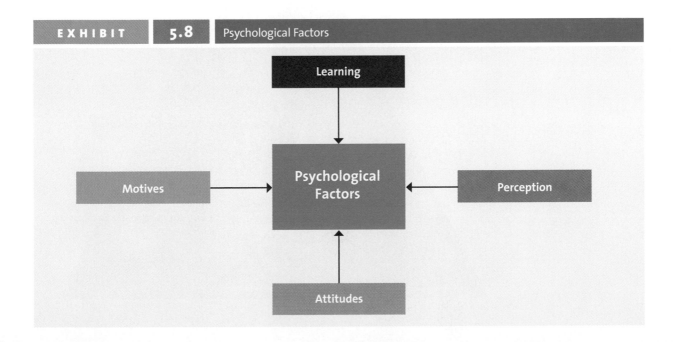

EXHIBIT | **5.8** | Psychological Factors

People have several types of motives. One of the best known paradigms for explaining these motive types was developed by Abraham Maslow more than 30 years ago.[19] A variation on the paradigm, called the **PSSP hierarchy of needs**, argues that people are motivated to satisfy higher-level human needs as the lower-level needs are taken care of.[20] As illustrated in Exhibit 5.9, PSSP stands for **P**hysiological, **S**afety, **S**ocial, and **P**ersonal needs. As our more basic needs (physiological and safety) are fulfilled, we turn to satisfying our more advanced needs (social and personal).

Physiological needs deal with the basic biological necessities of life—food, drink, rest, and shelter. Although for most people in developed countries these basic needs are generally met, there are those in both developed and less-developed countries who are less fortunate. However, everyone remains concerned with meeting these basic needs. Marketers seize every opportunity to convert these needs into wants by reminding us to eat at Taco Bell, drink milk, sleep on a Beautyrest mattress, and stay at a Marriott.

EXHIBIT	**5.9**	PSSP Hierarchy of Needs

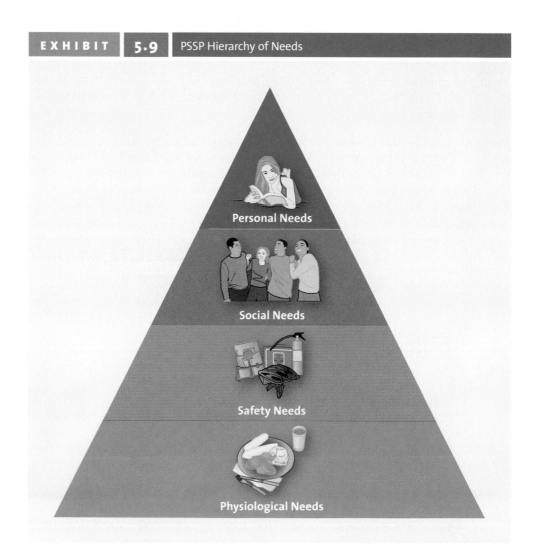

Safety needs pertain to protection and physical well-being. The marketplace is full of products and services that are designed to make you safer, such as airbags in cars and burglar alarms in homes, or healthier, such as vitamins and organic meats and vegetables.

Social needs relate to our interactions with others. Haircuts and makeup make you look more attractive, and deodorants prevent odor. Greeting cards help you express your feelings toward others.

Finally, **personal needs** allow people to satisfy their inner desires. Yoga, meditation, health clubs, and many books appeal to people's desires to grow or maintain a happy, satisfied outlook on life.

Which of the PSSP needs applies when a consumer purchases a magazine? Magazines such as *Weight Watchers*, for instance, help satisfy *physiological* needs like how to eat healthy, but also *personal* needs like how to be happy with one's life. Magazines like *Family Circle,* on the other hand, provide tips on how to make the home a *safer* place to live. Finally, magazines such as *Weddings* help satisfy *social* needs since it provides instructions on topics such as how to prepare invitations so friends and family will be properly informed and no one will be offended. Many of these magazines can fulfill several PSSP needs simultaneously. Good marketers add value to their products or services and thereby nudge people up the PSSP hierarchy.

Which PSSP needs do these magazines fulfill?

Attitude

We have attitudes about almost everything. For instance, we like this class, but we don't like the instructor. We like where we live, but we don't like the weather. An **attitude** is a person's enduring evaluation of his or her feelings about and behavioral tendencies toward an object or idea. Attitudes are learned and long lasting, and they might develop over a long period of time, though they can also abruptly change. For instance, you might like your instructor for much of the semester—until she returns your first exam. The one thing attitudes have in common for everyone is their ability to influence all decisions and actions in a person's life.

An attitude consists of three components. The **cognitive** aspect reflects what we believe to be true, the **affective** component involves what we feel about the issue at hand—our like or dislike of something—and the **behavioral** component comprises the action(s) we undertake with regard to that issue. For example, Ed and Jill Fern see an advertisement for a Volvo that shows a family of five driving down the road, the kids strapped into their car seats and mom and dad talking in the front. An announcer lists the features included with each model, as well as government safety ratings that indicate Volvo is the safest brand on the road in its class. On the basis of this advertisement, Ed and Jill believe that the government statistics must be true and that the car is therefore safe (cognitive component). Watching the happy family looking comfortable while driving this safe car allows Ed and Jill to feel that they would like to have this car for their family (affective).

People buy Volvos because they believe they are safe (cognitive component of an attitude), because they like them (affective), and because they have many convenient dealerships to visit (behavioral).

Thus encouraged, they go to the Volvo dealership closest to them to make a purchase (behavioral).

Ideally, agreement exists among these components. When there is incongruence among the three however, cognitive dissonance occurs. Suppose, for instance, that though Ed and Jill believe the Volvo is safe and like the car, they buy another brand because it is cheaper. It is likely that they will experience the discomfort of buyers' remorse.

Although attitudes are pervasive and usually slow to change, the important fact from a marketer's point of view is that they can be influenced and perhaps changed through persuasive communications and personal experience. Marketing communication—through salespeople, advertisements, free samples, or other such methods—can attempt to change what people believe to be true about a product or service (cognitive) or how they feel toward it (affective). If the marketer is successful, the cognitive and affective components work in concert to affect behavior. Continuing with our example, suppose that prior to viewing the ad, Ed and Jill thought that a Toyota Camry was the safest car on the road, but they liked the looks of the Volvo. The ad positively influenced the cognitive component of their attitude toward Volvo, making it consistent with the affective component.

Perception   Another psychological factor, **perception,** is the process by which we select, organize, and interpret information to form a meaningful picture of the world. Perception influences our acquisition and consumption of goods and services because it assigns meaning to such things as color, symbols, taste, and packaging. Culture, tradition, and our overall upbringing determine our perceptual view of the world. For instance, Jill has always wanted a Volvo because her best friend in college had one, and they had a great time driving across the country together one summer. However, based on his past experiences, Ed has a different perception. Ed thinks Volvos are slow, stodgy, unfashionable, and meant to be driven by little old ladies with gray hair—though they are safe! Volvo has worked hard in recent years to overcome this long-standing, negative perceptual bias that Ed and many others hold by creating faster cars with more stylish designs and using promotion to reposition the brand to portray a more positive image.

Learning   Learning refers to a change in a person's thought process or behavior that arises from experience and takes place throughout the consumer decision process. For instance, after Eva recognized that she needed a movie rental service, she started looking for ads and searching for reviews and articles on the Internet. She learned from each new piece of information, so that her thoughts about the services were different than before she had read anything. In addition, she liked the selection that was available through Netflix. She learned from this experience, and it became part of her memory to be used in the future, possibly so she could recommend the service to her friends.

Learning affects both attitudes and perceptions. Throughout the buying process, Eva's attitudes shifted. The cognitive component changed for her when she learned that no other service had so many classic movies available. Once she started getting movies, she realized how much she liked the service, which indicates the affective component, then subscribed to it—the behavioral component.

Each time she was exposed to information about or the service itself, she learned something different that affected her perception of the service. Before she tried it, Eva hadn't realized how fun it was to find exactly the movie she wanted to rent; thus, her perception of the service changed through learning.

A person's perceptions and ability to learn are affected by their societal experiences, which we discuss next.

Social Factors

Exhibit 5.10 illustrates that the consumer decision process is influenced by psychological factors—such as motivation, attitudes, perception, and learning—that exist within the person. But the decision process is also influenced by the external, social environment, which consists of the customer's family, reference groups, and culture. (See Exhibit 5.11.)[21]

Family   Many purchase decisions are made about products or services that the entire family will consume or use. Thus, firms must consider how families make purchase decisions and understand how various family members might influence these decisions.

When families make purchase decisions, they often consider the needs of all the family members. In choosing a restaurant, for example, all the family members may participate in the decision making. In other situations however, different members of the family may take on different roles. For example, the husband and teenage child may look through car magazines and *Consumer Reports* to search for information about a new car. But once they arrive at the dealership, the husband and wife, not the child, decide which model and color to buy, and the wife negotiates the final deal.

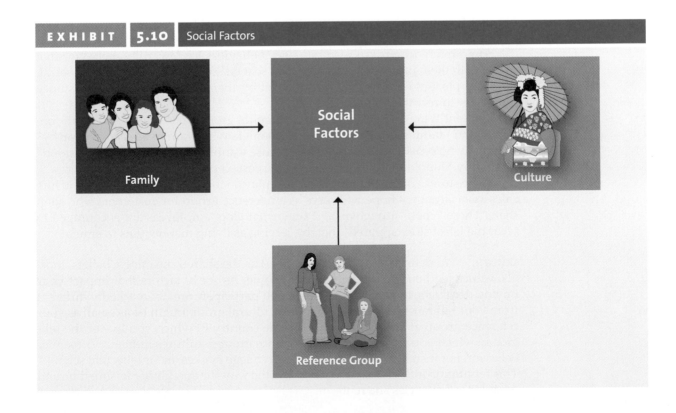

EXHIBIT   5.10   Social Factors

Family

Social Factors

Culture

Reference Group

Family members often influence buying decisions.

Despite that example, children and adolescents play an important role in family buying decisions. For instance, kids in the United States spend over $200 billion on personal items such as snacks, soft drinks, entertainment, and apparel. They directly influence the purchase of another $300 billion worth of items such as food, snacks, beverages, toys, health and beauty aids, clothing, accessories, gifts, and school supplies. Their indirect influence on family spending is even higher—$500 billion for items such as recreation, vacations, technology, and even the family car.[22]

Influencing a group that holds this much spending power is vitally important. Traditional food retailers are already caught in a squeeze between Wal-Mart, which lures low-end customers, and specialty retailers like Whole Foods, which target the high end. Knowing how children influence food buying decisions is a strategic opportunity for traditional supermarkets and their suppliers to exploit. Getting this group to prefer one store, chain, or product over another can make a difference in the bottom line, as well as in the chances for survival in a difficult marketplace.[23]

Reference Groups   A reference group is one or more persons whom an individual uses as a basis for comparison regarding beliefs, feelings, and behaviors. A consumer might have various reference groups, including family, friends, co-workers, or famous people the consumer would like to emulate. These reference groups affect buying decisions by (1) offering information, (2) providing rewards for specific purchasing behaviors, and (3) enhancing a consumer's self-image.

Reference groups provide information to consumers directly through conversation or indirectly through observation. For example, Eva received valuable information from a friend about Netflix. On another occasion, Eva heard one of her film history professors praising the virtues of Netflix during a lecture, which solidified her attitude about the service.

Some reference groups also influence behaviors by rewarding behavior that meets with their approval or chastising those who engage in behavior that doesn't. For example, smokers are often ostracized by their friends and made to smoke outside or in restricted areas.

By identifying and affiliating with reference groups, consumers can create, enhance, and maintain their self-image. Customers who want to be seen as "earthy" might buy Birkenstock sandals, whereas those wanting to be seen as "high fashion" might buy Manolo Blahnik shoes, as we discussed previously in this chapter.

Some stores, like Abercrombie & Fitch, play on these forms of influence and hire sales associates they hope will serve as a reference group for customers who shop there. These "cool," attractive, and somewhat aloof employees are encouraged to wear the latest store apparel—thereby serving as living mannequins to emulate.

Culture   We defined culture in Chapter 3 as the shared meanings, beliefs, morals, values, and customs of a group of people. As social factors that impact your buying decisions, the cultures in which you participate are not markedly different from your reference groups. That is, your cultural group might be as small as your reference group at school or as large as the country in which you live or the religion in which you participate. Like reference groups, cultures influence consumer behavior. For instance, the culture at Eva's college evokes an "intellectual school." This reputation influences, to some extent, the way she spends her leisure time and what types of movies she rents.

Situational Factors

Psychological and social factors typically influence the consumer decision process the same way each time. For example, your motivation to quench your thirst usually drives you to drink a Pepsi, and your reference group at the workplace coerces you to wear appropriate attire. But sometimes, situational factors, or factors specific to the situation, override, or at least influence, psychological and social issues. These situational factors are related to the purchase and shopping situation, as well as to the temporal state, as illustrated in Exhibit 5.11. Entrepreneurial Marketing 5.1 describes a rental car company that is desirable only in certain situations.

Purchase Situation   Customers may be predisposed to purchase certain products or services because of some underlying psychological trait or social factor, but these factors may change in certain purchase situations. For instance, Samantha Crumb considers herself a thrifty, cautious shopper—someone who likes to get a good deal. But her best friend is getting married, and she wants to buy the couple a silver tray. If the tray were for herself, she would probably go to Crate & Barrel or possibly even Wal-Mart. But since it is for her best friend, she went to Tiffany & Co. Why? To purchase something fitting for the special occasion of a wedding.

Shopping Situation   Consumers might be ready to purchase a product or service but be completely derailed once they arrive in the store. Marketers use several techniques to influence consumers at this choice stage of the decision process. Consider the following techniques:

■   *Store atmosphere*. Some retailers and service providers have developed unique images that are based at least in part on their internal environment, also known as their atmospherics.[24] Research has shown that, if used in concert

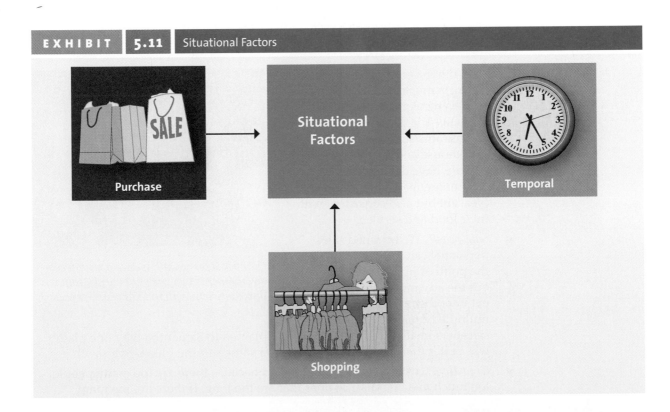

EXHIBIT   5.11   Situational Factors

Entrepreneurial Marketing 5.1

Zipcar—The Urban Rent-a-Car[25]

Estimates show that car ownership for every 1,000 persons living in the United States is 1,100—or 1.1 cars per person. And whether it's your basic "A to B" functional car or a luxury status symbol, we all seem to believe that a car is a necessity for daily life. So why is it that in cities such as Seattle, Boston, and Washington, DC, consumers are skipping the car payments, forgoing car insurance, and choosing to share cars with their neighbors?

During a trip to Berlin, Zipcar founder Robin Chase observed cars, parked around the city, that could be rented by the hour. When she returned to Boston, a city notorious for its parking congestion, Chase designed and instituted a similar concept. Keeping the specific needs of Boston consumers in mind, Chase employed Internet and wireless data transmission to ease reservation headaches and placed Zipcars at strategically chosen spots around the city. Membership in Zipcar costs $75 dollars per year and requires a valid driver's license, credit card, and Internet access. The cars rent for $8.50 to 12.50 per hour, including mileage and gasoline. Members simply make online reservations through the Web site, and within approximately two minutes, the information is transmitted via a wireless

Zipcars are great for people who don't need a car every day.

network to a chip inside the car. At the car, the member swipes a membership card over the windshield to unlock the doors and retrieve the key, which is tethered to a wire beside the ignition.

Zipcar has grown to include more than 10,000 members, with 250 cars in Boston, New York, and Washington, DC. The firm is also expanding beyond urban areas to college campuses and suburbs—such as the University of North Carolina at Chapel Hill and Arlington, Virginia—that are seeking alternatives to car congestion.

with other aspects of a retailer's strategy, music, scent, lighting, and even color can positively influence the decision process.[26] Restaurants such as Outback Steakhouse and The Cheesecake Factory have developed internal environments that are not only pleasant but also consistent with their food and service.

Outback Steakhouse has developed internal environments that are not only pleasant but also consistent with their food and service.

- *Salespeople.* Well-trained sales personnel can influence the sale at the point of purchase by pointing out the advantages of one item over another and encouraging multiple purchases. The salesperson at Tiffany, for instance, explained to Samantha why one platter was better than the next and suggested some serving pieces to go with it.

- *Crowding.* Customers can feel crowded because there are too many people, too much merchandise, or lines that are too long. If there are too many people in a store, some people become distracted and may even leave.[27] Others have difficulty purchasing if the merchandise is packed too close together. This issue is a particular problem for shoppers with mobility disabilities.

■ *In-store demonstrations.* The taste and smell of new food items may attract people to try something they normally wouldn't. Similarly, some fashion retailers offer "trunk shows," during which their vendors show their whole line on a certain day. During these well-advertised events, customers are often enticed to purchase that day because they get special assistance from the salespeople and can order merchandise that the retailer otherwise does not carry.

In-store demonstrations entice people to buy.

■ *Promotions.* Retailers employ various promotional vehicles to influence customers once they have arrived in the store. For instance, an unadvertised price promotion can alter a person's preconceived buying plan. Multi-item discounts, such as "buy 1, get 1 free" sales, are popular means to get people to buy more than they normally would. Finally, because many people regard clipping coupons from the newspaper as too much trouble, some stores make coupons available in the store.

■ *Packaging.* It is difficult to make a product stand out in the crowd when it competes for shelf space with several other brands. This problem is particularly difficult for consumer packaged goods, such as groceries and health and beauty products. Marketers therefore spend millions of dollars designing and updating their packages to be more appealing and eye catching.

Temporal State Our state of mind at any particular time can alter our preconceived notions of what we are going to purchase. For instance, some people are "morning people," whereas others function better at night. In turn, a purchase situation may have different appeal levels depending on the time of day and the type of person the consumer is. Mood swings can even alter consumer behavior. Suppose Samantha received a parking ticket just prior to shopping at Tiffany. It is likely that she would be less receptive to the salesperson's influence than if she came into the store in a good mood. Her bad mood may even cause her to have a less positive postpurchase feeling about the store.

As we've seen, people's lives are lived in different contexts, humans are not machines, and consumer decisions simply are not made in vacuums.

Summing Up

1. **When purchasing a product or a service, do you spend a lot of time considering your decision?**

   The answer to how much time a consumer spends making a purchasing decision depends on the product or service being purchased. Some purchasing decisions require limited problem solving because the perceived risk of the purchase is low or the consumer has previous experience purchasing the product or service. Impulse and habitual purchases fall in this category. Sometimes, however, consumers enter into extended problem solving because the perceived risk of the purchase is great.

2. **What steps do you go through when you decide to buy a product or service?**

   Consumers generally start their decision process by recognizing that they must buy something to satisfy a need or want. Sometimes the needs are simple; I need food because I am hungry. Often, however, they become more complex; I want to buy my girlfriend an engagement ring.

Once they recognize the need, consumers start searching for information. Generally, the more important the purchase, the more time and effort the consumer will spend on the search process. Firms facilitate this search by providing promotional materials and personal selling. Once they have enough information, consumers can evaluate their alternatives and make a choice.

In the next step of the decision process, consumers purchase and use the product or service. But the process doesn't simply stop there. After the sale, the consumer is either satisfied with the purchase or experiences postpurchase dissonance. Every marketer wants satisfied customers, but when instead they are confronted with dissatisfied customers who are in some way unsure about their purchase, marketers must proactively turn the situation around. If they don't, the customer may be gone for good.

3. What determines how much time consumers will search for information before buying a product or a service?

A variety of factors affect consumers' searches for information about a potential purchase. First, they consider the time and effort associated with searching versus the benefits derived from the search. Second, people who have an internal locus of control—those who believe they have control over the outcomes of their actions—are more likely to spend time searching for information than those with an external locus of control. Third, consumers who perceive a high performance, financial, or psychological risk associated with the purchase will spend relatively more time searching for information than those

who do not. Finally, consumers will spend more time searching for information for specialty goods than for shopping or convenience goods, respectively.

4. How can understanding consumers' behavior help marketers sell products or services?

First and foremost, firms must design their products and services to meet their customers' wants and needs, but understanding certain aspects of consumer behavior can help as well. For instance, it is important to understand people's motives (i.e., what drives them to buy), their attitudes (i.e., how they feel about a product or service), and their perceptions (i.e., how information about that product or service fits into their worldview). Knowledge about these psychological characteristics helps firms design and provide products and services that their customers want and need.

In addition, people don't live in a vacuum. Consumers are influenced by their family, their reference groups, and their culture. Understanding these social groups and people's roles within them provides important insights into consumers' buying behavior. Finally, though consumers already carry a host of psychological and social factors along with them on a shopping expedition, certain other factors can influence a purchase at the point of sale. For instance, customers might change their buying behavior because the purchase situation is different than the one they are used to. Also, things can happen to customers, both positive and negative, once they are in a store that might alter their preconceived notion of what they plan to purchase. Finally, people can be just plain finicky, and being in an unusually good or extremely bad mood can also alter a purchase decision. The more firms understand these psychological, social, and situational factors, the more likely they will be to influence purchase decisions.

Key Terms

- affective component, 135
- attitude, 135
- behavioral component, 135
- cognitive component, 135
- compensatory decision rule, 127
- consumer decision rules, 127
- convenience goods/services, 125
- culture, 138
- decision heuristics, 127
- determinant attributes, 126
- evaluative criteria, 126
- evoked set, 126

- extended problem solving, 120
- external locus of control, 124
- external search for information, 123
- financial risk, 124
- functional needs, 121
- habitual decision making, 120
- impulse buying, 120
- internal locus of control, 124
- internal search for information, 123
- learning, 136

- limited problem solving, 119
- motive, 133
- need recognition, 121
- negative word of mouth, 131
- noncompensatory decision rule, 127
- perception, 136
- performance risk, 124
- personal needs, 135
- physiological needs, 134
- postpurchase dissonance, 130
- PSSP hierarchy of needs, 134

Marketing Applications

1. Describe two products: one you just went and purchased without much thought and one that took some deliberation on your part. Why did you spend a different amount of time and effort deciding on your purchases of the two products?

2. Assume you are in the market to buy a new car. What kind of car would you consider? What type of need(s) would you be satisfying if you purchased that particular type of car?

3. Explain the factors that affect the amount of time and effort that a consumer might take when choosing an optometrist for contact lenses. How would your answer change if the consumer were looking for contact lens cleaning solution?

4. When evaluating different alternatives for a Saturday night outing at a fine restaurant, explain the difference between the universal set, the retrieval set, and the evoked set. From which set of alternatives will the consumer most likely choose the restaurant?

5. What can retailers do to make sure they have satisfied customers after the sale is complete?

6. Tazo makes a blend of exotic green teas, spearmint, and rare herbs into a tea called Zen. Using the PSSP hierarchy of needs, explain which need(s) are being fulfilled by this tea.

7. Identify and describe the three social factors that influence the consumer decision process. Provide an example of how each of these might influence the purchase of the necessary products and services for a family vacation.

8. Nike has developed a new shoe for long-distance runners designed to minimize wear and tear on the joints and tendons. Develop a theme for an advertising strategy that ensures all three components of attitude are positively covered.

9. What can a marketer do to positively influence a situation in which a consumer is ready to buy but has not yet done so?

10. You were recently hired by a retail and catalog company that promotes itself as an American firm selling only American made goods. The products featured in advertising and in the catalogs tell the stories of the firms that produced the goods in the United States. The sales response to the firm's Made in America position has been incredible and growth has been impressive. One day while speaking to a vendor, you find out a shipment of merchandise will be delayed since the product is coming from overseas and is late. A few days later you hear a similar story. As it turns out, the firm just barely earns the Made in the USA label. Though technically the products meet a standard to be classified as American made, you worry that the firms is not being truthful to its customers. You decide to write a letter to the VP of Marketing detailing your concerns. What would you put in the letter?

Toolkit

CONSUMER BEHAVIOR

Jill is trying to decide, once and for all, which soft drink company is her favorite. She has created a chart to help her decide. She has rated Coca-Cola, Pepsi-Cola, and Jones Soda in terms of price, taste, variety, and packaging. She has also assessed how important each of these four attributes is in terms of her evaluations. Please use the toolkit provided at www.mhhe.com/grewal-levy to determine which cola Jill will choose using a compensatory model. Which cola would she choose using a noncompensatory model? If you were Jill, which model would you use, the compensatory or the noncompensatory. Why?

Net Savvy

1. Visit the Harley-Davidson USA Web site (www.harley-davidson.com) and review the information provided about its Harley Owners Group (H.O.G.). Describe the efforts the company makes to maintain customer loyalty through its programs. What are the benefits to H.O.G. members? Discuss how these measures might be effective in creating value for members.

2. Customers use a variety of methods to provide feedback to companies about their experiences. Planetfeedback.com was developed as one such venue. Visit its Web site (www.planetfeedback.com) and identify the types of feedback that customers can provide. Look over the feedback about Ford, and summarize some of the most recent comments. What is the ratio of positive to negative comments about Ford during the last year or so? Describe the effect these comments might have on customer perceptions of Ford.

Chapter Case Study

THE SMART CAR PREPARES TO ENTER THE U.S. MARKET[28]

All the rage in crowded cities in Western Europe, the smart car brand will finally make its way across the Atlantic. Although various models are available elsewhere, an entirely new model is being introduced into the U.S. market: the smart SUV. According to Scott Keogh, General Manager at smart USA, the company expects to sell 25,000 smart cars to U.S. consumers in its first year.

Company Background[29]

The smart car was conceived in 1994 through a joint venture between Mercedes-Benz and SMH, the Swiss manufacturer of Swatch watches, and named for "**S**watch, **M**ercedes, and **art.**" Engineered with the environment in mind, the car originally was to use electric power or hybrid technology but ultimately was produced to consume either gasoline or diesel power, though it still achieves "green" status because of its anticorrosion undercoat and the powder coating on its steel body, which avoid polluting with wastewater and solvents. The body also features already colored, molded plastic panels to eliminate the need for paint booths and their resulting emissions.

The smart car was designed as a part of an overall transportation strategy for Europe's bustling big cities. To support efforts to reduce congestion, the smart car was to be used to reach local destinations, whereas longer trips would rely on rail and air transportation. For example, the Swiss have integrated smart cars into their transportation system to the point that consumers can have smart cars, rather than taxis, awaiting them at 40 different train stations.

EXHIBIT C5.1   Smart Models Available in the U.K.

The World Market for Smart

Wholly owned by DaimlerChrysler, smart cars are currently sold in 30 countries, including Germany, Italy, Switzerland, Australia, Canada, Hong Kong, Israel, Japan, Lebanon, Mexico, South Africa, Taiwan, Turkey, and the United Kingdom.

Because it manufactures a variety of models, the company provides a user-friendly smart configuration tool on its Web sites (www.smart.com) so potential buyers can design their own cars. (See Exhibit C5.1 for an example of the smart configuration tool for the U.K. market.)

As the world's smallest car, smart has earned the affectionate nicknames the electric razor on wheels, a glorified go-cart, high fashion by Hot Wheels, and a rolling backpack, to cite a few. Driving it has been likened to driving in a telephone booth, though some view it more as a high-tech toy whose cabin is part cockpit, part playpen. An article in *Money* magazine told readers to "Think of it as the T-shirt of cars: cute, comfy and cheap."[30] But beyond the teasing, the smart car has also been referred to as "an environmentalist's own rolling Kyoto treaty"[31] because of its ability to get 60 miles per gallon, its low emissions, and the recyclability of 85 percent of the materials used in its production. In markets in which gasoline costs upwards of $5 a gallon, the car has real appeal, especially among the eclectic crowd, with its hip, cool image. According to Keogh, the smart car is "a unique car for people who really want to stand out."[32] (See Exhibit C5.2 for an example of how the company conveys its hip image.)

One of the hallmarks of the smart car is its size. Its dimensions—eight feet long, five feet wide, and five feet tall—puts it five feet shorter and a foot narrower than the Volkswagen Beetle. Originally the smart car was intended only for the narrow streets of crowded European cities, where two-seaters are common, parking spaces are very scarce, and these cars navigate tight spots and squeeze into the tiniest of parking spots. When pulled in nose-to-curb, three of them can fit into one parallel parking space.

Although it only sports a three-cylinder, 50- to 60-horsepower engine, the smart car is reported to purr like a kitten and offer some spunk. In addition to front and optional side airbags, air conditioning, remote central locking, and electric windows, smart car buyers can change their car's colors if they purchase interchangeable snap-on body panels. When the mood hits, the owner pulls off the black panels, snaps on the red, and makes a whole new fashion statement.

EXHIBIT | **C5.2** | Smart Car—A Hip Image

The U.S. Market

In the recent past, small cars have had a difficult time making big inroads into the U.S. automobile market. American consumers like the luxury and safety provided by their large, massive horsepower cars, SUVs, and trucks—even when fuel prices skyrocket—partly because they are accustomed to a more sparsely populated geography, except for those U.S. consumers who live in sprawling metropolitan areas. Although uniquely styled cars like the PT Cruiser, Volkswagen Beetle, and Mini Cooper have managed to get a piece of the limelight, they appeal only to small niches in the market.

Rumors have abounded for years about the possible introduction of smart cars to the U.S. market. Various issues prevented the sale of the original models, such as the fear that they would never sell in sufficient numbers to be viable, their high price tag by American standards, and the difficulty of making them compliant with EPA regulations. In addition, U.S. auto safety advocates voiced serious concerns about the crashworthiness of the small vehicles in a market in which big vehicles rule the road.

The smart SUV destined for the U.S. market will be developed by Mitsubishi and produced in DaimlerChrysler's Juiz de Fora, Brazil, manufacturing facility. A cross between a car and an SUV (though a particularly small SUV by American standards), the smart will sport permanent all-wheel drive. The jury remains out about how well it will be accepted because the features demanded by Americans may differ drastically from those demanded by Europeans and Asians. Selected Mercedes-Benz dealerships throughout the United States will sell the smart cars from separate showrooms they are required to build to market the car.

Questions

1. Identify and discuss the type of decision process that consumers go through when purchasing this type of product. How have smart cars created value?

2. Identify the determinant attributes that might set the smart car apart from competing makes and models. What attributes might be of concern to consumers?

3. What are some differences between the U.S. market and other world markets that might make it tougher to sell the smart car to U.S. consumers?

4. Explain whether you think the smart car will be a success in the United States. Support and defend your position.

6

QUESTIONS

- How do B2B firms segment their markets?

- How does B2B buying differ from consumer buying behavior?

- What factors influence the B2B buying process?

- How has the Internet changed B2B marketing?

Business-to-Business Marketing

Think about the jeans in your closet. You probably bought them from a store in the course of a business-to-consumer (B2C) transaction. But from whom did the company that manufactured your jeans, say Seven for All Mankind, buy the components needed to get those jeans ready for you? Seven for All Mankind needed to buy the raw materials, like denim and thread. It also had to buy sewing machines to make the jeans and washers and dryers to help give them that popular vintage look. To age your new jeans further, Seven for All Mankind even had to buy little rocks to put into the dryers, along with some knives and sanders. When the company purchased these materials, they were shipped to the Seven for All Mankind factory on trucks or by rail. These very transactions—purchasing the materials and transportation, designing the patterns for cutting and manufacturing the fabric—are managed by computer systems that were developed by and purchased from software engineers and consultants. Then, once the jeans have been produced, they must be transported to and sold by retailers. In each of these transactions, one business sells to another, which makes each a B2B transaction. B2C transactions only occur when a business, typically a retailer, sells to a consumer.

■ ■ ■

Imagine how many B2B transactions took place before Jessica Simpson was able to buy these destroyed denim jeans.

Business-to-business (B2B) marketing refers to the process of buying and selling goods or services to be used in the production of other goods and services, for consumption by the buying organization, and/or for resale by wholesalers and retailers. Therefore, B2B marketing involves manufacturers, wholesalers, and service firms that market goods and services to other businesses but not to the ultimate consumer. The distinction between a B2B and a B2C transaction is not the product or service itself; rather, it is the ultimate *user of* that product or service. Had your jeans been sold to an industrial supply firm, which then sold them to a custodial firm whose employees would wear them on the job, the transaction would still be a B2B transaction because the jeans are being used by a business rather than by an individual household consumer.

Another major difference between the typical B2B and B2C transaction is the role of the salesperson. While salespeople are an important component of the communications mix for B2C transactions like real estate, insurance, jewelry, consumer electronics, and high-end apparel, most fast moving consumer goods (FMCG) found in grocery and discount stores are not sold with the aid of salespeople. On the other hand, in most B2B sales, the salesperson is an integral component of the transaction.

The demand for B2B sales is often derived from the B2C sales in the same supply chain. More specifically, **derived demand** is the linkage between consumers' demand for a company's output and its purchase of necessary inputs to manufacture or assemble that particular output. For instance, the demand for raw denim used to make Seven for all Mankind jeans is derived from the sale of the jeans to consumers.

In this chapter, we will look at the different types of B2B markets and examine the B2B buying process with an eye toward how it differs from the B2C buying process, which we discussed in Chapter 5. Several factors influence the B2B buying process, and we discuss these as well. Finally, the chapter concludes with a discussion about the role of the Internet and its influence on the way B2B marketing is conducted.

B2B Markets

Just like organizations that sell directly to final consumers in B2C transactions, B2B firms focus their efforts on serving specific target markets to create value for those customers.[1] For instance, AT&T has dedicated business units that serve business customers within each of its targeted markets, which are segmented by market size. The products geared toward small businesses offer basic voice services, packaged plans, and no long-term contracts. Medium-sized firms also can choose from networked voice, data, and information processing services, and they receive usage discounts when they sign up for longer term commitments. For its largest customers, AT&T provides everything from professional services to corporate calling cards.[2]

Some firms find it more productive to focus their efforts and resources on key business customers rather than on the ultimate consumer. The consumer products giant Procter & Gamble (P&G), for instance, has found that working closely with its retailers by reducing the number of its distributors by 80 percent enables it to provide much better service to those retailers and to achieve far better profits.[3] Companies such as P&G gain economies of scale by employing fewer, larger distributors that can add value in the form of logistics services (e.g., inventory management) that in turn will save the reseller money and thereby reduce costs for the end consumer.[4]

In our jeans example, we described two types of B2B organizations: manufacturers/producers and resellers. However, institutions and governments also may be involved in B2B transactions. We now describe each of these B2B organizations and how the government classifies them. (See Exhibit 6.1.)

Manufacturers or Producers

Some of the biggest business-to-business buyers are manufacturers and producers. They buy raw materials, components, and parts that allow them to manufacture their own goods. For example, Hewlett-Packard (HP) uses a variety of components to make its computer products, including plastic for its exterior cases, interior components, and packaging. Given its high sales volume, HP must manage its supply and demand chains closely to minimize any shortages or overages. Therefore, HP created a private Internet market that connects the company with its plastics suppliers so it can consolidate plastic purchases and efficiently communicate with other supply chain areas.[5] The improvement in the information flow engendered by this private Internet market has cut 25 percent off the time it takes HP to receive the merchandise, 30 percent off plastic costs, and a significant portion off its internal administrative costs.[6]

Ted and his firm use AT&T business systems to help market and distribute his healthy beverages.

Resellers

Resellers are marketing intermediaries that resell manufactured products without significantly altering their form. For instance, wholesalers and distributors buy jeans from Seven for all Mankind and sell them to retailers—a B2B transaction, and retailers in turn resell those same jeans to the ultimate consumer—a B2C transaction—wholesalers, distributors, and retailers are all resellers.

Institutions

Institutions, such as hospitals, educational organizations, and religious organizations, also purchase all kinds of goods and services. For instance, with an annual budget of $40 million for textbooks alone, the Chicago Public School system certainly qualifies as an institution with significant buying power.[7] However, like

EXHIBIT | **6.1** | B2B Markets

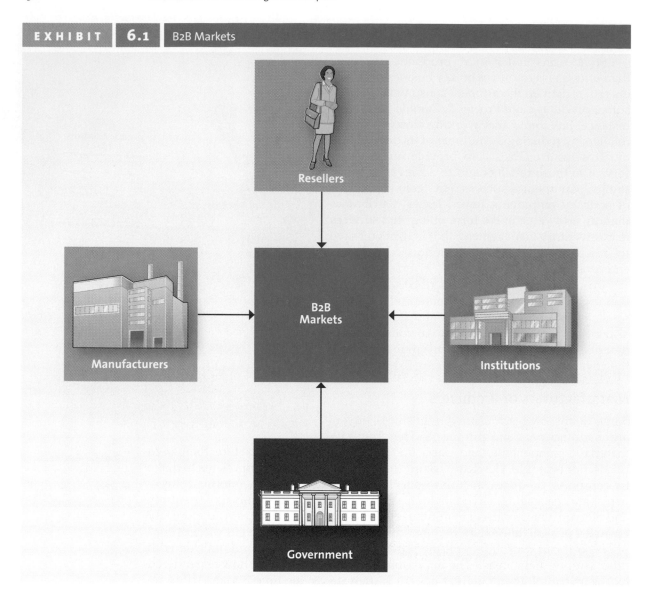

most other not-for-profit institutions, the Chicago Public Schools face very tight budgets, and their textbook procurement method badly needed an overhaul. The school administrators recently realized that 30 percent of all book orders contained 10 or fewer books, which meant they missed any bulk discounts and suffered price discrepancies on 44 percent of their orders. They first revised their procurement strategy by centralizing control. They also set up an internal clearinghouse so that schools looking to buy certain textbooks and other schools looking to dispose of the same textbooks could complete the transaction seamlessly. These relatively simple changes are expected to save the schools approximately 33 percent of their annual book budget. With such success, the school system is applying these lessons to other purchasing activities, including capital construction, equipment and supplies, and food and janitorial services.

Government

In most countries, the central government tends to be one of the largest purchasers of goods and services. For example the U.S. Federal Government spends about $2.1 trillion annually on procuring goods and services.[8] If you add in the amount state and local governments spend, these numbers reach staggering proportions. Specifically, with its approved $401.7 billion war budget in the fiscal year 2005, the Pentagon represents a spending force to be reckoned with,[9] especially when it comes to aerospace and defense (A&D) manufacturers, some of the Pentagon's largest suppliers of products. Because the Pentagon represents such an important customer for most of these manufacturers, they have recognized the need to provide it with excellent value. Therefore, over the next five years A&D manufacturers will spend $618 million to make their supply networks more efficient and responsive to the government.[10]

The U.S. government spends over $4 billion a year on aerospace and defense for everything from nuts and bolts to this F-14 Tomcat jetfighter.

B2B Classification System

The U.S. Bureau of the Census collects data about business activity in the United States through its classification scheme, which categorizes all firms into a hierarchical set of six-digit **North American Industry Classification System (NAICS) codes**.[11] Since the 1930s, the United States had used the Standard Industrial Classification (SIC) system, but the new NAICS, developed jointly with Canada and Mexico, provides comparable statistics about business activity in all of North America.

As the NAICS codes have evolved, more subcategories have been added to each sector. Consider, for example, the evolution of the telecommunications category shown in Exhibit 6.2. Under the 1987 SIC codes, telecommunications fell within the "Transportation, Communications and Utilities" sector, whose subcategories included telephones, telegraphs, and broadcasting. Today, though, with

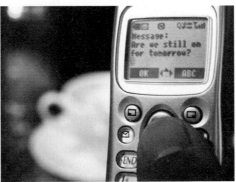

Which NAICS codes are used for these products?

EXHIBIT 6.2	Evolution of Telecommunications: NAICS Codes	
1987 SIC	**2002 NAICS**	**2002 Subcategories**
48 Communication 481 Telephone 4812 Radio Telephone	51 Information 517 Telecommunications 5172 Wireless telecommunications carriers (except satellite)	51721 Wireless telecommunication (except satellite) 517211 Paging ■ Beeper (i.e., radio pager) communication carriers ■ Paging services ■ Radio paging services communication carriers ■ Two-way paging communication carriers 517212 Cellular and other wireless communication ■ Cellular telephone communication carriers ■ Cellular telephone services ■ Mobile telephone communication carriers ■ Personal communication services (PCS) ■ Ship-to-shore broadcasting communication carriers ■ Telecommunications carriers, cellular ■ Telephone communications carriers, wireless (except satellite) ■ Wireless data communication carriers (except satellite) ■ Wireless telephone communications carriers (except satellite)

Source: http://www.census.gov/epcd/naics02/SICN02E.HTM#S48. Accessed September 4, 2006.

the rapid evolution of technology, telecommunications falls under a new sector know as "Information," which comprises publishing, motion pictures, broadcasting, Internet publishing, telecommunications, Internet service providers, and so on.[12] Older subcategories, such as telegraphs, have been updated as "wired communication," and emerging technologies, such as cellular communications, have their own category as "cellular and other wireless communication."[13]

The NAICS classification system can be quite useful to B2B marketers for segmenting and targeting their markets. Suppose, for instance, that a high-tech telecommunications components manufacturer has developed a new product that will significantly speed data transmission. Which of the types of firms listed under NAICS classification 51721 (wireless telecommunication) would be the most worthwhile to pursue as customers? To answer this question, the components manufacturer would first do research, probably using interviews conducted by company sales representatives, to determine which types of firms would find the new component most useful for their products. Then, using the NAICS data collected by the U.S. Census Bureau, the manufacturer could assess the number, size, and geographical dispersion of firms within each type, which might indicate both the product's potential and the types of firms that constitute the target market.

These different types of B2B markets and their distinct classifications lead to another way in which they differ from B2C markets, namely, how the B2B buying process differs from the process for B2C products and services.

The Business-to-Business Buying Process

The B2B buying process (Exhibit 6.3) parallels the B2C process, though it differs in many ways. Both start with need recognition, but the information search and alternative evaluation steps are more formal and structured in the B2B process. Typically, B2B buyers specify their needs in writing and ask potential suppliers to submit formal proposals, whereas B2C buying decisions are usually made by in-

| EXHIBIT | 6.3 | Business-to-Business Buying Process |

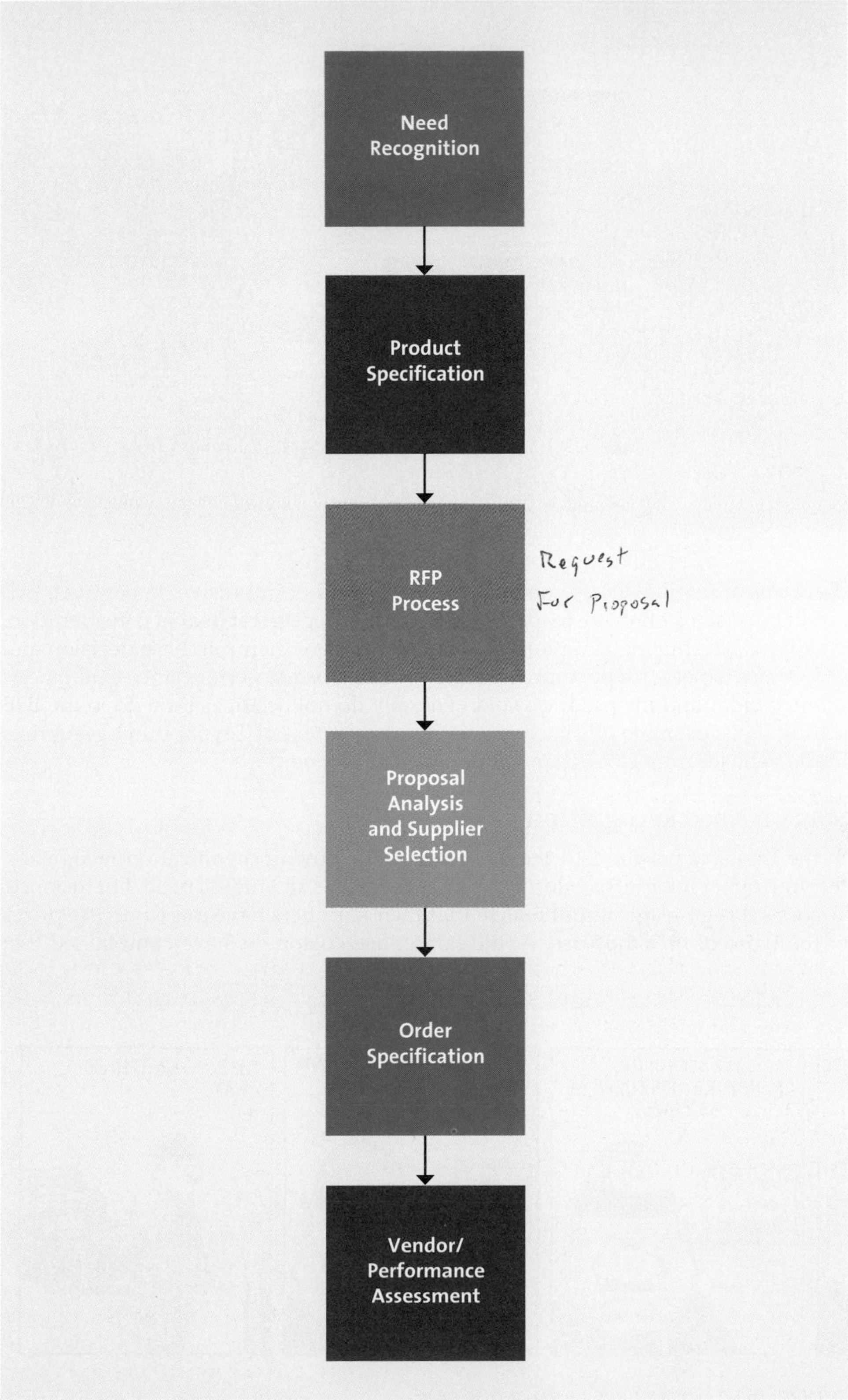

Need
Recognition

Product
Specification

RFP
Process

*Request
For Proposal*

Proposal
Analysis
and Supplier
Selection

Order
Specification

Vendor/
Performance
Assessment

Toyota recognized the need to change tire supplier when customers complained that their current supplier's tires did not perform adequately on snow-packed and off-the-road surfaces.

dividuals or families and sometimes are unplanned or impulsive. In contrast, B2B buying decisions often are made by committees after a great deal of consideration. Finally, in B2C buying situations, customers evaluate their purchase decision and sometimes experience postpurchase dissonance. Formal performance evaluations of the vendor and the products sold generally do not occur, as they do in the B2B setting. Let's examine all six stages within the context of Toyota purchasing tires for its vehicles from Goodyear, Dunlop, and Firestone.[14]

Stage 1: Need Recognition

In the first stage of the B2B buying process, the buying organization recognizes, through either internal or external sources, that it has an unfilled need. For instance, Toyota's design teams might realize that their suppliers have increased the prices of the types of tires they use. At the same time, customers have complained that

In B2B transactions it is important to seek information to recognize a need.

the tires they are currently using do not work very well on their all-wheel-drive vehicles. Toyota's own driving tests on snow-packed and off-the-road surfaces also indicate the need for a change. Through suppliers' salespeople, tradeshow demonstrations, ads in trade journals, Internet searches, and white papers, the company also has become aware of the benefits of different tire manufacturers.

Stage 2: Product Specifications

After recognizing the need, the organization considers alternative solutions and comes up with potential specifications that suppliers might use to develop their proposals to supply the product. Because a significant share of Toyota vehicles are made and sold in North America, the company has made a strong commitment to engaging in long-term, mutually beneficial relationships with North American suppliers. In 2004, for instance, it spent nearly $13 billion for parts and materials from hundreds of North American suppliers and business partners.[15] Rather than working in a vacuum to determine its specifications for the new tires, Toyota's design teams and engineers actually go on site to vendors' plants to develop the specifications for prototypes with their experts.

Stage 3: RFP Process

The **request for proposals (RFP)** is a common process through which buying organizations invite alternative suppliers to bid on supplying their required components. The purchasing company may simply post its RFP needs on its Web site, work through various B2B linkages (which we discuss later in this chapter), or contact potential suppliers directly. Toyota, for example, has set up ToyotaSupplier.com so current and potential suppliers can get information on its purchasing policies and relevant news articles.[16]

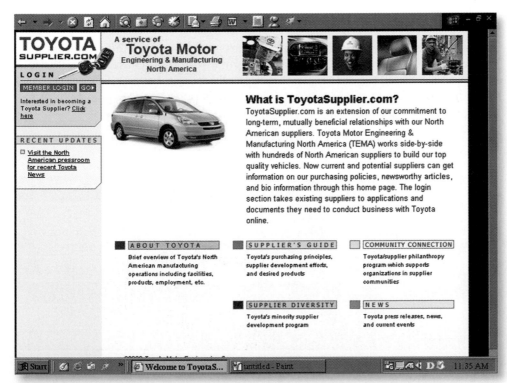

ToyotaSupplier.com is used to post RFPs so current and potential suppliers can get information on its purchasing policies and relevant news articles.

Stage 4: Proposal Analysis, Vendor Negotiation, and Selection

The buying organization, in conjunction with its critical decision makers, evaluates all the proposals it receives in response to its RFP. Firms are likely to narrow the process to a few suppliers, often those with which they have existing relationships, and discuss key terms of the sale, such as price, quality, delivery, and financing. Some firms have a policy that requires them to negotiate with several suppliers, particularly if the product or service represents a critical component or aspect of the business. This policy keeps suppliers on their toes; they know that the buying firm can always shift a greater portion of its business to an alternative supplier if it offers better terms. For example, because Toyota negotiates with Dunlop and Firestone as well, Goodyear knows that it cannot grow lax in the benefits it offers. In the end, Toyota decides to purchase from Goodyear because it has the best combination of strength of brand, ability to deliver, product quality, and ease of ordering.

In Step 4: Proposal Analysis, Vendor Negotiation, and Selection, Toyota decides to purchase from Goodyear because it has the best combination of strength of brand, ability to deliver, product quality, and ease of ordering.

Stage 5: Order Specification

In the fifth stage, the firm places its order with its preferred supplier (or suppliers). The order will include detailed description of the goods, prices, delivery dates, and, in some cases, penalties if the order is not filled on time. The supplier then will send an acknowledgement that it has received the order and fill it by the specified date. For Toyota, this description includes the specific sizes and number of tires it wants, the price it will agree to pay for those tires, the date it expects to receive them, and the result if the wrong tires are delivered or delivered after the due date.

Stage 6: Vendor Analysis

Just as occurs in the consumer buying process, firms analyze their vendors' performance so they can make decisions about their future purchases. The difference is that, in a B2B setting, this analysis is typically more formal and objective. Let's consider how Toyota might evaluate Goodyear's performance, as in Exhibit 6.4, using the following steps:

1. The buying team develops a list of issues that it believes are important to consider in the evaluation of the vendor.

EXHIBIT 6.4	Evaluating a Vendor's Performance		
(1) Key Issues	**(2) Importance Score**	**(3) Vendor's Performance**	**(4) Importance × Performance**
Strength of brand	.30	5	.15
Meets delivery dates	.20	4	.8
Product quality	.40	5	2.0
Ease of ordering	.10	3	.3
Total	1.0		4.6

2. To determine how important each of these issues (in column 1) is, the buying team assigns an importance score to each (column 2). The more important the issue, the higher a score it will receive, but the importance scores must add up to 1. In this case, the buying team believes that product quality and strength of brand are most important, whereas meeting the delivery dates and the ease of ordering are less important.

3. In the third column, the buying team assigns numbers that reflect its judgments about how well the vendor performs. Using a five-point scale, where 1 equals "poor performance" and 5 equals "excellent performance," the buying team decides that Goodyear has fairly high performance on all issues except ease of ordering.

4. To get the overall performance of the vendor, in the fourth column, the team combines the importance of each issue and the vendor's performance scores by multiplying them together. Note that Goodyear performed particularly well on the most important issues. As a result, when we add the importance/performance scores in column 4, we find that Goodyear's overall evaluation is quite high—4.6 on a 5-point scale!

Factors Affecting the Buying Process

The six-stage B2B buying process may be influenced by three factors within the purchasing organization: the buying center, the buying organization's philosophy or corporate culture, and the buying situation.

The Buying Center

In most large organizations, several people typically are responsible for the buying decisions. These **buying center** participants can range from employees who have a formal role in purchasing decisions (i.e., the purchasing or procurement department) to members of the design team that is specifying the particular equipment or raw material needed to employees who will be using a new machine that is being ordered. All these employees are likely to play different roles in the buying process, which vendors must understand and adapt to in their marketing and sales efforts.

We can categorize six different buying roles within a typical buying center (Exhibit 6.5). One or more people may take on a certain role, or one person may take on more than one of the following roles: "(1) **initiator**, the person who first

Many people are involved in making B2B purchasing decisions.

EXHIBIT **6.5** The Buying Center Roles

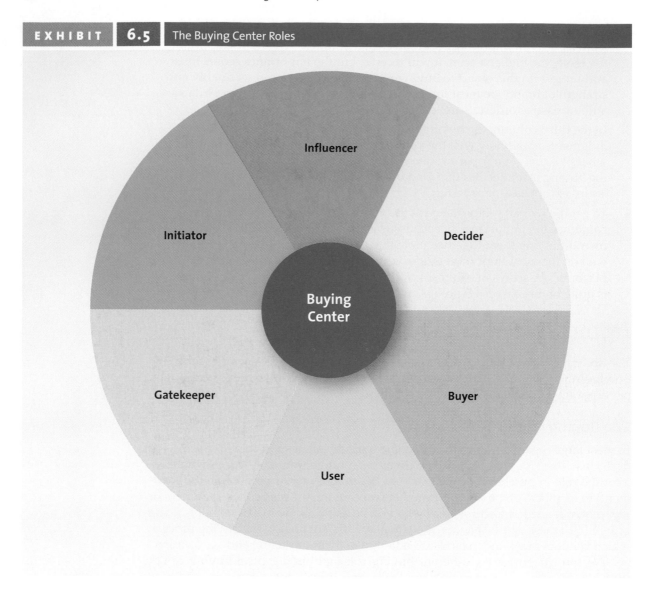

suggests buying the particular product or service; (2) **influencer,** person whose views influence other members of the buying center in making the final decision; (3) **decider,** the person who ultimately determines any part of or the entire buying decision—whether to buy, what to buy, how to buy, or where to buy; (4) **buyer,** the person who handles the paperwork of the actual purchase; (5) **user,** the person(s) who consumes or uses the product or service; and (6) **gatekeeper,** the person(s) who controls information or access, or both, to decision makers and influencers."[17]

To illustrate how a buying center operates, consider purchases made by a hospital. Where do hospitals obtain their x-ray machines, syringes, and bedpans? Why are some medical procedures covered in whole or in part by insurance, whereas others are not? Why might your doctor recommend one type of allergy medication instead of another?

The Initiator—Your Doctor   When you seek treatment from your physician, he or she *initiates* the buying process by determining the products and services that will best address and treat your illness or injury. For example, say that you fell backwards off your snowboard and, in trying to catch yourself, shattered your elbow. You require surgery to mend the affected area, which includes the insertion of several screws to hold the bones in place. Your doctor promptly notifies the hospital to schedule a time for the procedure and specifies the brand of screws she wants on hand for your surgery.

The Influencer—The Medical Device Supplier, the Pharmacy   For years, your doctor has been using ElbowMed screws, a slightly higher-priced screw. Her first introduction to ElbowMed screws came from the company's sales representative, who visited her office to demonstrate how ElbowMed screws were far superior to those of its competition. Your doctor recognized ElbowMed as a good value. Armed with empirical data and case studies, ElbowMed's sales rep effectively *influenced* your doctor's decision to use that screw.

The Decider—The Hospital   Even though your doctor requested ElbowMed screws, the hospital ultimately is responsible for *deciding* whether to buy El-bowMed screws. The hospital supplies the operating room, instrumentation, and surgical supplies, and therefore, the hospital administrators must weigh a variety of factors to determine if the ElbowMed screw is not only best for the patients but also involves a cost that is reimbursable by various insurance providers.

The Buyer   The actual *buyer* of the screw will likely be the hospital's materials manager, who is charged with buying and maintaining inventory for the hospital in the most cost-effective manner. Whereas ElbowMed screws are specific to your type of procedure, other items, such as gauze and sutures, may be purchased through a group purchasing organization (GPO), which obtains better prices through volume buying.

The User—The Patient   Ultimately though, the buying process for this procedure will be greatly affected by the *user,* namely, you and your broken elbow. If you are uncomfortable with the procedure or have read about alternative procedures that you prefer, you may decide that ElbowMed screws are not the best treatment.

The Gatekeeper—The Insurance Company   Your insurer may believe that El-bowMed screws are too expensive and that other screws deliver equally effective results and therefore refuse to reimburse the hospital in full or in part for the use of the screws.

   In the end, the final purchase decision must take into consideration every single buying center participant. Ethical Dilemma 6.1 examines how the "influencer" (the pharmaceutical sales representative and pharmaceutical companies) influences the "decider" (the physician) on purchases made by the "user" (the patient.)

Organizational Culture

A firm's **organizational culture** reflects the set of values, traditions, and customs that guide its employees' behavior. The firm's culture often comprises a set of unspoken guidelines that employees share with one another through various work situations. For example, a new employee might be told that the workday begins at 9:00 a.m.; however, in observing coworkers, he or she learns that most arrive at 8:30 a.m. and thus decides to start arriving earlier.

   Organizational culture can have a profound influence on purchasing decisions, and corporate buying center cultures might be divided into four general

Ethical Dilemma 6.1   How Does the Doctor Know Best?

The pharmaceutical industry is constantly introducing new drugs and new uses for existing drugs. Thus doctors have to constantly update their knowledge of pharmaceuticals and what they are prescribed for. One of the key information sources for doctors on changes in the pharmaceutical industry is the sales representatives who visit with the doctors. A recent study found that doctors want detailed information about drug safety, pricing, and prescribing in addition to information about new drugs. The doctors also want to understand the difference between the new drug and the old drug.

Unfortunately the study found that the sales representatives often do not provide all of this data to the doctors. The sales reps instead focus on the benefits of their new drugs while not volunteering pricing information, side effect data, or comparisons with existing products. Even safety data was found to be skewed toward placing the new drugs in a favorable light. To make matters worse, the study found that when competitors' products were mentioned to doctors they were generally discussed in unfavorable terms.

Perhaps an even more troubling finding of the study was that doctors who were frequently visited by sales representatives often chose to treat patients with drug therapies and not alternative nondrug therapies even if researchers consider the nondrug therapy superior. These doctors were also less likely to prescribe the generic equivalents to costly branded drugs. In other words, the sales representatives are having a dramatic impact on the doctors' choice in treatment of their patients.[18]

What, if anything, should be done about the behavior of pharmaceutical sales representatives? What incentives could doctors or the medical community provide to encourage pharmaceutical companies to provide doctors with the desired information, while limiting their influence over patient care?

From an ethical perspective, what information should pharmaceutical sales representatives provide to doctors?

types: autocratic, democratic, consultative, and consensus, as illustrated in Exhibit 6.6. Knowing which buying center culture is prevalent in a given organization helps the seller decide how to approach that particular client, how and to whom to deliver pertinent information, and to whom to make the sales presentations.

In an **autocratic buying center**, though there may be multiple participants, one person makes the decision alone, whereas the majority rules in a **democratic buying center. Consultative buying centers** use one person to make a decision but solicit input from others before doing so. Finally, in a **consensus buying center**, all members of the team must reach a collective agreement that they can support a particular purchase.[19]

Cultures act like living, breathing forces that change and grow, just as organizations do. Even within some companies, culture may vary by geography, by division, or by functional department. Whether you are a member of the buying center

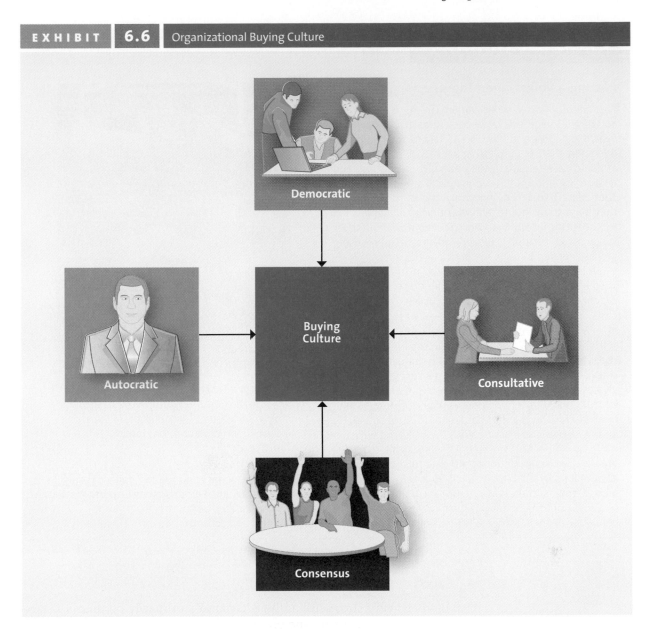

EXHIBIT 6.6 Organizational Buying Culture

Democratic

Autocratic

Buying Culture

Consultative

Consensus

or a supplier trying to sell to it, it is extremely important to understand its culture and the roles of the key players in the buying process. Not knowing the roles of the key players in that case would waste a lot of time—both yours and the buying center's—and could even alienate the real decision maker. Adding Value 6.1 examines how Volkswagen works with their suppliers to put a Volkswagen together.

Buying Situations

The type of buying situation also affects the B2B decision process. Most B2B buying situations can be categorized into three types: new buys, modified rebuys, and straight rebuys. (See Exhibit 6.7.) To illustrate the nuances between these three buying situations, we portray how Dell Inc. develops relationships with some of its business customers after first targeting them.

Adding Value 6.1

Putting a Volkswagen Together[20]

The German-based Volkswagen Group, which owns and distributes the Audi, Bentley, Bugatti, Lamborghini, Seat, Skoda, VW, and VW Commercial brands, noted at one point that its purchasing agents spent 70 percent of their time searching for, analyzing, validating, and forwarding information about parts and components. That meant that they had only about 30 percent of their time to devote to activities that would add value to the firm, which was an unacceptable limitation. What could VW do? It recognized that its purchasing process needed to be made far more efficient.

Volkswagen now manages its own Internet-based private network that links more than 5,000 suppliers of roughly $77 billion worth of components, automotive parts, and indirect raw materials—equal to 70 percent of Volkswagen's annual revenue. With its new integrated software system iPAD, or Internal Purchasing Agent Desk, Volkswagen has cut processing time dramatically. With iPAD, purchasing agents receive product descriptions directly from suppliers online, so the search process, which used to take two hours, is now complete in nine minutes. Moreover, whereas agents used to spend, on average, 60 minutes per order, they now spend only 20.

In addition to improving its internal processes, Volkswagen has maintained a strong relationship with its suppliers by setting up online tools to track invoices and payments and allowing suppliers to log on to its secure "Supplier Cockpit" Web site to find information pertinent to their products. Other online tools, includ-

Volkswagen's software system, iPad, has cut order processing time from two hours to nine minutes since VW's purchasing agents receive product descriptions directly from suppliers online.

ing a catalog, auction, and request for proposals (RFP), are readily available. Perhaps most important though, Volkswagen focuses on continually promoting its close partnerships and collaboration with its vendors.

Dell has been very successful in the B2B market, primarily because it is flexible, maintains a customer focus, and provides complete product solutions at value prices. Dell uses strong sales relationships and database marketing to understand what its customers want and how to fulfill those wants. First, Dell advertises heavily to educational and government institutions during the second and third quarters of the year, which coincide with the start of their buying cycle. Second, Dell's salespeople understand the financial and resource constraints that these groups face, so it offers complete packages of software, hardware, and IT services and provides installers who not only set up the equipment but also remove old hardware. Third, Dell works closely with its buyers to obtain feedback and solicit help from its product development teams so that production is geared toward customer needs. Fourth, Dell divides its accounts into three categories: acquisition, development, and retention. Working with key decision makers, the company maintains consistent contact with each account and maximizes every dollar it allocates toward technology spending.[21]

EXHIBIT **6.7** | Buying Situation

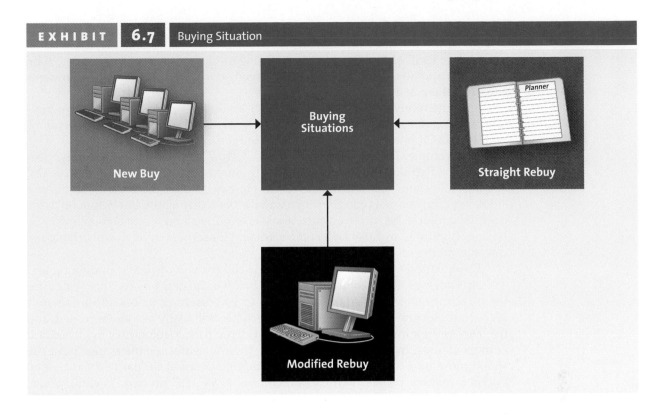

In a **new buy** situation, a customer purchases a good or service for the first time,[22] which means the buying decision is likely to be quite involved because the buyer or the buying organization does not have any experience with the item. In the B2B context, the buying center is likely to proceed through all six steps in the buying process and involve many people in the buying decision. Typical new buys might range from capital equipment to components that the firm previously made itself but now has decided to purchase instead.

Derek Welch, Chief Technology Officer of Douglas County School Systems, became involved in an instructive major new buy. When he took over his job, he inherited 3,300 disparate computers, both Apples and PCs, at 27 locations, many of which used different operating systems. To replace the existing equipment, Welch very much wanted to work with a single vendor. His choice of Dell PCs resulted in a 29 percent reduction of tech support calls from Douglas County Schools. The school system then went on to buy an additional 2,500 new computers.[23]

In a **modified rebuy,** the buyer has purchased a similar product in the past but has decided to change some specifications, such as the desired price, quality level, customer service level, options, or so forth. Current vendors are likely to have an advantage in acquiring the sale in a modified rebuy situation, as long as the reason for the modification is not dissatisfaction with the vendor or its products.

John Clarke, Chief Information Officer of UC Irvine's Graduate School of Management, had a different problem than the one that faced Derek Welch. He didn't need to buy all new equipment; he just had to modify an existing system. Because many UC Irvine students live off campus, the university needed a means to reach and communicate with students who might not be able to come to class. The school therefore converted a standard teleconferencing classroom into a streaming media education center, and Clarke installed Dell servers to work with Dell notebook PCs issued to the students. Even sessions with teaching assistants (TAs) were streamed using other Dell servers. Today, the streaming media program supports more than 37 classes, and all sessions have been archived so that current and future students can view them at any time.[24]

Straight rebuys occur when the buyer or buying organization simply buys additional units of products that had previously been purchased. A tremendous amount of B2B purchases are likely to fall in the straight rebuy category.

For example, John Stryker, Director of Technology and Information Services at Bay City Public Schools, had a relatively easy task: network more than 11,000 users in 17 school districts in six weeks. He had worked with Dell before on a similar rollout and was considering using the company again, but before he made his final decision, he surveyed current users and found high satisfaction levels. So he leased more than 1,000 Dell computers and 20 servers to be rapidly deployed throughout the schools.[25]

These varied types of buying situations call for very different marketing and selling strategies. The most complex and difficult is the new buy because it requires the buying organization to make changes in its current practices and purchases. As a result, several members of the buying center will likely become involved, and the level of their involvement will be more intense than in the case of modified and straight rebuys. In new buying situations, buying center members also typically spend more time at each stage of the B2B buying process, similar to the extended decision making process that consumers use in the B2C process. In comparison, in modified rebuys, the buyers spend less time at each stage of the B2B buying process, similar to limited decision making in the B2C process (see Chapter 5).

Dell sold 2,500 computers to the Douglas County School System. Is this a new buy, a modified new buy, or a straight rebuy?

In straight rebuys, however, the buyer is often the only member of the buying center involved in the process. Similar to a consumer's habitual purchase, straight rebuys often enable the buyer to recognize the firm's need and go directly to the fifth step in the B2B buying process, skipping the product specification, RFP process, and proposal analysis and supplier selection steps.

Regardless of the situation, more and more firms have begun to use the Internet to help facilitate buying for both buyers and sellers. Let's look at the various ways in which the Internet has transformed B2B marketing.

Role of the Internet in Business-to-Business Marketing

As consumers, we often use the Internet to research products and buy them for ourselves, our family, and our friends. In a similar fashion, the B2B market has been radically altered in recent years through Internet technologies. For instance, the Internet has become the communication mode of choice, and sometimes of necessity, for connecting divisions and employees located in dispersed locations. Consider a salesperson on a sales call far from his or her company headquarters. By logging in to the company's database, the salesperson can quickly find information about product availability and order status and even consult with his or her supervisors about important negotiating points, such as price and discounts.

The Internet is equally useful for communications between businesses through private exchanges and auctions. (See Exhibit 6.8.) A **private exchange** occurs when

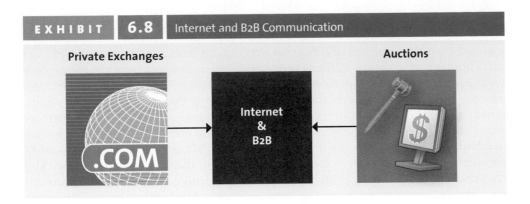

EXHIBIT 6.8 Internet and B2B Communication

Private Exchanges

.COM

Internet & B2B

Auctions

$

a specific firm (either buyer or seller) invites others to participate in online information exchanges and transactions. These exchanges help streamline procurement or distribution processes. Like Toyota with its ToyotaSource.com, as discussed at the beginning of this chapter, IBM, General Motors, Ford, General Electric, Wal-Mart, and other large firms have formed private exchanges and included their key suppliers. Some, such as IBM and GE, even have mandated that their suppliers must deal with them primarily through such online exchanges, which provide the primary benefits of tremendous cost savings through the elimination of periodic negotiations and routine paperwork, as well as the ability to form a supply chain that can respond quickly to the buyer's needs.

For example, as we said earlier in this chapter, Dell's suppliers derive their demand from the sales information Dell provides to them. The suppliers in turn can provide needed component orders quickly and without requiring extensive inventory stockpiles.[26] Because products and the prices of computer parts change rapidly through continuous innovation, the lack of an extensive inventory helps Dell keep its finished computer prices in sync with the declining prices of the component parts. These savings can be passed on to consumers as lower prices, which provides Dell with a very competitive position in the marketplace.

At another level, manufacturers and suppliers can work together to design better products.[27] Manufacturers and retailers collect detailed information about their customers' preferences and other market trends, which they can share with those key suppliers involved in product design. This collaborative design process results in products that more closely match customer needs, thus creating and delivering higher customer value.

Private exchanges have also formed on the manufacturer-to-retailer side of the supply chain. For example, P&G's private network collects information from the cash register (the point of sale) and electronically transfers it back through P&G's distributors to corporate headquarters.[28] By analyzing this information, P&G can track sales of its numerous products to determine the exact demand for each. This demand information then can be transmitted back to suppliers so that the supply side is coordinated as well.

Furthermore, B2B transactions have increasingly turned to online auctions, whether English or reverse. In an **English auction**, goods and services are simply sold to the highest bidder. Thus, if a PC manufacturer has a number of unsold PCs, it can auction them through an exchange (perhaps even through eBay) and sell them to the buyer that bids the highest price for them. In the **reverse auction**, however, the buyer

Using reverse auctions, firms like Dell are able to lower their procurement and component costs since they provide specifications to a group of sellers, who then bid down the price until Dell accepts a specific bid.

provides specifications to a group of sellers, who then bid down the price until the buyer accepts a specific bid. Firms like Dell, HP, Motorola, Palm, and Sun have lowered their procurement and component costs by using reverse auctions.[29]

Thus, in various ways, B2B marketing both differs from and mirrors the process we detailed in Chapter 5, on consumer behavior (B2C). The market segmentation process in B2B selling reflects the collective nature of the consumers in this field, whether they be manufacturers, resellers, institutions, or governments. Furthermore, though the buying process should look familiar and markedly similar to that in Chapter 5, it contains some unique aspects in its six stages, which makes sense considering the many factors that come into play in the B2B buying process. The constitution of the buying center (autocratic, democratic, consultative, or consensus), the culture of the purchasing firm, and the context of the buying situation (new buy, modified rebuy, straight rebuy) all influence the B2B buying process in various ways, which means that sellers must be constantly aware of these factors if they want to be successful in their sales attempts. Finally, just as it is seemingly everywhere we look, the Internet has radically changed some elements of the B2B world, increasing the frequency of both private electronic exchanges and auctions.

Summing Up

1. How do B2B firms segment their markets?

The basic principles behind market segmentation remain the same for both B2B and consumer markets. Specifically, B2B firms want to divide the market into groups of customers with different needs, wants, or characteristics and that therefore might appreciate products or services geared especially toward them. On a broad level, B2B firms divide the market into four types: manufacturers or producers, resellers, institutions, and government. Manufacturers purchase materials to make other objects or to help run their businesses, such as computer and telephone systems. Resellers are primarily wholesalers, distributors, or retailers that sell the unchanged products. Institutions typically include nonprofit organizations such as hospitals, schools, or churches. Finally, governments purchase all types of goods and services, but in the United States, defense is among the largest expenditures. To assist in their market segmentation, B2B businesses can use the NAICS, developed by the U.S. federal government in conjunction with Canada and Mexico, to identify potential customers by type and then develop marketing strategies to reach them.

2. How does B2B buying differ from consumer buying behavior?

At first glance, the B2B buying process looks similar to the consumer process described in Chapter 4. It starts with need recognition and ends with an evalu-

ation of the product's or service's performance. But it is really quite different, primarily because of its formality. For instance, in the second stage, product specifications, the buying group spells out very specific requirements for the products or services it wants to purchase. Then, in the RFP process of the third stage, the buying firm announces its need for a product or service and solicits formal proposals. In the fourth stage, buyers analyze the various proposals and negotiate a deal. Unlike the consumer process, the fifth stage, in which the B2B firm places the order, is very formal and spells out every detail of the sales contract.

3. What factors influence the B2B buying process?

In B2B situations, it is likely that several people, organized into a buying center, will be involved in making the purchase decision. The vendor must understand the relationships among the participants of the buying center to be effective. A firm's organizational culture can also influence the decision process. For instance, if a firm is trying to sell to a young, high-tech computer component manufacturer, it might be advised to send salespeople who are fluent in technology-speak and can easily relate to the customer. Finally, the buying process depends to a great extent on the situation. If a firm is purchasing a product or service for the first time, the process is much more involved than if it is engaging in a straight rebuy.

4. How has the Internet changed B2B marketing?

The Internet has done more to change the way B2B marketing is conducted than any previous innovation has. Not only has the Internet made it easier for people to communicate within firms, it also facilitates the transfer of information among companies. Buyers can purchase products and services over the Internet through private exchanges, which are set up by one firm that invites other participants, and through B2B Internet auctions. These exchanges and auctions have created opportunities to streamline the procurement process, opened up markets to new buyers and sellers, and provided for more competitive market pricing.

Key Terms

- autocratic buying center, 162
- business-to-business (B2B) marketing, 150
- buyer, 160
- buying center, 159
- consensus buying center, 162
- consultative buying center, 162
- decider, 160
- democratic buying center, 162
- derived demand, 150
- English auction, 167
- gatekeeper, 160
- influencer, 160
- initiator, 159
- modified rebuy, 165
- new buy, 165
- North American Industry Classification System (NAICS) codes, 153
- organizational culture, 161
- private exchange, 166
- request for proposals (RFP), 157
- resellers, 151
- reverse auction, 167
- straight rebuy, 166
- user, 160

Marketing Applications

1. Provide an example of each of the four key types of B2B organizations.

2. What are the major differences between the consumer buying process discussed in Chapter 4 and the B2B buying process discussed in this chapter?

3. Mazda is trying to assess the performance of two manufacturers that could supply music systems for its vehicles. Using the information above, determine which manufacturer Mazda should use.

4. Assume you have written this textbook and are going to attempt to sell it to your school. Identify the six members of the buying center. What role would each play in the decision process? Rank them in terms of how much influence they would have on the decision, with 1 being most influential and 6 being least influential. Will this ranking be different in other situations?

5. Provide an example of the three types of buying situations that the bookstore at your school might face when buying textbooks.

Performance Evaluation of Brands			
Issues	**Importance Weights**	**Manufacturer A's Performance**	**Manufacturer B's Performance**
Sound	0.4	5	3
Cost	0.3	2	4
Delivery time	0.1	2	2
Brand cache	0.2	5	1
Total	1		

Notes: Performance is rated on a scale of 1–5, where 1 = poor and 5 = excellent.

6. Describe the organizational culture at your school or job. How is it different than the one at the last school you attended or the last job you had?

7. Nike manufactures shoes and sportswear. How has the Internet changed the way this company communicates with its suppliers and retail customers?

8. You have just started to work in the purchasing office of a major oil processing firm. The purchasing manager has asked you to assist in writing an RFP for a major purchase. The manager gives you a sheet detailing the specifications for the RFP. While reading the specifications you realize that they have been written to be extremely favorable to one bidder. How should you handle this situation?

Toolkit

B2B VENDOR ANALYSIS

Help David evaluate two software vendors. He has created a chart to help him decide which one to pick. He has rated the two vendors on brand strength, timeliness of deliveries, product quality, and ease of ordering. His firm is generally most interested in quality and then in timeliness. Reputation is somewhat important. The ease of ordering is least important. Please use the toolkit provided at www.mhhe.com/grewal-levy to specify the importance weights and help David pick the best software vendor.

Net Savvy

1. Suppose you were working for Volkswagen. How would you use the North American Industry Classification System (NAICS) to assess the number of potential suppliers for tires? What is the NAICS classification code for tires? (You will have to do some research on the Internet to uncover this information.)

2. A number of years ago Levi Strauss & Co. experimented with direct sales to consumers from its Web site. That experiment failed primarily because of the protests from Levi's largest retail customers, especially Sears. Today Levis maintains its Web site and refers consumers from its Web site directly to retailers. Go to www.levis.com, click on the link for the United States and then on "where to buy." What do you find when you click this link? What happens when you click on the retailers' Web link? How is this type of linking beneficial to both Levis and to the various retailers? Now suppose you are seeking to purchase a specific product: women's, petite, boot cut jeans. What information does the Levi's Web site provide?

Chapter Case Study

WEYERHAEUSER: SERVING THE HOME BUILDING INDUSTRY[30]

Overview

With its annual sales of over $20 billion and 55,000 employees in 18 countries around the world, Weyerhaeuser has grown into one of the largest integrated forest products companies in the world. Its principal operations involve growing and harvesting trees and manufacturing, distributing, and selling forest products. Weyerhaeuser is currently the world's largest producer of softwood lumber and pulp.

Weyerhaeuser's wood products businesses produce and sell softwood lumber, plywood, and veneer; oriented strand board and composite panels; hardwood lumber; and engineered lumber products. These products are sold primarily through the company's sales organizations and building materials distribution business, though Weyerhaeuser targets large builders in particular with its National Builder Program. As partners with a leader in the worldwide

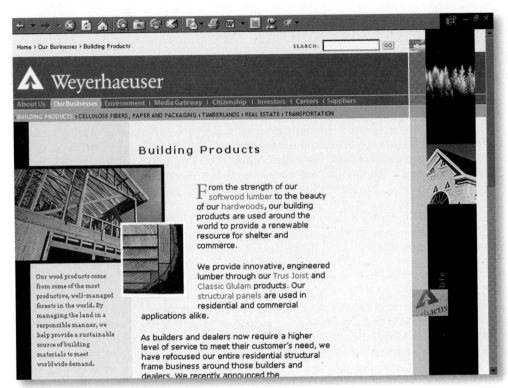

Weyerhaeuser, one of the largest integrated forest products companies in the world, is involved in growing and harvesting trees and manufacturing, distributing, and selling forest products.

forest products industry, members are offered the convenience of a single reliable source for quality building supplies. Moreover, the program offers customized features and value-added services designed to meet each builder's unique needs, such as [31]

- Access to Weyerhaeuser's in-depth product expertise and technical support.
- Input on product development to engineer greater value.
- Ongoing communication updates to enhance sales and profitability.
- Relationships at the executive level with key decision makers.
- Shared opportunities in e-commerce, environmental stewardship, joint marketing, and safety training.

Factors Affecting the Industry

In the wood products industry, changes in the political landscape in the past several years have affected environmental and land-use policies that regulate logging. In the late 1990s, logging on federal lands was cut back when the nesting areas of the spotted owl were made off-limits to loggers. Further restrictions were imposed due to additional concerns about other species. As a result, within the span of 10 years, the timber harvest on federal lands dropped by 75 percent.

Environmental concerns also fostered the growth of environmental certification and labeling for wood products as a means to ensure that the wood was harvested in an environmentally responsible way that sustains the forest ecosystem. These environmental concerns also led to the creative use of waste materials, like using wood byproducts as fuel to provide mills with electricity. Other scrap materials have been marketed to consumers as dyed mulch and shrink-wrapped bundles of firewood.

In addition to these environmental influences, some key technological advances have favorably affected the manufacturing of wood products for building. For example, the use of new technology and automation have greatly improved productivity, and computerized controls and laser scanners have maximized the amount of lumber obtained from a log, thus increasing output while consuming less wood.

The Building Construction Market

Housing is a major part of the U.S. economy, representing roughly 15 percent of the gross national product.[32] The largest volume items purchased by home builders are typically lumber and plywood, which represent roughly one-third of the total cost of the materials used to build a home.[33] The home construction industry also is highly cyclical, though repair and remodeling efforts are somewhat less so than new construction. The vibrancy of the industry varies along with several key factors, such as the overall health of the U.S. economy; demand levels for new home construction, improvements, and repairs; and the volume of home sales. During the first several years of the twenty-first century, the industry experienced strong growth after a pronounced lull; residential construction permits and starts reached record highs, largely fueled by low interest rates. Despite the threat of increasing interest rates, continued growth in the single residence home building construction market is anticipated in the next several years.

Although the industry is dominated by small firms, the largest builders represent a significant portion of new home sales. According to the most current government data, the top 1 percent of builders account for 40 percent of all new residential housing starts, and 1 percent of builders account for 34 percent of all new multifamily housing starts.[34] Industry concentration is likely to increase in the future through the increasing number of mergers and acquisitions.

For large wood products manufacturers like Weyerhaeuser, meeting the high expectations of large builders effectively is a business cornerstone. Because lumber represents a substantial portion of the total costs for builders, builders are careful to develop strong relationships with those manufacturers that can provide them with a good value for their money. Although the most important factor is obtaining competitively priced materials, builders also value product availability, speedy delivery, reliable products, and the ability to install quickly and efficiently.

Questions

1. Describe how you would expect large home building companies to purchase wood products from companies like Weyerhaeuser. Use the steps in the B2B buying process discussed in the chapter to facilitate your discussion.

2. Builders often consider wood products to be commodities, so companies like Weyerhaeuser work hard to provide additional value to gain a competitive advantage in the marketplace. Describe some ways that Weyerhaeuser provides greater value to its customers than its competitors can. (It might help to review its Web site at www.weyerhaeuser.com.)

3. Identify the environmental factors discussed in the case that have influenced the industry during the past decade or so. What additional environmental factors might be important to the lumber industry, and how would they affect its B2B operations?

7

Global Marketing

With $47 billion in annual sales, half of which is earned outside the United States, and a portfolio of products used more than 2 billion times daily, Procter & Gamble (P&G) has been ranked by *Forbes* magazine as the U.S. firm with the highest brand value.[1] In the United States, P&G has the top-selling products in any number of consumer product categories, including laundry detergent (Tide), toothpaste (Crest), and disposable diapers (Pampers), just to name a few.

When P&G decided to enter the Chinese market with its Head & Shoulders shampoo, it did so with the knowledge that it had a strong market position in the United States, offered its products for sale in most of the world, and, according to its marketing research results, would be well received in the Chinese market. Although the product looked like a winner, doing business in China is not easy. The Chinese government requires that foreign companies must have a local partner, and firms must meet and address quite a few regulatory hurdles.

Thus, P&G decided to partner with the Hong Kong–based Hutchinson and Whampoa and a factory by the name of Guangzhou Soap. Procter & Gamble brought its technological expertise in producing high-quality consumer products to the factory, not only to assist in the production of Head & Shoulders but also to facilitate the R&D of other products for the Asian market. The company also began developing strong ties with local and regional government officials to make the entry process as smooth as possible.

The next step was to determine the correct marketing mix. Two-thirds of the Chinese population earns less than $25 per month, and the product had to be packaged and priced to be accessible for this average consumer. Forgoing its usual bottle, P&G packaged Head & Shoulders in single-use packets, which made the shampoo affordable and

Head and Shoulders has become the best selling shampoo in China.

practical. The launch was a success. In three years, Head & Shoulders had become the top-selling shampoo in China, and P&G has since been able to repeat its success with a host of other products in China and throughout the rest of Asia.

Why was P&G so successful in China, where so many others have failed? The answer is its three-pronged approach. First, the company introduced world-class technology in both its production and its R&D. Second, it cultivated strong relationships with government officials at the national and, more important, the provincial and local levels. Third, P&G developed a strong local organization by partnering with a local producer and building a network of local distributors. These steps, combined with the leveraging of its knowledge of brand building in other parts of the world, enabled P&G to succeed in introducing more of its brands successfully into China.

The increasing globalization of markets affects not only large U.S. corporations like P&G that go in search of new markets but also small and medium-sized businesses that increasingly depend on goods produced globally to deliver their products and services. Most people don't think about how globalization impacts their daily lives, but just take a minute and read the labels on the clothing you are wearing right now. Chances are that most of the items, even if they carry U.S. brand names, were manufactured in another part of the world.

In the United States, the market has evolved from a system of regional market-places to national markets to geographically regional markets (e.g., Canada and the United States together) to international markets and finally to global markets. Globalization refers to the processes by which goods, services, capital, people, information, and ideas flow across national borders. Global markets are the result of several fundamental changes, such as reductions or eliminations of trade barriers by country governments, the decreasing concerns of distance and time with regard to moving products and ideas across countries, the standardization of laws across borders, and globally integrated production processes.[2]

Each of these fundamental changes has paved the way for marketing to flourish in other countries. The elimination of trade barriers and other governmental actions, for instance, allows goods and ideas to move quickly and efficiently around the world, which in turn facilitates the quick delivery of goods to better meet the needs of global consumers. When examining countries as potential markets for global products, companies must realize that these different countries exist at very different stages of globalization. The World Bank ranks countries according to their degrees of globalization on the basis of a composite measure that examines whether the factors necessary to participate in the global marketplace are present. Countries that score well on the scale represent the best markets for globalized products and services; those lowest on the scale represent the most troublesome markets.

Most Americans tend to take access to global products and services for granted. When we walk into Starbucks, we expect to find our favorite Jamaican Blue Mountain coffee ground and ready for us. But think about the process through which coffee came from a mountainside in Jamaica to your town. Or how a $3 Sri Lankan–made keychain could be produced, transported halfway around the world, and sold for so little money. These are the questions we will be examining in this chapter.

We begin by looking at the growth of the global economy and the forces that led to it. We'll see how firms assess the potential of a given market, make decisions to go global, and—as P&G did in the opening vignette—choose which products to sell globally. Then we explore how to build the marketing mix for global products and consider some of the ethical and legal issues of globalization.

Growth of the Global Economy: Globalization of Marketing and Production

Changes in technology, especially communications technology, have been the driving force for growth in global markets for decades. The telegraph, radio, television, computer, and, now, Internet increasingly connect distant parts of the world. Today, communication is instantaneous. Sounds and images from across the globe are delivered to TV sets, radios, and computers in real time, which enables receivers in all parts of the world to observe how others live, work, and play.

The globalization of production, also known as offshoring, refers to manufacturers' procurement of goods and services from around the globe to take advantage of national differences in the cost and quality of various factors of production (e.g., labor, energy, land, capital).[3] Although originally focused on relocating manufacturing to lower cost producer countries, the practice of offshoring has now grown to include the products of the knowledge economy: medical services, financial services, technological services, and consulting. The growth of cities such as Bangalore, India, for instance, demonstrate the rapid progression of the globalization of production of both products and services.[4]

Many goods and services are provided from other countries, an activity known as offshoring. At this call center in Delhi, India, experts provide information to an Internet service provider in the U.K.

Bangalore is now home to divisions of GE, Intel, IBM, and a growing number of technology and service firms. Companies in Bangalore provide a broad range of options to customers, including software development, programming, and R&D, as well as customer call centers and help lines. Many consumers have been surprised by disclosures in the media about accounting firms in Bangalore that complete U.S. tax returns or Indian radiologists who read x-rays taken of U.S. patients and digitally transmitted to India.[5]

By globalizing production, companies can lower their total production costs and improve their overall competitive position because they are able to offer higher quality products at lower costs—that is, a better value for the consumer. Yet offshoring leads to a paradox: the problem of invisible beneficiaries and very visible losers.[6] As Exhibit 7.1 indicates, U.S. software industry employees who have lost their jobs to offshoring are the visible losers, and the consumers who now benefit from the lower cost goods in the marketplace are the invisible winners. Also, the new software industry employees in India are now able to better afford U.S. made goods, which is a boost to the U.S. economy.

The growth of global markets also has been facilitated by organizations that are designed to oversee their functioning. Perhaps the most important of these organizations is represented by the **General Agreement on Tariffs and Trade (GATT).** The purpose of the GATT was to lower trade barriers, such as high tariffs on imported goods and restrictions on the number and types of imported products that inhibited the free flow of goods across borders. In 1948, 23 countries agreed to 45,000 tariff concessions that affected about one-fifth of world trade.[7] Over the years, successive rounds of trade negotiations have led to further reductions in trade barriers, as well as new rules designed to promote global trade further.

The original GATT also included the founding of the **International Monetary Fund (IMF),** but in 1994, the GATT was replaced by the **World Trade Organization (WTO).** The WTO differs from the GATT in that the WTO is an established institution based in Geneva, Switzerland, instead of simply an agreement. Furthermore,

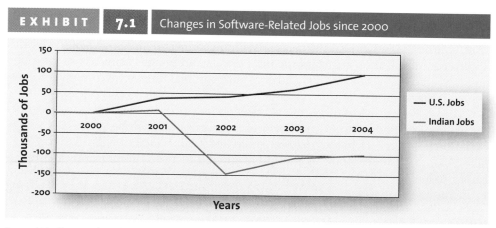

| EXHIBIT | 7.1 | Changes in Software-Related Jobs since 2000 |

Source: http://www.epi.org/issueguides/offshoring/figure12.gif

the WTO represents the only international organization that deals with the global rules of trade among nations. Its main function is to ensure that trade flows as smoothly, predictably, and freely as possible. The WTO also administers trade agreements, acts as a forum for trade negotiations, settles trade disputes, reviews national trade policies, and assists developing countries in their trade policy issues through technical assistance and training. Currently, the 148 members of the WTO account for 97 percent of global trade.[8]

As we noted, the original GATT established the IMF, whose primary purpose is to promote international monetary cooperation and facilitate the expansion and growth of international trade. Along with the IMF, the World Bank Group is dedicated to fighting poverty and improving the living standards of people in the developing world. It is a development bank that provides loans, policy advice, technical assistance, and knowledge-sharing services to low- and middle-income countries in an attempt to reduce poverty.[9] Thus, the key difference between the IMF and the World Bank is that the IMF focuses primarily on maintaining the international monetary system, whereas the World Bank concentrates on poverty reduction through low-interest loans and other programs. For instance, the World Bank Group is the largest external funding source of education and HIV/AIDS programs.

Both these organizations affect the practice of global marketing in different ways, but together, they enable marketers to participate in the global marketplace by making it easier to buy and sell, financing deserving firms, opening markets to trade, and raising the global standard of living, which allows more people to buy goods and services.

However, these organizations have been criticized by a diverse group of nongovernmental organizations, religious groups, and advocates for workers and the poor. The primary criticism of the World Bank is that it is merely a puppet of Western industrialized nations that use World Bank loans to assist their globalization efforts. Others argue that the World Bank loans too much money to third-world countries, which makes it almost impossible for these often debt-ridden nations to repay the loans.[10] Ethical Dilemma 7.1 discusses some of the more general criticisms of globalization.

Globalization obviously has its critics, and those critics very well may have a point. But globalization also has been progressing at a steady and increasing pace. With that development in mind, let's look at how firms determine in which countries to expand their operations.

The key difference between the IMF and the World Bank is that the IMF focuses primarily on maintaining the international monetary system, whereas the World Bank concentrates on poverty reduction through low-interest loans and other programs. In this photo, outgoing World Bank President James D. Wolfensohn, right, Development Committee Chairman Trevor Manuel, the Finance Minister of South Africa, center, and International Monetary Fund Managing Director Rodrigo de Rato, far left, speak with reporters at the IMF headquarters in Washington.

Assessing Global Markets

Because different countries, with their different stages of globalization, offer marketers a variety of opportunities, firms must assess the viability of various potential market entries. As illustrated in Exhibit 7.2, we examine four criteria necessary to assess a country market: economic analysis, infrastructure and technological analysis, government actions or inactions, and sociocultural analysis. Information about these four areas offers marketers a more complete picture of a country's potential as a market for products and services.

Ethical Dilemma 7.1   Globalization and Its Discontents

One of the most persuasive arguments antiglobalization groups use is that many of the problems related to globalization can be attributed to the seemingly insatiable appetite of countries in North America and Europe, as well as Japan and other industrialized nations, for natural resources, oil, gasoline, timber, food, and so forth.[11] These nations consume 80 percent of the world's resources but are home to only 20 percent of the population. Should firms in industrialized nations be able to utilize these natural resources at a disproportionate rate, regardless of whether their shareholders demand profitable growth?

As the industrialized West has put into place laws that protect workers' rights, workers' safety, and the environment, U.S. firms also have outsourced production to less developed countries that either have no such laws or don't enforce them. Without laws to protect workers and the environment, the factories that produce these goods often exploit both the workers and the environment of these countries. Industrialized nations obtain the goods they crave at low costs, but at what price do these goods come to the country that provides them?

In many parts of the world, the changes wrought by globalization have moved so fast that cultures have not had time to adapt. Many countries fear that the price for economic success and participation in the global market may be the loss of their individual identities and cultures. The challenge thus becomes whether economic needs should be allowed to outweigh cultural preservation.

Economic Analysis

The greater the wealth of a country, generally, the better the opportunity a firm will have in that particular country. A firm conducting an economic analysis of a country market must look at three major economic factors: the general economic environment, the population size and growth rate, and real income (see Exhibit 7-3).

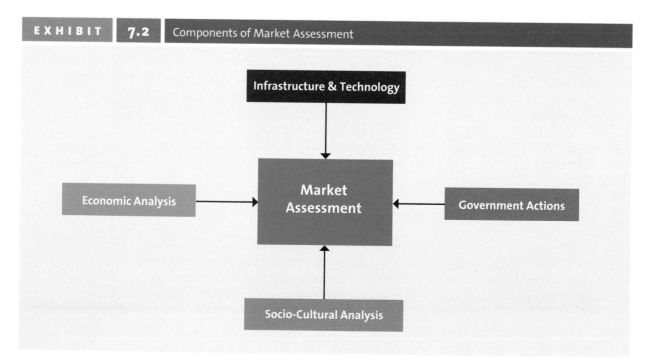

EXHIBIT 7.2 Components of Market Assessment

Evaluating the General Economic Environment   Generally, healthy economies provide better opportunities for global marketing expansions, and there are several ways a firm can measure the relative health of a particular country's economy. Each way offers a slightly different view, and some may be more useful for some products and services than for others.

To determine the market potential for its particular product or service, a firm should use as many measures as it can obtain. One measure is the relative level of imports and exports. The United States, for example, suffers a **trade deficit**, which means that the country imports more goods than it exports. For U.S. marketers, this deficit can signal the potential for greater competition at home from foreign producers. Firms would prefer to manufacture in a country that has a **trade surplus**, or a higher level of exports than imports, because it signals a greater opportunity to export products to more markets.

The most common way to gauge the size and market potential of an economy, and therefore the potential the country has for global marketing, is to use standardized measures of output. **Gross domestic product (GDP)**, the most widely used of these measures, is defined as the market value of the goods and services produced by a country in a year. **Gross national income (GNI)** consists of GDP plus the net income earned from investments abroad (minus any payments made to nonresidents who contribute to the domestic economy). In other words, U.S. firms that invest or maintain operations abroad count their income from those operations in the GNI but not the GDP.[12]

Another frequently used measure of an overall economy is the **purchasing power parity (PPP)**, a theory that states that if the exchange rates of two countries

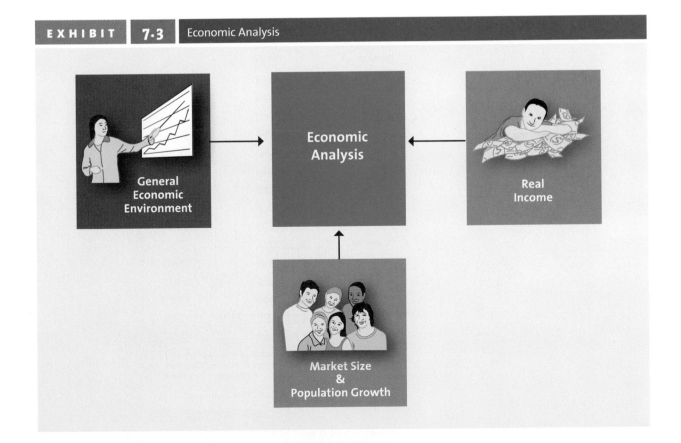

EXHIBIT 7.3   Economic Analysis

General Economic Environment

Economic Analysis

Real Income

Market Size & Population Growth

are in equilibrium, a product purchased in one will cost the same in the other, if expressed in the same currency.[13] A novel measure that employs PPP to assess the relative economic buying power among nations is *The Economist*'s Big Mac Index, which suggests that exchange rates should adjust to equalize the cost of a basket of goods and services, wherever it is bought around the world. Using McDonald's

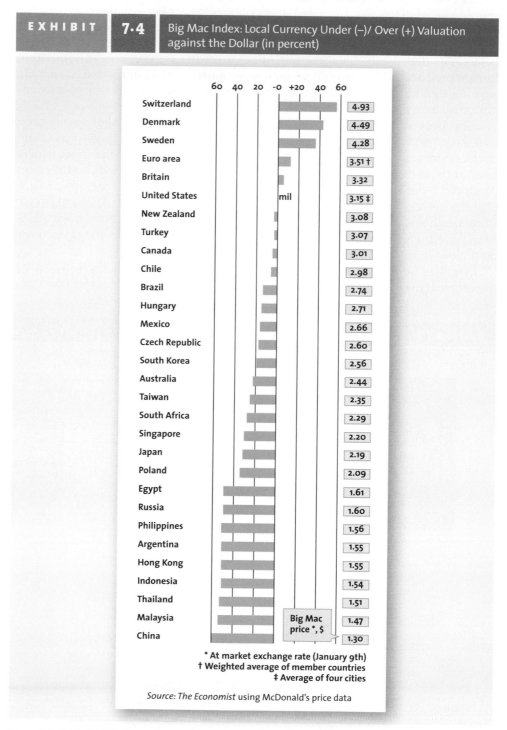

EXHIBIT 7.4 Big Mac Index: Local Currency Under (–)/ Over (+) Valuation against the Dollar (in percent)

Country	Big Mac price *, $
Switzerland	4.93
Denmark	4.49
Sweden	4.28
Euro area	3.51 †
Britain	3.32
United States	3.15 ‡
New Zealand	3.08
Turkey	3.07
Canada	3.01
Chile	2.98
Brazil	2.74
Hungary	2.71
Mexico	2.66
Czech Republic	2.60
South Korea	2.56
Australia	2.44
Taiwan	2.35
South Africa	2.29
Singapore	2.20
Japan	2.19
Poland	2.09
Egypt	1.61
Russia	1.60
Philippines	1.56
Argentina	1.55
Hong Kong	1.55
Indonesia	1.54
Thailand	1.51
Malaysia	1.47
China	1.30

* At market exchange rate (January 9th)
† Weighted average of member countries
‡ Average of four cities

Source: The Economist using McDonald's price data

Source: "Big Mac Index," *The Economist*, January 12, 2006, electronically accessed.

Big Mac as the market basket, Exhibit 7.4 shows that the cheapest burger is in China, where it costs $1.30, compared with an average American price of $3.15. This implies that the Chinese yuan is 59 percent undervalued.

These various measures help marketers understand the relative wealth of a particular country, though, as scholars have recently argued, they may not give a full picture of the economic health of a country because they are based solely on material output.[14] As a corollary measure to those described previously, the United Nations has developed the **human development index (HDI),** a composite measure of three indicators of the quality of life in different countries: life expectancy at birth, educational attainment, and whether the average incomes, according to PPP estimates, are sufficient to meet the basic needs of life in that country. For marketers, these measures determine the lifestyle elements that ultimately drive consumption (recall that Chapter 5, on consumer behavior, discussed the influence of lifestyle on consumption). The HDI is scaled from 0 to 1; those countries that score lower than .5 are classified as nations with low human development, those that score .5–.8 have medium development, and those above .8 are classified as having high human development. Exhibit 7.5 shows a map of the world with the various HDI scores.

These macroeconomic measures provide a snapshot of a particular country at any one point in time. Because they are standardized measures, it is possible to compare countries across time and identify those that are experiencing economic growth and increased globalization.

Although an understanding of the macroeconomic environment is crucial for managers facing a market entry decision, of equal importance is the understanding of economic measures of individual income and household size.

Evaluating Market Size and Population Growth Rate   Global population has been growing dramatically since the turn of the 20th century (see Exhibit 7.6). From a marketing perspective, however, growth has not been equally dispersed. Less-developed nations, by and large, are experiencing rapid population growth, while many developed countries are experiencing either zero or negative population growth. The countries with the highest purchasing power today may become less attractive in the future for many products and services because of stagnated growth.

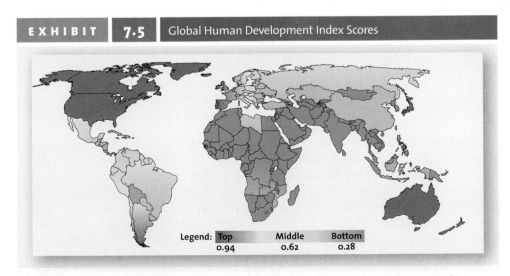

| **EXHIBIT** | **7.5** | Global Human Development Index Scores |

Legend: Top 0.94   Middle 0.62   Bottom 0.28

Source: http://www.nationmaster.com/red/graph/eco_hum_dev_ind-economy-human-development-index&int =-1&b_map=1#.

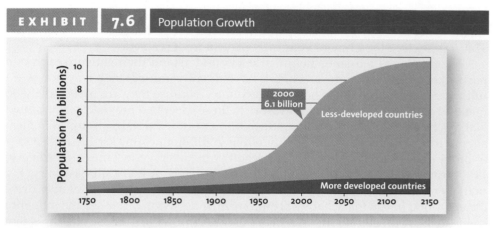

EXHIBIT 7.6 Population Growth

Source: http://www.prb.org/Content/NavigationMenu/PRB/Educators/Human_Population/Population_Growth/Population_Growth.htm

China's single-child policy means that there are four grandparents and two parents for every child, making the children's market very attractive.

Another aspect related to population and growth pertains to the distribution of the population within a particular region; namely, is the population located primarily in rural or urban areas? This distinction determines where and how products and services can be delivered. Long supply chains, in which goods pass through many hands, are necessary to reach rural populations and therefore add costs to products. In China, for instance, the previously overwhelmingly rural population is moving toward urban areas to meet the demand of the growing industrial manufacturing centers located outside China's major cities and along its coastal Pearl River Delta. This population shift will facilitate the delivery of goods and services and thereby make China an even more attractive country for global expansion.

Although China has the world's largest population, with more than 1 billion people, its population also is getting older, and the government's single-child policy has effectively capped its previously exponential population growth. Yet the single-child policy means that there are four grandparents and two parents for each child. This presents a very attractive market opportunity for firms such as toy retailers Wal-Mart and Toys R Us, known as Joyo in China. The market is especially strong for educational toys as well as quality toys with high safety ratings.[15]

Evaluating Real Income The adaptations that P&G made to its Head & Shoulders shampoo, as we described in the chapter's opening vignette, provide an excellent example of how a firm can make adjustments to an existing product to meet the unique needs of a particular country market. Coke and Pepsi are also making adjustments to their products and prices to be able to compete in India. For example, in the town of Jagadri in Northwest India, composed of 60,000 residents who are mostly farmers, Coke and Pepsi are battling for market share. Each firm has introduced repackaged products to win this market. Coke is producing a 200 ml. (6 oz.) bottle that sells for 12 cents at small shops, bus stops, and roadside stands in order to offer a more affordable alternative to Pepsi. Why battle for Jagadri? Because each firm knows that 70 percent of the Indian population, some 700 million people, still lives in rural areas and has incomes of less than $42 per month.[16] If they can win in Jagadri, they can win in other rural areas, and the only way to win is to make the product affordable.

Analyzing Infrastructure and Technological Capabilities

The next component of any market assessment is an infrastructure and technological analysis. **Infrastructure** is defined as the basic facilities, services, and installations needed for a community or society to function, such as transportation and communications systems, water and power lines, and public institutions like schools, post offices, and prisons. Marketers are especially concerned with four key elements of a country's infrastructure: transportation, distribution channels, communications, and commerce.

These four components are essential to the development of an efficient marketing system. First, there must be a system to transport goods throughout the various markets and to consumers in geographically dispersed marketplaces. Second, distribution channels must exist to deliver products in a timely manner and at a reasonable cost. Third, the communications system must be sufficiently developed to allow consumers access to information about the products and services available in the marketplace. Fourth, the commercial infrastructure consists of the legal, banking, and regulatory systems that allow markets to function. In the next section, we focus on how issues pertaining to the political and legal structures of a country can affect the risk that marketers face in operating in a given country.

Coke and Pepsi are battling for market share in India.

Analyzing Government Actions

Governmental actions, as well as the actions of nongovernmental political groups, can significantly influence firms' ability to sell goods and services, because they often result in laws or other regulations that either promote the growth of the global market or close off the country and inhibit growth. These issues include tariffs, quotas, boycotts, exchange controls, and trade agreements. (See Exhibit 7.7.)

Tariffs   A **tariff** (also called a **duty**) is a tax levied on a good imported into a country. In most cases, tariffs are intended to make imported goods more expensive and thus less competitive with domestic products,[17] which in turn protects domestic industries from foreign competition. In other cases, tariffs might be imposed to penalize another country

For a country to be a viable option for a new market entry, firms must assess its transportation, distribution channels, communications, and commercial infrastructure.

EXHIBIT | **7.7** | Government Actions

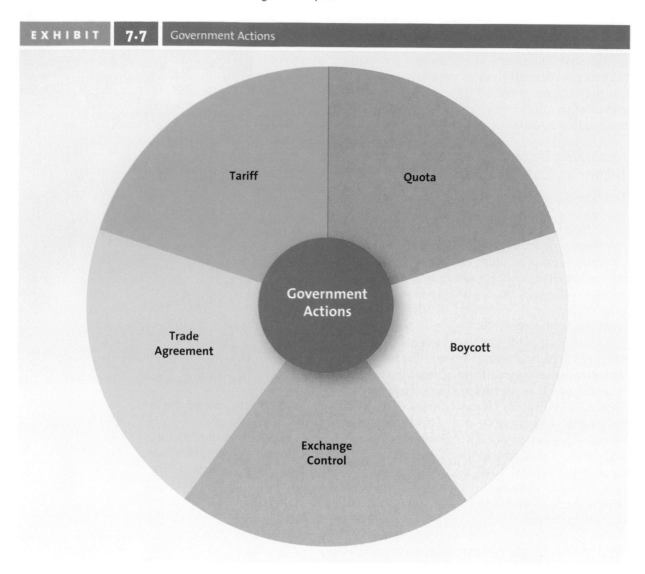

for trade practices that the home country views as unfair. In 2002, for example, the United States imposed a steep tariff on imported steel in response to the U.S. steel industry's claims that foreign countries were dumping low cost steel on the U.S. market:[18] selling it in the foreign market at a price that is lower than its domestic price or below its cost.[19]

Quotas   A quota designates the maximum quantity of a product that may be brought into a country during a specified time period. Many U.S. quotas on foreign-made textiles were eliminated in 2005, which reduced the cost of imported apparel products sold in the United States. Some firms have chosen to redistribute the bulk of these savings to consumers—in Wal-Mart's case, 75 percent of them—whereas others, such as Bebe, are planning to distribute only 25 percent and keep the rest as profit.[20]

However, tariffs and quotas also can impose a fundamental and potentially devastating blow on a firm's ability to sell products in another country. Tariffs artificially raise prices and therefore lower demand, and quotas reduce the availability

Many U.S. quotas on foreign-made textiles have been eliminated. Some firms have chosen to redistribute the bulk of these savings to consumers—in Wal-Mart's case (left), 75 percent of the savings; whereas other firms, such as Bebe (right), are planning to redistribute only 25 percent of the savings and keep the rest as profit.

of imported merchandise. Conversely, tariffs and quotas benefit domestically made products because they reduce foreign competition.

Boycott   A **boycott** pertains to a group's refusal to deal commercially with some organization to protest against its policies. Boycotts might be called by governments or nongovernmental organizations, such as trade unions or environmental groups. Although most are called by nongovernmental organizations, they still should be considered very political. The modern war in Iraq has led to increasing calls for boycotts of U.S. products and services by various countries. The long-term impact of such boycotts on the ability of U.S. firms to market in other countries, as a result of global antiwar sentiment, remains unknown. For a discussion of this issue, see Ethical Dilemma 7.2.

Exchange Control   **Exchange control** refers to the regulation of a country's currency **exchange rate,** the measure of how much one currency is worth in relation to another.[21] A designated agency in each country, often the Central Bank, sets the rules for currency exchange, though in the United States, the Federal Reserve sets the currency exchange rates. In recent years, the value of the U.S. dollar has decreased significantly compared with other important world currencies such as the euro and the pound sterling (UK). The fall of the dollar has had a twofold effect on U.S. firms' ability to conduct global business. For firms that depend on imports of finished products, raw materials that they fabricate into other products, or services from other countries, the cost of doing business has gone up dramatically. At the same time, buyers in other countries find the costs of U.S. goods and services much lower than they were before.

The decline of the value of the U.S. dollar against the Euro and other important world currencies has made imports to the U.S. more expensive, and exports from the U.S. less expensive.

A method of avoiding an unfavorable exchange rate is to engage in countertrade. **Countertrade** is trade between two countries where goods are traded for other goods and not for hard currency. For instance, the Philippine government has entered into a countertrade agreement with Vietnam. The Philippine International Trading Corp is importing rice and paying for half of it with fertilizer, coconuts, and coconut by-products.[23]

Ethical Dilemma 7.2   Protesting the War with the Wallet

Is "Made in the U.S.A" more a hindrance than a help in U.S. firms' efforts to penetrate the global marketplace?[22] According to the results of a recent survey of 8,000 consumers in five countries (Canada, China, France, Germany, Russia, and the United Kingdom), being an American firm may increasingly become a hindrance. The survey found that 20 percent of respondents from Europe and Canada stated that they were consciously avoiding purchasing U.S. products as a form of protest against U.S. foreign policy, especially its actions in Iraq.

The survey also asked the respondents if they were intentionally avoiding purchasing products from 40 U.S. corporations. Corporations viewed as being "more American" fared the worst. Sixty percent of respondents said that they would not buy Marlboro, and 48 percent claimed they would "definitely avoid" using American Express. The other brands that respondents stated they were "most avoiding" were Exxon-Mobile, AOL, Chevron, Texaco, United Airlines, Budweiser, Chrysler, Barbie Dolls, Starbucks, and General Motors. Adding to the bad news for U.S. corporations, 50 percent of the survey respondents stated they distrusted U.S. firms because of their perceived involvement in foreign policy.

Protesters in Manila boycott McDonald's and other U.S.-based firms to protest the U.S.-led war on Iraq.

The dilemma U.S. firms face is how to counter this negativity abroad but retain their patriotic reputation within the United States. Most of these quintessentially American firms operate through local partners and purchase from local suppliers in their global operations. So should these U.S. companies distance themselves from their U.S. identity? Should they highlight that boycotts harm local economies perhaps even more than they do the U.S. economy?

Trade Agreements   Marketers must consider the **trade agreements** to which a particular country is a signatory or the **trading bloc** to which it belongs. A trade agreement is an intergovernmental agreement designed to manage and promote trade activities for a specific region, and a trading bloc consists of those countries that have signed the particular trade agreement.[24]

Some major trade agreements cover two-thirds of the world's international trade: the European Union (EU), the North American Free Trade Agreement (NAFTA), Central America Free Trade Agreement (CAFTA), Mercosur, and the Association of Southeast Asian Nations (ASEAN).[25] These trade agreements are summarized in Exhibit 7.8. The EU represents the highest level of integration across individual nations, whereas the other agreements vary in their integration levels.

European Union   The EU is an economic and monetary union that currently contains 25 countries, as illustrated in Exhibit 7.9. Bulgaria and Romania head a

EXHIBIT	7.8	Trade Agreements
Name	**Countries**	
European Union	Austria, Belgium, Denmark, Finland, France, Germany, Greece, Ireland, Italy, Luxembourg, Netherlands, Portugal, Spain, Sweden, United Kingdom of Great Britain, and Northern Ireland. Ten countries joined the EU in 2004: Cyprus, the Czech Republic, Estonia, Hungary, Latvia, Lithuania, Malta, Poland, Slovakia, and Slovenia. Scheduled to be members (January 1, 2007): Bulgaria and Romania.	
NAFTA	United States, Canada, and Mexico.	
CAFTA	United States, Costa Rica, the Dominican Republic, El Salvador, Guatemala, Honduras, and Nicaragua.	
MERCOSUR	Full Members: Argentina, Brazil, Paraguay, Uruguay, and Venezuela.	
ASEAN	Brunei Darussalam, Cambodia, Indonesia, Laos, Malaysia, Myanmar, Philippines, Singapore, Thailand, and Vietnam.	

list of additional petitioners for membership, but they have not yet been granted full membership.[26] The European Union represents a significant restructuring of the global marketplace. By dramatically lowering trade barriers between member nations within the union, the complexion of the global marketplace has changed.

Having one currency, the euro, across Europe has simplified the way many multinational companies market their products. For instance, prior to the conversion to the euro on January 1, 1999, firms were unable to predict exchange rates. This made it difficult to set consistent prices across countries. After the euro replaced the traditional European currencies, stable prices resulted. Products could be preticketed for distribution across Europe. Patent requirements were simplified

The European Union has resulted in lowering trade barriers and strengthening global relationships among member nations.

EXHIBIT 7.9 EU Map

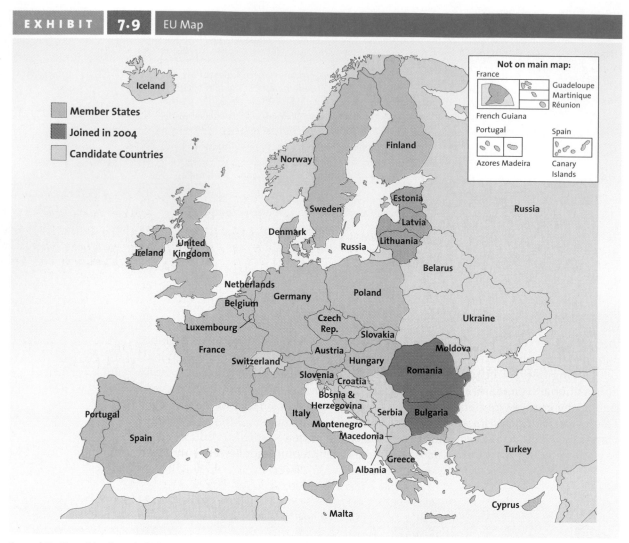

Source: http://en.wikipedia.org/wiki/European_Union, accessed Nov. 2, 2006.

since one patent application could cover multiple countries. Similarly the rules governing data privacy and transmission, advertising, direct selling, etc., have been streamlined and simplified, allowing seamless trade.

North American Free Trade Agreement (NAFTA)   NAFTA is limited to trade-related issues, such as tariffs and quotas, among the United States, Canada, and Mexico.

Central American Free Trade Agreement (CAFTA)   CAFTA is a trade agreement between the United States, Costa Rica, the Dominican Republic, El Salvador, Guatemala, Honduras, and Nicaragua.[27]

Mercosur.   Translated from the Spanish, Mercosur means the Southern Common Market. This group covers most of South America. In 1995, Mercosur member nations created the Free Trade Area of the Americas (FTAA), primarily in response to NAFTA.

Association of Southeast Asian Nations (ASEAN) Originally formed to promote security in Southeast Asia during the Vietnam War, ASEAN changed its mission to building economic stability and lowering trade restrictions among the six member nations in the 1980s.

These trading blocs affect how U.S. firms can conduct business in the member countries. Some critics contend that such blocs confer an unfair advantage on their member nations because they offer favorable terms for trade, whereas others believe they stimulate economies by lowering trade barriers and allowing higher levels of foreign investment.

Analyzing Sociocultural Factors

Understanding another country's culture is crucial to the success of any global marketing initiative. **Culture,** or the set of values, guiding beliefs, understandings, and ways of doing things shared by members of a society, exists on two levels: visible artifacts (e.g., behavior, dress, symbols, physical settings, ceremonies) and underlying values (thought processes, beliefs, and assumptions). Visible artifacts are easy to recognize, but businesses often find it more difficult to understand the underlying values of a culture and appropriately adapt their marketing strategies to them.[28]

One important cultural classification scheme that firms can use is Geert Hofstede's cultural dimensions concept, which sheds more light on these underlying values. Hofstede believes cultures differ on five dimensions:[29]

1. **Power distance:** Willingness to accept social inequality as natural.
2. **Uncertainty avoidance:** The extent to which the society relies on orderliness, consistency, structure, and formalized procedures to address situations that arise in daily life.
3. **Individualism:** Perceived obligation to and dependence on groups.
4. **Masculinity:** The extent to which dominant values are male oriented. A lower masculinity ranking indicates that men and women are treated equally in all aspects of society; a higher masculinity ranking suggests that men dominate in positions of power.[30]
5. **Time orientation:** Short- versus long-term orientation. A country that tends to have a long-term orientation values long-term commitments and is willing to accept a longer time horizon for, say, the success of a new product introduction.

To illustrate two of the five dimensions, consider the data and graph in Exhibit 7.10. Power distance is on the vertical axis and individualism is on the horizontal axis. Several Latin American countries cluster high on power distance but low on individualism; the United States, Australia, Canada, and the United Kingdom, in contrast, cluster high on individualism but low on power distance. Using this information, firms should expect that if they design a marketing campaign that stresses equality and individualism, it will be well accepted in the English-speaking countries, all other factors being equal. The same campaign, however, might not be as well received in Latin American countries.

Another means of classifying cultures distinguishes them according to the importance of verbal communication.[31] In the United States and most European countries, business relationships are governed by what is said and written down, often through formal contracts. In countries such as China and South Korea, however, most relationships rely on nonverbal cues, so that the situation or context

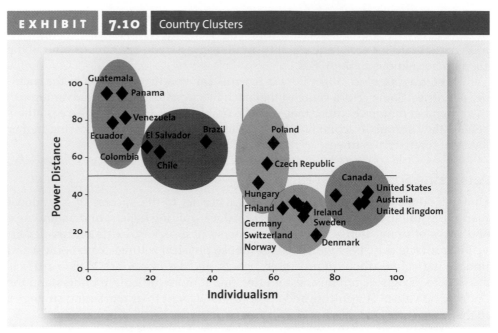

EXHIBIT   7.10   Country Clusters

Source: Based on data available at http://www.geert-hofstede.com. Data from: Geert Hofstede, *Culture's Consequences,* 2nd edition (Thousand Oaks, Sage 2001). Copyright © Geert Hofstede, reproduced with permission.

Business relationships in China often are formalized by just a handshake, and trust and honor are often more important than legal arrangements.

means much more than mere words. For instance, business relationships in China often are formalized by just a handshake, and trust and honor are often more important than legal arrangements.

Overall, culture affects every aspect of consumer behavior: why people buy, who is in charge of buying decisions, and how, when, and where people shop. After marketing managers have completed the four parts of the market assessment, they are better able to make informed decisions about whether a particular country possesses the necessary characteristics to be considered a potential market for the firm's products and services. In the next section, we detail the market entry decision process, beginning with a discussion of the various ways firms might enter a new global market.

Choosing a Global Entry Strategy

When a firm has concluded its assessment analysis of the most viable markets for its products and services, it must then conduct an internal assessment of its capabilities. As we discussed in Chapter 2, this analysis includes an assessment of the firm's access to capital, the current markets it serves, its manufacturing capacity, its proprietary assets, and the commitment of its management to the proposed strategy. These factors ultimately contribute to the success or failure of a market expansion strategy, whether at home or in a foreign market. After these internal market assessments, it is time for the firm to choose its entry strategy.

A firm can choose from many approaches when it decides to enter a new market, which vary according to the level of risk the firm is willing to take. Many firms actually follow a progression in which they begin with less risky strategies to enter their first foreign markets and move to increasingly risky strategies as they gain confidence in their abilities, as illustrated in Exhibit 7.11. We examine these different approaches that marketers take when entering global markets, beginning with the least risky.

Exporting   Exporting means producing goods in one country and selling them in another. This entry strategy requires the least financial risk but also allows for only a limited return to the exporting firm. Global expansion often begins when a firm receives an order for its product or service from another country, in which case it faces little risk because it can demand payment before it ships the merchandise. By the same token, it is difficult to achieve economies of scale when everything has to be shipped internationally. The Italian bicycle component manufacturer Campagnolo sells relatively small but expensive bicycle parts all over the world. Because its transportation costs are relatively small compared with the cost of the parts, the best way for it to service any market is to export from Italy.

Franchising   Franchising is a contractual agreement between a firm, the franchisor, and another firm or individual, the franchisee. A franchising contract allows the franchisee to operate a business—a retail product or service firm or a B2B provider—using the name and business format developed and supported by the franchisor. Many of the best-known retailers in the United States are also successful global franchisers, including McDonald's, Pizza Hut, Starbucks, Dominos Pizza, KFC, and Holiday Inn, all of which have found that global franchising entails lower risks and requires less investment than does opening units owned wholly by the firm. However, when it engages in franchising, the firm has limited control over the market operations in the foreign country, its potential profit is reduced because it must be split with the franchisee, and, once the franchise is established, there is always the threat that the franchisee will break away and operate as a competitor under a different name.

EXHIBIT **7.11** Entry Strategies

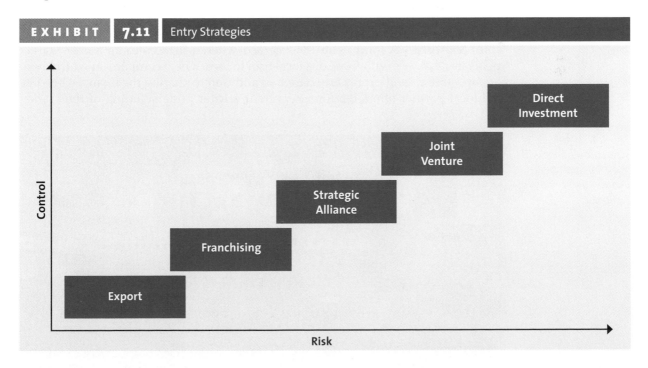

These franchise logos are recognized around the world.

Strategic Alliance   **Strategic alliances** refer to collaborative relationships between independent firms, though the partnering firms do not create an equity partnership; that is, they do not invest in one another. For example, Star Alliance constitutes one of the most complex strategic alliances in the world, with 15 airline members representing 16 countries: Air Canada, Air New Zealand, ANA (Japan), Asiana Airlines (South Korea), Austrian, BMI (United Kingdom), LOT Polish Airlines, Lufthansa (Germany), SAS Scandinavian Airlines (Denmark, Norway, and Sweden), Spanair (Spain), Singapore Airlines, Thai, United (United States), US Airways, and Varig (Brazil).[32]

What began as a series of bilateral agreements among five airlines grew over time into Star Alliance, which now acts as a separate legal entity in which each member is a stakeholder but no member is an equity owner in the others. Star Alliance coordinates the members on projects of mutual interest, such as helping members in their individual brand building efforts by creating value through their membership in the Alliance. This plan offers passengers benefits from individual airlines when they purchase from alliance partners. For instance, a US Airways frequent flier member could earn US Airways miles by flying Spanair. This alliance also allows seamless booking and other transactions across the Alliance membership.

Joint Venture   **A joint venture** is formed when a firm entering a new market pools its resources with those of a local firm to form a new company in which ownership, control, and profits are shared. In addition to sharing the financial burden, the local partner offers the foreign entrant greater understanding of the market

The Star Alliance is a strategic alliance with 15 airline members including LOT Polish Airlines.

Tesco, the U.K. supermarket chain has a joint venture in China in which it has purchased a 50 percent share in Ting Hsin—which owns and operates the 25-store hypermarket chain Hymall.

and access to resources such as vendors and real estate. Tesco, the U.K. supermarket, finance, telecom, and insurance superstar, has begun to enter China through a joint venture in which it has purchased a 50 percent share in Ting Hsin—which owns and operates the 25-store hypermarket chain Hymall—for $250 million dollars.[33] China usually requires joint ownership from entering firms, as do many other countries, though these restrictions may loosen as a result of WTO negotiations. Problems with this entry approach can arise when the partners disagree or if the government places restrictions on the firm's ability to move its profits out of the foreign country and back to its home country.

Direct Investment   **Direct investment** requires a firm to maintain 100 percent ownership of its plants, operation facilities, and offices in a foreign country, often through the formation of wholly owned subsidiaries. This entry strategy requires the highest level of investment and exposes the firm to significant risks, including the loss of its operating and/or initial investments. For example, a dramatic economic downturn caused by a natural disaster or war, political instability, or changes in the country's laws can increase a foreign entrant's risk considerably. Many firms believe that in certain markets, these potential risks are outweighed by the high potential returns; with this strategy, none of the potential profits must be shared with other firms. In addition to the high potential returns, direct investment offers the firm complete control over its operations in the foreign country.

ING Group, a financial services firm based in The Netherlands, decided to enter the U.S. market through a wholly owned subsidiary. Attracted by the United States' position as the world's largest financial services market, as well as regulations friendly to ING's desire to provide banking services, insurance, and asset management products (e.g., mortgages, investment accounts), ING began an aggressive entry into the U.S. market in 2000 and has not looked back since. Forgoing traditional bank branches, ING established ING Direct and operates purely online.

Although it began with online savings accounts, ING has expanded into investment accounts and online mortgage services and now has 1.5 million customers and more than $16 billion in assets in the United States—as well as an advertising campaign that gently pokes fun at people's lack of awareness about what the company does.[34]

As we noted, each of these entry strategies entails different levels of risk and rewards for the foreign entrant. But even after a firm has determined how much risk it is willing to take, and therefore how it will enter a new global market, it still must establish its marketing strategy, as we discuss in the next section.

Choosing a Global Marketing Strategy

Just like any other marketing strategy, a global marketing strategy includes two components: determining the target market(s) to pursue and developing a marketing mix that will sustain a competitive advantage over time. In this section, we examine marketing strategy as it relates specifically to global markets.

Target Market: Segmentation, Targeting, and Positioning

Global segmentation, targeting, and positioning (STP) is more complicated than local STP for several reasons. First, firms considering a global expansion have much more difficulty understanding the cultural nuances of other countries. Second, subcultures within each country also must be considered. Third, consumers often view products and their role as consumers differently in different countries.[35]

A product or service often must be positioned differently in different markets. For example, Tang, the fruit-flavored drink produced by Kraft, is positioned as a low-priced drink in the United States, but such a positioning strategy would not work in Brazil, where fresh orange juice already is a low-priced drink. Consequently, Kraft promotes a pineapple-flavored Tang and positions it as a drink for special occasions. In a similar fashion, McDonald's generally competes on convenience and low price, but in countries like China and India, where consumers already have lower-priced and more convenient alternatives, McDonald's positions itself as an "American" restaurant.[36]

Tropicana uses a global positioning strategy that stresses around the world that Tropicana is "fresh-squeezed Florida orange juice."

The most efficient route is to develop and maintain a global positioning strategy; one position means only one message to get out. For instance, Tropicana is the best-selling orange juice brand in the United States and owns 6 percent of the global juice market. Tropicana's parent company, PepsiCo, therefore takes a global positioning strategy that stresses around the world that Tropicana is "fresh-squeezed Florida orange juice."[37]

When it identifies its positioning within the market, the firm then must decide how to implement its marketing strategies using the marketing mix. Just as firms adjust their products and services to meet the needs of national target market(s), they must alter their marketing mix to serve the needs of global markets.

The Global Marketing Mix

During the early stages of globalization, in the 1950s and 1960s, large U.S. firms were uniquely positioned in the global marketplace because they had the unique skills necessary to develop, promote, and market brand name consumer products. In the 1970s and 1980s, however,

Japanese firms dominated the global marketplace because they could exploit their skills in production, materials management, and new product development. Today, retailers such as Wal-Mart, financial services firms such as Citicorp, and software firms such as Microsoft are dominating the newest stage of globalization by exploiting their technological skills.[38] In the following section, we explore the 4Ps (product, place, promotion, price) from a global perspective.

Global Product or Service Strategies   There are three potential global product strategies:

- Sell the same product or service in both the home country market and the host country.

- Sell a product or service similar to that sold in home country but include minor adaptations.

- Sell totally new products or services.

The strategy a firm chooses depends on the needs of the target market. The level of economic development, as well as differences in product and technical standards, helps determine the need for and level of product adaptation. Cultural differences such as food preferences, language, and religion also play a role in product strategy planning. For example, Frito-Lay discovered that the traditional cheese taste and bright orange color of Cheetos did not sell well in China, where cheese is not a traditional part of the diet. Therefore, it adapted Chinese Cheetos to offer a choice of either teriyaki or butter flavors.[39] Since that adaptation, Cheetos has been marketed in a variety of flavors and colors, including pink, strawberry-flavored snacks. The new product retained the Cheetos name though, because the Chinese character *qi duo* is pronounced "CHEE dwaugh" and means "new surprise."[40]

The level of economic development also affects the global product strategy because it relates directly to consumer behavior. For instance, consumers in developed countries tend to demand more attributes in their products than do consumers in less developed countries. In the United States, Honda does not offer its line of "urban" motorcycles, available in Mexico and China, because the product line resembles a motor scooter more than a motorcycle, which does not tend to appeal

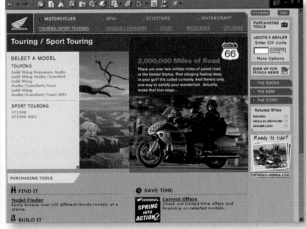

Honda adapts its product line to fit the needs of its customers. Their motorcycles in Mexico (left) are relatively inexpensive and designed for urban use. The much larger sport touring motorcycles sold in the U.S. (right) are designed for highway use.

Adding Value 7.1

MTV Conquers the World

You and millions of others around the globe might watch MTV tonight, but the MTV you see might not be the same as the one a college student in, say, Jakarta views.[42] MTV (Music Television) is now the world's leading youth brand, and can be seen in more than 374.7 million households in 164 countries via 34 channels in 18 languages. When MTV began its globalization efforts, it offered the same programming in every market. Similar to other global brands, MTV soon learned that offering a one size fits all product didn't meet the needs of its target segment, so while maintaining its unique personality and appeal to its target segment, MTV began establishing regional offices, especially in Asia. Today, approximately 80 percent of MTV's programming in Asia is local. This localized content provides an unprecedented venue for local musicians and musical traditions. For example, MTV Indonesia, with 13 million potential viewers, stumbled on one of its audiences' favorite shows, MTV Salam Dangdut, almost accidentally.

Salam Dangdut features Indonesia's most popular traditional music, Dangdut, in a show that originally aired simply as a gesture of appreciation for local culture. Ironically, Dangdut has long been unpopular in Indonesia's music industry, viewed as traditional music that was not exciting enough for a contemporary audience. It was only when MTV decided to air the program that local audiences began to appreciate the traditional music again. Young people, who had never been interested in music like Dangdut before, suddenly began seeing it as cool thanks to MTV's Generation Y–friendly approach.

The question of what to globalize and what to localize is always difficult to answer. But in this case, MTV seems to have hit a winning note.

to American consumers. Motorcycles sold in the United States have more horsepower and bigger frames and come with an array of options that are not offered in other countries.

Some firms also might standardize their products globally but use different promotional campaigns to sell them. The original Pringles potato chip product remains the same globally, as do the images and themes of the promotional campaign, with limited language adaptations for the local markets, though English is used whenever possible. However, the company does change Pringles' flavors in different countries, including paprika-flavored chips sold in Italy and Germany.[41]

Not just manufacturers must adapt their offering. On the service side, for example, MTV offers a mix of globally standardized and localized content to meet the needs of its diverse and varied markets (see Adding Value 7.1).

Despite the persistent differences across borders, marketers have found a growing convergence in tastes and preferences in many product categories. Starbucks is a good example of a company that has both influenced and exploited this global convergence in tastes. Even in China and Great Britain, traditional strongholds for tea marketers, coffee is quickly gaining as the beverage of choice.

Global Pricing Strategies Determining the selling price in the global marketplace is an extremely difficult task.[43] Many countries still have rules governing the competitive marketplace, including those that affect pricing. For example, in some countries, firms cannot charge prices lower than the local market prices, and price reductions can be taken only at certain times of the year or according to government-specified percentages. For firms such as Wal-Mart and other discounters, this restriction threatens their core competitive positioning as the lowest-cost provider in the market. Other issues, such as tariffs, quotas, anti-dumping laws, and currency exchange policies, can also affect pricing decisions.[44]

Competitive factors influence global pricing in the same way they do home country pricing, but because a firm's products or services may not have the same positioning in the global marketplace as they do in their home country, market prices must be adjusted to reflect the local pricing structure. Spain's fashion retailer Zara, for instance, is relatively inexpensive in the EU but moderately priced in North America. As the P&G Head & Shoulders example in the opening vignette indicates, significant economic factors often affect prices.

Global Distribution Strategies   Global distribution networks form complex value chains that involve middlemen, exporters, importers, and different transportation systems. These additional middlemen typically add cost and ultimately increase the final selling price of a product. As a result of these cost factors, constant pressure exists to shorten distribution channels wherever possible.

Distribution can be challenging in some countries if the transportation infrastructure is inadequate. In the Amazon jungle in Brazil, for instance, Avon products are sometimes delivered by canoe.

The number of firms with which the seller needs to deal to get its merchandise to the consumer determines the complexity of a channel. In most developing countries, manufacturers must go through many different types of distribution channels to get their products to end users, who often lack adequate transportation to shop at central shopping areas or large malls. Therefore, these consumers shop near their homes at small, family-owned retail outlets. To reach these small retail outlets, most of which are located far from major rail stations or roads, marketers have devised a variety of creative solutions. In the Amazon jungle in Brazil, for instance, Avon products are sometimes delivered by canoe. However, even if distribution channels present challenges, some products may be sold the same way in both foreign markets and the home country. For example, Dell distributes globally the same way it does in the United States— via the Internet.

Global Communication Strategies   The major challenge in developing a global communication strategy is identifying the elements that need to be adapted to be effective in the global marketplace. For instance, literacy levels vary dramatically across the globe. In Argentina, 3.8 percent of the adult population is illiterate, compared with 6 percent in the Philippines and a whopping 61 percent in Liberia.[45] Media availability also varies widely; some countries offer only state-controlled media. Advertising regulations differ too. In an attempt at standardization, the EU recently recommended common guidelines for its member countries regarding advertising to children and is currently reviewing a possible ban on "junk food" advertising.[46]

Differences in language, customs, and culture also complicate marketers' ability to communicate with customers in various countries. Language can be particularly vexing for advertisers. For example, in the United Kingdom, a thong is only a sandal, whereas in the United States, it can also be an undergarment. To avoid

Entrepreneurial Marketing 7.1

David versus Goliath in the Beer Wars

The Budvar brewery claims that Anheuser-Busch stole the name Budweiser and that its product is, in fact, the one and only true Budweiser.[50] Located in the Czech Republic, a member of the EU, Budvar brewery can trace its roots back 700 years. For years, the two Budweisers coexisted on opposite sides of the Atlantic in relative peace, though the first clash of the Budweisers occurred in 1911 at a trade fair. According to a Budvar spokesperson, the companies then reached an agreement to essentially divide the globe: "We wouldn't sell our beer north of the Panama Canal, and they wouldn't sell their beer in Europe."

After the fall of communism, both Budvar and Anheuser-Busch began to expand. Budvar began placing ads in the United Kingdom, and Anheuser-Busch started exporting to Europe. According to Anheuser-Busch, the company could no longer afford to ignore the lucrative European market.

Budvar argued that consumers expected "Budweiser" to be a premium product produced only by Budvar, and that Anheuser-Busch's Budweiser, which was in fact a shortened version of the name of the town in which Budvar was located, simply did not measure up to those standards. In response, Anheuser-Busch argued that Budweiser and Bud are global brand names associated with *its* product. It has invested hundreds of millions of dollars in the Budweiser and Bud names over the brands' 127-year histories, which has made them among the most valuable brand names in the world. The company believes its trademarks provide the foundation for its beer business, and it plans to protect them aggressively.

European countries have a long tradition of granting protections to local brands and regional products, making it difficult, if not impossible, for foreign manufacturers to enter the market. Thus far, the beer battle has

When you think of having a Bud, do you mean Budweiser or Budvar?

played out on a country-by-country basis and currently sits in an uneasy truce that involves some interesting compromises. Anheuser-Busch has national registrations for "Budweiser" or "Bud" in 20 of the 25 EU countries and sells 31 percent of its foreign beer (by volume) there. In many of these countries, the two Budweisers exist together on the shelves at the local store.

Budvar is presently looking to expand to the United States. The CEO of Budvar gives a wry chuckle when contemplating the possibility of a U.S. consumer mistakenly taking home a crate of the Czech beer and "accidentally" converting to Budvar.

Meanwhile, the WTO is examining the issue of regional and local product protections. Most indications suggest the WTO will deny both brewers' requests for exclusive use of the Bud and Budweiser names. It looks like the two products will remain side by side for years to come. In the long run, for Budvar, perhaps a little confusion will turn out to be a good thing.

the potential embarrassment that language confusion can cause, firms spend millions of dollars to develop brand names that have no preexisting meaning in any known language, such as Accenture (a management consulting firm) or Avaya (a subsidiary of Lucent Technologies, formerly Bell Labs).

Within many countries there are multiple variants on a language. For example in China where there are three main languages, firms such as Mercedes Benz adapted the name for each language. Thus, Mercedes-Benz is known by three Chinese names in Asia: Pronounced peng zee in Cantonese for Hong Kong; peng chi in Mandarin for Taiwan; and ben chi in Mandarin for mainland China. Other firms such as Nokia only use one name in China, pronounced nuo jee ya in Mandarin.[47]

As China continues to develop, having more than one name to represent a product or service will become increasingly inefficient.

Even with all these differences, many products and services serve the same needs and wants globally with little or no adaptation in their form or message. Firms whose products have global appeal, like Coca-Cola, can develop global advertising campaigns, an advantage that results in significant savings. According to Coca-Cola's advertising firm, McCann-Erickson, over a 20-year period, it saved Coca Cola $90 million by reusing advertisements it had already created and changing only a few elements for different local markets.[48]

However, other products require a more localized approach because of cultural and religious differences. In a classic advertisement for Longines watches, a woman's bare arm and hand appear, with a watch on her wrist. The advertisement was considered too risqué for Muslim countries, where women's bare arms are never displayed in public, but the company simply changed the advertisement to show a gloved arm and hand wearing the same watch.

Regulatory actions in the host country can also affect communication strategies. For example, the WTO has become involved in several cases that involve firms' rights to use certain names and affiliations for their products and promotions. Several products in the EU have established worldwide brand recognition on the basis of where they are made. For instance, the EU currently allows only ham made in Parma, Italy, to be called Parma ham and sparkling wine made in the Champagne region of France to be called Champagne. However, the EU has also refused to grant requests from non-EU countries for similar protection, notably Florida orange juice.[49] The WTO is expected to ask the EU to either remove all such protections or grant them to non-E.U. countries as well. In one case, similar arguments have even led to a global beer brawl, as we describe in Entrepreneurial Marketing 7–1.

Ethical Issues in Global Marketing

Although ethical issues abound domestically, an extra layer of complexity arises for global marketing. Firms that market globally must recognize that they are, in essence, visitors in another country and, as such, must be aware of the ethical concerns of their potential customers, both at home and abroad. In this section, we examine three areas of particular concern: environmental challenges, labor issues, and impact on host country culture.

Many developed countries produce almost two tons of household and industrial waste per person per year that requires proper disposal.

Environmental Concerns

Among the various **environmental concerns** that exist, people throughout the world are worried about the amount of waste being generated, especially in developed countries. Waste can include, but is not limited to, the excessive use of natural resources and energy, refuse from manufacturing processes, excess trash created by consumer goods packages, and hard-to-dispose-of products like tires, cell phones, and computer monitors.

Many developed countries produce almost two tons of household and industrial waste per person per year![51] Although developing countries do not produce nearly the same level of waste, much of the waste in these areas is not properly disposed of.

Global Labor Issues

Global labor issues, especially concerns about working conditions and wages paid to factory workers in developing countries, have become increasingly prominent.[52] Many large U.S. firms have been questioned by various groups, including nongovernmental organizations and human rights activists, about the degree to which workers the companies employs are paid less than a living wage or forced to work long hours in poor working conditions.[53]

Nike has been repeatedly questioned by a variety of groups about the working conditions in the manufacturing plants around the world that produce its products.[54] For the most part, Nike does not own the plants in which its goods are produced, so it must negotiate with factory owners to improve or ensure adequate working conditions and wages. In response to recent pressure, Nike has made a significant investment in its social responsibility initiatives, such as joining the Fair Labor Association, an organization dedicated to improving working conditions globally and creating a compliance program and code of conduct for its subcontractors. Nike's efforts have been recognized by the United Nations and other international organizations, and its program for contractors serves as a model for other firms. Nike admits it will never be perfect (with 600,000 contract workers in 900 factories in 50 countries, it is almost impossible to avoid some violations), but it is making the effort to bring its subcontractors into compliance with its labor standards.

Impact on Host Country Culture

When Western firms enter foreign markets, they must be cognizant of the host country's culture.

The final ethical issue involves **cultural imperialism,** or the belief that one's own culture is superior to that of other nations. Cultural imperialism can take the form of an active, formal policy or a more subtle general attitude.[55] Critics of U.S. firms entering foreign markets claim that U.S. products and services overwhelm the local culture, often replacing its foods, music, movies, and traditions with those of the West.

In Iran, for example, the ruling clerics have forbidden the celebration of Valentine's Day.[56] Despite strict Iranian laws regarding the interactions of men and women, especially unmarried men and women, Valentine's Day has become a popular holiday among the youth market. These Iranians were exposed to Valentine's Day through the Internet and satellite television, two information sources the government cannot control. Holiday-themed products arrive through underground distribution channels and are displayed in local shops. Risking legal action, florists, gift shops, and restaurants make special accommodations for the holiday. Many parents sponsor Valentine parties with both men and women in attendance. Apparently, there is no stopping love. Half the Iranian population is younger than 25 years of age, and this youth market has embraced the holiday and continues to celebrate it in traditional Western ways because it represents progress and modernization.

For other Iranians though, this type of celebration represents a threat to Iran's culture. Many U.S. firms find themselves squarely in the middle of this cultural conflict.[57] Various countries around the world encompass competing desires: the desire to modernize and participate in the global marketplace versus the desire to hold on to traditional cultural values and ways of life. There is no simple way to resolve these dilemmas. Firms that enter new markets simply must tread lightly to ensure that their business practices, products, and services do not create any unnecessary friction or offense in the host country.

Summing Up

1. What factors aid the growth of globalization?

Technology, particularly in communications, has facilitated the growth of global markets. Firms can communicate with their suppliers and customers instantaneously, easily take advantage of production efficiencies in other countries, and bring together parts and finished goods from all over the globe. International organizations such as the World Trade Organization, the International Monetary Fund, and the World Bank Group also have reduced or eliminated tariffs and quotas, worked to help people in less-developed countries, and facilitated trade in many areas.

2. How does a firm decide to enter a global market?

First, firms must assess the general economic environment. For instance, countries with a trade surplus, strong domestic and national products, growing populations, and income growth generally are relatively more favorable prospects. Second, firms should assess a country's infrastructure. To be successful in a particular country, the firm must have access to adequate transportation, distribution channels, and communications. Third, firms must determine whether the proposed country has a political and legal environment that favors business. Fourth, firms should be cognizant of the cultural and sociological differences between their home and host countries and adapt to those differences to ensure successful business relationships.

3. What ownership and partnership options do firms have for entering a new global market?

Firms have several options for entering a new country, each with a different level of risk and involvement. Direct investment is the most risky but potentially the most lucrative. Firms that engage in a joint venture with other firms already operating in the host country share the risk and obtain knowledge about the market and how to do business there. A strategic alliance is similar to a joint venture, but the relationship is not as formal. A less risky method of entering a new market is franchising, in which, similar to domestic franchise agreements, the franchisor allows the franchisee to operate a business using its name and strategy in return for a fee. The least risky method of entering another country is exporting.

4. What are the similarities and differences between a domestic marketing strategy and a global marketing strategy?

The essence of a global marketing strategy is no different than that of a domestic strategy. The firm starts by identifying its target markets, chooses specific markets to pursue, and crafts a strategy to meet the needs of those markets. However, additional issues make global expansion more difficult. For instance, should the product or service be altered to fit the new market better? Does the firm need to change the way it prices its products in different countries? What is the best way to get the product or service to the new customers? How should the firm communicate its product or service offering in other countries?

5. How do ethical issues impact global marketing practices?

In particular, firms must be cognizant of the impact their businesses have on the environment. When producing merchandise or employing service personnel in another country, they must be certain that the working conditions and wages are fair and adequate, even if the workers are employed by a third party. Finally, marketers must be sensitive to the impact their business has on the culture of the host country.

Key Terms

- boycott, 187
- countertrade, 187
- cultural imperialism, 202
- culture, 191
- direct investment, 195
- dumping, 186
- duty, 185
- environmental concerns, 201
- exchange control, 187
- exchange rate, 187
- exporting, 193
- franchisee, 193
- franchising, 193
- franchisor, 193

- General Agreement on Tariffs and Trade (GATT), 178
- global labor issues, 202
- globalization, 177
- globalization of production, 177
- gross domestic product (GDP), 181
- gross national income (GNI), 181
- human development index (HDI), 183
- infrastructure, 185
- International Monetary Fund (IMF), 178

- joint venture, 194
- offshoring, 177
- purchasing power parity (PPP), 181
- quota, 186
- strategic alliance, 194
- tariff, 185
- trade agreements, 188
- trade deficit, 181
- trade surplus, 181
- trading bloc, 188
- World Bank Group, 179
- World Trade Organization (WTO), 178

Marketing Applications

1. What is globalization? Why is it important for marketers to understand what globalization entails?

2. The World Trade Organization, World Bank, and International Monetary Fund all work in different ways to facilitate globalization. What role(s) does each organization play in the global marketplace?

3. Moots is a high-end bicycle manufacturer located in Steamboat Springs, Colorado. Assume the company is considering entering the U.K. and Chinese markets. When doing its market assessment, what economic factors should Moots consider to make its decision? Which market do you expect will be more lucrative for Moots? Why?

4. Now consider the political, economic, and legal systems of China versus the United Kingdom. Explain why you think one country might be more hospitable to Moots than the other.

5. Volkswagen sells cars in many countries throughout the world, including Mexico and Latin America. How would you expect its market position to differ in those countries compared with that in the United States?

6. What are the benefits of being able to offer a globally standardized product? What types of products easily lend themselves to global standardization?

7. What is cultural imperialism? Why would a recording company like Def Jam Records need to be aware of and sensitive to this issue?

8. Provide an example of a potentially ethically troubling practice by a non-U.S. firm doing business in the United States.

9. Many U.S. firms are relocating their production facilities and services overseas (outsourcing or offshoring). Why do you believe they are doing so? Do the benefits outweigh the potential losses of U.S. jobs? Why or why not?

10. Assume you work for a U.S.-based financial services firm that positions itself as having experts that personally manage the clients' accounts. The clients are unaware that most of the tax preparation work, the bookkeeping, and other record keeping are done by a company in India. The local office simply reviews the file and signs the cover letters. Yet as your manager pointed out, there is still only one person that *manages* each account. After recent news stories about the practice of offshoring sensitive transactions such as tax preparation, clients have been commenting about how grateful they are to have a local firm. What, if anything, should you tell your clients about the firm's practice of offshoring?

Net Savvy

1. For many small businesses, the idea of entering a foreign market is frightening. The U.S. national government, as well as most state governments, now offers assistance designed specifically for small business owners. One such organization is the Massachusetts Export Center. Visit its Web site at http://www.mass.gov/export/ and examine the types of services it provides for businesses. Now click on the trade statistics link. To what five countries did Massachusetts export the most? Do any of these countries surprise you?

2. McDonald's is now a global brand, yet in each country, it alters its products and promotions to accommodate local tastes. Go to www.mcdonalds.com and visit the U.S. site. Now click through to three non-Western countries. How are these three Web sites different from the U.S. site? What products are different? What promotional elements are different?

Chapter Case Study

IKEA TAKES ON THE WORLD, ONE COUNTRY AT A TIME

Entrepreneurial ideas can come from anyplace at anytime, and the founding of IKEA is a classic example of a happy accident. Ingvar Kamprad was just 17 years old in 1943 when, using money his father had given him, he began a household goods catalog. Realizing that his most profitable item was furniture, he began to focus on selling furniture in 1947. Who would have guessed in 1943 that his household goods catalog would one day become the world's largest furniture retailer, with annual sales of $12 billion to 286 million customers? IKEA now operates in 35 countries and is looking to expand both into more new markets and in the markets it currently serves. Kamprad realized that he had hit on a winning concept—the concept that still drives IKEA today.

It was a simple concept: Offer quality furniture at the lowest possible prices. According to the company's Web site, "The IKEA Concept is based on offering a wide range of well-designed, functional home furnishing products at prices so low that as many people as possible will be able to afford them. Rather than selling expensive home furnishings that only a few can buy, the IKEA Concept makes it possible to serve the many by providing low-priced products that contribute to helping more people live a better life at home."[58]

The combination of high quality and low price easily translates across global markets. To keep costs down, IKEA must always remain creative. It locates different steps of its production in different parts of the world to take advantage of the savings offered by buying less expensive products overseas. Perhaps the most innovative way IKEA has found to keep costs low is its choice to ship all of its products in flat packages, which keeps both shipping and storage costs to a minimum and also reduces damage during transit. Customers transport their flat purchases home and complete the final assembly themselves.

IKEA stores and the services it provides (or does not provide) differ from those of other furniture retailers.[59] The large, 15,000–35,000 square meter stores are divided into cheerfully decorated model rooms. Customers can lounge on the furniture. The stores are largely self-service, so customers are encouraged to measure the spaces in their homes before they come to the store. Huge price tags appear on the furniture itself, and cards with design tips are displayed in kiosks throughout the store. IKEA also offers elaborate childcare centers and restaurants with Swedish delicacies, like smoked salmon and lingonberry tarts.

Franchising has enabled IKEA to enter new markets but retain control over how those new outlets are organized and managed. Franchisees must demonstrate a firm commitment to the IKEA Concept and possess both extensive retail experience and enough financial resources to absorb the cost of constructing an IKEA store.

As IKEA enters each new market, it must make certain adjustments to its marketing mix. For example, to enter the U.S. market, it altered its European-style mattresses, which did not

Doing business in Russia has been a challenge for IKEA.

fit traditional American bed linens. Many Americans found the couches too hard and the dinnerware too small to accommodate their serving sizes. After it had made these necessary adjustments, IKEA took off in the United States.

Entering Russia required different adaptations. While they operate several stores across the country and a warehouse near Moscow, they have had problems getting local producers to deliver on time. Punitive tariffs designed to protect Russia's furniture industry from foreign competition can run as high as 80 percent. Russia's bureaucracy can also be difficult. Many contradictory laws make it almost impossible to follow every one.[60]

This combination of a commitment to its concept, an ability to take full advantage of globalized production, unique stores, carefully chosen franchisees, and the means to adapt the marketing mix to fit local needs have enabled IKEA to become a world-class furniture retailer.

Questions

1. Consumers' tastes for furniture typically vary from region to region within a country, from country to country, and across various demographic dimensions, such as age, income, and education. Yet, though IKEA's product line is fairly narrow, it has been successful in virtually every market it has entered. Who is IKEA's target market? Why does IKEA have such global appeal?

2. IKEA uses franchising to enter new markets. Are there any other entry strategies that would be appropriate for IKEA to use? Why or why not?

3. How is IKEA positioned relative to other furniture retailers?

8

QUESTIONS

- How does a firm decide what type of segmentation strategy to use—undifferentiated, differentiated, concentrated, or micromarketing?

- What is the best method of segmenting a market?

- How do firms determine whether a segment is attractive and therefore worth pursuing?

- What is positioning, and how do firms do it?

SECTION THREE

Targeting the Marketplace

Segmentation, Targeting, and Positioning

Shampoo sales in the United States have been decreasing since 1999.[1] Analysts blame this decrease, in part, on companies' slow response to market trends that are creating new market segments. Yet the natural and organic segment of the market has shown growth in the past few years, partially because the media has reported that many hair care products and cosmetics use harmful ozone pollutants and are capable of causing fertility problems.

France-based L'Oreal has seized the opportunity to pursue the customer segment interested in natural/organic products. Their Garnier Fructis line of shampoos and conditioners is made from fruit and vitamin extracts, a perfect match for all-natural enthusiasts. Garnier Fructis consistently places in the top 10 best-selling shampoos. It is the market leader in conditioners, which is a growing category that makes up 17 percent of the hair care market.

The "natural/organic" segment will prove to be a sustainable growth opportunity for many companies in the future as people become more aware of how their environment and the products they use affect their health. L'Oreal recognizes the opportunity Garnier Fructis has and the strength of the natural/organic segment. The company will continue to focus all three of its flagship brands—Garnier, L'Oreal Paris, and Maybelline New York—in the future by adapting the company's product and marketing mix to the changing market climate. Market segmentation, done properly, pays!

■ ■ ■

Make hair 5x smoother.*
Control frizz even with moisture in the air.

GARNIER
FRUCTIS
SLEEK & SHINE

The first long-lasting smoothing system **
with fruit micro-oils from Garnier.

- Nourishing fruit micro-oils help give
  long-lasting smoothness and frizz
  control, even with moisture in the air.
- Makes hair 5x smoother, 5x stronger
  and so much shinier.*

For hair that shines with all its strength.

GARNIER

*France-based
L'Oreal has seized
the opportunity to
pursue the customer
segment interested
in natural/organic
products with their
Garnier Fructis line
of shampoos and
conditioners that are
made from fruit and
vitamin extracts.*

Some people like conditioning shampoo, while others like oil reducing shampoo. Some people want a natural product; others care primarily about how well the product cleans. Still other people demand affordable shampoo, whereas some prefer it to be salon quality. More likely though, a group of people desires a shampoo that conditions, is affordable, and contains natural ingredients; whereas another group demands a shampoo that is salon quality, deep cleansing, and oil reducing. The many combinations of these three product attributes each potentially appeals to a different group of people.

In Chapter 1, we learned that marketing is about satisfying consumers' wants and needs. A company could make one type of shampoo and hope that every shampoo user would buy it, but that's the kind of mistake that has been leading the hair care industry into decline. Or, as we described in Chapter 2, the shampoo manufacturers could analyze the market to determine the different types of shampoo people want and then make several varieties that cater to the wants of specific groups. It is not enough just to make the product, however. Shampoo manufacturers such as L'Oreal must position their shampoos in the minds of their target market so those consumers understand why a particular shampoo meets their needs better than competitive brands do.

In Chapter 2, we described the steps involved in a marketing plan: The manager first defines the firm's mission and objectives and then performs a situation analysis. The third step of the marketing plan is to identify and evaluate opportunities by performing an STP (segmentation, targeting, and positioning) analysis—which makes up the topic of this chapter.

In the opening vignette, L'Oreal identified the various groups of shampoo users that would respond similarly to the firm's marketing efforts. These are also known as market segments. Those who like natural, affordable, conditioning shampoos are one market segment; people who prefer salon quality, deep cleansing, and oil reducing shampoo constitute a different segment. After evaluating each market segment's attractiveness, L'Oreal decided to concentrate its new product line on one group—its target market—because it believes it could satisfy their needs better than its competitors could. As we noted in Chapter 2, the process of dividing the market into groups of customers who have different needs, wants, or characteristics and who therefore might appreciate products or services geared especially for them is called market segmentation.

Once the target market was identified, L'Oreal had to convince the targeted group that when it comes to hair care products, their choice should be Garnier Fructis with its natural extracts. It is achieving this task by defining the marketing mix variables so that the target customers have a clear, distinctive, desirable understanding of what the product or services do or represent, relative to competing products—a process we described in Chapter 2 as market positioning. In particular, L'Oreal has designed a lifestyle advertising campaign that has positioned Garnier Fructis as the healthy choice versus its competitors. It has also

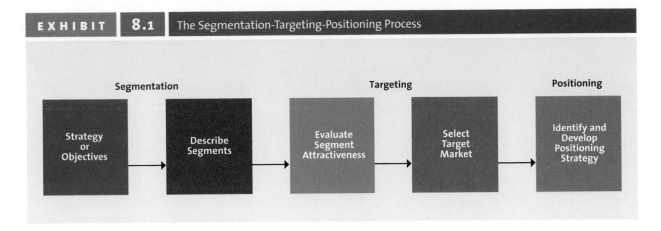

EXHIBIT 8.1 The Segmentation-Targeting-Positioning Process

Segmentation · Targeting · Positioning

Strategy or Objectives → Describe Segments → Evaluate Segment Attractiveness → Select Target Market → Identify and Develop Positioning Strategy

made sure that the shampoo is available almost anywhere its customers would want to buy it.

In this chapter, we discuss how a firm conducts a market segmentation or STP analysis (see Exhibit 8.1). We'll first discuss market segmentation, or how a segmentation strategy fits into a firm's overall strategy and objectives and which segments are worth pursuing. Then we discuss how to choose a target market or markets by evaluating each segment's attractiveness and, on the basis of this evaluation, choosing which segment or segments to pursue. Finally, we describe how a firm develops its positioning strategy.

Step 1: Establish Overall Strategy or Objectives

The first step in the segmentation process is to articulate the vision or the objectives of the company's marketing strategy clearly. The segmentation strategy must be consistent with and derived from the firm's mission and objectives, as well as its current situation—its strengths, weaknesses, opportunities, and threats (SWOT). L'Oreal's objective, for instance, is to increase sales in a declining industry. The company recognized its strengths were its brand name and its ability to place new products on retailers' shelves, but its primary weakness was that it didn't currently have a product line for the emerging market segments. Identifying this potentially large and profitable market segment before many of its mainstream competitors offered a great opportunity, though following through on that opportunity could lead to a significant threat: competitive retaliation. L'Oreal's choice to pursue environment and health conscious Americans thus is clearly consistent with its overall strategy and objectives.

Establishing a basic segmentation strategy is not always as easy and clear as it was for L'Oreal, however. Exhibit 8.2 illustrates several segmentation strategies. Sometimes it makes sense to not segment at all. In other situations, a firm should concentrate on one segment or go after multiple segments at once. Finally, some firms choose to specialize in their product or service line to meet the needs of very small groups—perhaps even one person at a time. We discuss each of these basic segmentation types next.

Undifferentiated Segmentation Strategy, or Mass Marketing   When everyone might be considered a potential user of its product, a firm uses an **undifferentiated segmentation strategy.** (See Exhibit 8.2 left.) If the product or service is perceived to provide the same benefits to everyone, there simply is no need to

EXHIBIT **8.2** Segmentation Strategies

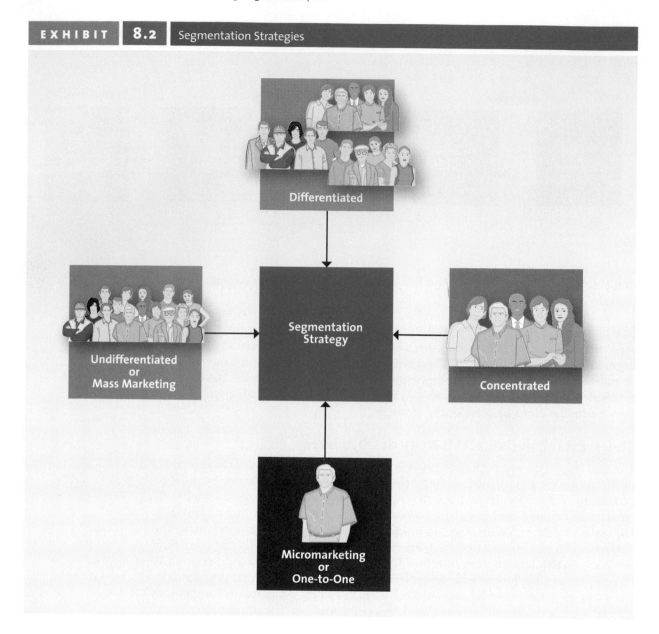

develop separate strategies for different groups. Although not a common strategy in today's complex marketplace, an undifferentiated strategy can be effective for very basic commodities, such as salt or sugar. However, even those firms that offer salt and sugar now are trying to differentiate their products.

An undifferentiated strategy also is common among smaller firms that offer products or services that consumers perceive to be indistinguishable, such as a neighborhood bakery. But again, more marketing-savvy entrepreneurs typically try to differentiate themselves in the marketplace. The corner bakery thus becomes "Le Croissant" or "Bagel Delight." By making their commodity-like products appear special, they add value for the customer and differentiate themselves from their competition.

What about gasoline? Everyone with a car needs it. Yet gasoline companies have vigorously moved from an undifferentiated strategy to a differentiated one by segmenting their market into low-, medium-, and high-octane gasoline users.

Differentiated Segmentation Strategy

Firms using a **differentiated marketing strategy** target several market segments with a different offering for each (see Exhibit 8.2 top). The Gap, for instance, employs three store formats—Banana Republic, The Gap, and Old Navy—to appeal to fashion-forward, traditional, and more price-sensitive segments, respectively. Beyond these three segments, The Gap has further differentiated the market into GapKids, babyGap, and GapBody.

Au Bon Pain (the place of good bread in French) is a national chain of bakeries found in urban and suburban crossroads, and even airports. They make their commodity-like products appear special by making them French.

In a similar fashion, adidas Group appeals to various segments through its various companies, including adidas Reebok, Rockport, and TaylorMade-adidas Golf lines of clothing and footwear.

Firms embrace differentiated segmentation because it helps them obtain a bigger share of the market and increase the market for their products overall. The more retail formats The Gap develops to reach different market segments, the more apparel and accessories it can and will sell. Offering several different shoe lines enables adidas to appeal to more potential customers than if it had just one line. Furthermore, providing products or services that appeal to multiple segments helps diversify the business and therefore lowers the company's overall risk. For example, if a line directed toward one segment is performing poorly, the impact on the firm's profitability can be offset by revenue from another line that continues to do well.

But a differentiated strategy can be expensive. Consider The Gap's investment in chinos alone. The firm must develop, manufacture, transport, store, and promote chinos separately for each of its store concepts.

rbk.com

The adidas Group uses a differentiated strategy to appeal to several markets with its adidas, Reebok, Rockport, and TaylorMade-adidas Golf brands. RbK, a division of Reebok, specializes in the fashion sneaker market.

Concentrated Segmentation Strategy

When an organization selects a single, primary target market and focuses all its energies on providing a product to fit that market's needs, it is using a **concentrated segmentation strategy** (see Exhibit 8.2 right). Entrepreneurial start-up ventures often benefit from using a concentrated strategy, which allows them to employ their limited resources more efficiently.

Have you ever shopped at Christopher & Banks?[2] Well, if you aren't 48 years old and the mother of two, live in a small town or the suburbs, and like polyester jumpers, flowered cardigans, and embroidered animals, then you aren't part of its target market. Christopher & Banks, a little-known chain of almost 500 stores that utilizes a very concentrated segmentation strategy, understands that its customers don't shop at The Gap, Chico's, or Ann Taylor.

To better understand its customers, Christopher & Banks asks women in focus groups where they eat, what cars they drive, and what their daily routines are. The responses have yielded some important insights. Customers want clothes that can be worn both at work and to a child's baseball game after work. To save time shopping, these women want merchandise that is designed to mix and match. Focus groups even look at photos of women and decide which one best represents the chain's target customer.

Firms like Lands' End are engaged in mass customization since they provide custom-made products to the masses.

Micromarketing[3]   Take a look at your collection of belts. Have you ever had one made to match your exact specifications? (If you're interested, try www.leather-goodsconnection.com.) When a firm tailors a product or service to suit an individual customer's wants or needs, it is undertaking an extreme form of segmentation called **micromarketing** or **one-to-one marketing** (see Exhibit 8.2 bottom). Small producers and service providers generally can tailor their offering to individual customers more easily, whereas it is far more difficult for larger companies to achieve this degree of segmentation. Nonetheless, companies like Dell and Lands' End have capitalized on Internet technologies to offer "custom-made" computers, dress shirts, chinos, and jeans. Firms that interact on a one-to-one basis with many people to create custom-made products or services are engaged in **mass customization,** providing one-to-one marketing to the masses.

Some consumers appreciate custom-made goods and services because they are made especially for them, which means they'll meet the person's needs exactly. But these products and services are typically more expensive than ready-made offerings and often take longer to obtain. For instance, you can get a pair of Lands' End chinos at Sears and wear them out of the store. The firm's custom chinos, in contrast, take three to four weeks to make and deliver.

The degree to which firms should segment their markets—from no segmentation to one segment to multiple segments to one-to-one segments—depends on the balance the firm wants to achieve between the added perceived customer value that segmentation can offer and its cost. Now let's take a look at how firms describe their segments.

Step 2: Describe Segments

The second step in the segmentation process is to describe the different segments, which helps firms better understand the profile of the customers in each segment,

EXHIBIT 8.3	Methods for Segmenting Markets
Segmentation Method	**Sample Segments**
Geographic	Continent: N. America, Asia, Europe, Africa Within U.S.: Pacific, mountain, central, south, mid-Atlantic, northeast
Demographic	Age, gender, income *, education, ethnicity*
Psychographic	Innovators, thinkers, achievers, experiencers, believers, strivers, makers, survivors
Benefits	Convenience, economy, prestige
Geodemographic	Urban, exurban, established, sophisticated townhouses, bohemians, affluent retirees
Loyalty	Not loyal, somewhat loyal, completely loyal

as well as the customer similarities within a segment and dissimilarities across segments. Soft-drink marketers, for instance, have broken up the carbonated beverage landscape into caffeinated or decaffeinated, regular (with sugar) or diet, and cola versus something else. This segmentation method is based on the benefits that consumers derive from the products.

As we see next, marketers also use geographic, demographic, psychographic, benefit, geodemographic, loyalty, and composite segmentation approaches. Examples of these are found in Exhibit 8.3.

Geographic Segmentation   **Geographic segmentation** organizes customers into groups on the basis of where they live. Thus, a market could be grouped by country (Germany, China), region (northeast, southeast), or areas within a region (state, city, neighborhoods, zip codes). Not surprisingly, geographic segmentation is most useful for companies whose products satisfy needs that vary by region.

Firms can provide the same basic goods or services to all segments even if they market globally or nationally, but better marketers make adjustments to meet the needs of smaller geographic groups. For instance, a national grocery store chain like Safeway or Albertson's runs similar stores with similar assortments in various locations across the United States. Within those similar stores though, a significant percentage of the assortment of goods will vary by region, city, or even neighborhood, depending on the different needs of the customers who surround each location.

Consider a new Super Saver store in Chicago, designed to cater specifically to the surrounding Hispanic neighborhood.[4] In the produce section, piles of shiny, green *pasilla* chiles sit beside paddle-shaped cactus leaves and bumpy, brown yucca roots. At the meat counter, a customer greets a clerk in Spanish and asks him to marinate some *arrachera* meat. Balloons in red, white, and green, the colors of the Mexican flag, decorate the grocery store, and pop star Marco Antonio Solis croons a love song over the piped-in music system.

Demographic Segmentation   **Demographic segmentation** groups consumers according to easily measured, objective characteristics such as age, gender, income, and education. These variables represent the most common means to define segments because they are easy to identify and because demographically segmented markets are easy to reach. For instance, if Kellogg's wants to advertise its Froot Loops cereal to kids, it easily determines that the best time for television

Firms like Gillette use an important demographic factor, gender, to sell different types of razors to men (Fusion ad on the left) and women (Venus ad on the right).

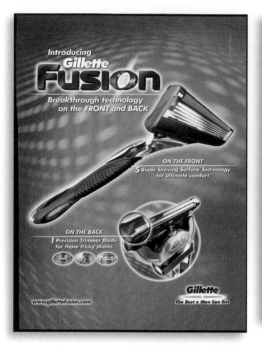

ads would be during cartoons shown on Saturday morning. By considering the viewer profiles of various TV shows, Kellogg's can find the ones that fit its target market's demographic profile.

One important demographic, gender, plays a very important role in how firms market products and services. For instance, TV viewing habits vary significantly between men and women. Men tend to channel surf—switching quickly from channel to channel—and watch primetime shows more often if they are action oriented and have physically attractive cast members. Women, in contrast, tend to view shows to which they can personally relate through the situational plot or characters and those recommended by friends.[5] Thus, a company like Gillette, which sells razors for both men and women, will consider the gender appeal of various shows when it buys advertising time on television.

However, demographics may not be useful for defining the target segments for other companies. For example, demographics are poor predictors of the users of activewear, such as jogging suits and athletic shoes. At one time, firms like Nike assumed that activewear would be purchased exclusively by young, active people, but the health and fitness trend has led people of all ages to buy such merchandise. Furthermore, relatively inactive consumers of all ages, incomes, and education find activewear more comfortable than traditional street clothes.

Psychographic Segmentation   Of the various methods for segmenting, or breaking down the market, **psychographics** is the one that delves into how consumers describe themselves. Usually marketers determine (through demographics, buying patterns, or usage) into which segment an individual consumer falls. But psychographics allows people to describe themselves using those characteristics that help them choose how they occupy their time (behavior) and what underlying psychological reasons determine those choices.[6] For example, a person might have a strong need for inclusion or belonging, which motivates him or her to seek out activities that involve others, which in turn influences the products he or she buys to fit in with the group. If a consumer becomes attached to a group that enjoys literary discussions, he or she is motivated to buy the latest books and spend time in stores such as Barnes & Noble. Such self-segmentation by the consumer could be very valuable knowledge for bookstore managers trying to find new ways of attracting customers. Determining psychographics involves knowing and understanding three components: self-values, self-concept, and lifestyles.

Self-values are goals for life, not just the goals one wants to accomplish in a day. In this context, they refer to overriding desires that drive how a person lives his or her life. Examples of self-value goals might include self-respect, self-fulfillment, or a sense of belonging. This motivating factor of psychographics enables people to develop self-images of how they want to be and then determine a way of life that will help them arrive at these ultimate goals. From a marketing point of view, the values help determine the benefits the target market may be looking for from a product. In this sense, the underlying, fundamental, personal need that pushes a person to seek out certain products or brands stems from his or her desire to fulfill a goal.

How does that underlying goal affect the individual? It does so through **self-concept,** or the image people have of themselves.[7] A person who has a goal to belong may see, or want to see, himself as a fun-loving, gregarious type whom people wish to be around. Marketers can make use of this image through communications that show their products being used by groups of laughing people who are having a good time. The connection emerges between the group fun and the product being shown and connotes a certain lifestyle.

Lifestyles, the third component of people's psychographic makeup, are the way we live.[8] If values provide an end goal and self-concept is the way one sees oneself in the context of that goal, lifestyles are how we live our lives to achieve goals. Someone with a strong sense of belonging who sees himself as a "people person" will probably live in a well-populated area that allows for many activities.

Marketers like Benetton want their ads to appeal to one's self-concept. "I'm like them, so I should buy their products."

Adding Value 8.1

Segmenting the Asthma Patient Market by Lifestyle

Consumer Health Sciences (CHS), a pioneer in offering consumer healthcare information to the pharmaceutical industry (http://www.chsinternational.com/), applied a lifestyle approach to segmenting the asthma patient market. As the chart below shows, it established five segments and differential strategies for reaching each.[9] For instance, because "Medical Buffs" trust doctors but also feel in control of their own health, they switch brands easily. So, to them, pharmaceutical firms must stress the superiority of their brand. To sustain the loyalty of this group, firms must develop strong relationships with these buffs.

CHS Asthma Patient Segmentation

Healthstyle Segment	Barriers to Adherence	Message for Patient	How to Reach
Disciples 20% ■ Trusting and highly compliant	Sometimes forget medication.	Reinforce physician's importance to managing treatment.	Traditional physician channels (physician is the audience).
Medical Buffs 23% ■ Strong adherents; trust doctors but feel in control of own health	Have strong brand ideas. First to switch to new brand—and first to switch to next.	Position treatment as patient–physician partnership. Stress superior efficacy of brand.	Heavy direct to consumer (DTC) appeals. Sustain brand loyalty through relationship marketing.
Naturalists 16% ■ Eschew pharmaceuticals in favor of holistic remedies	Distrust physicians and prescription medication. Anxious about side effects and long-term ramifications.	Position treatment as part of healthy living. Explain how drug works to assist body's natural function.	Guerilla marketing. Condition-specific Web site, nonbranded DTC ads.
Immortals 25% ■ Devil-may-care types; don't follow doctor's recommendations.	Ill informed and often in denial about condition and treatment options.	Deliver wake-up call. Clarify severity of condition and necessity of taking medication.	Patient-education materials via physician. Third-party service to make reminder calls.
Fatalists 19% ■ Feel health is out of their control; can't be counted on to comply	Feel hopeless, helpless. Not satisfied with healthcare. Resistant to taking prescription medication.	Convince them that with the physician's help, they can overcome symptoms.	Patient-education materials via physician. Third-party service to make reminder calls.

Source: Michael D. Lam, "Psychographic Demonstration," *Pharmaceutical Executive* 24, no. 1 (2004), pp. 78–82.

He likely will join clubs or partake in activities that attract like-minded people. Marketers thus have a built-in target group with similar interests and buying desires. An example of lifestyle segmentation is presented in Adding Value 8.1.

The most widely used psychographic tool is the **Value and Lifestyle Survey (VALS)**[10] conducted by SRI Consulting Business Intelligence. On the basis of their answers to the survey, consumers are classified into the eight segments in the two dimensions shown in Exhibit 8.4. On the vertical dimension, segments can be described by their resources, including their income, education, health, energy level, and degree of innovativeness. The upper segments have more resources and are more innovative; those on the bottom have fewer resources and are less innovative.

The horizontal dimension shows the segments' primary motivation. Consumers buy many products and services because of their primary motivations—that is, how they see themselves in the world and how that self-image governs their activities. The three universal primary motives are ideals, achievement, and self-expression. People who are primarily motivated by ideals are guided by knowledge and principles, whereas those who are motivated by achievement look for products and services that demonstrate success to their peers.

Firms are finding that psychographics are often more useful for predicting consumer behavior than are demographics. For instance, some college students and some day laborers may have similar demographics according to their income, but they spend that income quite differently because of their very different values and lifestyles.

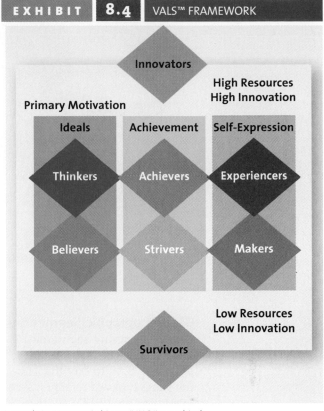

EXHIBIT 8.4 VALS™ FRAMEWORK

Source: http://www.sric-bi.com/VALS/types.shtml

There are limitations to using psychographic segmentation however. Psychographics are not as objective as demographics, and it is harder to identify potential customers. With demographics, for example, a firm like Nike can easily identify its customers as, say, men or women and then direct its marketing strategies to each group differently. It is much harder to identify and target thinkers versus makers. For these reasons, psychographic segmentation is often used in conjunction with other segmentation methods.[11]

Benefit Segmentation **Benefit segmentation** groups consumers on the basis of the benefits they derive from products or services. Because marketing is all about satisfying consumers' needs and wants, dividing the market into segments whose needs and wants are best satisfied by the product benefits can be very powerful. It is also relatively easy to portray a product's or service's benefits in the firm's communication strategies.

To illustrate benefit segmentation, consider Qoo, a ball-shaped character that dances across television screens in Japan, Korea, Taiwan, and Singapore, as well as a good-tasting health drink owned by Coca-Cola. The iconic Qoo character is a lovable yet mischievous symbol that reminds mothers of their own children while making children laugh. Using a benefit segmentation approach, Coca-Cola designed a product that parents would serve to their kids because it was healthy (the benefit) and their kids would drink because they loved the television character.

Using the VALS™ framework, it is a lot harder to identify "thinkers" (left) as opposed to "makers" (right) because "thinkers" are motivated by ideals, whereas "makers" are prompted to buy based on their need for self-expression.

Geodemographic Segmentation Because "birds of a feather flock together," **geodemographic segmentation** uses a combination of geographic, demographic, and lifestyle characteristics to classify consumers.[12] Consumers in the same neighborhoods tend to buy the same types of cars, appliances, and apparel and shop at the same types of retailers. Two of the most widely used tools for geographic segmentation are PRIZM (Potential Rating Index by Zip Market), developed by Claritas (www.claritas.com), and ESRI's (www.esri.com) Tapestry. Using detailed demographic data and information about the consumption and media habits of people who live in each U.S. block tract (zip code + 4), PRIZM can identify more than 60 geodemographic segments or neighborhoods, and Tapestry offers 65. Each block group then can be analyzed and sorted by more than 60 characteristics, including income, home value, occupation, education, household type, age, and several key lifestyle variables. The information in Exhibit 8.5 describes three PRIZM clusters.

Geodemographic segmentation can be particularly useful for retailers because customers typically patronize stores close to their neighborhood. Thus, retailers can use geodemographic segmentation to tailor each store's assortment to the preferences of the local community. This kind of segmentation is also useful for finding new locations; retailers identify their "best" locations and determine what type of people live in the area surrounding those stores, according to the geodemographic clusters. They can then find other potential locations where similar segments reside.

Loyalty Segmentation Firms have long known that it pays to retain loyal customers. Loyal customers are those who feel so strongly that the firm can meet their relevant needs best that any competitors are virtually excluded from their consideration; that is, these customers buy almost exclusively from the firm.[13] These loyal customers are the most profitable in the long term.[14] In light of the high cost of finding new customers and the profitability of loyal customers, today's companies are using **loyalty segmentation** and investing in retention and loyalty initiatives to retain their most profitable customers.

Airlines, for instance, definitely believe that all customers aren't created equal. At United Airlines, the customers who have flown the most miles with the

EXHIBIT 8.5	PRIZM CLUSTERS		
Cluster Name	**Boomtown Singles: Middle Income Young Singles**	**Hispanic Mix: Urban Hispanic Singles & Families**	**Gray Power: Affluent Retirees in Sunbelt Cities**
Description	This Cluster plays host to the youth of 100 fast-growing second cities in the south, Midwest, and west. They are young professionals and "techies" in public and private service industries who live in multiunit rentals, enjoy music, and vacation in the Caribbean.	This Cluster collects the nation's bilingual, Hispanic barrios, which are chiefly concentrated in the Atlantic metro corridor, Chicago, Miami, Texas, Los Angeles, and the southwest. These neighborhoods are populated by large families with many small children. They rank second in percentage of foreign-born members and are first in transient immigration.	This Cluster represents over two million senior citizens who have pulled up stakes and moved to the country or the Sunbelt to retire among their peers. Although these neighborhoods are found nationwide, almost half are concentrated in 13 retirement areas. They are health and golf fanatics with fat investment portfolios.
Age Groups	Under 24, 25–34	Under 24, 25–34	55–64, 65+

Source: http://www.tetrad.com/pcensus/usa/prizmlst.html#C1.

company, the "Premier Executive 1K," receive guaranteed reservations even on sold-out flights, priority check-in, special seating priorities, and priority waitlist status.[15] None of these special services are available to the occasional flyer.

Using Multiple Segmentation Methods   Although all segmentation methods are useful, each has its unique advantages and disadvantages. For example, segmenting by demographics and geography is easy because information about who the customers are and where they are located is readily available, but these characteristics don't help marketers determine their customer needs. Knowing what benefits customers are seeking or how the product or service fits a particular lifestyle is important for designing an overall marketing strategy, but such segmentation schemes present a problem for marketers attempting to identify specifically which customers are seeking these benefits. Thus, firms often employ a combination of segmentation methods, using demographics and geography to identify and target marketing communications to their customers, then using benefits or lifestyles to

Adding Value 8.2

Segmenting the Financial Services Market Using Demographics and Lifestyles[16]

LIMRA, a financial services research and consulting organization, surveyed its consumers to determine their personal financial objectives and the type of lifestyle they wanted when they retired. The survey yielded four identifiable segments for middle-income households, as described in the chart below.

Steve Hall is a financial consultant who is prospecting for new customers. What can he do with combined demographic and lifestyle LIMRA data? The demographic data can identify the type of people in a segment, how firms might reach these people through the media or other selling vehicles, and how profitable the segments may be. For instance, Steve has found a group of "Worker Bees" who are self-employed, over 40, and have relatively high incomes. The lifestyle data then can be used to help design products and promotional messages that are relevant to this group. For instance, Steve historically would study a customer's portfolio and his or her attitude toward taking financial risks before preparing a retirement package for that customer. But knowing the type of lifestyles to which these "Worker Bees" aspire when they retire enables the sales agent to better match customers' lifestyles and the financial planning process. Since the "Worker Bees" are very entrepreneurial and love to work, Steve designs a sales presentation that stresses how much money they need to save over the coming years to maintain their relatively modest lifestyle and enable them to continue to work as long as they wish or are physically able.

The financial services consulting firm, LIMRA targets four identifiable segments based on demographics and lifestyle data to best meet the needs of middle-income households getting ready to retire.

design the product or service and the substance of the marketing message. Adding Value 8.2 discusses how multiple segmentation methods can combine to develop a richer segmentation strategy for financial markets.

Step 3: Evaluate Segment Attractiveness

The third step in the segmentation process involves evaluating the attractiveness of the various segments. To undertake this evaluation, marketers first must determine whether the segment is worth pursuing using several descriptive criteria: Is the segment identifiable, substantial, reachable, responsive, and profitable (see Exhibit 8.6)?

Demographic and Retirement Lifestyle Segmentation for the Financial Services Market

	Pragmatic Planners	Worker Bees	Grand Thinkers	Status Quo
DEMOGRAPHIC CHARACTERISTICS	√ Single √ No dependent children √ Educated √ Moderate income √ Have discretionary income √ Under 45 years old	√ Couples √ Less formal education √ High income √ High investable assets √ Over 40 √ Self-employed	√ Couples √ Broad education levels √ Moderate incomes √ Broad age ranges	√ Couples √ With dependent children √ Less formal education √ Broad income range √ Over 40
PERCENTAGE OF MIDDLE-MARKET HOUSEHOLDS	30%	15%	34%	21%
RETIREMENT LIFESTYLE GOALS	√ Save to buy home √ Eliminate or reduce debt √ Save for retirement √ Maintain modest but comfortable standard of living √ Spend time with family √ Enjoy leisure activities	√ Start or expand business √ Save for retirement √ Maintain modest but comfortable living standard √ Start or run business √ Keep working in a capacity similar to today's	√ Save to buy home √ Protect family in case of death √ Eliminate or reduce debt √ Save for retirement √ Maintain modest but comfortable standard of living √ Spend time with family √ Enjoy leisure activities	√ Protect family in case of death √ Protect family in case of disability √ Eliminate or reduce debt √ Save for retirement √ Maintain modest but comfortable standard of living √ Spend time with family

Source: Pete Jacques, "Aspirational Segmentation," *LIMRA's MarketFacts Quarterly* 22 (Spring 2003), p. 2[0].

Identifiable Firms must determine who is within their market to be able to design products or services to meet their needs. It is equally important to ensure that the segments are distinct from one another because too much overlap between segments means that distinct marketing strategies aren't necessary to meet segment members' needs.

As noted earlier in this chapter, The Gap has identified several distinct segments to pursue. Recognizing that many of its core customers had families, The Gap opened GapKids and babyGap. Its research also indicated an opportunity to compete with The Limited Brands' Victoria's Secret in the women's intimate apparel market, so it opened GapBody. Finally, though The Gap is largely successful with middle-of-the-road customers, it was too expensive for some customers and

EXHIBIT **8.6** Evaluation of Segment Attractiveness

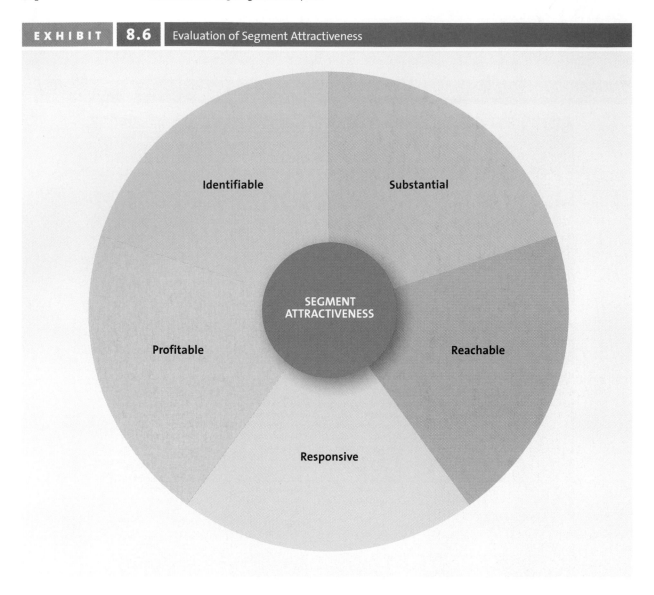

not fashion-forward enough for others. Its Old Navy and Banana Republic stores appeal better to these markets.

Substantial Once the firm has identified its potential target markets, it needs to measure their size. If a market is too small or its buying power insignificant, it won't generate sufficient profits or be able to support the marketing mix activities. Although The Gap had identified potential new target markets to pursue, it was imperative for the company to determine whether the market for women's intimate apparel was relatively small, in which case the company would fit the products into its regular stores. If the market was large, the products would require their own space. The Gap experimented cautiously with the new concept by first placing a section of intimate apparel in some of its stores. Over time, Gap managers realized the potential of the concept and began to roll out GapBody stores.

The Gap has identified several distinct segments to pursue. Two of its brands: Gap Kids (left) and Gap (right) appeal to different target markets.

Reachable   The best product or service cannot have any impact, no matter how identifiable or substantial the target market is, if that market cannot be reached (or accessed) through persuasive communications and product distribution. The consumer must know the product or service exists, understand what it can do for him or her, and recognize how to buy it.

Talbots, a chain of traditional apparel stores that also sells on the Internet and through catalogs, has a straightforward plan for reaching its target customers: college-educated women between 35 and 55 years of age with an average household income of $75,000 or more.[17] The company simply locates its new stores in places where it has gotten a lot of Internet and catalog business. Advertisements appear in media that are consistent with the lifestyle Talbots is trying to portray—traditional, conservative, and with good taste.

Firms trying to reach college students have a much more difficult time because students' media habits are quite diverse, and they generally are cynical about firms that try too hard to sell to them. High-end fashionable jeans companies, for instance, often underpromote their lines or promote them very subtly through traditional media because if their customers start to believe the brand is too mainstream, they won't buy it.

Responsive   For a segmentation strategy to be successful, the customers in the segment must react similarly and positively to the firm's offering. If, through the firm's distinctive competencies, it cannot provide products or services to that segment, it should not target it. For instance, suppose General Motors (GM) is considering introducing a line of cars to the large and very lucrative luxury car segment. People in this market are currently purchasing Ferraris, Porsches, BMWs, Audis, and top-of-the-line Lexuses. In contrast, GM has been somewhat successful competing for the middle-priced family-oriented car and light truck segments. (GM's Chevrolet Corvette is an exception.) Thus, though the luxury car segment meets all the other criteria for a successful segment, GM should not pursue it because the market probably will not be responsive to it.

Developing a market segmentation strategy over the Internet usually is somewhat easier than developing it for traditional channels. Adding Value 8.3 explains why.

Can GM be successful competing against Porsche, BMW, Audi, and Lexus?

Profitable   Marketers must also focus their assessments on the potential profitability of each segment, both current and future. Some key factors to keep in mind in this analysis include market growth (current size and expected growth rate), market competitiveness (number of competitors, entry barriers, product substitutes), and market access (ease of developing or accessing distribution channels and brand familiarity). Some straightforward calculations can help illustrate the profitability of a segment:[18]

Segment profitability = Segment size
    − Segment adoption percentage
    − Purchase behavior
    − Profit margin percentage
    − Fixed costs,

where

Segment size = Number of people in the segment.

Segment adoption percentage = Percentage of customers in the segment who are likely to adopt the product.

Purchase behavior = Purchase price × number of times the customer would buy the product ÷ service during a given time period.

Profit margin percentage = ((Selling price − variable costs) ÷ selling price).

Fixed costs = Fixed costs (e.g., advertising expenditure).

Several segments may appear to be equally profitable according to this formula. In some cases however, it is more accurate to evaluate the profitability of a segment over the lifetime of one of its typical customers. To address this issue, marketers consider factors such as how long the customer will remain loyal to the firm, the defection rate (percentage of customers who switch on a yearly basis), the costs of replacing lost customers (advertising, promotion), whether customers will buy more or more expensive merchandise in the future, and other such factors.[22]

Adding Value 8.3

Easy Does It with Internet-Based Segmentation[19]

Internet-based segmentation facilitates the implementation of segmentation strategies in several ways. First, it offers the possibility to cater to very small segments, sometimes as small as one customer at a time, very efficiently and inexpensively (e.g., mortgage and insurance sites that provide personalized quotes). A personalized Web site experience can be executed at a significantly lower cost than would be possible in other venues, such as in a retail store or over the phone, and sometimes even at negligible costs. For example, frequent fliers of American Airlines are able to check prices and choose special services online at a fraction of the cost that the company would incur for a phone or ticket counter interaction with an agent.[20]

Second, segmentation over the Internet simplifies the identification of customers and provides a great deal of information about them. Cookies, small text files a Web site places on a visitor's hard drive,[21] provide a unique identification of each potential customer who visits a Web site and detail how the customer has searched through the site. Marketers also can ask visitors to fill out an online registration form.

Third, through the Internet the company can make a variety of recommendations to customers on the basis of their site visit patterns and how they search the site. For example, Amazon.com and other e-tailers provide recommendations for related products to customers browsing and/or searching their site, which are based on matching their profiles to those of other customers. This tactic helps to boost sales of similar and complementary products.

Fourth, the marketing strategy can be customized in real time according to known data about the customer. For example, Staples can offer merchandise at different prices in different parts of the country by simply asking customers to enter their zip code.

However, the growth of Internet-based segmentation also has prompted increased consumer concerns and public policy mandates. Consumers are often worried about their privacy, especially when asked to identify themselves through site registrations or even by accepting cookies when visiting a site. Responding to both privacy concerns and industry self-regulations, most Internet sites now include privacy policies that clearly state what types of consumer information are collected and how that information is used. Consumers also are given a choice to "opt out" if they do not want their information shared with third parties or to be part of the firm's future marketing campaigns.

Although cookies themselves do not contain consumer-specific information, the use of consumer site visit information, along with data gathered from other sources, has potential legal consequences and may affect customer relationships. For example, when Amazon.com tried to offer different prices on the same day for certain DVDs, many observers criticized the practice as discrimination among consumer segments. Amazon argued that the price differences were the result of a pricing test being conducted; however, consumers and participants in chat forums like DVD Talk Forum disagreed. Many observers now contend that charging different prices to different customers is not bad as long as it is used to discount, rather than charge premium, prices.

For instance, Carhartt has been making rugged work clothes in the United States since 1889. Recently, a more affluent, urban, fashion-oriented customer has been attracted to the brand. Which of these two very different segments—buyers of traditional work clothes or fashion-forward consumers—will be more profitable to Carhartt in the long term? Even if the fashion-forward segment buys several of the more expensive items, Carhartt's appeal to that segment probably will be fleeting because these customers view their clothes as fashion rather than everyday work clothes.

Now that we've evaluated each segment's attractiveness (Step 3), we can select the target markets to pursue (Step 4.)

Which segment will be more profitable to Carhartt in the long run, a more fashion-forward segment inspired by movie stars like Tom Cruise in War of the Worlds *(left), or its traditional market for rugged work clothes (right)?*

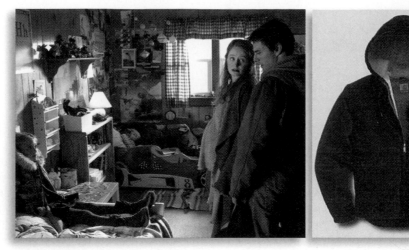

Step 4: Select Target Market

The fourth step in the STP process is selecting a target market. The key factor likely to affect this decision is the marketer's ability to pursue such an opportunity or target segment. Thus, as we mentioned in Chapter 2, a firm is likely to assess both the attractiveness of the opportunity (opportunities and threats based on the SWOT analysis, profitability of the segment) and its own competencies (strengths and weaknesses based on SWOT analysis) very carefully.

What could be a more undifferentiated market segment strategy than greeting cards? After all, they are available in grocery stores, discount stores, drug stores, and specialty card stores. Ninety percent of U.S. households purchase at least one greeting card per year. Everyone needs greeting cards from time to time, right? Then how does Hallmark, the U.S.'s largest greeting card company with more than $4.4 billion in annual sales and a brand recognized around the globe, segment its market?[23]

First, using a geographic segmentation strategy, Hallmark is continuing its global expansion, particularly to India and China. Also, it is using a benefit segmentation strategy by targeting those seeking the convenience of sending a card over the Internet. The industry was worried that e-cards, which are generally free, would negatively affect traditional card sales, but in fact the availability of e-cards has helped to boost sales. Hallmark.com has a link on its home page for Free-Cards to promote its brand name via the Internet. Internet users are exposed to traditional advertising, and Hallmark can sell and promote its movies made for the Hallmark Channel and sell gifts ornaments and other popular personal expression items. Exhibit 8.7 provides an illustration of how a firm like Hallmark might match its competencies with the attractiveness of various alternative segments and use this process to pick the best fit.

Sometimes firms' target market selection also can raise serious ethical concerns. Ethical Dilemma 8.1 examines the issue of marketing certain foods to children.

Step 5: Identify and Develop Positioning Strategy

The last step in developing a market segmentation strategy is positioning. Market positioning involves a process of defining the marketing mix variables so that target customers have a clear, distinctive, desirable understanding of what the product does or represents in comparison with competing products. This strategy can

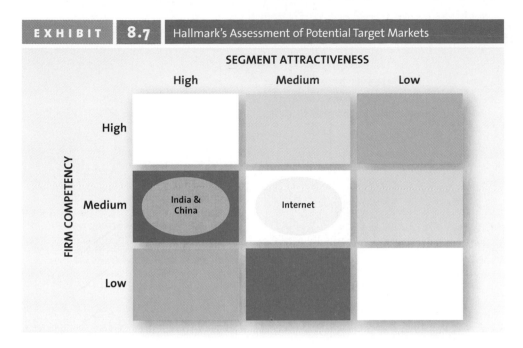

EXHIBIT 8.7 | Hallmark's Assessment of Potential Target Markets

be realized by communicating particular messages in persuasive communications and through different media.

Positioning strategies generally focus on either how the product or service affects the consumer or how it is better than competitors' products and services. When positioning against competitors, the objective is to play up how the brand being marketed provides the desired benefits better than do those of competitors. Firms thus position their products and services according to value, salient attributes, and symbols, and against competition (see Exhibit 8.8).

Value   Value is a popular positioning method because the relationship of price to quality is among the most important considerations for consumers when they make a purchase decision. Value positioning may open up avenues to attract new customer segments that the company previously had neglected. For example, while Proctor & Gamble's (P&G's) competitors, such as Unilever and Colgate, found success with lower-priced "value" products like Suave shampoo and Alberto VO5, P&G seemed to ignore that 80 percent of the world could not afford its products. In an attempt to correct this oversight, P&G company managers are now working globally to understand "price-sensitive customers" in various regions and sharing strategies to promote P&G products. For example, they've taken flagship products like Ivory soap and dropped the price 10–15 percent below that of rivals such as Dial. Moreover, once struggling premium products, like Daily Defense shampoo, have been relaunched at prices below 99 cents. Although the strategy hasn't yielded big numbers yet, it has slowed the market growth of competitive brands.[25]

Salient Attributes   One of the most common positioning strategies focuses on the product attributes that are most important to the target market. Volvo, the car company traditionally positioned for the safety-conscious driver, wants to stretch its safety image to one focused on driving performance and excitement. The company expects the positioning adjustment to be a long and concentrated effort, because so many of Volvo's boxier vehicles remain on the road today, which reinforces its more

EXHIBIT **8.8** Positioning Strategies

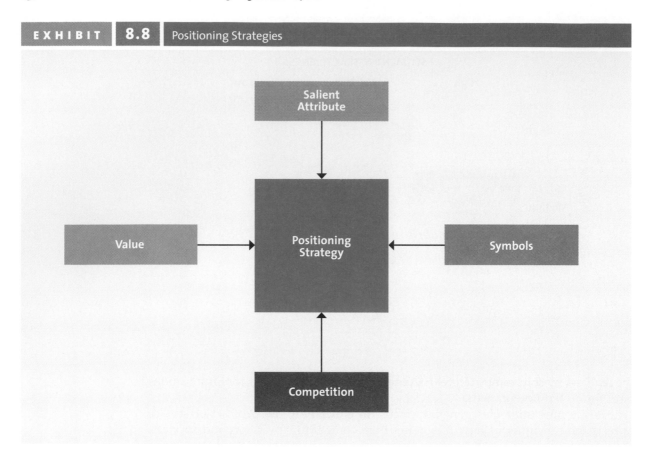

conservative image. Volvo's goal is not to abandon the safety notions associated with the brand but rather to expand its image to compete with other top luxury brands.[26] In a salient attributes success story, Nantucket Nectars was able to compete in the highly competitive beverage market by attracting a target market that wants quality and innovative drinks. (See Entrepreneurial Marketing 8.1.)

Can Volvo reposition its cars to be more exciting with higher performance without losing its traditional position that appeals to safety-conscious drivers?

Symbol A well-known symbol can also be used as a positioning tool. What comes to mind when you think of Colonel Sanders, the Jolly Green Giant, the Gerber Baby, or Tony the Tiger? Or consider the Texaco star, the Nike swoosh,

Ethical Dilemma 8.1 The Junk Food Wars[24]

The global rise in obesity among children has led to intense scrutiny of high fat, salt, sugar (HFSS) food products producers that pursue the market segment of young consumers. For example, carbonated soft drinks are an extremely popular product; average annual consumption reaches approximately 400 cans per person. Yet the nonprofit Center for Science in the Public Interest (CSPI) has labeled these products "liquid candy."

The CSPI recently called for new labeling requirements on HFSS foods so that consumers would realize that their overconsumption can contribute to a variety of health concerns, including obesity, diabetes, tooth decay, and osteoporosis, though CSPI is just one of many organizations now demanding changes or limitations in the way food is marketed, especially by targeting children.

Food marketers, grocers, and restaurant managers must now decide how to contend with the charges that their products contribute to public health problems. In response, many manufacturers have begun altering their product mix to focus on the health benefits of their products. For instance, General Mills has changed all of its cereals to whole grains, including its Trix and Lucky Charms children's brand cereals. Kraft Foods has identified products that it believes are nutritionally sound and grouped them together under the umbrella of its "Sensible Solutions" program. Sensible Solutions products are the only ones that will be targeted toward children and advertised during children's traditional viewing hours. Traditional Kraft favorites such as Oreos, Lunchables, and some Post cereals will not appear in ads during those times. In addition, Kraft is expanding its traditional lines with healthier sugar-free versions, such as sugar-free double chocolate and caramel creamy pudding, and vitamin fortified SuperMac & Cheese.

Whether these changes will have any impact on the complex problem of obesity in general and childhood obesity in particular is unknown. The dilemma for marketers is to choose between serving a viable target market with products that have been successful and are desired or to radically alter those products and how they are marketed to address the concerns expressed by CSPI and others.

or the Ralph Lauren polo player. These symbols are so strong and well known that they create a position for the brand that distinguishes it from its competition. Many such symbols are registered trademarks that are legally protected by the companies that developed them.

Competition   Firms can choose to position their products or services against a specific competitor or an entire product/service classification. For instance, 7-Up positioned its product as "the Uncola" to differentiate it from caramel-colored cola beverages like Pepsi and Coke. Goodrich tires were promoted as "the other guys," or the ones without the blimp, to set them apart from Goodyear tires. Marketers must be careful, however, that they don't position their product too closely to their competition. If, for instance, their package or logo looks too much like a competitor's, they might be opening themselves up to a trademark infringement lawsuit. For example, numerous store brands have been challenged for having packaging confusingly similar to that of national brands. Similarly, McDonald's sues anyone who uses the "Mc" prefix including McSleep Inns and McDental Services even though in the latter case there was little possibility that consumers would believe the fast food restaurant company would branch out into dental services. On the other hand, courts have allowed parody jeans for full figured women to be sold under the Lardasche label, despite the objections of Jordache jeans.

Entrepreneurial Marketing 8.1

Tom and Tom, the Juice Guys

Sometimes the best product ideas are happy accidents, as in the case of Nantucket Nectars.[27] Two friends, Tom First and Tom Scott, met at Brown University in 1985. After graduation, they moved to Nantucket, a small island off the coast of Massachusetts, determined not to take traditional jobs but still be successful. They began a company called Allserve, a floating convenience store catering to the needs of boaters in the harbor. One night in 1989, the Toms were messing around with a blender and various fruit combinations, trying to imitate a peach nectar drink they had enjoyed in Spain. Eventually, they hit upon a few winning combinations and decided to call their new products Nantucket Nectars. They realized there was a significant market segment looking for drinks that are innovative and use only the finest ingredients. The juice market is expected to grow over 1.5 percent annually through 2010 and nectar juices, which contain 30-99 percent real fruit juice, make up 8.3 percent of the total market.[28]

Tom and Tom began selling their juices through Allserve and, as they realized they had a big hit on their hands, soon decided to focus primarily on Nantucket Nectars. The first few years were difficult because quality ingredients cost more, which stretched their finances very thin. But the Toms were not willing to compromise on quality and maintained a positioning strategy of providing only top-quality juices. As the product line grew and sales increased, they decided to expand their market beyond Nantucket and distributed it in Washington, DC, and Boston. Their commitment to quality ultimately paid off; Nantucket Nectars kept growing.

The product line still focuses on using only top-quality ingredients but has expanded to include teas,

Solid marketing and entrepreneurship paid off for Tom and Tom. They sold Nantucket Nectars to Cadbury Schweppes in 2002.

organic blends of juices, and calcium-enhanced products. In 2002, with its $59 million in annual net sales, Tom and Tom sold Nantucket Nectars to the American division of Cadbury Schweppes for an undisclosed amount. They were able to develop products that appealed to a very lucrative segment of the packaged drink market. Their focused position to serve this market paid off. Not bad for two guys with a boat and a good idea.

The health conscious market is expected to continue to grow. In 2005 the U.S. Government Department of Agriculture's food pyramid was redesigned to call for more fresh fruits and vegetables.[29] A number of publicized studies argue that fresh fruits and vegetables can help prevent many health risks. Nantucket Nectars offers a variety of healthy choices including organic, 100 percent juice and light carbonated drinks to appeal to the healthier drinking trend.[30]

Now that we have identified the various methods by which firms position their products and services, we discuss the actual stages they go through in establishing that position.

Positioning Stages

When developing a positioning strategy, firms go through five important stages. Before you read about these stages though, examine Exhibit 8.9, a hypothetical perceptual map of the soft drink industry in the United States. A **perceptual map** displays, in two or more dimensions, the position of products or brands in the consumer's mind. We have chosen two dimensions for illustrative purposes: strong versus light taste (vertical) and fun versus healthy (horizontal). Also, though this industry is quite complex, we have simplified the diagram to include only a few players in the market. The position of each brand is denoted by a small circle, and the numbered asterisks denote consumers' **ideal points**—where a particular market segment's ideal product would lie on the map.

To derive a perceptual map such as this, marketers follow five steps.

1. **Determine consumers' perceptions and evaluations of the product or service in relation to competitors'.** Marketers determine their brand's position by asking consumers a series of questions about their and competitors' products. For instance, they might ask how the consumer uses the existing product or services, what items the consumer regards as alternative sources to satisfy his or her needs, what the person likes or dislikes about the brand in relation to competitors, and what might make that person choose one brand over another.

2. **Identify competitors' positions.** When the firm understands how its customers view its brand relative to competitors', it must study how those same competitors position themselves. For instance, POWERade ("Liquid Hydration") positions itself closely to Gatorade ("Is It In You?"), which means they appear next to each other on the perceptual map and appeal to target market 3. They are also often found next to each other on store shelves, are similarly priced, and are viewed by customers as sports drinks. Gatorade also knows that its sports drink is perceived to be more like POWERade than like its own Propel Fitness Water (located near target market 4), Coca-Cola (target market 1), or Sunkist orange juice (target market 2).

| EXHIBIT | 8.9 | Perceptual Map for U.S. Soft Drink Industry |

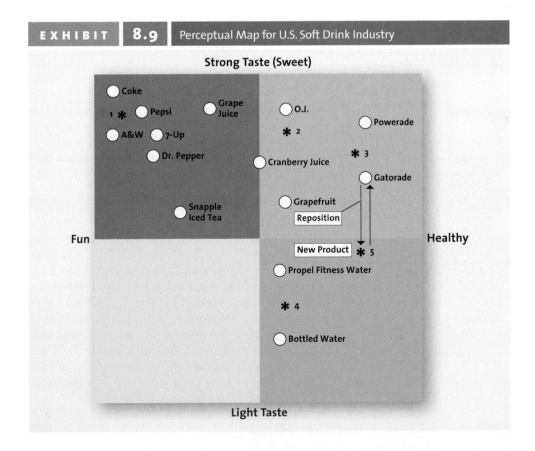

3. **Determine consumer preferences.** The firm knows what the consumer thinks of the products or services in the marketplace and their positions relative to one another. Now it must find out what the consumer really wants, that is, determine the "ideal" product or service that appeals to each market. For example, a huge market exists for traditional Gatorade, and that market is shared by POWERade. Gatorade also recognizes a market, depicted as the ideal product for segment 5 on the perceptual map, of consumers who would prefer a less sweet, less calorie-laden drink that offers the same rejuvenating properties as Gatorade. Currently, no product is adequately serving market 5.

4. **Select the position.** Continuing with the Gatorade example, the company has three choices to appeal to the "less sweet sports drink" target market 5. It could develop a new product to meet the needs of market 5. Alternatively, it could adjust or reposition its marketing approach—its product and promotion—to sell original Gatorade to market 5 (arrow pointing down from Gatorade to the ideal point for segment 5). Finally, it could ignore what target market 5 really wants and hope that consumers will be attracted to the original Gatorade because it is closer to their ideal product than anything else on the market (arrow pointing up from the ideal point for segment 5 to Gatorade).

5. **Monitor the positioning strategy.** Markets are not stagnant. Consumers' tastes shift, and competitors react to those shifts. Attempting to maintain the same position year after year can spell disaster for any company. Thus, firms must always view the first three steps of the positioning process as ongoing, with adjustments made in step four as necessary.

Has Chrysler repositioned its brand as a premium car without a premium price tag.

Repositioning

Sometimes firms try to change their positioning. For example, can Chrysler position itself as a premium product without a premium price tag? The car manufacturer seems to think so, moving away from its previous "Drive + Love" campaign that featured singer Celine Dion and into new ads that focus on features and benefits, alongside the suggested base price.

Chrysler is hoping to revive founder Walt Chrysler's 1924 philosophy: "I want to build a better-engineered car that outperforms my competition at half or a third of the price." Chrysler sales representatives are banking on building on the quality name offered by its parent company, Mercedes. The recent Chrysler 300 and Dodge Magnum use Mercedes-Benz parts, including their automatic transmissions and electronic stability control systems. Although Chrysler believes that its cars should speak for themselves, a little Mercedes name-dropping from the local affiliates seems to add some nice credibility to the overall product.[31] Most analysts agree, however, that it will take more than one product (Chrysler started its strategy with the Pacifica) to reposition Chrysler as a premium value supplier. Others also question whether people will actually believe a higher quality product can be cheaper than cars positioned in an identical fashion.

What do you think? Has Chrysler achieved its objective of being viewed as a premium car without a premium price tag?

Summing Up

1. How does a firm decide what type of segmentation strategy to use—undifferentiated, differentiated, concentrated, or micromarketing?

Most firms use some form of segmentation strategy. An undifferentiated strategy is really no segmentation at all and only works for products or services that most consumers consider to be commodities. The difference between a differentiated and a concentrated strategy is that the differentiated approach targets multiple segments, whereas the concentrated targets only one. Larger firms with multiple product/service offerings generally use a differentiated strategy; smaller firms or those with a limited product/service offering often use a concentrated strategy. Firms that employ a micromarketing or one-to-one marketing strategy tailor their product/service offering to each customer—that is, it is custom made. In the past, micromarketing was reserved primarily for artisans, tailors, or other craftspeople who would make items exactly as the customer wanted. Recently however, larger manufacturers and retailers have begun experimenting with custom-made merchandise as well. Service providers, in contrast, are largely accustomed to customizing their offering. Hair salons could not flourish if every customer got the same cut.

2. What is the best method of segmenting a market?

There is really no one "best" method to segment a market. Firms choose from various methods on the basis of the type of product/service they offer and their goals for the segmentation strategy. For instance, if the firm wants to identify its customers easily, geographic or demographic segmentation likely will work best. But if it is trying to dig deeper into why customers might buy its offering, then lifestyle, benefits, or loyalty segmentation work best. Geodemographic segmentation provides a nice blend of geographic, demographic, and psychographic approaches. Typically, a combination of several segmentation methods is most effective.

3. How do firms determine whether a segment is attractive and therefore worth pursuing?

Marketers use several criteria to assess a segment's attractiveness. First, the customer should be *identifiable*—companies must know what types of people are in the market so they can direct their efforts appropriately. Second, the market must be *substantial* enough to be worth pursuing. If relatively few people appear in a segment, it is probably not cost effective to direct special marketing mix efforts toward them. Third, the market must be *reachable*—the firm must be able to reach the segment through effective communications and distribution. Fourth, the firm must be *responsive* to the needs of customers in a segment. It must be able to deliver a product or service that the segment will embrace. Finally, the segment must be *profitable*, both in the near term and over the lifetime of the customer.

4. What is positioning, and how do firms do it?

Positioning is the "P" in the STP (segmentation, targeting, and positioning) process. It refers to how customers think about a product, service, or brand in the market relative to competitors' offerings. Firms position their products and services according to several criteria. Some focus on their offering's *value*—customers get a lot for what the product or service costs. Others determine the most *important attributes* for customers and position their offering on the basis of those attributes. The product's *use* can offer another positioning method. Cars, for example, can be positioned all the way from basic transportation (Toyota Corolla) to pure luxury (Bentley Continental). Symbols can also be used for positioning, though few products or services are associated with symbols that are compelling enough to drive people to buy. Finally, one of the most common positioning methods relies on the favorable comparison of the firm's offering with the products or services marketed by competitors.

Key Terms

- benefit segmentation, 219
- concentrated segmentation strategy, 213
- demographic segmentation, 215
- differentiated marketing strategy, 213
- geodemographic segmentation, 220

- geographic segmentation, 215
- ideal point, 233
- lifestyles, 217
- loyalty segmentation, 220
- mass customization, 214
- micromarketing, 214
- one-to-one marketing, 214
- perceptual map, 232

- psychographics, 216
- self-concept, 217
- self-values, 217
- undifferentiated segmentation strategy (mass marketing), 211
- Value and Lifestyle Survey (VALS), 218

Marketing Applications

1. You have been asked to identify various strategies for segmenting a market, which then will be used to choose one strategy for your sporting goods shop. List and discuss each of the overall strategies that can be used to develop a segmentation approach. Provide an example of each of the four strategies the sporting goods shop might use.

2. What overall segmentation strategy would you suggest for a small entrepreneur starting his own business? Justify why you would recommend that particular approach.

3. The concept of "mass customization" seems like a contradiction in terms. How and why would a retailer use mass customization?

4. A number of methods are used to segment markets. Identify the typical customer for each of the six methods discussed in the text.

5. You have been asked to evaluate the attractiveness of a group of identified potential market segments. What criteria will you use to evaluate those segments? Why are these appropriate criteria?

6. A small-business owner is trying to evaluate the profitability of different segments. What are the key factors you would recommend she consider? Over what period of time would you recommend she evaluate?

7. Think about the various hotel brands that you know (e.g., Marriott, Holiday Inn, Super 8). How do those various brands position themselves in the market?

8. Put yourself in the position of an entrepreneur who is developing a new product to introduce into the market. Briefly describe the product. Then, develop the segmentation, targeting, and positioning strategy for marketing the new product. Be sure to discuss (a) the overall strategy, (b) characteristics of the target market, (c) why that target market is attractive, and (4) the positioning strategy. Provide justifications for your decisions.

9. Think of a specific company or organization that uses various types of promotional material to market its offerings. (The Web, magazine ads, newspaper ads, catalogs, newspaper inserts, direct mail pieces, and flyers might all be sources for a variety of promotional materials.) Locate two or three promotional pieces for the company and use them as a basis to analyze the segment(s) being targeted. Describe the basic segmentation strategy reflected in these materials, and describe characteristics of the target market according to the materials. Be sure to include a copy of all the materials used in the analysis.

10. You have been hired recently by a large bank in its credit card marketing division. The bank has relationships with a large number of colleges and prints a wide variety of credit cards featuring college logos, images, and the like. You have been asked to oversee the implementation of a new program targeting the freshman class at the schools with which the bank has a relationship. The bank has already purchased the names and home addresses of the incoming freshman class. You have been told that no credit checks will be required for these cards as long as the student is over 18 years of age. The bank plans a first day of school marketing blitz that includes free hats, t-shirts, and book promotions, as well as free pizza, if the students simply fill out an application. Do you think it is a good idea to offer this program to these new students?

Toolkit

MARKET POSITION MAP ANALYSIS

Assume you are a brand manager for a major manufacturer. You have identified a number of market segments and are trying to understand how its products are positioned relative to other manufacturers'. Use the toolkit provided at www.mhhe.com/grewal-levy to conduct a Market Position Analysis.

Net Savvy

1. Go to the "My Best Segments" portion of the Claritas Web site, www.mybestsegments.com. Click on the tab that says "ZIP CODE LOOKUP," then enter your zip code to learn which segments are the top five in your zip code. Follow the links for each of the five most common PRIZM segments to obtain a segment description. Write up a summary of your results. Discuss the extent to which you believe these are accurate descriptions of the main segments of people who reside in your zip code.

2. Go to the SRI Consulting Business Intelligence Web site (http://www.sric-bi.com/VALS/presurvey.shtml), and click on the link to complete the VALS survey. After you submit your responses, a screen will display your primary and secondary VALS types. Click on the colored names of each segment to get additional information about them, and print out your results. Assess the extent to which these results reflect your lifestyle, and identify which characteristics accurately reflect your interests and activities and which do not.

Chapter Case Study

SODEXHO USA:[32] MASS CUSTOMIZATION IN THE COLLEGE FOOD SERVICE MARKET

In May 2004, Sodexho USA, the foodservice provider at Northwestern University, kicked off its second annual Global Chef program, a month-long international culinary residency that brings Sodexho chefs from around the world to the United States. During the event, Northwestern students were able to sample Indian dishes such as kabob, jinka tikka (grilled jumbo prawn with Indian spices), chicken tikka makhani, and kashmiri pulav rice (steamed rice with mixed dried fruits). Chef Placid Gomes, Sodexho's top chef in Oman, worked with local chefs and prepared the authentic Indian cuisine for students, faculty, and staff so that Sodexho could offer them a taste of authentic international cuisine.

Company Background

Sodexho USA, part of the Sodexho Alliance, is the leading provider of food and facilities management in the United States. With $5.8 billion in annual revenues and 110,000 employees, the company provides more than 1,800 organizations nationwide with food service. It offers customers a wide variety of products and services that range from large corporations to educational facilities to zoos and aquariums to the U.S. Marine Corp. The company prides itself on mass customization of its menus, which enables clients to design dining experiences that meet their needs. In particular, it has determined it can segment its college market to achieve happier customers.

Serving the College Market

Sodexho USA's Campus Services Division operates three distinct programs: one for college students using residential dining facilities, another for on-campus restaurants, and a third for its catering services. Through these programs, the company offers a broad range of service

Sodexho Campus Service segments its college market into six groups based on lifestyle characteristics.

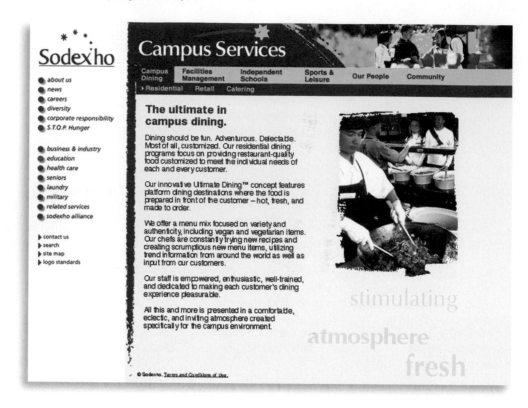

styles, price points, and menu selections, with customizable options to suit the needs of different groups.

Its food offerings are more than your standard college fare. Students on campuses served by Sodexho USA might enjoy roast beef with caramelized onions on a baguette or shrimp jambalaya with jalapeno cornbread rather than pita pockets and turkey sandwiches. The company's campus programs deliver international menus through a variety of ethnic food stations, bistro cuisine, and the Global Chef program.

These innovative food programs are the result of extensive research into student dining trends and preferences and are designed to better serve the company's foodservice markets. Realizing that customer segmentation would be an invaluable tool in this endeavor, Sodexho embarked on a strategy to isolate and understand different market segments. As a foundation for its research efforts, Sodexho started with secondary research from syndicated sources. It accessed the Student Monitor's Lifestyle and Media Survey, which identifies student trends and lifestyles, and partnered with Claritas. After gaining important insights from this research, marketers at Sodexho developed and administered questionnaires to thousands of students to learn more about their specific preferences, such as portion sizes, tastes, brands, price, and dining atmosphere.

These research efforts yielded some very useful results. One proprietary tool from these efforts, LifeSTYLING, allows the company to segment its markets using student zip codes. Life-STYLING has identified six unique segments: Metro Fusion, Main Streamers, Fun Express, Time Liners, Dream Catchers, and Trend Setters. Each segment has its own lifestyle characteristics that influence the consumers' preferences for menu items, specific brands, times they want to eat, and marketing materials. (See Exhibit C8.1.) Sodexho relies on this market information to customize the products and dining venues it offers to suit the specific tastes of different segments.

The company has found this segmentation approach useful in a variety of college settings. As Glenn Kvidahl, director of Indiana State University's dining services, describes:[34]

EXHIBIT c8.1	Sodexho's LifeSTYLING Segments[33]	
Segment	Characteristics	Budget
Metro Fusion	Value-conscious, convenience-driven Prefer ethnic and innovative food Seek new menu tastes such as vegan or sushi	Low
Main Streamers	Price- and value-driven Into comfort foods Quantity is important Prefer traditional food Prefer national fast-food brands	Low
Fun Express	Want variety Interested in ethnic foods Prefer innovative food Crave new, cutting-edge experiences	Medium
Time Liners	Convenience-oriented Prefer traditional foods Enjoy fast-food and value meals	Medium
Dream Catchers	Brand-conscious Spend more for what they want Enjoy active, fun, and healthy lifestyle Prefer ethnic, innovative, and traditional foods	Medium/High
Trend Setters	Seek authentic/unique experiences Look for cultural experiences Prefer ethnic and innovative food Image-conscious and high-end spenders	High

Through that research, they found that about 24 percent of the population at Indiana State are trend setters. They're a little more adventuresome in their tastes. They may like bagels but not plain bagels. They would rather have jalapeño bagels or blueberry scones. They like food with a twist—authentic pastas and sauces, vegetarian dishes. In the Commons, we didn't have a lot to attract that group. What we're trying to do with the Global Market Café is appeal to the trend setters.

At Sodexho, understanding the needs of different customer segments is part of everyday business. And that everyday business has proved a successful venture for both the company and the college students it serves.

Questions

1. Describe the type of segmentation strategy Sodexho uses to serve the college foodservice market. Provide support for your answer.

2. Why would a company like Sodexho go to the trouble of using these techniques to serve a captive market like college students? Can Sodexho be successful in using this mass customization approach?

3. Describe some of your experiences as a student with foodservice providers on college campuses. If your campus uses Sodexho, evaluate its performance relative to the description provided in the case. If your university does not use Sodexho, do you think that Sodexho would provide better value than the foodservice providers you have encountered?

9

Marketing Research and Information Systems

A s one of the largest casino operators in the world, Harrah's Entertainment runs more than 50 casinos in 13 states and five countries under a variety of brand names. Its facilities typically include hotel and convention space, restaurants, and entertainment facilities.[1] The company has another type of facility as well: It collects a vast amount of information about its millions of customers' preferences and gaming activities.

In a move to provide greater value to customers, thereby encouraging them to spend a greater portion of their time and money at its casinos, Harrah's assigned its managers to comb through this collected information using sophisticated analytical techniques called data mining. Contrary to the conventional wisdom, what they found when they looked at the data wasn't that the high rollers had the greatest lifetime value; it was average, middle-aged working people and seniors, like school teachers, machinists, and bankers, who meant the most to Harrah's bottom line. Analysis of the data revealed that these customers, who represent 26 percent of Harrah's customer base, bring in the lion's share (82 percent) of its revenues.

Then the analysis revealed that these customers weren't interested in the typical gaming incentives, like free rooms, food, and nongaming entertainment. So Harrah's developed a three-tiered incentive program that provides different levels of service to different customer segments, designated according to their level of play as Total Gold, Total Platinum, or Total Diamond program players. Customers can earn reward credits toward vacations, sporting events, and merchandise, but they also get more of what they want, namely, better service through shorter waits in line. While competing casino opera-

tors are trying to lure in customers by adding amenities like luxury spas, upscale shopping centers, and fabulous shows, Harrah's is garnering a very loyal following by catering to those who prefer to drop by after work to play the slots. The Total Gold customers must stand in regular lines at the reception desk and restaurants, whereas Total Platinum customers are directed into shorter lines, and the privileged Total Diamond customers bypass most lines altogether. The entire three-tier promotion, of course, was made very conspicuous, which made customers more interested in rising to the higher tiers. Harrah's use of marketing research was a real winner! With the recent acquisition of Caesars Entertainment Inc., Harrah's will have plenty of opportunity to expand its Total Rewards Program, customer information database and, of course, its revenue.[2]

Data mining techniques revealed that Harrah's most profitable customers were average middle aged working people and seniors like 84 year old Josephine Crawford who won more than $10 million at a Harrah's slot machine in Atlantic City, New Jersey.

■ ■ ■

As the Harrah's example shows, **marketing research** is a key prerequisite to successful decision making; it consists of a set of techniques and principles for systematically collecting, recording, analyzing, and interpreting data that can aid decision makers involved in marketing goods, services, or ideas.[3] When marketing managers attempt to develop their strategies, marketing research can provide valuable information that will help them make segmentation, positioning, product, place, price, and promotion decisions.

Firms invest billions of dollars in marketing research every year. For instance, as the largest U.S.-based marketing research firm, VNUNU earns annual worldwide revenues of almost 3 billion dollars.[4] Why do marketers find this research valuable? First, it helps reduce some of the uncertainty under which they constantly operate. Successful managers know when research might help their decision making and then take appropriate steps to acquire the information they need. Second, marketing research provides a crucial link between firms and their environments, which enables them to be customer oriented because they build their strategies using customer input and continual feedback. Third, by constantly monitoring their competitors, firms can respond quickly to competitive moves.

Politicians and not-for-profit organizations do research to understand their constituencies.

If you think market research is only applicable to corporate or retailing ventures, think again. Not-for-profit organizations and governments also use research to serve their constituencies better. The political sector has been slicing and dicing the voting public for decades to determine relevant messages for different demographics. Politicians desperately want to understand who makes up the voting public to determine how

to reach them. But not only do they want to know your political views; they also want to understand your media habits, such as what magazines you subscribe to, so they can target you more effectively.[5]

In this chapter, we examine how marketing information systems create value for firms and their customers. We also discuss some of the ethical implications of using the information marketing information systems collect, followed by a discussion of the overall marketing research process.

Using Marketing Information Systems to Create Better Value

In today's networked business world, marketers use increasingly sophisticated methods of gathering and employing marketing information to help them provide greater value to customers. A **marketing information system (MkIS)** is a set of procedures and methods that apply to the regular, planned collection, analysis, and presentation of information that then may be used in marketing decisions. An MkIS provides a means to accumulate information from sources both internal and external to the organization for the purpose of making it routinely available to managers for their more informed decision making. For example, Loews Cineplex, one of the largest movie theater chains in the world, contracted with Siebel, a leading provider of multichannel e-business applications software, to develop a system for selling group tickets at a discount to U.S. corporations, which they can use as employee rewards and incentives. Loews began selling discounted tickets to more than 16,000 companies and greatly improved its customer service, yielding a 17 percent sales growth from its top accounts.[6] This system also enabled the company to better meet the needs of its best business customers, thus improving the overall value of its offering.

Loews Cineplex used a marketing information system to learn the sales impact of group sales to the corporation.

Although an MkIS can be expensive, if used properly, it can be a valuable investment. Nowadays, companies usually find it necessary to go beyond using routine reports and must generate customized analyses. For example, Harrah's might be interested in comparing the number of guests drawn in by two different promotions targeted to the same specific geographic region of the country. By initiating a query of the number of guests from the set of zip codes that constitute the targeted area, an analyst could compare the effectiveness of each marketing program or take the analysis one step further and determine the total revenue generated from those guests, broken down into the amount they spent on gambling, accommodations, and other hotel services like restaurants, cocktail lounges, gift shops, and massage services. In this way, the MkIS helps the company determine which promotion addressed which aspects of the Harrah's experience that customers valued most.

Since the use of MkIS has become more widespread, organizations of all types have vast amounts of data available to them. One of the most valuable resources such firms have at their disposal is their rich cache of

Marketers use data mining techniques to determine what items people buy at the same time so they can be promoted and displayed together.

customer information and purchase history. However, it can be difficult to make sense of the millions and even billions of pieces of individual data, which are stored in large computer files called **data warehouses.** For this reason, firms find it necessary to use data mining techniques to extract valuable information from their databases. **Data mining** uses a variety of statistical analysis tools to uncover previously unknown patterns in the data or relationships among variables. Through data mining, for example, Harrah's found out that its most profitable customers weren't the high rollers whom they expected had the highest value. A gardening retailer might learn through its data mining that 25 percent of the time that customers buy a garden hose, they also purchase a sprinkler. Or an investment firm might use statistical techniques to group clients according to income, age, type of securities purchased, and prior investment experience. This categorization identifies different segments, to which the firm can offer valuable packages that meet their specific needs. The firm can tailor separate marketing programs to each of these segments. Data mining thus can be useful for a broad range of organizations, both public and private, for-profit and not-for-profit.

The Ethics of Using Customer Information

As we noted in Chapter 3, upholding strong business ethics requires more than a token nod to ethics in the mission statement. A strong ethical orientation must be an integral part of a firm's marketing strategy and decision making. In Chapter 3, we discussed how marketers have a duty to understand and address the concerns of the various stakeholders in the firm—recall Exhibit 3.5, an example of how various stakeholders' needs should be included in the decision process of a marketing research firm.

As technology continues to advance rapidly, especially in terms of a firm's ability to link data sets and build enormous databases that contain information on millions of customers, marketing researchers must be careful to not abuse their ability to access these data, which can be very sensitive. Recent security breaches at some of the United States' largest banks and credit-reporting services have shown just how easily this stored data can be abused. DSW, a chain of almost 200 shoe stores in the United States, has firsthand experience in credit fraud and damage control. It discovered that transaction information for 1.4 million credit cards and 96,000 checks was stolen from over 100 of its stores. As DSW Shoes learned, even customer account data is not safe from outside hackers intent on accessing it.[7] DSW did everything it could to minimize the damage and shore up the security breach. It reported the fraud immediately to authorities and card holder associations. It also brought in a security firm to investigate the problem and posted a customer alert. Nevertheless, in the long run, even though DSW did all that it could to minimize the damage to its image, some customers may decide to blame any ill effects they suffer, like identity theft or a ruined credit report, on it. Thus, the lesson for marketing researchers is to respect and protect the privacy of individual customers absolutely. From charitable giving to medical records to Internet tracking, consumers are more anxious than ever about preserving their fundamental right to privacy.

More and more, consumers want to be assured that they have control over the information that has been collected about them through various means, such as a Web site or product registration or rebate form. Consumers' anxiety has become so intense that the U.S. government has promulgated various regulations, such as the "junk fax prevention act" and "Do Not Call" and "Do Not Email" lists, to give citizens control over who contacts them.[8] When conducting marketing research, researchers must assure respondents that the information they provide will be treated as confidential and used solely for the purpose of research. Without such assurances, consumers will be reluctant to either provide honest responses to marketing research inquiries or even agree to participate in the first place.

Many firms voluntarily notify their customers that any information provided to them will be kept confidential and not given or sold to any other firm. Several organizations, including the Center for Democracy and Technology and the Electronic Privacy Information Center, have emerged as watchdogs over data mining of consumer information. In addition, national and state governments in the United States play a big part in protecting privacy. In addition to the "Do Not Call" and "Do Not Email" initiatives, companies now are required to disclose their privacy practices to customers on an annual basis. Therefore, marketers must adhere to legislative and company policies, as well as respect consumers' desires for privacy.[9]

Finally, it is extremely important to adhere to ethical practices when conducting marketing research. The American Marketing Association, for example, provides three guidelines for conducting marketing research: (1) It prohibits selling or fundraising under the guise of conducting research, (2) it supports maintaining research integrity by avoiding misrepresentation or the omission of pertinent research data, and (3) it encourages the fair treatment of clients and suppliers. Numerous codes of conduct written by various marketing research societies all reinforce the duty of the researcher to respect the rights of the subjects in the course of their research. The bottom line: Marketing research should be used only to produce unbiased, factual information.

The Marketing Research Process

Managers consider several factors before embarking on a marketing research project. First, will the research be useful; will it provide insights beyond what the managers already know and reduce uncertainty associated with the project? Second, is top management committed to the project and willing to abide by the results of the research? Related to both of these questions is the value of the research. Marketing research can be very expensive, and if the results won't be useful or management does not abide by the findings, it represents a waste of money.

Consider Whirlpool's approach to the European market for washing machines.[10] Although the findings of a major marketing research program indicated that there were significant regional differences in consumer preferences, managers stayed committed to their strategy of introducing the "World Washer," which could be sold in all EU markets. However, offering the same machine to different regions failed to address those different preferences in the marketplace, like Britons' preference to wash laundry more frequently using quieter machines than their neighbors in the rest of Europe. While the company maintained its "World Washer" strategy, its European competitors continued to innovate by responding to preferences in different regions.

Whirlpool Corporation
Building unmatched loyalty
one customer at a time.

While Whirlpool chose to pursue a "World Washer" strategy in Europe that was contrary to its own research findings, its European competitors continued to innovate by responding to preferences in different regions.

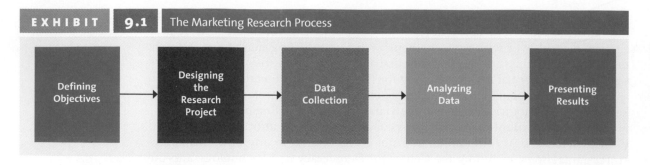

EXHIBIT   9.1   The Marketing Research Process

Defining Objectives → Designing the Research Project → Data Collection → Analyzing Data → Presenting Results

Although Whirlpool considered the research to be a worthwhile project, it was not particularly valuable to the firm because it chose to pursue a strategy that was contrary to its own research findings.

The marketing research process itself can be divided into five steps (see Exhibit 9.1).

Step 1: Defining the Objectives and Research Needs

Because research is both expensive and time consuming, it is important to establish in advance exactly what information is required to answer specific research questions and how that information should be obtained. Researchers assess the value of a project through a careful comparison of the benefits of answering some of their questions and the costs associated with conducting the research. For instance, going back to Whirlpool's European washing machine study, suppose the company had a choice of conducting in-depth interviews with several hundred washing machine owners at a cost of $200 per interview or doing an online survey with the same number of respondents but at a cost of only $2 per questionnaire. Which data collection method should Whirlpool use? Clearly the questionnaires are much less expensive, but the in-depth interviews provide richer information that would be virtually impossible to access through questionnaires. As this simple example shows, there are always value trade-offs in marketing research. Researchers can always design a more expensive study and eke out more and better information, but in the end, they should choose the method that will provide them with the information they need at the lowest cost.

Marketing research efforts and resources can be wasted if research objectives are poorly defined.[11] Poor design arises from three major sources: basing research on irrelevant research questions, focusing on research questions that marketing research cannot answer, or addressing research questions to which the answers are already known. For companies with track records of anticipating new technologies, fashions, or gadgets that consumers will demand, as well as the core competencies to deliver them in a timely manner, lengthy marketing research studies likely will not add significantly to the benefits of their own intuition. However, timely and focused marketing research could help them refine their ideas and prototypes. When researchers have determined what information they need to address a particular problem or issue, the next step is to design a research project to meet those objectives.

Step 2: Designing the Research Project

The second step in the marketing research project involves design. In this step, researchers identify the type of data needed and determine the type of research necessary to collect it. Recall that the objectives of the project drive the type of data needed, as outlined in Step 1. Let's look at how this second step works using a hypothetical example about marketing disposable razors.

Superior Razors, a marketer of a national brand of men's shaving products, sets out to evaluate its position in the marketplace relative to its competitors. The specific purpose of the marketing research is twofold: to determine current market share and to assess how that position will change in the next few years.

Identifying the type of data needed for the first purpose—determining market share—is fairly straightforward. It requires finding the company's sales during a particular time frame relative to total industry sales.

Identifying the type of data needed for the second purpose—assessing the extent to which the firm's market position will improve, stay the same, or deteriorate—is not as easy to obtain. For instance, the company's marketers might want to assess customers' brand loyalty, because if the company enjoys high levels of loyalty, the future looks rosier than if loyalty is low. Superior Razor's market share in relation to that of its competitors over time can also shed light on the future of its market position. The firm will want to know which firms have been gaining market share and which are losing.

The objective of Superior Razor's research project is to evaluate its position in the marketplace relative to its competitors.

Thus, after the firm has identified its specific objectives and needs, it must consider whether the data required are secondary or primary in nature, as illustrated in Exhibit 9.2.

Secondary Data **Secondary data** are pieces of information that have already been collected from other sources and usually are readily available. Census data, the company's sales invoices, and information from trade associations, the Internet, books, and journal articles are all readily available, free (or inexpensive) sources of secondary data.

EXHIBIT	9.2	Secondary Data vs. Primary Data

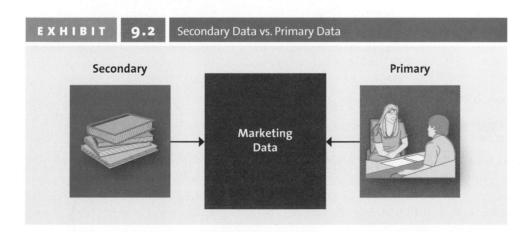

In addition, marketers can purchase **syndicated data**, which are data available for a fee from commercial research firms such as Information Resources Inc. (IRI), National Purchase Diary Panel, and ACNielsen. (Exhibit 9.3 contains information about various firms that provide syndicated data.) This type of information, in our hypothetical razor example, might include the prices of various razors, sales figures, growth or decline in the category, and advertising and promotional spending. Consumer packaged goods firms that sell to wholesalers may not have the means to gather pertinent data directly from the retailers that sell their products to the consumer, which makes syndicated data a valuable resource for them. Some syndicated data providers also offer information about shifting brand preferences and product usage in households, which they gather from consumer panels. Adding Value 9.1 describes the valuable information that IRI provides to its customers.

A marketing research project often begins with a review of the relevant secondary data, which provides both advantages and disadvantages. The data can be quickly accessed at a relatively low cost; the Census of Retail Trade and County Business Patterns, for example, provides data about sales of different types of retail establishments. These patterns may be the only accurate sources available to a small new business that wants to determine the size of its potential market. For such a firm, gathering accurate and comprehensive data on its own would be quite difficult.

At other times, however, secondary data are not adequate to meet researchers' needs. Because the data initially were acquired for some purpose other than

EXHIBIT 9.3	Syndicated Data Providers and Their Services
ACNielsen (www.acnielsen.com)	With its *Market Measurement Services*, the company tracks the sales of consumer packaged goods, gathered at the point of sale in retail stores of all types and sizes.
Information Resources Inc. (www.infores.com)	*InfoScan* store tracking provides detailed information about sales, share, distribution, pricing, and promotion across a wide variety of retail channels and accounts.
J.D. Power and Associates (www.jdpower.com)	Widely known for its automotive ratings, it produces quality and customer satisfaction research for a variety of industries.
Mediamark Research Inc. (www.mediamark.com)	Supplies multimedia audience research pertaining to media and marketing planning for advertised brands.
National Purchase Diary Panel (www.npd.com)	Tracking services provide information about product movement and consumer behavior in a variety of industries.
NOP World (www.nopworld.com)	The *mKids US* research study tracks mobile telephone ownership and usage, brand affinities, and entertainment habits of American youth between 12 and 19 years of age.
Research and Markets (www.researchandmarkets.com)	Promotes itself as a "one-stop shop" for market research and data from most leading publishers, consultants, and analysts.
Roper Center for Public Opinion Research (www.ropercenter.uconn.edu)	The *General Social Survey* is one of the nation's longest running surveys of social, cultural, and political indicators.
Simmons Market Research Bureau (www.smrb.com)	Reports on the products American consumers buy, the brands they prefer, and their lifestyles, attitudes, and media preferences.
Yankelovich (www.yankelovich.com)	The *MONITOR* tracks consumer attitudes, values, and lifestyles shaping the American marketplace.

IRI and the Value of Information[12]

Information Resources Inc. (IRI), one of the top U.S. research organizations, provides market research and analytical services to the consumer packaged goods, healthcare, and retail industries. For its clients—which include Anheuser-Busch, ConAgra, Johnson & Johnson, Philip Morris, and PepsiCo—IRI collects, monitors, and manages a variety of data in some of the most active research markets in the world, including the United States and Europe.

From appropriate channel usage to desired packaging, IRI tracks a host of data to deliver detailed findings that are designed to grow and enhance clients' operations. Recently, IRI published a report tracking 76 health and beauty care categories to show a channel-by-channel analysis of where, when, and how consumers spend their money on a per-household, per-store visit, and annual basis. To create this report, IRI collected point-of-sale data from almost 40,000 retail outlets throughout the country, then cross-referenced these data with data collected from the 70,000 households that make up the Consumer Network Household Panel and that IRI had armed with personal scanners to track their household purchases.

The findings from this research can be used to identify effective promotional activities, fine-tune cat-egory offerings, and predict shopping patterns. In this case, IRI noted that smoking cessation patches, which account for only 1.3 percent of household spending, still racked up an average of $42 per purchase, with drug stores averaging $45.50 at the register and supercent-ers averaging $34.40. Retailers and suppliers of these patches thus could recognize the profit potential of such products because of their relatively high ticket price and great likelihood that they will be purchased relatively frequently. If promotions could be directed toward patch users, they might also be used to draw traffic into the store.

Furthermore, IRI noted some interesting patterns with regard to seasonal spending. Seasonal candy sales, for instance, made up 28 percent of annual candy sales in the food, drug, and mass merchandise channels (excluding Wal-Mart). Most sales occurred during the last three weeks of the particular season (Halloween, Christmas, and Easter), which suggests that consumers are being encouraged to spend during these specific periods rather than spreading their purchases out over time. As these two examples show, IRI's research delivers actionable insights that businesses throughout the world value.

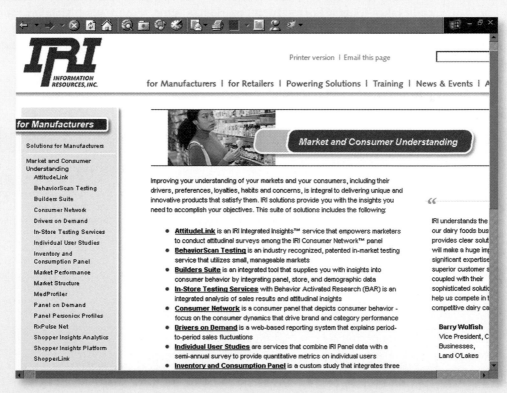

The homepage for IRI explains some of its many market research products.

The major advantage of using primary data like focus groups for market research is that it can be tailored to fit the pertinent research questions. But it usually is more expensive and takes longer to collect than secondary data.

the research question at hand, they may not be completely relevant. For instance, the U.S. Census is a great source for demographic data about a particular market area, and it can be easily accessed at a low cost. However, the data are collected only at the beginning of every decade, so they quickly become outdated. For example, if a firm were interested in opening a retail flooring store in the next year, it would have to rely on U.S. Census data collected in 2000. If it hoped to locate in an area where housing starts are projected to grow rapidly in the next several years, these data would be too old to provide much in the way of insights. Researchers must also pay careful attention to how the secondary data were collected; despite the great deal of data available on the Internet, easy access does not ensure that the data are trustworthy.

Primary Data   In many cases, the information researchers need is available only through **primary data,** or data collected to address specific research needs. Marketers collect primary data using a variety of means such as observing consumer behavior, conducting focus group interviews, or surveying customers using the mail, telephone, in-person interviews, or the Internet. Primary data collection can help eliminate some of the problems inherent to secondary data.

A major advantage of primary research is that it can be tailored to fit the pertinent research questions, though it also has its own set of disadvantages. For one thing, it is usually more costly to collect primary than secondary data, and the collection typically takes longer. Furthermore, marketers often require sophisticated training and experience to design and collect primary data that are unbiased, valid, and reliable. (For a summary of the advantages and disadvantages of each type of research, see Exhibit 9.4.)

Adding Value 9.2 shows how marketers are beginning to use Weblogs to gather additional types of information.

EXHIBIT 9.4	Advantages and Disadvantages of Secondary and Primary Data		
Type	**Examples**	**Advantages**	**Disadvantages**
Secondary Research	■ Census data ■ Sales invoices ■ Internet information ■ Books ■ Journal articles ■ Syndicated data	■ Saves time in collecting data because they are readily available ■ Reduces data collection costs	■ May not be precisely relevant to information needs ■ Information may not be as timely as needed ■ Sources may not be original and therefore usefulness is an issue ■ Methodologies for collecting data may not be relevant or may contain bias in the subject matter
Primary Research	■ Observed consumer behavior ■ Focus group interviews ■ Surveys	■ Specific to the immediate data needs and topic at hand ■ Offers behavioral insights generally not available from secondary research	■ Usually more costly to collect ■ Typically takes longer to collect ■ Often requires more sophisticated training and experience to design and collect unbiased, valid, reliable data

Adding Value **9.2**

Using Weblog Information

When information abounds, marketers take notice.[13] So it's not surprising that some marketers consider the 3.2 million Weblogs, or blogs, available worldwide as an alternate information channel. In these interactive, online journals, people write about all sorts of things, including their personal experiences, opinions, and hobbies.

Initially set up to connect individual users and allow them to post unedited commentaries on a variety of topics, blogs now provide a source of information that often is monitored and even used by corporate America. For example, Robert Scoble, an employee of Microsoft, runs one of the United States' most influential blogs, "the Scobleizer" (scoble.weblogs.com) Scoble posts comments daily on a variety of topics, including the world's largest pistachio factory and cheap dining spots in Shanghai. The majority of entries, however, center on technical issues, many of which include the pros and cons of his employer's products. Although

Scoble created the blog of his own accord, with a disclaimer stating that everything he posts is his own personal opinion and is not read or approved by his employer before it is posted,[14] Microsoft has benefited from the blog's ability to generate tech-savvy ideas to improve its products and track dissatisfaction among its users. Scoble even has been known to offer mild criticism of Microsoft that puts a human spin on the software giant.

Other companies are following suit. Verizon, for example, tracks various blogs and Web sites to find relevant news about its competitors. Hartford Financial Services tested blogs among mobile field managers and found that they can enhance service because they offer a means to track information and share it among several persons at the same time. DaimlerChrysler uses an internal blog to connect U.S. plants and enable managers to discuss and document problems and their resolutions.

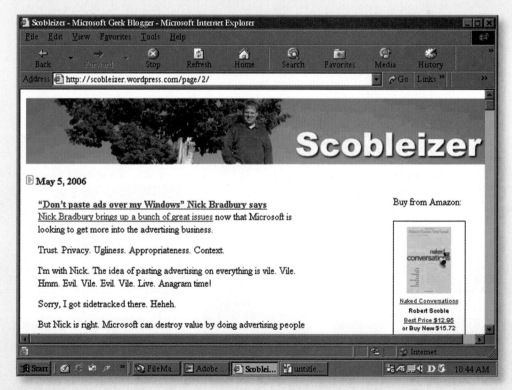

Web blogs like the Scobleizer can help firms get free information that can help it improve its products and identify dissatisfaction among its users.

Step 3: Data Collection Process

Data collection begins only after the research design process. Depending on the nature of the research problem, the collection can employ either exploratory or conclusive research.

As its name implies, **exploratory research** attempts to begin to understand the phenomenon of interest; it also provides initial information when the problem lacks any clear definition. Exploration can include informal methods, like reviewing available secondary data, or more formal methods that encompass qualitative research, such as observation techniques, in-depth interviews, focus groups, and projective techniques (see Exhibit 9.5).

If the firm is ready to move beyond preliminary insights, it likely is ready to engage in **conclusive research,** which provides the information needed to confirm those insights and which managers can use to pursue appropriate courses of action. For marketing researchers, because it is often quantitative in nature, conclusive research offers a means to confirm implicit hunches through surveys, formal studies such as specific experiments, scanner and panel data, or some combination of these. (See Exhibit 9.5 right.) In the case of formal research, it also enables the researcher to test his or her predictions.

Many research projects use exploratory research as the first phase of the research process and follow it up with conclusive research. Let's attempt to understand this progression by studying both methods in detail.

Exploratory Research Methods

Managers commonly use several exploratory research methods: observation, in-depth interviewing, focus group interviews, and projective techniques (Exhibit 9.5 left).

Observation   An exploratory research method, **observation** entails examining purchase and consumption behaviors through personal or video camera scrutiny. For example, researchers might observe customers while they shop or when they

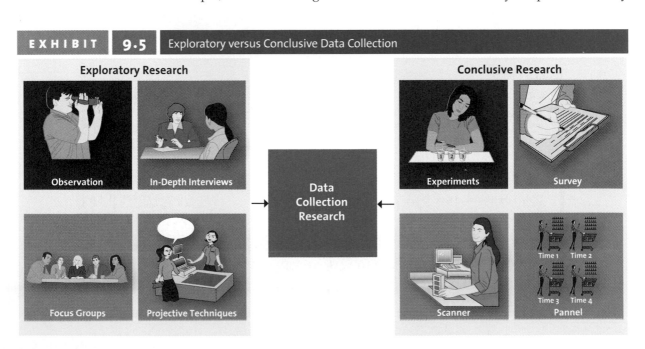

EXHIBIT 9.5   Exploratory versus Conclusive Data Collection

Exploratory Research — Observation, In-Depth Interviews, Focus Groups, Projective Techniques

Data Collection Research

Conclusive Research — Experiments, Survey, Scanner, Pannel (Time 1, Time 2, Time 3, Time 4)

go about their daily lives, during which processes they use a variety of products. Observation can last for a very brief period of time (e.g., two hours watching teenagers shop for clothing in the mall), or it may take days or weeks (e.g., researchers live with families to observe their use of products). When consumers are unable to articulate their experiences, observation research becomes particularly useful; how else could researchers determine which educational toys babies choose to play with or confirm purchase details that consumers might not be able to recall accurately? As Ethical Dilemma 9.1 describes, observational research can even be used to understand the differences among consumers of various beer brands

In-Depth Interviews

An **in-depth interview** is an exploratory research technique in which trained researchers ask questions, listen to and record the answers, and then pose additional questions to clarify or expand on a particular issue. For instance, in addition to simply watching teenagers shop for apparel, interviewers might stop them one at a time in the mall to ask them a few questions, such as: "We noticed that you went into and came out of Abercrombie & Fitch very quickly and without buying anything. Why was that?" If the subject responds that no one had bothered to wait on her, the interviewer might ask a follow-up question like, "Oh? Has that happened to you before?" or "Do you expect sales assistance there?" The results often provide insights that help managers better understand the nature of their industry, as well as important trends and consumer preferences, which can be invaluable for developing marketing strategies.

In-depth interviews provide quite a few benefits. They can provide an historical context for the phenomenon of interest, particularly when they include industry experts or experienced consumers. They also can communicate how people really feel about a product or service at the individual level, a level that rarely emerges from other methods that use group discussions. Finally, marketers can use the results of in-depth interviews to develop surveys.

Focus Group Interviews

In **focus group interviews,** a small group of persons (usually 8 to 12) comes together for an intensive discussion about a particular topic. Using an unstructured method of inquiry, a trained moderator guides the conversation on the basis of a predetermined general

Observation is an exploratory technique that entails examining purchase and consumption behaviors through personal or video camera scrutiny. In this case, a family is observed cooking a meal.

An in-depth interview is an exploratory research technique in which trained researchers ask questions, listen to and record answers, and then pose additional questions to clarify or expand on a particular issue.

Ethical Dilemma 9.1   Watching Consumers[15]

How does sitting in a mall or standing in a store checking out the people in the corner add up to bona fide market research? Well, for corporate ethnographers, Emma Gilding and Paco Underhill, it's just another day on the job. Gilding helped found Ogilvy & Mather's (O&M) Discovery Group; Paco Underhill created Envirosell.

Gilding's projects range from Miller Lite beer to Huggies diapers and a number of pharmaceutical products. The applicants go through a screening process that is based on a predetermined set of qualifications, such as age, gender, and amount of alcohol consumption. Those who qualify are paid to allow a camera crew, which documents their every move, to follow them during their daily routines for a day or more. Gilding is quick to point out that any unnatural behaviors the cameras may bring about soon subside as subjects fall into their normal routines. Furthermore, and importantly, study participants are fully informed and have given their consent to being the subjects of a marketing research study.

Envirosell has performed projects for firms ranging from Staples to Wells Fargo. For Staples, consumers were observed in 12 stores. They were videotaped at the stores for eight hours each research day to better understand how consumers actually moved around the various departments while they shopped, viewed signs, and interacted with sales associates. Researchers also conduct interviews with shoppers. Based on the results of these studies, Staples has rolled out a new store format designed around solving customer problems by combining service with self-service rather than just selling individual items. Staples associates can now provide a higher level of service in those areas that need it, and the new store format gives customers the tools to be self-sufficient if they choose to browse on their own.

Using ethnographic approaches, the research team can identify information that would not be accessible to them through more traditional marketing research means—a respondent to a simple questionnaire or those involved in an interview probably would not be able to provide insightful information into their pattern of walking through a store or a mall.

In some cases researchers obtain consent from the consumers they are watching and videotaping, and in other cases do not. The ethical dilemma for marketing researchers centers around whether using observational techniques in which the subjects are not informed that they are being studied, like viewing customers in a mall or a retail store, violates the rule of fair treatment. Observing uninformed consumers very well may lead to important insights that would not otherwise be discovered. But do the results justify the methodology?

Do you believe it is ethical for a firm to record the movements and activities of customers as they shop in a store? Would your opinion be different if the customers were informed that they were being watched?

outline of the topics of interest. Researchers usually record the interactions by video- or audiotape so they can carefully comb through the interviews later to catch any patterns of verbal or nonverbal responses.

In particular, focus groups gather qualitative data about initial reactions to a new or existing product or service, opinions about different competitive offerings, or reactions to marketing stimuli, like a new ad campaign or point-of-purchase display materials.

Lexus, for example, used focus groups to develop an advertising campaign for its ES 300 model. Finding the right message and determining the right medium to convey that message was imperative for the vehicle launch. Using extensive focus group testing with both current ES owners and owners of competitive models, Lexus set out to determine what "luxury" meant for consumers in their car purchases. Lexus owners saw luxury as "a personal oasis of tranquility and freedom." Armed with this information, Lexus initiated a targeted newspaper campaign that built on its "relentless pursuit of perfection" theme for the ES 300 launch.[16]

Virtual focus groups have started to make inroads into the market researchers' toolkit. Lego, for instance, invited over 10,000 kids to participate in a virtual focus group to get ideas for new products.[17] The participants saw short lists of proposed toys and clicked on the ones they liked. They ranked their choices and even suggested new ideas. These ideas were fed, in turn, to other potential customers and were rated against the ideas from Lego's own toy creators. The new suggestions, in turn, got creative juices flowing among still other potential customers. The resulting product, the Star Wars Imperial Destroyer, was different from anything else in Lego's 73-year history—it was Lego's largest and most expensive set ever, at 3,100 parts and a $300 price tag. Its first production run, planned to last a year, sold in less than five weeks.

Lego's Star Wars Imperial Destroyer, with 3,100 parts and a $300 price tag was designed with the help of virtual focus groups.

Projective Technique   A **projective technique** is a type of qualitative research in which subjects are provided a scenario and asked to express their thoughts and feelings about it. For example, consumers may be shown a cartoon that has a consumer looking at a shelf display in a supermarket with a text box above the consumer. The respondent would write in their thoughts on the issue in the text box. Thus, the cartoon allows the respondent to visualize the situation and project his/her thoughts or feelings by filling out the text box.

Conclusive Research Methods

Conclusive research can be descriptive in nature—such as when it profiles a typical user or nonuser of a particular brand according to a survey. It can also be experimental—such as when a soft-drink producer conducts a taste test to determine which formulation of a green, high caffeine drink is preferred by customers. Conclusive research can also be collected from the merchandise that is scanned at a store, or from a group of customers, known as a panel, who record all of their purchases. In this section, we will discuss each of these conclusive research techniques—survey, experiment, scanner, and panel.

Survey Research   A **survey** is a systematic means of collecting information from people that generally uses a questionnaire. A **questionnaire** is a form that features a set of questions designed to gather information from respondents and thereby accomplish the researchers' objectives. Individual questions on a questionnaire can be either unstructured or structured. **Unstructured questions** are open ended

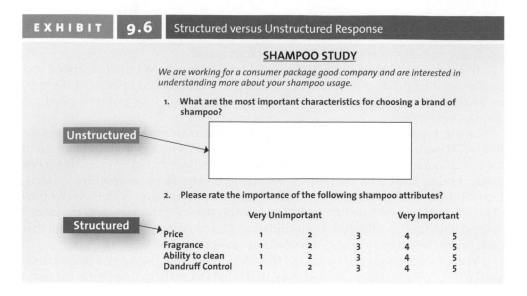

EXHIBIT 9.6 Structured versus Unstructured Response

SHAMPOO STUDY

We are working for a consumer package good company and are interested in understanding more about your shampoo usage.

1. **What are the most important characteristics for choosing a brand of shampoo?**

   Unstructured

2. **Please rate the importance of the following shampoo attributes?**

   Structured

	Very Unimportant				Very Important
Price	1	2	3	4	5
Fragrance	1	2	3	4	5
Ability to clean	1	2	3	4	5
Dandruff Control	1	2	3	4	5

and allow respondents to answer in their own words. An unstructured question like "What are the most important characteristics for choosing a brand of shampoo?" yields an unstructured response. However, the same question could be posed to respondents in a structured format by providing a fixed set of response categories, like price, fragrance, ability to clean, and dandruff control, and then asking respondents to rate the importance of each. **Structured questions** thus are closed-ended questions for which a discrete set of response alternatives, or specific answers, is provided for respondents to evaluate (see Exhibit 9.6).

Developing a questionnaire is part art and part science. The questions must be carefully designed to address the specific set of research questions. Moreover, for a questionnaire to produce meaningful results, its questions cannot be misleading in any fashion (e.g., open to multiple interpretations), and they must address only one issue at a time. Furthermore, they must be worded in vocabulary that will be familiar and comfortable to those being surveyed. More specifically, the questions should be sequenced appropriately: general questions first, more specific questions next, and demographic questions at the end. Finally, the layout and appearance of the questionnaire must be professional and easy to follow, with appropriate instructions in suitable places. For some tips on what *not* to do when designing a questionnaire, see Exhibit 9.7.

Marketing surveys can be conducted either online or offline, but online marketing surveys offer researchers the chance to develop a database quickly with many responses, whereas offline marketing surveys provide a more direct approach that includes interactions with the target market.

Web surveys have steadily grown as a percentage of all quantitative surveys. Although the Internet has not proven effective for online focus groups, online surveys have a lot to offer managers with tight deadlines,[18] including the following benefits:

■ **Response rates are relatively high.** Typical response rates run from 1 to 2 percent for mail and 10 to 15 percent for phone surveys. For online surveys, in contrast, the response rate can reach 30 to 35 percent, or even higher in business-to-business research.

EXHIBIT 9.7	What Not to Do When Designing a Questionnaire	
Issue	**Good Question**	**Bad Question**
Avoid questions the respondent cannot easily or accurately answer.	When was the last time you went to the grocery store?	How much money did you spend on groceries last month?
Avoid sensitive questions unless they are absolutely necessary.	Do you take vitamins?	Do you dye your hair?
Avoid double-barreled questions, which refer to more than one issue with only one set of responses.	1. Do you think John Kerry would make a good U.S. president? 2. Do you think John McCain would make a good U.S. president?	Do you think that John Kerry or John McCain would make a good U.S. president?
Avoid leading questions, which steer respondents to a particular response, irrespective of their true beliefs.	Please rate how safe you believe a Volvo is on a scale of 1 to 10, with 1 being not safe and 10 being very safe.	Volvo is the safest car on the road, right?
Avoid one-sided questions that present only one side of the issue.	To what extent do you feel fast food contributes to adult obesity? 1: Does not contribute, 5: Main cause	Fast food is responsible for adult obesity: Agree/Disagree
Avoid questions with implicit assumptions, which presume the same point of reference for all respondents.	Should children be allowed to drink Coca-Cola in school?	Since caffeine is a stimulant, should children be allowed to drink Coca-Cola in school?
Avoid complex questions and those that may seem unfamiliar to respondents.	What brand of wristwatch do you typically wear?	Do you believe that mechanical watches are better than quartz watches?

Source: Adapted from A. Parasuraman, Dhruv Grewal, and R. Krishnan, *Marketing Research,* 2nd ed. (Boston, MA: Houghton Mifflin, 2007), Ch. 10.

■ **Respondents may lie less.** Respondents lie in any medium. Have you ever wondered, for example, how many administrative assistants fill out mail surveys for their bosses? And what sort of answers they might give? Because the Internet has a higher perception of anonymity than telephone or mail contacts, respondents are more likely to be more truthful.

■ **It is inexpensive.** An average 20-minute phone interview can cost $30 to $40, compared with $7 to $10 for an online interview. Costs likely will continue to fall more as users become more familiar with the online survey process.

■ **Results are processed and received quickly.** Reports and summaries can be developed in real time and delivered directly to managers in simple, easy-to-digest reports, complete with color, graphics, and charts. Traditional phone or mail surveys require laborious data collection, tabulation, summary, and distribution before anyone can grasp their results.

Online marketing surveys enable researchers to develop a database quickly with many responses at a relatively low cost.

The Internet can also be used to collect data other than that available from quantitative surveys. If consumers give a firm permission to market to them, the firm can collect data about their usage of its Web site and other Internet applications. In addition, open-ended questionnaires can be used to collect more in-depth qualitative data.

Experimental research is a type of quantitative research that systematically manipulates one or more variables to determine which variable(s) have a causal effect on another variable. For example, suppose Cheesecake Factory is trying to determine the most profitable price for a new menu item. They put the item on the menu at four different prices in four different markets. In general, the more expensive the item, the less it will sell. But by running this experiment, they determine that the most profitable item is the second most expensive item. Evidently, some people believed the most expensive item was too expensive, so they didn't buy it. The two least expensive sold fairly well, but Cheesecake didn't make as much money on each item sold. In this experiment, we believe that the changes in price caused the changes in quantities sold, and therefore impacted profitability.

Scanner research is a type of quantitative research that uses data obtained from scanner readings of UPC codes at check-out counters. Whenever you go into your local grocery store, your purchases are rung up using scanner systems. The data from these purchases are likely to be acquired by leading marketing research firms, such as Information Resources Inc. or AC Nielsen. They use this information to help leading consumer package good firms (e.g., Kellogg's, Pepsi, and Sara Lee) assess what is happening in the marketplace. For example, a firm can determine what would happen to sales if they reduced their price by 10% in a given month. Did it increase, decrease or stay the same?

Panel research is a type of quantitative research that involves collecting information from a group of consumers (the panel) over time. The data collected from the panelists may be from a survey, or a record of purchases. This data provides consumer package good firms with a comprehensive picture of what individual consumers are buying or not buying. Thus, one key difference between scanner research and panel research is the nature of aggregation. Scanner research typically focuses on weekly consumption of a particular product at a given unit of analysis (e.g., individual store, chain, and region); whereas panel research focuses on the total weekly consumption of a particular person or group of people.

Regardless of how they do it though, collecting data can be an expensive process for entrepreneurs working on a shoestring budget. Entrepreneurial Marketing 9.1 suggests a host of avenues that they might pursue.

Step 4: Analyzing Data

The next step in the marketing research process—analyzing and interpreting the data—should be both thorough and methodical. To generate meaningful information, researchers analyze and make use of the collected data. In this context, data can be defined as raw numbers or other factual information that, on their own, have limited value to marketers. However, when the data are interpreted, they become **information**, which results from organizing, analyzing, and interpreting data and puts the data into a form that is useful to marketing decision makers. For example, a checkout scanner in the grocery store collects sales data about individual consumer purchases. Not until those data are categorized and examined do they provide information about which products and services were purchased together or how an in-store promotional activity translated into sales.

The purpose of converting data to information is to describe, explain, predict, and/or evaluate a particular situation. For example, an entrepreneur might learn that her core customers live in various suburbs around the outskirts of town. This piece of data takes on new meaning when she learns that none of these customers were drawn to her store by a clever and expensive recent direct mail campaign. By analyzing data she collected through a survey, she discovers that her core customers are working professionals who are drawn to the store when they walk by it on their way to and from work, not people from the upscale apartments in the downtown region that she targeted with her direct mail advertisements.

Data analysis might be as simple as calculating the average purchases of different customer segments or as complex as forecasting sales by market segment using elaborate statistical techniques. Coinstar, a worldwide leader in self-service coin counting, has begun analyzing marketing research in increasingly sophisticated ways. The company operates machines in more than 10,000 supermarkets in the United States, Canada, and the United Kingdom; consumers use the machines, which can count up to 600 coins per minute, to process large

Coinstar, a worldwide leader of self-service coin counting machines, uses sophisticated regression models to identify and rank potential locations for its machines.

volumes of change that they exchange for a voucher good for cash or groceries. Since it was founded in 1991, the company has tried to identify new and profitable locations on an ongoing basis as demand for its services continues to grow. When the company was small, coming up with "best guesses" of prime locations based on intuition worked out well, but Coinstar researchers recently developed regression models to identify and rank potential locations where it could locate its "green machines." This approach greatly improved Coinstar's ability to find prospective locations and forecast those that had the best potential for growth and profitability. The company can now capitalize on the estimated $7.7 billion in coins sitting in people's homes, waiting to be converted to paper money or grocery purchases.[19]

Step 5: Presenting Results

In the final phase in the marketing research process, the analyst prepares the results and presents them to the appropriate decision makers. A typical marketing research report includes an executive summary, the body of the report (which discusses the research objectives, methodology used, and detailed findings), the conclusions, the limitations, and appropriate supplemental tables, figures, and appendixes. To be effective, a written report must be short, interesting, methodical, precise, lucid, and free of errors.[20] Furthermore, the reports should use a style appropriate to the audience and devoid of technical jargon and include recommendations that managers can actually implement.

For example, when eBrain, a marketing research firm in Arlington, Virginia, surveyed 1,522 women regarding their consumer electronics experiences, the researchers found that they needed to report some rather startling results. Approximately three-quarters of those surveyed stated that they had received better service when they shopped with a man; 40 percent even claimed that they typically would only shop with men in tow. One of their biggest gripes was that service personnel were consistently condescending to them. Reporting these findings in a straightforward manner allowed the consumer electronics managers who received the report to implement some meaningful programs that acknowledged that women account for more than half of the $97 billion in consumer electronic sales each year and, beyond that figure, influence three-quarters of electronics purchases.

Several retailers responded accordingly.[21] Target paired up with Sony to offer a line of consumer electronics branded "Liv" that would attract the store's core market of women between the ages of 25 and 40 years. SoundTrack stores retrained its

Entrepreneurial Marketing 9.1

Marketing Research on a Shoestring Budget

Imagine your company needs some research conducted but has a relatively small budget. Fortunately, marketing research does not have to have a high price tag, though it always takes drive and knowledge. Here are some ways to uncover the information you and your company might need without breaking the bank.

Objective: What is it that you need to know?

- **Network.** Use your phone directory on your cell phone and call friends and professional colleagues. In most cases, researchers probably already know people in the industry who will be able to share their knowledge. They can help marketers determine what their objectives should be in upcoming research projects.

Customer Analysis: Who are your customers, and what do they want?

- **Customers.** Talk with current and prospective customers. Ask them the right questions, and they will provide the necessary answers. This approach is remarkably cheap because it entails only the researcher's labor, though it will require a large time commitment. Marketers need to take care how they ask the questions though; people tend to provide answers that they think the questioner wants or that seem socially acceptable.

- **Online.** Use a search engine like Google by simply typing in some appropriate keywords.

- **U.S. Census Bureau.** The U.S. Census Bureau is an important source of information. At www.census.gov, industry, demographic, and economic reports are all accessible for free. Although not known for its ease of use, the Web site offers a wealth of information.

Competitive Analysis: What are your competitors doing?

- **Web sites.** Visit competitors' Web sites, if they have them. Learn about their products and services, pricing, management team, and philosophies. Read their press releases. You can even infer what part of the business is thriving through reading their career pages.

- **SEC Filings.** If competitors are public, they are required to file 10K forms annually with the Securities Exchange Commission (SEC). Search for SEC filings using www.finance.yahoo.com or http://moneycentral.msn.com/home.asp, both of which provide sales and expense numbers, in addition to other important information in the footnotes.

- **Go there.** If competitors are smaller mom-and-pop stores, visit them. Hang out in front of the store armed with a pad and paper and count the number of people who walk in, then the percentage of people that walk out having purchased something. Use logic and judgment. Have the customers purchased items that appear to have higher profit margins? Find out where and what competitors are advertising.

- **NAICS Codes.** For a wider view of the competitive industry, review the North American Industry Classification System (NAICS) codes. The NAICS identifies companies operating in an industry sector with a six digit code. The government's Web site at www.census.gov/epcd/www/naics.html helps pinpoint the correct NAICS code and can generate an industry-specific report. For example, if you want to identify women's clothing stores, you would go to number 44812. The first two digits, 44, identify merchandise retailers (as would 45). The third digit breaks down the merchandise retailers further. For example, retailers selling clothing and clothing accessories are in classification 448, while general merchandise retailers are in classification 452. The fourth digit subdivides clothing and accessory retailers (448) into clothing stores (4481), shoe stores (4482), and jewelry and luggage stores (4483). The fifth digit provides a further breakdown into men's clothing stores (44811) and women's clothing stores (44812). The sixth digit (not shown here) is used to capture differences in the three North American countries using the classification scheme, the United States, Mexico, and Canada.

Classification by Type of Merchandise

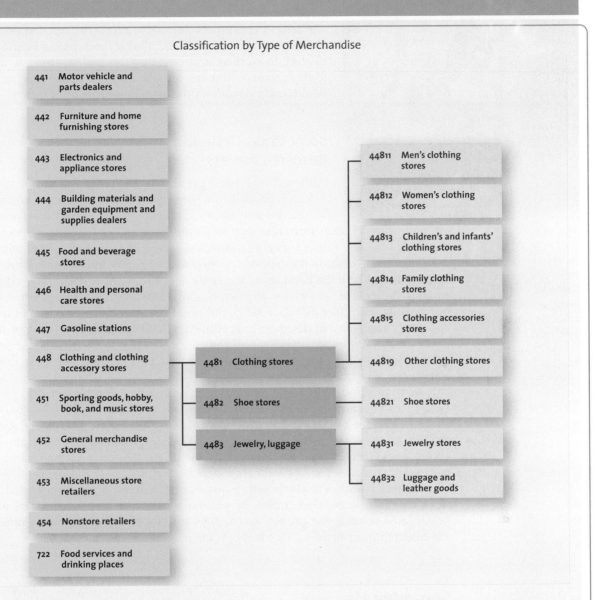

441	Motor vehicle and parts dealers
442	Furniture and home furnishing stores
443	Electronics and appliance stores
444	Building materials and garden equipment and supplies dealers
445	Food and beverage stores
446	Health and personal care stores
447	Gasoline stations
448	Clothing and clothing accessory stores
451	Sporting goods, hobby, book, and music stores
452	General merchandise stores
453	Miscellaneous store retailers
454	Nonstore retailers
722	Food services and drinking places

4481	Clothing stores
4482	Shoe stores
4483	Jewelry, luggage

44811	Men's clothing stores
44812	Women's clothing stores
44813	Children's and infants' clothing stores
44814	Family clothing stores
44815	Clothing accessories stores
44819	Other clothing stores
44821	Shoe stores
44831	Jewelry stores
44832	Luggage and leather goods

Focus Groups, Surveys, and Analyst Reports: What detailed information can you gather?

- **Be Specific.** Determine precisely what information is required; it is very costly to pay for research that does not assist in a decision or provide strategic direction.

- **Surveys.** Determine what form will provide the most value. Phone surveys cost about $40 per interview, mailings average from $5,000 to $15,000 for 200 responses, and e-mail surveys usually are much cheaper.

- **Focus Groups.** Although focus groups can be more expensive, there are ways to cut corners. Develop the questions in-house, and don't outsource the moderator or facility. It is important, however, to find the right participants.

- **Analyst Reports.** Prewritten reports, covering a broad price range and a wide variety of questions, are available for purchase from the hundreds of companies that write and sell reports. Two of the best known are www.forrester.com and www.hoovers.com.

Research indicates that 75 percent of women surveyed believed they received better service while shopping with a man for consumer electronics.

staff to stress product benefits rather than features and began to designate its delivery service as "Red Carpet" treatment, which meant literally that the deliverers would protect floor surfaces in consumers' homes. Circuit City opened two pilot stores under the name "Iris" that it intended to be more appealing to women, and Best Buy tailored its stores to appeal to its female customers. Finally, Radio Shack started offering health and relaxation products, known as its "Lifeline" product mix.

Some Final Thoughts on the Marketing Research Process

Although we have presented the stages of the marketing research process in a step-by-step progression, of course, research doesn't always happen that way. Sometimes, researchers go back and forth from one step to another as the need arises. For example, marketers may establish a specific research objective, which they follow with data collection and preliminary analysis. If they uncover new information during the collection step or if the findings of the analysis spotlight new research needs, they might redefine their objectives and begin again from a new starting point. A major automobile manufacturer once set out to identify consumer responses to its new company logo, only to discover in preliminary focus groups that some of the respondents thought the company had gone out of business! Clearly, those researchers had to regroup and set out in a different direction with an entirely different objective.

Another important step when embarking on a research project is to plan the entire project in advance. For example, when setting up a questionnaire, marketers should consider the data collection process and anticipate the types of analyses that might produce meaningful results for decision makers. For example, open-ended questions on a questionnaire can slow down the coding process and make it difficult to run some sophisticated statistical analyses. If the decision makers want a sophisticated analysis fast, a questionnaire filled with open-ended questions may not be the best choice. By planning the entire research process well in advance of starting the project, researchers can avoid unnecessary alterations to the research plan as they move through the process.

Summing Up

1. How do marketers use information systems to create greater value for customers?

A marketing information system (MkIS) is a set of procedures and methods for the regular, planned collection, analysis, and presentation of information that marketers can use to make marketing decisions. A MkIS provides a means to accumulate information from sources both internal and external to the organization, which then makes that information routinely available to managers for their informed decision making. In turn, a MkIS enables firms to understand what customers want better through analyses of their purchases. This specialized knowledge can translate into purchasing and promotion programs that are tailor-made for customers.

2. Can certain marketing research practices cause a firm to encounter ethical problems?

Marketing researchers have obligations to their subjects and to society to behave in an ethical manner. This responsibility means that marketing researchers must take every precaution to ensure the confidentiality of the data they collect from consumers and the privacy of study participants. Researchers should never misrepresent the purpose of a study; for example, a sales pitch should never be cast as a marketing research study. Finally, the results of research studies should be reported fully. If data or parts of the study are ignored, the results might be misinterpreted.

3. What are the necessary steps to conduct marketing research?

There are five steps in the marketing research process. The first step is to define objectives and research needs, which sounds so simple that managers often gloss over it. But this step is crucial to the success of any research project because, quite basically, the research must answer those questions that are important for making decisions. In the second step, designing the research project, researchers identify the type of data that are needed, whether primary or secondary, on the basis of the objectives of the project from Step 1, and then determine the type of research that enables them to collect those data. The third step involves deciding on the data collection process and collecting the data. Depending on the research objectives and the findings from the secondary data search, researchers will choose either exploratory or conclusive research. Exploratory research usually involves observation, in-depth interviews, or projective techniques, whereas if the project calls for conclusive research, the researchers

may perform a survey, an experiment, or use scanner, and panel data. The fourth step is to analyze and interpret the data, and the fifth and final step is to prepare the findings for presentation. Although these steps appear to progress linearly, researchers often work backward through the process as they learn at each step.

4. What are primary and secondary data, and when should each be used?

Secondary data are pieces of information that have been collected from other sources, such as the U.S. Census, internal company sources, the Internet, books, articles, trade associations, or syndicated data services. Primary data are data collected to address specific research needs, usually through observation, focus groups, interviews, surveys, or experiments. Research projects typically start with secondary research, which provides a background for what information is already known and what research has been done previously. Also, compared with primary research, secondary research is quicker, easier, and less expensive, and it requires less methodological expertise. However, secondary research likely was collected for reasons other than those pertaining to the specific problem at hand, which means the information may be dated, biased, or simply not specific enough to answer the research questions. Primary research, in contrast, can be designed to answer very specific questions, but it also can be expensive and time consuming.

Key Terms

- conclusive research, 252
- data mining, 244
- data warehouses, 244
- experimental research, 258
- exploratory research, 252
- focus group interview, 253
- in-depth interview, 253
- information, 258

- marketing information system (MkIS), 243
- marketing research, 242
- observation, 252
- panel research, 258
- primary data, 250
- projective technique, 255

- questionnaire, 255
- scanner research, 258
- secondary data, 247
- structured questions, 256
- survey, 255
- syndicated data, 248
- unstructured questions, 255

Marketing Applications

1. A large department store collects data about what its customers buy and stores these data in a data warehouse. If you were the store's buyer for children's clothing, what would you want to know from the data warehouse that would help you be a more successful buyer?

2. Identify a not-for-profit organization that might use marketing research, and describe one example of a meaningful research project that it might conduct. Discuss how this project would be useful to the organization.

3. Marketing researchers do not always go through the steps in the marketing research process in sequential order. Provide an example of a research project that might not follow this sequence.

4. A new men's clothing store is trying to determine if there is a significant market for its type of merchandise in a specific location where it is considering putting a store. Would it be most likely to use primary or secondary data, or a combination of the two, to answer this question?

5. A high-tech firm has just developed a new technology to correct bad vision without surgery or contact lenses. The company needs to estimate the demand for such a service. Would it use primary or secondary data, or a combination of the two?

6. A bank manager notices that by the time customers get to the teller, they seem irritated and impatient. She wants to investigate the problem further, so she hires you to design a research project to figure out what is bothering the customers. What type of research method would you recommend? Is it an exploratory or conclusive method?

7. Snapple has developed a new beverage, and it wants to determine if it should begin to market it throughout the United States. The company used two separate studies for the advertising campaign:
   - A focus group to identify the appropriate advertising message for the new beverage and
   - A survey to assess the effectiveness of the advertising campaign for the new Snapple beverage.

   Which study was exploratory and which was conclusive? What other studies would you recommend Snapple undertake?

8. Suppose your university wants to modify its course scheduling procedures to better serve students. What are some secondary sources of information that might be used to conduct research into this topic? Describe how these sources might be used. Describe a method you could use to gather primary research data about the topic. Would you recommend a specific order in obtaining each of theses types of data? Explain your answer.

9. Tony is planning to launch a new shampoo and is trying to decide what features and price would interest consumers. He sends a request for a proposal to four marketing research vendors, and three respond, as described in the table below.

   Which vendor should Tony use? Explain your rationale for picking this vendor over the others.

Vendor A	Vendor B	Vendor C
The vendor that Tony has used in the past, it estimates it can get the job done for $200,000 and in two months. The vendor plans to do a telephone-based survey analysis and use secondary data.	Tony's key competitor has used this vendor, which claims that it can get the job done for $150,000 and in one month. This vendor plans to do a telephone-based survey analysis and use secondary data. During a discussion pertaining to its price and time estimates, the vendor indicates it will draw on insights it has learned from a recent report prepared for one of Tony's competitors.	This well-known vendor has recently started to focus on consumer packaged good clients. It quotes a price of $180,000 and a time of one month. The vendor plans to conduct a Web-based survey analysis and use secondary data.

Net Savvy

1. Go to the Web site for the Gallup Organization (www. gallup.com), which administers public opinion polls. Search the site for results from any recent survey that is available for free. Print out the results. Identify the objective(s) of the survey. Discuss one of the major findings, and provide an interpretation of the data.

2. Visit the Eopinions.com Web site (www.eopinions. com), a clearinghouse for consumer reviews about different products and services. Think of a particular business with which you are familiar, and review the ratings and comments for that business. Discuss the extent to which this site might be useful to a marketer for that company who needs to gather market research about the company and its competitors. Identify the type of research this process involves— secondary or primary? Exploratory or conclusive?

Chapter Case Study

NIKE: GOING AFTER FEMALE CONSUMERS[22]

Nike is the top athletic shoe and apparel company in the world. It possesses a strong reputation in the industry, built largely around its association with world-class athletes like Michael Jordan, and its Nike swoosh is recognized around the world. But for a company named after the Greek goddess of victory, the company traditionally has failed to cater to female consumers as well as some of its smaller competitors have. Nike began to recognize that it could not survive without attracting women to its products, so it undertook a research effort to design a marketing offering that would attract female consumers.

Does Nike do a good job of marketing to women?

Nike Women

In the hypercompetitive market for athletic shoes and apparel, every company must jockey for market share. The market, though it can be segmented on many different bases, including age or gender and different types of sports, includes a significant proportion of customers who want the gear for their casual use, not as armor on the playing field.

The reality of the market is that 81 percent[23] of all athletic purchases are made by women, but for Nike, they represented only 20 percent of total sales.[24] To say Nike has totally ignored women is inaccurate; it offers an extensive line of products for women and girls. But none of its stores targeted women only. Its flagship Niketown stores, located in major metropolitan areas, appeal mainly to men with their in-your-face style, pulsating music, and jock bravado appeal. Even though Niketown stores carry merchandise for women, the strong drive to appeal to men had become a turnoff for many female customers. In the words of Fara Warner of *Fast Company:*

> Consider the San Francisco Niketown. The women's section is on the fourth floor. But getting there isn't a matter of taking a few escalators. At each floor, women looking for workout shoes or a yoga mat have to wade through displays on basketball, golf, and hockey to catch the next escalator up. The feel of the store is dark, loud, and harsh—in a word, male.[25]

Nike executives began to see the signs that the flagship brand, which stood for hyper-competitive athletes, was becoming associated only with men and totally failed to appeal to women. Realizing that something must change, Nike offered a horror film parody ad during the 2000 summer Olympic games, in which a female Olympian in a bra ran from an attacker. Female viewers quickly responded that the ad was in very poor taste and that they would be taking their business elsewhere. Among those put off by the ad were 30 celebrity women who contacted CEO Phil Knight directly. Nike needed help understanding the women's market. It turned to outside marketing researchers.

The results of focus group interviews in New York, Chicago, and Seattle conducted with active, working women, 21 to 34 years of age, showed that women viewed sports differently than men did. Sports were a normal part of their daily schedule, not a separate activity, and many women were motivated to try a sport or activity because of an emotional, inner drive.

The launch of the www.nikegoddess.com Web site in 2001 was a direct result of this research. On the site, Nike included a survey to learn more about its female consumers and soon discovered that women:[26] (1) wanted information that would motivate and inspire them; (2) craved new ideas for ways to do more in their lives because being active wasn't just something to do, it was something they were; and (3) participated in physical activities to get not just fit but emotionally stronger and more confident.

Questions

1. How should Nike use the information collected from the focus groups and the survey at www.nikegoddess.com to appeal to its female customers?

2. Propose two different research methods besides the focus groups and online survey that would enable Nike to answer the same research questions. Which method(s) would you use?

10

Product, Branding, and Packaging Decisions

Why do people buy jeans named after truck fuel and priced at $130 to $170 when they could buy Wrangler jeans at Wal-Mart for $14.94?[1] Because Diesel, with its provocative and irreverent ads that often parody the pretensions of upscale designers, aims to create value for its nonconformist customers who have grown disenchanted with the seeming emptiness promoted in other jeans ads.

Italian-based Diesel was created by Renzo Russo and a few partners. In 1985, after Russo bought out his partners, he began to build the business into the dominant global brand that exists today. The company's headquarters in Molvena, Italy, oversees its 17 subsidiaries and more than 2,500 employees worldwide. It now has a presence in over 80 countries and almost 50 company-owned stores.

Everything about Diesel is unique. Consider the in-store experience of shoppers, for example. The 40 different cuts and 50 different washes available wallpaper the shelves with no apparent directory or labeling to ease the shopping experience. This forces shoppers to depend on help from the sales staff, who are ever-present in the background. Unlike any other store experience, Diesel has found a way to create a closer connection between sales staff and customers and therefore between customers and the brand.

Its advertising is also different. The "Diesel–For Successful Living" campaign offered a spoof on the typical ways that fashion is advertised to upper-crust consumers. Although considered absurd and pointless to some, its advertising amuses its loyal consumer base by suggesting a seriousness that is obviously playful. For instance, a pamphlet circulated in Europe in 2003 declared that, according to company market research, "In the last 9

Everything Diesel does helps build its brand, including its advertising. Although considered absurd and pointless to some, its advertising amuses its loyal consumer base and makes them want to go out and buy jeans.

months the total amount received in tips by waitresses wearing Diesel jeans has tripled." Is this for real? The public doesn't ask, and it doesn't care. They just go out and buy Diesel jeans.

Everything Diesel does helps build its brand. Partnering with Warner Music International (WMI), it dared its loyal customers to part with their "most embarrassing" piece of music. In exchange for their donation, customers received a CD compiled of tracks from artists like Busta Rhymes, Lynyrd Skynyrd, and other WMI musicians. The 50,000 CDs were available only through Diesel Stores, and all the donated "embarrassing" CDs were auctioned off on eBay as a charity benefit.

Its innovative marketing campaigns were once considered company suicide by marketing professionals. Now they're considered ingenious. Diesel has taken its high-quality, high-priced jeans and created real panache, strong brand equity, high customer awareness, and intense loyalty.

■ ■ ■

As a key element of a firm's marketing mix (the 4Ps) strategies, product strategies, along with price, are central to the creation of value for the consumer. A **product** is anything that is of value to a consumer and can be offered through a voluntary marketing exchange. In addition to *goods,* such as toothpaste, or *services,* such as a haircut, products might also be *places* (e.g., Disney World), *ideas* (e.g., "stop smoking"), *organizations* (e.g., The American Red Cross), *people* (e.g., George Bush), or *communities* (e.g., MotleyFool.com) that create value for consumers in their respective competitive marketing arenas.

This chapter begins with a discussion of how firms adjust their product lines to meet and respond to changing market conditions. Then we turn our attention to branding—why are brands valuable to the firm, and what are the different branding strategies firms use? We also never want to underestimate the value of a product's packaging and label. These elements must send out a strong message from the shelf: Buy me! The final section of this chapter examines packaging and labeling issues.

Product Assortment and Product Line Decisions

The complete set of all products offered by a firm is called its **product assortment** or **product mix.** Colgate-Palmolive's product assortment is shown in Exhibit 10.1. The product assortment typically consists of various **product lines,** which are groups of associated items, such as items that consumers use together or think of as part of a group of similar products. Colgate-Palmolive's product lines include oral care, personal care, household care, fabric care, and pet nutrition.

Within each product line, there are often multiple product categories. A **product category** is an assortment of items that the customer sees as reasonable substitutes for one another. For example, in the oral care product line, Colgate-Palmolive offers several categories: toothpaste, toothbrushes, kid's oral care products, whitening products, floss, and oral first aid. Each category within a product line may use the same or different **brands,** which are the names, terms, designs, symbols, or any other features that identify one seller's good or service as distinct from those of other sellers.[2] For instance, Colgate-Palmolive offers several brands of toothbrushes (e.g., Plus, Whitening, Massager, Navigator).

EXHIBIT 10.1	Colgate-Palmolive Product Assortment				
	Product Lines				
	Oral Care	**Personal Care**	**Household Care**	**Fabric Care**	**Pet Nutrition**
Product Categories	*Toothpaste* (Colgate Total) *Toothbrush* (Colgate Plus) *Kids' products* (Colgate Barbie Bubble Fruit toothpaste) *Whitening products* (Colgate Simply White) *Floss* (Colgate Total Dental Floss) *Oral first aid* (Colgate Orabase)	*Deodorants* (Speed Stick) *Bar soap* (Irish Spring) *Body wash* (Soft Soap) *Hand wash* (Soft Soap) *Men's toiletries* (Skin Bracer Aftershave)	*Dishwashing liquid* (Palmolive) *Automatic dishwashing liquid* (Palmolive) *Household cleaners* (Ajax) *Dish wipes* (Palmolive)	*Laundry detergents* (Fab) *Fabric softener* (Suavitel)	Hill's Pet Nutrition, Inc.–subsidiary *Dog food* (Science Diet) *Cat food* (Science Diet)

Product assortments can also be described in terms of their breadth and depth. A firm's **product line breadth** (sometimes also referred to as variety) represents the number of product lines offered by the firm; Colgate-Palmolive has five. **Product line depth**, in contrast, is the number of categories within a product line. Within Colgate-Palmolive's oral care line, for example, there are several categories—toothpaste, toothbrushes, kids' products, and so forth. Its pet nutrition product line, however, comprises fewer categories and therefore has less depth.

Within each product category are a number of individual items called **stock keeping units** (SKUs), which are the smallest unit available for inventory control. Within the toothpaste category, for instance, Colgate-Palmolive offers 49 Colgate SKUs that represent various sizes, flavors, and configurations of Colgate Herbal White, Colgate Total, and Colgate Fresh Confidence.[3] The **category depth** is the number of SKUs within a category.

The decision to expand or contract product lines and categories depends on several industry-, consumer-, and firm-level factors. Among the industry factors, firms expand their product lines when it is relatively easy to enter a specific market (entry barriers are low) and/or when there is a substantial market opportunity.[4] When firms add new product categories and brands to their product assortments, they often earn significant sales and profits, as was the case with Doritos' Cool Ranch product line, Ford's Explorer line, and Chrysler's minivans.[5]

However, unchecked and unlimited product line extensions may have adverse consequences. Too much variety in the product assortment is often too costly to maintain, and too many brands may weaken the firm's brand reputation.[6] In the past several years, for example, Heinz has gone through a major restructuring, consolidating its global operations and increasing concentration on those products and markets that were doing well. In Europe, it reduced the number of different Heinz ketchup options (as indicated by the bottle designs available) from 24 to 12.[7]

Now let's look at why firms change their product mix's breadth, depth, or number of SKUs, as well as product line decisions for services.

Change Product Mix Breadth

Firms may change their product mix breadth by either adding to or deleting categories.

Increase Breadth   Firms often add new product categories to capture new or evolving markets, increase sales, and compete in new venues. After years of simply watching sports-utility vehicle (SUV) sales increase steadily, Porsche decided to enter the SUV market with its Porsche Cayenne. The vehicle, which debuted in 2003, attempts to live up to the performance standards and sporty image Porsche sports cars enjoy. Porsche's decision to extend to a new product category was no surprise, given that approximately 40 percent of Porsche sports car owners were buying SUVs as their second automobiles.[8]

Decrease Breadth   Sometimes it is necessary to delete entire product lines to address changing market conditions or meet internal strategic priorities. A few years ago, SC Johnson sold off many products in its skin care line, including its successful Aveeno brand, to Johnson & Johnson.[9] The firm no longer competes in the skin care business, though it remains a strong competitor in its original product lines, such as home cleaning (Pledge, Windex), air care (Glade), and home storage (Saran, Ziploc).[10]

Do you really need 450 hp to pick up diapers?
You ever run out of diapers?

The Cayenne Turbo

The Quikie Mart doesn't get any quicker. Cayenne Turbo. Seamless acceleration through all six gears. 0 to 60 in 5.2 seconds. The stability of Porsche Traction Management and Active Suspension. An SUV, but decidedly a Porsche when you need one most. Porsche. There is no substitute.

PORSCHE

Porsche increased its product mix breadth by adding the Cayenne SUV. It was a natural extension since 40 percent of Porsche sports car owners were buying SUVs as their second car.

Change Product Mix Depth

As with product line breadth, firms occasionally either add to or delete from their product line depth.

Increase Depth Firms may add new product lines or categories to address changing consumer preferences or preempt competitors while boosting sales. In 2003, Levi-Strauss introduced its Signature line of low-cost jeans to be sold through Wal-Mart. Later that year, the firm started selling the Signature line through Target as well.[11] The Signature line is priced at only $21 to $23 a pair, almost half the price of the popular Levi's 505 and 501 brands (the "red tab" line) sold through department stores.[12] The firm's decision was not only an attempt to get a much-needed sales boost but also a response to the new reality that powerful retailers like Wal-Mart and Macy's, not powerful manufacturers, now had the balance of power in the marketplace.[13]

Decrease Depth From time to time it is necessary to delete product lines or categories to realign resources. The decision to delete product lines is never taken lightly. Generally, substantial investments have been made to develop the brand and manufacture the products. Consumer goods firms, such as Procter & Gamble and Unilever, make pruning decisions regularly to eliminate unprofitable items and refocus their marketing efforts on more profitable items. For example, when executives at consumer goods giant Unilever noted flat sales and declining profits in 1999, they recognized they were carrying a lot of excess baggage. The company took decisive action to divest in 400 core brands, like Ragu pasta sauces, and reduce its portfolio of 1,600 brands. This move made Unilever more competitive with rivals like Procter & Gamble and freed up resources for future acquisitions, such as Ben & Jerry's Homemade Ice Cream.[14]

Change Number of SKUs

A very common and ongoing activity for many firms is the addition or deletion of SKUs in existing categories to stimulate sales or react to consumer demand. Fashion manufacturers and their retailers, for instance, change their SKUs every season. Generally, these changes are minor, such as a different color or fabric. Sometimes though, the change is more drastic, such as when jeans manufacturers lowered the waistline and flared the legs of their products.

Product Line Decisions for Services

Many of the strategies used to make product line decisions for physical products can also be applied to services. For instance, a service provider like a bank typically offers different product lines for its business and retail (consumer) accounts; those product lines are further divided into categories based on the needs of different target markets.

On the retail side, banks offer savings and checking accounts to individual consumers. The different types of accounts thus are equivalent to SKUs. Bank of America (BofA), one of the world's largest financial institutions that serves more than 33 million customers in the United States and additional customers in 150 other countries,[15] offers a variety of checking account products to meet the needs of its different target markets. For example, with Bank of America Advantage Checking®, customers who maintain higher balances are rewarded with preferred interest and free banking services. For customers older than 55 years of age, BofA offers Bank of America Advantage for Seniors®, which allows customers to invest in CDs and use up to $2,500 of their value, without early withdrawal penalties, for expenditures or emergencies. BofA even offers college accounts, like CampusEdge™ Checking, with low opening deposits and low fees.[16]

Branding

Branding provides a way for a firm to differentiate its product offerings from those of its competitors and can be used to represent the name of a firm and its entire product assortment (General Motors), one product line (Chevrolet), or a single item (Corvette). Brand names, logos, symbols, characters, slogans, jingles, and even distinctive packages constitute the various brand elements firms use,[17] which they usually choose to be easy for consumers to recognize and remember. For example, most consumers are aware of the Nike Swoosh logo and would recognize it even if the word "Nike" did not appear on the product or in an advertisement. Exhibit 10.2 summarizes these brand elements.

Value of Branding for the Customer and the Marketer

Brands add value to merchandise and services beyond physical and functional characteristics or the pure act of performing the service.[18] Let's examine some ways in which brands add value for both customers and the firm. (See Exhibit 10.3.)

Brands Facilitate Purchasing   Brands are often easily recognized by consumers and, because they signify a certain quality level and contain familiar attributes, brands help consumers make quick decisions.[19] When consumers see a brand like Honda, they immediately know what it is, its level of quality and engineering, its relative status, how much it generally costs, and, most important, whether they like it and want to buy it. Brands enable customers to differentiate one firm or

EXHIBIT 10.2	What Makes a Brand?
Brand Element	**Description**
Brand name	The spoken component of branding, it can either describe the product or service/product characteristics and/or be composed of words invented or derived from colloquial or contemporary language. Examples include Comfort Inn (suggests product characteristics), Saturn (no association with the product), or Avanade (invented term).
URLs (uniform resource locators) or domain names	The location of pages on the Internet, which often substitutes for the firm's name, such as Yahoo! and Amazon.
Logos and symbols	Logos are visual branding elements that stand for corporate names or trademarks. Symbols are logos without words. Examples include the Nike Swoosh and the Mercedes star.
Characters	Brand symbols that could be human, animal, or animated. Examples include the Pillsbury Doughboy and the Keebler Elves.
Slogans	Short phrases used to describe the brand or persuade consumers about some characteristics of the brand. Examples include State Farm's "Like A Good Neighbor" and Dunkin Donuts' "America Runs On Dunkin."
Jingles	Audio messages about the brand that are composed of words or distinctive music. Examples are Intel's four-note sound signature that accompanies the "Intel Inside" slogan.

Source: Kevin Lane Keller, *Strategic Brand Management*, 2d ed. (Upper Saddle River, NJ: Prentice Hall, 2003).

product from another. Without branding, how could we easily tell the difference between a Honda and a Toyota without looking very closely?

Brands Establish Loyalty   Over time and with continued use, consumers learn to trust certain brands. They know, for instance, that Band-Aid bandages always perform in the exact same way. Many customers become loyal to certain brands in much the same way that you or your friends likely have become loyal to your college. They wouldn't consider switching brands and, in some cases, feel a strong affinity to certain brands. For instance, Coca-Cola drinkers don't drink Pepsi, and wouldn't dare touch a Dr Pepper.

Brands Protect from Competition and Price Competition   Strong brands are somewhat protected from competition and price competition. Because such brands are more established in the market and have a more loyal customer base, neither competitive pressures on price nor retail-level competition is as threatening to the firm. For instance, Chemise LaCoste is known for its polo shirts. Although many similar brands are available and some retailers offer their own brands, LaCoste is perceived to be of superior quality, garners a certain status among its users, and can therefore command a premium price.

Brands Reduce Marketing Costs   Firms with well-known brands can spend relatively less on marketing costs than firms with little-known brands because the brand sells itself. People have become familiar with Target's red-and-white bull's-eye logo, so its advertisements don't need to explain who the company is or what it does. People just know.

Brands Are Assets   Brands are also assets that can be legally protected through trademarks and copyrights and thus constitute a unique ownership for the firm. Firms sometimes have to fight to keep their brands "pure." Rolex and other Swiss

| EXHIBIT | 10.3 | Value of Branding |

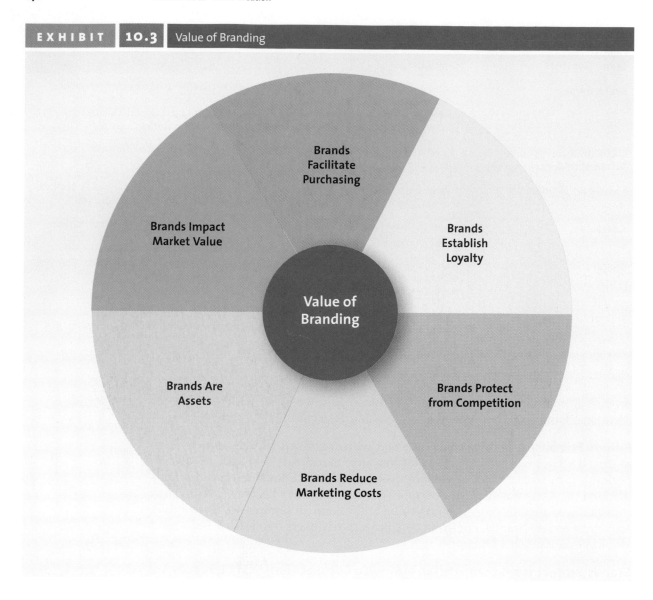

watch companies are ever watchful to ensure that the value of their brands is not diluted with counterfeit merchandise or sales through nonauthorized dealers.

Brands Impact Market Value   Having well-known brands can have a direct impact on the company's bottom line. The value of a brand can be calculated by assessing the earning potential of the brand over the next 12 months;[20] as some examples, the world's 10 most valuable brands appear in Exhibit 10.4.

Brand Equity

The value of a brand translates into brand equity, or the set of assets and liabilities linked to a brand that add to or subtract from the value provided by the product or service.[21] Like the physical possessions of a firm, brands are assets the firm can build, manage, and harness over time to increase its revenue, profitability, and overall value. Firms spend millions of dollars on promotion, advertising, and other

Ingeniously designed to help protect the things that need protecting.

At Honda, we continue to show our commitment to "Safety for Everyone" by developing new technologies designed to help protect you and your family in the event of an accident. Regardless of the size or price of your Honda.* By studying the dynamics of collisions between vehicles, our engineers created the

ACE helps absorb frontal-collision energy.

Advanced Compatibility Engineering™ (ACE™) body structure. It's a unique design that helps spread the energy of a frontal collision throughout the body. ACE is only from Honda and comes standard on the all-new Civic. In the future, ACE will come standard on many of our models as they evolve. After all, we made a promise to help keep all of our drivers and passengers safe.

Safety for Everyone.   **HONDA**
The Power of Dreams

*Does not include specialty vehicles: Honda Insight, Honda S2000 and Acura NSX. © 2005 American Honda Motor Co., Inc. safety.honda.com

When customers see an ad for Honda, they immediately make associations with familiar attributes, like safety, to help them make quick decisions.

marketing efforts throughout a brand's life cycle. These marketing expenditures, if done carefully, result in greater brand recognition, awareness, and consumer loyalty for the brand.

Polo/Ralph Lauren has mastered the art of building brand equity by defining its own version of value. The name Polo/Ralph Lauren, the ubiquitous polo player, and associated brands like Polo/Ralph Lauren Purple Label, RLX, and Polo Jeans Co. have engendered a loyal following throughout North America and the rest of the world. Ralph Lauren merchandise can command prices 50 to 100 percent higher than similar-quality merchandise from lesser known and appreciated designers and manufacturers. The brand, under the tight control of its parent company, has been licensed for tabletop, bed and bath, furniture, paints, broadloom, and gift items.[22] These licensed products are manufactured and distributed by firms other than Polo/Ralph Lauren, but the brand association earns them greater value.

How do we know how "good" a brand is, or how much equity it has? Experts look at four aspects of a brand to determine its equity: brand awareness, perceived value, brand associations, and brand loyalty. (See Exhibit 10.5.)

Brand Awareness   **Brand awareness** measures how many consumers in a market are familiar with the brand and what it stands for and have an opinion about that brand. The more aware or familiar customers are with a brand, the easier

EXHIBIT	10.4	The World's 10 Most Valuable Brands	
Rank	Brand	Country of Ownership	Brand Value in 2004 ($ Billions)
1	Coca-Cola	U.S.	67
2	Microsoft	U.S.	59.9
3	IBM	U.S.	56.2
4	GE	U.S.	48.9
5	Intel	U.S.	32.3
6	Nokia	Finland	30.1
7	Toyota	Japan	27.9
8	Disney	U.S.	27.8
9	McDonald's	U.S.	27.5
10	Mercedes	Germany	21.8

Source: The Business Week/Interbrand Annual Ranking of the 2006 Best Global Brands, http://www.ourfishbowl.com/images/press_releases/IB_Press_Release_BGB06.pdf

their decision-making process will be. Familiarity matters most for products that are bought without much thought, such as soap or chewing gum. However, brand awareness is also important for infrequently purchased items or items the consumer has never purchased before. If the consumer recognizes the brand, it probably has attributes that make it valuable.[23] For those who have never purchased a Toyota, for instance, just being aware of the brand can help facilitate a purchase. Certain brands gain such predominance in a particular product market over time that they

These brands have such predominance in their product market that the brand name is used as the generic product category.

EXHIBIT | **10.5** | Brand Equity

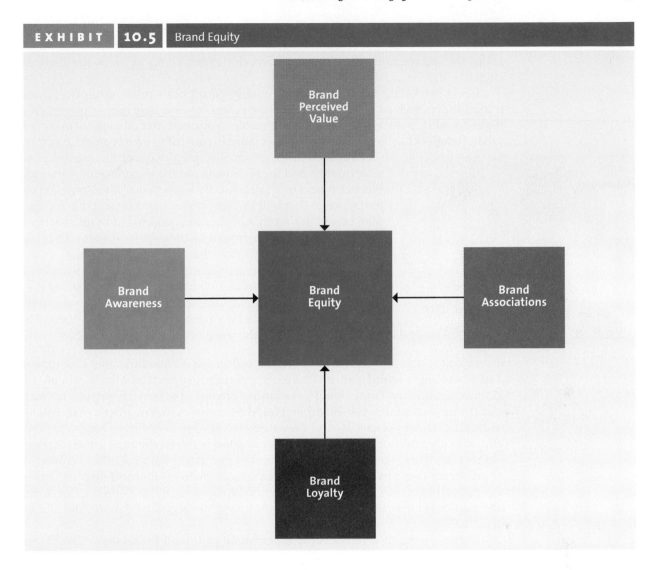

become synonymous with the product itself; that is, the brand name starts being used as the generic product category. Examples include Kleenex tissue, Clorox bleach, Xerox copiers, Band-Aid adhesive bandages, and Rollerblade skates. Companies must be vigilant in protecting their brand names, because if they are used so generically, over time, the brand itself can lose its trademark status.

Marketers create brand awareness through repeated exposures of the various brand elements (brand name, logo, symbol, character, packaging, or slogan) in the firm's communications to consumers. Such communication media include advertising and promotions, personal selling, sponsorship and event marketing, publicity, and public relations[24] (see Chapters 17–19). Because consumer awareness is one of the most important steps in creating a strong brand, firms are willing to spend tremendous amounts of money advertising the brand, including more than $2 million for just one 30-second spot on television during the Super Bowl.

Perceived Value Brand awareness alone does not ensure a strong brand. Consumers could be aware of a brand but have a negative opinion of its value or of the firm's reputation. **Perceived value**, therefore, is the relationship between a product or service's benefits and its cost. Customers usually determine the offering's value in relationship to that of its close competitors. If they feel an inexpensive brand is about the same quality as a premium brand, the perceived value of the cheaper choice is high.

Good marketing raises customers' quality perceptions relative to price; thus, it increases perceived value. Many customers tend to associate higher prices with higher quality, but they also have become more informed and perceptive in recent years. Retailers like Target and Kohl's specialize in providing great value. Certainly, merchandise at these stores is not always of the highest possible quality, and the apparel is not the most fashion-forward. But customers don't necessarily want to buy a wastebasket or paring knife that will last for 50 years and be suitable for display in a living room, nor do they need to show up at school looking like they came from a fashion-show runway. Instead, they want products to do what they were designed to do and be available at a reasonable price. SuperCuts, a national haircutting chain, provides "hip haircuts at an affordable price"—usually one-half to one-third salon prices. Its customers perceive the chain to be a great value because the haircut is better than good and the price is more than reasonable.

SuperCuts, a national haircutting chain, provides its customers with a great value because the haircut is better than good and the price is more than reasonable.

Brand Associations   Brand associations reflect the mental links that consumers make between a brand and its key product attributes, such as a logo, slogan, or famous personality. These brand associations often result from a firm's advertising and promotion efforts. For example, Wal-Mart conveys its low prices with advertising that stresses price cuts and the slogan "Everyday Low Prices." Associations with specific attributes help create differentiation between the brand and its competitors, as when Volvo stresses that its cars are made with consumer safety in mind. Firms also attempt to create specific associations for their brands with positive consumer emotions, such as fun, friendship, good feelings, family gatherings, and parties. State Farm Insurance advertises that "like a good neighbor, State Farm is there."

Firms sometimes even develop a personality for their brands, as if the brand were human. Brand personality refers to such a set of human characteristics associated with a brand,[25] which has symbolic or self-expressive meanings for consumers.[26] Brand personality elements include male, female, young, old, fun-loving, and conservative, as well as qualities such as fresh, smooth, round, clean, or floral.[27] McDonald's has created a fun-loving, youth-oriented brand personality with its golden arches, brightly lit and colored restaurants, exciting and youthful packaging and advertising, and spokesperson and mascot Ronald McDonald, the clown.

Brand Loyalty   Brand loyalty occurs when a consumer buys the same brand's product or service repeatedly over time rather than buying from multiple suppliers within the same category.[28] Therefore, brand-loyal customers are an important source of value for firms. First, such consumers are often less sensitive to price. In return, firms sometimes reward loyal consumers with loyalty or customer relationship management (CRM) programs, such as points customers can redeem for extra discounts or free services, advance notice of sale items, and invitations to special events sponsored by the company. Second, the marketing costs of reaching loyal consumers are much lower because the firm does not have to spend money on advertising and promotion campaigns to attract these customers. Loyal consum-

Life goes by in the blink of an eye, so now is the time to talk to your State Farm agent about Life Insurance. You've trusted us with your car and home, you can count on us for Life Insurance, too. To make sure you're keeping up, see your State Farm agent or visit us at statefarm.com® today.

STATE FARM
Auto
Life   Fire
INSURANCE ®

LIKE A GOOD NEIGHBOR, STATE FARM IS THERE.®
Providing Insurance and Financial Services

What do YOU think of when you hear, "like a good neighbor…"?

ers simply do not need persuasion or an extra push to buy the firm's brands. Third, a high level of brand loyalty insulates the firm from competition because, as we noted in Chapter 2, brand-loyal customers do not switch to competitors' brands, even when provided with a variety of incentives.

Firms can manage brand loyalty through a variety of CRM programs. They create associations and clubs to provide a community feeling among loyal customers,[29] like Harley-Davidson's Harley Owners Group (HOG), which the company formed in 1983 so Harley owners could meet with other owners in their communities. As we described in Chapter 4, more than 1,000 HOG chapters worldwide host a total of almost 1 million members. Other firms, like airlines, hotels, long-distance telephone providers, credit card companies, and retailers, have developed frequent buyer/user programs to reward their loyal customers. The better CRM programs attempt to maintain some continuous contact with loyal customers by sending them birthday cards or having a personal sales associate contact them to inform them of special events and sales.

Adding Value 10.1 illustrates how difficult it is to build a brand from scratch, especially in a global setting.

Branding Strategies

Firms institute a variety of brand-related strategies to create and manage key brand assets, such as the decision to own the brands, establishing a branding policy, extending the brand name to other products and markets, cooperatively using the brand name with that of another firm, and licensing the brand to other firms.

Adding Value 10.1

Building a Brand from Scratch in the United States

Shanghai Tang, an upscale apparel brand and retailer was founded in 1994 and has become China's first global, upscale brand. As China's 1.3 billion people enter the capitalistic marketplace, opportunities are flourishing not only for established Western brands and businesses to enter China, but for Chinese to expand beyond their borders.

On November 21, 1997 at 6:18 p.m., a time chosen by a feng shui advisor, Shanghai Tang opened its Madison Avenue doors across from the upscale retailer, Barney's. The grand opening was a success, but the store missed its target of attracting the stylish shoppers on New York's most stylish streets. Eighteen months later Shanghai Tang moved down the street to a smaller and cheaper storefront. The firm learned that it needed to be more modern. Shanghai Tang's first U.S. store attempted to sell silver rice bowls and traditional Chinese dress to the American public. However, its customers wanted high-end fashion with subtle Chinese touches, not purely Chinese ornamentation. Also, to compete in the world of posh designers and finicky customers, the company needed to develop a consistent brand that included wearable clothing that is continually changing to keep customers intrigued and coming back.

Joanne Ooi, Shanghai Tang's creative director, quickly realized that to succeed it had to be a blended East/West brand. For each collection she researches a theme and then disperses the fundamental items that encapsulate the theme to her designers around the world. For the fall/winter 2005 collection, for instance, the theme was Beijing's Forbidden City. She extracted symbols from the emperor's robe, such as the sun,

Have you ever heard of Shanghai Tang? Well, it's no wonder. They are relatively new to the U.S. Next time you are on Madison Avenue in New York, check it out.

moon, and five-clawed dragon and suggested accents of brocade, jade, and fur. It is important to Ooi that each item has an element of prestige, but also is wearable.

These changes have paid off, as the firm reports solid sales in its new Madison Avenue store. While Shanghai Tang plans to open five new stores a year in the world's most fashionable cities, it is still focusing its efforts on the Asian market; its hometown presence in Asia makes up 70 percent of its stores. Shanghai Tang is owned by Richemont, a luxury brand group managing brands such as Cartier and Mont Blanc.

Source: Linda Tischler, "The Gucci Killers," *Fast Company,* January, 2006 (102), p. 42, www.richemont.com.

Brand Ownership

Brands can be owned by any firm in the supply chain, whether manufacturers, wholesalers, or retailers. There are three basic brand ownership strategies: manufacturer or national brands, private label or store brands, and generic brands. (See Exhibit 10.6.) **Manufacturer brands** are owned and managed by the manufacturer, are also known as **national brands,** and include Nike, Mountain Dew, Kitchenaid, and Marriott. The majority of the brands marketed in the United States are manufacturer brands. Manufacturing firms spend millions of dollars each year to promote their brands. For example, Procter & Gamble spends about $100 million in media expenditures annually to promote its Tide brand of liquid and powdered detergents.[30] By owning their brands, manufacturers retain more control over their marketing strategy, are able to choose the appropriate market

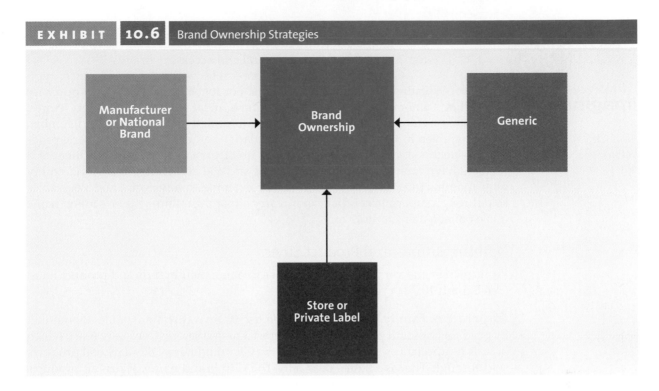

EXHIBIT **10.6** Brand Ownership Strategies

segments and positioning for the brand, and can build the brand and thereby create their own brand equity.

Brands that are owned and managed by retailers, in contrast, are called **private-label** or **store brands.** Some manufacturers prefer to make only private-label merchandise because the costs of national branding and marketing are prohibitive, whereas other firms manufacture both their own brand and merchandise for other brands or retailers. For instance, Whirlpool sells appliances under its own name and also makes them for Sears under the Kenmore brand. Wholesalers also sometimes develop private-label brands. President's Choice, a private label developed and marketed by Canada's largest food distributor, Loblaw Companies, is extremely successful in Canada and parts of the United States.[31] President's Choice is positioned as a premium, high-quality private label with moderate prices.[32] Private-label brands are particularly common in supermarkets, discount stores, and drug stores. Their popularity among consumers depends on several

President's Choice, a private label developed and marketed by Canada's largest food distributor, Loblaw Companies, is successfully positioned as a premium, high-quality private label with moderate prices.

factors, including consumer preferences for a lower-cost brand and the trust consumers have in the store and its brand. Such private-label brands, especially those marketed by large chains such as Wal-Mart and Costco, are fast gaining in popularity and consumer loyalty. Recently, Wal-Mart's private-label Ol' Roy dog food sales surpassed those of Nestlé's Purina to make it the world's top-selling dog food.[33]

Private-label brands have also gained popularity in apparel and other categories found in department and specialty stores. Nordstrom, for instance, provides several store brands, including

imagination at work

All of General Electric's brands carry the GE brand name, so they all benefit from the brand awareness associated with the corporate name.

Preview, Essentials, and Premier. Specialty retailers, such as The Gap and Victoria's Secret, stock only their own labels and rank among the top 20 most recognized apparel and accessory brands.[34]

Generic products are those sold without brand names, typically in commodities markets. For instance, shoppers can purchase unbranded salt, grains, produce, meat, or nuts in grocery stores. Hardware stores often sell unbranded screws, nuts, and lumber. However, even in these markets, the popularity and acceptance of generic products has declined. Consumers question the quality and origin of the products, and retailers have found better profit potential and the ability to build brand equity with manufacturer and store brands. For example, many fruits and vegetables sold through supermarket chains now carry either the manufacturer's brand name (Dole bananas) or the store's.

Naming Brands and Product Lines

Firms use several very different strategies to name their brands and product lines. (See Exhibit 10.7.)

Corporate or Family Brand   A firm can use its own corporate name to brand all its product lines and products, such as the General Electric Company (GE), which brands its appliances prominently with the GE brand name. Similarly, all products sold through The Gap stores bear only The Gap brand name. When all products are sold under one corporate or family brand, the individual brands benefit from the overall brand awareness associated with the family name.

Corporate and Product Line Brands   A firm also could use combinations of the corporate and product line brands to distinguish its products. For example, Kellogg's uses its family brand name prominently on its cereal brands (e.g., Corn

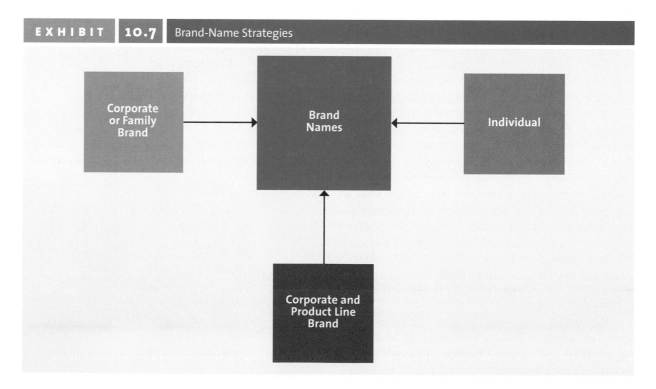

EXHIBIT 10.7 Brand-Name Strategies

Corporate or Family Brand → Brand Names ← Individual

Corporate and Product Line Brand → Brand Names

Depending on the brand, sometimes Kellogg's uses its family brand name prominently on its cereal brands, while other times the individual brand's name is more prominently displayed on the package.

Flakes, Froot Loops, Rice Krispies). In other cases, the individual brand's name is more prominently displayed on the package than the Kellogg's name, as in the case of Pop-Tarts, Eggo, Cheez-Its, and Nutri-Grain. In addition, Kellogg's owns other brands, such as Keebler, that are not overtly associated with the family brand.

Individual Brands   A firm can use individual brand names for each of its products. For example, in its house and home products line, Procter & Gamble markets various detergent products (Tide, Gain, Cheer, Downy, Febreze), paper products (Bounty, Charmin), household cleaners (Mr. Clean, Swiffer), and dishwashing products (Cascade, Dawn, Joy). Furthermore, it markets brands in various other product lines, such as personal and beauty products (Olay, Old Spice, Secret, Cover Girl), health and wellness products (Prilosec OTC, Glide, Puffs), baby products (Pampers, Luvs), and pet nutrition and care products (Iams).[35]

Choosing a Name   Although there is no simple way to decide how to name a brand or a product line, the more the products vary in their usage or performance, the more likely it is that the firm should use individual brands. For instance, Harley-Davidson has partnered with the Buell Motorcycle Company since 1993 and owned the firm since 1998. Yet Buell has retained its individual brand name and unique identity because the product lines are so different. Harleys are generally cruisers and touring bikes, whereas Buells are sportsbikes. Customers looking for one won't generally be interested in the other.

Brand Extension

A brand extension refers to the use of the same brand name for new products being introduced to the same or new markets.[36] The dental hygiene market, for instance, is full of brand extensions; Colgate, Crest, and Butler all sell toothpaste, toothbrushes, and other dental hygiene products. Brand extensions are also common in global expansions. For example, Coca-Cola, Nike, and Levi's are sold the world over under the same name. In some cases, firms use the same wording and lettering in their logos when extending their brands globally.

There are several advantages to using the same brand name for new products. First, because the brand name is already well established, the firm can spend less in developing consumer brand awareness and brand associations for the new product.[37] Gillette's Braun brand started selling kitchen appliances (coffeemakers, toasters, food processors, blenders, juicers) in the United States , then extended into various other product categories, including shaving (dry razors, beard care), beauty care products (cordless hair stylers), oral care products (power toothbrushes), and steam irons.[38]

Crest uses a brand extension strategy since they use the same brand name for many related products.

Second, if the brand is known for its high quality, that perception will carry over to the new product. Following its success in the PC market, Dell extended its brand name to monitors, printers, handheld computers, digital juke boxes, LCD televisions, servers, and network switches, among other products.[39]

Third, the marketing costs for a new product by an established brand are lower because consumers already know and understand the brand. Moreover, consumers who have adopted the core brand are more likely to try the extension.

Fourth, when brand extensions are used for complementary products, a synergy exists between the two products that can increase overall sales. For example, Frito-Lay markets both chips and dips under its Frito-Lay and Doritos brand names.[40] When people buy the chips, they tend to buy the dips as well.

Fifth, successful brand extensions can boost the sales of the parent or core brand because adopters of the extended brand may now try the parent brand, if they are not already using it. For example, consumers who had not used the Neutrogena brand before trying the Neutrogena On-the-Spot Acne Patch might be encouraged to try Neutrogena moisturizing lotion, especially if their experience with the acne patch has been positive.[41]

Not all brand extensions are successful, however. Some can dilute brand equity.[42] **Brand dilution** occurs when the brand extension adversely affects consumer perceptions about the attributes the core brand is believed to hold.[43] For example, Cadbury's association with fine chocolates and candy was weakened when the company extended its brand name to mainstream food products such as mashed potatoes and soups.[44] If the brand extension is very similar to the core brand, it even could cause cannibalization of sales from the core brand. Entrepreneurial Marketing 10.1 examines the rise and extension of Sir Richard Branson's brand, Virgin.

To prevent the potentially negative consequences of brand extensions, firms must consider the following caveats:

- Marketers should carefully evaluate the fit between the product class of the core brand and that of the extension.[45] If the fit between the product categories is high, consumers will consider the extension credible, and the brand association will be stronger for the extension.

- Firms should carefully evaluate consumer perceptions of the attributes of the core brand and seek out similar attributes for the extension because brand-specific associations are very important for extensions.[46] For example, if HP printers were associated with reliability, performance, and value, consumers would expect the same brand-specific attributes in other products that carried the HP brand name.

- Firms should refrain from extending the brand name to too many products and product categories to avoid diluting the brand and damaging brand equity.

- Firms should consider whether the brand extension will be distanced from the core brand, especially if the firm wants to use some but not all of the existing brand associations. When Marriott introduced its budget line of hotels, it downplayed the Marriott name, calling the new chain Fairfield Inn. And did you even know that Marriott International owns 99 percent of the Ritz-Carlton chain of luxury hotels? Not many people do, and that ignorance is by the company's design. The information is buried on the Ritz-Carlton's Web page.[47]

Entrepreneurial Marketing 10.1

Exploring Virgin Territories

Sir Richard Branson's first business venture was a magazine called *Student*, launched in 1968 when he was only 17.[48] Two years later, he started a mail-order record company called Virgin, but the business was adversely affected by a postal strike the very next year. He then opened his first Virgin record store, followed by a recording studio and a record label. In 1984, Branson started Virgin Atlantic Airways. The Virgin label can now be found on a broad array of product categories and markets, including health clubs (Virgin Active), book publishing (Virgin Books), travel and tourism (Virgin Holidays, Virgin Express, Virgin Limobike, Virgin Trains), cell phones (Virgin Mobile), and cosmetics (Virgin Cosmetics), to name a few. These product categories currently enjoy group sales of over $8 billion and maintain approximately 35,000 employees.[49]

The Virgin name has been placed on products and product categories far removed from its core businesses: air travel and music stores (the firm sold its record business to Thorn EMI in 1992). These developments have challenged the conventional wisdom that successful brand extensions must occur in similar product categories. However, Virgin's core emphasis on value has made most of its extensions successful. Some believe that the success of the Virgin brand extensions is due not to the quality of any particular Virgin product but to the characteristics associated with the family brand—being irreverent, entertaining, and unconventional.

Although it may appear that there are no limits to extending the Virgin brand name, the firm experienced some failures, especially in the alcoholic and cola beverages markets. Its brand of vodka was a failure, and Virgin Cola failed in the United States and achieved only

Sir Richard Branson has successfully extended the Virgin brand beyond its core businesses of air travel and music stores. One of his latest ventures is Virgin Home Loans.

a 3 percent market share in the United Kingdom. The primary risk that Virgin runs from extending its brand too far is not being able to satisfy all its customers of all its brands. As long as the customer has a nice flight on Virgin Atlantic, he or she may try Virgin Mobile. But if that same person has a bad experience with his or her cell phone contract, Virgin Atlantic—and the other Virgin brands—may lose a customer forever.

Cobranding

Cobranding is the practice of marketing two or more brands together, on the same package or promotion. Primarily due to credit card companies, such as Visa and MasterCard, the practice has greatly increased in the past decade. Airlines were among the first to cobrand with credit card companies (such as the United Visa Card), but recently, firms in other industries, such as banking, retail, and restaurants, have begun forming similar alliances. Starbucks was the first in the quick-service restaurant industry to offer its own Starbucks credit card in alliance with Visa.[50]

Cobranding enhances consumers' perceptions of product quality[51] by signaling "unobservable" product quality through links between the firm's brand and a well-known quality brand. For example, NutraSweet's claim to be a sugar substitute that was safe and left no aftertaste got a boost after both Coca-Cola and Pepsi started offering products that contained it. The cobranding of Intel, with its "Intel Inside" logo, helped boost the brand reputations of PC manufacturers that chose to use Intel chips.

Cobranding can also be a prelude to an acquisition strategy. FedEx entered into a cobranding arrangement with Kinko's, whereby it provided FedEx delivery services at Kinko's retail outlets.[52] Then in early 2004, FedEx acquired Kinko's for an estimated $2.4 billion and has begun rebranding Kinko's as FedEx Kinko's.[53]

However, there are, of course, some risks to cobranding, especially when customers for each of the brands are vastly different. For example, the Burger King and Häagen-Dazs cobranding strategy failed because the customer profiles for each brand were too different.[54] Cobranding may also fail if the brands' owners cannot resolve financial disputes about revenue or royalty sharing.[55] Finally, the firms that own the brands may change their priorities, as a result of which the cobranded product may no longer be available. In this scenario, the customer relationships and loyalty created with the cobranded product would be lost.[56]

Brand Licensing

Brand licensing is a contractual arrangement between firms, whereby one firm allows another to use its brand name, logo, symbols, and/or characters in exchange for a negotiated fee.[57] Brand licensing is common for toys, apparel, accessories, and entertainment products, such as video games; in the United States alone, it generates more than $100 billion in retail sales per year.[58] The firm that provides the right to use its brand (licensor) obtains revenues through royalty payments from the firm that has obtained the right to use the brand (licensee). These royalty payments sometimes take the form of an upfront, lump-sum licensing fee or may be based on the dollar value of sales of the licensed merchandise.

Several aspects of a brand can be licensed. Popular apparel designers, such as Ralph Lauren, Calvin Klein, and Eddie Bauer, and luxury goods manufacturers often license the right to use their brand name on a variety of products. The Porsche name is used by Grundig radios and also appears on watches, luggage sets, and tennis rackets. The computer world has even capitalized on the Porsche brand name with the game *Need for Speed: Porsche Unleashed*. One very popular form of licensing is the use of characters created in books and other media. Such entertainment licensing has generated tremendous revenues for movie studios like Disney, Lucas Films (think of the *Star Wars* memorabilia), and New Line (licensor of *Lord of the Rings* toys and collectibles), as well as for comic book publishers such as Marvel Entertainment Inc. (*Spider-Man*). A long-standing staple of licensing has been major league sports teams that play in the NBA, NFL, or NHL, as well as various collegiate sports teams.

Licensing is an effective form of attracting visibility for the brand and thereby building brand equity while also generating additional revenue. There are, however, some risks associated with it. For the licensor, the major risk is the dilution of its brand equity through overexposure of the brand, especially if the brand name and characters are used inappropriately.[59]

Consider, for instance, the famous—or possibly infamous—alligator shirt. In 1933, the company founded by Frenchman David Lacoste (the licensor), famous as a tennis player and for his nickname "the alligator," entered into a licensing agreement with Andre Gillier (the first licensee) to produce a high-quality, white, knit shirt with a ribbed collar, short sleeves, and a crocodile emblazoned on the right breast. The line expanded to include other casual apparel items, and in 1966, the

The famous tennis player Rene "the alligator" Lacoste (left in 1927 photo) co-founded a firm that made a white, knit shirt, with an alligator emblazoned on the right breast. The brand is still sold today (right) at Lacoste boutiques and stores like Neiman Marcus.

Lacoste name was licensed to American manufacturer Izod (the second licensee). Alligator-emblazoned apparel could be found in better department stores and country club golf and tennis shops into the late 1980s. But Izod also began to sell the alligator apparel in discount stores, and quality and sales suffered. The alliance continued until 1992, when Lacoste severed its ties with Izod. Lacoste has since regained its prestige image and can be found in boutiques and exclusive specialty department stores around the world.[60]

Licensors also run the risk of improperly valuing their brand for licensing purposes or entering into the wrong type of licensing arrangement. For example, Marvel Entertainment Inc.'s previous deals with movie studios for the use of its comic book characters were "undervalued," because the firm took lump-sum licensing fees up-front rather than pegging its royalty fees to sales. As a result, the firm probably left money on the table for deals on the first *X-Men* and *Blade* films.[61] In entertainment licensing, both licensors and licensees run the risk that characters based on books and movies will be only a fad. Moreover, the success or failure of merchandise based on movies is directly affected by the success or failure of the movie itself.[62]

Brand Repositioning

Brand repositioning or **rebranding** refers to a strategy in which marketers change a brand's focus to target new markets or realign the brand's core emphasis with changing market preferences.[63] As manufacturers were driving prices of appliances down and steel was pushing material costs up, Whirlpool began to see its appliances become a commodity. The company needed an innovation that would justify higher prices and increase its market share. Whirlpool's design chief fought against traditional mind sets and brought in usability researchers, graphic artists and engineers to design new appliances. The Duet is a result of one of these teams. It is a matching set of stylish washers and dryers that demands the highest price in the front-loading washer/dryer market and owns 20 percent of the front-loading

Whirlpool has successfully repositioned its washer/dryer market with the newly designed Duet line. It is so stylish that it has been displayed in Paris's Louvre Museum and has won a design award from the Smithsonian.

washer/dryer market. Whirlpool has brought appliances into a realm that previously didn't exist. Appliances can be "cool". Paris's Louvre Museum has exhibited Whirlpool's next-generation concept products and the Smithsonian awarded Whirlpool its annual National Design Award in corporate achievement.[64]

The growth of new marketing opportunities also may spur firms to reposition their brands. The growing youth segment, its purchasing power, and its increasing influence on household purchasing decisions has made firms in various industries sit up and take notice. Surf detergent's advertising, showing "laundry time" as an unpleasant chore but better than being in the dentist's chair, was targeted toward the youth segment and represented a welcome change from the rational "cleans better" message of most laundry detergents.[65] Since buying the Elizabeth Arden unit from Unilever in 2000, FFI Fragrances has repositioned several of the firm's cosmetics lines to attract younger consumers, using celebrities such as Kate Beckinsale, Kirsten Dunst, Sarah Jessica Parker, and Catherine Zeta-Jones in its advertisements.[66] Some magazines have also been repositioned, moving from the overcrowded young teen segment to slightly older teens, such as *YM*'s repositioning of its publication to cater to 19-year-olds.[67]

Repositioning can change the quality image of the brand too. In the U.S. wine market, Gallo's brand reputation and market share of almost 25 percent was built on an image of cheap wines that came in jugs with screw tops.[68] However, as consumers began buying more premium wines, Gallo repositioned itself as a quality wine producer—pricing up; promoting a young, fun, hip image in its advertisements; and seeking the endorsements of wine competition judges, celebrities, and restaurant employees.[69]

Repositioning also breathes life into old brands. Such revitalization sometimes can result from changing the packaging and/or altering the characteristics of the brand.[70] Aqua Velva aftershave lotion changed its packaging to a more convenient bottle, and Arm & Hammer started advertising a variety of uses for its baking soda, including deodorizing refrigerators.[71]

Although repositioning can improve the brand's fit with its target segment or boost the vitality of old brands, it is not without costs and risks. Firms often need to spend tremendous amounts of money to make tangible changes to the product and packages, as well as intangible changes to the brand's image through advertising. These costs may not be recovered if the repositioned brand and messages are not credible to the consumer or if the firm has mistaken a fad for a long-term market trend.

Packaging

Packaging is an important brand element with more tangible or physical benefits than the other brand elements because packages come in different types and offer a variety of benefits to consumers, manufacturers, and retailers. The **primary package** is the one the consumer uses, such as the toothpaste tube. From the primary package, consumers typically seek convenience in terms of storage, use, and consumption.

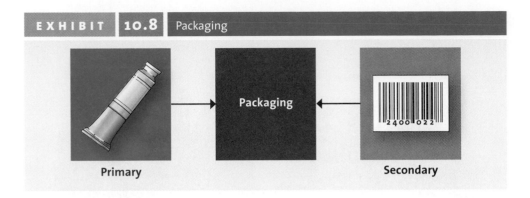

EXHIBIT 10.8 | Packaging

Primary → Packaging ← Secondary

The **secondary package** is the wrapper or exterior carton that contains the primary package and provides the UPC label used by retail scanners, see Exhibit 10.8. Consumers can use the secondary package to find additional product information that may not be available on the primary package. Similar to primary packages, secondary packages add consumer value by facilitating the convenience of carrying, using, and storing the product.[72]

Retailers' priorities for secondary packaging, however, differ: They want convenience in terms of displaying and selling the product. For customers, Labatt Blue's Blue Light Mountain Pack beer container of 20 cans offers a triangular shape and convenient handle-like slots for carrying it from the store; for retailers, the packaging offers the means to easily stack the containers into various mountain shapes in the retailer's display.[73] The secondary package can also be an important marketing tool for the manufacturer if it is used to convey the brand's positioning. Cosmetics giant Estée Lauder considers the secondary package to be primarily about brand image, so its packages portray a modern, sophisticated look that is immediately recognizable.[74]

In addition, secondary packages often may be packed into larger cartons, pallets, or containers to facilitate shipment and storage from the manufacturer to the retailer. These shipping packages benefit the manufacturer and the retailer in that they protect the shipment during transit; aid in loading, unloading, and storage; and allow cost efficiencies due to the larger order and shipment sizes.

Because all these packages are critical to the firm's brand positioning and shelf appeal, many innovations in design and materials have occurred in the past few decades. Some examples include[75]

- **Stand-up, reclosable zipper pouches.** Capri Sun's stand-up pouch juice drink took the lead; now a variety of products and pouch types are available, including pouches with reclosable zippers.
- **Aluminum beverage cans.** First introduced in 1965, cans dominated the beverage market by 1985. Even some water and energy drink brands now are available in aluminum cans.
- **Ring-pull cans.** First supplied by Alcoa to Pittsburgh Brewing Co. for its Iron City brand, the ring-pull is now a standard feature of all beverage cans, as well as several other types of food cans, including soups and nuts.
- **Aseptic drink bottles.** TetraPak and IP provided designs and machinery that increased the shelf life of beverages without refrigeration. They are used primarily by juice marketers.

Innovative packages can enhance a product's positioning and shelf appeal. Consider: reclosable packages, child-resistant/senior-friendly packages, ring-pull aluminum cans, aseptic drink bottles and twist-off tops.

- **Child-resistant/senior-friendly packages.** Products that are harmful to children under the age of five years, such as drugs and medicines, solvents, chemicals, and pesticides, now are packaged with child-resistant tops. In 1995, the Consumer Products Safety Council amended the child-resistant packaging protocol so that older adults could easily open such packaging.

Product Labeling

The label for Dannon Yogurt highlights seven specific benefits.

Labels on products and packages provide information the consumer needs for his or her purchase decision and consumption of the product. In that they identify the product and brand, labels are also an important element of branding and can be used for promotion. The information required on them must comply with general and industry-specific laws and regulations, including the constituents or ingredients contained in the product, where the product was made, directions for use, and/or safety precautions.

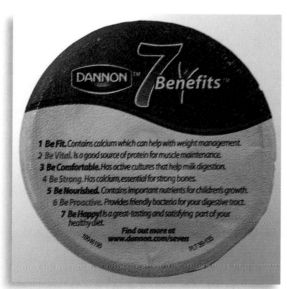

Many labeling requirements stem from various laws, including the Federal Trade Commission Act of 1914, the Fair Packaging and Labeling Act of 1967, and the Nutrition Labeling Act of 1990. Several federal agencies, industry groups, and consumer watchdogs carefully monitor product labels. The Food and Drug Administration is the primary federal agency that reviews food and package labels and ensures that the claims made by the manufacturer are true. Recently, the Food Safety and Inspection Service of the U.S. Department of Agriculture required that all raw meat and poultry products be labeled to provide nutrition information.[76]

Ethical Dilemma 10.1   Why Is Food More Fattening in the United States Than in the United Kingdom?

How is it that an American jar of mayonnaise has double the saturated fat of a jar sold in London?[78] The culprit is soy oil, a genetically altered ingredient used to make mayonnaise in the United States. In the United Kingdom, however, putting soy oil into a product poses a problem: Genetically modified food has become a serious issue for consumers. Consumer protests have led to the adoption of new labeling requirements that are designed to alert consumers to the presence of genetically modified ingredients. Unwilling to incur the wrath of consumers, Hellmann's and other mayonnaise manufacturers substitute vegetable oil for soy oil in the United Kingdom and anywhere else that requires a descriptive label. Vegetable oil is lower in saturated fats, which leads to the difference between a jar of mayonnaise in the two countries.

For food manufacturers, it is not just consumer protests that are causing product changes; there are also increasing concerns about the global rise in obesity. Many countries are investigating whether to regulate the marketing of food products or require products deemed "unhealthy" or "junk food" to carry warning labels. In response, manufacturers are scrambling to reformulate certain products to be lower in fat, salt, sugar, and calories. Some products are promoting these new changes, such as calcium enriched Kraft Macaroni & Cheese and General Mills' whole grain cereals.

For food marketers, the reality is that tastes vary in every country. Some countries prefer sweeter products and others sour. Some prefer salty or spicy versus bland. Therefore, the recipes and ingredients used in food products are carefully chosen and tested to match consumer preferences, as well as to meet shipping and shelf life considerations.

To address consumers' heightened sensitivity to health concerns, some firms, in a questionable attempt to make products appear healthier, have played games with the serving sizes listed on the label. Thus, one label for a candy bar might list information as it pertains to one serving, considered to be the entire bar, whereas the label for another candy bar also lists the information for one serving, but defines a serving as half the bar. Although not inaccurate, this type of labeling has the potential to mislead consumers into thinking a product is healthier than it truly is. Companies also might tout the health benefits of their products while downplaying less attractive product attributes. For example, some consumer packaged goods manufacturers advertise that their products are low fat, but in order to make them still taste good, they add sugar and/or salt.

Should firms provide full disclosure on labels and try to make products healthier, or should they make products that they think consumers want and let them make their own health decisions?

Manufacturers' claims on labels also can be subject to criticisms by various consumer groups. In the United Kingdom, the consumer watchdog group ITC ruled that Danone's Shape yogurt was not "virtually fat free," as its label claimed. The Dairy Industry Federation guidelines state that only products containing less than 0.3 grams of fat per every 100 grams could be called "virtually fat free," but Danone's Shape yogurt contained three times that amount.[77]

Ethical Dilemma 10.1 illustrates the problems food manufacturers face with regard to the types of ingredients they use in their products, as well as the associated labeling concerns. These concerns are further compounded when the products are sold across international borders.

A product label is much more than just a sticker on the package; it is a communication tool. Many of the elements on the label are required by laws and regulations (i.e., ingredients, fat content, sodium content, serving size, calories), but other elements of the label remain within the control of the manufacturer. How manufacturers use labels to communicate the benefits of their products to consumers varies by the product. For example, the label for Dannon yogurt highlights the fact that yogurt contains calcium. Many other products highlight other specific ingredients, vitamin content, or nutrient content (e.g., iron). This focus signals to consumers that the product offers these benefits. Although often overlooked, the importance of the label as a communication tool should not be underestimated.

Summing Up

1. **How do firms adjust their product lines to changing market conditions?**

   Market conditions change. New opportunities arise, others mature and die. Competition may become more intense or competitors may move on to pursue other opportunities. Firms grow their product lines by adding either new product categories or new SKUs within a product category. The decision to add products should be made carefully. Excessive product line expansions can confuse consumers and dilute the appeal of the brand's core products. Sometimes, products or product lines become unprofitable, the firm's priorities change, or consumer preferences shift. When this happens, firms must prune their product lines by deleting items or possibly even entire product categories.

2. **Why are brands valuable to firms?**

   Brands facilitate the consumer search process. Some customers are loyal to certain brands, which essentially protects those brands from competition. In addition, brands are valuable in a legal sense, in that trademarks and copyrights protect firms from counterfeiters and knockoff artists. Firms with well-known brands can spend relatively less on marketing because the brand and its associations help sell the product. Finally, brands have real market value as a company asset.

3. **How do firms implement different branding strategies?**

   Firms use a variety of strategies to manage their brands. First, they must decide whether to offer national, private-label, or generic brands. Second, they have a choice of using an overall corporate brand or a collection of product line or individual brands. Third, to reach new markets or extend their current market, they can extend their current brands to new products. Fourth, firms can cobrand with another brand to create sales and profit synergies for both. Fifth, firms with strong brands have the opportunity to license their brands to other firms. Sixth and finally, as the marketplace changes, it is often necessary to reposition a brand.

4. **How do a product's packaging and label contribute to a firm's overall strategy?**

   Like brands, packaging and labels help sell the product and facilitate its use. The primary package holds the product, and its label provides product information. The secondary package provides additional consumer information on its label and facilitates transportation and storage for both retailers and their customers. Labels have become increasingly important to consumers because they supply important safety, nutritional, and product usage information.

Key Terms

- brand, 271
- brand association, 280
- brand awareness, 277
- brand dilution, 286
- brand equity, 276
- brand extension, 285
- brand licensing, 288
- brand loyalty, 280
- brand personality, 280
- brand repositioning (rebranding), 289
- category depth, 272
- cobranding, 287
- corporate and product line brands, 284
- corporate brand (family brand), 284
- generic, 284
- individual brands, 285
- manufacturer brands (national brands), 282
- perceived value, 279
- primary package, 290
- private label (store brands), 283
- product, 270
- product assortment, 271
- product category, 271
- product line breadth, 272
- product line depth, 272
- product lines, 271
- product mix, 271
- secondary package, 291
- stock keeping units (SKUs), 272

Marketing Applications

1. Prepared foods at Whole Foods Market, the world's largest retailer of organic foods, are very profitable. To make them even more profitable, suggest two strategies that would alter the product mix breadth and depth.

2. Suppose you have just been hired by a jewelry manufacturer as a marketing consultant. The manufacturer has been making private-label jewelry for 75 years but is thinking about developing its own brand of jewelry. Discuss the advantages and disadvantages of such a strategy.

3. Identify a specific brand that has developed a high level of brand equity. What specific aspects of that brand establish its brand equity?

4. Are you loyal to any brands? If so, pick one and explain why you believe you are loyal, beyond that you simply like the brand. If not, pick a brand that you like and explain how you would feel and act differently toward the brand if you were loyal to it.

5. Ford Motor Company owns several brands: Ford, Lincoln, Mercury, Mazda, Volvo, Jaguar, Land Rover, and Aston Martin. Within each brand are many models, each of which has a unique identifying name. Wouldn't it be easier to just identify them all as Fords? Justify your answer.

6. Identify a specific company that has recently introduced a new brand extension to the marketplace. Discuss whether you believe the brand extension example you provided will benefit or harm the firm.

7. The Chicago Marathon is cobranded with LaSalle Bank (www.chicagomarathon.com). What are the benefits and potential liabilities of such a partnership from each group's point of view?

8. Do you think all food sold in a grocery store should have an ingredient and nutrition label? Consider the perspectives of consumers, the manufacturer, and the store.

9. You are hired by a small bakery that is interested in distributing its product through supermarkets. The market for the bakery's products has been steadily growing and it is time to expand distribution now that the bakery has expanded its production capacity. You have an appointment with the manager of a local grocery chain. The manager is familiar with the bakery's products and is excited about the possibility of having them in the store. He presents the contract and you notice a $10,000 fee for stocking the product. When you ask about the fee, you are told it is simply the cost of doing business and that the bigger bakeries are not in favor of adding your product line to the chain. You know that the bakery cannot afford to pay the fee. What should you do now?

Net Savvy

1. Visit the Procter & Gamble Web site (www.pg.com). Identify and briefly describe its different *product lines*. Now identify one of its *product categories*, and discuss the *product line breadth* of that particular category. Be sure to justify your answers.

2. Interbrand Corporation is a leading brand consultancy firm headquartered in New York that conducts research on the monetary value of different brands.

Visit the company's Web site (www.interbrand.com) and access the most recent "Best Global Brands" survey. Identify the top five brands, their brand values, and their countries of origin. Describe changes in the rankings of these firms from the previous year. Identify the brands with the greatest increase and the greatest decrease in terms of percentage change in brand value from the previous year.

Chapter Case Study

BAND-AID® BRAND PRODUCTS:[79]
BUILDING ON THE VALUE OF THE BRAND[80]

Part of global giant Johnson & Johnson's Consumer Products Company, Band-Aid® is widely known as a leader in the wound care market. With its dominant share of the market, the brand is widely recognized and respected by consumers and health care professionals alike. Known as an innovator of wound care products, the company continues to introduce new products that exploit creative technologies, one of which led *Good Housekeeping* magazine to name Band-Aid® Brand Liquid Bandage a "Good Buy" award winner. From its early beginnings to today, the company has excelled at providing value to its customers and demonstrated that people across the world can trust the brand.

The Brand Begins

Necessity is the mother of invention, and in the case of Band-Aid® the saying applies. Back in 1920, when Earl Dickson came home from his cotton-buying job at Johnson & Johnson, he would always find a hot meal that his wife Josephine had prepared for him. He also found visible burns and cuts on Josephine from her kitchen labors, which prompted Earl to piece together gauze squares and adhesive tape to cover her wounds. Soon, Earl decided to prepare ready-made bandages in this fashion, with pieces of gauze at intervals along the tape so that Josephine could cut the premade strip and tend to her wounds throughout the day. When the product was first launched in the market, the bandages were made by hand, were not sterile, and had annual sales of just $3,000.

The Company Today

Today, Band-Aid® products are machine-made and completely sterile. A visit to the company's Web site (www.bandaid.com) revels the distance Band-Aid® has come from the early tape and gauze product, as well as the modern demand for over-the-counter first-aid products in a variety of categories.

In keeping with its long history of product innovations, the company continues to invest in new product development and marketing (Exhibit C10.1). Band-Aids® come in a host of styles, including those with popular characters for kids; uniquely shaped bandages for various parts of the body; antibiotic Band-Aids® to help fight germs; waterproof products with aloe to treat burns; scar-healing strips; bandages in clear plastic, stretchy cloth, and round and square shapes; and treated and untreated pads. Moreover, the Band-Aid® franchise has expanded to include various ointments, gauze, tapes, and kits for a plethora of first-aid needs. For example, One-Step Cleansing + Infection Protection Foam antiseptic cleans and heals wounds without the need for antibiotic ointment; Calamine Spray dries rashes from poison ivy; Bug-Bite Relief Patches relieve itching and prevent scratching; and FIRST AID TO GO!® Mini First-Aid Kits include essential travel-sized products.

Band-Aids come in a variety of sizes and styles. These packages are made for children.

But new product introductions by Band-Aid® don't come cheap; of the $28 million marketing budget for 2003, $17 million was earmarked for three new product extensions. Advanced Healing Blister Block, a round, waterproof cushioning strip to heal and prevent foot blisters, received $7 million in marketing support to tout its ability to promote fast, natural healing. Finger Care Tough Strips obtained a marketing budget of $5 million and was rolled out as an extension of regular finger care products. Finally,

EXHIBIT	C10.1	Examples of Band-Aid® Product Innovations

Year	Product Innovation
1920	Band-Aid® brand adhesive bandages—3" wide and 18" long—introduced to the market
1924	First machine-made, sterile bandages
1940	Packaging adds red strings to open bandage packages
1951	Plastic strips
1956	Decorated bandages
1958	Sheer vinyl bandages
1994	Sport-strip bandages
1997	Antibiotic adhesive bandages with ointment on the pad
2000	Advanced healing strips for wound care
2001	Liquid bandage that promotes fast healing
2003	Scar-healing technology that fades red and raised scars

Source: www.bandaid.com.

Extra Large Tough Strips were also supported with $5 million for marketing.[81] Previous years' launches were similarly supported, including Liquid Bandages ($7 million), Water Block Bandages ($8 million), and Hurt-Free Antiseptic Wash ($5 million).

The company is in an enviable position. People around the world see the value of Band-Aid® products to heal, prevent, and repair minor nicks, cuts, scrapes, wounds, and bruises. Continued product innovations and line expansions likely will help the company continue to be the most recognized name in tape, bandages, and gauze.

Questions

1. Visit the company's Web site (www.bandaid.com) and identify and describe the different product lines that it markets. How would you describe its product line breadth?
2. Review the different product categories in each of the company's product lines. Which has the greatest breadth? Which has the least?
3. Look at the new products that the company offers. Identify which are extensions of the Band-Aid® brand name and which are not. Discuss the extent to which the brand extensions might dilute brand equity.
4. Review the company's products designed for children. To what extent do these use manufacturer (national) branding? Private-label (store) branding? Licensed branding? Justify your answers. What added value do these products offer compared with regular Band-Aid® protection products?

11

Developing New Products

W hen you run out of ideas, "who you gonna call?"[1] Many companies turn to IDEO, a design firm based in Palo Alto, California, for help. IDEO helps its clients generate new product and service ideas for industries as diverse as healthcare, toys, and computers. Among the many IDEO design successes have been the Palm V, the TiVo recorder, Polaroid's I-Zone camera, the Steelcase Leap chair, Crest's stand-up toothpaste tube, and Oral-B toothbrushes for children. The firm's designs have won numerous awards from various prestigious organizations and industrial design associations.

IDEO employs anthropologists, graphic designers, engineers, and psychologists whose special skills help foster creativity and innovation, which the firm puts to work for clients such as Procter & Gamble and Kaiser Permanente, the largest HMO in the United States, for which IDEO designed a new work environment. To name just a few, it also has worked with firms such as Nestlé, Hewlett-Packard, Vodafone, Samsung, AT&T Wireless, NASA, and the BBC.

In addition, IDEO does not just create products; it designs a better consumer experience. To do so, it follows five steps:

1. Observation. IDEO's cognitive psychologists, sociologists, and anthropologists work with their corporate clients to understand consumer experiences through various methods, including observing the consumer and interviewing both users and nonusers of the product.

2. Brainstorming. IDEO facilitates brainstorming sessions, in which a group gets together to generate new product or service ideas.

3. Prototyping. A prototype is a rough version of the physical product or a preliminary definition of a new service. Instead of actually making a physical product in this step, the team uses video technology to simulate the product or service.

4. Refining. Through further brainstorming and cooperation with the client, IDEO narrows the number of possible alternatives for the new product or service and develops actual prototypes.

5. Implementation. Finally, IDEO coordinates all resources, including engineering, design, and marketing, to create the new product or service.

■ ■ ■

Imagine living 200 years ago. You cook your meals on a stove fueled by coal or wood. As a student, you do your homework by hand, illuminated only by candlelight. You get to school on foot, by horseback, or in a horse-drawn carriage, if you're really fortunate. Your classroom is small and basic, and you have very few classmates. The professor simply lectures and writes on a chalkboard.

Fast forward to today. You finish your homework on a personal computer with word-processing software that appears to have a mind of its own and can correct your spelling automatically. Your climate-controlled room has ample electric light. While you work on your computer, you can also be talking with a friend using the hands-free headset of your wireless phone. On your way to school, in your car, you pick up fast food from a convenient drive-through window while listening to a mixture of songs recorded recently and more than 40 years ago, which are broadcast through the air from a satellite. When you arrive at college, you sit in a 200-person classroom in which you can plug in your laptop and take notes on your computer while the professor lectures with the aid of PowerPoint presentations.

None of these products were available a few years ago.

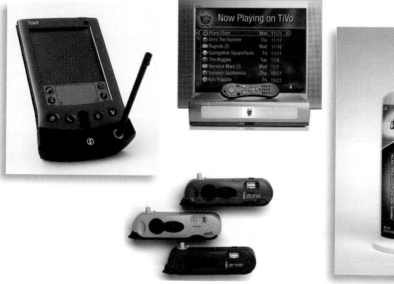

Our lives are defined by the many new products and services developed through scientific and technological advances and refined either with the help of companies like IDEO or by firms' internal product development teams. Whereas scientific research opens up the world of ideas, technological research transforms these ideas into interesting and useful services, tangible products, and processes.

This is the second chapter that deals with the first P in the marketing mix: product. Continuing our discussion from the preceding chapter, we explore how companies such as IDEO add value to firms' product and service offerings through innovation. We also look at how firms develop new products and services. We conclude the chapter with an examination of how new products and services are adopted by the market and how firms change their marketing mix as the product or service moves through its life cycle.

Innovation and Value

Innovation is the process by which ideas are transformed into new products and services that will help firms grow. Without innovation and its resulting new products and services, firms would have only two choices: continue to market current products to current customers or take the same product to another market with similar customers.

Although innovation strategies may not work in the short run, overriding long-term reasons compel firms to introduce new products and services. First, as they add new products to their offerings, firms can create and deliver value more effectively by satisfying the changing needs of their current and new customers or simply by keeping customers from getting bored with the current product or service offering. For example, Unilever's Dove Beauty Bar product line successfully extended the brand into hair, face, and skin care lines, all under the Dove umbrella. Today, Dove loyalists can enjoy not only bar soap but also antiperspirants and deodorants, moisturizing lotions, cleansers, toners, shampoo, conditioner, and much more.[2]

By adding new products, Unilever's Dove brand creates and delivers value more effectively by satisfying the changing needs of its current and new customers or simply by keeping customers from getting bored with its current product offerings.

Second, the longer a product exists in the marketplace, the more likely it is that the market will become saturated. Without new products or services, the value of the firm will ultimately decline.[3] Suppose, for instance, that Reebok adopted a strategy of producing the same sneakers year after year. Because many people don't actually wear out their shoes within a year, they would have no incentive to buy new ones. But people tend to get tired of the same old shoes and seek variety.[4] By introducing new lines several times a year, Reebok is able to sustain its growth.

Third, the portfolio of products that innovation can create helps the firm diversify its risk and therefore enhances firm value better than a single product can.[5] If some products in a portfolio are doing poorly, others may be doing well. Firms with multiple products are better able to withstand external shocks, including changes in consumer preferences or intensive competitive activity. For this reason, firms like 3M demand that a specific percentage of their sales each year must come from new products introduced within the previous few years.

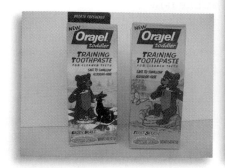

Have you ever heard of any of these products? No wonder. They all failed. Orajel (left) was a "fluoride-free" toothpaste targeted towards young children. Dunk-A-Balls cereal (center) was shaped like basketballs so children could play with them before eating them. The Garlic Cake (right) was supposed to be served as an hors d'oeuvre. But the company forgot to mention potential usage occasions to consumers, so people wondered why they would want to eat one.

Fourth, in some industries, such as the arts and software, most sales come from new products. For example, a motion picture generates most of its theater, DVD, and cable TV revenues within a year of its release. Consumers of computer software and video games demand new products in much the same way that fashion mavens demand new apparel styles.

The degree to which a new product or service adds value to the firm and for customers also depends on how new it really is. When we say a "new product," we don't necessarily mean that the product has never existed before; these completely new-to-the-market products represent fewer than 10 percent of all new product introductions each year. It is more useful to think of the degree of newness of a product on a continuum from "new-to-the-world"—as WiFi was a few years ago—to "slightly repositioned," such as the repositioning of Kraft's Capri Sun brand of ready-to-drink beverages, repackaged in a bigger pouch to appeal more to teens.

New product introductions, especially new-to-the-world products that create new markets, can add tremendous value to firms. These new products, also called **pioneers** or **breakthroughs**, establish a completely new market or radically change both the rules of competition and consumer preferences in a market.[6] Some examples of pioneers include minicomputers, the Intel microprocessor, Canon's desktop photocopiers, Microsoft's Windows operating system, eBay's online auction model, and the PalmPilot.[7]

Pioneers have the advantage of being **first movers**; as the first to create the market or product category, they become readily recognizable to consumers and thus establish a commanding and early market share lead. Studies also have found that market pioneers can command a greater market share over a longer time period than later entrants can.[8]

This finding does not imply, however, that all pioneers succeed.[9] In many cases, imitators capitalize on the weaknesses of pioneers and subsequently gain advantage in the market. Because pioneering products and brands face the uphill task of establishing the market alone, they pave the way for followers, which can spend less marketing effort creating demand for the product category and instead focus directly on creating demand for their specific brand. Also, because the pioneer is the first product in the market, it often has a less sophisticated design and may be priced relatively higher, leaving room for better and lower priced competitive products. The majority of new products are failures: As many as 95 percent of all consumer goods fail, and products across all markets and industries suffer failure rates of 50 to 80 percent.[10]

Even if they succeed, new-to-the-world products are not adopted by everyone at the same time. Rather, they diffuse or spread through a population in a process known as diffusion of innovation.

Diffusion of Innovation

The process by which the use of an innovation—whether a product or a service—spreads throughout a market group, over time and over various categories of adopters, is referred to as **diffusion of innovation**.[11] The theory surrounding diffusion of innovation helps marketers understand the rate at which consumers are likely to adopt a new product or service. It also gives them a means to identify potential markets for their new products or services and predict their potential sales, even before they introduce the innovations.

As the diffusion of innovation curve in Exhibit 11.1 shows, the number of users of an innovative product or service spreads through the population over a period of time and generally follows a bell-shaped curve. A few people buy the product or service at first, then increasingly more buy, and finally fewer people buy as the degree of the diffusion slows. These purchasers can be divided into five groups according to how soon they buy the product after it has been introduced.

EXHIBIT	11.1	Diffusion of Innovation Curve

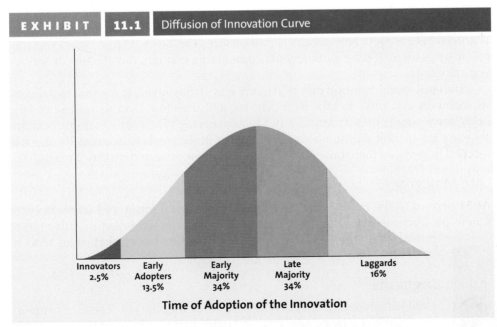

Source: Adapted from Everett M. Rodgers, *Diffusion of Innovation* (New York: The Free Press, 1983).

Innovators

Innovators are those buyers who want to be the first on the block to have the new product or service. These buyers enjoy taking risks and are regarded as highly knowledgeable. You probably know someone who is an innovator—or perhaps you are one for a particular product or service category. For example, the person who stood in line for days to be sure to get a ticket for the very first showing of the latest Harry Potter movie is an innovator in that context. Firms that invest in the latest technology, either to use in their products or services or to make the firm more efficient, also are considered innovators. Typically, innovators keep themselves very well informed about the product category by subscribing to trade and specialty magazines, talking to other "experts," searching the Internet, and attending product-related forums, seminars, and special events. Typically, innovators represent only about 2.5 percent of the total market for any new product or service.

However, these innovators are crucial to the success of any new product or service because they help the product gain market acceptance. Through talking and spreading positive word of mouth about the new product, they prove instrumental in bringing in the next adopter category, known as early adopters.

Early Adopters

The second subgroup that begins to use a product or service innovation is the early adopters. They generally don't like to take as much risk as innovators but instead wait and purchase the product after careful review. Early adopters tend to enjoy novelty and often are regarded as the opinion leaders for particular product categories.

This group, which represents about 13.5 percent of all buyers in the market, acts as opinion leaders who spread the word. As a result, early adopters are crucial for bringing the other three buyer categories to the market. If the early adopter group is relatively small, the number of people who ultimately adopt the innovation likely will also be small.

Early Majority

The early majority, which represents approximately 34 percent of the population, is crucial because few new products and services can be profitable until this large group buys them. If the group never becomes large enough, the product or service typically fails.

The early majority group differs in many ways from buyers in the first two stages. Its members don't like to take as much risk and therefore tend to wait until "the bugs" are worked out of a particular product or service. When early majority customers enter the market, the number of competitors in the marketplace usually also has reached its peak, so these buyers have many different price and quality choices.

Late Majority

Laggards may never adopt a new product or service.

At 34 percent of the market, the late majority is the last group of buyers to enter a new product market; when they do, the product has achieved its full market potential. By the time the late majority enters the market, sales tend to level off or may be in decline.

Laggards

Laggards make up roughly 16 percent of the market. These consumers like to avoid change and rely on traditional products until they are no longer available.[12] In some cases, laggards may never adopt a certain product or service.

Using the Diffusion of Innovation Theory

Using the diffusion of innovation theory, firms can predict which types of customers will buy their new product or service immediately after its introduction, as well as later as the product gets more and more accepted by the market. With this knowledge, the firm can develop effective promotion, pricing, and other marketing strategies to push acceptance among each customer group. However, because different products diffuse at different rates, marketers must understand what the diffusion curve for the new product looks like, as well as the characteristics of the target customers in each stage of the diffusion. The speed with which products diffuse depends on several product characteristics, illustrated in Exhibit 11.2.

Relative Advantage   If a product is perceived to be better than substitutes, then the diffusion will be relatively quick. Many believe, for example, that Starbucks' meteoric rise to success is because it is a superior substitute to doughnut or traditional coffee shops.

Compatibility   Similarly, the ritual of "having a coffee" is well ingrained in many cultures, including American culture. "Having a coffee" is consistent with people's

EXHIBIT	11.2	Factors Affecting Product Diffusion

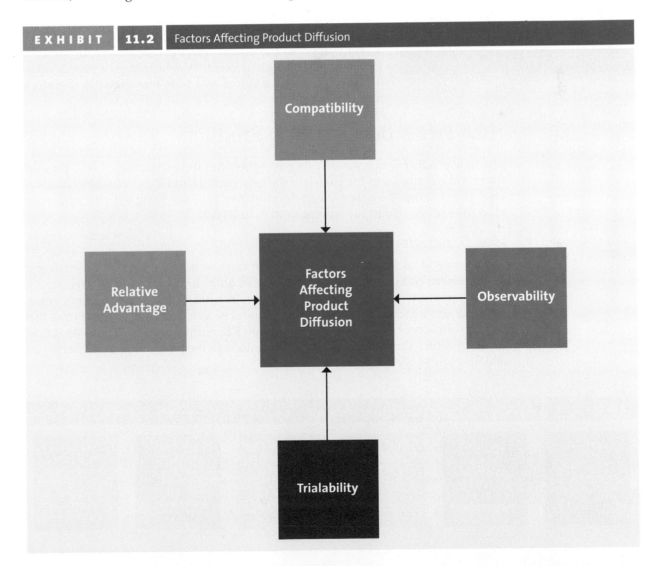

What has made Starbucks so successful? It has a strong relative advantage to other coffee venues. It is compatible with people's current behavior. Products and locations are easily observable by others. It is not complex and is easy to try.

past behavior, their needs, and their values. Since people are accustomed to drinking coffee, it has been relatively easy for Starbucks to acquire customers in the United States. The diffusion has been much slower in countries like China and Japan, where tea has been the traditional drink.

Observability   The ubiquitous Starbucks logo can be easily seen on cups in and around Starbucks stores. When products are easily observed, their benefits or uses are easily communicated to others, thus enhancing the diffusion process. A botox treatment to reduce wrinkles, on the other hand, is not easily observed by others and therefore has diffused more slowly.

Complexity and Trialability   Products that are relatively less complex are also relatively easy to try. These products will generally diffuse more quickly than those that are not. Purchasing a tall nonfat latte, for instance, is a lot easier than purchasing a new car with a GPS system.

The diffusion of innovation theory thus comes into play in the immediate and long-term aftermath of a new product or service introduction. But before the introduction, firms must actually develop those new offerings. Therefore, in the next section, we detail the process by which most firms develop new products and services and how they initially introduce them into the market.

How Firms Develop New Products

The new product development process begins with the generation of new product ideas and culminates in the launch of the new product and the evaluation of its success. The stages of the new product development process, along with the important objectives of each stage, are summarized in Exhibit 11.3.

Idea Generation

To generate ideas for new products, a firm can use its own internal research and development (R&D) efforts, collaborate with other firms and institutions, license technology from research-intensive firms, brainstorm, research competitors' products and services, and/or conduct consumer research, see Exhibit 11.4. Firms that want to be pioneers rely more extensively on R&D efforts, whereas those that tend to adopt a follower strategy are more likely to scan the market for ideas. Let's look at each of these idea sources.

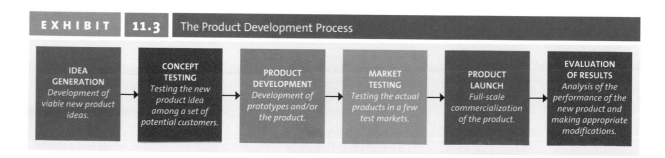

EXHIBIT 11.3   The Product Development Process

IDEA GENERATION	CONCEPT TESTING	PRODUCT DEVELOPMENT	MARKET TESTING	PRODUCT LAUNCH	EVALUATION OF RESULTS
Development of viable new product ideas.	*Testing the new product idea among a set of potential customers.*	*Development of prototypes and/or the product.*	*Testing the actual products in a few test markets.*	*Full-scale commercialization of the product.*	*Analysis of the performance of the new product and making appropriate modifications.*

EXHIBIT	11.4	Sources of Ideas

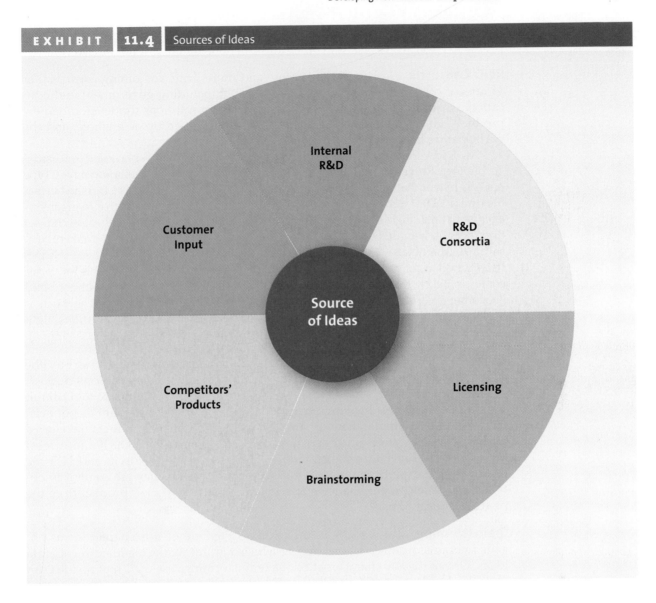

Internal Research and Development   Many firms have their own R&D departments, in which scientists work to solve complex problems and develop new ideas.[13] Historically, firms such as IBM in the computer industry, Rubbermaid in the consumer goods industry, 3M in the industrial goods industry, and Merck and Pfizer in the pharmaceuticals industry have relied on R&D development efforts for their new products. In other industries, such as software, music, and motion pictures, product development efforts also tend to come from internal ideas and investments.

The product development costs for these firms are quite high, and the resulting new product or service has a good chance of being a technological or market breakthrough. Firms expect such products to generate enough revenue and profits to make the costs of R&D worthwhile; however, R&D investments generally are considered continuous investments, so firms may lose money on a few new products. In the long run though, these firms are betting that a few extremely successful new products, often known as blockbusters, can generate enough revenues and profits to cover the losses from other introductions that might not fare so well.

R&D Consortia   In recent years, more and more firms are joining consortia, or groups of other firms and institutions, possibly including government and educational institutions, to explore new ideas or obtain solutions for developing new products. Here, the R&D investments come from the group as a whole, and the participating firms and institutions share the results.

An R&D consortium led by the Taiwanese government–sponsored Industrial Technology Research Group (ITRG) currently is working on developing a new type of DVD player that will play a red laser-based optical disk known as a forward versatile disc (FVD).[14] Disks created with the FVD system can store as much as 6 gigabytes of content on a single side. The consortium of 29 Taiwanese firms—including chip set designers such as Mediatek, DVD player makers such as BenQ, and disk makers such as CMC Magnetics—has begun marketing FVD players by offering them with 10 free movies to consumers in China and Taiwan at a total price of $160. This low price comes in below the production costs, but the consortium hopes it will attract rapid consumer acceptance. Compared with HD-DVD players, which may cost as much as $1,000 when they eventually are introduced, the FVD system offers consumers high-definition content at a very affordable price.

Licensing   For many new scientific and technological products, firms buy the rights to use the technology or ideas from other research-intensive firms through a licensing agreement. This approach saves the high costs of in-house R&D, but it means that the firm is banking on a solution that already exists but has not been marketed. For example, many pharmaceutical firms license products developed by biotechnology firms such as Amgen, Biogen, and Genentech. Because most biotechnology firms are smaller, tend to be very research focused, and lack the resources and expertise to market their own innovations, they are content to obtain some development financing and royalties on sales of their product from the pharmaceutical firms.[15]

Brainstorming   As we saw in the opening vignette of this chapter, firms engage in brainstorming sessions during which a group works together to generate ideas. One of the key characteristics of a brainstorming session is that no idea can be immediately accepted or rejected. The moderator of the session may channel participants' attention to specific product features and attributes, performance expectations, or packaging, but only at the end of the session do the members vote on the best ideas or combinations of ideas. Those four to eight ideas that receive the most votes are carried forward to the next stage of the product development process.

Competitors' Products   A new product entry by a competitor may trigger a market opportunity for a firm, which can use reverse engineering to understand the competitor's product and then bring an improved version to market. **Reverse engineering** involves taking apart a product, analyzing it, and creating an improved product that does not infringe on the competitors' patents, if any exist. This copycat approach to new product development is widespread and practiced by even the most research-intensive firms. Copycat consumer goods show up in grocery and drugstore products, as well as in technologically more complex products like automobiles and computers.

Customer Input   Listening to the customer is essential for successful idea generation.[16] Prior studies have found that as much as 85 percent of all new business-to-business (B2B) product ideas come from customers.[17] Because customers for B2B products are relatively few in number, firms can follow their use of products closely and survey them often for suggestions and ideas to improve those products. The firm's design and development team then works on these suggestions, sometimes in consultation with the customer. This joint effort between the selling firm and the customer significantly increases the probability that the customer eventually will buy the new product.

In the food and beverage industry, in which new product failure rates are as high as 78 percent, Kraft minimizes its risk through a careful new product development process that includes consumer research. Kraft's Tombstone Mexican-Style Pizza was developed after research revealed that Mexican cuisine and pizza were both favorites among teenage boys. Kraft also routinely holds "innovation weeks," during which all employees are encouraged to create new product ideas, and "idea fairs," in which key suppliers and key customers present new product ideas to the firm.[18]

One successful customer input approach is to analyze **lead users**, those innovative product users who modify existing products according to their own ideas to suit their specific needs.[19] These lead users have customized the firm's products; other customers might wish to do so as well. Thus, studying lead users helps the firm understand general market trends that might be just on the horizon. Manufacturers and retailers of fashion products often spot new trends by noticing how trendsetters have altered their clothing and shoes. For instance, designers of high-fashion jeans distress their products in different ways depending on signals they pick up "on the street." One season, jeans appear with whiskers, the next holes, the next paint spots. Products developed by paying attention to lead users include Gatorade, protein-based shampoo, Liquid Paper correction fluid, mountain bikes, chocolate milk, desktop publishing, and the World Wide Web.

At the end of the idea-generation stage, the firm should have several ideas that it can take forward to the next stage: concept testing.

These innovative consumers are called lead users *because they modify existing products according to their own ideas to suit their specific needs.*

Concept Testing

Ideas with potential are developed further into **concepts**, which in this context refer to brief written descriptions of the product; its technology, working principles, and forms; and what customer needs it would satisfy.[20] A concept might also include visual images of what the product would look like.

Concept testing refers to the process in which a concept statement is presented to potential buyers or users to obtain their reactions. These reactions enable the developer to estimate the sales value of the product or service concept, possibly make changes to enhance its sales value, and determine whether the idea is worth further development.[21] If the concept fails to meet customers' expectations, it is doubtful it would succeed if it were to be produced and marketed. Because concept testing occurs very early in the new product introduction process, even before a real product has been made, it helps the firm avoid the costs of unnecessary product development.

Ethical Dilemma 11.1 Should Cosmetics Firms Test Products on Animals?

Cosmetics testing on animals has been a primary issue for animal right activists for years.[26] As public opposition to animal testing increases, so do many companies' declarations that they "do not test products on animals". However, such statements can be misleading because even though the whole product may not have been tested on animals, the individual ingredients may have been. To help clarify any confusion, companies can apply to the Coalition for Consumer Information on Cosmetics (CCIC), a national group formed by eight animal welfare group members such as the American Humane Association and the Doris Day Animal League, and be certified as "cruelty free." They then can purchase the trademarked Leaping Bunny Logo for use on their labels from CCIC.

One of the founding principles of The Body Shop, and one that has resonated well with its customers is that its products are free of animal testing. Another major cosmetics manufacturer, Procter & Gamble, has eliminated animal testing on more than 80 percent of its products. It uses a combination of vitro testing, computer modeling, and historical data to determine the safety of new products and ingredients. These methods are more expensive than more traditional methods, but P&G claims that the results are better. If performed correctly, new chemicals can either be dropped from consideration or pushed forward in as little as three days compared to the six months previously required for animal testing.

Animal welfare groups continue to influence the use of animal testing in the cosmetics industry by using propaganda, pressure from consumers, and lobbying legislatures; and the industry continues to push back citing consumer choice, expense, and free trade.

The European Union has passed a ban on animal testing altogether. Beginning in 2009, any cosmetic tested on animals, even in other parts of the world, cannot be sold in the European Union. However, the cosmetic industry is worried that this ban will not only affect their companies' sales, but also their customers' ability to find the products they want. The E.U. cosmetics industry successfully lobbied for an extension on certain areas of toxicity testing to provide more time to find alternatives. The cosmetic industry believes it will be difficult to find alternative testing methods in time, and if they cannot, then they will have fewer ingredients to make the products consumers want.

The issues involved in animal testing for cosmetics are complex. At the broadest level, should firms be allowed to develop products that customers want, even if there is some potential harm to the environment or to those animals that share the environment with humans? More specifically, should firms be allowed to test products on animals, even when those products are not specifically designed to improve the health and well-being of their human users? After all, these products may make their users more attractive, but they will not save their lives. Does the testing that is performed endanger the lives or health of the animals?

The concept for an electric scooter might be written as follows:

The product is a lightweight electric scooter that can be easily folded and taken with you inside a building or on public transportation. The scooter weights 25 pounds. It travels at speeds of up to 15 miles per hour and can go about 12 miles on a single charge. The scooter can be recharged in about two hours from a standard electric outlet. The scooter is easy to ride and has simple controls—just an accelerator button and a brake. It sells for $299.[22]

Concept testing progresses along the research techniques described in Chapter 9. The firm likely starts with exploratory research, such as in-depth interviews or focus groups, to test the concept, after which it can undertake conclusive research through Internet or mall-intercept surveys. Video clips on the Internet might show a virtual prototype and the way it works so that potential customers can evaluate the product or service.[23] In a mall-intercept survey, an interviewer would provide a description of the concept to the respondent and then ask several questions to obtain his or her feedback.

The most important question pertains to the respondent's purchase intentions were the product or service made available. Marketers also should ask whether the product would satisfy a need that other products currently are not meeting. Depending on the type of product or service, researchers might also ask about the expected frequency of purchase, how much customers would buy, whether they would buy it for themselves or as a gift, when would they buy, and whether the price information (if provided) indicates a good value. In addition, marketers usually collect some demographic information so they can analyze which consumer segments are likely to be most interested in the product.

Some concepts never make it past this stage, particularly if respondents seem uninterested. Those that do receive high evaluations from potential consumers, however, move on to the next step, product development.

Product Development

Product development or product design entails a process of balancing various engineering, manufacturing, marketing, and economic considerations to develop a product's form and features or a service's features. An engineering team develops a product prototype that is based on research findings from the previous concept testing step, as well as their own knowledge about materials and technology. A prototype is the first physical form or service description of a new product, still in rough or tentative form, that has the same properties as a new product but is produced through different manufacturing processes—sometimes even crafted individually.[24]

Product prototypes are usually tested through alpha and beta testing. In alpha testing, the firm attempts to determine whether the product will perform according to its design and whether it satisfies the need for which it was intended.[25] Rather than using potential consumers, alpha tests occur in the firm's R&D department. For instance, Ben & Jerry's Ice Cream alpha tests all its proposed new flavors on its own employees at its corporate headquarters in Vermont. It may be a great job, but it also sounds rather fattening!

Many people, consumer groups, and governmental agencies are concerned when alpha testing involves tests on animals, particularly when it comes to pharmaceuticals and cosmetics. Ethical Dilemma 11.1 discusses these concerns in the United States and the European Union.

In contrast, beta testing uses potential consumers, who examine the product prototype in a "real use" setting to determine its functionality, performance, potential problems, and other issues specific to its use. The firm might develop several prototype products that it gives to users, then survey those users to determine whether the product worked as intended and identify any issues that need resolution.

When it comes to these product design details, computer companies have taken great initiatives. Adding Value 11.1 explores the factors that make Apple Computer's iMac G5 desktop computer an excellent product design.

Beta testing uses potential consumers who examine a product prototype in a "real use" setting to determine its functionality, performance, potential problems, and other issues specific to its use.

Adding Value 11.1

Designing Apple's iMac G5 Desktop Computer

What makes a good industrial product design? Apple Computer's iMac G5 desktop computer has all of the properties of good design. It may look like a flat panel screen, but it is far more than that: Its two-inch width conceals the entire CPU. Convenient ports are located on the back, with a combination CD/DVD drive on the side of the screen. Furthermore, the iMac follows the key rules of design:[27]

- **Utility.** The product should be safe and easy and intuitive to use. Each feature must convey its function clearly to the user.[28] The iMac's compact design fits the utility needs of users well. Not only are all controls visible and intuitive, but the unit itself can be moved easily to suit the user's needs.

- **Appearance.** The form, line, proportion, and color must be integrated into a pleasing whole. Experts and consumers alike believe the G5 is one of the most aesthetically appealing desktops manufactured so far.

- **Ease of Maintenance.** Product design must facilitate ease of maintenance and repair. The G5 appears so simple that it seems as if nothing could go wrong with it.

- **Good Value.** The relationship between what the customer receives and what the product costs should be significant and obvious to consumers. Apple computers have never been known to fall at the low end of the price scale. Yet the iMac's base price, when it was introduced in September 2004, was only $1,299, quite comparable to other desktops of similar power and performance.

- **Communication.** The product should communicate the corporate design philosophy and mission through its visual qualities. Because the iMac G5 looks like a larger version of Apple's extremely popular iPod music player in its cradle, it reflects Apple's corporate design theme: modern, simple, and on the cutting edge.

Source: http://www.apple.com/imac/ (accessed October 29, 2004).

Market Testing

The firm has developed its new product or service and tested the prototypes. Now it must test the market for the new product with a trial batch of products. These tests can take two forms: premarket testing or test marketing.

Premarket Tests   Firms conduct premarket tests before they actually bring a product or service to market to determine how many customers will try and then continue to use the product or service according to a small group of potential consumers. One popular proprietary premarket test version is called BASES II, conducted by the research firm ACNielsen. During the test, potential customers are exposed to the marketing mix variables, such as the advertising, then surveyed and given a sample of the product to try.[29] After some period of time, during which the potential customers try the product, they are surveyed about whether they would buy/use the product again. This second survey indicates an estimation of the probability of a consumer's repeat purchase. From these data, the firm generates a sales estimate for the new product that enables it to decide whether to introduce the product, abandon it, redesign it before introduction, or revise the marketing plan. An early evaluation of this sort—that is, before the product is introduced to the whole market—saves marketers the costs of a nationwide launch if the product fails.

Sometimes firms simulate a product or service introduction,[30] in which case potential customers view the advertising of various currently available products or services along with advertising for the new product or service. They receive money to buy the product or service from a simulated environment, such as a mock Web page or store, and respond to a survey after they make their purchases. This test thus can determine the effectiveness of a firm's advertising as well as the expected trial rates for the new product.

Test Marketing   A method of determining the success potential of a new product, **test marketing** introduces the offering to a limited geographical area (usually a few cities) prior to a national launch. A test marketing effort uses all the elements of the marketing mix: It includes promotions like advertising and coupons, just as if the product were being introduced nationally, and the product appears in targeted retail outlets, with appropriate pricing. On the basis of the results of the test marketing, the firm can estimate demand for the entire market.

Test marketing costs more and takes longer than premarket tests, which may provide an advantage to competitors that could get a similar or better product to market first. For this reason, some firms, such as Newman's Own Organic, launch new products (e.g., its Fig Newmans™) without extensive consumer testing and rely instead on intuition, instincts, and guts.[31]

However, test marketing offers a key advantage: The firm can study actual consumer behavior, which is more reliable than a simulated test. Kraft, for instance, test marketed its Freshmade Creations refrigerated meal kits in the Midwest in the United States, and Coca-Cola test marketed its smaller eight-ounce soda cans for Coke, Diet Coke, Sprite, and Vanilla Coke in the Chicago area and some Wisconsin stores.[32] Movies often are released first in "select cities" in just a few theaters to test their market potential.

Coca-Cola test marketed its smaller eight-ounce soda cans for Coke, Diet Coke, and other flavors in the Chicago area and some Wisconsin stores.

Many firms use BehaviorScan to improve the probability of success during the test marketing phase of a new product introduction. BehaviorScan utilizes consumer panel data collected passively at the point of sale in stores and through home scanning to measure individual household first time trial and repeat purchases. New products are placed in stores within 1 week of introduction, rather than the typical 8- to 12-week period. Since more sales data are collected in a shorter period of time than conventional test marketing methods, first-year sales can be estimated after just 16 to 24 weeks in the test market.[33] Once the market demand is estimated, the product is released nationally.

Product Launch

If the market testing returns with positive results, the firm is ready to introduce the product to the entire market. This most critical step in the new product introduction requires tremendous financial resources and extensive coordination of all aspects of the marketing mix. If the new product launch is a failure, it may be difficult for the product—and perhaps the firm—to recover. Some products show great promise through their launches, though, as Exhibit 11.5 describes.

So what does a product launch involve? First, on the basis of the research it has gathered on consumer perceptions and the tests it has conducted, as well as any

EXHIBIT	11.5	Top New Products[34]	
		Kellogg Drink'n Crunch Portable Cereals	An inner cup contains the cereal and the outer cup contains the milk. The cereal and milk do not mix so the cereal does not get soggy.
		Hershey Foods' Swoops Candy Slices	Six potato chip shaped candy slices are packed in a cup
		Minute Maid Premium Heart Wise Orange Juice	Each 8-oz serving of the orange juice contains 1 gram of plant sterols that can reduce cholesterol levels.
		Pam for Baking with Flour	One-step product combining no-stick Pam with flour so that there is less cleanup
		Aquafresh Floss 'N' Cap Fluoride Toothpaste	The cap of the toothpaste contains floss.

Source: www.biz-architect.com/consumer_products.htm.

competitive considerations, the firm confirms its target market(s) and decides how the product will be positioned. Then the firm finalizes the remaining marketing mix variables for the new product, including the marketing budget for the first year.[35]

Promotion   The test results help the firm determine an appropriate integrated marketing communications strategy.[36] For products that are somewhat complex or conceptually new, marketers may need to provide for more consumer education about the product's benefits than they would for simpler and more familiar products. For technical products, technical support staff must be trained to answer any customer questions that may arise immediately after the launch.

Place   The firm must have an adequate quantity of products available for shipment and to keep in stock at relevant stores. The product offering should also be as complete as possible. For example, a firm launching a new printer should ensure it has an adequate supply of the related cartridges or toners.

Price   The firm needs to ensure that they get the price right. It is sometimes easier to start with a higher price and offer promotions (coupons, rebates, etc.) and then over time to lower the price than it is to introduce the new product at a low price and then try to raise it.

Timing   The timing of the launch may be important, depending on the product.[37] Hollywood studios typically release movies targeted toward general audiences (i.e., those rated G or PG) during the summer when children are out of school. New automobile models traditionally are released for sale during September, and fashion products are launched just before the season of the year for which they are intended.

Evaluation of Results

After the product has been launched, marketers must undertake a critical post-launch review to determine whether the product and its launch were a success or failure and what additional resources or changes to the marketing mix are needed, if any. Firms measure the success of a new product by three interrelated factors: (1) its satisfaction of technical requirements, such as performance; (2) customer acceptance; and (3) its satisfaction of the firm's financial requirements, such as sales and profits.[38] If the product is not performing sufficiently well, poor customer acceptance will result, which in turn leads to poor financial performance. The new product development process, when followed rationally and sequentially, helps avoid such domino-type failures. The product life cycle, discussed in the next section, helps marketers manage their products' marketing mix during and after its introduction.

The Product Life Cycle

The **product life cycle** defines the stages that new products move through as they enter, get established in, and ultimately leave the marketplace and thereby offers marketers a starting point for their strategy planning. Exhibit 11.6 illustrates a typical product life cycle, including the industry sales and profits over time. In their life cycles, products pass through four stages: introduction, growth, maturity, and decline. When innovators start buying the product, the product enters the **introduction stage** of its life cycle. In the **growth stage,** the product gains acceptance, demand and sales increase, and competitors emerge in the product category. In the **maturity stage,** industry sales reach their peak, so firms try to rejuvenate their products by adding new features or repositioning them. If these efforts succeed, the product achieves new life.[39] If not, it goes into **decline** and eventually exits the market.

Not every product follows the same life cycle shape; many products stay in the maturity period for a very long time. For example, "white good" categories, such as clothes washers, dryers, and refrigerators, have been in the maturity stage for a very long time and will remain there indefinitely until a superior product comes along to replace them.

The product life cycle also offers a useful tool for managers to analyze the types of strategies that may be required over the life of their products. Even the strategic emphasis of a firm and its marketing mix (4Ps) strategies can be adapted from insights about the characteristics of each stage of the cycle, as we summarize in Exhibits 11.6 and 11.7.

Let's look at each of these stages in depth.

Introduction Stage

The introduction stage for a new, innovative product or service usually starts with a single firm, and innovators are the ones to try the new offering. Some new-to-the-world products and services that defined their own product category and industry

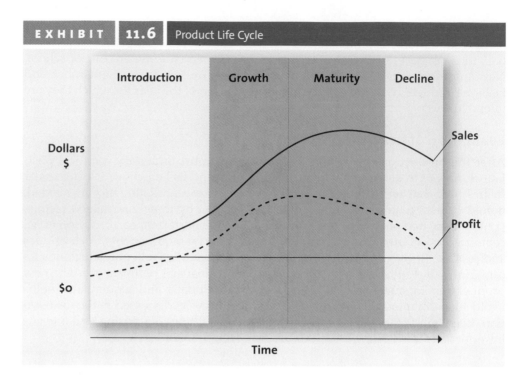

EXHIBIT 11.6 Product Life Cycle

EXHIBIT 11.7 Characteristics of Different Stages of the Product Life Cycle

	Introduction	Growth	Maturity	Decline
Sales	Low	Rising	Peak	Declining
Profits	Negative or low	Rapidly rising	Peak to declining	Declining
Typical consumers	Innovators	Early adopters and early majority	Late majority	Laggards
Competitors (number of firms and products)	One or few	Few but increasing	High number of competitors and competitive products	Low number of competitors and products

include the telephone (invented by Alexander Graham Bell in 1876), the transistor semiconductor (Bell Laboratories in 1947), the Walkman portable cassette player (Sony in 1979), and the Internet browser (Netscape in 1994). Sensing the viability and commercialization possibilities of this market-creating new product, other firms soon enter the market with similar or improved products at lower prices. The same pattern holds for less innovative products like apparel, some CDs, or even a new soft drink flavor. The introduction stage is characterized by initial losses to the firm due to its high start-up costs and low levels of sales revenue as the product begins to take off. If the product is successful, firms may start seeing profits toward the end of this stage.

Growth Stage

The growth stage of the product life cycle is marked by a growing number of product adopters, rapid growth in industry sales, and increases in both the number of competitors and the number of available product versions.[40] The market becomes more segmented and consumer preferences more varied, which increases the potential for new markets or new uses of the product or service.[41] Innovators start rebuying the product, and early majority consumers enter.

These new-to-the-world products defined their own product category and industry. The telephone (left) was invented in 1876, and the Sony Walkman (right) came out in 1979.

Also during the growth stage, firms attempt to reach new consumers by studying their preferences and producing different product variations—varied colors, styles, or features—which enables them to segment the market more precisely. The goal of this segmentation is to ride the rising sales trend and firmly establish the firm's brand, so as not to be outdone by competitors. For example, there are now several firms that produce DVD players for both broad mass-market applications and specialized markets, such as those in which consumers use them with computers, on the road, or to record homemade movies. With these many available product options, industry sales have risen rapidly; more than 50 percent of households in the United States and parts of Europe have now adopted DVD players.[42] Simultaneously, the average price of DVD players has gone down sharply, which provides tremendous consumer value. For the Thanksgiving holiday season sale, for example, Wal-Mart offered DVD players for as little as $29, causing a consumer stampede in some stores.[43]

As firms ride the crest of increasing industry sales, profits in the growth stage also rise because of the economies of scale associated with manufacturing and marketing costs, especially promotion and advertising. At the same time, firms that have not yet established a stronghold in the market, even in narrow segments, may decide to exit in what is referred to as an "industry shakeout." Adding Value 11.2 describes TiVo's move from the introduction to growth stage of the product life cycle.

Maturity Stage

The maturity stage of the product life cycle is characterized by the adoption of the product by the late majority and intense competition for market share among firms. Marketing costs (e.g., promotion, distribution) increase as these firms vigorously defend their market share against competitors. At the same time, they face intense competition on price as the average price of the product falls substantially compared with the shifts during the previous two stages of the life cycle. Lower prices and increased marketing costs begin to erode the profit margins for many firms. In the later phases of the maturity stage, the market has become quite saturated, and practically all potential customers for the product have already adopted the product. Such saturated markets are prevalent in developed countries; in the United States, most consumer packaged goods found in grocery and discount stores are already in the maturity stage.

Firms may pursue several strategies during this stage to increase their customer base and/or defend their market share, such as entry into new markets and market segments and developing new products.

Adding Value 11.2

"TiVo"-ing the Consumer[44]

The digital video recorder (DVR) enables consumers to choose what television shows to watch and when, to pause and rewind whenever they want, and even to get an instant replay of their favorite TV shows. Silicon Valley–based TiVo Inc. has been the pioneer and dominant brand in this market since the introduction of DVRs in 1999. TiVo's unit, a box that sits atop consumers' television sets, can record as many as 140 hours of TV programming on its hard drive using the MPEG-2 format that records video onto DVDs. Each night, the unit dials into a server and downloads weeks' worth of program information from the consumer's cable or satellite provider. Consumers pay for the initial unit as well as a monthly subscription fee.

TiVo's primary competitors include satellite providers, such as Dish Network, and cable providers, such as Time Warner and Comcast. Currently, DVR penetration in the United States is approximately 3.5 million households,

of which 1.6 million use TiVo. According to Forrester Research, the DVR market will grow rapidly; by 2006, almost 25 million households likely will have adopted it.

TiVo's challenge therefore is to get consumers not only to adopt the technology but also to prefer its brand of DVRs. The firm already has ties with DirecTV, a satellite TV provider, through which it has obtained almost all of its subscribers. The firm faces significant challenges from cable providers, which can bundle their DVR with attractive promotions for various cable packages and programs. In response, TiVo plans to woo customers by providing better consumer information; selectively distributing through electronics retailers that can better promote the product, such as Best Buy; keeping the technology and installation process as simple as possible; and entering into partnerships with other manufacturing firms, such as Sony, that may use the TiVo software in their devices.

Entry into New Markets or Market Segments   Because the market is saturated at this point, firms may attempt to enter new geographical markets, including international markets (as we discussed in Chapter 7), that may be less saturated. For example, Whirlpool has started manufacturing washing machines for Brazil, China, and India that it prices lower than those it sells in the United States to attract the large consumer base of lower-income consumers in these countries.[45] In many developing economies, the large and growing proportion of middle-class households is just beginning to buy the home, kitchen, and entertainment appliances that have been fairly standard in U.S. households for several decades. In India alone, the roughly 487 million middle-class consumers will spend $420 billion on a variety of consumer products in the next four years.[46]

Just a few years ago, baby wipes accounted for most of the sales of personal wipes. Firms have seen the opportunity to enter new markets, so products have proliferated.

However, even in mature markets, firms may be able to find new market segments. Emerging new trends or changes in consumer tastes may fragment mature markets, which would open new market opportunities. As the popularity of the Internet increased, for example, firms such as Expedia, Orbitz, Priceline, and Travelocity found that they could provide the easy access and convenience of online bookings for air travel, hotel stays, and car rentals. Consumers who prefer such access and conve-

nience, as well as the ability to compare prices across different service providers, increasingly are using the Internet to make their travel plans.

New market opportunities also may emerge through simple product design changes, such as in the market for "wipes." Just a few years ago, baby wipes accounted for most of the sales of personal wipes, but Procter & Gamble's Oil of Olay Facial Cleansing Cloths and Unilever's Ponds Age-Defying wipes have recently gained significant market share.[47] In the household sector, products such as P&G's Swiffer, the electrostatic wipe for mopping floors, have expanded the market greatly. Clorox has added premoistened Armor All wipes to its do-it-yourself car cleaning line[48] and the Clorox® ToiletWand™ for consumers who don't enjoy unsightly and unsanitary toilet brushes hanging around in their bathrooms.[49] Although the household cleaning and cosmetic markets are both well established and mature, marketers working in these product categories saw trends early and moved to create new products that offer value for consumers.

Development of New Products   Despite market saturation, firms continually introduce new products with improved features or find new uses for existing products because they need constant innovation and product proliferation to defend market share during intense competition. Firms such as 3M, P&G, and Hewlett-Packard, for instance, continuously introduce new products. Innovations by such firms ensure that they are able to retain or grow their respective market shares.

The NanoCar is one billionth the size of a regular car and is used to conduct research on a molecular scale.

Sometimes new products are introduced by less-than-famous companies. Consider, for instance, the NanoCar, which is one-billionth the size of a regular automobile. Although not appropriate for a Sunday drive, it is fully functioning with parts such as axles, a laser-based security system to prevent theft or tampering, and an electrostatic motor to get it around. It is used to conduct research on a molecular scale to help unravel the mystery of atomic sciences.[50] Even in a product category as old as shoes, entrepreneurs like Mario Moretti Polegato keep coming up with new innovations, as we discuss in Entrepreneurial Marketing 11.1.

Decline Stage

Firms with products in the decline stage either position themselves for a niche segment of diehard consumers or those with special needs or they completely exit the market. The few laggards that have not yet tried the product or service enter the market at this stage. Take vinyl long-playing records (LPs) for example. In an age of CDs and Internet-downloaded music in MP3 and other formats, it may seem surprising that vinyl records are still made and sold. But though the sales of vinyl LPs have been declining in the past 15 years, about 2 million still are sold in the United States each year. Granted, this is a miniscule number compared with the 800 million CDs sold each year, but diehard music lovers prefer the unique sound of a vinyl record to the digital sound of CDs and music in other formats. Because the grooves in vinyl records create sound waves that are similar to those of a live performance, and therefore provide a more authentic sound, nightclub DJs, discerning music listeners, and collectors prefer them. Even some younger listeners have been buying vinyl records, influenced perhaps by their parents' collections, the sound, or simply the uniqueness of an LP.

Aiding this continued demand is the fact that there are simply too many albums of music from the predigital era that are available only on vinyl. It may take

Entrepreneurial Marketing 11.1

Geox, the Holy Shoe[51]

Mario Moretti Polegato was attending a wine convention in Reno, Nevada, in the early 1990s when, due to the heat and his allergies, he found he needed to poke holes in the soles of his shoes to let air circulate around his feet. When he went back to Italy, Polegato decided to work further on this idea for staying cool and soon left his family wine business to manufacture his innovation: Geox shoes. The name Geox is derived from "Geo," Greek for Earth, and "x," to suggest a technological feel.

Polegato took his innovative idea for "breathable" or "ventilated" shoes to leading manufacturers such as Fila, Nike, Adidas, and Timberland. None was interested. But when Polegato introduced Geox shoes himself in Europe, despite an otherwise saturated shoe market, the brand was a big hit. Now sold in the firm's own chain of stores and in the United States through upscale retail chains, Geox sells approximately 10 million pairs of shoes annually and plans to expand to 150 stores in Italy and 100 overseas.

Mario Moretti Polegato created Geox ventilated shoes to keep his feet cool in hot weather.

many years, maybe even decades, for all the music from earlier generations to be digitized. Until that time, turntable equipment manufacturers, small record-pressing companies such as Music Connection in Manhattan, and new and emerging record companies, such as Premier Crue Music, continue to have a market that demands their LPs.[52]

The Shape of the Product Life Cycle Curve

In theory, the product life cycle curve is assumed to be bell shaped with regard to sales and profits. In reality, however, each product or service has its own individual shape; some move more rapidly through their product life cycles than others, depending on how different the product or service is from products currently in the market and how valuable it is to the consumer. New products and services that consumers accept very quickly have higher consumer adoption rates very early in their product life cycles and move faster across the various stages.

For example, DVD players and DVDs moved much faster than VCRs across the life cycle curve and have already reached the maturity stage, likely because consumers, who already owned VCRs, were accustomed to recording TV shows and playing prerecorded movies and programs. It also was easy to switch VCR customers to DVD technology because DVDs were more durable and had better resolution than videotapes. Finally, prices for DVDs and DVD players dropped more quickly and drastically than did VCR prices, which made the new technology a better value.

Strategies Based on Product Life Cycle: Some Caveats

Although the product life cycle concept provides a starting point for managers to think about the strategy they want to implement during each stage of the life cycle of a product, this tool must be used with care. The most challenging part of applying the product life cycle concept is that managers do not know exactly what shape each product's life cycle will take, so there is no way to know precisely what stage a product is in. If, for example, a product experiences several seasons of declining sales, a manager may decide that it has moved from the growth stage to decline and stop promoting the product. As a result, of course, sales decline further. The manager then believes he or she made the right decision because the product continues to follow a predetermined life cycle. But what if the original sales decline was due to a poor strategy or increased competition—issues that could have been addressed with positive marketing support? In this case, the product life cycle decision became a self-fulfilling prophecy, and a growth product was doomed to an unnecessary decline.[53]

Fortunately, new research, based on the history of dozens of consumer products, suggests that the product life cycle concept is indeed a valid idea, and new analytical tools now provide "rules" for detecting the key turning points in the cycle.[54] In the pharmaceutical industry, where breakthrough innovations are few and far between, firms use the product life cycle to identify the consumer promotions needed at each stage to get the most out of their existing brands.[55]

Summing Up

1. How can firms create value through innovation?

New products and services keep current customers coming back for more and induce new customers into the market. Multiple products and services also help diversify the firm's portfolio, thus lowering its overall risk and enhancing its value. Although risky, new-to-the-world products have tremendous potential because they are the first in the market to offer something that has never before been available.

2. What is the diffusion of innovation theory, and how can managers use it to make product line decisions?

The diffusion of innovation theory can help firms predict which types of customers will buy their products or services immediately upon introduction, as well as later as it gains more acceptance in the market. The firm can then develop marketing strategies to encourage acceptance among each customer group. Diffusion of innovation also can help predict sales.

3. How do firms create new products and services?

When firms develop new products, they go through several steps. First, they generate ideas for the product or service using several alternative techniques, such as internal research and development, R&D consortia, licensing, brainstorming, tracking competitors' products or services, or working with customers. Second,

firms test their concepts by either describing the idea of the new product or service to potential customers or showing them images of what the product would look like. Third, the design process entails determining what the product or service will actually include and provide; fourth, firms test market their designs. Fifth, if everything goes well in the test market, the product is launched. Sixth, firms must evaluate the new product or service to determine its success.

4. What is a product life cycle, and how can the concept be applied to product line decisions?

The product life cycle helps firms make marketing mix decisions on the basis of the product's stage in its life cycle. In the introduction stage, companies attempt to gain a strong foothold in the market quickly by appealing to innovators. During the growth stage, the objective is to establish the brand firmly. When the product reaches the maturity stage, firms compete intensely for market share, and many potential customers already own the product or use the service. Eventually, most products enter the decline phase, during which firms withdraw marketing support and eventually phase out the product. Knowing where a product or service is in its life cycle helps managers determine its specific strategy at any given point in time.

Key Terms

- alpha testing, 311
- beta testing, 311
- breakthrough, 302
- concept, 309
- concept testing, 309
- decline stage, 315
- diffusion of innovation, 303
- early adopter, 304
- early majority, 304

- first movers, 302
- growth stage, 315
- innovation, 301
- innovator, 304
- introduction stage, 315
- laggard, 304
- late majority, 304
- lead user, 309
- maturity stage, 315

- pioneer, 302
- premarket test, 312
- product development, 311
- product design, 311
- product life cycle, 315
- prototype, 310
- reverse engineering, 308
- test marketing, 313

Marketing Applications

1. Some people think that a product should be considered "new" only if it is completely new to the market and has never existed before. Describe or give examples of other types of new products.

2. Apple has introduced a new iPod with a video feature. How quickly do you think this product will diffuse among the U.S. population? Describe the types of people that you expect will be in each of the diffusion of innovation categories.

3. Are there any advantages for companies that are the first to introduce products that create new markets? Justify your answer. If you see advantages, explain why some new products still fail.

4. Identify and describe the ways that companies generate new product ideas. Which of these ways involve the customer? How can firms assess the value of the ideas that customers generate?

5. Describe an example of a new product or service that is targeted at the college student market. Using the concept testing discussion in the chapter, describe how you would conduct a concept test for this product or service.

6. Various portable MP3 players are currently available in the market. How might the design and value provided by MP3 players make this product more appealing to consumers than, say, portable cassette or CD players?

7. Mazda is about to introduce a new model and is currently in the market testing phase of the new product development process. Describe two ways that Mazda might conduct initial market testing prior to launching this new model.

8. Gateway has just introduced a new notebook PC. As the manager responsible for this product, how would you assess its success? Why do you believe these issues are important?

9. What type of shampoo do you use? What stage of the product life cycle is it in? Is the shampoo manufacturer's marketing strategy—its 4Ps—consistent with the product's stage in its life cycle? Explain.

10. In what stage of the product life cycle is a new model of a Palm PDA? Is Palm's marketing strategy—its 4Ps—consistent with the product's stage in its life cycle? How is it different from that of the shampoo in the previous question? Explain.

11. You have recently been hired by a cosmetics company in the product development group. The firm's brand is a top-selling, high-end line of cosmetics. The head of the development team has just presented research that shows the "tween" girls, aged 11 to 15, are very interested in cosmetics and have the money to spend. The decision is made to create a line of tween cosmetics based on the existing adult line. As the product moves through development you begin to notice that the team seems to lean toward a very edgy and sexual theme for the line, including naming the various lines "envy," "desire," "prowess," and "fatal attraction." You begin to wonder, is this concept too much for girls in the targeted age group?

1. Go to http://www.hotproductnews.com and search for an interesting new product. Is this an innovative, new-to-the-world product? Discuss the extent to which the new product has the properties outlined in Adding Value 11.1 as important for new product design and development.

2. The automotive industry is constantly adding new and different products into cars and trucks. Conduct an Internet or library database search for innovative new automotive technologies. Choose products that fit each stage of the product life cycle, and justify your choices.

Chapter Case Study

MARKETING APPLE'S IPOD:[56] MUSIC TO YOUR EARS[57]

Whether it starts with a dream, an idea, or a thought, the road to marketing success is often long and requires research, planning, product alterations, and creative contemplations, which makes it all the more rare to witness the success of the iPod, the brainchild of Apple founder Steve Jobs, who got his product designed, built, and on shelves in less than a year. The cool product of choice for listening to and trading the latest sounds, the iPod has expanded to various models that music enthusiasts have quickly bought up during its brief existence. Furthermore, its introduction and subsequent acceptance has spawned an entire industry comprised of companies that market compatible accessories. Despite some initial problems with its battery life, the product is going strong, driving the majority of Apple's revenue growth. iPod thus is a prime example of successful marketing.

The Product Concept

Launched in October 2001, iPod was the first portable music player with the capability to download and store thousands of songs digitally. Its sales have reached over 4 million per year. The concept started off in response to consumer wants and in an environment that was ready for a product that would change the tide in the practice of pirating digital forms of music. Jobs saw the need for a good quality player that would allow its users to legally download and customize their music and to trade songs. In less than three years, his invention had already been termed "a cultural phenomenon" by *Brandweek* magazine.

This is not to say the road to success was without hurdles. Jobs had to persuade the major music labels to allow their artists' songs to be downloaded for 99 cents each, or about $9.99 per album. After being burned by sites like Roxio's Napster, which allowed peer-to-peer downloading for free, the music industry was hesitant to open its doors to such a proposal. Jobs sold the idea to the recording industry by making sure it would get its cut and relying on his credibility as a well-known name in computers and the head of Pixar Animation Studios. iPod owners would purchase songs via Apple's iTunes Music Store software, accessed through the iMac. The concept represented a cultural change for how people would access, purchase, and listen to music. The support of the industry soon became overwhelming; iTunes now offers more than 1 million tracks, representing 5 major music labels and 600 independents.

Making It Happen

Being first in the market with a very desirable product meant Jobs was able to command upward of $400 for the 40GB (10,000 songs stored) iPod model. More than 1,000 accessories have been rolled out, including car adaptors, custom carrying cases, and home speakers.

When other companies realized the power of the iPod, they began cobranding with Apple so that they could get a piece of the action. Hewlett-Packard, Bose, Volkswagen of America, and BMW—which built adaptors into some of its cars' stereo systems—are just a few examples. Other smaller companies marketed iPod accessories, allowing Apple to extend the iPod's

reach even further in the retail market. Even U2 got into the game, working with Apple to offer an iPod specific to the band.

The iPod's most distinguishing feature, according to Apple's advertising agency, was the white cord that connects the player to the earphones and that identifies iPod users as they go about their daily business, whether that means walking across campus, dancing down the sidewalk, or driving in their BMWs. Anyone can spot a member of the iPod "club." The introductory multimedia advertising campaign therefore focused on a simple, silhouetted dancing figure with a highlighted iPod and earphones.

Apple has a new iPod, which in addition to playing 15,000 songs and displaying 25,000 photos on a 2.5-inch color screen, can play videos. Customers can purchase music videos, short films from Pixar Animation, and TV shows like *Desperate Housewives* and *Lost*. There is concern among some network affiliates that this "off TV" viewing will hurt ratings and this certainly may ultimately be true, but the video iPod is an example of the paradigm shift that has been developing.

The Future

The iPod has been such a success that some industry analysts claim Apple would be better off as a marketer of entertainment and consumer electronics rather than a computer company. As CEO, Jobs has a reputation in the marketplace for his creative genius and for personally seeing new products successfully from the initial idea to the product launch. He has been credited with an uncanny ability to spot the next revolutionary innovation that will change the landscape of the marketplace. That's a tough reputation to maintain. Will the company morph into a small electronics marketer? Will it take a different direction in the not-so-distant future? The answer depends on so many factors that it defies speculation. For the time being, Apple will enjoy its recent successes and prepare for the next big thing.

Apple's iPod commands an impressive share of the hard-drive based music player market, hovering around 90 percent. However, iPod is seeing a few serious competitors from other companies. Samsung's Z5 and Sony's new Walkman have earned some recognition and sales. However, they have some of the same problems other portable players are running into—there are not as many accessories for them as for iPod, their synchronization with the computer to upload songs is not nearly as effortless, and their ease of use is still lagging behind the simple language developed by Apple. Some analysts suggest that the mini player sector will see more competition in the future as it becomes a casual market and price competition begins. But they expect that iPod will still dominate the larger memory portable player market. Its brand recognition is growing each year as more companies are cobranding their products to make iPod easier to use, cooler to own, and more visible than ever.

Questions

1. One critical factor that affects the market potential for a product innovation is the ability to offer a differentiated product that delivers unique and superior value to customers. Discuss the extent to which Apple successfully accomplished this with the iPod and with its subsequent introductions, like the iPod shuffle and the iPod nano.

2. How would you classify the iPod today in terms of its stage in the product life cycle? Why?

3. Provide a description of what you think each type of adopter would be for an iPod. Do you think we are seeing late majority adopters or laggards yet?

12

Services: The Intangible Product

Why would someone pay $2 or more for a cup of tea when it costs only pennies to buy a Lipton tea bag and put it in a cup of hot water?[1] Because companies like Peet's Coffee and Tea have learned to create value by adding great customer service and premium products. Peet's, known as the "grandfather of specialty coffee," was started by Alfred Peet in 1966 a few blocks away from University of California, Berkeley. Although its primary business is coffee, Peet's managers know that if everything they sell—including tea—isn't as good as it can be, business will suffer.

Peet's first priority is educating its staff. In addition to knowing how to brew tea, employees need to know about the beverage they're serving. How are green, black, and oolong teas grown and processed? How do they differ? How do they taste? What about their caffeine content? Every store also has a training guide who is particularly knowledgeable about the tea and coffees, and whose responsibility it is to teach and instill a passion in their co-workers about the different products they sell. If the employees don't know the answer to a customer's question, they find out by asking their training guide, the store manager, or the home office.

The best way to sell tea is to drink it. At Peet's, training employees to taste different teas gives them the confidence and knowledge to be good tea emissaries. Besides initial and ongoing product and service training, Peet's hosts in-store tastings for customers at least once a month as well as weekly sampling to highlight special offering teas. At the in-store tastings, Peet's employees guide customers to taste, compare, and learn about different teas.

At Peet's Coffee and Tea, the staff is provided in-depth product knowledge to serve their customers better than the competition.

Consuming tea can be a very personal experience, so Peet's employees are encouraged to interact with customers. For instance, they might ask drinkers to describe their favorite tea and how it tastes, then use those details to suggest new, alternative teas. All of the teas available on Peet's menu can also be purchased by the pot at the beverage counter so that customers can taste the tea before purchasing a larger amount for home brewing. To help ensure that the customer has a pleasant experience with the tea once they are at home, each package is accompanied by brewing instructions—how much tea should be used, how long it should brew for optimal taste, and how hot the water should be. Peet's has figured out that the key to its success is not just good coffee and tea but excellent service delivered by knowledgeable employees.

Peet's offers an example of a firm that provides excellent service as well as products. Whereas a **service** is any intangible offering that involves a deed, performance, or effort that cannot be physically possessed,[2] **customer service** specifically refers to human or mechanical activities firms undertake to help satisfy their customers' needs and wants. By providing good customer service, firms add value to their products or services.

Exhibit 12.1 illustrates the continuum from a pure service to a pure product. Most offerings, like Peet's, lie somewhere in the middle and include some service and some product. As we noted in Chapter 2, even those firms that are engaged primarily in selling a product, like an apparel store, typically view service as a method to maintain a sustainable competitive advantage. This chapter moves on to take an inclusive view of services as anything from pure service businesses to a business that uses service as a differentiating tool to help it sell physical products.

Economies of developed countries like the United States have become increasingly dependent on services. For example, service industries like retail and information services account for about two-thirds[3] of the U.S. gross domestic product (GDP) and the lion's share of U.S. jobs. This dependence and the growth of service-oriented economies in developed countries have emerged for several reasons.

First, it is generally less expensive for firms to manufacture their products in less-developed countries. Even if the goods are finished in the United States, some of their components likely were produced elsewhere. In turn, the proportion of service production to goods production in the United States, and other similar

EXHIBIT	12.1	The Service–Product Continuum

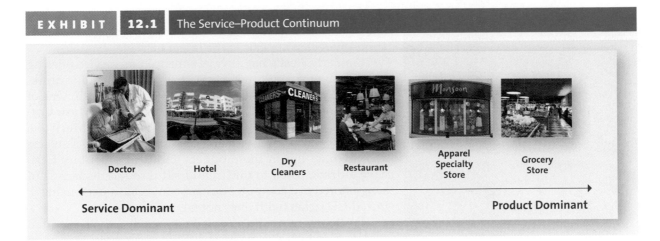

Doctor   Hotel   Dry Cleaners   Restaurant   Apparel Specialty Store   Grocery Store

Service Dominant   **Product Dominant**

economies, has steadily increased over time. Second, household maintenance activities, which many people performed by themselves in the past, have become quite specialized. Food preparation, lawn maintenance, house cleaning, laundry and dry cleaning, hair care, and automobile maintenance all are often performed by specialists in the modern economy.

Third, people place a high value on convenience and leisure. Most households have little time for the household maintenance tasks mentioned in the previous point, and many are willing to pay others to do their chores. Fourth, as the U.S. population ages, the need for healthcare professionals—not only doctors and nurses but also assisted living facilities and nursing homes—also increases. Along the same lines, an ever greater number of retired Americans are traveling more and utilizing various forms of leisure services.

As the population ages, the need for healthcare professionals increases.

Services Marketing Differs from Product Marketing

The marketing of services differs from product marketing because of the four fundamental differences involved in services: They are intangible, inseparable, variable, and perishable.[4] See Exhibit 12.2. This section examines these differences and discusses how they affect marketing strategies.

Intangible

As the title of this chapter implies, the most fundamental difference between a product and a service is that services are intangible—they cannot be touched, tasted, or seen like a pure product can. When you get a physical examination, you see and hear the doctor, but the service itself is intangible. This intangibility can prove highly challenging to marketers. For instance, it makes it difficult to convey the benefits of services—try describing whether the experience of visiting your dentist was good or bad and why. Healthcare service providers (e.g., physicians, dentists) offer cues to help their customers experience and perceive their

At Starbucks' "Hear Music Coffeehouses," customers can buy CDs, have a drink, listen to music and create personalized, mixed-CDs.

Since services are intangible, healthcare service providers must create visual images to promote and sell their services.

service more positively, such as a waiting room stocked with television sets, beverages, and comfortable chairs to create an atmosphere that appeals to the target market.

Similarly, Peet's has always enhanced its service offering by providing a comfortable and cozy atmosphere for drinking coffee, working, reading, or chatting with friends. One of Peet's competitors, Starbucks, has launched "Hear Music Coffeehouses," fully integrated cafés and music stores. Much like a regular Starbucks, this wholly owned subsidiary is warm and inviting, but in these outlets, customers can buy CDs, have a drink, listen to music, and sift through thousands of songs stored in a computer database to create a personalized, mixed-CD jacket (with liner notes even!).[5]

Furthermore, a service can't be shown directly to potential customers, which also makes it difficult to promote. Marketers must therefore creatively employ symbols and images to promote and sell services, like Walt Disney World does in using its advertising to evoke images of happy families and nostalgic memories of Mickey Mouse and previous visits to the theme park. Professional medical services provide appropriate images of personnel doing their jobs in white coats surrounded by high-tech equipment. Educational institutions promote the quality of their services by touting their famous faculty and alumni, as well as their accreditations. They also often use images of happy students sitting spellbound in front of a fascinating professor or going on to lucrative careers of their own.

Because of the intangibility of services, the images marketers use reinforce the benefit or value that a service provides. Professional service providers, such as doctors, lawyers, accountants, and consultants, depend heavily on consumers' perceptions of their integrity and trustworthiness. Yet the promotional campaigns some of these professionals use have been criticized by their peers and consumer welfare groups. Ethical Dilemma 12.1 discusses the tension created when service providers use marketing tactics to attract clients to their service but still attempt to maintain a perception of integrity and trustworthiness.

Inseparable Production and Consumption

Another difference between services and products is that services are produced and consumed at the same time; that is, service and consumption are **inseparable**. Because service production can't be separated from consumption, astute service marketers provide opportunities for their customers to get directly involved in the service. Healthcare providers have found, for instance, that the more control they allow their patients in determining their course of treatment, the more satisfied those patients are.[6]

Because the service is inseparable from its consumption, customers rarely have the opportunity to try the service before they purchase it. And after the service has been performed, it can't be returned. Imagine telling your dentist that you want a "test" cavity filled before he or she starts drilling a real one. Because the purchase risk in these scenarios can be relatively high, services sometimes provide extended

| EXHIBIT | 12.2 | Core Differences between Services and Goods |

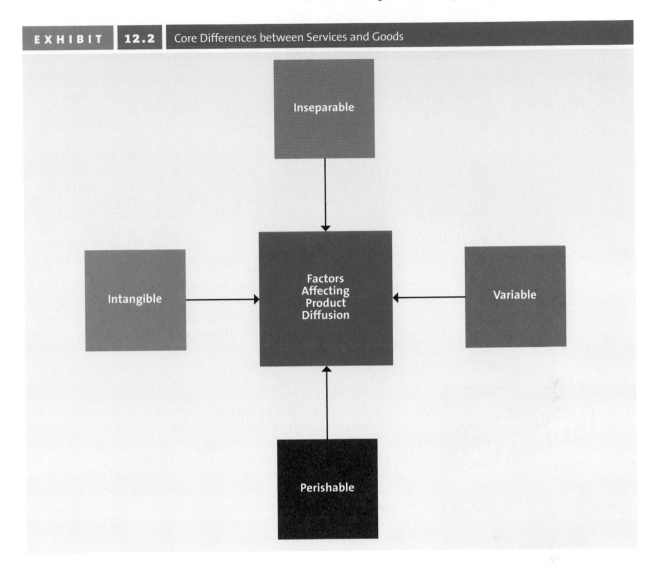

warranties and 100 percent satisfaction guarantees, such as those offered by many hotels (e.g., Comfort Inn, Comfort Suites, Quality Inn, Sleep Inn, Clarion, MainStay Suites). More specifically, these hotel chains post claims along the lines of the following: "If you are not satisfied with your accommodations or our service, please advise the front desk of a problem right away and give them an opportunity to correct the situation. If the hotel staff is unable to satisfy you, they will give you up to one night's free stay."[7]

Variable

The more humans are needed to provide a service, the more likely there is to be **variability** in the service's quality. A hair stylist may give bad haircuts in the morning because he or she went out the night before, yet that stylist still may offer a better service than the undertrained stylist working in the next station over. A restaurant, which offers a mixture of services and products, generally can control its food quality but not the variability in food preparation or delivery. If a consumer

Ethical Dilemma 12.1   Ambulance Chasers?

At one time lawyers in many states were prohibited from advertising their services because many believed that marketing by lawyers would undermine the integrity of the profession. Over time, the laws were repealed. But in the face of the advertising that has ensued, many are questioning whether the marketing tactics of some lawyers have gone too far.

The term "ambulance chaser" usually is used derogatorily to refer to lawyers who solicit clients when they are stressed or their ability to make rational decisions is limited, such as just after a car accident. The term was coined when some personal injury lawyers literally followed ambulances and offered legal services to the injured parties. Critics of lawyers who market their services point to the aggressive advertising and promotional programs these attorneys use, which often prey on potential clients' vulnerabilities after they have been injured or in some way been negatively impacted by the actions of others. The lawyers who market themselves this way claim they are providing a valuable service to society.

For practicing lawyers and other professionals, the ethical dilemma is how to balance their need to gain clients through marketing with their need to retain an image of professionalism and integrity. Can marketing be used to communicate the benefits of legal services without preying on the vulnerabilities of consumers?

Enterprise Rent-A-Car reduces their service variability through training and standardization. You get the same great service everywhere you go.

has a problem with a product, it can be replaced, redone, destroyed, or, if it is already in the supply chain, recalled. In many cases, the problem can even be fixed before the product gets into consumers' hands. But an inferior service can't be recalled; by the time the firm recognizes a problem, the damage has been done.

As we noted in the opening vignette, marketers like Peet's strive to reduce their service variability through training and standardization. Enterprise Rent-A-Car, for instance, has worked to standardize its service delivery across the United States and, to that end, provides extensive training to its associates. Go to any Enterprise outlet at any airport, and chances are you will be greeted in the same personalized way. The airport shuttle drivers will load and unload your bags. When you get off the shuttle, you will be greeted by name, and your car will be ready to go in minutes. This smooth and pleasant service transaction is the result of the company's very specific service standards and excellent training program.

Marketers also can use the variable nature of services to their advantage. A micromarketing segmentation strategy can customize a service to meet customers' needs exactly (see Chapter 8). A consulting company in the Boston area called Geek Housecalls will come to your home or office and take care of any repair or service your PC might need—setting up a network, cleaning your hard drive, or even tutoring you on the operation of a particular program. Each customer's needs are different, so Geek Housecalls employs a cadre of consultants who possess a variety of skills. Clients are matched with their very own "personal geek" on the basis of their needs, which allows for a fully personalized service offering.

Such micromarketing can be expensive to deliver though, particularly for a firm that offers multiple services. Consumers also may get confused or even irritated if they must pay for each little service. Imagine a hotel that charged separately

Adding Value 12.1

Adding Convenience through Self-Checkout Machines[9]

Thought of as a gimmick when they were first introduced in 1995, self-checkout machines have gained converts and are heading into more arenas. The machines are multiplying in grocery and discount stores at blistering speed. Wal-Mart, Kroger, Farmer Jack, Sam's Club, Costco, and Meijer already use them; Walgreens, the nation's largest drugstore chain, is testing them. Even libraries nationwide are installing self-checkout machines for books.

Self-checkouts are successful and increase customer loyalty because they appeal to those shoppers who want to move on quickly and believe they can zip through their checkouts faster by using the machines. Some experts say the reason customers think self-checkout is faster is that they are active when using it, unlike waiting for a cashier, which leaves customers with nothing to do and may make it seems as though time is dragging. Others contend that self-checkout actually does save between 15 seconds and 15 minutes, depending on the size of an order.

If customers like the machines, so will retailers. Industry experts say each machine costs about $90,000 and handles 15 to 40 percent of the daily transactions of stores that maintain them. Although expensive, the machines reduce labor expenses; one cashier can oversee the operation of four to eight self-checkouts. And the machines don't have to be trained, nor do they ever come to work with a bad attitude.

Do self-checkout machines increase or reduce consumers' perception of service?

for each bed, towel, bar of soap, use of the TV, and lap in the swimming pool. Instead, service providers usually bundle their services into one package and charge a single price. For example, Club Med resorts offer all-inclusive amenity packages for one price, which includes, for example, a flight from New York to Club Med Turkoise Island and then accommodations, meals, snacks, bar service, and sports and entertainment activities once you arrive for about $1,400 for seven nights—include a friend for just $400 more![8]

In an alternative approach, some service providers tackle the variability issue by replacing people with machines. For simple transactions like getting cash, using an ATM is usually quicker and more convenient—and less variable—than waiting in line for a bank teller. Adding Value 12.1 describes how some retailers and other service providers have begun to provide additional value with their self-checkout machines.

Computer crashing? Network down? Call Geek Housecalls.

When firms offer multiple services like Club Med, they often bundle the services under one price.

The technological delivery of services can cause additional problems. Some customers either do not embrace the idea of replacing a human with a machine for business interactions or have problems using the technology. In other cases, the technology may not perform adequately, such as self-checkout scanners that fail to scan all merchandise or ATMs that run out of money or are out of order.

The Internet has reduced service variability in several areas. Prior to the mid-1990s, customers engaged in one-on-one interactions when they purchased travel items (e.g., airlines, hotel, rental car), concert and movie tickets, insurance, mortgages, and merchandise. Today, these purchases can be made directly via the Internet, and if the customer wants more information than is available online, Web sites provide ways to contact customer service personnel by e-mail or telephone.

Beyond online benefits, the Internet has also reduced in-store service variability. At Staples, for instance, in-store kiosks provide information, prices, availability, and product information to customers. They represent a useful supplement for salespeople, who can't possibly be knowledgeable about every aspect of the many high-tech products the company carries.

Perishable

Services are **perishable** in that they cannot be stored for use in the future. You can't stockpile a yoga class like you could a six-pack of beer, for instance. The perishability of services provides both challenges and opportunities to marketers in terms of the critical task of matching demand and supply. As long as the demand for and the supply of the service match closely, there is no problem, but unfortunately, this perfect matching rarely occurs. A ski area, for instance, can be open as long as there is snow, even at night, but demand peaks on weekends and holidays, so ski areas often offer less expensive tickets during off-peak periods to stimulate demand. Airlines, cruise ships, movie theaters, and restaurants confront similar challenges and attack them in similar ways.

As we have seen, providing great service is not easy, and it requires a diligent effort to analyze the service process piece by piece. In the next section, we examine

Since services are perishable, service providers like ski areas offer less expensive tickets at night to stimulate demand.

what is known as the Gaps Model, which is designed to highlight those areas where customers believe they are getting less or poorer service than they should (the gaps) and how these gaps can be closed.

Providing Great Service: The Gaps Model

Customers have certain expectations about how a service should be delivered. When the delivery of that service fails to meet those expectations, a service gap results. The Gaps Model (Exhibit 12.3) is designed to encourage the systematic examination of all aspects of the service delivery process and prescribe the steps needed to develop an optimal service strategy.[10]

As Exhibit 12.3 shows, there are four service gaps:

1.   The **knowledge gap** reflects the difference between customers' expectations and the firm's perception of those customer expectations. Firms can close this gap by matching customer expectations with actual service through research.

2.   The **standards gap** pertains to the difference between the firm's perceptions of customers' expectations and the service standards it sets. By setting appropriate service standards and measuring service performance, firms can attempt to close this gap.

3.   The **delivery gap** is the difference between the firm's service standards and the actual service it provides to customers. This gap can be closed by getting employees to meet or exceed service standards.

4.   The **communication gap** refers to the difference between the actual service provided to customers and the service that the firm's promotion program promises. If firms are more realistic about the services they can provide and manage customer expectations effectively, they generally can close this gap.

EXHIBIT   12.3   Gaps Model for Improving Service

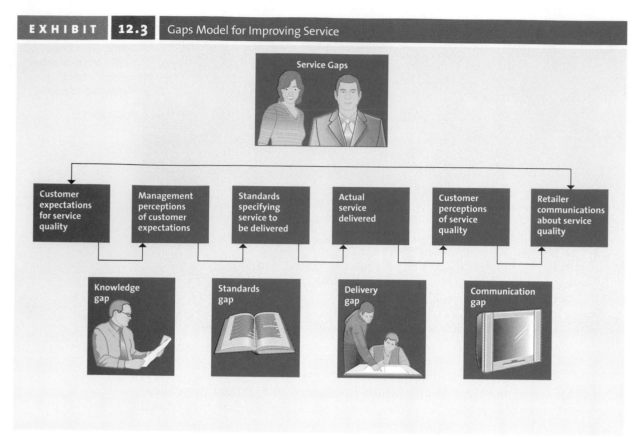

Source: Michael Levy and Barton Weitz, *Retailing Management*, 6th ed. (Burr Ridge, IL: McGraw-Hill, 2007). Adapted from Valerie Zeithaml, A. Parasuraman, and Leonard Berry, *Delivering Quality Customer Service* (New York: The Free Press, 1990) and Valerie Zeithaml, Leonard Berry, and A. Parasuraman, "Communication and Control Processes in the Delivery of Service Quality," *Journal of Marketing* 52, no. 2 (April 1988), pp. 35–48.

What service gaps did Marcia experience while on vacation at the Paradise Motel in Maine?

As we discuss the four gaps subsequently, we will apply them to the experience that Marcia Kessler had with a motel in Maine. She saw an ad for a package weekend that quoted a very reasonable daily rate and listed the free amenities available at Paradise Motel: free babysitting services, a piano bar with a nightly singer, a free Continental breakfast, a heated swimming pool, and newly decorated rooms. When she booked the room, Marcia discovered that the price advertised was not available during the weekend, and a three-day minimum stay was required. After checking in with a very unpleasant person at the front desk, Marcia and her husband found that their room appeared circa 1950 and had not been cleaned. When she complained, all she got was "attitude" from the assistant manager. Resigned to the fact that they were slated to spend the weekend, she decided to go for a swim. Unfortunately, the water was "heated" by Booth Bay and stood at around 50 degrees. No one was using the babysitting services because there were few young children at the resort. It turns out the piano bar singer was the second cousin of the owner, and he couldn't carry a tune, let alone play the piano very well. The Continental breakfast must have come all the way from the Continent, because everything was stale and tasteless. Marcia couldn't wait to get home.

The Knowledge Gap: Knowing What Customers Want

An important early step in providing good service is knowing what the customer wants. For example, the motel offered babysitting services, but most of its customers did not have kids, had not brought them on their trip, or simply did not want to use the service. Had the motel known that no one would take advantage of this service, it might have trained the babysitters to get the rooms cleaned in time for the guests' arrival.

To reduce the knowledge gap, firms must understand the customers' expectations. To understand those expectations, firms undertake customer research and increase the interaction and communication between managers and employees.

Understanding Customer Expectations Customers' expectations are based on their knowledge and experiences.[11] Marcia's expectations were that her room at the motel in Maine would be ready when she got there, the swimming pool would be heated, the singer would be able to sing, and the breakfast would be fresh. If the resort never understood her expectations, it is unlikely it would ever be able to meet them.

Expectations vary according to the type of service. Marcia's expectations might have been higher, for instance, if she were staying at a Ritz-Carlton rather than the Paradise Motel. At the Ritz, she might expect employees to know her by name, be aware of her dietary preferences, and have placed fresh fruit of her choice and fresh-cut flowers in her room before she arrived. At the Paradise Motel, she would expect easy check-in/checkout, easy access to a major highway, a clean room with a comfortable bed, and a TV.

People's expectations also vary depending on the situation. Marcia may be satisfied with both the preceding hotel properties, depending on the circumstances. If she were traveling on business, the Paradise Motel might be fine, but if she were celebrating her 10th wedding anniversary, she probably would prefer the Ritz. Regardless of these choices, however, the service provider needs to know and understand the expectations of the customers in its target market.

Evaluating Service Quality To meet or exceed customers' expectations, marketers must determine what those expectations are. Yet because of their intangibility, the **service quality**, or customers' perceptions of how well a service meets or exceeds their expectations, often is difficult for customers to evaluate.[12] Customers generally use five distinct service dimensions to determine overall service quality: reliability, responsiveness, assurance, empathy, and tangibles (Exhibit 12.4).

If you were to apply the five service dimensions to your own decision-making process when you selected a college—which provides the service of education—you might find results like those in Exhibit 12.5.

If your expectations include an individualized experience at a state-of-the-art institution, perhaps University B is a better alternative for you. But if you are relying heavily on academic performance and career placement from your university experience, then University A might be a better choice. If a strong culture and tradition are important to you, University A offers this type of environment. What were your expectations, and how did your university choices fall within these service dimensions?

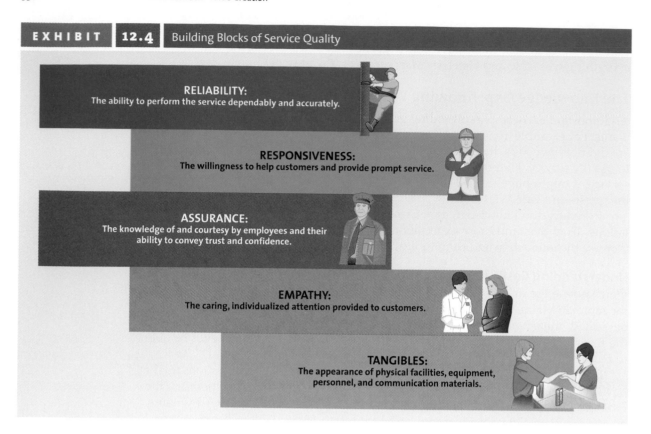

EXHIBIT 12.4   Building Blocks of Service Quality

RELIABILITY:
The ability to perform the service dependably and accurately.

RESPONSIVENESS:
The willingness to help customers and provide prompt service.

ASSURANCE:
The knowledge of and courtesy by employees and their
ability to convey trust and confidence.

EMPATHY:
The caring, individualized attention provided to customers.

TANGIBLES:
The appearance of physical facilities, equipment,
personnel, and communication materials.

Marketing Research: Understanding Customers   Marketing research (see Chapter 9) provides a means to better understand consumers' service expectations and their perceptions of service quality. This research can be extensive and expensive, or it can be integrated into a firm's everyday interactions with customers. Today, most service firms have developed voice-of-customer programs and employ ongoing marketing research to assess how well they are meeting their customers' expectations.

A systematic **voice-of-customer (VOC) program** collects customer inputs and integrates them into managerial decisions. For instance, when Bank of America talks about the success of its online bill payment feature, it quickly cites its VOC program as essential to the widespread user acceptance it enjoys; the bank has captured 50 percent of the entire e-payment market. Its VOC program entails a complex polling system, coupled with technology enhancements, that allows Bank of America to gather and collate data points from various channels and thus closely gauge responses to its new products and services. Bank of America is so committed to listening to its customers that it was one of the first to offer free bill payment services. Other enhancements stemming from the program include an overview page that integrates frequently used functions, single-point access, and e-statements that customers can access for a full year's history through the bank's Web site.[13]

Another means to evaluate how well firms perform on the five service quality dimensions (Exhibit 12.4), the concept of the zone of tolerance refers to the area between customers' expectations regarding their desired service and the minimum

EXHIBIT 12.5	Collegiate Service Dimensions	
	University A	**University B**
Reliability	Offers sound curriculum with extensive placement services and internships.	Curriculum covers all the basics but important courses are not always available. Career placement is haphazard at best.
Responsiveness	Slow to respond to application. Very structured visitation policy. Rather inflexible with regard to personal inquiries or additional meetings.	Quick response during application process. Open visitation policy. Offers variety of campus resources to help with decision making.
Assurance	Staff seems very confident in reputation and services.	Informal staff who convey enthusiasm for institution.
Empathy	Seems to process student body as a whole rather than according to individual needs or concerns.	Very interested in providing a unique experience for each student.
Tangibles	Very traditional campus with old-world look and feel. Facilities are manicured. Dorm rooms are large, but bathrooms are a little old.	New campus with modern architecture. Campus is less manicured. Dorm rooms are spacious with newer bathrooms.

level of acceptable service—that is, the difference between what the customer really wants and what he or she will accept before going elsewhere.[14] To define the zone of tolerance, firms ask a series of questions about each service quality dimension that relate to

- The desired and expected level of service for each dimension, from low to high.
- Customers' perceptions of how well the focal service performs and how well a competitive service performs, from low to high.
- The importance of each service quality dimension.

Pooch Palace rates higher than Goth Kennel on all Service Quality Dimensions, and is within the zone of tolerance on all dimensions except responsiveness, where it is outside the zone on the high side.

Exhibit 12.6 illustrates the results of such an analysis for the Pooch Palace dog kennel. The rankings on the left are based on a nine-point scale, on which 1 is low and 9 is high. The length of each box illustrates the zone of tolerance for each service quality dimension. For instance, according to the length of the reliability box, customers expect a fairly high level of reliability (top of the box), but will also only accept a fairly high level of reliability (bottom of the box). On the other end of the scale, customers expect a high level of assurance (top of the box), but will accept a fairly low level (bottom of the box). This is expected since the customers were also asked to assign an important score to the five service quality dimensions so that the total equals 100 percent. Looking at the average importance score, we conclude that reliability is relatively important to these customers, but assurance is not. So customers have a fairly narrow zone of tolerance for service dimensions that are fairly important to them, and a wider range of tolerance for those service dimensions that are less important. Also note that Pooch Palace always rates higher than its primary competitor, Goth Kennels, on each dimension.

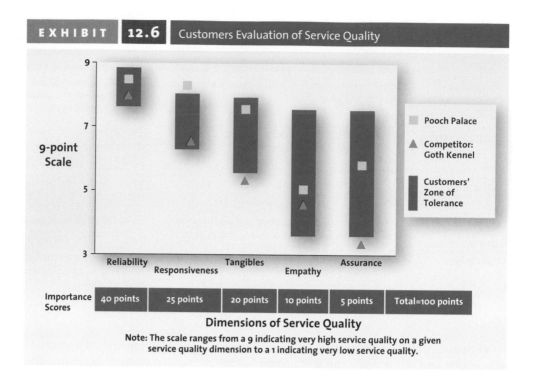

EXHIBIT 12.6 Customers Evaluation of Service Quality

9-point Scale

- ■ Pooch Palace
- ▲ Competitor: Goth Kennel
- ■ Customers' Zone of Tolerance

Reliability · Responsiveness · Tangibles · Empathy · Assurance

Importance Scores	40 points	25 points	20 points	10 points	5 points	Total=100 points

Dimensions of Service Quality

Note: The scale ranges from a 9 indicating very high service quality on a given service quality dimension to a 1 indicating very low service quality.

Also note that Goth Kennels scores below the zone of tolerance on the tangibles dimension, meaning that customers are not willing to accept the way the kennel looks and smells. Pooch Palace, in contrast, performs above the zone of tolerance on the responsiveness dimension—maybe even too well. The kennel may wish to conduct further research to verify which responsiveness aspects it is performing so well, and then consider toning those aspects down. For example, being responsive to customers' desires to have a 24-hour drop-off and pick-up capability can be expensive and may not add any further value to the company itself because customers would accept more limited times.

A very straightforward and inexpensive method of collecting consumers' perceptions of service quality is to gather them at the time of the sale. Service providers can ask customers how they liked the service—though customers often are reticent to provide negative feedback directly to the person who provided the service—or distribute a simple questionnaire. The company must take care not to lose much of this information, which can happen if there is no effective mechanism for filtering it up to the key decision makers. Furthermore, in some cases, customers cannot effectively evaluate the service until several days or weeks later. Automobile dealers, for instance, often call their customers a week after they perform a service like an oil change to assess their service quality.

Another excellent method for assessing customers' expectations is making effective use of customer complaint behavior. Even if complaints are handled effectively to solve customers' problems, the essence of the complaint is too often lost on managers. For instance, a large PC retailer responded to complaints about the lack of service from salespeople and issues with products by providing an e-mail address for people to contact the service department. This proved to be difficult when the problem is that the computer isn't working.[15]

Entrepreneurial Marketing 12.1

The Key to One's Heart (and Stomach) Is Good Food and Great Service[16]

Phil Romano is a household name, or at least his businesses are. Romano began his entrepreneurial life in 1963 in Lake Park, Florida with a small Italian restaurant named Gladiator. Fifteen years later and in San Antonio he had added Fuddruckers and Macaroni Grill to his portfolio. Romano is a nationally recognized entrepreneur and restaurateur. He is the only person to have created six national restaurant concepts. In addition to Fuddruckers and Macaroni Grill (now owned by Brinker International), there is Spageddies, Cozymats, Rudy's Country Store and BBQ and eatZi's Market and Bakery. These concepts produce over $1 billion in sales each year.

Romano doesn't operate all these restaurants himself. In fact, he dislikes the day-to-day management. He recognizes that it takes a team effort of knowledgeable people dedicated to the art of providing excellent service quality.

These concept restaurants were created with the goal that they should service the customer first, have an identifiable point of difference, and then consider profit. For example, Fuddruckers is his personal attempt to fulfill a great desire for the perfect hamburger. The hamburgers here are made from daily ground 100 percent beef, fresh baked buns, and a choice of condiments, all prepared in the customers' view.

Romano's credentials, if not impressive by themselves, have won him several even more impressive

Phil Romano started Fuddruckers and several other chain restaurants.

titles and awards. In 2000 he was named one of the top 20 restaurateurs. In 1995 he was named "Innovator of the Year," and in 1996 his concept eatZi's Market Bakery was a "Hot Concept of the Year." Also, in 1997 *Advertising Age* named Romano one of the "top 100 innovative and inspiring marketers who have most successfully established or repositioned a brand."

Romano's mind is never at rest. He says there are "so many [restaurant concepts] I want to do. And when I'm going to do it, it's going to have a real point of difference."

Even firms with the best formal research mechanisms in place must put managers on the front lines occasionally to interact directly with the customers. Unless the managers who make the service quality decisions know what their service providers are facing on a day-to-day basis, and unless they can talk directly to the customers with whom those service providers interact, any customer service program they create will not be as good as it could be. Entrepreneurial Marketing 12.1 provides a glimpse into how important service quality is to the success of restaurants.

The Standards Gap: Setting Service Standards

Say the Paradise Motel in Maine set out to determine its customers' service expectations and gained a pretty good idea of them. Its work is still far from over; the next step is to set its service standards and develop systems to ensure high-quality service. How can it make sure that every room is cleaned by 2:00 p.m.? That the food is checked for freshness and quality every day? The manager needs to set

Service providers, like this housekeeper at a hotel, generally want to do a good job, but they need to be trained to know exactly what a good job entails.

an example of high service standards, which will permeate throughout the organization, and the employees must be thoroughly trained not only to complete their specific tasks but also in how to treat guests.

Achieving Service Goals through Training To deliver consistently high-quality service, firms must set specific, measurable goals based on customers' expectations; to help ensure that quality, the employees should be involved in the goal setting. For instance, for the Paradise Motel, the most efficient process would be to start cleaning rooms at 8:00 a.m. and finish by 5:00 p.m. But many guests want to sleep late, and new arrivals want to get into their room as soon as they arrive, often before 5:00. So a customer-oriented standard would mandate that the rooms get cleaned between 10:00 a.m. and 2:00 p.m.

Service providers generally want to do a good job, as long as they know what is expected of them. Motel employees should be shown, for instance, exactly how managers expect them to clean a room and what specific tasks they are responsible for performing. In general, more employees will buy into a quality-oriented process if they are involved in setting the goals. For instance, suppose an employee of the motel refuses to clean the glass cups in the rooms because she believes that disposable plastic cups are relatively inexpensive and more hygienic. If management listens to and makes the change, it should make the employees all the more committed to the other tasks involved in cleaning rooms.

For frontline service employees, pleasant interactions with customers do not always come naturally. Although people can be taught specific tasks related to their jobs, it is simply not enough to tell employees to "be nice" or "do what customers want." A quality goal should be specific: Greet every customer/guest you encounter with "good morning/afternoon/evening, Sir or Miss." Try to greet customers by name.

In extreme cases, such training becomes even more crucial. From long ticket lines to cancelled flights to lost baggage, customer service incidents are on the rise in the airline industry. Faced with mounting complaints, airlines are responding with better employee training geared toward identifying and defusing potentially explosive situations. For example, Northwest Airlines has implemented a "Customer First" training program for its ground operations, customer service agents, flight attendants, and pilots that mandates specific performance measures and standardized practices throughout Northwest's service areas. Policies for service during delays, such as providing snacks on board or trucking food out to waiting planes and offering status updates every 15 minutes, have given employees the tools and guidelines they need to better service their customers.[17]

Commitment to Service Quality Service providers take their cues from management. If managers strive for excellent service, treat their customers well, and demand the same attitudes from everyone in the organization, it is likely employees will do the same. Take for example Les Schwab, the 85-year-old founder of Les Schwab Tire Centers in Portland, Oregon. Unlike its competitors, Les Schwab is legendary for its focus on customer service—service that has resulted in a $1 billion empire. In addition to traditions like "free beef month," in which customers receive steaks with the purchase of four tires in March, Les Schwab provides its employees with a generous profit-sharing plan that rewards them when stores succeed. In many cases, store managers earn six figures and retire as millionaires.

Schwab also believes in rewarding loyalty by promoting only from within; such a sense of partnership has fostered an environment in which stores compete to take care of the customers the fastest and receive the most complimentary letters. For Cook, his clear understanding of the link between customer satisfaction and his own prosperous future means that he was ready to stop to help a woman stranded on the side of the road with a flat tire. After putting on her temporary tire, he directed her toward a Schwab Tire Center, where his buddies fixed her flat tire for free.[18]

The Delivery Gap: Delivering Service Quality

The delivery gap is where "the rubber meets the road," where the customer directly interacts with the service provider. Even if there are no other gaps, a delivery gap always results in a service failure. Marcia experienced several delivery gaps at the Paradise Motel: the unclean room, the assistant manager's attitude, the unheated swimming pool, the poor piano bar singer, and the stale food.

Delivery gaps can be reduced when employees are empowered to act in the customers' and the firm's best interests and supported in their efforts so they can do their jobs effectively.[19] Technology can also be employed to reduce delivery gaps. (See Exhibit 12.7.)

Empowering Service Providers   In this context, **empowerment** means allowing employees to make decisions about how service is provided to customers. When frontline employees are authorized to make decisions to help their customers, service quality generally improves.[20] Best Buy, for instance, has reengineered its organizational structure to empower employees to be more involved in the day-to-day running of the business and to make adjustments as necessary. The new

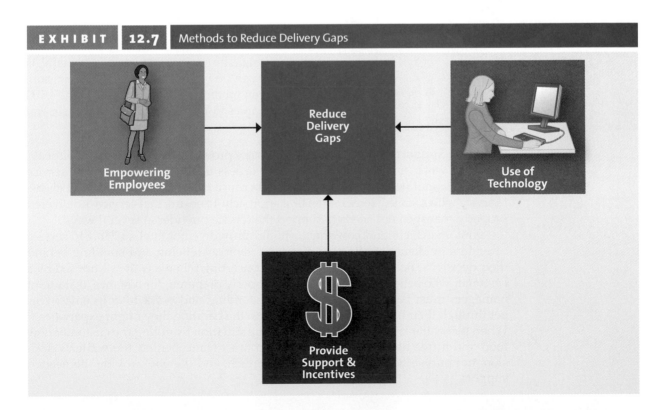

EXHIBIT 12.7 Methods to Reduce Delivery Gaps

Empowering Employees → Reduce Delivery Gaps ← Use of Technology

Provide Support & Incentives

employee-centric culture has helped Best Buy significantly lower its employee turnover rate. Happy employees make for happy customers.[21]

However, empowering service providers can be difficult and costly. In cases in which the service is very repetitive and routine, such as at a fast-food restaurant, it might be more efficient and easier for service providers to follow a few simple rules. For instance, if a customer doesn't like his hamburger, ask him what he would like instead or offer him a refund. If an exceptional circumstance that does not fit the rules arises, then a manager should handle the issue.

Empowerment becomes more important when the service is more individualized. Suppose a man purchased an expensive wristwatch and accidentally dropped and broke it before he even left the store. The sales associate who waited on him should be empowered to do whatever it takes to satisfy him and to take responsibility for the problem rather than to turn it over to someone else.

The Container Store is successful, in part, because it empowers its employees to help solve customers' storage and organization problems.

The Container Store, a chain of stores located across the United States, sells multifunctional storage and organization products that save customers space and, ultimately, time.[22] But just having lots of cool stuff in which customers can put their own stuff isn't the only reason The Container Store is so successful; it also empowers its employees to help solve customers' storage and organization problems. People don't generally know exactly what they need when they enter the stores, but they know they want to clean up their messy garage or store their sweaters for the summer. Sales associates at The Container Store receive 235 hours of training in their first year, as well as additional training throughout their careers, on not only product information but also ways to help customers. The training excites the associates and sparks their creativity for finding solutions. What about a ceiling-mounted bike rack in the garage? Perhaps a six-shelf hanging bag to keep your sweaters in the closet and out of your dresser? The approach seems to be working. The chain is financially successful, is involved in an ongoing multiple-store expansion, and has been on the top of *Fortune* magazine's 100 Best Companies to Work for in America for several years running.

Providing Support and Incentives A service provider's job can often be difficult, especially when customers are unpleasant or less than reasonable. But the service provider cannot be rude or offensive just because the customer is. The old cliché, "Service with a smile," remains the best approach. To ensure that service is delivered properly, management needs to support the service provider in several ways.

First, managers and coworkers should provide emotional support to service providers by demonstrating a concern for their well-being and standing behind their decisions. Because it can be very disconcerting when a waiter is abused by a customer who believes her food was improperly prepared, for instance, restaurant managers must be supportive and understanding and work to help employees get through their often emotional reaction to the berating they might experience.[23] When the waiter is empowered to rectify the situation by giving the customer new food and a free dessert, the manager also must stand behind the waiter's decision, not punish her for giving away too much, and thereby provide the needed support.

Second, service providers require instrumental support—the systems and equipment—to deliver the service properly. Many retailers provide similarly state-of-the-art instrumental support for their service providers. In-store kiosks help sales associates provide more detailed and complete product information and enable them to make sales of merchandise that is either not carried in the store or temporarily out of stock.

Third, the support that managers provide must be consistent and coherent throughout the organization. Patients expect physicians to provide great patient care using state-of-the-art procedures and medications, but because they are tied to managed-care systems (health maintenance organizations or HMOs), many doctors must squeeze more people into their office hours and prescribe less optimal, but less expensive, courses of treatment. These conflicting goals can be so frustrating and emotionally draining on physicians and other healthcare providers that some have found work outside of medicine.

Conflicting service goals also can occur within an organization. For instance, inventory managers might restrict purchasing levels to lower the company's inventory investment, but that attempt at greater efficiency causes salespeople stress because they are out of stock of merchandise their customers want. Managers therefore must balance the sometimes conflicting needs of inventory managers and salespeople by providing clear guidance and oversight in attending to the expectations of customers.

Fourth, a key part of any customer service program is providing rewards to employees for excellent service. Numerous firms have developed a service reputation by ensuring that their employees recognize the value the firm places on customer service. Nordstrom, for example, offers its VIP club and "Employee of the Month" service awards. The retailer encourages associates or their managers to stand up and recount their great customer service episodes from the past week.[24] One associate in Denver won the service award for selling shoes to a teenager whose feet were different sizes; to save the sale and please the customer, the associate took one shoe from one box and another from another box and sold the teen the mixed pair.

Use of Technology   Technology has become an increasingly important method for facilitating the delivery of services. Since the mid-1990s, with the widespread usage of the Internet, firms have invested heavily in technologies that have enabled customers to buy more quickly, more easily, and with more information than in the past. Electronic kiosks, for instance, have found their way into many service venues. Ticketing kiosks at airports allow customers to get boarding passes and seat assignments, often in less than a minute. Many hotels, including Marriott, have installed self–check-in kiosks that enable customers to charge their rooms, encode and dispense key cards, and secure identification.[25]

Web-enabled services have also changed the way firms do business with other companies. By 2007, 70 percent of all service centers likely will support Web-based service applications. Already, Cisco Systems, the leading supplier of networking equipment and networking management for the Internet, receives in excess of 80 percent of new orders electronically and resolves more than 80 percent of its customer issues through self-service mechanisms.[26]

Using technology to facilitate service delivery can provide many benefits, such as access to a wider variety of services, a greater degree of control by the customer over the services, and the ability to obtain information. Management also benefits from the increased efficiency in service processes through reduced servicing costs, and, in some cases, can develop a competitive advantage over less service-oriented competitors.[27]

The advent of Web-enabled service thus is changing customers' perceptions about the availability and types of services offered, though those attitudes vary. Some customers embrace technology, while others resent it. Many multichannel retailers have experienced a new Web-related service challenge: abandoned shopping carts on Internet sites. This technology-related issue signals that customers may have become disappointed, frustrated, or angry while shopping and have decided to take their money elsewhere.[28]

The Communications Gap: Communicating the Service Promise

The communications gap pertains to the difference between the service promised and the service actually delivered. A customer of a California Internet provider was convinced to cancel her service to sign up with a new one after hearing advertisements for "great service" at a lower cost. During the first three weeks of the service she was only able to access the Internet half a dozen times because of technology failures. She was further disappointed because when she called technology support she had to pay long distance rates since an 800 number was not available to her. When she did call she was told to call back because no one was in that department at the moment. She expected reliable service and helpful customer representatives, but instead received spotty service at best, as well as difficult and expensive technology support.[29]

Although firms have difficulty controlling service quality because it can vary from day to day and provider to provider, they do have control over how they communicate their service package to their customers. If a firm promises more than it can deliver, customers' expectations won't be met. An advertisement may lure a customer into a service situation once, but if the service doesn't deliver on the promise, the customer will never return. Dissatisfied customers also are likely to tell others about the underperforming service, using word of mouth or, increasingly, the Internet, which has become an important channel for dissatisfied customers to vent their frustrations.

The communications gap can be reduced by managing customer expectations. Suppose you need an operation, and the surgeon explains, "You'll be out of the hospital in five days and back to your normal routine in a month." You have the surgery and feel well enough to leave the hospital three days later. Two weeks after that, you're playing tennis again. Clearly, you will tend to think your surgeon is a genius. However, regardless of the operation's success, if you had to stay in the hospital for 10 days and it took you two months to recover, you would undoubtedly be upset.

Promising only what you can deliver, or possibly even a little less, is an important way to control the communications gap.[30] For instance, when Federal Express first issued its next-day delivery guarantee—"absolutely, positively there by 10:30 a.m."—it achieved a competitive advantage until others matched its promise. Now Federal Express often gives next-day service when the customer has paid only for second-day service. If the package arrives on the second day, it meets expectations. If it arrives a day early, it exceeds them.

A relatively easy way to manage customer expectations considers both the time the expectation is created and the time the service is provided. Expectations typically are created through promotions, whether in advertising or personal selling. For instance, if a salesperson promises a client that an order can be delivered in one day, and that delivery actually takes a week, the client will be disappointed.

However, if the salesperson coordinates the order with those responsible for the service delivery, the client's expectations likely will be met.

Customer expectations can also be managed when the service is delivered. For example, recorded messages can tell customers who have telephoned a company how many minutes they will have to wait before the next operator is available. Business-to-business sellers automatically inform online customers of any items that are out of stock. Whether online or in a store, retailers can warn their customers to shop early during a sale because supplies of the sale item are limited. People are generally reasonable when they are warned that some aspect of the service may be below standards. They just don't like surprises!

Service Recovery

Despite a firm's best efforts, sometimes service providers fail to meet customer expectations. When this happens, the best course of action is to attempt to make amends with the customer and learn from the experience. Of course, it is best to avoid a service failure altogether, but when it does occur, the firm has a unique opportunity to demonstrate its customer commitment.[31] Effective service recovery efforts can significantly increase customer satisfaction, purchase intentions, and positive word of mouth, though customers' postrecovery satisfaction levels usually fall lower than their satisfaction level prior to the service failure.[32]

The Paradise Motel in Maine could have made amends with Marcia Kessler after its service failures if it had taken some relatively simple, immediate steps: The assistant manager could have apologized for his bad behavior and quickly upgraded her to a suite and/or given her a free night's lodging for a future stay. The motel could also have given her a free lunch or dinner to make up for the bad breakfast. None of these actions would have cost the motel much money. Yet by not taking action, it lost Marcia, who over the next few years could have been responsible for several thousand dollars in sales, as a customer forever. Furthermore, Marcia is likely to spread negative word of mouth about the motel to her friends and family because of its failure to recover. Quite simply, effective service recovery entails (1) listening to the customer, (2) providing a fair solution, and (3) resolving the problem quickly.[33] (Exhibit 12.8)

When a service failure occurs, like receiving a poor meal at a restaurant, a firm's goodwill can be recovered by giving the customer a free dessert.

Listening to the Customer

Firms often don't find out about service failures until a customer complains. Whether the firm has a formal complaint department or the complaint is offered directly to the service provider, the customer must have the opportunity to air the complaint completely, and the firm must listen carefully to what he or she is saying.

Customers can become very emotional about a service failure, whether the failure is serious (a botched surgical operation) or minor (the wrong change at a restaurant). In many cases, the customer may just want to be heard, and the service provider should give the customer all the time he or she needs to "get it out." The very process of describing a perceived wrong to a sympathetic listener is therapeutic in and of itself. Service providers therefore should welcome the opportunity to be that sympathetic ear, listen carefully, and appear anxious to rectify the situation to ensure it doesn't happen again.[34]

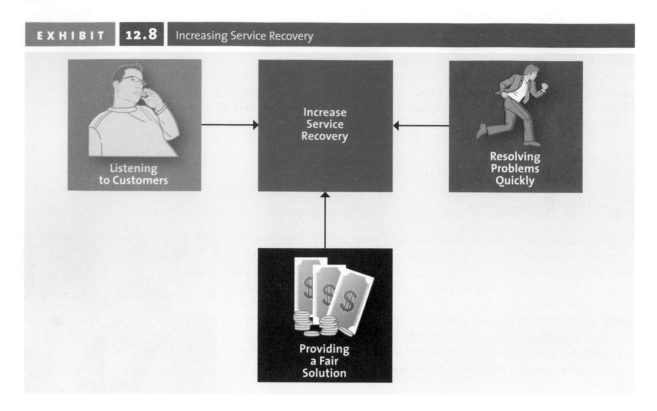

| EXHIBIT | 12.8 | Increasing Service Recovery |

Finding a Fair Solution

Most people realize that mistakes happen. But when they happen, customers want to be treated fairly, whether that means distributive or procedural fairness.[35] Their perception of what "fair" means is based on their previous experience with other firms, how they have seen other customers treated, material they have read, and stories recounted by their friends.

Distributive Fairness   Distributive fairness pertains to a customer's perception of the benefits he or she received compared with the costs (inconvenience or loss). Customers want to be compensated a fair amount for a perceived loss that resulted from a service failure. If, for instance, a person arrives at the airport gate and finds her flight is overbooked, she may believe that taking the next flight that day and receiving a travel voucher is adequate compensation for the inconvenience. But if no flights are available until the next day, the traveler may require additional compensation, such as overnight accommodations, meals, and a round-trip ticket to be used at a later date.[36]

The key to distributive fairness, of course, is listening carefully to the customer. One customer, traveling on vacation, may be satisfied with a travel voucher, whereas another may need to get to the destination on time because of a business appointment. Regardless of how the problem is solved, customers typically want tangible restitution—in this case, to get to their destination—not just an apology. If providing a tangible restitution isn't possible, the next best thing is to assure the customer that steps are being taken to prevent the failure from recurring.

A mother approached Buck Rogers, who was the general manager of the Daytona Cubs minor league baseball team, to inform him that a rowdy patron near her and her young child had been swearing constantly during the game. Rogers immediately offered to change her seat, but the mother did not find this offer sufficient because she believed she could probably hear the swearing fan from anywhere in the ballpark. The woman indicated she would never come back. Trying to find an acceptable solution and not lose the fan, Rogers offered her a free admission to another game and told her that when she returned, her son could throw out the first pitch. The end result of this quick thinking: The woman and her son returned many times.[37]

Procedural Fairness   With regard to complaints, **procedural fairness** refers to the perceived fairness of the process used to resolve them. Customers want efficient complaint procedures over whose outcomes they have some influence. Furthermore, customers tend to believe they have been treated fairly if the service providers follow specific company guidelines, though rigid adherence to rules can have deleterious effects. CVS, the largest drugstore chain in the United States, requires a manager's approval for every return, no matter how small. This process can take several minutes and therefore can irritate everyone in the checkout line. In this case, the procedure the company uses to handle a return may overshadow potential positive outcomes. Therefore, as we noted previously, service providers should be empowered with some flexibility to solve customer complaints.

When handling returns or other services issues, it is important to use procedures that are perceived to be fair by the customers.

Consider the local convenience store that sells both cigarettes and alcohol. The storeowner has implemented a policy that everyone under 30 years of age who attempts to purchase these items must show valid identification. If the store clerks comply, the customers see and accept it as part of the purchasing protocol and perceive it as fair for everyone. If a customer clearly looks over 40 years of age, however, it is doubtful that he or she is under 21 years old, and giving the store clerk a little discretion about asking for identification can avoid a service failure.

Resolving Problems Quickly

The longer it takes to resolve a service failure, the more irritated the customer will become and the more people he or she is likely to tell about the problem. To resolve service failures quickly, firms need clear policies, adequate training for their employees, and empowered employees. Health insurance companies, for instance, have made a concerted effort in recent years to avoid service failures that occur because customers' insurance claims have not been handled quickly or to the customers' satisfaction. USAA, a member-owned financial services organization that caters to members of the military and their families, employs telephone representatives who work directly with "action agents" within the organization to resolve customer complaints and identify service failures quickly. Its efforts have paid off; USAA has an annual customer renewal rate of 98 percent[38] and owns and manages more than $73 billion in assets for more than 5 million members.[39]

The CREST Method of Resolving Service Failures

The CREST method refers to an acronym that, when carefully implemented, can help resolve service failures.

- C: "Calm the customer" by actively listening and empathizing.
- R: "Repeat the problem" so that the customer knows he or she was heard and understood. For example, respond "Now, Mrs. Jones, you paid your mortgage on time, but still were assessed the penalty fee, is that correct?"

- ■ E: Use "empathy statements," such as, "Yes, Mrs. Jones, I can see your point. I would feel the same way."
- ■ S: "Solve the problem" by indicating what action will be taken to resolve the issue. Say, for example, "I will contact Dave in our mortgage area, and call you this afternoon."
- ■ T: Make a "timely response" to ensure that the problem is resolved in a defined span of time that is acceptable to both parties.[40]

It may seem overly simple, but to recover effectively from service failures, firms must not only listen to the customers' complaints but act on them. It is the implementation of this simple rule that offers firms such challenges.

Summing Up

1. How does the marketing of services differ from the marketing of products?

First and foremost, services are intangible—they can't be seen or touched—which makes it difficult to describe a service's benefits or promote it to others. Service providers attempt to reduce the impact of the service's intangibility by enhancing its delivery with more tangible attributes, like a nice atmosphere or price benefits. Second, services are produced and consumed at the same time. Third, services are more variable than products, though service providers attempt to reduce this variability through standardization, training, service bundling, and technology. Fourth, because consumers can't stockpile services, marketers provide incentives to stagger demand over time.

2. Why is it important that service marketers know what customers expect?

A knowledge gap occurs when marketers don't understand what their customers want. They may not be providing customers enough or the right service, in which case customers will be disappointed. To understand customer expectations, marketers analyze service quality through comprehensive studies and by interacting with customers.

3. What can firms do to help employees provide better service?

First, firms should provide training to employees regarding how to do their job and interact with customers. Second, they need to demonstrate a strong commitment to service and lead through example. Third, they can empower service providers to solve service issues and problems. Fourth, they should provide employees with both emotional support and the tools they need to do a good job. Fifth, the service program should be consistent throughout the organization. Sixth, service providers need incentives that encourage them to do a good job.

4. What should firms do when a service fails?

In the best-case scenario, the service does not fail in the first place. But failures are inevitable, and when they do happen, the firm must make amends to the customer. Listen carefully to the customer. Let the customer air his or her complaint. Find a fair solution to the problem that not only compensates the customer for the failure but also follows procedures that the customer believes are fair. Resolve the problem quickly.

Key Terms

- ■ communication gap, 335
- ■ customer service, 328
- ■ delivery gap, 335
- ■ distributive fairness, 348
- ■ empowerment, 343
- ■ inseparable, 330

- ■ intangible, 329
- ■ knowledge gap, 335
- ■ perishable, 334
- ■ procedural fairness, 349
- ■ service, 328
- ■ service gap, 335

- ■ service quality, 337
- ■ standards gap, 335
- ■ variability, 331
- ■ voice-of-customer (VOC) program, 338
- ■ zone of tolerance, 338

Marketing Applications

1. Those companies from which you purchase products and services are not pure sellers of services, nor are they pure sellers of products. What services does a department store provide? What goods does a dentist provide?

2. You have been sitting in the waiting room of your doctor's office for an hour. With the knowledge that products are different than services, develop a list of the things the office manager could do to improve the overall service delivery. Consider how the office might overcome problems associated with the tangibility, separability, variability, and perishability of services.

3. You have conducted a zone of tolerance analysis for a local dry cleaner. You find that the length of the reliability and responsiveness boxes are much greater than those of the other three service quality dimensions. You also find that the dry cleaner is positioned above the zone box on reliability but below the box on responsiveness. What should you tell the manager of the dry cleaner to do?

4. Design a simple system for collecting customer information about the services of your dry cleaner client.

5. Think back to your last job. What training did your employer provide regarding how to interact with customers and provide good customer service? What could your employer have done to prepare you better to interact with customers?

6. Provide a specific situation in which a service provider could have avoided a service failure if he or she had been empowered by an employer to do so. What should that person have done?

7. What types of support and incentives could your university provide advisors to help make them more attentive to students' needs?

8. What technologies do you use that help facilitate your transactions with a specific retailer or service provider? Would you rather use the technology or engage in a face-to-face relationship with a person? How, if at all, would your parents' answer be different to these two questions?

9. A local health club is running a promotional campaign that promises you can lose an inch a month off your waist if you join the club and follow its program. How might this claim cause a communications gap? What should the club do to avoid a service failure?

10. Suppose the health club didn't listen to your advice and ran the promotional campaign as is. A new member has come in to complain that not only did he not lose inches off his waist, he actually gained weight. How should the health club manager proceed?

11. You are hired by a career consulting firm that promises to market new graduates to high-paying employers. The firm provides potential clients with an impressive client list. It charges the clients a fee, and then a separate finders fee if the client gets a position. The firm aggressively markets its services and has a large client base. You learn that the firm simply takes any submitted resumés and posts them to a variety of online job search engines. The firm never actually contacts any firms on its clients' behalf. The CEO, himself a recent college grad, tells you that the firm never promises that firm will contact potential employees themselves, only that they have access to and will distribute clients' resumés. What do you think of the career consulting firm's practices?

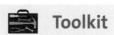 **Toolkit**

SERVICES ZONE OF TOLERANCE

Use the Toolkit provided at www.mhhe.com/grewal-levy to assess the Zone of Tolerance for several service providers.

Net Savvy

1. What services does JetBlue (www.jetblue.com) offer? Compare its services to those offered by American Airlines (www.aa.com) using the five service quality dimensions (tangibility, responsiveness, reliability, assurance, and empathy).

2. Evaluate the ease with which you can make hotel reservations using Marriott's (www.marriott.com) Internet reservation system. Marriott subscribes to the BBBOnline Privacy Program. What is this program? Why do you believe that Marriott includes its seal on its Web site?

Chapter Case Study

WEGMANS SERVICES ITS EMPLOYEES—AND ITS CUSTOMERS TOO[41]

For many grocery stores, meeting customers' needs is what they do.[42] For Wegmans, exceeding customers' needs and expectations is who it is and how it operates. In an industry in which 84 percent of consumers don't believe that traditional supermarkets can provide anything different from nontraditional grocers such as Wal-Mart, Wegmans has developed a strong and loyal customer base.

From its start in Rochester, New York, privately owned Wegmans has expanded in the past 90 years to reach customers in New York, New Jersey, Pennsylvania, Virginia, and, most recently, Maryland. By any count, Wegmans is successful. Its sales per square foot are $9.29, fifty percent higher than the industry average. Considering that its new stores are 130,000 square feet each—three times the size of a typical supermarket—Wegmans must be doing something right. In 2004, Wegmans received 7,000 letters, half of which were requests for a store to be built in a new community. When the Dulles store in Virginia opened, more than 15,500 customers, typical traffic for a week in a typical supermarket, came through on opening day.

Wegmans believes that the key to great service is happy and professionally trained employees.

Wegmans respects and services both its customers and its employees. When it earned *Fortune*'s coveted "Best Company to Work for" Award, Wegmans noted that part of its success as a retailer stems from its success as an employer. In the past 20 years, Wegmans has paid more than $54 million in college scholarships to both full-time and part-time employees. On a different educational front, employees who work in the meat and fish departments must graduate from a "university" program that takes between 30 and 55 hours and gives employees knowledge that assists them in furthering their careers.

Furthermore, because Wegmans prides itself on its customer service and satisfaction, it gives its employees power to assist customers in any way they see fit, without the approval of a supervisor. For example, one customer purchased the largest turkey Wegmans had for Thanksgiving and then discovered it was too large to cook at home. A Wegmans' employee cooked the turkey for the customer without charge.

In another case, a woman was looking for a particular item in the store. When the employee couldn't find the location of the item immediately, the customer said, "Go on back to whatever you were doing." A few minutes later, the employee found the customer in another section of the store and exclaimed, "There you are! I finally found it!" The employee took the time away from her current task to help a customer, even after she was no longer expected to be of assistance.

By the same token, Wegmans works hard to maintain certain standards. A customer survey told Wegmans that customers found its checkout experience superior to that of competing retailers. However, through its own investigations, Wegmans determined that its current alcohol and tobacco policy left too much to the discretion of underage cashiers. For the benefit of customers and the safety of the community's youth, Wegmans implemented a 100 percent proof policy in New York. This policy means that everyone, regardless of their apparent age, must present identification to purchase alcohol or tobacco. In addition, cashiers no longer have to worry about peer pressure or making an incorrect judgment call and insulting the customer.

Wegmans offers far more than you would find in a traditional supermarket—a real service bonanza. Drop off your child at the in-store daycare center. Saunter through the bookstore for Oprah's newest book club recommendation. Drop off your dry cleaning and overdue video rental. Pick up your dry cleaning. When you tire of browsing the flower and international newspaper sections, you can finally start on your grocery list, but before you run through the checkout, don't forget to pick up that bottle of champagne the cheese shop attendant told you would complement the white Castello cheese he handpicked for you.

Wegmans may sell many of the same products as other grocery retailers, but it's not the same. Employees at every level work to service the customer and exceed their needs and expectations. As a result, Wegmans' store count is growing at a steady pace, and so is its loyal customer base.

Questions

1. Using the building blocks of service quality (Exhibit 12.4) and, as discussed in this chapter, evaluate Wegmans.

2. Compare Wegmans' service quality performance with that of another grocery store in your town.

3. Using the Gap Model, identify the service gaps you noticed in your local grocery store. How might the store close those gaps?

13

Pricing Concepts for Establishing Value

"*You get what you pay for!*" "*Why pay more? They're all the same.*"

You've no doubt heard both these views and may even espouse one or the other of them from time to time when you shop.[1] So, which is it? When it comes to lunch, do you buy McChicken, Burger King's Tendergrill Chicken Sandwich, a bucket of KFC, or Panera Bread's Fontega Chicken sandwich? Each appeals to a different set of consumer preferences and beliefs about pricing. Is it better to spend the extra money to get a better product? Or should you save your money because the products are basically the same? Is Panera Bread's really that much better? Does it matter?

These different philosophies about price reflect the concept of value. Panera Bread® started out as a bakery-café called Saint Louis Bread Co. in 1981 with the notion that suburbanites wanted a healthy and delicious sandwich. The price reflects its intrinsic value. The bread is baked fresh at each store from dough that contains no trans fats. The chicken it serves is hormone and antibiotic free, and every two months the chain introduces a new item to invigorate the menu. The average Panera Bread patron spends nearly $4.00 more than the typical quick-serve meal to both eat healthfully and to enjoy the softer and more upscale ambience in the restaurants. Panera Bread has seemingly found the right price point and offers a great value because Panera Bread is on *BusinessWeek*'s Hot Growth ranking of small companies and net income is growing at an average annual rate of 50 percent.

In essence, if consumers value the brand and the potential benefits a higher price might signify, they likely will buy a sandwich at Panera Bread. However, a consumer who

Are you willing to pay more for this Panera Bread's Fontega Chicken Panini than for other fast-food chicken sandwiches?

values lower prices will likely purchase a McChicken or Tender-grill. Thus, knowing how consumers arrive at their perceptions of value is critical to developing successful pricing strategies. Nonetheless, a good pricing strategy must consider other factors as well, which is why developing one is a formidable challenge to all firms. Do it right, and the rewards to the firm will be substantial. Do it wrong, and failure will be swift and severe. But even if a pricing strategy is implemented well, consumers, economic conditions, markets, competitors, government regulations, and even a firm's own products change constantly—and that means that a good pricing strategy today may not remain an effective pricing strategy tomorrow.

A lot rides on marketers setting the right price, so we take two chapters to explain the role of price in the marketing mix. First, in this chapter, we explain what "price" is as a marketing concept, why it is important, how marketers set pricing objectives, and how various factors influence price setting. In the next chapter, we extend this foundation by focusing on specific pricing strategies that capitalize on capturing value.

Imagine that a consumer realizes that to save money on a particular item, she will have to drive an additional 20 miles. She may judge that her time and travel costs are not worth the savings, so even though the price tag is higher at a nearby store, she judges the overall cost of buying the product there to be lower. To include aspects of price such as this, we define price as the overall sacrifice a consumer is willing to make to acquire a specific product or service. This sacrifice usually includes the money that must be paid to the seller to acquire the item, but it also may involve other sacrifices, whether nonmonetary, like the value of the time necessary to acquire the product or service, or monetary, like travel costs, taxes, shipping costs, and so forth, all of which the buyer must give up to take possession of the product.[2] As we discuss subsequently, price also provides information about the quality of products and services.

Previously, we have defined value as the relationship between the product's benefits and the consumer's costs, which highlights the same relationship. Consumers judge the benefits the product delivers against the sacrifice necessary to obtain it, then make a purchase decision based on this overall judgment of value. Thus, a great but overpriced product can be judged as low in value and may not sell as well as an inferior but well-priced item. In turn, we cannot define price without referring to the product or service associated with it. The key to successful pricing is to match the product or service with the consumer's value perceptions.

That key raises a related question: If firms can price their products or services too high, can they price them too low as well? Quite simply, yes. Although price represents the sacrifice consumers make to acquire the product or service, it also provides information to consumers. A price set too low may signal low quality, poor performance, or other negative attributes about the product or service. Would you trust your looks to a plastic surgeon advertising rhinoplasty surgery (commonly referred to as a nose job) for only $299.99? We discuss this connection in further detail when we talk about specific pricing strategies in the next chapter, but for now, note that consumers don't necessarily want a low price all the time or for all products. Rather, they want high value, which may come with a relatively high or low price, depending on the bundle of benefits the product or service delivers.

However, because price is the only element of the marketing mix that does not generate costs, but instead generates revenue, it is important in its own right. Every other element in the marketing mix may be perfect, but with the wrong price, sales simply will not occur. Research has consistently shown that consumers usually rank price as one of the most important factors in their purchase decisions.[3]

As half of the value equation, price serves another important role. If the firm wants to deliver value and value is judged by the benefits relative to the cost, then pricing decisions are absolutely critical to the effort to deliver value.

Knowing that price is so critical to success, why don't managers put greater emphasis on it as a strategic decision variable? Price is the most challenging of the four Ps to manage, partly because it is often the least understood. Historically, managers have treated price as an afterthought to their marketing strategy, setting prices according to what competitors were charging or, worse yet, by adding up their costs and tacking a desired profit on to set the sales price. Prices were rarely changed except in response to radical shifts in market conditions. Even today pricing decisions are often relegated to standard rules of thumb that fail to reflect our current understanding of the role of price in the marketing mix.

For example, retailers sometimes use a 100 percent markup rule, otherwise known as "keystoning." That is, they simply double what they paid for the item when they price it for resale. Yet what happens if the store receives a particularly good deal from the manufacturer on an item? If consumers are not sensitive to

At IKEA, one can infer that a higher price means higher quality.

price changes for the product, should marketers blindly pass this lower price on to consumers? Why lower the price if it will not stimulate more sales? In this case, it might be better for the store not to follow its standard markup practice and instead take the additional profit. Similarly, if the store's cost for an item goes up and consumers are particularly sensitive to price increases for that product, the store might want to take less than 100 percent markup.

Moreover, managers have held an overly simplistic view of the role of price, considering it simply the amount of money a consumer must part with to acquire a product or service. We now know that price is not just a sacrifice but an information cue as well. That is, consumers use the price of a product or service to judge its quality.[4] Price is a particularly powerful indicator of quality when consumers are less knowledgeable about the product category. For example, most college students know little about upholstered furniture, so if a student found himself in an IKEA store and had to make a decision about which sofa to purchase, he might judge the quality of the various sofas according to their prices and assume that a higher price means higher quality.

In summary, marketers should view pricing decisions as a strategic opportunity to create value rather than as an afterthought to the rest of the marketing mix. Price communicates to the consumer more than how much a product or service costs; it can signal quality, or lack thereof. Let us now turn to the five basic components of pricing strategies.

The Five Cs of Pricing

Successful pricing strategies are built through the five critical components found in Exhibit 13.1.

We examine these components in some detail because each makes a significant contribution to formulating good pricing decisions.[5] To start, the first step is to develop the company's pricing objectives.

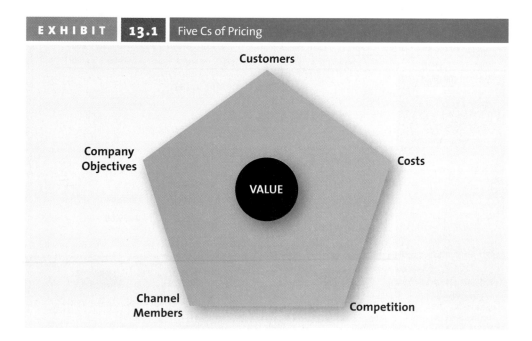

EXHIBIT 13.1   Five Cs of Pricing

Customers

Company Objectives

Costs

VALUE

Channel Members

Competition

Company Objectives

By now, you know that different firms embrace different goals. These goals should spill down to the pricing strategy, such that the pricing of a company's products and services should support and allow the firm to reach its overall goals. For example, a firm with a primary goal of very high sales growth will likely have a different pricing strategy than a firm with the goal of being a quality leader.

Each firm then embraces an objective that seems to fit with where management thinks the firm needs to go to be successful, in whatever way they define success. These specific objectives usually reflect how the firm intends to grow. Do managers want it to grow by increasing profits, increasing sales, decreasing competition, or building customer satisfaction?

Company objectives are not as simple as they might first appear; they often can be expressed in slightly different forms that mean very different things. Exhibit 13.2 introduces some common company objectives and corresponding examples of their implications for pricing strategies. These objectives are not always mutually exclusive, because a firm may embrace two or more noncompeting objectives.

Profit Orientation   Even though all company methods and objectives may ultimately be oriented toward making a profit, firms implement a **profit orientation** specifically by focusing on target profit pricing, maximizing profits, or target return pricing.

- Firms usually implement **target profit pricing** when they have a particular profit goal as their overriding concern. To meet this targeted profit objective, firms use price to stimulate a certain level of sales at a certain profit per unit.

- The **maximizing profits** strategy relies primarily on economic theory. If a firm can accurately specify a mathematical model that captures all the factors required to explain and predict sales and profits, it should be able to identify the price at which its profits are maximized. Of course, the problem with this approach is that actually gathering the data on all these relevant factors and somehow coming up with an accurate mathematical model is an extremely difficult undertaking.

- Other firms are less concerned with the absolute level of profits and more interested in the rate at which their profits are generated relative to their investments. These firms typically turn to **target return pricing** and employ pricing strategies designed to produce a specific return on their investment, usually expressed as a percentage of sales.

EXHIBIT 13.2	Company Objectives and Pricing Strategy Implications
Company Objective	**Examples of Pricing Strategy Implications**
Profit-oriented	Institute a companywide policy that all products must provide for at least an 18 percent profit margin to reach a particular profit goal for the firm.
Sales-oriented	Set prices very low to generate new sales and take sales away from competitors, even if profits suffer.
Competitor-oriented	To discourage more competitors from entering the market, set prices very low.
Customer-oriented	Target a market segment of consumers who highly value a particular product benefit and set prices relatively high (referred to as premium pricing).

Sales Orientation   Firms using a **sales orientation** to set prices believe that increasing sales will help the firm more than will increasing profits. For example, a new health club might focus on unit sales, dollar sales, or market share and therefore be willing to set a lower membership fee and accept less profit at first to focus on and generate more unit sales. In contrast, a high-end jewelry store might focus on dollar sales and maintain higher prices. This store relies on its prestige image, as well as the image of its suppliers, to provoke sales. Even though it sells fewer units, it can still generate high dollar sales levels.

Finally, some firms may be more concerned about their overall market share than about dollar sales per se (though these foci often go hand in hand) because they believe that market share better reflects their success relative to the market conditions than do sales alone. A firm may set low prices to discourage new firms from entering the market, encourage current firms to leave the market, take market share away from competitors—all to gain overall market share. For instance, the discount airlines Ireland's Ryan Air and U.S. low-cost leader Southwest regularly lower their fares to rates below their competition's prices to gain market share. Note that in all instances, however, profits are of lesser concern; the focus is on increasing sales.

Want to fly from London to Milan? You can do it on Ryan Air for 19€ or about $24.

Adopting a market share objective does not always imply setting low prices. Rarely is the lowest-price offering the dominant brand in a given market. Heinz Ketchup, Philadelphia Brand Cream Cheese, Crest toothpaste, and Nike athletic shoes have all dominated their markets, yet all are premium-priced brands. Thus, companies can gain market share simply by offering a high-quality product at a fair price as long as they use effective communication and distribution methods to generate high-value perceptions among consumers. Although the concept of value is not overtly expressed in sales-oriented strategies, it is at least implicit because for sales to increase, consumers must see greater value.

Competitor Orientation   When firms undertake a **competitor orientation**, they strategize according to the premise that they should measure themselves primarily against their competition. Some firms focus on **competitive parity**, which means they set prices that are similar to those of their major competitors. Another competitor-oriented strategy, **status quo pricing**, changes prices only to meet those of competition. Value is only implicitly considered in competitor-oriented strategies, in the sense that competitors may be using value as part of their pricing strategies, so copying their strategy might provide value.

Customer Orientation   A **customer orientation** explicitly invokes the concept of value. Sometimes a firm may attempt to increase value by focusing on customer satisfaction and setting prices to match consumer expectations. Or a firm can use a "no-haggle" price structure to make the purchase process simpler and easier for consumers, thereby lowering the overall price and ultimately increasing value. For example, Saturn has relied on a "no-haggle" price policy, as depicted in Exhibit 13.3, since it began selling cars.

Firms also may offer very high-priced, "state-of-the-art" products or services in full anticipation of limited sales. These offerings are designed to enhance the company's reputation and image and thereby increase the company's value in the

EXHIBIT	**13.3**	Saturn's Pricing Policy

A Different Experience

It's no secret that most people dread shopping for a car. Which is why Saturn retailers are continually finding ways to make buying and servicing your vehicle more pleasant. In addition to the now famous no-hassle, no-haggle sales policy, many Saturn retailers continue to improve the retail experience with additions like family-room-style waiting areas, computer terminals and children's play areas.

minds of consumers. For example, Paradigm, a Canadian speaker manufacturer, produces what many audiophiles consider a high-value product, offering speakers priced as low as $189 per pair. However, Paradigm also offers a very high-end pair of speakers for $6,000. Although few people will spend $6,000 on a pair of speakers, this "statement" speaker communicates what the company is capable of and can increase the image of the firm and the rest of its products—even that $189 pair of speakers. Setting prices with a close eye to how consumers develop their perceptions of value can often be the most effective pricing strategy, especially if it is supported by consistent advertising and distribution strategies.

After a company has a good grasp on its overall objectives, it must implement pricing strategies that enable it to achieve those objectives. As the second step in this process, the firm should look toward consumer demand to lay the foundation for its pricing strategy.

Customers

When firms have developed their company objectives, they turn to understanding consumers' reactions to different prices. The second C of the five Cs of pricing is the most important, in that it captures the essence of marketing: the customers. Consumers want value, and as you likely recall, price is half of the value equation.

Can you tell the difference between the $6000 and the $189 Paradigm speaker?

Adding Value 13.1

Musicians Look for Value in Their Axes

Possibly the most famous name in electric guitars, Fender has left its mark on country, rock, blues, jazz, and most every other genre of music since Leo Fender built the first guitar in 1951 in his small radio repair shop.[6] Often referred to as an "axe," the electric guitar became increasingly popular during the next two decades as rock and country music, both of which generally position the electric guitar as the focal instrument, established themselves in the mainstream. The original Telecaster model, along with the Stratocaster introduced in 1954, has dominated the rock and country scenes. But along with this growth came higher and higher costs due to the labor-intensive process and the high cost of materials required to build a high-quality musical instrument—even resale values of used Fender guitars remained significant. For the professional, ever increasing prices were simply a cost of doing business. But students learning how to play guitar, young musicians just starting out, hobbyists, and other musicians who were priced out of owning a Fender guitar pressured the company to lower its prices or introduce cheaper models.

Fender listened. First it tried to cut corners and introduced new models, like the Fender Mustang, which was built to a smaller scale and used less costly parts. Although the price of the Mustang guitar was lower, it still did not begin to reach the price range many customers were demanding.

John Frusicante of the Red Hot Chili Peppers uses a Fender Stratocaster.

In 1982, Fender finally capitalized on its previous purchase of a Japan-based music string manufacturer, V.C. Squier, and introduced a separate, budget-priced line of similar guitars under the Squier brand name. Made in Japan using automated manufacturing, lower-cost labor, and less expensive parts, Squier guitars could be priced very aggressively and yet still be profitable for Fender and its dealers. They offered a look very similar to and performance only a notch below the original Fender guitars. Today, an American-made standard Fender Stratocaster lists for $1,327.99, whereas a similar Squier Stratocaster® model ranges from $150 to $250.

To determine how firms account for consumers' preferences when they develop pricing strategies, we must first lay a foundation of traditional economic theory that helps explain how prices are related to demand (consumers' desire for products) and how managers can incorporate this knowledge into their pricing strategies. But first read through Adding Value 13.1, which considers how Fender listened to customers' demands for a high-value guitar.

Demand Curves and Pricing   A **demand curve** shows how many units of a product or service consumers will demand during a specific period of time at different prices. Although we call them "curves," demand curves can be either straight or curved, as Exhibit 13.4 shows. Of course, any static demand curve assumes that everything else remains unchanged. For example, marketers creating a demand curve must assume that the firm will not increase its expenditures on advertising and that the economy will not change in any significant way.

Exhibit 13.4 illustrates the common downward-sloping demand curve in which, as price increases, demand for the product or service decreases. In this case,

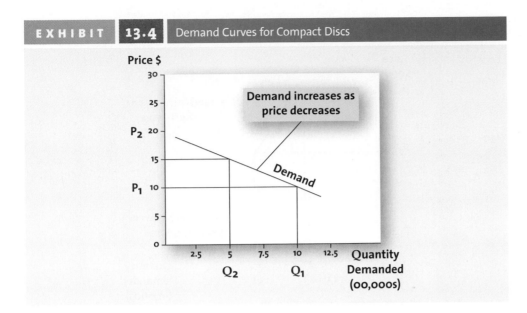

EXHIBIT **13.4**   Demand Curves for Compact Discs

consumers will buy more CDs as the price decreases. We can expect to uncover a demand curve similar to this one for many, if not most, products and services.

The horizontal axis measures the quantity demanded for the CDs in units and plots it against the various price possibilities indicated on the vertical axis. Each point on the demand curve then represents the quantity demanded at a specific price. So, in this instance, if the price of a CD is $10 per unit ($P_1$), the demand is 1,000,000 units (Q_1), but if the price were set at $15 ($P_2$), the demand would only be 500,000 units (Q_2). The firm will sell far more CDs at $10 each than at $15 each. Why? Because of the greater value this price point offers.

Knowing the demand curve for a product or service enables a firm to examine different prices in terms of the resulting demand and relative to its overall objective. In our preceding example, the music retailer will generate a total of $10,000,000 in sales at the $10 price ($10 × 1,000,000 units) and $7,500,000 in sales at the $15 price ($15 × 500,000 units). In this case, given only the two choices of $10 or $15, the $10 price is preferable as long as the firm wants to maximize its sales in terms of dollars and units. But what about a firm that is more interested in profit? To calculate profit, it must consider its costs, which we cover in the next section.

Interestingly enough, not all products or services follow the downward-sloping demand curve for all levels of price depicted in Exhibit 13.4. Consider **prestige products or services,** which consumers purchase for their status rather than their functionality. The higher the price, the greater the status associated with it and the greater the exclusivity, because fewer people can afford to purchase it. Most important, in this case, a higher price also leads to a greater quantity sold—up to a certain point. When customers value the increase in prestige more than the price differential between the prestige product and other products, the prestige product attains the greater value overall.

Exhibit 13.5 illustrates a demand curve for a hypothetical prestige service, like a Caribbean cruise. As the graph indicates, when the price increases from $1,000 ($P_1$) to $5,000 ($P_2$), the quantity demanded actually increases from 200,000 (Q_1) to 500,000 (Q_2) units. However, when demand rises above 500,000 units and the price increases to $8,000 ($P_3$), the demand then decreases to 300,000 (Q_3) units.

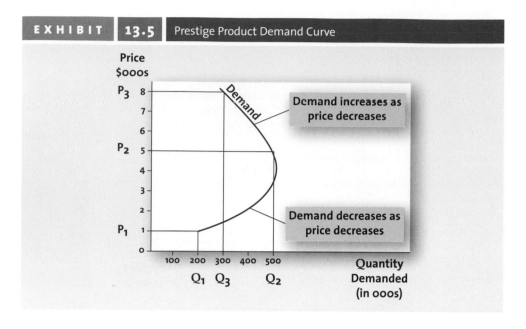

EXHIBIT | **13.5** | Prestige Product Demand Curve

Although the firm likely will earn more profit selling 300,000 cruises at $8,000 each than 500,000 cruises at $5,000 each, we do not know for sure until we bring costs into the picture. However, we do know that more consumers are willing to book the cruise as the price increases initially from $1,000 to $5,000 and that most consumers will choose an alternative vacation as the price increases further from $5,000 to $8,000.

We must consider this notion of consumers' sensitivity to price changes in greater depth. But first, review Entrepreneurial Marketing 13.1, which examines the unusual strategy of JetBlue's founder David Neeleman: generating substantial demand by offering low prices and high service—value squared!

Price Elasticity of Demand Although we now know something about how consumers react to different price levels, we still need to determine how consumers respond to actual changes in price. These responses vary depending on the product or service. For example, consumers are generally less sensitive to price increases for necessary items, like milk, because they have to purchase the items even if the

Consumers are less sensitive to the price of milk (left) than to steak (right). When the price of milk goes up, demand does not fall significantly because people still need to buy milk. However, if the price of steak rises beyond a certain point, people will buy less because they can turn to the many substitutes for steak.

Entrepreneurial Marketing 13.1

JetBlue Provides Value[2]

Founder David Neeleman launched JetBlue Airways in 2000, flying out of New York.[7] When JetBlue first got its start, many experts were skeptical. It was a market of cutthroat pricing, but founder David Neeleman was undeterred. Neeleman had already started several companies; sold his first regional airline, Morris Air, to Southwest Airlines in 1993; and helped launch a second successful airline in Canada. While other airlines generally offer either low price/low service or higher price/ somewhat higher service, Neeleman determined to take a rather unusual and risky approach to establishing value and to create JetBlue as a low-priced/high-service airline. It provides value.

Since Neeleman knew he couldn't compete with traditional airlines on all service dimensions, he decided to concentrate on those aspects of airline service that customers desired most and had not yet found in the marketplace: low prices but with a focus on comfort and customer satisfaction. According to Neeleman, "They said we'd never find quality employees, that no one would want to fly domestically from New York's JFK, and that we'd never be able to offer both low fares and a product that includes new planes, leather seats, and live satellite TV with DirecTV® programming." In just a few years though, JetBlue grew from one route (New York's JFK to Ft. Lauderdale, Florida) to servicing more than 30 cities.[8]

On average, JetBlue planes fly with 83.2 percent capacity, the highest load factor (percentage of seats filled) of any major U.S. carrier. JetBlue's value proposition of low prices and high service thus appears to have proven very successful. JetBlue offers its everyday low fares using a simple four-tiered structure, determined according to the number of days (14, 7, 3, or, for walk-up customers, 0) in advance customers purchase their tickets. A customer who walks up to the airport counter to purchase a ticket to fly the same day will pay twice as much as one who purchases a ticket 14 days in advance. Unlike other carriers, which generally require at least a one-night stay for fliers to receive lower fares, all JetBlue's tickets are one-way. Tickets can be changed for a $25 fee or $20 if the change occurs via the company's Web site.

JetBlue historically has beat competitor pricing by up to 40 percent for advance ticket purchases and 70 percent for walk-up tickets. Part of the reason it is able to price its flights so far below the rest of the market is its low-cost structure and concentration on efficiency. The Internet, its largest selling channel, accounts for more than 75 percent of sales. This history has given JetBlue a great deal of confidence in its operations and pricing structure; the company plans to expand its fleet to more than 430 planes by 2015. A formidable force, JetBlue has found a way to be profitable and successful in an industry that is facing widespread cutbacks and bankruptcies.

David Neeleman, founder of JetBlue, created a successful approach to providing customer value: low prices AND high service.

price climbs. When the price of milk goes up, demand does not fall significantly because people still need to buy milk. However, if the price of steak rises beyond a certain point, people will buy less because they can turn to the many substitutes for this cut of meat. Marketers need to know how consumers will respond to a price increase (or decrease) for a specific product or brand so they can determine whether it makes sense for them to raise or lower prices.

Price elasticity of demand measures how changes in a price affect the quantity of the product demanded. Specifically, it is the ratio of the percentage change in quantity demanded to the percentage change in price. We can calculate it with the following formula:

$$\text{Price elasticity of demand} = \frac{\% \text{ change in quantity demanded}}{\% \text{ change in price}}.$$

The demand curve provides the information we need to calculate the price elasticity of demand. For instance, what is the price elasticity of demand if we increase the price of our CD from $10 to $15?

$$\% \text{ change in quantity demanded} = \frac{(1{,}000{,}000 - 500{,}000)}{1{,}000{,}000} = 50\%, \text{ and}$$

$$\% \text{ change in price} = \frac{(\$10 - \$15)}{10} = -50\%, \text{ so}$$

$$\text{Price elasticity of demand} = \frac{50\%}{-50\%} = -1.$$

Thus, the price elasticity of demand for our CD is –1.

In general, the market for a product or service is price sensitive (or **elastic**) when the price elasticity is less than –1, that is, when a 1 percent decrease in price produces more than a 1 percent increase in the quantity sold. In an elastic scenario, relatively small changes in price will generate fairly large changes in the quantity demanded, so if a firm is trying to increase its sales, it can do so by lowering prices. However, raising prices can be problematic in this context, because doing so will lower sales. To refer back to our grocery examples, a retailer can significantly increase its sales of filet mignon by lowering its price because filets are elastic.

The market for a product is generally viewed as price insensitive (or **inelastic**) when its price elasticity is greater than –1, that is, when a 1 percent decrease in price results in less than a 1 percent increase in quantity sold. Generally, if a firm must raise prices, it is helpful to do so with inelastic products or services because in such a market, fewer customers will stop buying or reduce their purchases. However, if the products are inelastic, lowering prices will not appreciably increase demand; customers just don't notice or care about the lower price.

Consumers are generally more sensitive to price increases than to price decreases.[9] That is, it is easier to lose current customers with a price increase than it is to gain new customers with a price decrease. Also, the price elasticity of demand usually changes at different points in the demand curve unless the curve is actually a straight line, as in Exhibit 13.4. For instance, a prestige product or service, like our Caribbean cruise example in Exhibit 13.5, enjoys a highly inelastic demand curve up to a certain point so that price increases do not affect sales significantly. But when the price reaches that certain point, consumers start turning to other alternatives because the value of the cruise has finally been reduced by the extremely high price.

American consumers have experienced the full force of this elasticity phenomenon during the past few years as the U.S. dollar has lost ground to other major world currencies, particularly the Euro. In 2000, the exchange rate was $0.90 for a Euro; in 2007, the currencies had traded places, and the exchange rate was over $1.27. Therefore, a German-made Mercedes Benz that may have cost $39,000 in 2005 would have cost $55,000 in 2007 if Mercedes didn't absorb any of the cost of the currency devaluation. While American consumers have seen the value of products made in other countries, particularly the higher-priced West-

ern European countries, erode with the dollar, Europeans have begun to perceive shopping in the United States to be like one big bargain basement.

This German-made Mercedes Benz is much more expensive in the U.S. today than it was in 2005 due to significant devaluation of the U.S. dollar.

Factors Influencing Price Elasticity of Demand
We have illustrated how price elasticity of demand varies across different products and at different points along a demand curve, as well as how it can change over time. What causes these differences in the price elasticity of demand? We discuss a few of the more important factors next.

Income Effect   Generally, as people's income increases, their spending behavior changes: They tend to shift their demand from lower-priced products to higher-priced alternatives. That is, consumers buy hamburger when they're stretching their money but steak when they're flush. Similarly, they may increase the quantity they purchase and splurge on a movie a week instead of one per month. In turn, when the economy is good and consumers' incomes are rising overall, the price elasticity of steak or movies may actually drop, even though the price remains constant. Conversely, when incomes drop, consumers turn to less expensive alternatives or purchase less. This **income effect** refers to the change in the quantity of a product demanded by consumers due to a change in their income.

Substitution Effect   The **substitution effect** refers to consumers' ability to substitute other products for the focal brand. The greater the availability of substitute products, the higher the price elasticity of demand for any given product will be. For example, there are many close substitutes for the various brands of peanut butter. If Skippy raises its prices, many consumers will turn to Jif, Peter Pan, or another brand because they are more sensitive to price increases when they can easily find lower-priced substitutes. Extremely brand-loyal consumers, however, are willing to pay a higher price, up to a point, because in their minds, Skippy still offers a better value than the competing brands, and they believe the other brands are not adequate substitutes.

If there are many close substitutes for a product, customers will be sensitive to small price changes, and the product will be highly price elastic. If, for instance, Skippy raises its price, many customers will switch to another brand.

Keep in mind that marketing plays a critical role in making consumers brand loyal. And because of this brand loyalty and the lack of what consumers judge to be adequate substitutes, the price elasticity of demand for some brands is very low. For example, Polo/Ralph Lauren sells millions of its classic polo shirt at $65 while shirts of equal quality but without the polo player logo sell for much less. Getting consumers to believe that a particular brand is unique, different, or extraordinary in some way makes other brands seem less substitutable, which in turn increases brand loyalty and decreases the price elasticity of demand.

Cross-Price Elasticity   Cross-price elasticity is the percentage change in the quantity of Product A demanded compared with the percentage change in price in Product B. For example, when the price of DVD players dropped rapidly in the years 2000–2004, the demand for DVDs also increased rapidly. We refer to products like DVDs and DVD players as complementary products, which are products whose demands are positively related, such that they rise or fall together. In other words, a percentage increase in the quantity demanded for Product A results in a percentage increase in the quantity demanded for Product B.[10] However, when the price for DVD players dropped, the demand for VCRs went down, so DVD players and VCRs are substitute products because changes in their demand are negatively related. That is, a percentage increase in the quantity demanded for Product A results in a percentage decrease in the quantity demanded for Product B.[11] In addition, the Internet, specifically shopping bots like www.MySimon.com and www.Bizrate.com, have made it much easier for people to shop for substitutable products like consumer electronics, which likely has affected the price elasticity of demand for such products.[12]

Prior to this point, we have focused on how changes in prices affect how much customers buy. Clearly, knowing how prices affect sales is important, but it cannot give us the whole picture. To know how profitable a pricing strategy will be, we must also consider the third C, costs.

Costs

To make effective pricing decisions, firms must understand their cost structures so they can determine the degree to which their products or services will be profitable at different prices. In general, prices should *not* be based on costs because consumers make purchase decisions based on their perceived value; they care little about the firm's costs to produce and sell a product or deliver a service. Consumers use just the price they must pay and the benefits they may receive to judge value; they will not pay a higher price for an inferior product simply because the firm cannot be as cost efficient as its competitors.

If, for instance, a CD were available at both Borders and Wal-Mart, located on the same block, most consumers would buy it at Wal-Mart, where it likely will be priced lower. But many consumers see additional benefits to shopping at Borders because it has a bigger assortment, they can find their choice more easily, or they enjoy buying a CD while sipping a latte they have purchased from the same place. If these consumers did not value these benefits, Borders would not survive at that location.

Although companies incur many different types of costs as a natural part of doing business, there are two primary cost categories: variable and fixed.

Variable Costs   Variable costs are those costs, primarily labor and materials, that vary with production volume. As a firm produces more or less of a good or service, the total variable costs increase or decrease at the same time. Because each unit of the product produced incurs the same cost, marketers generally express variable costs on a per-unit basis. Continuing with our CD example, the variable costs include the labor needed to burn each CD; the costs of the blank CDs, jewel cases, and labels; and royalties paid to the artist. Each of these costs is incurred each time the producer makes a new CD.

In the service industry, variable costs are far more complex. A hotel, for instance, incurs certain variable costs each time it rents a room, including the costs associated with the labor and supplies necessary to clean and restock the room.

Note that the hotel does not incur these costs if the room is not booked. Suppose that a particular hotel calculates its total variable costs to be $10 per room; each time it rents a room, it incurs another $10 in variable costs. If the hotel rents out 100 rooms on a given night, the total variable cost is $1,000 ($10/room × 100 rooms).

In either case, however, variable costs tend to change depending on the quantity produced. If a record producer creates five CDs, it must pay for each CD and likely a set amount of time for a person to burn them. If it makes 500, though, it can probably get the discs at a lower price by buying in bulk, and the time required to burn the additional CDs likely is not significantly more. Similarly, a very large hotel will be able to get quantity discounts on most, if not all, the incidentals it needs to service the room because it purchases such a large volume. However, as the hotel company continues to grow, it may be forced to add more benefits for its employees or increase wages to attract and keep long-term employees. Such changes will increase its overall variable labor costs and affect the total variable cost of cleaning a room. Thus, though not always the case, variable costs per unit may go up or down (for all units) with significant changes in volume.

Fixed Costs   Fixed costs are those costs that remain essentially at the same level, regardless of any changes in the volume of production. Typically, these costs include items such as rent, utilities, insurance, administrative salaries (for executives and higher-level managers), and the depreciation of the physical plant and equipment. Across reasonable fluctuations in production volume, these costs remain stable; whether the producer makes 5 or 500 CDs, the rent it pays for the building in which it burns the CDs remains unchanged.

Total Cost   Finally, the total cost is simply the sum of the variable and fixed costs. For example, in one year, our hypothetical hotel incurred $100,000 in fixed costs. We also know that because the hotel booked 10,000 room nights, its total variable cost is $100,000 (10,000 room nights × $10/room). Thus, its total cost is $200,000.

Next, we illustrate how to use these costs in simple analyses that can inform managerial decision making about setting prices.

Break-Even Analysis and Decision Making

A useful technique that enables managers to examine the relationships among cost, price, revenue, and profit over different levels of production and sales is called the break-even analysis. Central to this analysis is the determination of the break-even point, or the point at which the number of units sold generates just enough revenue to equal the total costs. At this point, profits are zero.

How do we determine the break-even point? Although profit, which represents the difference between the total cost and the total revenue (total revenue or sales = selling price of each unit sold × number of units sold) can indicate how much money the firm is making or losing at a single period of time, it cannot tell managers how many units a firm must produce and sell before it stops losing money and at least breaks even.

Exhibit 13.6 presents the various cost and revenue information we have discussed in a graphic format. The graph contains three curves (recall that even though they are straight, we still call them curves): fixed costs, total costs, and total revenue. The vertical axis measures the revenue or costs in dollars, and the horizontal axis measures the quantity of units sold. The fixed cost curve will always appear as a horizontal line straight across the graph because fixed costs do not change over different levels of volume.

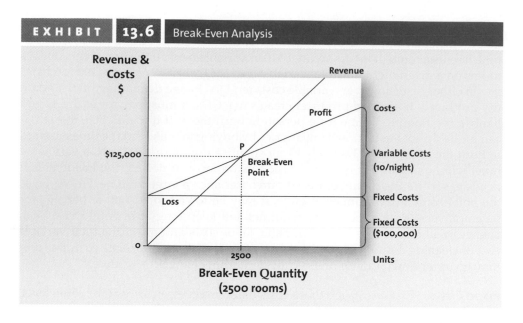

EXHIBIT | 13.6 | Break-Even Analysis

Break-Even Quantity
(2500 rooms)

The total cost curve starts where the fixed cost curve intersects the vertical axis. When volume is equal to zero (no units are produced or sold), the fixed costs of operating the business remain and cannot be avoided. Thus, the lowest point the total costs can ever reach is equal to the total fixed costs. Beyond that point, the total cost curve increases by the amount of variable costs for each additional unit, which we calculate by multiplying the variable cost per unit by the number of units, or quantity.

Finally, the total revenue curve increases by the price of each additional unit sold. To calculate it, we multiply the price per unit by the number of units sold. The formulas for these calculations are as follows:

$$\text{Total variable cost} = \text{Variable cost per unit} \times \text{Quantity}$$

$$\text{Total cost} = \text{Fixed cost} + \text{Total variable cost}$$

$$\text{Total revenue} = \text{Price} \times \text{Quantity}$$

We again use the hotel example to illustrate these relationships. Recall that the fixed costs are $100,000 and the variable costs are $10/room rented. If the rooms rent for $50 per night, how many rooms must the hotel rent over the course of a year to break even? If we study the graph carefully, we find the break-even point at 2,500, which means that the hotel must rent 2,500 rooms before its revenues equal its costs. If it rents fewer rooms, it loses money; if it rents more, it makes a profit. To determine the break-even point in units mathematically, we must introduce one more variable, the **contribution per unit**, which is the price less the variable cost per unit.

In this case,

$$\text{Contribution per unit} = \$50 - \$10 = \$40$$

Therefore, the break-even point becomes

$$\text{Break-even point (units)} = \frac{\text{Fixed costs}}{\text{Contribution per unit}}.$$

In this case,

$$\text{Break-even point (units)} = \frac{\$100{,}000}{\$40} = 2{,}500 \text{ room nights.}$$

When the hotel has crossed that break-even point of 2,500 rooms, it will then start earning profit at the same rate of the contribution per unit. So if the hotel rents 4,000 rooms—1,500 rooms more than the break-even point—its profit will be $60,000 (1500 rooms × $40 contribution per unit).

Let's extend this simple break-even analysis to show how many units a firm must produce and sell to achieve a target profit. Say the hotel wanted to make $200,000 in profit each year. How many rooms would it have to rent at the current price? In this instance, we need only add the targeted profit to the fixed costs to determine that number:

$$\text{Break-even point (units)} = \frac{(\text{Fixed costs} + \text{Target profit})}{\text{Contribution per unit}}, \text{ or}$$

$$7{,}500 \text{ rooms} = \frac{(\$100{,}000 + \$200{,}000)}{\$40}.$$

Although a break-even analysis cannot actually help managers set prices, it does help them assess their pricing strategies because it clarifies the conditions in which different prices may make a product or service profitable. It becomes an even more powerful tool when performed on a range of possible prices for comparative purposes. For example, the hotel management could analyze various prices, not just $50, to determine how many hotel rooms it would have to rent at what price to make a $200,000 profit.

Naturally, however, there are limitations to a break-even analysis. First, it is unlikely that a hotel has one specific price that it charges for each and every room, so the price it would use in its break-even analysis probably represents an "average" price that attempts to account for these variances. Second, prices often get

In a hotel, the cost of the physical structure, including the lobby (left) is fixed—it is incurred even if no rooms are rented. The costs of towels and sheets (right) are variable—the more rooms that are rented, the more the costs.

reduced as quantity increases because the costs decrease, so firms must perform several break-even analyses at different quantities.

Third, a break-even analysis cannot indicate for sure how many rooms will be rented or, in the case of products, how many units will sell at a given price. It only tells the firm what its costs, revenues, and profitability will be given a set price and an assumed quantity. To determine how many units the firm actually will sell, it must bring in the demand estimates we discussed previously.

Competition

Because the fourth C, competition, has a profound impact on pricing strategies,[13] we use this section to focus on its effect, as well as on how competitors react to certain pricing strategies. There are three levels of competition—oligopolistic, monopolistic, and pure—and each has its own set of pricing challenges and opportunities. (Exhibit 13.7)

When a market is characterized by oligopolistic competition, only a few firms dominate. Firms typically change their prices in reaction to competition to avoid upsetting an otherwise stable competitive environment. Often cited examples of oligopolistic markets include the soft drink market and the market for education at elite universities (where tuition represents the price).

Sometimes reactions to prices in oligopolistic markets can result in a price war, which occurs when two or more firms compete primarily by lowering their prices. Firm A lowers its prices; Firm B responds by meeting or beating Firm A's new price.

EXHIBIT 13.7 Competition

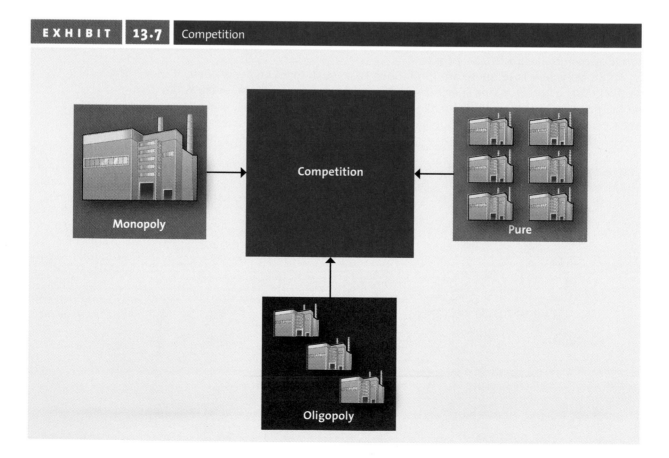

Ethical Dilemma 13.1 Do Protectionist Laws Hurt or Help Consumers?[16]

Protectionist laws keep some companies from conducting business in a particular region or line of business, which in effect gives a monopoly to those firms already operating in the area. The Wright Amendment is one of those laws. It prevents airlines from connecting Dallas Love Field (DAL) in Dallas, Texas, to any point outside the seven states surrounding Texas. Since Love Field is the corporate headquarters and primary hub for Southwest Airlines, many believe that the Wright Amendment provides an unfair and potentially monopolistic advantage to rival American Airlines, which operates one-third of the flights in and out of the much larger Dallas/Fort Worth (DFW) airfield. For instance, there are no direct Southwest flights from Boston to Dallas. To fly the normally very competitively priced Southwest, you would have to fly from nearby Providence, Rhode Island, or Manchester, New Hampshire, and change planes at least once. The need for connecting flights makes a trip on Southwest from the Boston area to the Dallas area much more expensive than it would be if there were direct flights.

A recent study indicates that if Southwest were able to fly from any location directly into DAL, it would save all roundtrip passengers flying in and out of the Dallas/Fort Worth area $688 million per year. Exhibit 13.8 shows the ticket prices of American Airlines flight routes with comparable mileage with and without Southwest competition. So, for instance, an American Airlines flight from DFW to Memphis and DFW to New Orleans has similar mileage. But American Airlines competes with Southwest with a direct flight from DFW to New Orleans, and the ticket price is significantly less than the DFW to Memphis flight where a direct flight into DAL on Southwest does not exist.

Clearly, it is in American Airlines' best interest to keep the Wright Amendment that limits Southwest's destinations out of DAL. But is it ethical to limit competition in order to protect a lucrative market from another business? Would allowing pure competition initiate a price war between American and Southwest that would drive prices so low that neither airline could operate routes out of the Dallas area profitably?

| **EXHIBIT** | **13.8** | American Airlines Ticket Prices on Flight Routes with Comparable Mileage with and without Southwest Competition from Dallas–Fort Worth Airport |

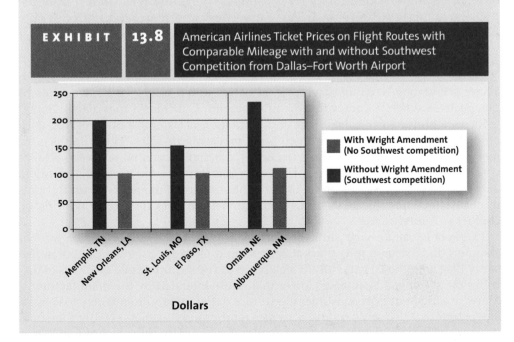

Firm A then responds with another new price, and so on. Price wars often appear in the airline industry when a low-cost provider like JetBlue enters a market in which established carriers already exist. But what motivates firms to enter price wars?[14] In the airline example, the new entrants might want to gain market share, whereas the established airlines drop their prices to preserve their market share. Other reasons include avoiding the appearance of being insensitive to consumers and simply overreacting to a price decrease offered by competitors. In many cases, companies do not need to respond to price cuts with price cuts of their own[15] because consumers do not buy solely on the basis of price. Better service, higher quality, and brand loyalty might be used as competitive strategies instead.

Monopolistic competition occurs when there are many firms competing for customers in a given market but their products are differentiated. When so many firms compete, product differentiation rather than a strict pricing competition tends to appeal to consumers. Thus, when Apple entered the hotly contested MP3 player market, it not only priced the iPod at a premium level, but its positioning focused on the product's smart design, cool looks, and convenience. Sometimes laws create monopolistic competition as is the case with American Airlines in the Dallas/Fort Worth market. See Ethical Dilemma 13.1 for details.

The Colombia Coffee Growers Association invented Juan Valdez to decommoditize their product in the face of pure competition.

With **pure competition,** different companies that consumers perceive as substitutable sell commodity products. In such markets, price usually is set according to the laws of supply and demand. For example, wheat is wheat, so it does not matter to a commercial bakery whose wheat it buys. However, the secret to pricing success in a pure competition market is not necessarily to offer the lowest price because doing so might create a price war and erode profits. Instead, some firms have brilliantly decommoditized their products. For example, coffee beans used to be regarded as all the same, and then Juan Valdez and the Colombian Coffee Growers Association made their "100% Colombian" coffee special, ensuring that coffee drinkers now know the difference between their beans and everything else.

When a commodity can be differentiated somehow, even if simply by a sticker or logo, there is an opportunity for consumers to identify it as distinct from the rest, and in this case, firms can at least partially extricate their product from a pure competitive market.

Channel Members

Channel members—manufacturers, wholesalers, and retailers—can have different perspectives when it comes to pricing strategies. Consider a manufacturer that is focused on increasing the image and reputation of its brand but working with a retailer that is primarily concerned with increasing its sales. The manufacturer may desire to keep prices higher to convey a better image, whereas the retailer wants lower prices and will accept lower profits to move the product, regardless of consumers' impressions of the brand. Unless channel members carefully communicate their pricing goals and select channel partners that agree with them, conflict will surely arise.

Channels can be very difficult to manage, and distribution outside normal channels does occur. A **gray market,** for example, employs irregular but not necessarily illegal methods; generally, it legally circumvents authorized channels of distribution to sell goods at prices lower than those intended by the manufacturer.[17] Many manufacturers of consumer electronics therefore require retailers to sign an agreement that demands certain activities (and prohibits others) before they may become authorized dealers. But if a retailer has too many high-definition TVs in stock, it may sell them at just above its own cost to an unauthorized discount dealer. This move places the merchandise on the street at prices far below what authorized dealers can charge, and in the long term, it may tarnish the image of the manufacturer if the discount dealer fails to provide sufficient return policies, support, service, and so forth.

To discourage this type of gray market distribution, some manufacturers, such as Fujitsu, have resorted to large disclaimers on their Web sites, packaging, and other communications to warn consumers that the manufacturer's product warranty becomes null and void unless the item has been purchased from an authorized dealer.[18]

Television sets and other consumer electronics are commonly sold in the gray market.

Macro Influences on Pricing

Thus far, we have focused mainly on product- and firm-specific factors—the five Cs—that influence pricing. Now we turn to the broader factors that have a more sweeping effect on pricing in general. In this section, we consider the Internet and various economic factors.

The Internet

The shift among consumers to acquiring more and more products, services, and information online has made them more price sensitive and opened new categories of products to those who could not access them previously. Gourmet foods, books, music, movies, and electronics are just a few of the product categories that present a significant online presence. Because they have gained access to rare cheeses, breads, meats, spices, and confections, consumers are demanding more from their local grocery stores in terms of selection and variety and have become more sensitive about prices. Furthermore, consumers' ability to buy electronics at highly discounted prices online has pushed bricks-and-mortar stores to attempt to focus consumers' attention on prepurchase advice and expertise, consulting services, and after-sales service—and away from price.

The Internet also has introduced search engines that enable consumers to find the best prices for any product quickly, which again increases their price sensitivity and reduces the costs associated with finding lower-price alternatives.[19] Not only do consumers know more about prices, they know more about the firms, their products, their competitors, and the markets in which they compete.

Another implication of the Internet for prices has been the growth of online auction sites such as eBay. Gone are the days when sellers had to offer their unwanted items to local buyers at "fire sale" prices. Although there certainly are good deals to be had on eBay, many items can fetch a premium price because bidders tend to get caught up in the bidding process. Also, unique and special interest items, which previously required professional appraisals before their value could be established, now have millions of potential bidders clearly articulating a value for everything from a seven-carat canary diamond engagement ring selling for $189,000 to a 1960 Porsche 356 Roadster selling for $86,500. Today, many consumers use eBay's prior auction section to determine the prices at which products have sold in the past and establish a value for new offerings.

H&M has introduced disposable chic and cross-shopping to middle America's shopping habits.

Economic Factors

Two interrelated trends that have merged to impact pricing decisions are the increase in consumers' disposable income and status consciousness. Some consumers appear willing to spend money for products that can convey status in some way. Products once considered only for the very rich, such as Rolex watches and Mercedes-Benz cars, are now owned by more working professionals. Although such prestige products are still aimed at the elite, more and more consumers are making the financial leap to attain them.

At the same time, however, a countervailing trend finds customers attempting to shop cheap. The popularity of everyday low price retailers like Wal-Mart and Target and extreme value stores such as Dollar General among customers who can afford to shop at department and specialty stores illustrates that it is cool to save a buck. Retailers like Old Navy and H&M also have introduced disposable chic and cross-shopping into middle America's shopping habits. In this context, **cross-shopping** is the pattern of buying both premium and low-priced merchandise or patronizing both expensive, status-oriented retailers and price-oriented retailers. These stores offer fashionable merchandise at great values—values so good that if items last for only a few wearings, it doesn't matter to the customers. The net impact of these contradictory trends on prices has been that some prestige items have become more expensive, whereas many other items have become cheaper.

Finally, the economic environment at local, regional, national, and global levels influences pricing. Starting at the top, the growth of the global economy has changed the nature of competition around the world. Many firms maintain a presence in multiple countries—products get designed in one country, the parts are manufactured in another, the final product assembled in a third, and after-sales service is handled by a call center in a fourth. By thinking globally, firms can seek out the most cost-efficient methods of providing goods and services to their customers.

On a more local level, the economy still can influence pricing. Competition, disposable income, and unemployment all may signal the need for different pricing strategies. For instance, rural areas are often subjected to higher prices because it costs more to get products there and because competition is lower. Similarly, retailers often charge higher prices in areas populated by people who have more disposable income and enjoy low unemployment rates.

By thinking globally, firms can seek out the most cost-efficient methods of providing goods and services to their customers.

Summing Up

1. Why should firms pay more attention to setting prices?

Price is the only element of the marketing mix that generates revenues. It is also half the value equation. Although costs and other factors should be taken into consideration when setting prices, the most important factor is how the customer views the price in relationship to what he or she receives.

2. What is the relationship between price and quantity sold?

Generally, when prices go up, the quantity sold goes down. Sometimes, however—particularly with prestige products and services—demand actually increases with price. Furthermore, some products and services are more elastic, or sensitive, to price than others. This degree of elasticity also changes at various price levels. Consumers' sensitivity to price is influenced by how expensive a product or service is and whether substitute or complementary products or services are available.

3. Why is it important to know a product's break-even point?

Break-even analysis offers a flexible tool that provides managers with an understanding of the relationships among prices, costs, revenues, and profits at different demand levels. It also indicates the conditions in which different prices can make a product or service profitable. However, a break-even analysis cannot provide managers with "the best" price because it does not include demand estimates at different price points.

4. Who wins in a price war?

A price war occurs when two or more firms compete by sequentially lowering their prices. The question of who wins depends on what the firms are trying to accomplish. If a firm wants to gain market share and is strong enough to sustain price cuts, it has a good chance of victory. But competing firms may risk financial peril if they lower their prices or lose significant market share if they don't. Often, however, it is the consumer who wins. If competitors match each other's price cuts, there are no market share gains, and the consumer just gets a lower price.

5. How has the Internet changed the way some people use price to make purchasing decisions?

Because it is so easy to get information on the Internet, people generally have become more aware of and sensitive to price. This trend has forced both manufacturers and retailers to become more price competitive. Some consumers even know more about the relative value of different products than the firms from which they are buying. Online auctions like eBay not only provide consumers with the relative value of millions of products but also enhance their value by establishing a global market for products that would have been geographically limited in the past.

Key Terms

Marketing Applications

1. You and your two roommates are starting a pet grooming service to help put yourself through college. There are two other well-established pet services in your area. Should you set your price higher or lower than that of the competition? Justify your answer.

2. One roommate believes the most important objective in setting prices for the new pet grooming business is to generate a large profit, while keeping an eye on your competitors' prices; the other roommate believes it is important to maximize sales and set prices according to what your customers expect to pay. Who is right and why?

3. Assume you have decided to buy an advertisement in the local newspaper to publicize your new pet grooming service. The cost of the ad is $1,000. You have decided to charge $40 for a dog grooming, and you want to make $20 for each dog. How many dogs do you have to groom to break even on the cost of the ad? What is your break-even point if you charge $50 per dog?

4. Have you ever purchased a higher-priced product or service just because you thought the quality was better than that of a similar, lower-priced product or service? What was the product or service? Do you believe you made a rational choice?

5. How does the fluctuating value of the Euro affect the price of German cars sold in the United States?

6. On your weekly grocery shopping trip, you notice that the price of hamburger meat has gone up 50 cents a pound. How will this price increase affect the demand for hamburger meat, ground turkey, and hamburger buns? Explain your answer in terms of the price elasticity of demand.

7. Zinc Energy Resources Co., a new division of a major battery manufacturing company, recently patented a new battery that uses zinc-air technology. The unit costs for the zinc-air battery are: The battery housing is $8, materials are $6, and direct labor is $6 per unit. Retooling the existing factory facilities to manufacture the zinc-air batteries amounts to an additional $1 million in equipment costs. Annual fixed costs include sales, marketing, and advertising expenses of $1 million; general and administrative expenses of $1 million; and other fixed costs totaling $2 million. Please answer the following questions.

   a. What is the total per-unit variable cost associated with the new battery?

   b. What are the total fixed costs for the new battery?

   c. If the price for the new battery was set at $35, what would the break-even point be?

8. How do pricing strategies vary across markets that are characterized by monopolistic, oligopolistic, and pure competition?

9. Suppose you are in the market for a new Panasonic DVD player. You see one advertised at a locally owned store for $100 less than it costs at Best Buy. The salesperson at the local store tells you that the DVD came from another retailer in the next state that had too many units of that model. Explain who benefits and who is harmed from such a gray market transaction: you, Panasonic, Best Buy, the local store?

10. Has the Internet helped lower the price of some types of merchandise? Justify your answer.

11. Though not illegal, many firms operating over the Internet have been experimenting with charging different consumers different prices for the same product or service. Since stores in different parts of the country might have different prices, some Web sites require zip codes information before providing prices . Why would retailers charge different prices in different markets or zip codes? Is it ethical for retailers to do so? Is it a good business practice?

Toolkit

BREAK-EVEN ANALYSIS

A shoe manufacturer has recently opened a new manufacturing plant in Asia. The total fixed costs are $50 million. They plan to sell the shoes to retailers for $50, and their variable costs (material and labor) are $25 per pair. Calculate the break-even volume. Now see what would happen to the break even if the fixed costs were increased to $60 million due to the purchase of new equipment, or the variable costs were decreased to $20 due to a new quantity discount provided by the supplier. Please use the toolkit provided at www.mhhe.com/grewal-levy to experiment with changes in fixed cost, variable cost, and selling price to see what happens to break-even volume.

Net Savvy

1. Several different pricing models can be found on the Internet. Each model appeals to different customer groups. Go to www.eBay.com and try to buy this book. What pricing options and prices are available? Do you believe that everyone will choose the least expensive option? Why or why not? Now go to www.Amazon.com. Is there more than one price available for this book? If so, what are those prices? If you had to buy another copy of this book, where would you buy it, and why would you buy it there?

2. Prices can vary depending on the market being served. Because Dell sells its computers directly to consumers all around the world, the Dell Web site makes it easy to compare prices for various markets. Go to www.dell.com. Begin on the Dell USA site and determine the price of a Dimension 3000 desktop computer. Next go to the Dell United Kingdom Web site and another country of your choice to find the price of the same computer. (If you need to convert currency to U.S. dollars, go to www.xe.com.) How does the price of the desktop computer vary? What would account for these differences in price?

Chapter Case Study

FINDING THE BEST PRICE: BIZRATE VERSUS EBAY[20]

Economists point to auction Web sites such as eBay as the best means to represent the value of any given product, because the price is determined solely by the value that the consumer attaches to it. That is, the value of the item is accurately reflected in the price paid. Thus, the prices paid for items on eBay must be some of the lowest prices available, right?

Recently, various Internet search engines, such as www.shopzilla.com, www.pricegrabber.com, and www.pricescan.com, have gained popularity. Perhaps one of the most popular is www.bizrate.com.

Do auction Web sites or price search engines really give consumers the lowest price? To address this question, we performed searches using both Bizrate and eBay for two specific products: a Sony model DCR-DVD 101 DVD camcorder and a Yamaha receiver, model HTR 5790. At bizrate.com, we found 17 stores that sold the Yamaha receiver at prices ranging from a high of $719 to a low of $495. For the Sony camcorder, we found 51 stores offering it at prices from $800 to $449.

Product	Bizrate		eBay	
	Low	**High**	**Low**	**High**
Yamaha receiver	$495	$719	$495	$550
Sony DVD camcorder	$449	$800	$480	$774

At eBay, the prices for the Yamaha receiver started at $550 and moved down to $495; the Sony camcorder prices ranged from $774 to $480.

Thus, it appears from analyzing these two products alone that the lowest prices are available through both channels, but the high-end prices are lower at eBay. eBay displays similar products together on the same page, which may explain why the range of prices found on eBay is narrower than that on Bizrate.

Questions

1. How has the Internet changed price competition for well-known, branded products?

2. Would the nature of price competition on the Internet be different if we had looked for commodities or esoteric luxury products?

3. Do you think this accessibility to detailed price comparisons has reduced price competition, such that all sellers price at the same level?

4. What assumptions do you tend to make about a product that seems priced very low? Very high?

14

LET THERE BE Q

Strategic Pricing Methods

H ave you ever thought about what makes those huge-screen TVs possible?[1] At the heart of the technology is a light machine that uses Digital Light Processing™ (DLP), a method owned by Texas Instruments (TI) that enables the design and manufacture of highly accurate, high-quality displays of video reproductions at reasonably low costs. Although also used in commercial theaters, DLP technology has been a significant advancement for the home theater market because it offers large, bright, vivid, accurate pictures. Each new generation of the DLP chip provides consumers with blacker blacks, higher resolutions, better color fidelity, and overall better pictures.

Pricing a new technology like DLP can be both difficult and dangerous. Should the firm price the chips high initially, signaling to the market the high quality and sophistication of the technology? Certainly, this choice would give TI a high margin on each chip and help the company recover its high research and development investments. Alternatively,

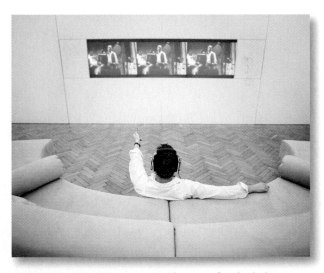

How did Texas Instruments set the price for the light machine that helps produce the accurate high-quality displays in big-screen TVs?

should TI take a more aggressive approach and price it very low, knowing that the per-unit cost to manufacture the chip will likely drop rapidly as accumulated volume grows? This approach may increase the market even faster, because consumers who normally would not consider buying a large-screen television may find themselves able to afford one.

Initially, TI priced the chips very high because most projectors using DLP were targeted at industrial and educational markets. Demand remained high, and with each new and improved version of DLP, TI slashed the prices of the older versions to get rid of the inventory. Each subsequent generation then was priced more aggressively to compete with alternative technologies that were improving and providing substantial competition. With these lower prices, the market for DLP-based big-screen televisions began to open up and grow. And by 2004, TI had generated $750 million in DLP sales.

■ ■ ■

Coming up with the "right" price is never easy, as the DLP example shows. If TI had decided to price the DLP at a low point initially, how would it have affected future sales—both its own and of potential competitors? We examine these and other pricing strategies in this chapter.

The previous chapter was devoted to examining what "price" is, why it is important, how marketers set pricing objectives, and the factors that influence prices. In this chapter, we extend that foundation by focusing on specific pricing strategies that capitalize on capturing value, as well as the psychological aspects of pricing that convey value. We also examine the implications of various pricing strategies and some of the more important legal and ethical issues associated with pricing.

Pricing Strategies

Firms embrace different objectives, face different market conditions, and operate in different manners; thus, they employ unique pricing strategies that seem best for the particular set of circumstances in which they find themselves. Even a single firm needs different strategies across its products and services and over time as market conditions change. The choice of a pricing strategy thus is specific to the product/service and target market. Although firms tend to rely on similar strategies when they can, each product or service requires its own specific strategy because no two are ever exactly the same in terms of the marketing mix. Cost-based, competitor-based, and value-based strategies are discussed in this section (see Exhibit 14.1).

Cost-Based Methods

As their name implies, **cost-based pricing methods** determine the final price to charge by starting with the cost. Cost-based methods do not recognize the role that consumers or competitors' prices play in the marketplace. Although relatively

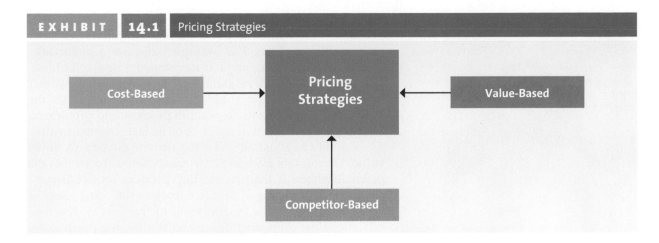

EXHIBIT **14.1** Pricing Strategies

simple, compared with other methods used to set prices, cost-based pricing requires that all costs can be identified and calculated on a per-unit basis. Moreover, the process assumes that these costs will not vary much for different levels of production. If they do, the price might need to be raised or lowered according to the production level. Thus, with cost-based pricing, prices are usually set on the basis of estimates of average costs.

Competitor-Based Methods

Most firms know that consumers compare the prices of their products with the different product/price combinations competitors offer. Thus, using a **competitor-based pricing method,** they may set their prices to reflect the way they want consumers to interpret their own prices relative to the competitors' offerings. For example, setting a price very close to a competitor's price signals to consumers that the product is similar, whereas setting the price much higher signals greater features, better quality, or some other valued benefit.

This Ferrari Scaglietti uses premium pricing.

Another competitor-based method is **premium pricing,** which means the firm deliberately prices a product above the prices set for competing products to capture those consumers who always shop for the best or for whom price does not matter. For example, can a $250,000 Ferrari be that much better than a $230,000 Ferrari? Regardless, some consumers will want to pay the additional $20,000 to get what they perceive as the very best.

Value-Based Methods

Value-based pricing methods include approaches to setting prices that focus on the overall value of the product offering as perceived by the consumer. Consumers determine value by comparing the benefits they expect the product to deliver with the sacrifice they will need to make to acquire the product. Of course, different consumers perceive value differently. So how does a manager use value-based pricing methods? We consider two key approaches.

Improvement Value Method With the first method, the manager must estimate the improvement value of a new product or service. This **improvement**

Is the improvement value on this new cell phone sufficiently greater than competitive products that Motorola can charge a higher price for it?

value represents an estimate of how much more (or less) consumers are willing to pay for a product relative to other comparable products. For example, suppose a major telecommunications company has developed a new cell phone. Using any of a host of research methods—such as consumer surveys—the manager could get customers to assess the new product relative to an existing product and provide an estimate of how much better it is, or its improvement value.

Exhibit 14.2 illustrates how to calculate the improvement value. Consumers evaluate how much better (or worse) the new cell phone is than an existing product on five dimensions: clarity, coverage, security, battery life, and ease of use. According to the respondents to the survey, the new cell phone has 20 percent more clarity than the comparison phone. These consumers also weight the importance of the five attributes by allocating 100 points among them to indicate their relative importance; for the clarity dimension, this weighting is .40. When the manager multiplies the improvement weight by the relative importance percentage, clarity (20% × 0.40) emerges with a weighted factor of 8 percent. The marketer repeats the process for each benefit and sums the weighted factors to arrive at an approximation of the improvement value of the new product from customers' point of view. In this illustration, the improvement value is equal to 21 percent, so if the other cell phone costs $100, the firm should be able to charge customers a value-based price as high as $121 ($100 × 1.21).

Cost of Ownership Method   Another value-based method for setting prices determines the total cost of owning the product over its useful life. Using the cost of ownership method, consumers may be willing to pay more for a particular product because, over its entire lifetime, it will eventually cost less to own than a cheaper alternative.[2]

Exhibit 14.3 illustrates the concepts associated with value-based pricing in terms of the total cost of ownership method. Consider, for example, a carpet manufacturing company that needs to set a price for its new high-grade commer-

EXHIBIT 14.2	Improvement Value		
Incremental Benefits	**Improved Value**	**Benefit Weight**	**Weighted Factor**
Clarity	20%	0.40	8%
Range	40%	0.20	8%
Security	10%	0.10	1%
Battery	5%	0.20	1%
Compatibility	30%	0.10	3%
Overall		1.00	21%

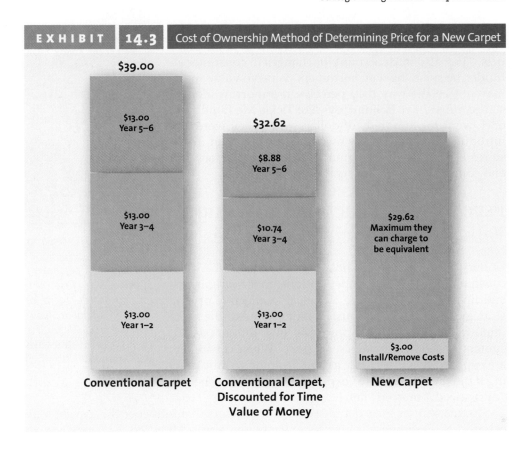

EXHIBIT | **14.3** | Cost of Ownership Method of Determining Price for a New Carpet

$39.00

$13.00
Year 5–6

$13.00
Year 3–4

$13.00
Year 1–2

Conventional Carpet

$32.62

$8.88
Year 5–6

$10.74
Year 3–4

$13.00
Year 1–2

**Conventional Carpet,
Discounted for Time
Value of Money**

$29.62
Maximum they
can charge to
be equivalent

$3.00
Install/Remove Costs

New Carpet

cial carpet.[3] Its conventional commercial carpeting has an average lifespan of two years, and the costs per square yard are as follows:

$10.00 per square yard

+ 2.00 installation

+ 1.00 removal of old carpet
_____

$13.00 every two years.

The newly introduced carpet lasts for six years; the installation and removal costs are the same. Because the conventional carpet requires installation and removal three times in six years, its total cost over that time is $39.00 per yard. However, we must also discount the payments over the six years by the prevailing interest rate (because the consumer does not have to spend the money immediately, this discount represents the time value of money), which in our illustration is 10 percent. Therefore, the consumer's discounted spending becomes $32.62 over the six years. Because the new carpet requires the $2.00 installation and $1.00 removal only once in the six years and the time value of money does not come into play (the customer must pay all the money immediately), the company can charge as much as $29.62 per yard ($32.62 – 3.00) for the new carpet. But it might choose to charge less and pass some of the savings on to customers as an incentive to buy the new carpet.

Although value-based pricing strategies can be quite effective, they also necessitate a great deal of consumer research to be implemented successfully. Sellers must know how consumers in different market segments will attach value to the benefits delivered by their products. They also must account for changes in consumer attitudes because the way customers perceive value today may not be the way they perceive it tomorrow. For instance, must-have holiday toys like Tickle Me Elmo dolls once went for hundreds of dollars when they were first introduced. They are now available for less than $35 at stores like Wal-Mart. Therefore, firms must be actively and constantly engaged in consumer research.

What is a Tickle Me Elmo doll worth? It depends on customers' perception of value. When first introduced, they went for hundreds of dollars. Now they are available for less than $35.00 at stores like Wal-Mart.

Psychological Factors Affecting Value-Based Pricing Strategies

Understanding the psychology underlying the way consumers arrive at their perceptions, make judgments, and finally invoke a choice is critical to effective pricing strategies, so marketers must examine some of the more important psychological processes that influence consumers' reactions to and use of price. When consumers are exposed to a price, they assign meaning to it by placing it into a category, like "expensive," "a deal," "cheap," "overpriced," or even "fair."

In this section, we examine some of the factors that influence this psychological process of adding meaning to, or evaluating, price.[4] But first, let's look at how two men with incredible vision started a type of retailing that is based on very inexpensive merchandise in Entrepreneurial Marketing 14.1.

Consumers' Use of Reference Prices

A **reference price** is the price against which buyers compare the actual selling price of the product and that facilitates their evaluation process. In some cases, the seller itself provides an **external reference price,** a higher price to which the consumer can compare the selling price to evaluate the deal.[6] Typically, the seller labels the external reference price as the "regular price" or an "original price." When consumers view the "sale price" and compare it with the provided external reference price, their perceptions of the value of the deal will likely increase.[7] In the advertisement in Exhibit 14.4, Sears has provided an external reference price, in smaller print and labeled "Reg.," to indicate that $24.99 is the regular price of Lee jeans. In addition, the advertisement highlights the current "sale" price of $21.99. Thus, the external reference price suggests to consumers that they are getting a good deal and will save money.

Consumers may also rely on an **internal reference price** to judge a price offering by accessing price information stored in their memory—perhaps the last price they paid or what they expect to pay.[8] For instance, when a consumer has been seated in a restaurant and first views the price of a large pepperoni pizza, she only has her internal reference price for comparison. If the price of the pizza on the menu is $12 and the consumer's internal reference price is $10 because she recalls that as the price she usually pays for a large pepperoni pizza at another restaurant, she may judge the menu price as high.

Entrepreneurial Marketing 14.1

Turning $1 into a Million

Cal Turner Sr. and Leon Levine are entrepreneurs who helped invent a new type of retail format—extreme value retailers.[5] Turner founded Dollar General in 1939 and Levine founded Family Dollar in 1959. Both used the concept that everything in the store should be really cheap—a dollar at Dollar General and $2 at Family Dollar. Today, these extreme value retailers have higher price points, but they still provide extreme value to their customers.

Many value retailers, particularly Family Dollar and Dollar General, target low-income consumers, whose shopping behavior differs from typical discount store or warehouse club customers. For instance, although these consumers demand well-known national brands, they often can't afford to buy large-size packages. Since this segment of the retail industry is growing rapidly, vendors often create special smaller packages for them. Today, however, higher-income consumers are increasingly patronizing extreme value retailers for the thrill of the hunt. Some shoppers see them as an opportunity to find some hidden treasure among the basic merchandise.

Although known for nonfood items, both chains now carry food, and even some perishable food items. Although price is the main reason that customers shop at these stores, convenience is also a factor. The stores are strategically placed close to neighborhoods so few customers have to drive more than five minutes to reach one. The stores are relatively small compared to discount stores like Wal-Mart or Target, so customers can find what they need, save money, and get out. Many customers are doing much more of their weekly shopping at these stores because even though the variety of items is limited, so is the price—in a good way.

From a single store started by their founders Turner and Levine, Dollar General has grown to over 8,000 stores and Family Dollar has over 6,000 stores. That is a lot of convenience and a lot of savings.

People love to shop at Family Dollar stores because its merchandise is inexpensive, the stores are conveniently located and easy-to-shop, and occasionally treasures may be found among the basics.

A more complex element of reference prices is the relationship among them. That is, external reference prices influence internal reference prices.[9] When consumers are repeatedly exposed to higher reference prices, their internal reference prices shift toward the higher external reference prices, assuming their initial internal reference price was not too far away from it. The net effect is that consumers will perceive the product or service in question to have a relatively lower selling price, and it therefore becomes a better deal in their perceptions.

Everyday Low Pricing (EDLP) versus High/Low Pricing

With an everyday low pricing (EDLP) strategy, companies stress the continuity of their retail prices at a level somewhere between the regular, nonsale price and the deep-discount sale prices their competitors may offer.[10] By reducing consumers' search costs, EDLP adds value; consumers can spend less of their valuable time comparing prices, including sale prices, at different stores. For example, Wal-Mart relies on EDLP to communicate to consumers that, for any given group of often purchased items, its prices are lower than those of any other company in that market. This claim does not necessarily mean that every item that consumers may purchase will be priced lower at Wal-Mart than anywhere else—in fact, some competitive retailers will offer lower prices on some items. However, on average market baskets, Wal-Mart's prices tend to be lower overall.

Alternatively, some retailers prefer a high/low pricing strategy, which relies on the promotion of sales, during which prices are temporarily reduced to encourage purchases. In the end, which consumers prefer which strategy depends on how those consumers evaluate prices and quality. Some prefer not to expend the time to find the lowest price and favor EDLP as an efficient way to get low, even if not the very lowest, prices. Alternatively, other consumers may relish the challenge of getting the lowest price or be so price sensitive that they are willing to expend the time and effort to seek out the lowest price every time.

But even this categorization gets more complicated, in that it needs to include quality perceptions as well. Some consumers perceive that stores that use EDLP carry lower quality goods, whereas high/low pricing stores tend to carry better quality items. In part, this perception forms because consumers view the initial price at a high/low store as the reference price. In the end, however, the consumer's decision, once again and as always, comes down to value.

Odd Prices

Have you ever wondered why prices rarely end in round amounts, like $3.00 or $23.00? In various product categories, odd prices, or those that end in odd numbers, usually 9, are very common, such as $11.99, $3.98, $7.77, and $3.99. Although

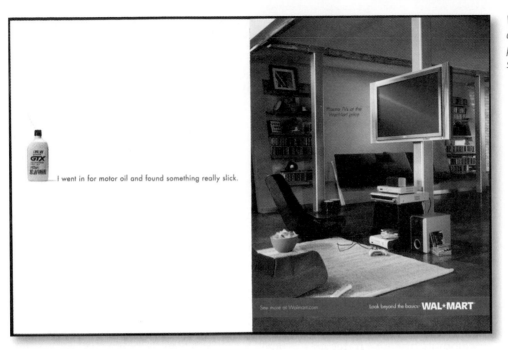

Wal-Mart relies on an everyday low price (EDLP) pricing strategy.

not documented, most marketers believe that odd pricing got its start as a way to prevent sales clerks from just pocketing money. Because the price was odd, the clerk would have to open the cash register for change, which required that the sale be rung up on the register.

Today, it seems that odd pricing simply may be so traditional that sellers are afraid to round off their prices for fear that consumers will respond negatively. Also, some sellers may believe that consumers mentally truncate the actual price, making the perceived price appear lower than it really is. For example, if the price is $21.99, consumers may focus more on the $21 than on the 99 cents, which may cause them to perceive the price as significantly lower than $22.00, even though that difference is only a penny. Another explanation is that consumers infer that an odd price must have been precisely calculated to wind up with such an odd result. Thus, the price must be fair, because the seller obviously could have rounded it up and taken in a little more money for each item. The main finding from research on the odd pricing approach is that odd prices signal to consumers that the price is low.[11]

Odd prices signal to consumers that the price is low.

The bottom line is that if sellers want to suggest a deal to be had, odd prices may be appropriate. However, odd prices also can suggest low quality.[12] Some consumers may perceive higher value because of the low price (especially if quality is less important to them than price), whereas others may infer lower value on the basis of the low-quality image the odd price suggests (especially if price is less important to them than quality).

The Price–Quality Relationship

Imagine that you have an important date tonight, and you are cooking a special, romantic, Italian dinner. You go to the grocery store to buy the food and realize that your recipe for the antipasto appetizer calls for Lupini beans (a large bean usually imported from Italy). You've never even heard of Lupini beans, much less purchased or used them in a recipe. Luckily, the store has three different brands of Lupini beans. But how do you choose which brand to buy? The three choices are priced at $3.99, $3.79, and $3.49. Are you going to risk the success of this dinner to save a mere $.50 on a can of beans? Probably not. Without other information to help you make a choice, you will likely go for the $3.99 can of beans because, like most consumers, you believe that they must be of higher quality because they cost more.

But not all consumers rely on price to judge quality. When consumers know the brands, have had experience with the products, or have considerable knowledge about how to judge the quality of products objectively, price becomes less important.[13] The store, brand name, product warranties/guarantees, and where the product was produced also represent information consumers use to judge quality. Nonetheless, price generally plays a critical role in consumers' judgments of quality.[14]

Given these various psychological pricing factors that come into play for consumers, marketers must consider how they function when they set prices. In the next section, we discuss how to apply psychological factors in the pricing decisions for new products.

New Product Pricing

Developing pricing strategies for new products is one of the most challenging tasks a manager can undertake. When the new product is just another "me-too" product, similar to what already appears on the market, this job is somewhat easier because the product's approximate value has already been established. But when the new product is truly innovative, or what we call "new to the world," determining consumers' perceptions of its value and pricing it accordingly becomes far more difficult.

Consider, for example, the value to consumers of innovations like the polio vaccine, cell phones, the Internet, satellite radio, or air bags. Air bags, for one, can prevent serious life-long disabilities and even save lives. How do car manufacturers attach value to benefits like those? To make it even more complex, automobile companies had to consider the value of an air bag that never deploys. Although difficult assessments to make, good marketing research can uncover the value of an innovation in the eyes of the consumer. Therefore, we turn our attention to two distinct pricing strategies for new products: skimming and penetration.

Price Skimming

In many markets, and particularly for new and innovative products or services, innovators and early adapters (see Chapter 11) are willing to pay a higher price to obtain the new product or service. This strategy, known as **price skimming**, appeals to these segments of consumers who are willing to pay the premium price to have the innovation first. Do you recall, among your friends, who owned the first cell phone that had the ability to take pictures, send e-mail and instant messages, and maintain MP3 storage? Whoever it was, that person was likely in the top segment of the cell phone market, which made him or her willing to pay the very highest prices when these product enhancements were first introduced. After this high-price market segment becomes saturated and sales begin to slow down, companies generally lower the price to capture (or skim) the next most price sensitive market segment, which is willing to pay a somewhat lower price. This process can continue until the demand for the product has been satisfied, even at the lowest price points.

For price skimming to work, the product or service must be perceived as breaking new ground in some way, offering consumers new benefits currently unavailable in alternative products. When they believe it will work, though, firms use skimming strategies for a variety of reasons. Some may start by pricing relatively high to signal high quality to the market. Others may decide to price high at first to limit demand, which gives them time to build their production capacities. Similarly, some firms employ a skimming strategy to try to quickly earn back some of the high research and development investments they made for the new product. Finally, firms employ skimming strategies to test consumers' price sensitivity. A firm that prices too high can always lower the price, but if the price is initially set too low, it is almost impossible to raise it without significant consumer resistance.

For a skimming pricing strategy to be successful, competitors cannot be able to enter the market easily; otherwise, price competition will likely force lower prices and undermine the whole strategy. Competitors might be prevented from entering the market through patent protections, their inability to copy the innovation (because it is complex to manufacture, its raw materials are hard to get, or the product relies on proprietary technology), or the high costs of entry.

The publishers of the Harry Potter novels use a price skimming strategy: They set the price high when the book is first introduced, then lower the price significantly to maintain sales.

Skimming strategies also face a significant potential drawback in the relatively high unit costs often associated with producing small volumes of products. Therefore, firms must consider the trade-off between earning a higher price and suffering higher production costs.

Price skimming also can cause some discontent for consumers. Those who purchase early and pay a higher price may feel somewhat cheated when the prices drop. For instance, when introduced, the latest Harry Potter novel sold millions of copies for $29.99. Within weeks though, it could be purchased for about $20.00. To avoid negative responses, some firms differentiate their products in some way. For example, publishers generally release a new book first in hard cover and later in soft cover at a lower price.

Market Penetration Pricing

Instead of setting the price high, firms using a market penetration strategy set the initial price low for the introduction of the new product or service. Their objective is to build sales, market share, and profits quickly. In direct opposition to a skimming strategy, the low market penetration price encourages consumers to purchase the product immediately rather than waiting for the price to drop. Although it is not always the case, many firms expect the unit cost to drop significantly as the accumulated volume sold increases, an effect known as the experience curve effect. With this effect, as sales continue to grow, the costs continue to drop, allowing even further reductions in the price.

In addition to offering the potential to build sales, market share, and profits, penetration pricing discourages competitors from entering the market because the profit margin is relatively low. Furthermore, if the costs to produce the product drop because of the accumulated volume, competitors that enter the market later will face higher unit costs, at least until their volume catches up with the early entrant.

Similar to a skimming strategy, a penetration strategy has its drawbacks. First, the firm must have the capacity to satisfy a rapid rise in demand—or at least be able to add that capacity quickly. Second, low price does not signal high quality. Of course, a price below their expectations decreases the risk for consumers to purchase the product and test its quality for themselves. Third, firms should avoid a penetration pricing strategy if some segments of the market are willing to pay more for the product; otherwise, the firm is just "leaving money on the table." Adding Value 14.1 illustrates how the skimming and penetration pricing strategies are used in the world of high fashion.

Pricing Tactics

It is important to distinguish clearly between pricing strategies and pricing tactics. A *pricing strategy* is a long-term approach to setting prices broadly in an integrative effort (across all the firm's products) based on the five Cs (company objectives, costs, customers, competition, and channel members) of pricing discussed in Chapter 13. **Pricing tactics**, in contrast, offer short-term methods to focus on select components of the five Cs. Generally, a pricing tactic represents either a short-term response to a competitive threat (e.g., lowering price temporarily to meet a competitor's price reduction) or a broadly accepted method of calculating a final price for the customer that is short-term in nature. We separate our discussion of pricing tactics into those aimed at intermediaries in a business-to-business (B2B) setting and those directed at end consumers.

Business-to-Business Pricing Tactics and Discounts

The pricing tactics employed in B2B settings differ significantly from those used in consumer markets. Among the most prominent are seasonal and cash discounts, allowances, quantity discounts, and uniform delivered versus zone pricing. (See Exhibit 14.5.)

Seasonal Discounts   A **seasonal discount** is an additional reduction offered as an incentive to retailers to order merchandise in advance of the normal buying season. For instance, Lennox may offer its air conditioning dealers an additional

EXHIBIT 14.5	Business-to-Business Pricing Tactics
Tactic	
Seasonal discounts	An additional reduction offered as an incentive to retailers to order merchandise in advance of the normal buying season.
Cash discounts	An additional reduction that reduces the invoice cost if the buyer pays the invoice prior to the end of the discount period.
Allowances	Advertising or slotting allowances (additional price reductions) offered in return for specific behaviors. **Advertising allowances** are offered to retailers if they agree to feature the manufacturer's product in their advertising and promotional efforts. **Slotting allowances** are offered to get new products into stores or to gain more or better shelf space.
Quantity discounts	Providing a reduced price according to the amount purchased.
Uniform delivered versus zone pricing	**Uniform delivered price:** shipper charges one rate, no matter where the buyer is located. **Zone price:** different prices depending on the geographical delivery area.

Adding Value 14.1

Price Skimming versus Market Penetration in the World of High Fashion[15]

A young socialite walks down Manhattan's 5th Avenue with a $5,000 silk Hermes scarf from France to perfectly complement her $20 peek-a-boo tank top she purchased at Zara. Style is no longer dictated by price, but both the price skimming designers such as Valentino and Chanel and the stores using a penetration pricing strategy such as Spain-based Zara and Sweden-based H&M are successful.

H&M and Zara carefully observe the styles and trends of the designer brands and then quickly and efficiently turn out very similar lines in their own stores at a very affordable price. Because of their very efficient supply chains, they are often able to beat the designers' fashions to the stores. To combat the new stores offering lower-priced, but well-designed clothing, high-end designers design their accessories and clothing with details that cannot be duplicated at a low cost. They use alligator skin,

mink, and very fine stitching. Much of their merchandise is hand sewn. These designers are continually trying to find the next big fashions and get them into their customers' hands before their competitors using penetration pricing learn to copy the design and make it cheaply.

Both the affordable stylized clothes of H&M and Zara and the expensive and extravagant lines of Hermes, Valentino, and Chanel sell well. The masses can afford H&M and Zara, and those who value the detail and cutting-edge design of designers like Chanel pay the price. Karl Lagerfeld has designed a ready-to-wear line for H&M and still is in charge of Chanel couture. People have lined up around the block to buy both collections. The middle-of-the-road stores with average designed clothes and average prices are the ones that are struggling. They are neither hip and inexpensive nor expensive and elaborate.

Can you tell the difference between the relatively inexpensive Karl Lagerfeld designed fashions at H&M (left) and the very expensive couture fashions from Valentino (right)?

seasonal discount if they place their orders and receive delivery before April 1, prior to the warm months when air conditioner sales are highest. If it can ship earlier in the season, Lennox can plan its production schedules more easily and lessen its finished goods inventory. Its dealers, however, must weigh the benefits of a larger profit because of the discount versus the extra cost of carrying the inventory for a longer period of time.

Cash Discounts   A cash discount reduces the invoice cost if the buyer pays the invoice prior to the end of the discount period. Typically, it is expressed in the form of a percentage, such as 3/10, n/30, or "3%, 10 days, net 30," all of which mean the buyer can take a 3 percent discount on the total amount of the invoice if the bill is paid within 10 days of the invoice date; otherwise the full, or net, amount is due within 30 days. Why do B2B sellers offer cash discounts to customers? By encouraging early payment, they benefit from the time value of money. Getting money earlier rather than later enables the firm to either invest the money to earn a return on it or avoid borrowing money and paying interest on it. In both instances, the firm is better off financially.

Allowances   Another pricing tactic that lowers the final cost to channel members is allowances, such as advertising or slotting allowances, offered in return for specific behaviors. An advertising allowance offers a price reduction to channel members if they agree to feature the manufacturer's product in their advertising and promotional efforts. Slotting allowances are fees paid to retailers simply to get new products into stores or to gain more or better shelf space for their products. Some argue that slotting allowances are unethical because they put small manufacturers that cannot readily afford allowances at a competitive disadvantage. Demanding large slotting allowances could be considered a form of bribery—"paying off" the retailer to get preferential treatment.

Quantity Discounts   A quantity discount provides a reduced price according to the amount purchased. The more the buyer purchases, the higher the discount and, of course, the greater the value.

A cumulative quantity discount uses the amount purchased over a specified time period and usually involves several transactions. This type of discount particularly encourages resellers to maintain their current supplier because the cost to switch must include the loss of the discount. For example, automobile dealers often attempt to meet a quota or a sales goal for a specific time period, such as a quarter or a year. If they meet their quotas, they earn discounts on all the cars they purchased from the manufacturer during that time period in the form of a rebate check. For this very reason, you will often find good deals on cars at the end of a quarter or fiscal year. If the dealership can just sell a few more cars to meet its quota, the rebate earned can be substantial, so taking a few hundred dollars less on those last few cars is well worth the opportunity to receive a rebate check worth many times the amount of the losses.

A noncumulative quantity discount, though still a quantity discount, is based only on the amount purchased in a single order. It therefore provides the buyer with an incentive to purchase more merchandise immediately. Such larger, less frequent orders can save manufacturers order processing, sales, and transportation expenses. For example, a jeans store might get a 40 percent discount off the manufacturer's suggested retail price for placing a $500 order; a 50 percent discount for an order of $501–$4,999, and a 60 percent discount for an order of greater than $5,000.

Uniform Delivered versus Zone Pricing   These pricing tactics are specific to shipping, which represents a major cost for many manufacturers. With a **uniform delivered pricing** tactic, the shipper charges one rate, no matter where the buyer is located, which makes things very simple for both the seller and the buyer. **Zone pricing**, however, sets different prices depending on a geographical division of the delivery areas. For example, a manufacturer based in New York City might divide the United States into seven different zones and use different shipping rates for each zone to reflect the average shipping cost for customers located therein. This way, each customer in a zone is charged the same cost for shipping. Zone pricing can be advantageous to the shipper because it reflects the actual shipping charges more closely than uniform delivered pricing can.

Pricing Tactics Aimed at Consumers

When firms sell their products and services directly to consumers, rather than to other businesses, the pricing tactics they use naturally differ. In this section, we analyze some tactics for products and services aimed directly at consumers: price lining, price bundling, and leader pricing. (Exhibit 14.6)

Price Lining   When marketers establish a price floor and a price ceiling for an entire line of similar products and then set a few other price points in between to represent distinct differences in quality, the tactic is called **price lining**.

Consider the specific price lines used by Brooks Brothers. The firm prices its sport coats and blazers at three price points, $398, $498, and $598—or good, better, and best. The lowest-priced line of blazers, at $398, still communicates a high level of quality compared with blazers offered by competitors, such as department stores, that are priced even lower. The two higher-priced lines then communicate even higher levels of quality. Note that Brooks Brothers offers both $498 and $598 versions of its classic two-button blazer. The more expensive blazer is described as follows:

> An elegant look in pure lightweight wool. Classically detailed with double besom pockets and a back center vent. Darted and slightly fitted through the chest. Full signature navy lining with green trim.

Compare that description to that for the lower-priced, $498 version:

> Meticulously tailored in Italy from refined Super 100s wool blended with cashmere. Darted front. Back center vent. Finished with gold-tone buttons. Fully lined.

From these descriptions, it is difficult to determine which is the better jacket, but the price makes it very clear, with little room for ambiguity!

EXHIBIT 14.6	Pricing Tactics Aimed at Consumers
Tactic	
Price Lining	Establishing a price floor and a price ceiling for an entire line of similar products and then setting price points in between to represent distinct differences in quality.
Price Bundling	Pricing of more than one product for a single, lower price.
Leader Pricing	Building store traffic by aggressively pricing and advertising a regularly purchased item, often priced at or just above the store's cost.

Jewel grocery stores practice price lining. Its private label (left) has the lowest price; Smuckers (right) has a higher price; and the St. Dalfour brand from France (middle) has the highest price.

Price Bundling   When firms are stuck with a slow moving item, to encourage sales, they sometimes will "bundle" it with a faster moving item and price the bundle below what the two items would cost separately. Sometimes, however, firms bundle products together just to encourage customers to stock up so they won't purchase competing brands, encourage trial of a new product, or provide an incentive to purchase a less desirable product or service to obtain a more desirable one in the same bundle. This practice of selling more than one product for a single, lower price is called **price bundling**.

We present a price bundling example in Exhibit 14.7. Imagine we have two products to offer for sale, A and B. The first column designates four different customers, A–D. Each subsequent column indicates the average price that each of these customers is willing to pay for Product A alone, Product B alone, and finally the total revenue if they purchase both A and B. If we price Product A at $7 and Product B at $4, the total revenue would be $22, because only customers A and C

EXHIBIT 14.7		An Illustration of Price Bundling				
Customer	**Willing to Pay for Product A**	**Buy Product A at $7**	**Willing to Pay for Product B**	**Buy Product B at $4**	**Revenue for Products A & B**	**Buy Bundle at $9**
A	8	Yes	1	No	9	Yes
B	3	No	6	Yes	9	Yes
C	8	Yes	7	Yes	15	Yes
D	5	No	2	No	7	No
Sell at	7		4		9	

Sell at $7 and $4; Overall Revenue = $22

Sell bundle at $9; Overall Revenue = $27

would buy Product A (revenue = $14) and only customers B and C would buy Product B (revenue = $8). However, if we bundled both products at a price of $9, our total revenue would be $27, because customers A, B, and C would all pay $9 for both items.

Leader Pricing   Leader pricing is a tactic that attempts to build store traffic by aggressively pricing and advertising a regularly purchased item, often priced at or just above the store's cost. The rationale behind this tactic argues that, while in the store to get the great deal on, say, milk, the consumer will also probably pick up other items he or she needs. The store has priced these items at higher profit margins, so their purchase will more than cover the lower markup on the milk. Imagine the marketing potential of various combinations of products; the store uses leader pricing on cocktail sauce, which gives employees the perfect opportunity to ask, "How about a pound of fresh shrimp to go with the cocktail sauce you're purchasing?"

Stores like Aldi use a pricing tactic called leader pricing to build store traffic by aggressively pricing and advertising regularly purchased items, often at or just above the store's cost.

Consumer Price Reductions

The final price a customer pays for a product or service often has been adjusted from the original price because marketers have used various techniques designed to enhance value. Some of these techniques include markdowns, quantity discounts, coupons, and rebates. (Exhibit 14.8)

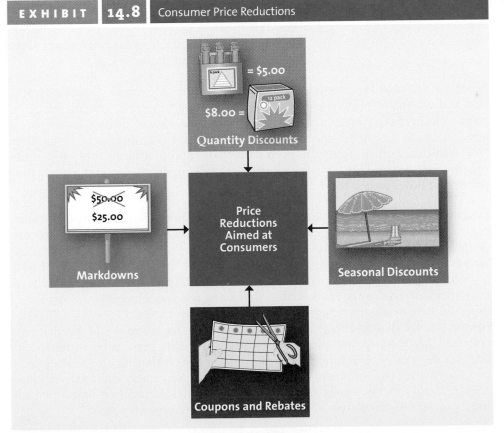

EXHIBIT 14.8   Consumer Price Reductions

Markdowns   Markdowns are the reductions retailers take on the initial selling price of the product or service.[16] An integral component of the high/low pricing strategy we described previously, markdowns enable retailers to get rid of slow moving or obsolete merchandise, sell seasonal items after the appropriate season, and match competitors' prices on specific merchandise. Retailers must get rid of merchandise that isn't selling because holding on to such items hurts the retailer's image and ties up money in inventory that could be used more productively elsewhere.

Retailers also use markdowns to promote merchandise and increase sales. Particularly when used in conjunction with promotions, markdowns can increase traffic into the store, which many retailers view as half the battle. Once customers are in the store, retailers always hope they will purchase other products at regular prices.

Quantity Discounts for Consumers   We have already discussed how firms use quantity discounts in the B2B marketplace, but the most common implementation of a quantity discount at the consumer level is the size discount. For example, there are three sizes of General Mills' popular cereal Cheerios—10-, 15-, and 20-

Customers get a size discount for buying larger sizes. With Cheerios, the larger the box, the less it costs per ounce.

ounce boxes priced at approximately $3.89, $4.49, and $5.99, respectively. The larger the quantity, the less the cost per ounce, which means the manufacturer is providing a quantity discount. The goal of this tactic is to encourage consumers to purchase larger quantities each time they buy. In turn, these consumers are less likely to switch brands and often tend to consume more of the product, depending on the product usage characteristics. Typically, buying a larger package of toilet tissue does not mean consumers will use it faster, but buying a larger box of cereal may encourage them to eat more of it or eat it more often.[17]

Seasonal Discounts   Seasonal discounts are price reductions offered on products and services to stimulate demand during off-peak seasons. You can find hotel rooms, ski lift tickets, snowmobiles, lawn mowers, barbeque grills, vacation packages, flights to certain destinations, and Christmas cards at discounts during their "off" seasons. Some consumers even plan their buying around these discounts, determined to spend the day after Christmas stocking up on discounted wrapping paper and bows for the following year.

Coupons and Rebates   Coupons and rebates both provide discounts to consumers on the final selling price. However, for the coupon, the retailer handles the discount, whereas the manufacturer issues the refund in the case of the rebate, which is defined as a portion of the purchase price returned to the buyer in the form of cash.

The goal of coupons is to prompt consumers to try a product, reward loyal customers, or encourage repurchases. By saving the consumer money, firms add value to their products. A segment of the market, the diehard "coupon clippers," devote a great deal of time and effort to searching for, clipping, and redeeming coupons. Many coupon clippers have streamlined this process by using the Internet, which offers entire forums dedicated to coupon sharing and management (e.g., www.couponforum.com). Nonetheless, many consumers dislike the cumbersome coupon process, so redemption rates on coupons average less than 2 percent. In response, coupon distribution has been declining in recent years.[18]

Rebates can be even more frustrating for consumers, but the idea is similar. Whereas a coupon provides instant savings when presented, a rebate promises savings, usually mailed to the consumer at some later date, only if the consumer carefully follows the rules. The "hassle factor" for rebates thus is higher than for coupons; the consumer must first buy the item during a specified time period, then mail in the required documentation—which usually includes the original sales receipt—and finally wait four to six weeks (or more!) for a check to arrive. Although consumers may believe this process adds value when the potential rebate is, say, $50, they might question whether a rebate for a couple of dollars is worth their time and effort. From the marketer's viewpoint, however, rebates offer greater control than do coupons and provide the firm with valuable customer information. Also, consumers may consider the rebate during their purchase decision process but then never redeem it—an added bonus for the seller.

With so many different pricing strategies and tactics, it is no wonder that unscrupulous firms find ample opportunity to engage in pricing practices that can hurt consumers. We now take a look at some of the legal and ethical implications of pricing.

Legal Aspects and Ethics of Pricing

Prices tend to fluctuate naturally and respond to varying market conditions. Thus, though we rarely see firms attempting to control the market in terms of product quality or advertising, they often engage in pricing practices that can unfairly reduce competition or harm consumers directly through fraud and deception. A host of laws and regulations at both the federal and state levels attempt to prevent unfair pricing practices, but some are poorly enforced, and others are difficult to prove.

Deceptive or Illegal Price Advertising

Although it is always illegal and unethical to lie in advertising, a certain amount of "puffery" is typically allowed (see Chapter 18). But price advertisements should never deceive consumers to the point of causing harm. For example, a local car dealer's advertising that it had the "best deals in town" would likely be considered puffery. In contrast, advertising "the lowest prices, guaranteed" makes a very specific claim and, if not true, can be considered deceptive.

Deceptive Reference Prices Previously, we introduced external reference prices, which create reference points for the buyer against which to compare the selling price. If the reference price is bona fide, the advertisement is informative. If the reference price has been inflated or is just plain fictitious, however, the advertisement

Is this a legitimate sale, or is the retailer using deceptive reference prices?

is deceptive and may cause harm to consumers. But it is not easy to determine whether a reference price is bona fide. What standard should be used? If an advertisement specifies a "regular price," just what qualifies as regular? How many units must the store sell at this price for it to be a bona fide regular price—half the stock? A few? Just one? Finally, what if the store offers the item for sale at the regular price but customers do not buy any? Can it still be considered a regular price? In general, if a seller is going to label a price as a regular price, the Better Business Bureau suggests that at least 50 percent of the sales have occurred at that price.[19]

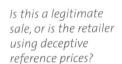

Loss Leader Pricing   As we discussed previously, leader pricing is a legitimate attempt to build store traffic by pricing a regularly purchased item aggressively but still above the store's cost. **Loss leader pricing** takes this tactic one step further by lowering the price *below* the store's cost. Some states prohibit loss leader pricing by requiring some minimum markup, but such laws are difficult to enforce. No doubt you have seen "buy one, get one free" offers at grocery and discount stores. Unless the markup for the item is 100 percent of the cost, these sales obviously do not generate enough revenue from the sale of one unit to cover the store's cost for both units, which means it has essentially priced the total for both items below cost. Yet we find such sales all the time, even though they may be illegal.

Bait and Switch   Another form of deceptive price advertising occurs when sellers advertise items for a very low price without the intent to really sell any. This **bait-and-switch** tactic is a deceptive practice because the store lures customers in with a very low price on an item (the bait), only to aggressively pressure these customers into purchasing a higher-priced model (the switch) by disparaging the low-priced item, comparing it unfavorably with the higher-priced model, or professing an inadequate supply of the lower-priced item. Again, the laws against bait-and-switch practices are difficult to enforce because salespeople, simply as a function of their jobs, are always trying to get customers to trade up to a higher-priced model without necessarily deliberately baiting them. The key to proving deception centers on the intent of the seller, which is also difficult to prove.

Predatory Pricing

When a firm sets a very low price for one or more of its products with the intent to drive its competition out of business, it is using **predatory pricing**. Predatory pricing is illegal under both the Sherman Act and the Federal Trade Commission Act because it constrains free trade and represents a form of unfair competition. It also tends to promote a concentrated market with a few dominant firms (an oligopoly).

But again, predation is difficult to prove. First, one must demonstrate intent, that is, that the firm intended to drive out its competition or prevent competitors from entering the market. Second, the complainant must prove that the firm charged prices lower than its average cost, an equally difficult task.

Price Discrimination

Is this price discrimination illegal?

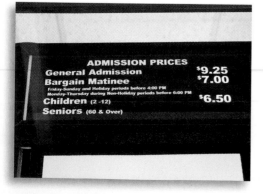

There are many forms of price discrimination, but only some of them are considered illegal under the Clayton Act and the Robinson-Patman Act. When firms sell the same product to different resellers (wholesalers, distributors, or retailers) at different prices, it can be considered **price discrimination**; usually, larger firms receive lower prices.

We have already discussed the use of quantity discounts, which is a legitimate method of charging different prices to different customers on the basis of the quantity they purchase. The legality of this tactic stems from the assumption that it costs less to sell and service 1,000 units to one customer than 100 units to 10 customers. But quantity discounts must be available to all customers and not be structured in such a way that they consistently and obviously favor one or a few buyers over others. Subtle forms of price discrimination, such as rebates, free delivery, advertising allowances,

Ethical Dilemma 14.1   Oh Yes, It's Ladies' Night ... No More

Despite the enduring popularity of Kool and the Gang's 1979 hit, it may not be ladies' night anymore in several states. In 2004, New Jersey became the latest state to fall in the battle to outlaw ladies' nights in bars.[21] Traditionally, bars have chosen one night per week and designated it "ladies' night," the night when women are admitted either for free or at a reduced rate and, once inside, served drinks at reduced prices. A New Jersey man named David Gillespie went to the Coastline bar on one ladies' night and was charged a $5 admission and full price for drinks; when he requested the discounted ladies' night prices, he was refused.

Gillespie sued under New Jersey's Law Against Discrimination and won. Essentially, the courts found that because the bar offered public accommodation, it could not discriminate in either entry or service on the basis of gender. Coastline did not argue that higher prices were being charged to men but instead offered in its defense that the difference in prices had a legitimate business purpose and no intent of hostility toward men. In fact, it argued, 80 percent of the patrons in the bar on ladies' night were men.

Other similar arguments have been made successfully in court, but not in this case. Regardless of motive, the practice was deemed to discriminate purely on the basis of gender. The court's decision opens the doors for reviews of other types of discount pricing programs, such as children's or senior prices in restaurants.

The decision has met with mixed reviews. The former Governor of New Jersey, James McGreevey, issued a written statement denouncing it as "bureaucratic nonsense," and an "overreaction that reflects a complete lack of common sense and good judgment." One TV commentator cried "Is there nothing sacred?" For now, however, the law stands, and it is ladies' night no more.

Putting aside your own potential gender biases for a moment, do you agree with the governor or the court? Is this a real case of discrimination that should be protected under the law or an effective pricing strategy?

Should bars be allowed to have "ladies' night" when women are admitted either for free or at a reduced rate and, once inside, served drinks at reduced prices? Is this illegal price discrimination?

and other methods used to lower the price without actually changing the invoice, are specifically prohibited by the Robinson-Patman Act. It is, however, perfectly legitimate to charge a different price to a reseller if the firm is attempting to meet a specific competitor's price. In addition, a barter agreement, in which buyers and sellers negotiate a mutually agreed upon price, is commonplace and absolutely legal in retail settings such as car sales and collectibles markets.

Furthermore, the Robinson-Patman Act does not apply to sales to end consumers, at which point many forms of price discrimination occur. For example, students and seniors often receive discounts on food and movie tickets, which is perfectly acceptable under federal law. However, a series of recent court decisions in 10 states has caused some sellers to rethink the meaning of price discrimination. These 10 states have now banned "ladies' nights" in bars because the practice violates the rights of men and compromises various state antidiscrimination statutes (see Ethical Dilemma 14.1).

Price Fixing

Price fixing is the practice of colluding with other firms to control prices. Recently, the five largest music companies—Universal Music, Sony Music, Warner Music, BMG Music, and EMI—and three of the largest music retailers—Musicland Stores, Trans World Entertainment, and Tower Records—agreed to pay $67.4 million and distribute $75.7 million in CDs to public and nonprofit groups to settle a lawsuit for alleged price fixing during the late 1990s.[20]

This particular case of price fixing is especially interesting because it includes both horizontal and vertical price fixing. Horizontal price fixing occurs when competitors that produce and sell competing products collude, or work together, to control prices, effectively taking price out of the decision process for consumers. In this particular case, prosecutors alleged that horizontal price fixing had occurred among the record companies, which specified pricing terms associated with the sale and distribution of CDs. Vertical price fixing occurs when parties at different levels of the same marketing channel (e.g., manufacturers and retailers) collude to control the prices passed on to consumers. In the music industry case, prosecutors alleged that the music companies colluded with music retailers to maintain retail prices for CDs.

Whereas horizontal price fixing is clearly illegal under the Sherman Antitrust Act, vertical price fixing falls into a gray area. In 1997, Supreme Court Justice Sandra Day O'Connor rendered a decision that vertical price fixing does not always violate antitrust laws.[22] Thus, the practice of vertical price fixing is not always illegal but rather must be reviewed on a case-by-case basis to determine its legality.

As these legal issues clearly demonstrate, pricing decisions involve many ethical considerations. In determining both their pricing strategies and their pricing tactics, marketers must always balance their goal of inducing customers, through price, to find value and the need to deal honestly and fairly with those same customers. Whether another business or an individual consumer, buyers can be influenced by a variety of pricing methods; it is up to marketers to determine which of these methods works best for the seller, the buyer, and the community.

Summing Up

1. **How should firms set their prices?**

The various methods of setting prices each have their own set of advantages and disadvantages. The fixed percentage and markup approaches are quick and easy but fail to reflect the competitive environment or consumer demand. Although it is always advisable to be aware of what competitors are doing, using competitor-based pricing should not occur in isolation without considering consumers' reactions. Taking a value-based approach to pricing, whether the

improvement value or the total cost of ownership, in conjunction with these other methods provides a nicely balanced method of setting prices.

2. **What psychological factors affect the way consumers make pricing decisions?**

Customers take different perspectives and use different sources to set a particular value for a product or service. For instance, some use the manufacturer's suggested retail price as a reference point, whereas others prefer to consider the total prices of all their purchases at a particular store. These latter customers tend to prefer stores that use an everyday low pricing strategy because the average prices of their purchases likely will be low. For those customers who equate price with quality—the higher the price, the higher the quality—a high/low strategy is appealing because they can not only gauge quality by the initial higher price but also use it as their reference price. For almost all customers though, odd prices, like those that end in 9, tend to signal a good deal.

3. In what conditions should a price skimming or a market penetration strategy be used?

When firms use a price skimming strategy, the product or service must be perceived as breaking new ground or customers will not pay more than what they pay for other products. Firms use price skimming to signal high quality, limit demand, recoup their investment quickly, and/or test people's price sensitivity. Moreover, it is easier to price high initially and then lower the price than vice versa. Market penetration, in contrast, helps firms build sales and market share quickly, which may discourage other firms from entering the market. Building demand quickly also typically results in lowered costs as the firm gains experience making the product or delivering the service.

4. What tactics do sellers use to reduce prices to retailers? To consumers?

Pricing tactics can be divided into those that affect resellers like retailers and those that affect consumers. On the B2B side, seasonal discounts give retailers an incentive to buy prior to the normal selling season, cash discounts prompt them to pay their invoices early, and allowances attempt to get retailers to advertise the manufacturer's product or stock a new product. In addition, quantity discounts can cause retailers to purchase a larger quantity over a specific period of time or with a particular order. Finally, zone pricing bases the cost of shipping the merchandise on the distance between the retailer and the manufacturer—the farther away, the more it costs. On the consumer side, marketers can use price lining to indicate different quality levels to consumers or bundle products to offer lower prices than those charged if the products were purchased separately. To get customers into their stores, retailers also price certain products or services at very low prices, with the hope that these same customers will also buy other, more profitable items. In some methods similar to those used in B2B contexts, sellers offer seasonal and quantity discounts to individual buyers as well. Finally, coupons and rebates offer consumers additional price reductions.

5. How can firms avoid legal and ethical problems when setting or changing their prices?

There are almost as many ways to get into trouble by setting or changing a price as there are pricing strategies and tactics. Three of the most common legal issues pertain to advertising deceptive prices. Specifically, if a firm compares a reduced price with a "regular" or reference price, it must actually have sold that product or service at the regular price. In many states, advertising the sale of products priced below the retailer's cost constitutes an unfair competitive practice, as does bait-and-switch advertising. Charging different prices to different customers is sometimes, but not always, illegal, whereas any collusion among firms to fix prices is always illegal.

Key Terms

- advertising allowance, 396
- bait and switch, 402
- cash discount, 396
- competitor-based pricing method, 385
- cost-based pricing method, 384
- cost of ownership method, 386
- coupon, 400
- cumulative quantity discount, 396
- everyday low pricing (EDLP), 390
- experience curve effect, 393
- external reference price, 388
- high/low pricing, 390
- horizontal price fixing, 404
- improvement value, 385
- internal reference price, 388
- leader pricing, 399
- loss leader pricing, 402
- markdowns, 400
- market penetration strategy, 393
- noncumulative quantity discount, 396
- odd prices, 390
- predatory pricing, 402
- premium pricing, 385
- price bundling, 398
- price discrimination, 402
- price fixing, 404
- price skimming, 392
- pricing lining, 397
- pricing tactics, 394
- quantity discount, 396
- reference price, 388
- seasonal discount, 394
- size discount, 400
- slotting allowances, 396
- uniform delivered pricing, 397
- value-based pricing method, 385
- vertical price fixing, 404
- zone pricing, 397

Marketing Applications

1. Suppose you have been hired as the pricing manager for a grocery store chain that typically adds a fixed percentage onto the cost of each product to arrive at the retail price. Evaluate this technique. What would you do differently?

2. Some high fashion retailers, notably H&M and Zara, sell what some call "disposable fashion"—apparel priced so reasonably low that it can be disposed of after just a few wearings. Here is your dilemma: You have an important job interview and need a new suit. You can buy the suit at one of these stores for $199 or at Brooks Brothers for $500. Of course, the Brooks Brothers suit is of higher quality and will therefore last longer. How would you use the two value-based approaches described in this chapter to determine which suit to buy?

3. Consider the last purchase you made on sale. How did you use external and internal reference prices to determine the product's value? Do you believe the external reference price was deceptive? Why or why not?

4. Identify two stores at which you shop, one of which uses everyday low pricing and another that uses a high/low pricing strategy. Do you believe that each store's chosen strategy is appropriate for the type of merchandise it sells and the market of customers to whom it is appealing? Justify your answer.

5. As the product manager for Puma running shoes, you are in charge of pricing new products. Your product team has developed a revolutionary new shoe that is so technologically advanced and different that you believe it will be difficult for your competition to copy it easily. Should you adopt a skimming or a penetration pricing strategy? Justify your answer.

6. What is the difference between a cumulative and a noncumulative quantity discount?

7. If you worked for a manufacturing firm located in Oregon and shipped merchandise all over the United States, which would be more advantageous, a zone or a uniform delivered pricing policy? Why?

8. Coupons and rebates benefit different channel members. Which would you prefer if you were a manufacturer, a retailer, and a consumer? Why?

9. Suppose the president of your university got together with the presidents of all the universities in your athletic conference for lunch. They discussed what each university was going to charge for tuition the following year. Are they in violation of federal laws? Explain your answer.

10. Imagine that you are the newly hired brand manager for a T-shirt company whose new line is about to come out. Because of a major fashion magazine's very positive review of the line, the company wants to reposition the brand as a premium youth brand. Your boss asks what price you should charge for the new T-shirt line. The current line, considered mid-range retail, is priced at $20. What steps might you undertake to determine what the new price should be?

11. You have been hired by a regional supermarket chain as the soft drink buyer. Your shelves are dominated by national firms like Pepsi and Coke. The chain imposes a substantial slotting fee to allow new items to be added to their stock selection. Management reasons that it costs a lot to add and delete items, and besides these fees are a good source of revenue. A small minority-operated local firm produces several potentially interesting soft drinks, all with natural ingredients, vitamins, reduced sugar, and a competitive price—and they also happen to taste great. You'd love to give the firm a chance, but its managers claim the slotting fee is too high. Should your firm charge slotting fees? Are slotting fees fair to the relevant shareholders—customers, stockholders, vendors?

Net Savvy

1. Go to couponsaver.com (http://www.couponsurfer.com/) and identify five of the products featured.

   ■ How effective are coupons for selling these products? Why?

   ■ What are the benefits to the seller of using couponsaver.com over other integrated marketing communication options?

   ■ How do you think couponsaver.com makes money?

Chapter Case Study

FUJITSU GENERAL AMERICA INC.[23]

Fujitsu General America Inc. is a subsidiary of Fujitsu General Limited, which is headquartered in Kawasaki, Japan. A large conglomerate that includes the manufacturer of Fujitsu consumer electronics, the company has been in business since 1935. In 1993, Fujitsu introduced the world's first color plasma display: 21 inches (measured diagonally) for $25,000. In January 1997, Fujitsu introduced the first large-format, flat-panel plasma display at a price of $13,999. By the spring of 1997, the *Stereophile Guide to Home Theater*[24] still had not listed any plasma screens in its "Recommended Components" section, where it cites home theater products worthy of consideration for purchase—nor, for that matter, had it mentioned plasma screens anywhere else in the magazine.

It wasn't until September 1998, almost two years later, that the magazine finally reviewed any plasma monitors, including Fujitsu's latest 42-inch model, the 4204, priced at $10,999 (introduced in January 1998), as well as the higher-priced Philips 42-inch model at $15,000 and the lower-priced Mitsubishi 40-inch model at $10,000. Fujitsu's version offered 852 × 480 resolution, was 6 inches thick, weighed in at 87 pounds, and could not reproduce high-definition television. Nonetheless, the magazine's reviewer selected the Fujitsu as the clear choice "in terms of both cost and performance. It offers an impressive picture, the most advanced electronics, and the best black-level rendition."[25] The plasma screen went on to become the world's best selling.

In June 1999, Fujitsu announced a price reduction on the 4203 to $6,995, noting "Since introducing the 4203 in January 1998, one of our primary objectives has been to make this model more affordable." According to Michael Gleason, National Sales Manager of Fujitsu General America, "This considerable price move is attainable because of our factory's ability to minimize costs, especially on this model, which they have been producing for over 18 months."

Later in 1999, the firm introduced a new 42-inch plasma display model, the 4221, that was only 3.3 inches thick and had a host of new features and capabilities, including the ability to produce high-definition television with 1024 × 1024 resolution. The price was set at $15,999, apparently to invoke a premium pricing strategy, position the company in the competitive landscape as the high-price/quality leader, and signal high quality to consumers. Reviewed by *Stereophile Guide to Home Theater* in summer 2000, this model led the author to conclude that "Fujitsu's Plasmavision SlimScreen PDS 4221 is easily the finest plasma display I have ever reviewed."[26]

At some point in January or February 2001, the price of the 4221 fell to $13,999. Then, in March 2001, Fujitsu announced price reductions on most of its plasma displays, including a $4,000 reduction in the latest version of the 42" high-definition model (4222) from $13,999 to $9,999. In June, it announced the next generation (4241) with more features, improved quality, and a new price of $8,995. In just four months in 2001, the price had dropped by almost half. Another successor model (4242) was introduced in July 2001 at $9,995, slightly higher than the previous model. Apparently, Fujitsu had inventory of the old model to sell and did not want to be forced to discount it, as it would be if it had brought the new model out at the same price.

By April 2003, the latest version of the high-definition, 42-inch plasma monitor was priced at $7,999; by January 2005, the replacement model was priced at $6,995, a much slower decrease per year over these three and a half years than consumers experienced during the first few years.

Questions

1. Does it make sense for Fujitsu to keep using a skimming pricing strategy? Justify your position. If the company were to change to a penetration strategy, what issues would it need to wrestle with?

2. When new technologies move through the marketplace, the process is called the "diffusion of innovation." Plasma technology seems to be gaining acceptance; what, other than lower prices, has influenced consumers' perceptions of value of the plasma displays?

3. Does the price–quality relationship hold for the market for plasma displays? Why or why not?

15

QUESTIONS

- What is supply chain management?

- How do supply chains add value?

- How does a supply chain work?

- How is a supply chain designed?

- How is a supply chain managed?

SECTION SIX

Value Delivery: Designing the Channel and Supply Chain

CHAPTER 15   Supply Chain Management
CHAPTER 16   Retailing

Supply Chain Management

Zara International, Inc. (www.zara.com), a fast-growing Spanish apparel retailer and an inexpensive but chic subsidiary of Inditex (Industria de Diseño Textil, Galicia, Spain), operates about 820 fashionable clothing stores in 60 countries (including 9 in the United States).[1] The chain takes in annual sales of more than $3 billion—an impressive number for a company founded only 30 years ago. The first Zara shop opened its doors in 1975 in La Coruña in the northwestern region of Spain's Galicia. Nearby is Zara's ultramodern headquarters and its 500,000 square meter distribution center that supplies all its stores.

In a tribute to Zara's "with it" image, according to *Vogue*, even French customers of Zara stores identify Zara as being of French origin. Various fashion pages continue to feature celebrities like Cindy Crawford shopping at a Zara store in Canada; Chelsea Clinton visiting the Zara store in Ankara, Turkey; the children of the Spanish royal family purchasing regularly at the Zara store on Madrid's upscale Velazquez Street; and tourist buses making sightseeing stopovers at the Zara store on Paseo de Garcia in Barcelona. Today Zara shops can be found in upscale neighborhoods such as New York's 5th Avenue, Paris's Champs Elysées, London's Regent Street, and Tokyo's Shibuya Shopping Centre.

Inditex (www.inditex.com), which owns and operates Zara, is made up of almost 100 companies that all deal with activities related to textile design, production, and distribution. Inditex also operates seven other chains: Kiddy's Class, Pull and Bear, Massimo Dutti, Bershka, Stradivarius, Oysho, and Zara Home. But Zara International is the largest and the oldest of its chains, providing close to 80 percent of its revenues.

Although Zara competes with local retailers in most of its markets, analysts consider its three closest competitors to be The Gap, Sweden's Hennes & Mauritz (H&M), and

Zara's advanced supply chain and information systems enable it to get its relatively inexpensive high fashion apparel to stores in New York (left) and Paris (right) in a matter of a few weeks.

Italy's Benetton. There are, however, important differences in the ways the four firms operate. The Gap and H&M own most of their stores but outsource all their manufacturing. In contrast, Benetton has invested relatively heavily in manufacturing, but licensees run its stores. Zara not only owns a majority of its stores, it also produces a majority of its own clothes, mostly at its ultramodern manufacturing complex in northwestern Spain. In another departure from the pack, Zara makes over 40 percent of its own fabric—far more than most of its rivals.

From its base in Spain, Zara also operates its own worldwide distribution network. Controlling the supply chain gives Zara flexibility that its competitors can only dream about. It also allows Zara to operate with minimal inventory buildups because its stores get deliveries twice a week, and newly supplied items rarely remain on the retail shelves for more than a week. In this sense, Zara has one of the most sophisticated supply chains of any apparel retailer. Zara takes only four to five weeks to design a new collection and then about a week to manufacture it. Its competitors, by comparison, need an average of six months to design a new collection and another three weeks to manufacture it. How does Zara do it?

The company derives its competitive advantage from an astute use of information and technology. All its stores are electronically linked to the headquarters in Spain. Store managers, together with a fleet of sharp-eyed, design-savvy trend spotters on Zara's staff, routinely prowl fashion hot spots such as university campuses and happening nightclubs. Their job is to function as the company's eyes and ears, to spot the next wave. Using wireless handheld devices, they send images back to corporate headquarters so that designers can produce blueprints for close-at-hand manufacturers to start stitching, resulting in garments that will be hanging in Zara stores within weeks.

In effect, Zara's designers have real-time information when they make decisions, with the commercial team, about the fabric, cut, and price of a new line of garments. This combination of real-time information sharing and internalized production means that Zara can work with almost no stock and still have new designs in its stores twice a week. Customers love the results of this high-velocity operation: They queue up in long lines at Zara's stores on designated delivery days, a phenomenon dubbed "Zaramania" by the press.

■ ■ ■

In this chapter, we discuss the third P, place, which includes all activities required to get the right products to the right customer when that customer wants it. Students of marketing often overlook or underestimate the importance of place in the marketing mix simply because it happens behind the scenes. Yet place, or supply chain management as it is commonly called, adds value for customers because it gets products to customers efficiently—quickly and at low cost.

As we noted in Chapter 1, **supply chain management** refers to a set of approaches and techniques firms employ to efficiently and effectively integrate their suppliers, manufacturers, warehouses, stores, and transportation intermediaries into a seamless value chain in which merchandise is produced and distributed in the right quantities, to the right locations, and at the right time, as well as to minimize systemwide costs while satisfying the service levels their customers require.[2] As we learned in the opening vignette, Zara employs a completely integrated supply chain because the company owns or at least has considerable control over each phase. As a result, it is able to conceive of, design, manufacture, transport, and ultimately sell high-fashion apparel much more quickly and efficiently than any of its major competitors.

Exhibit 15.1 shows a simplified supply chain, in which manufacturers make products and sell them to retailers or wholesalers. The exhibit would be much more complicated if we had included suppliers of materials to manufacturers and all of the manufacturers, wholesalers, and stores in a typical supply chain. **Wholesalers** are firms that buy products from manufacturers and resell them to retailers, and retailers sell products directly to consumers. Manufacturers ship to a wholesaler, or, in the case of many multistore retailers, to the retailer's distribution center (as is the case for Manufacturer 1 and Manufacturer 3) or directly to stores (Manufacturer 2).

Although Exhibit 15.1 shows the typical flow of manufactured goods, many variations to this supply chain exist. Some retail chains, like Home Depot and Costco, function as both retailers and wholesalers; they act as retailers when they sell to consumers directly and as wholesalers when they sell to other businesses, like building contractors or restaurant owners. When manufacturers such as Dell or Avon sell directly to consumers, they are performing both production and retailing activities. When Dell sells directly to a university or business, it becomes a business-to-business (B2B) transaction, but when it sells to the students or employees individually, it is a B2C (business-to-consumer) operation.

Supply Chain, Marketing Channels, and Logistics Are Related

People often talk about supply chain management, marketing channel management, and logistics management as if they were the same thing. A **marketing channel** is the set of institutions that transfer the ownership of and move goods

EXHIBIT | **15.1** | Typical Supply Chain

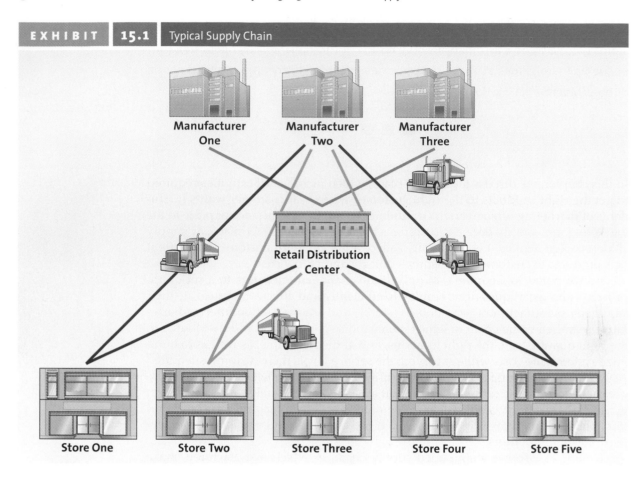

from the point of production to the point of consumption; as such, it consists of all the institutions and marketing activities in the marketing process.[3] Thus, a marketing channel and a supply chain are virtually the same.

Logistics management describes the integration of two or more activities for the purpose of planning, implementing, and controlling the efficient flow of raw materials, in-process inventory, and finished goods from the point of origin to the point of consumption. These activities may include, but are not limited to, customer service, demand forecasting, distribution communications, inventory control, materials handling, order processing, parts and service support, plant and warehouse site selection, procurement, packaging, return goods handling, salvage and scrap disposal, traffic and transportation, and warehousing and storage.[4] Therefore, logistics management is that element of supply chain management that concentrates on the movement and control of the physical products; supply chain management as a whole also includes an awareness of the relationships among members of the supply chain or channel and the need to coordinate efforts to provide customers with the best value.

So, are marketing channel management, supply chain management, and logistics management the same or different? To answer this question, we must look at how firms have handled these activities in the past. Marketing channel management traditionally has been the responsibility of marketing departments, under the direction of a marketing vice president. Logistics was traditionally the responsibility of operations, under a vice president of operations. Although their goals were similar, they often saw solutions differently, and sometimes they worked in conflict. For instance, the marketing department's goal might have been to make sales, whereas logistics wanted to keep costs low. Firms have come to realize there is tremendous opportunity in coordinating marketing and logistics activities not only within a firm but also throughout the supply chain. Thus, because supply chain management takes a systemwide approach to coordinating the flow of merchandise, it includes both channel management and logistics and is therefore the term that we use in this chapter.

Supply Chains Add Value

Why would a manufacturer want to use a wholesaler or a retailer? Don't these supply chain members just cut into their profits? Wouldn't it be cheaper for consumers to buy directly from manufacturers? In a simple agrarian economy, the best supply chain may in fact follow a direct route from manufacturer to consumer: The consumer goes to the farm and buys food directly from the farmer. But how will the food get cooked? The consumer doesn't know how to make a stove, nor does she have the materials to do so. The stove maker who has the necessary knowledge must buy raw materials and components from various suppliers, make the stove, and then make it available to the consumer. If the stove maker isn't located near the consumer, the stove must be transported to where the consumer has access to it. To make matters even more complicated, the consumer may want to view a choice of stoves, hear about all their features, and have the stove delivered and installed.

How many companies are involved in making and getting a stove to your kitchen?

Each participant in the supply chain thus adds value. The components manufacturer helps the stove manufacturer by supplying parts and materials. The stove maker then turns the components into the stove. The transportation company gets the stove to the retailer. The retailer stores the stove until the customer wants it, educates the customer about product features, and delivers and installs the stove. At each step, the stove becomes more costly but also more valuable to the consumer.

Exhibit 15.2A and B show how using supply chain partners can provide value overall. Exhibit 15.2A shows three manufacturers, each of which sells directly to three consumers in a system that requires nine transactions. Each transaction costs money—for example, the manufacturer must fill the order, package it, write up the paperwork, and ship it—and each cost is passed on to the customer. Exhibit 15.2B shows the same three manufacturers and consumers, but this time they go through a retailer. The number of transactions falls to six, and as transactions are eliminated, the supply chain becomes more efficient, which adds value for customers by making it more convenient and less expensive to purchase merchandise.

Supply Chain Management Streamlines Distribution

Supply chain management offers the 21st century's answer to a host of distribution problems faced by firms. As recently as the early 1990s, even the most innovative firms needed 15 to 30 days—or even more—to fulfill an order from the warehouse to the customer. The typical order-to-delivery process had several steps: order creation, usually using a telephone, facsimile, or mail; order processing, using a manual system for credit authorization and assignment to a warehouse; and physical delivery. Things could, and often did, go wrong. Ordered goods were not available. Orders were lost or misplaced. Shipments were misdirected. These mistakes lengthened the time it took to get merchandise to customers and potentially made the entire process more expensive.

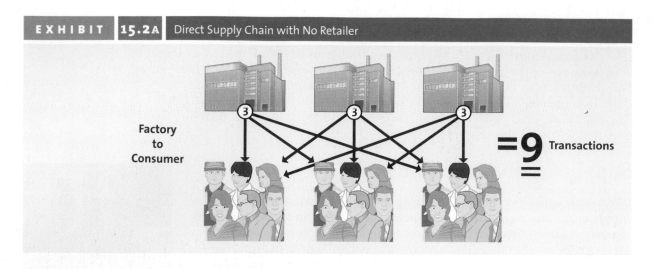

EXHIBIT 15.2A Direct Supply Chain with No Retailer

Factory to Consumer

=**9** Transactions

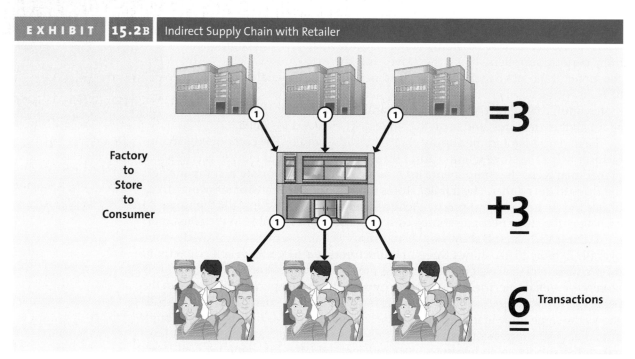

EXHIBIT 15.2B Indirect Supply Chain with Retailer

Factory to Store to Consumer

=**3**

+**3**

6 Transactions

Faced with these predicaments, firms began stockpiling inventory at each level of the supply chain (retailers, wholesalers, and manufacturers), but keeping inventory where it is not needed becomes a huge and wasteful expense. Take, for instance, the troubled U.S. airline industry. Bankrupt USAirways took drastic steps to reduce its spare inventory of replacement parts by more than $100 million, or 24 percent of its annual maintenance budget. Prior to the cut, the firm was carrying $500 million in extra inventory to support its 279 mainline jets and spending $130 million annually on new parts or parts repair. Similarly, Delta Airlines decreased its maintenance costs by roughly 51 percent by implementing an inventory management system. Between 2001 and 2002, Delta's maintenance expenses dropped 11 percent, saving the company $90 million.[5]

Supply Chain Management Affects Marketing

Every marketing decision is affected by and has an effect on the supply chain. When products are designed and manufactured, how and when the critical components reach the factory must be coordinated with production. The sales department must coordinate its delivery promises with the factory or distribution centers. A **distribution center,** a facility for the receipt, storage, and redistribution of goods to company stores or customers, may be operated by retailers, manufacturers, or distribution specialists.[6] Furthermore, advertising and promotion must be coordinated with those departments that control inventory and transportation. There is no faster way to lose credibility with customers than to promise deliveries or run a promotion and then not have the merchandise when the customer expects it. Entrepreneurial Marketing 15.1 describes how entrepreneur Michael Dell got into the computer business and developed his firm into one that provides better value to customers with great supply chain management.

Five interrelated activities emerge in supply chain management: making information flow, making merchandise flow, managing inventory, designing the supply chain, and managing the relationships among supply chain partners. In the next few sections, we examine each of these activities.

Making Information Flow

Information flows from the customer to stores, to and from distribution centers, possibly to and from wholesalers, to and from product manufacturers, and then on to the producers of any components and the suppliers of raw materials. To simplify our discussion and because information flows are similar in other supply chain links and B2B channels, we shorten the supply chain in this section to exclude wholesalers, as well as the link from suppliers to manufacturers. Exhibit 15.3 illustrates the flow of information that starts when a customer buys a Sony DVD player at Best Buy. The flow follows these steps:

Flow 1 (Customer to Store): The sales associate at Best Buy scans the **Universal Product Code (UPC)** tag, the black-and-white bar code found on most merchandise, on the DVD player packaging, and the customer receives a receipt.

Flow 2 (Store to Buyer): The point-of-sale (POS) terminal records the purchase information and electronically sends it to the buyer at Best Buy's corporate office. The sales information is incorporated into an inventory management system to aid in planning future purchases and promotions.

Flow 3 (Store to Manufacturer): The purchase information from each Best Buy store is typically aggregated by the retailer as a whole, which creates an order for new merchandise and sends it to Sony. The buyer at Best Buy may also communicate directly with Sony to get information and negotiate prices, shipping dates, promotional events, or other merchandise-related issues.

Flow 4 (Store to Manufacturer): If the merchandise is reordered frequently, the ordering process can become automatic and virtually bypass the buyer.

Flow 5 (Store to Distribution Center): Stores also communicate with the Best Buy distribution center to coordinate deliveries and check inventory status.

In Flow 3, the retailer and manufacturer exchange business documents through a system called electronic data interchange (EDI).

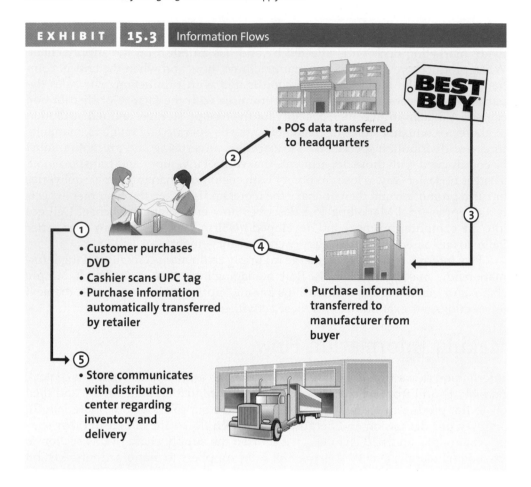

EXHIBIT 15.3 Information Flows

① • Customer purchases DVD
• Cashier scans UPC tag
• Purchase information automatically transferred by retailer

② • POS data transferred to headquarters

④ • Purchase information transferred to manufacturer from buyer

⑤ • Store communicates with distribution center regarding inventory and delivery

Electronic Data Interchange

Electronic data interchange (EDI) is the computer-to-computer exchange of business documents from a retailer to a vendor and back. In addition to sales data, purchase orders, invoices, and data about returned merchandise can be transmitted back and forth.

Many retailers now require vendors to provide them with notification of deliveries before they take place using an **advanced shipping notice,** an electronic document that the supplier sends the retailer in advance of a shipment to tell the retailer exactly what to expect in the shipment. If the advanced shipping notice is accurate, the retailer can dispense with opening all the received cartons and checking in merchandise. In addition, EDI enables vendors to transmit information about on-hand inventory status, vendor promotions, and cost changes to the retailer, as well as information about purchase order changes, order status, retail prices, and transportation routings.

Typically, EDI is transmitted over the Internet through either intranets or extranets. **Intranets** are secure communication systems contained within one company, such as between buyers and distribution centers. In contrast, an **extranet** is a collaborative network that uses Internet technology to link businesses with their suppliers, customers, or other businesses. These extranets are typically private and secure, in that they can be accessed only by certain parties. Thus, some but not all manufacturers would have access to a retailer's extranet.

Entrepreneurial Marketing 15.1

Dell Gets You What You Want

As a college student, Michael Dell declared that he wanted to beat IBM.[7] In 1983, he began conducting business out of his dorm room at the University of Texas in Austin, selling custom-made PCs and components. A year later, with $1,000 in start-up capital, Dell officially set up his business and left school. "Being an entrepreneur wasn't on my mind," insists Dell. "What was on my mind was the opportunity I saw ahead, which was so compelling." This single-minded focus has been translated into one of the most innovative and efficient supply chain management systems in not just the computer industry but the world.

The company builds roughly 50,000 made-to-order computers a day and carries just four days' worth of parts inventory. Online sales account for nearly half of its orders. Using state-of-the-art technology, Dell monitors every aspect of the supply chain, including supplier report cards that compare individual performance to preset criteria.

Creating value then continues on the customer side. For example, Dell may find that demand for 60 gig hard drives is exceeding supply. Rather than delay deliv-

Michael Dell makes made-to-order computers on this assembly line.

ery, the firm offers 80 gig hard drives at promotional prices and works with suppliers to keep inventory levels of the 60 gig drives from becoming too low. Likewise, in reviewing its inventory and service for repair, Dell introduced real-time and historical reporting that has dropped its repair time from 43 to 17 days.[8]

Especially through extranets, EDIs have gone beyond merely communicating order and shipping information. Suppliers, through the Internet, can describe and show pictures of their products, and buyers can issue requests for proposals. The two parties then can electronically negotiate prices and specify how the product will be made and how it should look.

Toy giant Hasbro, for example, launched an EDI initiative to improve its order processing. Before its EDI, roughly 70 percent of all incoming orders filtered through 100 vendors in Asia. Each order was sent from the vendor to the appropriate manufacturer, and the manufacturer manually reviewed all vendor requests. When exceptions or delays occurred, the process became laborious because of the numerous faxes and phone calls needed to resolve any issue. After Hasbro implemented an EDI for its manufacturers, 80 percent of the orders needed no human interaction at all. As a result, the Asian operations were able to absorb a 100 percent increase in their order volume without any additional resources.[9]

Hasbro makes toys and games like this "Risk Star Wars—Clone Wars Edition," but they communicate efficiently with their vendors with EDI.

CPFR   Popular in the grocery and drug industries, collaboration, planning, forecasting, and replenishment (CPFR) is an inventory management system that uses an EDI through which a retailer sends sales information to a manufacturer. The manufacturer then can create a computer-generated sales forecast and delivery schedule, on which both firms agree.

A CPFR system can significantly improve inventory management. Wal-Mart and Sara Lee, Kimberly-Clarke and Kmart, and Nabisco and Wegmans Grocery, among others, have collaboratively engaged in pilot programs to test CPFR applications.[10]

Here's how CPFR works: Partnering with Wegmans Grocery, a chain of stores in New York, New Jersey, and Pennsylvania, Nabisco tested CPFR for 22 of the Planters Nut SKUs it offered in each store. Both parties developed a joint business plan according to their marketing objectives and historical sales performance. The Nabisco sales manager and the Wegmans buyer then developed a rolling 13-week sales forecast that included sales and promotional forecasts generated from historical data captured by Nabisco. Meanwhile, a Nabisco customer service representative monitored the order process. Although the shipments were based on the original forecasts, the representative could easily adjust the orders according to actual demand.

The Nabisco–Wegmans CPFR pilot test has been considered a great success. For the six months the pilot ran, Planters' sales increased 53 percent, while the average inventory in stores decreased.[11]

Making Merchandise Flow

Exhibit 15.4 illustrates different types of merchandise flows[12]

1. from Sony to Best Buy's distribution centers, or
2. from Sony directly to stores.
3. If the merchandise goes through distribution centers, it is then shipped to stores
4. and then to the customer.

Inbound Transportation

Because its distribution centers typically are quite busy, a dispatcher—the person who coordinates deliveries to Best Buy's distribution centers—assigns a time slot for each shipment of DVD players to arrive. If the truck misses the time slot, it is fined. Although many manufacturers pay transportation expenses, some retailers negotiate with their vendors to absorb this expense. These retailers believe they can lower net merchandise cost and control their merchandise flow better if they negotiate directly with truck companies and consolidate shipments from many vendors.

Receiving and Checking

Receiving refers to the process of recording the receipt of merchandise as it arrives at a distribution center or store. Checking is the process of going through the goods upon receipt to ensure they arrived undamaged and that the merchandise ordered was the merchandise received.

In the past, checking merchandise was a very labor-intensive and time-consuming process, but today, many distribution systems using EDI are designed

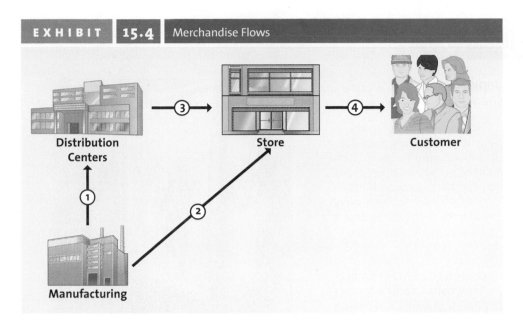

EXHIBIT | **15.4** | Merchandise Flows

Distribution Centers

Store

Customer

Manufacturing

to minimize, if not eliminate, these processes. The advance shipping notice tells the distribution center what should be in each box. The recipient scans the UPC label on the shipping carton or the radio frequency identification (RFID) tag, which identifies the carton's contents, and those contents then are automatically counted as being received and checked. **Radio frequency identification (RFID) tags** are tiny computer chips that automatically transmit to a special scanner all the information about a container's contents or individual products. Adding Value 15.1 explains how the U.K. retailer Marks & Spencer has begun to make use of RFID tags.

Storing and Cross-Docking

There are three types of distribution centers: traditional, cross-docking, and combinations. A **traditional distribution center** is a warehouse in which merchandise is unloaded from trucks and placed on racks or shelves for storage. When the merchandise is needed in the stores, a worker goes to the rack, picks up the item, and places it in a bin. A conveyor system or other material-handling equipment transports the merchandise to a staging area, where it is consolidated and made ready for shipment to stores.

The second type, called a **cross-docking distribution center,** is one to which vendors ship merchandise prepackaged in the quantity required for each store. The merchandise already contains price and theft detection tags. Because the merchandise is ready for sale, it goes straight to a staging area rather than into storage. When all the merchandise going to a particular store has arrived in the staging area, it is loaded onto a truck, and away it goes.

Most modern distribution centers are neither pure warehouse nor pure cross-docking systems but instead combine the two. It is difficult for a firm to operate without some storage facilities, even if merchandise is stored for only a few days. For instance, some merchandise, such as tent stakes at L.L. Bean,

RFID tags make receiving and checking merchandise accurate, quick, and easy.

Adding Value 15.1

RFID Tracks Merchandise through Marks & Spencer

The U.K. department and grocery retailer Marks & Spencer is experimenting with RFID tags to replace bar-coded identification tags on all its apparel. Each RFID tag has a unique number, as opposed to bar codes, which only provide unique product numbers for each SKU.[13] This enables Marks & Spencer to track every item from the time the vendor receives it to the time it leaves the store. Tags are removed at the time of sale to protect customers' privacy.

About as large as a pinhead, RFID tags consist of an antenna and a chip that contains an electronic product code that stores far more information about a product than bar (UPC) codes can. The tags also act as passive tracking devices, signaling their presence over a radio frequency when they pass within a few yards of a special scanner. The tags have long been used in high-cost applications, such as automated highway toll systems and security identification badges.

The prospect of affordable tags is exciting supply chains everywhere. If every item in a store were tagged, RFID technology could be used to locate mislaid products, deter theft, and even offer customers personalized sales pitches through displays mounted in dressing rooms. Ultimately, tags and readers could replace bar codes and checkout labor altogether. Customers could just walk through a door equipped with a sensor, which would read all the tags electronically and charge the purchases directly to the customer's credit card.

When placed on merchandise, RFID tags can be used to deter theft and locate mislaid merchandise.

The main value of RFID is that it eliminates the need to handle items individually by enabling distribution centers and stores to receive whole truckloads of merchandise without having to check in each carton. Still, the watchword, for both retailers and manufacturers of consumer products, is caution. For most supply chain members, long-term investments in RFID technology are still too risky and expensive. Experts believe it will be 5 to 10 years before RFID tags are prevalent on most consumer products.

In a cross-docking distribution center, merchandise moves from vendors' trucks to the retailer's delivery trucks in a matter of hours.

has relatively slow sales but must be carried because it rounds out an assortment. These items are good candidates for storage in a distribution center, even if the rest of the merchandise is cross-docked. Also, no matter how good a sales forecasting system may be, sometimes the merchandise arrives before it is needed in the stores. In these cases, the retailer must have a system to store the merchandise temporarily.

Getting Merchandise Floor-Ready

Floor-ready merchandise is merchandise that's ready to be placed on the selling floor immediately. Getting merchandise floor-ready entails ticketing, marking, and, in the case of apparel, placing garments on hangers. **Ticketing and marking** refers to creating price and identification labels and placing them on the merchandise. It is more efficient for a retailer to perform these activities at a distribution center than in its stores because the work is time consuming and messy. Some retailers force their suppliers to ship merchandise floor-ready, thus totally eliminating this expensive, time-consuming process for themselves.

Shipping Merchandise to Stores

Shipping merchandise to stores is quite complex for multistore chains. A Best Buy distribution center will run approximately 100 trucks to its stores per day. To handle such complex transportation problems, distribution centers use a sophisticated routing and scheduling computer system that considers the rate of sales in the store, road conditions, and transportation operating constraints to develop the most efficient routes possible. As a result, stores receive an accurate estimated time of arrival, and the supply chain maximizes vehicle use.

Inventory Management through Just-In-Time Systems

Customers demand specific SKUs, and they want to be able to buy them when needed. If, for instance, you want to buy a pair of size 10 Nike Zoom Elite 8, you probably aren't going to purchase a size 9 Nike Air Moray Slide sandals just because the retailer is out of the shoes you want. At the same time, firms can't afford to carry more than they really need of an SKU, because to do so is very expensive. Suppose, for instance, a shoe store carries $1 million worth of inventory at its own expense. Experts estimate that it would cost between 20 and 40 percent of the value of the inventory, or $20,000 to $40,000 per year, to hold that inventory! So firms must balance having enough inventory to satisfy customer demands with not having more than they need.

To help reconcile these seemingly conflicting goals, many firms have adopted just-in-time (JIT) inventory systems. **Just-in-time inventory systems**, also known as **quick-response** (QR) systems in retailing, are inventory management systems designed to deliver less merchandise on a more frequent basis than traditional inventory systems. The firm gets the merchandise "just-in-time" for it to be used in the manufacture of another product, in the case of parts or components, or for sale

Retailers must have the inventory to satisfy your exact needs. If you want a pair of Nike's Air Zoom Elite shoes in size 10 (left), you aren't going to purchase a size 9 Air Moray Slide sandals (right).

when the customer wants it, in the case of consumer goods. The JIT systems lower inventory investments, but product availability actually increases.

To illustrate a JIT system, consider how the supply chain works at Procter & Gamble. Previously, P&G would use data supplied by retailers to forecast sales and plan production. The company would produce a lot of each item at a time and then store the merchandise until retailers ordered it. Today, it has implemented a five-step process to embrace a JIT approach. Managers start with demand data, which they obtain directly from their retailers. They work closely with these retailers to develop sales forecasts and shipping schedules that better align P&G's production with demand at the retail store. This effort reduces both excess inventory and out-of-stock situations. Most important for JIT, P&G produces just enough to meet demand. To achieve this balance, the company has moved from producing every product once a month to a system in which it produces every item every day, which it then delivers to the customer the following day.[14]

Benefits of a JIT System

The benefits of a JIT system include reduced lead time, increased product availability, and lower inventory investment.

Reduced Lead Time By eliminating the need for paper transactions by mail, overnight deliveries, or even faxes, the EDI in the JIT system reduces **lead time**, or the amount of time between the recognition that an order needs to be placed and the arrival of the needed merchandise at the seller's store, ready for sale. Because the vendor's computer acquires the data automatically, no manual data entry is required on the recipient's end, which reduces lead time even more and eliminates vendor recording errors. Even better, the shorter lead times further reduce the need for inventory because the shorter the lead time, the easier it is for the retailer to forecast its demand.

Celestica Inc., a manufacturer of electronics equipment for Hewlett-Packard, IBM, and Nortel Networks, relies heavily on its supply chain partners to communicate with and manage its Chinese operations efficiently and thereby to reduce its lead times. The supply chain partners link Celestica with local suppliers and transportation companies using EDI and supervise 10 distribution centers located within five minutes of Celestica's manufacturing facilities. The end result? Shortened lead times and increased responsiveness.[15]

Zara doesn't need to carry a lot of inventory on hand because their JIT inventory system insures quick delivery of needed merchandise.

Increased Product Availability and Lower Inventory Investment In general, as a firm's ability to satisfy customer demand by having stock on hand increases, so does its inventory investment; that is, it needs to keep more backup inventory in stock. But with JIT, the ability to satisfy demand can actually increase while inventory decreases. Because the firm can make purchase commitments or produce merchandise closer to the time of sale, its own inventory investment is reduced. Firms also need less inventory because they're getting less merchandise in each order, but they receive shipments more often. Inventory is even further reduced because the firms aren't forecasting sales quite as far into the future. For instance, fashion retailers that don't use QR must make purchase commitments as much as six months in advance and receive merchandise well ahead of actual sales, whereas QR systems align deliveries more closely with sales.

The ability to satisfy customer demand by keeping merchandise in stock also increases in JIT systems as a result of the more frequent shipments. For instance, if a Zara store runs low on a medium-sized, Kelly green sweater, its QR system ensures a shorter lead time than those of more traditional retailers. As a result, it's less likely that the Zara store will be out of stock for its customers before the next sweater shipment arrives.

Costs of a JIT System

Although firms achieve great benefits from a JIT system, it is not without its costs. The logistics function becomes much more complicated with more frequent deliveries. With greater order frequency also come smaller orders, which are more expensive to transport and more difficult to coordinate.

Therefore, JIT systems also require a strong commitment by the firm and its vendors to cooperate, share data, and develop systems like EDI and CPFR. Successful JIT systems require not only financial support from top management but also a psychological commitment to partnering with vendors. In some cases, larger firms even pressure their less powerful supply chain partners to absorb many of these expensive logistics costs.

Designing Supply Chains

Supply chains are composed of various entities that are buying, such as retailers or wholesalers; selling, such as manufacturers or wholesalers; or helping facilitate the exchange, such as transportation companies. Like interactions between people, these relationships can range from close working partnerships to one-time arrangements. In almost all cases though, they occur because the parties want something from one another. For instance, Home Depot wants hammers from Stanley Tool Company, Stanley wants an opportunity to sell its tools to the public, and both companies want UPS to deliver the merchandise.

Each member of the supply chain performs a specialized role. If one member believes that another isn't doing its job correctly or efficiently, it usually can replace that member. So, if Stanley isn't getting good service from UPS, it can switch to Fed

The Home Depot and Stanley Tool Company have a mutually beneficial partnership. The Home Depot buys tools from Stanley because their customers find value in Stanley products. Stanley sells tools to Home Depot because they have established an excellent market for its products.

Ex. Likewise, if Home Depot believes its customers don't perceive Stanley tools to be a good value, it may buy from another tool company. Home Depot could even decide to make its own tools or use its own trucks to pick up tools from Stanley. However, even if a supply chain member is replaced, the function it performed remains, so someone needs to complete it.

In this section, we examine how supply chains are structured, as well as the appropriate level of distribution intensity.

Supply Chain Structure

When a firm is just starting out or entering a new market, it doesn't typically have the option of designing the "best" supply chain structure—that is, of choosing whom it buys from or to whom it sells. A new retailer selling children's clothing, for instance, will be primarily concerned about getting the right assortment and needs to scout the market to get just the right mix. Some manufacturers won't want to sell to this new retailer initially because its credit isn't established or the manufacturers already have enough of their products represented by other retailers in the area. The problem can be equally daunting for manufacturers entering a new market, whose primary concern will be to find retailers that want to take a chance on their line. When choosing retailers to whom to sell, the manufacturer should consider where the end customer expects to find the product, as well as some important retailer characteristics.

Customer Expectations   Supply chain management is an integral part of any marketing strategy. And another key part of any strategy is to determine customer expectations. From a retailer's perspective, it is important to know from which manufacturers its customers want to buy. Manufacturers, in contrast, need to know where their target market customers expect to find their products and those of their competitors. As we see in the hypothetical example in Exhibit 15.5, the children's apparel manufacturer OshKosh B'Gosh currently sells to Dillard's Department Stores, Federated Department Stores, and Sears (red arrows). Its competitor Carter's sells to Dillard's and Federated but also to JCPenney (green arrows). A survey of young parents shows the firm that OshKosh's customers expect to find its clothes at Kohl's, Dillard's, Federated, and JCPenney (blue box). On the basis of this information, Osh-Kosh decides to start selling at Kohl's and JCPenney but stop selling at Sears.

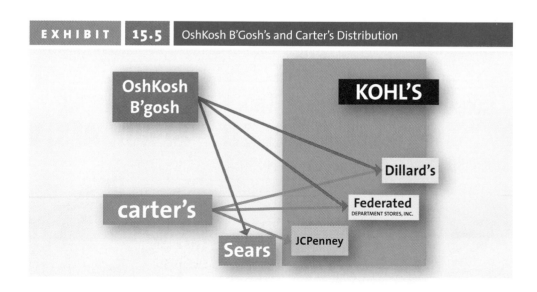

EXHIBIT   **15.5**   OshKosh B'Gosh's and Carter's Distribution

Customers generally expect to find certain products at some stores but not at others. For instance, OshKosh would not choose to sell to Neiman Marcus or Dollar General because its customers would not expect to shop at those stores for children's clothing. Instead, Neiman Marcus might carry imported clothing from France, and Dollar General will probably offer bargain closeouts. But OshKosh's customers definitely expect to find its clothing offerings at major department stores.

Supply Chain Member Characteristics   Several factors pertaining to the supply chain members themselves will help determine the supply chain structure. Generally, the larger and more sophisticated the channel member, the less likely that it will use supply chain intermediaries. A small specialty toy manufacturer will probably use a group of independent salespeople to help sell its line, whereas a large manufacturer like Mattel will use its own sales force. In the same way, an independent grocery store might buy merchandise from a wholesaler, but Wal-Mart, the world's largest grocer, only buys directly from the manufacturer. Larger firms often find that by performing the supply chain functions themselves, they can gain more control, be more efficient, and save money.

Distribution Intensity

When setting up distribution for the first time or introducing new products, firms decide the appropriate level of **distribution intensity**—the number of supply chain members to use at each level of the supply chain. Distribution intensity commonly is divided into three levels: intensive, exclusive, and selective. (See Exhibit 15.6.)

EXHIBIT 15.6 Distribution Intensity

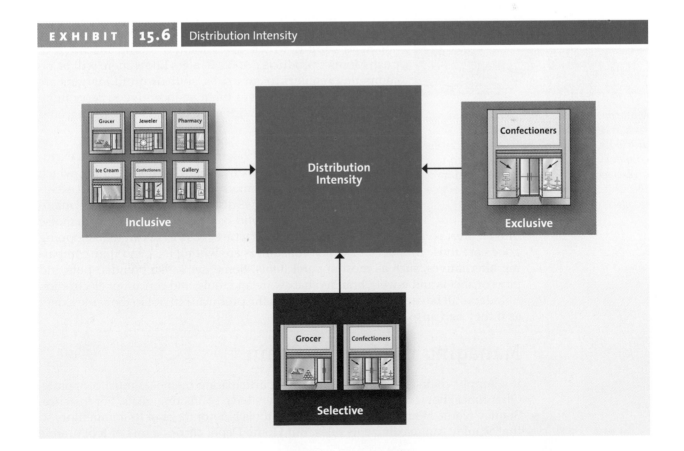

Most consumer packaged goods companies, such as Pepsi (top), strive for intensive distribution—it wants to be everywhere. But cosmetics firms like Estée Lauder (bottom) use an exclusive distribution strategy by limiting their distribution to a few select, higher-end retailers in each region.

Intensive Distribution   An **intensive distribution** strategy is designed to get products into as many outlets as possible. Most consumer packaged goods companies, such as Pepsi, P&G, Kraft, and most other nationally branded products found in grocery and discount stores, strive for and often achieve intensive distribution. Pepsi, for instance, wants its product available everywhere—grocery stores, convenience stores, restaurants, and vending machines. The more exposure it gets, the more it sells.

Exclusive Distribution   Manufacturers also might use an exclusive distribution policy by granting **exclusive geographic territories** to one or very few retail customers so no other customers in the territory can sell a particular brand. Exclusive distribution can benefit manufacturers by assuring them that the most appropriate customers represent their products. Cosmetics firms like Estée Lauder, for instance, limit their distribution to a few select, higher-end retailers in each region. They believe that if they sell their products to drug stores, discount stores, and grocery stores, this distribution would weaken their image.

In cases of limited supply or when a firm is just starting out, providing an exclusive territory to one customer helps ensure enough inventory to offer the customer an adequate selection. For instance, Moots is a limited production titanium bicycle manufacturer in Steamboat Springs, Colorado. By granting exclusive territories, it guarantees its retailers adequate supply, which gives them a strong incentive to push Moots's products. Moots dealers know there will be no competing retailers to cut prices, so their profit margins are protected, which also gives them an incentive to carry more inventory and use extra advertising, personal selling, and sales promotions.

Selective Distribution   Between the intensive and exclusive distribution strategies lies **selective distribution,** which uses a few selected customers in a territory. Similar to exclusive distribution, selective distribution helps a seller maintain a particular image and control the flow of merchandise into an area, so many shopping goods manufacturers use it. Recall that shopping goods are those products for which consumers are willing to spend time comparing alternatives, such as most apparel items, home items like branded pots and pans or sheets and towels, branded hardware and tools, and consumer electronics. Retailers still have a strong incentive to sell the products but not to the same extent as if they had an exclusive territory.

Managing the Supply Chain

If a supply chain is to run efficiently, the participating members must cooperate. Oftentimes, however, supply chain members have conflicting goals. For instance, Stanley wants Home Depot to carry all its tools but not those of its competitors so that Stanley can maximize its sales. But Home Depot carries a mix of tool brands so it can maximize the sales in its tool category. When supply chain members are not in agreement about their goals, roles, or rewards, **supply chain** or **channel conflict** results.

Supply chain conflict can be resolved through a good negotiation process. But when the issues can't be worked out, relationships can fall apart, and the firms may go their separate ways. In other cases, conflict may lead to a stronger supply chain. In the mid-1980s, Procter & Gamble was having trouble selling to Wal-Mart; in their relationship, there was no sharing of information, no joint planning or sales forecasting, and no systems coordination. So Sam Walton ventured out on a canoe trip with Lou Pritchett, P&G's vice president of sales. On this trip, they started a process of examining how the two firms could mutually profit by working together. The conflict thus ultimately resulted in a much stronger partnership between the two firms in which they currently work together to establish sales forecasts and determine how to best restock P&G merchandise on Wal-Mart's shelves. All parties benefit. Customers get lower prices and high product availability, and because P&G produces according to demand, there is less need for backup stock, so its salespeople spend less time in the stores. Finally, Wal-Mart achieves higher sales with a lower inventory investment.[16]

There are two non–mutually exclusive ways to manage a supply chain: coordinate the channel using a vertical marketing system or develop strong relationships with supply chain partners.

Managing Supply Chains through Vertical Marketing Systems

Although conflict is likely to occur in any supply chain, it is generally more pronounced when the supply chain members are independent entities. Supply chains that are more closely aligned, whether by contract or ownership, share common goals and therefore are less prone to conflict.

In an **independent** or **conventional supply chain**, the several independent members—a manufacturer, a wholesaler, and a retailer—each attempt to satisfy their own objectives and maximize their own profits, often at the expense of the other members, as we portray in Exhibit 15.7.

None of the participants has any control over the others. For instance, the first time Zara purchases cotton fabric from Tessuto e Colore in Northern Italy, both parties try to extract as much profit from the deal as possible, and after the deal has been consummated, neither party feels any responsibility to the other. Over time, Zara and Tessuto might develop a relationship in which their transactions become more routinized and automatic, such that Zara depends on Tessuto for fabric, and Tessuto depends on Zara to buy a good portion of its output. This scenario represents the first phase of a **vertical marketing system,** which is a supply chain in which the members act as a unified system, as in Exhibit 15.7. There are three types, or phases, of vertical marketing systems, each with increasing levels of formalization and control. The more formal the vertical marketing system, the less likely conflict will ensue.

Zara and Tessuto e Colore in Northern Italy might develop a vertical marketing system in which transactions have become routinized and automatic, such that Zara depends on Tessuto for fabric, and Tessuto depends on Zara to buy a good portion of its output.

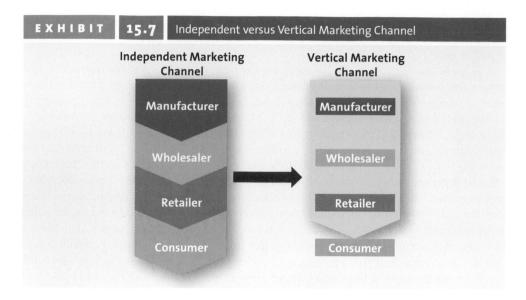

EXHIBIT 15.7   Independent versus Vertical Marketing Channel

Administered Vertical Marketing System   The Zara/Tessuto supply chain relationship offers an example of an administered vertical marketing system. In an **administered vertical marketing system,** there is no common ownership and no contractual relationships, but the dominant channel member controls the channel relationship. In our example, because of its size and relative power, Zara imposes some control over Tessuto; it dictates, for instance, what Tessuto should make and when it should be delivered. Zara also has a strong influence over the price. If either party doesn't like the way the relationship is going, however, it can simply walk away.

Contractual Vertical Marketing System   Over time, Zara and Tessuto may formalize their relationship by entering into contracts that dictate various terms, such as how much Zara will buy each month, at what price, and the penalties for late deliveries. In **contractual vertical marketing systems** like this, independent firms at different levels of the supply chain join together through contracts to obtain economies of scale and coordination and to reduce conflict.[17]

Franchising is the most common type of contractual vertical marketing system; franchising companies and their franchisees account for $1 trillion in annual U.S. retail sales—an astonishing 40 percent of all retail sales in this country—and employ more than 8 million people, or more than 7 percent of total nonagricultural employment in the United States.[18] **Franchising** is a contractual agreement between a franchisor and a franchisee that allows the franchisee to operate a retail outlet using a name and format developed and supported by the franchisor. Exhibit 15.8 lists the United States' top franchises. These rankings, determined by *Entrepreneur* magazine, are created using a number of objective measures, such as financial strength, stability, growth rate, and size of the franchise system.[19]

In a franchise contract, the franchisee pays a lump sum plus a royalty on all sales in return for the right to operate a business in a specific location. The franchisee also agrees to operate the outlet in accordance with the procedures prescribed by the franchisor. The franchisor typically provides assistance in locating and building the business, developing the products or services sold, management training, and advertising. To maintain the franchisee's reputation, the franchisor also makes sure that all outlets provide the same quality of services and products.

EXHIBIT 15.8		Top Franchises		
Rank	Franchise	Type	Start-Up Costs	Number of U.S. Outlets
1	Subway	Submarine sandwiches & salads	$86K–213K	17,012
2	Curves	Women's fitness & weight-loss centers	$36.4K–42.9K	6,651
3	Quizno's	Submarine sandwiches, soups, salads	$208.4K–243.8K	2,179*
4	7-Eleven	Convenience store	$65K–227K	3,827
5	Jackson Hewitt	Tax preparation services	$47.4K–75.2K	4,330
6	UPS Store	Postal/business/communications services	$145.8K–247.5K	3,788
7	McDonald's	Hamburgers, chicken, salads	$506K–1.6M	11,629
8	Jani-King	Commercial cleaning	$11.3K–34.1K+	8,506
9	Dunkin' Donuts	Donuts & baked goods	$255.7K–1.1M	4,140
10	Baskin-Robbins	Ice cream & yogurt	$145.7K–527.8K	2,604

Source: http://entrepreneur.com/franzone/rank/0,6584,12-12-F5-2004-0,00.html

A franchise system combines the entrepreneurial advantages of owning a business with the efficiencies of vertical marketing systems that function under single ownership (a corporate system, as we discuss next). Franchisees are motivated to make their stores successful because they receive the profits, after they pay the royalty to the franchisor. The franchisor is motivated to develop new products, services, and systems and to promote the franchise because it receives royalties on all sales. Advertising, product development, and system development are all done efficiently by the franchisor, with costs shared by all franchisees.

Corporate Vertical Marketing System   Because Zara deals with "fast fashion," it is imperative that it have complete control over the most fashion-sensitive items. So Zara manufactures these items itself and contracts out its less fashionable items to other manufacturers.[20] The portion of its supply chain that Zara owns and controls is called a corporate vertical marketing system. Because Zara's parent company Inditex owns the manufacturing plants, warehouse facilities, retail outlets, and design studios, it can dictate the priorities and objectives of that supply chain, and thus conflict is lessened.

Managing Supply Chains through Strategic Relationships

There is more to managing supply chains than simply exercising power over other members in an administered system or establishing a contractual or corporate vertical marketing system. There is also a human side.

In a conventional supply chain, relationships between members often are based on the argument over the split of the profit pie—if one party gets ahead, the other party falls behind. Sometimes this type of transaction is acceptable if the parties have no interest in a long-term relationship. For instance, if Cole Haan sees a fad for very narrow white belts, it may only be interested in purchasing from a particular vendor once. In that case, it might seek to get the best one-time price, even if it means the supplier will make very little money and therefore might not want to sell to Cole Haan again.

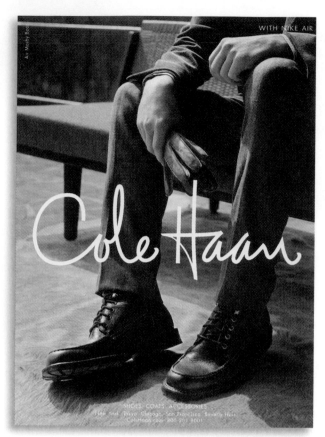

Cole Haan tries to develop strategic partnerships with its suppliers based on mutual trust, open communications, common goals, and credible commitments.

More often than not, however, firms seek a **strategic relationship**, also called a **partnering relationship,** in which the supply chain members are committed to maintaining the relationship over the long term and investing in opportunities that are mutually beneficial. In a conventional or administered supply chain, there are significant incentives to establishing a strategic relationship, even without contracts or ownership relationships. Both parties benefit because the size of the profit pie has increased, so both the buyer and the seller increase their sales and profits. These strategic relationships are created explicitly to uncover and exploit joint opportunities, so members depend on and trust each other heavily; share goals and agree on how to accomplish those goals; and are willing to take risks, share confidential information, and make significant investments for the sake of the relationship. Successful strategic relationships require mutual trust, open communication, common goals, and credible commitments as illustrated in Exhibit 15.9.[21]

Mutual Trust Mutual trust holds a strategic relationship together. Trust is the belief that a partner is honest (i.e., reliable, stands by its word, sincere, fulfills obligations) and benevolent (i.e., concerned about the other party's welfare). When vendors and buyers trust each other, they're more willing to share relevant ideas, clarify goals and problems, and communicate efficiently. Information shared between the parties thus becomes increasingly comprehensive, accurate, and timely. For instance, a CPFR system for mutual inventory forecasting would not be possible without mutual trust.

With trust, there's also less need for the supply chain members to constantly monitor and check up on each other's actions because each believes the other won't take advantage, even given the opportunity. The RFID systems that enable sealed cartons to be checked into a distribution center without being opened also would be impossible without mutual trust. However, though RFID tags can greatly enhance efficiency in a supply chain and though they rely on trust in that supply chain, they pose serious privacy concerns for consumers, as we discuss in Ethical Dilemma 15.1.

Open Communication To share information, develop sales forecasts together, and coordinate deliveries, Cole Haan and its suppliers maintain open and honest communication. This maintenance may sound easy in principle, but most businesses don't tend to share information with their business partners. But open, honest communication is a key to developing successful relationships because supply chain members need to understand what is driving each other's business, their roles in the relationship, each firm's strategies, and any problems that arise over the course of the relationship.

Common Goals Supply chain members must have common goals for a successful relationship to develop. Shared goals give both members of the relationship an

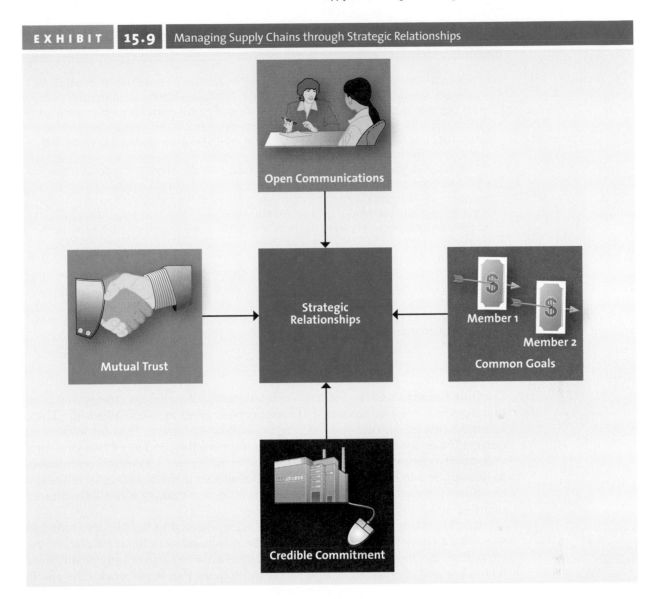

EXHIBIT 15.9 Managing Supply Chains through Strategic Relationships

incentive to pool their strengths and abilities and exploit potential opportunities together. Such commonality also offers an assurance that the other partner won't do anything to hinder the achievement of those goals within the relationship.

For example, Cole Haan and its local suppliers recognize that it is in their common interest to be strategic partners. Cole Haan needs the QR local manufacturers afford, and those manufacturers recognize that if they can keep Cole Haan happy, they will have more than enough business for years to come. With common goals, both firms have an incentive to cooperate because they know that by doing so, both can boost sales. For instance, if Cole Haan needs a special production run to make an emergency shipment to New York, the suppliers will work to meet the challenge. If one of Cole Haan's suppliers has difficulty getting a particular fabric or financing its inventory, it is in Cole Haan's best interest to help it because they are committed to the same goals in the long run.

Ethical Dilemma 15.1   Can RFIDs Keep a Secret?

Although RFIDs (radio frequency identification devices) can provide a lot of value for a company by streamlining the supply chain, they also strike fear in some consumers when they are used on individual items.[22] Retailers of higher-priced or theft-prone items particularly like RFID tags, which enable them to easily track the merchandise's whereabouts. They also facilitate warranty services and recalls because the tag has information about when the item was purchased, where, and by whom.

So, suppose you buy a notebook computer with an affixed RFID tag. As the item is scanned at the point of sale (POS), the retailer adds personal information to the database, such as your name, when the item was purchased, the selling price, and your purchase history with the retailer. This information then might be read by an unauthorized reader, such as another retailer in the mall. Also, in the same way that RFID tags track the whereabouts of a carton of merchandise, the tag can pinpoint your location after the sale as you carry your new computer around campus.

Some people thus are concerned that RFID tags will encroach on their personal privacy. They believe that once the product is purchased, it belongs to them, and information regarding its use is no one's business except their own. Companies manufacturing RFID tags therefore are developing countermeasures to these potential concerns, such as a kill function that disables the tag at the checkout point.

Credible Commitments   Successful relationships develop because both parties make credible commitments to, or tangible investments in, the relationship. These commitments go beyond just making the hollow statement, "I want to be your partner"; they involve spending money to improve the products or services provided to the customer.[23] For example, if Cole Haan makes a financial commitment to its suppliers to help them develop state-of-the-art manufacturing facilities and computer systems for improved communication, it is making a credible commitment—putting its money where its mouth is.

Just like many other elements of marketing, managing the supply chain can seem like an easy task at first glance: Put the merchandise in the right place at the right time. But the various elements and actors involved in a supply chain create its unique and compelling complexities and require that firms work carefully to ensure they are achieving the most efficient and effective chain possible.

Summing Up

1. What is supply chain management?

Supply chain management refers to the effort to coordinate suppliers, manufacturers, warehouses, stores, and transportation intermediaries so that the merchandise the customer wants is produced in the right quantities and sent to the right locations at the time the customer wants it. Logistics concentrates on the movement and control of the products, whereas supply chain management includes the managerial aspects of the process as well.

2. How do supply chains add value?

Without a supply chain, consumers would be forced to find raw materials, manufacture products, and somehow get them to where they could be used, all on their own. Each supply chain member adds value to the product by performing one of these functions. Supply chain management also creates value for each firm in the chain and helps bind together many company functions, including manufacturing, inventory management, transportation, advertising, and marketing.

3. How does a supply chain work?

For a supply chain to operate properly, the flow of information and merchandise must be coordinated, and supply chain members must work together to their mutual benefit. In more sophisticated supply chains, information flows seamlessly between supply chain members through EDI. Many of the best supply chains use a JIT or QR inventory management system, which provides the right amount of inventory just when it is needed. The JIT systems thus improve product availability and reduce inventory investments.

4. How is a supply chain designed?

Sometimes, particularly when firms are starting out, supply chain members cannot choose their ideal partners but instead take the partners they can get to obtain the materials or customers they need. In general, the larger and more sophisticated the supply chain member, the more likely it will perform some supply chain activities itself rather than using third-party intermediaries. Firms that want as much

market exposure as possible use intensive distribution, whereas firms that either want to maintain an exclusive image or are not large enough to sell to everyone tend to use an exclusive distribution strategy. Somewhere in the middle lies a selective distribution strategy.

5. How is a supply chain managed?

The more closely aligned the supply chain members are with each other, the less likely there will be significant conflict. An administered supply chain occurs when a dominant and powerful supply chain member has control over the other members. In a contractual supply chain (e.g., franchising), coordination and control are dictated by contractual relationships between members. Corporate supply chains can operate relatively smoothly because one firm owns the various levels of the chains. Supply chains also can be effectively managed through strong relationships developed with supply chain partners. To create such relationships, the partners must trust each other, communicate openly, have compatible goals, and be willing to invest in each other's success.

Key Terms

- administered vertical marketing system, 428
- advanced shipping notice, 416
- checking, 418
- collaboration, planning, forecasting, and replenishment (CPFR), 418
- contractual vertical marketing system, 428
- corporate vertical marketing system, 429
- cross-docking distribution center, 419
- dispatcher, 418
- distribution center, 415
- distribution intensity, 425

- electronic data interchange (EDI), 416
- exclusive geographic territories, 426
- extranet, 416
- floor-ready merchandise, 420
- franchising, 428
- independent (conventional) supply chain, 427
- intensive distribution, 426
- intranet, 416
- just-in-time inventory systems, 421
- lead time, 422
- logistics management, 412
- marketing channel, 411

- quick response, 421
- radio frequency identification (RFID) tags, 419
- receiving, 418
- selective distribution, 426
- strategic relationship (partnering relationship), 430
- supply chain conflict (channel conflict), 427
- supply chain management, 411
- ticketing and marking, 421
- traditional distribution center, 419
- universal product code (UPC), 415
- vertical marketing system, 427
- wholesaler, 411

Marketing Applications

1. Describe supply chain management by identifying the major activities that it involves. Identify several ways that supply chain management adds value to a company's offerings, with regard to both consumers and business partners.

2. Discuss the similarities and differences among the concepts of supply chains, marketing channels, and logistics.

3. In what ways can the flow of information be managed in the supply chain? How can the ready flow of information increase a firm's operating efficiencies?

4. Describe how B2B transactions might employ EDI to process purchase information. Considering the information discussed in Chapter 6 about B2B buying situations, determine which buying situation (new task, modified rebuy, or straight rebuy) would most likely align with the use of EDI technology. Justify your answer.

5. What are the differences between the use of a traditional distribution center and one that relies on cross-docking? Discuss the extent to which one is more efficient than the other, being sure to detail your reasoning.

6. Discuss the advantages to a retailer like Sports Authority of expending the time and effort to get merchandise floor-ready at either the point of manufacture or in the distribution center rather than having retail store staff members do it in the stores. Provide the logic behind your answer.

7. A JIT inventory system appears to be an important success factor for Zara. Choose a local retailer and examine the advantages and disadvantages of its use of a JIT system. Do you believe it should use JIT? Why?

8. Give an example of a retailer that participates in an independent (conventional) supply chain and one involved in a vertical marketing system. Discuss the advantages and disadvantages of each.

9. For each of the following consumer products, identify the type of vertical marketing system used, and justify your answer: (a) Keebler Cookies sold through grocery stores, (b) Krispy Kreme donuts sold through franchises, and (c) www.polo.com by Ralph Lauren.

10. Why would a big company like Nike want to develop strategic partnerships with locally owned running stores? Describe what Nike would have to do to maintain such relationships.

11. You are hired as an assistant brand manager for a popular consumer product. One day in an emergency meeting, the brand manager informs the group that there is a problem with one of the suppliers and that he has decided to send you over to the manufacturing facilities to investigate the problem. When you arrive at the plant you learn that a key supplier has become increasingly unreliable in terms of quality and delivery. You ask the plant manager why they don't switch suppliers since this is becoming a major problem for your brand. He informs you that the troubled supplier is his cousin whose wife has been very ill, and he just can't switch right now. What course of action should you take?

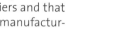

Net Savvy

1. Dell is considered exemplary in its ability to manage its supply chain efficiently. Log on to the company's Web site (www.dell.com) and go through the process of configuring a computer to purchase. Print out a copy of the computer system you have designed, making note of the delivery date and price. Describe how Dell has revolutionized computer sales and delivery. Is there any indication that Dell has partnered with other companies to sell peripheral equipment like printers or scanners? How would this partnership add value to customers?

2. The opening vignette for this chapter highlighted ways that Zara International, a division of Inditex, successfully manages its supply chain. Visit Inditex's Web site (www.inditex.com) and review the company's commitment to social responsibility, particularly the section that pertains to its code of conduct. Considering the discussion in this chapter about strategic relationships, how does Inditex address the factors necessary for mutually beneficial partnerships according to its code of conduct?

Chapter Case Study

WAL-MART: PIONEER IN SUPPLY CHAIN MANAGEMENT[24]

Wal-Mart dominates the retailing industry in terms of its sales revenue, its customer base, and its ability to drive down costs and deliver good value to its customers. After all, the world's largest corporation takes pride in having received numerous accolades for its ability to continuously improve efficiency in the supply chain while meeting its corporate mandate of offering customers Everyday Low Prices.

Tight inventory management is legendary at Wal-Mart through its just-in-time techniques, some of which are homegrown, that allow the firm to boast one of the best supply chains in the world. Wal-Mart has not only transformed its own supply chain but influenced how vendors throughout the world operate. For example, retailers everywhere are now placing much more emphasis on vendors' on-time and accurate deliveries. To meet these requirements, vendors have had to upgrade their inventory management and delivery systems to ensure they are doing business the way their large retailer customers prefer.[25] Recognized for its ability to obtain merchandise from global sources, Wal-Mart also pioneered the strategy of achieving high levels of growth and profitability through its precision control of manufacturing, inventory, and distribution. Although the company is not unique in this regard, it is by far the most successful and most influential corporation of its kind and has put into practice various innovative techniques.

And when Wal-Mart does something, it does it on a massive scale. Wal-Mart's computer system, for example, is second only to that of the Pentagon in storage capacity. Its information systems analyze more than 10 million daily transactions from point-of-sale data and distribute their analysis in real time both internally to its managers and externally via a satellite network to Wal-Mart's many suppliers, who use the information for their production planning and order shipment.

Much of the popularity of supply chain management has been attributed to the success of Wal-Mart's partnership with Procter & Gamble. During the 1980s, the two collaborated in building a software system that linked P&G to Wal-Mart's distribution centers, taking advantage of advances in the world's telecommunications infrastructure. When a Wal-Mart store sold a particular P&G item, the information flowed directly to P&G's planning and control systems. When the inventory level of P&G's products at Wal-Mart's distribution center got to the "reorder point," the system automatically alerted P&G to ship more products; this information in turn helped P&G plan its production. Wal-Mart was also able to track when a P&G shipment arrived at one of its distribution warehouses, which enabled it to coordinate its own outbound shipments to stores. Both Wal-Mart and P&G realized savings from the better inventory management and order processing, savings that in turn were passed on to Wal-Mart's consumers through its low everyday prices.

Wal-Mart's Innovations

Wal-Mart has pioneered many innovations in the purchase and distribution processes of the products it sells. As many as 20 years ago, Wal-Mart drove the adoption of UPC bar codes throughout the retail industry; it also pioneered the use of electronic data interchange (EDI) for computerized ordering from vendors. Its hub-and-spoke distribution network ensures goods are brought to distribution centers around the country and then directed outward to thousands of stores, each of which are within a day's travel. Through the use of cross-docking, one of its best-known innovations, goods get trucked to a distribution center from suppliers and then are immediately transferred to trucks bound for stores, without ever being placed into storage.[26] In addition, Wal-Mart uses a dedicated fleet of trucks to ship goods from warehouses to stores in less than 48 hours, as well as to replenish store inventories about twice a week. Thus, with flow-through logistics, the company speeds the movement of goods from its distribution centers to its retail stores around the world.

Today the retail giant continues to push the supply chain toward greater and greater efficiency. It has well-established systems for the continuous replenishment of merchandise, vendor-managed inventory, cross-docking, strategic collaborations with producers in the manufacturing planning cycle, order and delivery, and direct shipments from manufacturers. It also strives to apply new technologies. For example, by the end of 2006, Wal-Mart had all suppliers place RFID (radio frequency identification) tags on all pallets and cases it received.[27] Its continuous use of innovations thus leads to lower inventory and operating costs, which enables Wal-Mart to keep its costs in check.

Wal-Mart furthermore has made an art of managing the flow of products and information among its suppliers, distribution centers, and individual stores through technology, the application of which allows for precision control of logistics and inventory. It's this type of innovation that has put Wal-Mart at the top of the retailing game. Not all organizations can pull this approach off so well; Wal-Mart is a unique case in which a single, very powerful firm took primary responsibility for improving performance across its own supply chain. By developing a superior supply chain management system, it has reaped the rewards of higher levels of customer service and satisfaction, lower production and transportation costs, and more productive use of its retail store space. Fundamentally, it boils down to Wal-Mart's ability to link together suppliers, manufacturers, distributors, retail outlets, and, ultimately, customers, regardless of their location. Although operational innovation isn't the only ingredient in Wal-Mart's success, it has been a crucial building block for its strong competitive position.

Questions

1. How does an individual firm like Wal-Mart "manage" a supply chain, particularly considering that supply chains include multiple firms with potentially conflicting objectives? Describe some of the conflicts that could arise in such a circumstance.

2. What are some of the ways that Wal-Mart's supply chain management system has provided it the benefits of higher levels of product availability and lower merchandise acquisition and transportation costs? Provide specific examples of each benefit.

16

QUESTIONS

■ What will make retailers successful in the future?

■ How do retailers create value for customers?

■ How has the Internet changed the way consumers shop for some products?

■ Which types of retailers are winning, and at whose expense?

Retailing

Urban Outfitters Inc. has successfully made "unique design" the anthem for all three of its retail brands: Urban Outfitters, Anthropologie, and Free People.[1] As the flagship brand, Urban Outfitters caters to young adults and college students with 10,000-square-foot stores that house edgy styles and slightly funky home décor. No two stores are exactly alike. Employees hand-write sale signs, and the locally salvaged and refurbished furniture creates a distinctive personality for each retail location. Urban Outfitters' drive for style runs from the store floor to the corporate level.

For example, an assistant buyer was surfing the Internet one day when she came across a small T-shirt operation called Classic Sports Logos (www.classicsportslogos.com). Liking the shirts, she soon made a deal with its owner to let Urban Outfitters sell Classic's faux-vintage shirts with defunct sports team logos. Urban Outfitters now carries Classic Sports Logo's T-shirts in many of its locations and on its Web site.

For slightly older, fashion-conscious women, Anthropologie sells clothing, home and garden accessories, and children's goods. The highly individualistic stores were first launched in 1992 and have grown to more than 70 retail locations. Every Anthropologie store employs two full-time representatives to check the aesthetic value of all displays and create the proper suburban character and ambience. Compared with the mandatory sweater display at the front of every The Gap store, Anthopologie's is an unusual and effective approach, and in 2003, Anthropologie accounted for 43 percent of Urban Outfitters Inc.'s total sales.

Classic Sports Logos faux-vintage t-shirts can be found at Urban Outfitters stores and on their Web site.

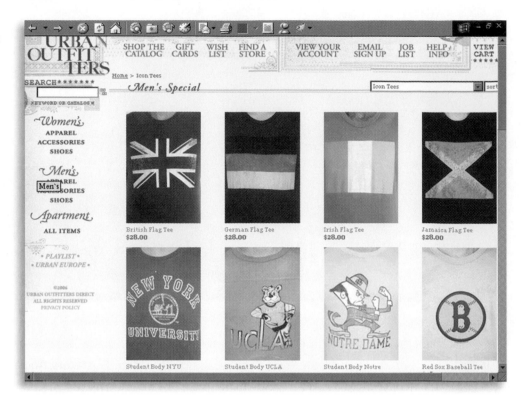

Free People is the third brand of Urban Outfitters Inc., and it targets contemporary young women. Until 2003, when the first Free People store opened, the brand sold exclusively through retail and catalog wholesalers. The store's ultimate goals are to act as a display model for department store wholesalers and increase brand awareness. Urban Outfitters now produces its own catalog, and all three brands are planning on additional store openings in the future.

■ ■ ■

Retailing sits at the end of the supply chain, where marketing meets the consumer. Regardless of how good a firm's strategy is or how great the product or service is, if it isn't available when the customer wants it, where he or she wants it, at the right price, and in the right size, color, and style, it simply won't sell. It is primarily the retailer's responsibility to make sure that these customers' expectations are fulfilled.

Retailing is defined as the set of business activities that add value to products and services sold to consumers for their personal or family use. Our definition includes products bought at stores, through catalogs, and over the Internet, as well as services like fast-food restaurants, airlines, and hotels. Some retailers claim they sell at "wholesale" prices, but if they sell to customers for their personal use, they are still retailers, regardless of how low their prices may be. **Wholesalers** (see Chapter 15), in contrast, are those firms engaged in buying, taking title to, often storing, and physically handling goods in large quantities, then reselling the goods (usually in smaller quantities) to retailers or industrial or business users.

Retailing today is changing, both in the United States and around the world. No longer do manufacturers rule many marketing channels, as they once did. Retailers like Wal-Mart, Carrefour (a French hypermarket), Home Depot, Kroger, and Metro (a German retail conglomerate)[2]—the largest retailers in the world—dictate to their suppliers what should be made, how it should be configured, when it should be delivered, and, to some extent, what it should cost. These retailers are clearly in the driver's seat.

Retailing in the aggregate is a big business. Virtually every penny you spend, except for taxes, goes to retailers. Food, rent, clothing, tuition, insurance, and haircuts are all either retail services or goods provided by retailers. Even nonprofit organizations like the Salvation Army, Goodwill Industries, and the Museum of Fine Arts have retail operations. American retail sales in 2005 were $4.1 trillion.[3] In 2002, there were more than 1 million retail firms in the United States, and at least 95 percent of those ran only one store.[4] Retailing also serves as one of the nation's largest employers—11.5% of the U.S. workforce works in retail.[5]

Even nonprofit organizations like Goodwill Industries have retail operations.

In the next section, we explain how retailing has evolved into its current structure. Then, we examine how retailers create value by implementing marketing strategies, which leads us to a discussion of how the Internet has transformed the way some retailers do business. We conclude with a discussion of the various types of retailers.

The Changing Retail Landscape

Various theories have been developed to explain the structure and evolution of the retail industry.[6] One view of how retail institutions may evolve is the Big Middle, which we depict in Exhibit 16.1.[7]

The Big Middle refers to that part of the market in which the most successful retailers compete because the biggest potential customer base resides there. A firm does not have to be in the Big Middle to be successful in the short term, and successful firms typically do not start there. Great new retailers often start out with an innovative format or products, offer a low-price advantage (usually achieved through operational excellence through great supply chain management), or both.[8] Over time, the most successful "innovative" and "low-price" competitors drift into the Big Middle. Customers become loyal to these Big Middle retailers partially because they provide them with what they need and what they are accustomed to: good customer service and excellent loyalty programs.

Although the Big Middle is a desirable goal, due to its great profit potential, it is also the most dangerous and competitive retailing space. Firms get to the Big Middle through innovations in products or formats or operational excellence that

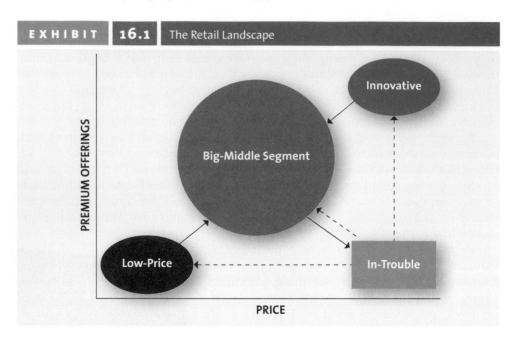

EXHIBIT 16.1 The Retail Landscape

lead to great value. But once there, newly Big Middle retailers must constantly audit, fine tune, and, in many cases, change their innovative or operational skills to maintain their position. Over time, Big Middle customers will be lured away by other retailers that offer innovative products or formats, a lower price, or both. Retailers who offer none of these are in trouble.

The retail-market structure shown in Exhibit 16.1, containing Innovative, Big Middle, and Low-Price segments, has remained constant throughout the decades, but the retail players in each segment have changed. For instance, in the 1980s, the Big Middle contained primarily traditional department stores like Macy's, as well as JCPenney and Sears. The innovative stores were Best Buy, Home Depot, and The Gap, and the low-price stores included Wal-Mart, Kmart, and Target.

Today, customers have shifted, retailers have changed, or both. Now, the Big Middle encompasses the 1980s' "low-price" leaders, Wal-Mart and Target. At the same time, Home Depot, Best Buy, and The Gap, although still innovative, have moved into the Big Middle as well. The once-dominant traditional department stores and some national chains have become secondary players.

The retailers posing a threat to the current structure by offering greater value are extreme value retailers (which we discuss later in the chapter), and innovators are generally e-retailers. It's not clear who will be the next Big Middle entrants, but the situation will certainly continue to change.

To maintain their positions in the Big Middle, retailers must understand their strengths and weaknesses, continually keep an eye on their target segments and competition, and do anything and everything they can to retain loyal customers. If they don't, someone else will.

How Do Retailers Create Value?

Imagine trying to buy a suit for a job interview without being able to visit a retailer. You would have to figure out exactly what size, color, and style of suit you wanted. Then you'd have to contact various manufacturers, whether in person, by phone, or over the Internet, and order the suit. Assuming it fit you reasonably well, you might still need to take it to a tailor to have the sleeves shortened. Then you'd have to go through the same process for a shirt or blouse, accessories, and shoes. It would not be very convenient.

Retailers like Men's Wearhouse create value by pulling it all together for you. The store offers a broad selection of suits, shirts, ties, and other accessories that it has carefully chosen in advance. You can see, touch, feel, and try on each item while in the store. You can buy one suit or shirt at a time or buy several shirts to go with your new suit. Finally, the store provides a salesperson to help you coordinate your outfit and a tailor to make the whole thing fit perfectly.

A battle for survival lies ahead for many U.S. retailers,[9] arising from a basic structural change taking place in the industry. Now and in the future, success for U.S. retailers will mean learning how to compete in a value-driven world. Remember, value doesn't just mean low price. It means getting more benefit for the money. Retailers that provide great value, like Target, Costco, and Dollar General, were once known largely as a destination for monthly stock-up trips only. But today, they have penetrated the weekly shopping routine. Consumers of all ages, nearly all income groups, and practically all segments have undertaken the "shift to value."

Two related factors explain this dramatic shift that prioritizes value. First, consumers have fundamentally changed their reference points for both price and quality, such that they have been trained to expect significantly lower prices from many retailers. In addition, as many people's lifestyles have become more casual, consumers have begun to redefine quality from "good" to just "good enough" for particular items and occasions, such as their casual weekend wardrobe. As their definition of quality changes, so does their definition of value. Second, some retailers that used to be known primarily for their low prices have outexecuted their competition and moved beyond price as their sole point of differentiation, often offering assortment, convenience, and in-store experiences comparable to those of their more upscale competitors. Today, Target is also known for its style, Costco its hidden treasures, and Dollar General its convenience.

Value retailers—those in the Big Middle—continue to improve their "shopability," providing more convenient store layouts and shopping experiences that make the task faster and easier. Value retailers are rapidly expanding, bringing more types of retailers and store locations under fire. To date, the majority of regional and national retailers have not yet felt the full force of the value retailers. But the most vulnerable, the smaller, undifferentiated regional chains, have consistently lost out to value retailers when they arrive in the local market. These regional chains will likely be absorbed by larger chains or remain stranded, with limited growth outside their core geographies.

Men's Wearhouse creates value by helping men put it all together. Their wardrobe consultants provide expert fashion advice, and their tailors make sure everything fits properly.

Target provides customers with a good value—people get a lot for what they have to pay. Target is also known for its style.

Using the Four Ps to Create Value in Retailing

Like other marketers, retailers perform important functions that increase the value of the products and services they sell to consumers. We now examine these functions, classified into the four Ps.

Product

A typical grocery store carries 20,000 to 30,000 different items; a regional department store might carry as many as 200,000. Providing the right mix of merchandise and services that satisfies the needs of the target market is one of retailers' most fundamental activities. Offering assortments gives customers choice. But to reduce transportation costs and handling, manufacturers typically ship cases of merchandise to retailers, such as cartons of mayonnaise or boxes of blue shirts. Because customers generally don't want or need to buy more than one of the same item, retailers break the cases and sell customers the smaller quantities they desire.

Manufacturers don't like to store inventory because their factories and warehouses are typically not available to customers. Consumers don't want to store more than they need because it takes up too much space. Neither group likes to store inventory that isn't being used because doing so ties up money that could be used for something else. Retailers thus provide value to both manufacturers and customers by performing the storage function, though many retailers are beginning to push their suppliers to hold the inventory until they need it. (Recall our discussion of JIT inventory systems in Chapter 15.)

You can only get I.N.C private-label apparel at Macy's.

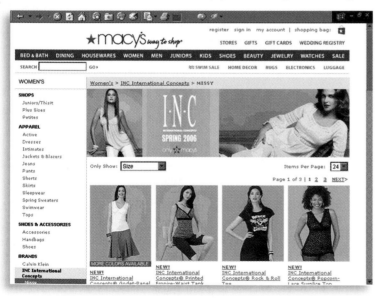

It is difficult for retailers to distinguish themselves from their competitors through the merchandise they carry because competitors can purchase and sell many of the same popular brands. So many retailers have developed **private-label brands** (also called **store brands**), which are products developed and marketed by a retailer and available only from that retailer. For example, if you want an I.N.C. dress, you have to go to Macy's. Ethical Dilemma 16.1 deals with the outsourcing challenges faced by numerous private-label retailers.

Price

Price helps define the value of both the merchandise and the service, and the general price range of a particular store helps define its image. Although both Banana Republic and Old Navy are owned by The Gap, their images could not be more different. Banana Republic prices its merchandise to attract young professionals, whereas Old Navy aims to satisfy trendy, price-sensitive consumers.

Price must always be aligned with the other elements of the retail mix: product, promotion, place, personnel, and presentation. For instance, you would not expect to pay $20 for a candy bar sold in your local grocery store, but a limited-edition candy bar, made of fine Belgian dark chocolate, packaged in a gold-plated keepsake box, sold at Neiman Marcus, might be a real steal at $20.

Ethical Dilemma 16.1 Whence to Outsource?[10]

Retailers must provide good customer value and still make a profit. Increased competition, stateside labor costs, and energy and material costs have forced many retailers to contract with manufacturers in countries with lower cost structures to make their private-label merchandise. But it is difficult to control what goes on in a factory that the firm doesn't own in a country thousands of miles away from the firm's home office. Let's consider some of the problems facing prominent U.S.-based retailers.

The Gap is leading the way in disclosing the working conditions in its suppliers' factories. In May 2004, it released a report ranking its suppliers on how well they were abiding by The Gap's code of conduct. However, the news was not as good as the company had hoped; it determined that "few factories, if any, are in full compliance all the time." This full disclosure came about after The Gap settled a class-action lawsuit, along with 21 other retailers, filed by sweatshop workers in Saipan. The Gap maintains that the lawsuit was unfair because it was grouped with other retailers, such as Target and JCPenney. Regardless, The Gap and 100 other U.S. and EU multinational companies have united with six leading anti-sweatshop groups to create a universal set of labor standards and a cheaper, more efficient inspection system to promote them. For many human rights activists, the absence from this group of some retail powerhouses, such as Wal-Mart and Target, is deeply troubling.

In a class-action lawsuit covering 100,000–500,000 workers spanning six countries, such as China, Nicaragua, and Bangladesh, Wal-Mart has been accused of overlooking substandard work conditions at suppliers' factories, such as pay withholdings, beatings, and firings based on employees' suspected union activity. Wal-Mart's logo, "Always Low Prices," spans its corporate culture, not just its signage, which means constant pressure to slash costs and prices has demanded that its suppliers lower their costs even further. But the bad publicity arising from this lawsuit has taken a toll on Wal-Mart's image. Wal-Mart retaliated with an advertising campaign that attempted to repair the damage, but critics point out that the retail giant monitors its own plants without assistance from Social Accountability International (SAI), a nonprofit international organization whose mission is to promote human rights for workers around the world,[11] or any other antisweatshop groups involved in enforcing labor standards. These critics freely express their skepticism that Wal-Mart can police itself. Despite all the controversy, Wal-Mart refuses to release its labor reports, as The Gap does, or the names of the factories in which its products are made.

Even Mickey Mouse confronts this issue. Many people associate the Walt Disney Company solely with theme parks and movies, but it also runs a gigantic private-label business. Think of all those little stuffed dolls and toys! The National Labor Committee released a report about Disney citing the below-standard working conditions in two Chinese Disney factories—conditions including lack of overtime pay, exceeding the legal overtime limit by 569 percent, and maternity rights violations. Disney responded immediately that "the appropriate actions to remediate violations found" would be taken. But in all cases, retailers must address some key questions:

- Is a U.S.-based retailer responsible for human rights violations that take place in a factory it does not own and in a country in which it does not operate?
- What can retailers do to ensure that the merchandise they purchase is made in factories that are safe and clean and that the employees of those factories are treated humanely and paid a fair wage?

Promotion

Retailers know that good promotion, both within their retail environments and throughout the mass media, can mean the difference between flat sales and a growing consumer base. Advertising in traditional media such as newspapers, magazines, and television continues to be important to get customers into the stores. Once in the store, however, retailers use displays and signs, placed at the point of purchase or in strategic areas such as the end of aisles, to inform customers and stimulate purchases of the featured products.

Store credit cards and gift cards are more subtle forms of promotion that also facilitate shopping. Retailers also might offer pricing promotions—such as coupons, rebates, in-store or online discounts, or perhaps buy-one-get-one-free offers—to attract consumers and stimulate sales. These promotions play a very important role in driving traffic to retail locations, increasing the average purchase size, and creating opportunities for repeat purchases. But retail promotions also are valuable to customers; they inform customers about what is new and available and how much it costs.

In addition to more traditional forms of promotion, many retailers are devoting more resources to their overall retail environment as a means to promote and showcase what the store has to offer. Their displays of merchandise, both in the store and in windows, have become an important form of promotion. Since many shopping activities can be rather mundane, those retailers who can distinguish themselves with unusual and exciting store atmospherics add value to the shopping experience. Bass Pro Shops Outdoor World in Lawrenceville, Georgia, for instance, offers a 30,000-gallon aquarium stocked with fish for casting demonstrations, an indoor archery range, and a 43-foot climbing wall. These features enhance customers' visual experiences, provide them with educational information,

Bass Pro Shops Outdoor World in Lawrenceville, Georgia, uses its 43-foot climbing wall as a way to promote its store.

and enhance the store's sales potential by enabling customers to "try before they buy."

A variety of factors influence whether customers will actually buy once they are in the store, some of which are quite subtle. Consumers' perceptions of value and their subsequent patronage are heavily influenced by their perceptions of the store's "look and feel." Music, color, scent, and crowding can also significantly impact the overall shopping experience.[12] Therefore, the extent to which stores offer a more pleasant shopping experience fosters a good mood, resulting in greater spending.

Personal selling and customer service representatives are also part of the overall promotional package. Retailers must provide services that make it easier to buy and use products, and retail associates, whether in the store, on the phone, or over the Internet, provide customers with information about product characteristics and availability. They can also facilitate the sale of products or services that consumers perceive as complicated, risky, or expensive, such as an air conditioning unit or a diamond ring. In some retail firms, these salesperson and customer service functions are being augmented, or even replaced, by technology used through in-store kiosks, the Internet, or self-checkout lanes.

The knowledge retailers can gain from their store personnel and customer relationship management (CRM) databases

JCPenney's just4me. com site enables petite, tall, and plus-sized women to create a virtual model and "try on" clothing that is designed to look good on them.

is key for developing loyal customers and operating loyalty programs. Traditionally, retailers treated all their customers the same way, but today, the most successful retailers concentrate on providing more value to their best customers. Using direct salesperson contact, targeted promotions, and services, they attempt to increase their **share of wallet**—the percentage of the customer's purchases made from that particular retailer—with their best customers. For instance, Internet retailers can use consumer information to provide a level of personal service that previously was available only through expensive salespeople in the best specialty stores. JCPenney's just4me.com site enables petite, tall, and plus-sized women to create a virtual model and "try on" clothing that is designed to look good on them.

Place

Retailers already have realized that convenience is a key ingredient to success, and an important aspect of this success is convenient locations.[13] As the old cliché claims, the three most important things in retailing are "location, location, location." Many customers choose stores on the basis of where they are located, which makes great locations a competitive advantage that few rivals can duplicate. For instance, once Starbucks saturates a market by opening in the best locations, it will be difficult for Peet's to break in to that same market—where would it put its stores?

In pursuit of better and better locations, retailers are experimenting with different options to reach their target markets. The United States' largest drugstore retailer, Walgreens, has begun to open free-standing stores, unconnected to other

To make their locations more convenient, Walgreens has begun to open free-standing stores, unconnected to other retailers, so the stores can offer a drive-up window for customers to pick up their prescriptions.

retailers, so the stores can offer a drive-up window for customers to pick up their prescriptions. Other stores, like Brookstone, have opened stores where they have a captive market: airports.

Internet and Electronic Retailing

In this section, we discuss the most important innovation in retailing since point-of-sale terminals began scanning UPC (universal product codes) tags in grocery stores more than 20 years ago—electronic, Internet, or simply e-retailing. Prior to 2000, some retailing experts predicted the demise of traditional stores, or **bricks-and-mortar retailers,** as they often are called. These experts argued that everyone would start buying everything over the Internet. Of course, these prophets of doom were wrong, but we have learned several important lessons about what works and what doesn't for e-retailing.

At the core of any business strategy is the ability to develop a sustainable competitive advantage.[14] Some aspects of a retailer's strategy are more sustainable than others, whether for e-retailers or bricks-and-mortar players. For instance, when retailers offer pure commodities (building supplies, office supplies) or quasi-commodities (books, CDs), competitors can easily match their offering in terms of both assortment and price.[15] Therefore, a sustainable advantage is difficult for e-retailers of pure commodities to maintain unless the perceived service associated with buying online outweighs the benefits of shopping in a store. For instance, Amazon.com enhances the shopping experience by providing reviews and making suggestions based on customers' past purchases. Furthermore, many more products are likely to be available at Amazon than in any single store. Whereas some products, such as apparel, can be difficult for customers to purchase over the Internet because of their need to touch, feel, and try on such retail offerings, Entrepreneurial Marketing 16.1 tells how Jeff Bezos started Amazon.com in 1995 and turned it into a worldwide Internet marketplace.

With the Internet's low entry costs and constantly improving search engines and shopping bots, smaller niche sources for hard-to-find products, collectibles, and hobbies can expand their **trade area**—the geographical area that contains the potential customers of a particular retailer or shopping center—from a few city blocks to the world. These retailers may have established storefronts, or they may play only in the Internet space. Senzatempo, which means "without time" in Italian, is an eclectic store for watches and home furnishings that opened in 1991 on Miami Beach. It started as a vintage watch store but has become a very diverse gallery. Originally, the furniture and other items—brought in from the personal collections of the owners, Massimo Barracca and Matthew Bain—were used simply as decoration and for the comfort of customers while they examined the watches. But when people started to ask about the furnishings, and got mad when they found out they weren't for sale, the store expanded beyond watches. In 1997, Barracca and Bain took their watches onto the Internet under the name watchcommander.com. Now they sell famous brands like Patek Philippe and Vacheron & Constantin, some of which may have been manufactured 50 to 70 years ago, to collectors all over the world.[17]

The Internet has facilitated market expansions by traditional retailers as well. Not only can a customer in Zurich shop online at jcrew.com or Barney's New York (Barneys.com), but a Staples customer can buy a computer online and pick it up at the store. Consumers who shop at **multichannel retailers**—retailers that sell merchandise in more than one retail channel (i.e., store, catalog, and Internet)—

Entrepreneurial Marketing **16.1**

Bezos Builds Amazon.com[16]

Jeffrey P. Bezos boasts an impressive resume. He graduated from Princeton *summa cum laude* in electrical engineering and computer science and is a member of Phi Beta Kappa. He was the youngest vice president of FITEL and senior vice president of D.E. Shaw & Co. But none of these resumé builders compare to his Amazon.com, one of the world's top retail Internet sites.

While driving with his wife Mackenzie from Texas to Seattle, Bezos formulated his business plan for an extensive, one-stop Internet catalog for books. Seattle was the hub of choice due to its proximity to two major book wholesalers and a well-stocked pool of computer talent. Once they arrived, Bezos transformed the garage of his rented house into an office, using doors for tables, lots of extension cords, and three Sun microstations.

In July 1995, one year after he arrived in Seattle, Bezos contacted 300 volunteer testers to purchase books. When the computer code proved viable, he asked them to spread the word. By September 1995, Amazon.com was selling $20,000 worth of books a week. Then in 1997, Amazon.com went public. Original investors were warned there was a 70 percent chance they would never see their investment again, but with his goal to dominate the retail book business, Bezos was confident in Amazon.

Bezos's vision was to create "the world's most customer-centric company. The place where people come to find and discover anything they might want to buy online." As CEO and majority insider shareholder of Amazon.com, he has worked hard to fulfill his dream. Amazon.com has diversified its offerings by partnering with clothing companies such as The Gap, Nordstrom,

Jeff Bezos, founder, CEO and chairman of Amazon.com holds the company's first sign, quickly spray-painted prior to an interview with a Japanese television station in 1995.

and Lands' End. Cobranding sites with Toys 'R' Us and Borders have spread its Web presence even further.

Through cobranding, partnering, and employing the services of Amazon.com's subsidiaries, Amazon has grown into a retail giant. Operational sites function in various countries, including the United States, France, Japan, United Kingdom, Germany, and Canada. And Jeff Bezos was the one who created the direction and the ideology that has allowed Amazon.com to spread this far, this fast, and this successfully.

typically buy more than those who shop in only one retail channel. In addition to increasing sales by expanding the current customer base and attracting new customers, an electronic channel enables retailers to collect information about what people looked at or purchased when they visited the Web site, which the retailer then can use to plan inventories, promotions, and loyalty programs. Furthermore, multichannel retailers can achieve economies of scale by coordinating their buying and logistics activities across channels and consolidating their marketing information and activities.

From customers' points of view, e-stores offer the convenience of a wide selection, available at any time, that they can view from the comfort of their home or office and that can be delivered right to their door. However, e-stores cannot always fulfill all their needs and often have more difficulty providing personalized human

The Internet has enabled firms like Senzatempo.com, also known as Watch Commander, to sell its vintage wristwatches to discerning collectors around the world.

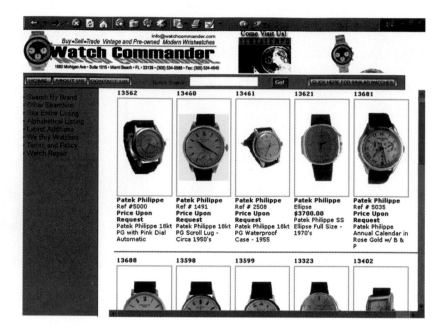

contact, prepurchase trial or experience, and low-cost after-sales service (including returns) than their bricks-and-mortar competitors. We summarize the factors that help and hinder the growth and success of e-retailing in Exhibit 16.2.

So what is in store for the future of electronic retailing? There are, and will continue to be, three major categories of e-retailers: Internet niche, large Internet-only, and traditional retailers with Internet offerings. Internet niche retailers are those like Senzatempo that offer specific items to interested customers around the world. The second group of large, Internet-only retailers is limited in number, though several quite successful stores exist in this group, such as Amazon.com

Consumers that shop at multichannel retailers—retailers that sell merchandise in more than one retail channel such as a J.Crew store (left), catalog (middle), and Internet (right))—typically buy more than those who shop in only one retail channel.

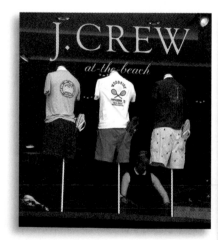

EXHIBIT 16.2	Internet Helpers and Hinderers[18]
Internet Helpers	
Product Category	Standardized and uniquely branded products easier to purchase via Internet.
Access to Information	Consumers can conveniently peruse the entire assortment and obtain product information.
Accessibility	Consumers can access an e-retailer from anywhere Internet service is available.
Convenience	The Internet is open 24 hours a day, seven days a week. Provides tremendous convenience to consumers.
Internet Hinderer	
Lack of Trial	Internet is deficient in offering pre-trial experience and evaluation.
Lack of Interpersonal Trust	Internet retailing is inherently limited in its ability to offer high-trust persuasive communication.
Lack of Instant Gratification	Usually time delay between purchase and obtaining merchandise or service.
Loss of Privacy and Security	Less perceived privacy and security concerns while shopping in an e-retailing environment.
Lack of In-Store Shopping Experience	Perceived as a less entertaining environment.
High Shipping and Handling Costs	Costs of shipping and handling add considerably to the costs of fulfillment in Internet retailing.

and Bluefly.com. Much of the positive discussion regarding the future of Internet retailing centers on the third group, the large traditional retailers that have opened Internet stores, such as Officedepot.com, JCPenney.com, Sears.com, and REI.com. These and many other well-known multichannel retailers have found that customers seem to recognize the potential of having the option to shop in stores, on the Internet, and possibly through a catalog.

Types of Retailers

In the next few sections, we examine the various types of retailers, identify some major players, and discuss some of the issues facing each type. (See Exhibit 16.3.)

Food Retailers

Not too long ago, people shopped for food primarily at traditional grocery stores. Today, however, you can buy food at drugstores, discount stores, warehouse clubs, and convenience stores. Pharmacy chains like Walgreens offer milk, bread, and even fresh fruit in some locations.[19] Wal-Mart, Kmart, and Target all provide supercenters whose product mix contains 30 to 40 percent food items. Food sales represent about 50 percent of the total sales in warehouse clubs like Costco, BJ's Wholesale Club, and Sam's Club. Convenience stores now offer more than a Slurpee and gasoline. Sheetz convenience stores, which originated in Pennsylvania, now employ three chefs so they can offer made-to-order subs, sandwiches, and salads. Some stores even include a coffee bar that allows customers to order custom coffee drinks using touchscreens similar to those used to order food.[20] And of

| EXHIBIT | 16.3 | Types of Retailers |

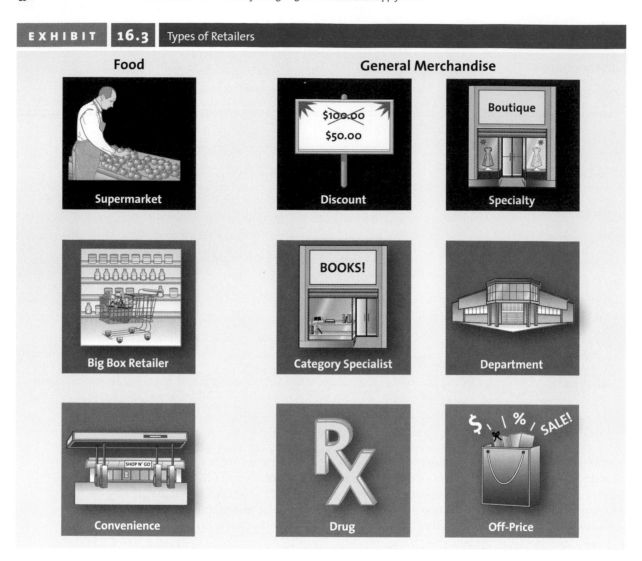

course, restaurants also compete for consumers' food dollars. The characteristics of the three major categories of food retailers—conventional supermarkets, big-box food retailers, and convenience stores—are summarized in Exhibit 16.4.

All this competition can mean trouble for traditional grocery stores. Yet some continue to thrive because they are conveniently located, make shopping easy, have fair prices, and find special products and services that are important to their customers. Adding Value 16.1 describes how Whole Foods effectively competes on selection and service.

General Merchandise Retailers

The main types of general merchandise retailers are discount stores, specialty stores, category specialists, department stores, drugstores, off-price retailers, and extreme value retailers. Many of these general merchandise retailers sell through multiple channels, such as the Internet and catalogs, as we discussed previously in this chapter.

EXHIBIT 16.4	Retailer Characteristics	
Category	**Description**	**Examples**
Conventional Supermarket	Offer groceries, meat, and produce with limited sales of nonfood items, such as health and beauty aids and general merchandise, in a self-service format.	Safeway is a popular supermarket in the western United States; Shaw's is common on the East Coast.
Big-Box Food Retailers	Come in three types: supercenters, hypermarkets, and warehouse clubs. Larger than conventional supermarkets, they carry both food and nonfood items.	Supercenters and warehouse clubs are popular in the United States, whereas hypermarkets tend to flourish in Europe and South America. Hypermarkets (Carrefour) and warehouse clubs (Costco) generally carry a greater percentage of food.
Convenience Stores	Provide a limited number of items at convenient locations in small stores with speedy checkout.	Stores such as 7-Eleven generally charge higher prices than most other types of food stores. Most convenience stores also sell gasoline, which accounts for more than 55 percent of their annual sales.

Discount Stores   A **discount store** offers a broad variety of merchandise, limited service, and low prices. Wal-Mart and Target dominate the discount store industry in the United States and vie for similar target markets. But because their competencies are slightly distinct, they both can thrive. Wal-Mart pioneered the everyday low-price concept, and its efficient operations have allowed it to offer the lowest-priced basket of merchandise in every market in which it competes—which doesn't necessarily mean that Wal-Mart has the lowest price on every item in every market. But it does try to be the lowest across a wide variety. Target, in contrast, has concentrated on merchandising. Opting for quality and style, Target is known for providing a good value without being cheap.

Specialty Stores   **Specialty stores** concentrate on a limited number of complementary merchandise categories in relatively small stores. For example, Payless ShoeSource is the largest specialty family footwear retailer in the Western Hemisphere. Payless stores feature fashionable, quality footwear and accessories for women, men, and children at affordable prices in a self-selection format. Exhibit 16.4 provides examples of other major U.S. specialty store chains.

Stores like Home Depot are known as category specialists because they offer a narrow variety but a deep assortment of merchandise.

Category Specialists   A **category specialist** offers a narrow variety but a deep assortment of merchandise. Some are like large specialty stores, such as Williams-Sonoma (home and kitchen tools) or Barnes & Noble (books); others resemble discount stores in appearance and have similar low prices but offer a more concentrated assortment of goods, such as Circuit City (consumer electronics) or Lowe's (home improvement). Most category specialists use a self-service approach, but some, like Home Depot or Men's Wearhouse, provide extensive customer service. Because category specialists offer such an extensive assortment in a particular category, they

Adding Value 16.1

Whole Foods Is at the Top of the Food Chain

Most products found at grocery stores are seen by customers as commodities, items that are somewhat substitutable. Convenient locations and price has traditionally been the two most important criteria for choosing where to shop. In the last few years, however, the grocery store business has been revolutionizing by the low prices offered by discount chains like Wal-Mart and Target and big box warehouse clubs such as Costco. Since these new large grocery retail formats can provide low prices because of their large buying power, it is difficult for traditional grocery stores to compete. To survive, they must find other strategies to sustain their profitability.

Whole Foods is one grocery chain that is positioned on service, and their high quality, somewhat unique merchandise, and not on price. Many Whole Foods enthusiasts actually refer to it as "Whole Paycheck." At Whole Foods, shoppers have access to over 700 varieties of wine and a bakery that has almost everything covered in chocolate, called the "Chocolate Enrobing Station."[21] They offer high quality organic produce, natural meat, and extensive selection of unique and ethnic foods from around the world.

Partially due to Whole Foods' success, other more traditional grocery chains are adding extensive organic food sections. But Whole Foods isn't worried, at least not now. John Mackey, chairman and CEO of Whole Foods says, "[Wal-Mart] is going to pick up a few hundred SKUs, but we've got 30,000 of them."[22] They are providing luxury in groceries similar to Apple Inc. or Starbucks.

Not only does it offer a wide assortment of great products, but it provides the customer service to warrant its relatively higher prices. Its employees have a thorough understanding of the products, which creates additional value for the customer. Whole Foods has become a lifestyle choice for its thousands of loyal customers. One doesn't just stop there to pick up a gallon of milk. Instead, they browse the beautiful displays of products, and experience the wholeness of environmentally friendly products.

---

can so overwhelm the category that other retailers have difficulty competing; in these cases, the specialists are frequently called **category killers.**

Department Stores   **Department stores** refer to those retailers that carry many different types of merchandise (broad variety) and lots of items within each type (deep assortment), offer some customer services, and are organized into separate departments to display their merchandise. Department stores often resemble a collection of specialty shops, including women's, men's, and children's clothing and accessories; home furnishings and furniture; and kitchenwares and small appliances.

The largest department store chains in the United States are JCPenney, Federated Department Stores (Macy's and Bloomingdale's), and Sears Holding Company (Sears and Kmart). Department store chains are very diverse. Some, like Sears, JCPenney, and Kohl's, carry relatively inexpensive products and compete closely with discount stores, whereas others, like Neiman Marcus, Bloomingdale's, and Saks Fifth Avenue, sell expensive, exclusive merchandise and compete with high-end specialty store chains. Macy's tends to fall somewhere in the middle.

Department stores have lost market share to specialty stores, discount stores, and category specialists in recent years. They seem to have gotten stuck in the middle, between those retailers that provide a better value at lower prices and those that offer more complete and fashionable assortments and better customer service, according to consumer perceptions. But they are fighting back with a vengeance. Several stores have begun placing a greater emphasis on high-fashion, private-label merchandise than in the past.

EXHIBIT 16.5	Specialty Store Retailers	
Accessories	**Electronics/Software/Gifts**	**Optical**
Claire's	Radio Shack	LensCrafters
	Electronics Boutique	Pearle Vision
	Sharper Image	
Apparel	**Food Supplements**	**Shoes**
The Gap	GNC	Foot Locker
The Limited		Payless Shoe Source
Charming Shoppes		Famous Footwear
Abercrombie & Fitch	**Furniture**	
JoAnn Stores	Ethan Allen	
Talbots	Haverty	
Auto Parts	**Jewelry**	**Sporting Goods**
AutoZone	Zales	Hibbett
Pep Boys	Tiffany	Sports Authority

Macy's private brand, INC, has proven to be the fastest growing brand in all its stores and its carries some big names like BCBG and Polo Jeans Co.[23] INC is positioned to grow even more as Macy's moves into former department store locations as a result of Federated's buyout of May Department Stores. Additionally, Macy's is continually reevaluating its customers' shopping experiences and innovating to improve it. It has wider aisles to accommodate baby carriages and the dressing rooms are larger with better lighting. Macy's is also increasing shipment frequency to provide a continuous flow of new merchandise. The more comfortable atmosphere and continually changing product selection will encourage customers to return and spend, which gives Macy's a leg to stand on in a world of specialty stores and category specialists.

Drugstores   Drugstores are specialty stores that concentrate on health and personal grooming merchandise, though pharmaceuticals often represent more than 60 percent of their sales. The largest drugstore chains in the United States—CVS, Walgreens, and Rite Aid[24]—face a major challenge because of the low margins they earn on prescription drugs; health insurance companies and government programs pay most of the cost of many prescriptions, and the health insurance companies negotiate substantially lower prices with drugstores. These drugstores therefore are attempting to make up for their lost profits on prescriptions by concentrating their efforts on nonpharmaceutical products. General merchandise has long been a staple in drugstores, but food, and particularly fresh food like milk and fruit, are relatively new additions to their assortment.[25]

Off-Price Retailers   Off-price retailers offer an inconsistent assortment of merchandise at relatively low prices. They typically buy from manufacturers or other retailers with excess inventory or at the end of a season for one-fifth to one-fourth the original wholesale price. Because of the way these retailers buy, customers can never be confident that the same type of merchandise will be in stock each time they visit the store. Different bargains also will be available on each visit. To improve their offerings' consistency, some off-price retailers complement their opportunistically bought merchandise with merchandise purchased at regular wholesale prices.

Adding Value 16.2

What Kind of Retailer Is Save-A-Lot?[26]

Save-A-Lot, which claims that its food prices are as much as 40 percent lower than those of conventional supermarkets, recently added general merchandise to its stores. This wholly owned subsidiary of the grocery retailer SUPERVALU is enjoying explosive growth, high inventory turnovers, and low operating costs, all at once.

Although Save-A-Lot, which has increased its selling space by about 10 percent per year, operates more than 1,200 stores across the country, analysts think that number could easily double or triple in just a few more years. Behind Wal-Mart Supercenters, it is the fastest growing retail chain in the United States. Save-A-Lot also is starting to roll out "combo" stores that sell both groceries and fixed-price general merchandise; analysts believe these stores will generate the bulk of SUPERVALU's sales and profit growth for the foreseeable future.

SUPERVALU's focus on maintaining a limited assortment has proven tremendously successful for food retailers in other countries as well. Save-A-Lot combines the pricing power and efficiency of a Wal-Mart Supercenter with the small-store environment of a convenience store. Each store averages about 12,000 to 15,000 square feet, whereas conventional supermarkets range from 50,000 to 100,000 square feet.

Is Save-A-Lot a grocery store, a general merchandise store, or an extreme value retailer?

Save-A-Lot carries about 1,250 items but only the best selling brands of each category. Its limited assortment strategy allows the company to sell products quickly and avoid getting stuck with excess inventory that eats into its profit margins. Furthermore, though customers still bag their own purchases, SUPERVALU has invested millions of dollars into sprucing up existing Save-A-Lot stores. And Save-A-Lot has launched its first national branding campaign, including television and print ads and a new logo.

In addition to their low prices, the key to off-price retailers' success is the treasure hunt environment they create. Similar to wholesale clubs like Costco, they are known for selling unexpected items at very low prices. For instance, Big Lots sells a seven-piece, solid-wood, sleigh bedroom set for $999, which is approximately one-fourth of what it would cost from a traditional furniture store.[27]

Extreme value retailers are a subset of off-price retailers and one of the fastest growing retailing segments. **Extreme value retailers** are general merchandise discount stores found in lower-income urban or rural areas. They are much smaller than traditional discount stores, usually less than 9,000 square feet. The largest are Dollar General and Family Dollar Stores,[28] but for an interesting amalgam of an off-price and a food retailer, see Adding Value 16.2, which discusses the example of Save-A-Lot.

Summing Up

1. **What will make retailers successful in the future?**

   Retailers that become market leaders start out by being very innovative, providing a low price, or both. Over time, they come to occupy the Big Middle, the part of the market that provides value for the majority of consumers. If these retailers are able to maintain their innovative or value edge, retain loyal customers, and stay a step ahead of their competition, they'll remain in the Big Middle. Otherwise, they will simply falter and fade away. The next wave of value-oriented retailers may be extreme value retailers and/or innovative entrants coming from specialty and e-retailing.

2. **How do retailers create value for customers?**

   Retailers provide customers with a choice of merchandise in the quantities they want to buy and services that facilitate the sale and use of those products. They offer convenient locations to shop and an atmosphere and presentation that enhance the shopping experience. Promotions, both in the store and outside, provide customers with information. Finally, price provides signals to the customer about the image of the store, its merchandise, and its services.

3. **How has the Internet changed the way consumers shop for some products?**

   Customers feel particularly comfortable buying commodities and branded merchandise over the Internet because they can easily judge quality and compare prices. Other products that require consumers to touch or feel them are more difficult. The Internet has expanded the market for many retailers, from small, specialty niche retailers to large global retailers. The group of retailers that appears to be benefiting the most from the Internet channels is multichannel retailers, who can better determine what their customers want and provide them with convenient shopping options.

4. **Which types of retailers are winning, and at whose expense?**

   Traditional food retailers are facing stiff competition from all sides—supercenters, drugstores, convenience stores, and restaurants. Some are successfully meeting this competition by honing their assortments, offering specialized services, and taking advantage of their great locations. Discount stores are being dominated by Wal-Mart and Target. Many category specialists continue to be strong and innovative, though some of these also have had to compete head-to-head with Wal-Mart on price. Department stores continue to maintain market share, despite the strong competition from virtually every other form of general merchandise retailer. Many are creating strong private-label merchandise programs and experimenting with various exciting strategies to help retain their customers. Because of their smaller size and convenient locations, drugstores are stealing market share from food and convenience stores. Finally, due to customers' increasing desire for value, off-price retailers have become one of the fastest growing segments in retailing.

Key Terms

- big-box food retailer, 452
- bricks-and-mortar retailer, 448
- category killer, 454
- category specialist, 453
- convenience store, 452
- conventional supermarket, 452
- department store, 454
- discount store, 453
- drugstore, 455
- extreme value retailer, 456
- general merchandise retailer, 452
- multichannel retailers, 448
- off-price retailer, 455
- private-label brands, 444
- retailing, 440
- share of wallet, 447
- specialty store, 453
- store brands, 444
- trade area, 448
- wholesaler, 441

Marketing Applications

1. How have retail institutions evolved over time according to the Big Middle concept? Provide an example of a specific retailer that operates within each of the categories identified in the model.

2. Why don't traditional department stores have the same strong appeal to American consumers that they once enjoyed during their heyday in the last half of the twentieth century? Discuss which types of retailers are now competing with department stores.

3. What do retailers do to increase the value of products and services for consumers? Discuss the extent to which bricks-and-mortar retailers are threatened by Internet-only retailers with regard to these factors.

4. Some argue that retailers can be eliminated from the distribution channel because they only add costs to the final product without creating any value-added services in the process. Do you agree with this perspective? Is it likely that consumers will make most purchases directly from manufacturers in the near future? Provide justification for your answers.

5. Many years ago, the corporations that sold gasoline made the strategic move to include a substantial offering of food items. Today, it is rare to find a gas station that does not sell food items. Into which category of food retailer did these service stations fall? Do you think this was a prudent strategic direction for these corporations? Explain your logic.

6. What is a trade area? What has happened to the trade area for small and medium-sized retailers since the emergence of widespread usage of the Internet as a channel for serving current and potential customers?

7. Identify three categories of products especially suited for sale on the Internet. Identify three categories that are not currently suitable for sale on the Internet. Justify your choices.

8. How does Staples.com or Officedepot.com provide value to their customers beyond the physical products that they sell? Identify some of the ways that the companies have overcome the inhibitors to successful Internet retailing.

9. What options do you have for purchasing food in your town? Under what circumstances would you shop at each option? What about a family with two young children?

10. You can purchase apparel at a discount store, specialty store, category specialist, off-price retailer, department store, or Internet-only store. From which of these types of stores do you shop? Explain why you prefer one type over another.

11. Suppose you are the confectionary buyer for a regional chain of grocery stores. The store policy is to charge a "substantial" slotting fee for the placement of new items. Slotting fees were originally designed to cover the costs of placing new products on the shelves, such as adjustments to computer systems and realignment of warehouse and store space. Over the years, these fees have become larger, and they are now a significant source of revenue for the chain. A local minority-owned manufacturer of a popular brand of specialty candy would like to sell to your chain, but claims that the slotting fee is too high and does not reflect the real cost of adding their candy. Discuss the ethical implications of such a policy. What should the chain do?

Net Savvy

1. Companies like L.L.Bean have expanded their offerings beyond their original channels to sell through multiple channels. Visit the company's Web site (www.llbean.com) and determine in which channels it operates (Web, stores, and/or catalog). Discuss the advantages of using a multichannel strategy over a single channel strategy.

2. Using either your own experience or that of a friend, select a familiar Internet Web site that engages in some form of retailing. Evaluate that Web site in terms of its helpers and hinderers (Exhibit 16.2), and summarize the extent to which you think the site is successful in sustaining a retailing Web presence.

STAPLES, INC.[29]

Staples operates in the highly competitive, $240 billion office products market, which historically has been served by traditional office products retailers. These traditional retailers purchase a significant portion of their merchandise from wholesalers that purchase merchandise from manufacturers. Traditional office supply retailers often employ commissioned salespeople who use the wholesaler's catalog to present their business customers with products to select.

But due to their ability to sell at lower prices, mass merchandisers, warehouse clubs, and discount retailers have taken market share away from these traditional retailers, and the industry has grown substantially in the past two decades with the emergence of office supply superstores like Staples, Office Depot, and Office Max. In addition, mail order firms, contract stationery businesses, electronic commerce wholesalers, and manufacturers that sell directly to the consumer all compete for sales. However, though the office products business has changed in recent years, a significant portion of the market is still served by small retailers.

Regardless, the superstores have dramatically changed the landscape of the office supply industry. First, they greatly expanded the use of the retail store format to distribute office supply products, capitalizing in part on the significant increase in the number of home offices. Prior to the mid-1980s, office supply customers primarily placed their orders through commissioned salespeople. Second, an even more recent change in this industry has been the greater use of the Internet for ordering office supply products. These changes have resulted in a very price-competitive market for office supplies, dominated by a small number of providers.

Company Background

Originally opened in 1986 by executive-turned-entrepreneur Tom Stemberg, Staples sales exceeded $16 billion in 2005.[30] Staples has been credited with pioneering the high-volume office products superstore concept. By evolving its original mission of slashing the costs and eliminating the hassles of running an office, to making it easy to buy office products, Staples has become the world's largest office products company.

To distinguish itself in this competitive industry, Staples strives to provide a unique shopping experience to customers in all its market segments. Central to maintaining customer satisfaction is developing strong customer relationship skills and broad knowledge about office products in all associates hired by the company. Therefore, Staples includes formal training as an integral part of the development of its associates. Another truly important aspect of customer service is the availability of merchandise. In the office supply industry, customers have very specific needs, such as finding an ink cartridge for a particular printer, and if the store is out of stock of a needed item, the customer may never come back.

Staples uses various channels of distribution to address the needs of its different segments. Smaller businesses are generally served by a combination of retail stores, catalog, and the Internet. Retail operations focus on serving the needs of consumers and small businesses, whereas the catalog and Internet operations focus on customers who need delivery of their office products and other specialized services. The typical Staples retail store has approximately 7,000 stockkeeping units (SKUs), but Staples.com offers about 45,000 SKUs.

Staples believes that the Internet channel has helped it increase its sales while reducing its overhead costs. It has developed three standalone Web sites: Staples.com, a public Web site; Quill.com, an e-commerce site for medium-sized businesses; and StaplesLink.com, a secure, customized, e-commerce procurement Web site for large customers with contracts with Staples. In addition, the company has placed Staples.com kiosks in its stores so that customers can make purchases of any product, even if they are not stocked in the store. Customers can pay for these purchases at the register or through Staples.com and have the product delivered to their home or business. This multichannel approach allows Staples to increase its productivity by stocking only fast-moving items in stores but not sacrificing product availability.

Multichannel Integration

Staples' overall goal has been to become the leading office products and service provider by combining its existing experience, extensive distribution infrastructure, and customer service expertise with Web-based information technology. As a result, the integration of different channels of distribution into one seamless customer experience has been of particular interest to the company. Staples, like many other multichannel retailers, has found that many customers use multiple channels to make their Staples purchases and that sales increase when customers use more than one channel (customers that shop two channels spend twice as much as a single-channel shopper; a tri-channel shopper spends about three times as much as a single-channel shopper). Therefore, the greater the number of channels a particular customer shops, the greater the overall expenditure he or she is likely to make.

Staples faces several challenges in integrating its channels of distribution, most of which are related to its Internet channel. First, it must consider the extent to which the Internet may cannibalize its retail store sales. The most attractive aspect of the Internet is its potential to attract new customers and sell more to existing customers. But if overall sales are flat, that is, if online retailing only converts retail store sales to Internet sales, Staples suffers increased overhead costs and poorer overall productivity. Second, Staples must be concerned about the stock position of its retail stores compared with that of alternative channels. Since a retail store cannot carry as much merchandise as the Internet channel, the challenge is keeping an appropriate balance between minimizing stockouts and avoiding the proliferation of too many SKUs in the retail stores.

Questions

1. Assess the extent to which Staples has developed a successful multichannel strategy. What factors have contributed to its success?

2. What are the advantages and disadvantages of using kiosks as a part of its approach?

3. How should Staples assess which SKUs to keep in its stores?

17

QUESTIONS

- How do customers perceive marketing communications?

- Why are some media channels growing while others are shrinking?

- How should firms plan for and measure integrated marketing communications (IMC) success?

- Why are some governmental agencies and consumer groups concerned about certain innovative IMC strategies?

SECTION SEVEN

Value Communication

Integrated Marketing Communications

How does a car company known for extremely safe but somewhat boring cars introduce a sporty new performance model?[1] This was the problem facing Volvo when it introduced the S60. Volvo's marketing agency, Euro RSCG MVBMS, had to come up with an innovative way to engage consumers and force them to question their own assumptions about Volvo.

The agency found inspiration in an unlikely place: interactive television polls. More and more, television audiences, especially those who view sports programs, are being asked to share their opinions on a variety of issues by calling in or logging on to a Web site during the program. On the basis of its prior success with interactive polls during sporting events, the agency determined to launch the Volvo campaign during the NCAA championship basketball tournament. Therefore, it designed commercials, aired during games, to grab consumers' attention and build brand awareness; the ads also ended with basketball-themed questions (e.g., "Which would you rather have, a good offense or a good defense?") and prompted viewers to visit and answer questions on a dedicated Web site. Once viewers had logged on to the site, the agency would try to get them to agree to continue the conversation by offering the chance to enter two sweepstakes—one for the new S60 and one for tickets to the following year's NCAA tournament—in exchange for answering a few questions about their current and future car buying plans. The goal was to change people's assumptions; the sweepstakes entries allowed consumers to continue the conversation if they so desired by opting in to receive e-mail and other communications from Volvo.

VOLVO S60

An integrated marketing communication program that includes television advertising, direct marketing, public relations, customer relationship management (CRM), Web sites, mobile phones, and other new communication technologies seeks to convince consumers that the new Volvo S60 is both safe and sporty.

The campaign required a mix of traditional and nontraditional promotional tools. The integrated marketing communication plan that resulted included television advertising, direct marketing, public relations, customer relationship management (CRM), Web sites, mobile phones, and other new communication technologies. The central positioning for the campaign, regardless of the media format, was that Volvo could be both safe and sporty.

The results from combining these promotional elements into one integrated marketing campaign were impressive. Compared with previous campaigns, Volvo determined that the S60 campaign was more successful at both getting consumers to opt in for further marketing communications and increasing brand awareness and purchase intentions.

The campaign's success thus demonstrates that each element of an integrated marketing communication (IMC) strategy must have a well-defined purpose and support and extend the message delivered by all the other elements. In Volvo's case, these various tools helped create awareness and interest about both the performance and the safety aspects of the S60—just as the company had hoped.

■ ■ ■

Throughout this book, we have focused our attention on how firms create value by developing products and services. In Chapters 10, 11, and 12, we also focused on how they deliver value to customers. However, consumers are not likely to come flocking to new products and services unless they are aware of them. Therefore, marketers must consider how to communicate the value of a new product and/or service—or more specifically, the value proposition—to the target market. The Volvo S60 example illustrates how a firm can develop a communication strategy to demonstrate the value of its product, but let's begin our subsequent consideration by examining what IMC is, how it has developed, and how it contributes to value creation.

Integrated marketing communications (IMC) represents the Promotion P of the four Ps. It encompasses a variety of communication disciplines—general advertising, personal selling, sales promotion, public relations, direct marketing, and electronic media—in combination to provide clarity, consistency, and maximum communicative impact.[2] Rather than consisting of separated marketing communication elements with no unified control, IMC programs regard each of the firm's marketing communications elements as part of a whole, each of which offers a different means to connect with the target audience. This integration of

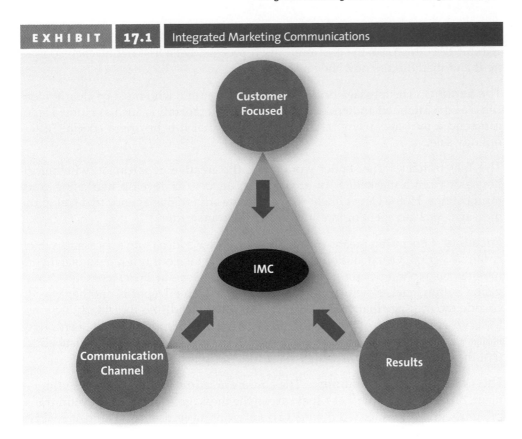

elements provides the firm with the best means to reach the target audience with the desired message, and it enhances the value story by offering a clear and consistent message.

There are three elements in any IMC strategy: the consumer, the channels through which the message is communicated, and the evaluation of the results of the communication, as we depict in Exhibit 17.1. This chapter is organized around these three elements. In the first section, the focus is on *consumers*, so we examine how consumers receive communications, whether via media or other methods, as well as how the delivery of that communication affects a message's form and contents. The second section examines the various *communication channels* that make up the components of IMC and how each is used in an overall IMC strategy. The third section considers how the level of complexity in IMC strategies leads marketers to design new ways to measure the *results* of IMC campaigns. The chapter concludes with a discussion of some legal and ethical issues arising from the use of these new forms of marketing communications.

Communicating with Consumers

As the number of communication media has increased, the task of understanding how best to reach target consumers has become far more complex. In this section, we examine a model that describes how communications go from the firm to the consumer and the factors that affect the way the consumer perceives the message. Then we look at how marketing communications influence consumers—from making them aware that a product or service exists to moving them to buy.

The Communication Process

Exhibit 17.2 illustrates the communication process. Let's first define each component and then discuss how they interact.

The Sender   The message originates from the **sender,** who must be clearly identified to the intended audience. For instance, an organization such as Home Depot can send a message, using its distinctive logo, that it is having a special "after-holiday sale."

The Transmitter   The sender works with the creative department, whether in-house or from a marketing (or advertising) agency, to develop marketing communications. Home Depot likely works with its advertising agency to develop the message. Such an agent or intermediary is the **transmitter.**

Encoding   **Encoding** means converting the sender's ideas into a message, which could be verbal, visual, or both. Home Depot may take out full-page ads in every major newspaper proclaiming: "Amazing Holiday Deals at 25 Percent Off!" A television commercial showing people shopping at Home Depot is another way to encode the message that "there are great deals to be had." As the old saying goes, a picture can be worth a thousand words. But the most important facet of encoding is not what is sent but rather what is received. Home Depot shoppers must believe that the sale is substantial enough to warrant a trip to a store.

The Communication Channel   The **communication channel** is the medium—print, broadcast, the Internet—that carries the message. Home Depot could transmit through television, radio, and various print advertisements, and it realizes that the media chosen must be appropriate to connect itself (the sender) with its desired recipient. So Home Depot might advertise on HGTV and in *Better Homes and Gardens.*

The Receiver   The **receiver** is the person who reads, hears, or sees and processes the information contained in the message and/or advertisement. The sender, of

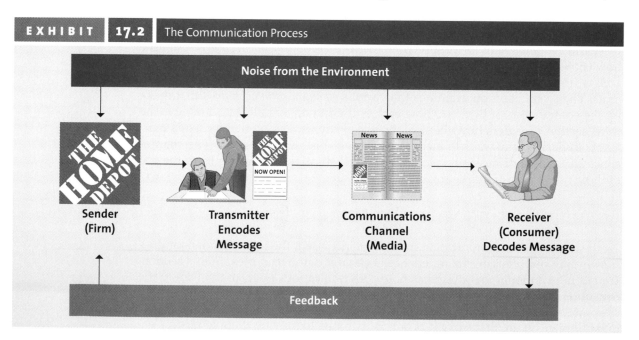

EXHIBIT **17.2** The Communication Process

Noise from the Environment

Sender (Firm)

Transmitter Encodes Message

Communications Channel (Media)

Receiver (Consumer) Decodes Message

Feedback

course, hopes that the person receiving it will be the one for whom it was originally intended. For example, Home Depot wants its message received and decoded properly by people who are likely to shop in its stores. **Decoding** refers to the process by which the receiver interprets the sender's message.

Which component of the communication process exemplifies this Home Depot ad?

Noise   **Noise** is any interference that stems from competing messages, a lack of clarity in the message, or a flaw in the medium, and it poses a problem for all communication channels. Home Depot may choose to advertise in newspapers that its target market doesn't read, which means the rate at which the message is received by those to whom it has relevance has been slowed considerably. As we have already defined, encoding is what the sender intends to say, and decoding is what the receiver hears. If there is a difference between them, it is probably due to noise.

Feedback Loop   The **feedback loop** allows the receiver to communicate with the sender and thereby informs the sender whether the message was received and decoded properly. Feedback can take many forms: a customer's purchase of the item, a complaint or compliment, the redemption of a coupon or rebate, and so forth. If Home Depot observes an increase in store traffic and sales, its managers know that their intended audience received the message and understood that there were great after-holiday bargains to be found in the store.

How Consumers Perceive Communication

The actual communication process is not as simple as the model in Exhibit 17.2 implies. Each receiver may interpret the sender's message differently, and senders often adjust their message according to the medium used and the receivers' level of knowledge about the product or service.

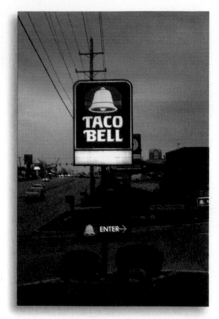

Receivers decode messages differently. What does the Taco Bell sign mean to you?

Receivers Decode Messages Differently   Each receiver decodes a message in his or her own way, which is not necessarily the way the sender intended. Different people shown the same message will often take radically different meanings from it. For example, what does the image on the left convey to you?

If you are a user of this brand, it may convey satisfaction. If you recently went on a diet and gave up your favorite Mexican food, it may convey dismay or a sense of loss. If you have chosen to be a non-user, it may convey some disgust. If you are a recently terminated employee, it may convey anger. The sender has little, if any, control over what meaning any individual receiver will take from the message.[3]

Senders Adjust Messages According to the Medium and Receivers' Traits   Different media communicate in very different ways. So marketers make adjustments to their messages and media depending on whether they want to communicate with suppliers, shareholders, customers, or the general public.[4] Kellogg's would not, for instance, send the same message to its shareholders in a targeted e-mail as it would to its consumers on Saturday morning TV.

The AIDA Model

Clearly, IMC is not a straightforward process. After being exposed to a marketing communication, consumers go through several steps before actually buying or taking some other action. There is not always a direct link between a particular marketing communication and a consumer's purchase.

To create effective IMC programs, marketers must understand how marketing communications work. Generally, marketing communications move consumers stepwise through a series of mental stages, for which there are several models. The most common is the **AIDA model** (Exhibit 17.3),[5] which suggests that **A**wareness leads to **I**nterests, which lead to **D**esire, which leads to **A**ction. At each stage, the

Senders must adjust messages according to the receivers' traits. Kellogg's, for instance, uses different ads to target kids (left) and its retail customers (right).

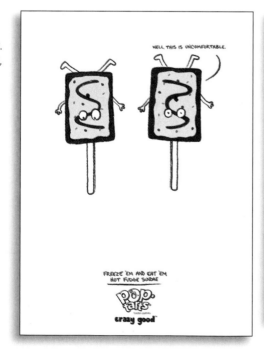

EXHIBIT **17.3** The AIDA Model

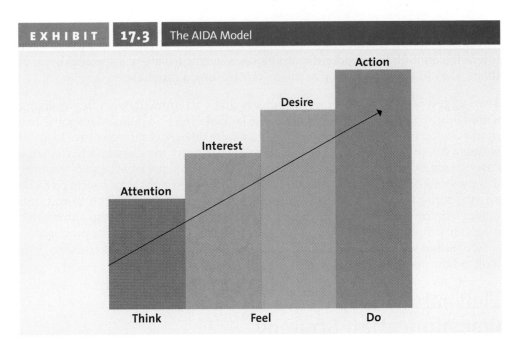

consumer makes judgments about whether to take the next step in the process. Customers actually have three types of responses, so the AIDA model is also known as the "think, feel, do" model. In making a purchase decision, consumers go through each of the AIDA steps to some degree, but the steps may not always follow the AIDA order. For instance, during an impulse purchase, a consumer may "feel" and "do" before he or she "thinks."

Awareness   Even the best marketing communication can be wasted if the sender doesn't gain the attention of the consumer first. When Ford introduced the redesigned F-150 truck, its first step was to make consumers aware of the new design. So the company placed television ads, radio spots, and Internet and print advertising to reach its desired target audience. This multichannel approach increased the likelihood that the message would be received because even if one of the communication channels were missed or ignored, odds remain good that another would catch the potential customer's attention.

Interest   Once the consumer is aware that the company or product exists, communication must work to increase his or her interest level. It isn't enough to let people know that the product exists; consumers must be persuaded that it is a product worth investigating. Marketers do so by ensuring that the ad's message includes attributes that are of interest to the target audience. To appeal to a customer who likes the great outdoors, Ford's ads for the F-150 show scenes of it performing under extraordinary circumstances. Through these communications, consumers' interest must be piqued enough that they do something about it.

Desire   After the firm has piqued the interest of its target market, the goal of subsequent IMC messages should move the consumer from "I like it" to "I want it." For instance, Ford might devise a communication strategy that offers special financing to make the F-150 appear to be a particularly good deal or highlight special options that make the truck seem unique.

Action   The ultimate goal of any marketing communication is to drive the receiver to action. If the message has caught consumers' attention and made them interested enough to consider the product as a means to satisfy a specific desire of theirs, they likely will act on that interest by making a purchase.

The Lagged Effect   Sometimes consumers don't act immediately after receiving a marketing communication because of the **lagged effect**—a delayed response to a marketing communication campaign. It generally takes several exposures to an ad before a consumer fully processes its message.[6] In turn, measuring the effect of a current campaign becomes more difficult because of the possible lagged response to a previous one.[7] Suppose you purchased a Ford F-150 right after hearing a radio ad sponsored by a local dealer. The radio ad may have pushed you to buy, but other communications from Ford, such as television ads and articles in automotive magazines that you saw weeks earlier, probably also influenced your purchase.

Now that we've examined various aspects of the communication process, let's look at how specific media are used in an IMC program.

Elements of an Integrated Marketing Communication Strategy

For any communications campaign to succeed, the firm must deliver the right message to the right audience through the right media. Reaching the right audience is becoming more difficult, however, as the media environment grows more complicated.

Advances in technology have led to satellite radio, wireless technology, pop-up and banner ads on Web sites, brand-sponsored Web sites, PDA messaging, and text messaging, all of which vie for consumers' attention. Print media have also grown and become more specialized. In 1970, 6,690 magazines were published in the United States; today, there are 15,000 magazines, 11,000 journals, 9,000 newspapers, 12,000 newsletters, and 10,000 catalogs.[8]

This proliferation of media has led many firms to shift their promotional dollars from advertising to direct marketing, Web site development, product placements, and other forms of promotion in search of the best way to deliver messages to their target audiences. Media fragmentation has also occurred on television. Networks are dedicated to certain types of sports (Outdoor Life Network, Golf Channel), children (Nickelodeon), ethnic minorities (Black Family Channel, Univision), and classic movies (AMC, Turner Classic Movies). Each of these channels allows IMC planners to target their desired audience narrowly. Entrepreneurial Marketing 17.1 describes a television channel just for women.

We now examine the individual elements of IMC and the way each contributes to a successful IMC campaign (see Exhibit 17.4). Some elements—advertising, personal selling, and sales promotion—appear in detail in subsequent chapters; we discuss them only briefly here.

Advertising

Perhaps the most visible of the IMC components, **advertising** is a paid form of communication from an identifiable source, delivered through a communication channel, and designed to persuade the receiver to take some action, now or in the future.[9] In Chapter 18, we discuss the purpose of advertising and its various types, but for now, we note that advertising is extremely effective for

Entrepreneurial Marketing 17.1

Oxygen: The Network for Women[10]

It is difficult to determine what kind of television programs appeal to today's woman, but even after it identifies such promising prospects, a network still faces a key challenge: convincing her to take time out of her jam-packed schedule to sit and watch. The founders of the Oxygen network Geraldine Laybourne, who had built Nickelodeon; Oprah Winfrey, the talk show host and founder of HARPO Productions; and Marcy Carsey, Tom Werner, and Caryn Mandabach, the owners of vastly successful independent television companies, knew there was definitely an unmet need in the marketplace for a "network for women." But starting a new network and then convincing modern women to tune in represented an enormous undertaking.

The Oxygen network remained in the red for the first five years after it began in 1998. To reverse this trend, executives began to pay greater attention to the target market and restructure programming toward more entertainment. Women indicated that they wanted fun, but fun and entertainment that acknowledged their intelligence and modern responsibilities—family, careers, and so forth. In support of this shift, Oxygen launched an advertising campaign to promote its individual content and spirit and feature network stars rather than pop icons like Madonna, as its previous advertising had done.

As a form of media outlet itself, Oxygen televises its own ads and maintains an On-Air Promotion department to ensure it communicates a consistent message in all its televised ads. It also relies on various public relations efforts that appeal to its target audience. The network-sponsored Mentors' Walk, for example, enables young female viewers to register to partner with an experienced female mentor in their selected career field, with whom they can discuss their concerns and get advice during a stroll through New York's Central Park. The network's Web site communicates the same message: support of young, professional women through entertainment, programming, sweepstakes contests, archived content, and games.

After its initial difficulties, the network achieved access to more than 56 million cable households. It airs

Oxygen founders from left to right: Marcy Carsey, Oprah Winfrey, Geraldine Laybourne, and Caryn Mandabach.

more original programming than any other network targeted at women. The appeal that Oxygen consistently attempts to communicate in all its advertising and promotional material is that it gives women "a place to have fun that respects their intelligence and doesn't take itself too seriously," according to CEO Geraldine Laybourne. With this approach, Laybourne has led her company to sales of more than $46.5 million annually.

EXHIBIT 17.4 Integrated Marketing Communications

creating awareness of a product or service and generating interest. Mass advertising can entice consumers into a conversation with marketers, just as it did for the Volvo S60. However, advertising must break through the clutter of other messages to reach its intended audience. And as marketers attempt to find ways to reach their target audiences, advertising has become increasingly pervasive. Not so long ago, the majority of many firms' promotional budgets was spent on advertising. Since the 1990s, however, advertising's share of total promotional dollars has fallen as the budgets for other forms of sales promotion, especially direct marketing, have increased, resulting in a more balanced approach to the use of marketing communications elements.

Personal Selling

Personal selling is the two-way flow of communication between a buyer and a seller that is designed to influence the buyer's purchase decision. Personal selling can take place in various settings: face-to-face, video teleconferencing, on the telephone, or over the Internet. Although consumers don't often interact with professional salespeople, personal selling represents an important component of many IMC programs, especially in business-to-business (B2B) settings.

The cost of communicating directly with a potential customer is quite high compared with other forms of promotion, but it is simply the best and most efficient way to sell certain products and services. Customers can buy many products and services without the help of a salesperson, but salespeople simplify the buying process by providing information and services that save customers time and effort. In many cases, sales representatives add significant value, which makes the added expense of employing them worthwhile. We devote Chapter 19 to personal selling and sales management.

Sales Promotions

Sales promotions are special incentives or excitement-building programs that encourage the purchase of a product or service, such as coupons, rebates, contests, free samples, and point-of-purchase displays. Marketers typically design these incentives for use in conjunction with other advertising or personal selling programs. Many sales promotions, like free samples or point-of-purchase displays, are designed to build short-term sales, though others, like contests and sweepstakes, have become integral components of firms' CRM programs as means to build customer loyalty. We discuss such sales promotions in Chapter 18.

Direct Marketing

The component of IMC that has received the greatest increase in aggregate spending recently is **direct marketing,** or the sales and promotional techniques that deliver promotional materials individually to potential customers.[11] The direct marketing toolkit contains a variety of marketing communication initiatives, including telephone, mail, program-length television commercials (infomercials), catalogs, the Internet, and e-mail, as well as newer communication technologies such as PDAs, podcasts, and cell phones. All these initiatives address the customer in very different ways. In our Volvo example, many such direct marketing initiatives were crucial to the initial success of its IMC plan, and many others were used only after consumers had identified themselves to Volvo as wanting to continue their conversation. Unlike mass media, which communicate to a wide audience, direct marketing allows for personalization of the message, a key advantage.

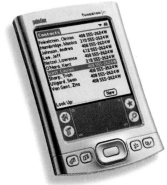

The increased use of customer databases has enabled marketers to identify and track consumers over time and across purchase situations, which has contributed to the rapid growth of direct marketing. Marketers have been able to build these databases thanks to consumers' increased use of credit and debit cards, store-specific credit and loyalty cards, and online shopping, all of which require the buyer to give the seller personal information that becomes part of its database. Because firms understand customers' purchases better when they possess such information, they can more easily focus their direct marketing efforts appropriately. In Adding Value 17.1, we offer some details about how firms can use this information to market to customers one at a time.

Public Relations (PR)

Public relations is the organizational function that manages the firm's communications to achieve a variety of objectives, including building and maintaining a positive image, handling or heading off unfavorable stories or events, and maintaining positive relationships with the media. Public relations activities support the other promotional efforts by the firm by generating "free" media attention. For example, for the Volvo S60 campaign, columnists who cover the auto industry had to be induced to write about the S60, and car enthusiast Web masters received information about the S60 to list on their sites. This media attention was crucial if the S60 was to be successfully promoted as a cutting-edge vehicle that used advanced safety technology and offered a sleek redesign.

Good PR has always been an important success factor. Yet in recent years, the importance of PR has grown as the cost of other forms of marketing communications has increased. At the same time, the influence of PR has become

Direct marketers now use PDAs and cell phones to reach potential customers.

Adding Value 17.1

One-to-One Marketing

One-to-one marketing is more than a direct marketing tool;[12] it is the total integration of sales, marketing, production, and finance into one system that offers seamless interactions with customers. For instance, if an existing customer comes to a firm with a request or calls with a concern, a good one-to-one marketing system can fill the request or solve the problem immediately because the firm already has an electronic file of that customer that contains his or her purchase information, preferences, and some personal data, like birthdays. Successful one-to-one marketing programs also segment customers so that the best customers receive the attention they deserve. Paying close attention to the most loyal customers is valuable to those customers because they get special treatment; it creates value for the firm because loyal customers are typically the most profitable segment.

Sky Alland Marketing's (http://www.skyalland.com/) system is an excellent example of how to implement a one-to-one marketing program. An outsourced customer care company, Sky Alland receives contracts from firms to handle their customer relationships. When Sky

Alland calls a customer, it captures the entire conversation in its database. For instance, Ford might hire the firm to check on new car owners' satisfaction. If a customer complains that her sunroof is leaking, that information automatically gets flagged and sent to the dealer so that the problem can be remedied without the consumer having to make another phone call. The database is detailed enough that when the Sky Alland representative contacts an individual customer, the entire contents of their last interaction is available. The rep therefore can answer previously asked questions and share other relevant information.

One-to-one programs create a win–win situation for customers and the firm. Customers get their needs addressed efficiently; firms are able to gather large amounts of data about customers, including their needs and wants, purchase intentions, and levels of satisfaction. This information enables the firm to develop products and services that offer higher value to customers, which in turn gives those customers an incentive to remain loyal to the firm.

---

more powerful as consumers have become increasingly skeptical of marketing claims made in other media.[13] In many instances, consumers view media coverage generated through PR as more credible and objective than any other aspects of an IMC program, because the firm does not "buy" the space in print media or time on radio or television.

Yoplait's Save Lids to Save Lives promotional and PR campaign enhances its image while supporting a worthwhile cause.

Yoplait's Save Lids to Save Lives campaign and Champion's Program both illustrate how a well-orchestrated IMC effort using a combination of promotional and PR campaigns can enhance a firm's image while supporting a worthwhile cause.[14] The Save Lids to Save Lives campaign was designed not only to sell yogurt but also to create a positive association between the brand and a social cause, in this case, breast cancer awareness. This form of promotional campaign is called **cause-related marketing,** which refers to commercial activity in which businesses and charities form a partnership to market an image, product, or service for their mutual benefit.[15] In the Save Lids to Save Lives campaign, Yoplait donates a set monetary amount for each special pink yogurt lid that consumers send in to the Susan G. Komen Breast Cancer Foundation.[16]

Integrally linked to the Save Lids to Save Lives campaign is Yoplait's Champion's Program, another PR campaign. The goal of the nationwide Champion's Program is to identify and

EXHIBIT 17.5	Elements of a Public Relations Toolkit
PR Element	**Function**
Publications: Brochures, special purpose single-issue publications such as books	Inform various constituencies about the activities of the organization and highlight specific areas of expertise.
Video and audio: Programs, public service announcements	Highlight the organization or support cause-related marketing efforts.
Annual reports	Give required financial performance data and inform investors and others about the unique activities of the organization.
Media relations: Press kits, news releases, speeches, event sponsorships	Generate news coverage of the organization's activities or products/services.
Electronic media: Web sites, e-mail campaigns	Web sites can contain all the previously mentioned toolbox elements, while E-mail directs PR efforts to specific target groups.

recognize "ordinary people doing extraordinary things" in the fight against breast cancer. The 25 individual champions' stories appear in local media, and the program itself often makes the national media. Both initiatives thus are extremely successful in expanding consumers' knowledge about Yoplait's social commitments, as well as Yoplait's brand awareness.[17]

Another very popular PR tool is event sponsorship. **Event sponsorship** occurs when corporations support various activities (financially or otherwise), usually in the cultural or sports and entertainment sectors. For example, Rollerblade USA, the maker of Rollerblade in-line skates, sponsors Skate-In-School, a program it developed with the National Association for Sport and Physical Education (NAPSE) to promote the inclusion of rollerblading in physical education curricula.

Firms often distribute a PR toolkit to communicate with various audiences. Some toolkit elements are designed to inform specific groups directly, whereas others are created to generate media attention and disseminate information. We depict the various elements of a PR toolkit in Exhibit 17.5.

These kids have benefited from an event sponsorship program co-sponsored by Rollerblade USA and the National Association for Sport and Physical Education. The program provides equipment and training to schools.

Electronic Media

The Internet has had a dramatic impact on how marketers communicate with their customers. The tools range from simple e-mail and Web site content to far more interactive features like corporate blogs.

Corporate Blogs   Corporate blogging has risen from obscure, random company postings to a valuable Web addition in virtually no time. A **blog (Web log)** contains periodic posts on a common Web page. As a new form of marketing communication, a well-received blog can create positive word of mouth, customer loyalty, valuable feedback, and tangible economic results, whereas a poorly received blog may lead to backlash, decreased customer trust, and tangible but negative economic returns.[18] Corporate blogs that connect with customers also prompt sales increases because the company can respond directly to customers' comments.

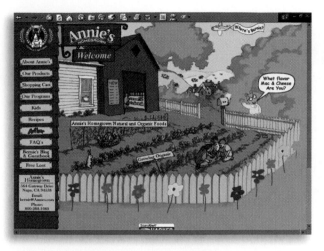

Annie's Homegrown uses its blog to test its new organic food product ideas and share information about organic farming and other subjects in which its customers might be interested.

Annie's Homegrown uses its blog to test its new organic food product ideas and share information about organic farming and other subjects in which its customers might be interested. The company mascot, Bernie the Rabbit of Approval, authors Annie's blog. Despite expert warnings against character blogs, this approach has served to attract children to Annie's site and product line.

Insincere postings or fake blogs that are actually disguised advertising campaigns are problematic. By its very nature, a blog is transparent and contains authors' honest observations, which can help customers determine their trust and loyalty levels. Anything less than total honesty will break that bond and damage the relationship. When handled appropriately though, blogs can serve as trusted platforms for damage control. For instance, the vice chairperson of General Motors started a blog to dispel rumors that the company would discontinue its Pontiac and Buick brands.[19]

Online Games   One particularly successful way to reach younger consumers is through short online games that allow consumers to interact with the site and possibly other players. In line with its hipster image, young male target market, and claim that it is "uniquely designed to attract the ladies," Tag Body Spray includes on its Web site a game in which visitors take on the role of a male character who must get past various virtual roadblocks—the family dog, parents, a younger brother—to gain access to the female "honey" who will find his Tag-enhanced scent appealing. Other games appeal to even younger customers, such as Neopet, a site we discuss in the later "Stealth Marketing" section.[20]

Visitors to the Tag Body Spray Web site can view this game in which visitors take on the role of a male character who must get past various virtual roadblocks—the family dog, parents, a younger brother—to gain access to the female "honey" who will find his Tag-enhanced scent appealing.

Text Messaging   Using the Internet in novel ways also has led to the growth of text messaging (or short message service [SMS]) as an increasingly important way for marketers to communicate with younger consumers. Recent experiments using text messaging have yielded some impressive results. An average SMS campaign generates a 15 percent response rate, compared with less than half that amount for direct mail. Research also shows that 94 percent of all advertising text messages are read, 23 percent of SMS advertisements are forwarded or shown to other users, and 8 percent of those consumers reply to the text message.[21]

Over time, technology will continue to improve, and other new means of communicating with consumers will be added to the IMC channel mix. For now, let's look at how the components of IMC fit together with results-driven elements to achieve the organization's strategic objectives.

Results-Driven Elements: Planning for and Measuring IMC Success

We begin by examining how marketers set strategic goals before implementing any IMC campaign. After they have established those goals, marketers can set the budget for the campaign and choose the measurement tools they will use to evaluate whether it has achieved its strategic objectives.

Goals

As with any strategic undertaking, firms need to understand the outcome they hope to achieve before they begin. These goals can be short-term, such as generating inquiries, increasing awareness, and prompting trial. Or they can be long-term in nature, such as increasing sales, market share, and customer loyalty. Selling S60s was the primary and long-term goal of the Volvo campaign, but in the short term, Volvo wanted to establish brand awareness and purchase intentions. Thus, the campaign was designed to get consumers' attention first through television ads during the NCAA tournament, then to encourage viewers to log on to the S60 Web site.

These goals, both short- and long-term, should be explicitly defined and measured. They constitute part of the overall promotional plan, which is usually a subsection of the firm's marketing plan. Another part of the promotional plan is the budget.

Budget

Firms use a variety of methods to plan their marketing communications budgets. Because all the methods of setting a promotional budget have both advantages and disadvantages, no one method should be used in isolation.[22]

The **objective-and-task method** determines the budget required to undertake specific tasks to accomplish communication objectives. To use this method, marketers first establish a set of communication objectives, then determine which media best reach the target market and how much it will cost to run the number and types of communications necessary to achieve the objectives. This process—set objectives, choose media, and determine costs—must be repeated for each product or service. The sum of all the individual communication plan budgets becomes the firm's total marketing communications budget. In addition to the objective-and-task method, various **rule-of-thumb methods** can be used to set budgets (see Exhibit 17.6).

These rule-of-thumb methods use prior sales and communication activities to determine the present communication budget. Although they are easy to implement, they obviously have various limitations, as noted. Clearly, budgeting is not a simple process. It may take several rounds of negotiations among the various managers, who are each competing for resources for their own areas of responsibility.

Measuring Success

Once a firm has decided how to set its budget for marketing communications and its campaigns have been developed and implemented, it reaches the point that it must measure the success of the campaigns. Each step in the IMC process can be measured to determine how effective it has been in motivating consumers to move to the next step in the buying process. However, recall that the lagged effect

EXHIBIT 17.6	Rule-of-Thumb Methods	
Method	**Definition**	**Limitations**
Competitive parity	The communication budget is set so that the firm's share of communication expenses equals its share of the market.	Does not allow firms to exploit the unique opportunities or problems they confront in a market. If all competitors use this method to set communication budgets, their market shares will stay approximately the same over time.
Percentage-of-sales	The communication budget is a fixed percentage of forecasted sales.	Assumes the same percentage used in the past, or by competitors, is still appropriate for the firm. Does not take into account new plans (e.g., to introduce a new line of products in the current year).
Affordable budgeting	Marketers forecast their sales and expenses, excluding communication, during the budgeting period. The difference between the forecast sales and expenses plus desired profit is reserved for the communication budget. That is, the communication budget is the money available after operating costs and profits have been budgeted.	Assumes communication expenses do not stimulate sales and profit.

influences and complicates marketers' evaluations of a promotion's effectiveness, as well as the best way to allocate marketing communications budgets. Because of the cumulative effect of marketing communications, it may take several exposures before consumers are moved to buy, so firms cannot expect too much too soon. They must invest in the marketing communications campaign with the idea that it may not reach its full potential for some time. In the same way, if firms cut marketing communications expenditures, it may take time before they experience a decrease in sales.

When measuring IMC success, the firm should examine when and how often consumers have been exposed to various marketing communications. Specifically, they use measures of *frequency* and *reach* to gauge consumers' *exposure* to marketing communications. For most products and situations, a single exposure to a communication is hardly enough to generate the desired response. Therefore, marketers measure the **frequency** of exposure—how often the audience is exposed to a communication within a specified period of time. The other measure used to measure consumers' exposure to marketing communications is **reach**, which describes the percentage of the target population exposed to a specific marketing communication, such as an advertisement, at least once.[23] Marketing communications managers usually state their media objectives in terms of **gross rating points**

(GRP), which represents reach multiplied by frequency (GRP = reach × frequency).

GRP can be measured for print, radio, or television, but when comparing them, they must refer to the same medium. Suppose that Seven for all Mankind, the maker of Seven Jeans, places five advertisements in *Elle* magazine, which reaches 50 percent of the "fashion forward" target segment. The total GRP generated by these five magazine advertisements is 50 reach × 5 advertisements = 250 GRP. Now suppose Seven Jeans includes 15 television ads as part of the same campaign, run during the program *Lost*, which has a rating of 9.2. The total GRP generated by these 15 advertisements is 138 (9.2 × 15 = 138). However, advertisements typically appear during more than one television program, so the total GRP equals the sum of the GRP generated by each program.

Although GRP is an adequate measure for television and radio advertisements, assessing the effectiveness of any Web-based communications efforts in an IMC campaign generally requires **Web tracking software** to indicate how much time viewers spend on particular Web pages and the number of pages they view. **Click-through tracking** measures how many times users click on banner advertising on Web sites. **Online couponing** is a promotional Web technique in which consumers print a coupon directly from a site and then redeem the coupon in a store. Another promotional Web technique is **online referring,** in which consumers fill out an interest or order form and are referred to an offline dealer or firm that offers the product or service of interest. All these methods can be easily measured and assessed.

Online coupons like this one from barnes&noble.com can be printed directly from a site and then redeemed in a store.

As IMC programs become more sophisticated, measurement is not the only concern. There are a host of legal and ethical issues that marketers need to worry about, so in the last section, we examine some current legal and ethical IMC issues.

Legal and Ethical Issues in IMC

Integrated marketing communications brings together many diverse forms of communication under one umbrella. But in the United States, each form of communication media traditionally has been regulated separately. For example, cigarette advertising was banned from television and radio in 1969 under the Public Health Smoking Act but could still appear in print and on billboards, and cigarette companies still sponsored various entertainment and sporting events. However, after 1997, cigarette companies voluntarily agreed to remove cigarette advertising from billboards and end all sponsorship of sports and entertainment events in the United States.[24] For now, cigarette advertising is permitted only in print media and online. In Chapter 18, we detail the various agencies that regulate the different forms and media for advertising in the United States. In this section, we discuss some controversies surrounding commercial speech and new forms of potential deception.

What Is Commercial Speech?

When IMC brings all these different media together, it often employs a mix of commercial and noncommercial speech, which the United States legally distinguishes. However, the courts are starting to have a difficult time determining which is which. **Commercial speech**[25] is defined as a message with an economic motivation, that is, to promote a product or service, to persuade someone to purchase,

Ethical Dilemma **17.1** Is It Deceptive to Disguise the Message Sender?

The quest for innovative ways to reach consumers has led companies to promote some confusion about who the sender of a message really is. Traditionally, the sender of any commercial message had to be identified, and the message was required to indicate that it was a commercial or promotional message.[26] With new media like Web sites, however, it can become extremely difficult for consumers to know whether a message is commercial. If consumers don't know they are viewing a promotional message, they may be unable to evaluate its claims properly, and deception could ensue. The Federal Trade Commission (FTC) defines **deceptive advertising** as being a representation, omission, act, or practice that is likely to mislead consumers acting reasonably under the circumstances.

Consider the promotion mix Lion's Gate Films used for the horror movie *Godsend*, which included a Web site (http://www.godsendinstitute.org/) along with traditional movie promotions. However, the Web site never clearly indicates that it was designed to promote a movie. The film *Godsend* is about cloning, and if you did a Google search for "cloning," the Web page for the Godsend Institute—not a real institute but rather the setting for the film—would appear in the results list.

The site is very professional and looks very much like a Web site for a legitimate fertility clinic, including online tours of the facilities and testimonials from parents who had been patients at the center. Family snapshots supposedly portray the children Godsend has cloned from dying siblings. The effect is dramatic—and completely fake. Nowhere on the site is there a disclaimer stating its true purpose. Tom Ortenberg, president of film releasing for Lion's Gate, stated that the *Godsend* site is "a million dollar idea" built for only about $10,000, in that the site resulted in millions of hits and generated a lot of publicity.[27]

This and other similar Web sites have sparked controversy primarily because of their realism and lack of clear promotional message. Many believe that a Web site is deceptive if it does not make clear that the site is actually promoting a product. But is it deceptive or just clever marketing? This challenge remains an open question for now. In the meantime, other movies and television programs, such as *Lost*, have begun using the tactic of creating false Web sites.

and so on. Marketers can only make commercial claims that are fact based, not mere opinions. A statement such as "our product X is superior to our competitor's product Y" must be substantiated.

Noncommercial speech, in contrast, is a message that does not have an economic motivation and therefore is fully protected under the First Amendment. Firms can express matters of opinion, such as when the president of the firm tells an audience, "Our company makes the best products," without needing to offer substantiation for the claim as long as those claims are not designed with an economic motivation.

Advertising and direct marketing are forms of commercial speech, whereas PR is not. For instance, in *Kasky* v. *Nike*, Nike claimed that a letter to the editor written by its CEO was part of a PR campaign and thus not an advertising message.[28] Unfortunately for Nike, the California courts felt otherwise and found that Nike's letter was an advertisement and qualified as commercial speech, which meant that the claims made in the letter had to be substantiated. In relation to another similar concern, Ethical Dilemma 17.1 raises the issue of whether it is deceptive to disguise the sender of a message.

Stealth Marketing

The *Godsend* Web site is just one example of a growing number of "stealth" promotional campaigns. Stealth marketing is a strategy used to attract consumers using promotional tactics that deliver a sales message in unconventional ways, often without the target audience knowing that the message even has a selling intent.[29] Stealth marketing can take many forms and use many different communication channels, and as marketers find more innovative ways to communicate with their target markets, they have crossed

into uncharted waters. Consumers thus are starting to lose confidence that they can distinguish a commercial message from a noncommercial one.

Marketers have also begun to employ actual consumers to be, in essence, salespeople for the brand. For example, the makers of Al Fresco chicken sausage began paying consumers to take the product to barbeques or similar types of gatherings and discuss it with other guests.[30] The partygoers were not informed that they were being given a sales pitch, paid for by Al Fresco. Al Fresco's goal was to turn these parties into a launching point for viral marketing, a marketing phenomenon that encourages people to pass along a marketing message to other potential consumers.[31] There are no current regulations on viral campaigns; the laws that cover deceptive practices have never had to address this new form of marketing.

The use of online games also has been quite effective at getting children's attention and drawing them to firms' Web sites—as well as at drawing criticism from children's media watchdog groups. These groups believe that the Web sites do not inform children that the games contain branded messages. One of the most controversial is www.neopet.com, which offers games sponsored by various corporations. By signing up to receive offers from these sponsors, site users get assistance in taking care of their Neopet, a virtual animal they adopt when they register with the site.[32] They can earn points by taking consumer surveys or feeding their Neopet McDonald's products. Young girls, who make up most of the site's visitors, spend an average of 3.5 hours a month on the site.

As sites like Neopet become more popular with children, children's media watchers begin to ask: Can children distinguish between entertainment and commercial content?[33] For now, again, there are no formal regulations for children's Web sites other than those designed to protect children's privacy online. However, U.S. regulators are examining the practices used on these sites to determine whether any current regulations are being violated and whether such practices need to be regulated. In the meantime, marketers will continue their quest to find more innovative ways to reach their target audiences using both traditional and nontraditional methods.

Do you believe that stealth marketing strategies directed toward children like the one used by Neopet is ethical? Should the government regulate media in which children may not be able to distinguish between entertainment and commercial content?

Summing Up

1. How do customers perceive marketing communications?

On the surface, marketing communications look simple: People become aware of a product or service, then grow interested, then desire it, and finally take an action such as purchasing it. But it isn't quite that simple. First, there is the cumulative effect of marketing communications. Ads from the past, for instance, help influence consumers' actions in the future. Second, everyone interprets commercial messages differently, thus making it difficult for a marketer to be assured that a particular, clear signal is getting through. Third, to be effective, marketers must adjust their messages to fit the media and the receiver's knowledge level.

2. Why are some media channels growing while others are shrinking?

In the past, most of a firm's promotional budget was spent on advertising. Although advertising still demands a sizable portion, other media channels have taken up a substantial chunk of the total budget. Direct marketing expenditures are growing because the number of direct marketing media options has increased in recent years. While outbound telephone calls remain a popular form of direct marketing, mail, infomercials, alternative media such as catalogs, the Internet, e-mail, and other new communication technologies such as PDAs and cell phones are all expanding. Public relations also has become increasingly important as other media forms become more expensive and as consumers grow more skeptical of commercial messages. Finally, the Internet has spawned some innovative new ways to promote products and services.

3. How should firms plan for and measure IMC success?

Planning an IMC budget should encompass a combination of factors. The process could start by setting the overall IMC budget as a percentage of sales. Then, the firm might examine what other firms are spending on similar product categories. When it gets down to planning the budget for individual product categories or items, the firm should set its objectives for the campaign and allocate enough money to meet those objectives.

Marketers rely on a mix of traditional and nontraditional measures to determine IMC success. Because potential customers generally need to be exposed to IMC messages several times before they will buy, firms estimate the degree to which customers are exposed to a message by multiplying frequency (the number of times an audience is exposed to a message) by reach (the percentage of the target population exposed to a specific marketing communication). Measuring Internet IMC effectiveness requires different measures, such as click-through tracking that measures how many times users click on banner advertising on Web sites.

4. Why are some governmental agencies and consumer groups concerned about certain innovative IMC strategies?

If a message is designed to promote or sell a product or service, it is generally considered commercial speech, but if the message has no promotional or selling intent, it is fully protected by the First Amendment. The line becomes blurred, however, when normally noncommercial venues are used to sell something. Another practice that is causing a stir emerges when the sender of a commercial message is not clearly identified. Activities such as bogus Web sites or certain stealth marketing programs, in which the identity of the sponsor of an activity or event is intentionally kept from prospective customers, can be considered deceptive promotional practices.

Key Terms

- advertising, 470
- AIDA model, 468
- blog (weblog or Web log), 475
- cause-related marketing, 474
- click-through tracking, 479
- commercial speech, 479
- communication channel, 466
- deceptive advertising, 480
- decoding, 467
- direct marketing, 473
- encoding, 466
- event sponsorship, 475

- feedback loop, 467
- frequency, 478
- gross rating points, 478
- integrated marketing communications (IMC), 464
- lagged effect, 470
- noise, 467
- noncommercial speech, 480
- objective-and-task method, 477
- online couponing, 479
- online referring, 479

- personal selling, 472
- public relations, 473
- reach, 478
- receiver, 466
- rule-of-thumb methods, 477
- sales promotions, 473
- sender, 466
- stealth marketing, 481
- transmitter, 466
- viral marketing, 481
- Web tracking software, 479

Marketing Applications

1. The designer jean company Juicy Couture has embarked on a new IMC strategy. It has chosen to advertise on the NBC *Nightly News* and in *Time* magazine. The message is designed to announce new styles for the season and uses a 17-year-old woman as the model. Evaluate this strategy.

2. Using the steps in the AIDA model, explain why a potential consumer in Question 1 who views Juicy Couture's advertising may not be ready to go out and purchase a new pair of jeans.

3. Suppose Heinz has just come out with a new product called Samores—crunchy peanut butter with chocolate chips and graham crackers. How would you expect this product's IMC program to differ from that for its regular plain peanut butter?

4. It's holiday time, and you've decided to purchase a jewelry item for the person of your choice at Tiffany & Co. Evaluate how Tiffany's advertising, personal selling, public relations, and electronic media might influence your purchase decision. How might the relative importance of each of these IMC elements be different if your parents were making the purchase?

5. Suppose you saw your instructor for this course being interviewed on TV about the impact of a big storm on an upcoming holiday's sales. Is this interview part of your college's IMC program? If so, do you believe it benefits the college? How?

6. A retail store places an ad in the local newspaper for capri pants. The sales of the featured pants increase significantly for the next two weeks; sales in the rest of the sportswear department go up as well. What do you think are the short- and long-term objectives of the ad? Justify your answer.

7. As an intern for Michelin tires, you have been asked to develop an IMC budget. The objective of the IMC strategy is to raise Michelin's market share by 5 percent in the United States in the next 18 months. Your manager explains, "It's real simple; just increase the budget 5 percent over last year's." Evaluate your manager's strategy.

8. What makes marketing communication deceptive? What are the features of stealth marketing campaigns that make them vulnerable to charges of deception?

9. You were sitting in the school cafeteria yesterday, and a young man from your marketing class, whom you don't know well, asked if he could sit down. He then started telling you about this very cool new Microsoft product that helps you organize your class notes. Although you recognize the merit in the product, you later find out that he works for Microsoft. Do you believe his action constitutes an ethical IMC strategy? How will it affect your attitude toward Microsoft and the potential that you will purchase the product?

Net Savvy

1. Visit http://www.thephelpsgroup.com/default.asp to view the Web site of the Phelps Group, a well-known IMC consulting firm. The site contains a lot of information about what IMC is and how it can be used effectively by a wide variety of companies. Of particular interest is the case studies section. Locate the case studies link, read the current case, and discuss the following: What were the goals of the IMC campaign? Which IMC components were used in that particular campaign? How do those components contribute to the success of the IMC campaign in achieving its stated goals?

2. The Direct Marketing Association is the primary source of information about direct marketing activities for both academics and practitioners. The Web site for the DMA, at http://www.the-dma.org/, contains a wealth of information about direct marketing practices and self-regulation. How many different target markets does the DMA address on its home page? Click on the "For Consumers" tab. What services does the DMA provide for consumers? Why do you think it offers those services? Now return to the home page and click on the "Industry Home Pages." How many different industry segments does the Web site address? Were there any surprises in this list? Pick five segments and discuss how these industries use direct marketing.

Chapter Case Study

CASE: SCION COMMUNICATES VALUE WITH ITS INNOVATIVE IMC CAMPAIGN[34]

Toyota's campaign for its new Scion line was designed to both inform and persuade 20-something buyers that the car meets their needs. In catering to this target market, Scion chose to rely heavily on nontraditional media efforts, perhaps because buyers between 16 and 24 years of age purchase only around 850,000 new cars a year (6 percent of the total market). By the year 2010, however, 63 million people from this age group will be driving. Despite their obvious interest in this age demographic, car manufacturers have largely failed to design cars that appeal to these finicky buyers. Scion was keenly aware of Honda's effort to attract the young market with the boxy Element, which, despite its flashy marketing campaign, attracted more 40-somethings than 20-somethings. So what do these young buyers want?

The same thing they have always wanted: price and value. Scion decided to enter this market with a comprehensive strategy: a car that is a good value for the money but also one that speaks directly to young consumers, which meant Scion had to know what cars would mean to them. Scion researchers found that 16- to 24-year-olds like customization, so the Scion comes with options like illuminated cup holders, colored door-lock covers, and red and gray steering wheels,[35] which allow Scion buyers to create "their" car.

Want tC?
Check out the 2005 160 hp Scion tC at wanttC.com

Now that Scion believes it has the vehicle this segment wants, it must face the challenge of communicating it to these buyers. Although the Camry is the top-selling U.S. brand, Scion sold only 106,000 of its 1.5 million new vehicles to drivers younger than 25 years. To reach them, Scion had to break away from its traditional IMC strategy.

It began by identifying promising geographic markets that might contain 20-something opinion leaders. Using "street teams," Scion visited nightclubs, malls, and art galleries handing out free stuff—key chains, T-shirts, and so forth—featuring the Scion name and Web address. With this approach, consumers could feel as though they had "discovered the brand," not that the brand had been pushed on them,[36] and then they would ideally inform others about the Scion.

In California, the agency also tried innovative methods such as skywriting, projecting images onto buildings, and building life-sized sand sculptures of the Scion. Less than 1 percent of the California promotional budget was spent on traditional advertising. In addition, Scion offered camera-equipped Scions for test drives so consumers could film themselves while driving and e-mail the clips to friends. Of the 4,000 people who filmed their test drives in California, 1,100 then asked to see a dealer.[37]

Nationally, the company also used feature films, including the 22-minute *On the D.L.*, which Scion entered in the prestigious Tribeca Film Festival. Featuring two 30-something musicians on their quest to obtain drivers' licenses, the film was cut into five-minute clips and placed on different Web sites. Furthermore, Scion undertook PR activities, like sponsoring the Sprite Liquid Mix Tour and the Scion DJ Contest, to drive interest in the brand. Refusing to leave any stone unturned, Scion even hired several dozen young adults to wear temporary forehead tattoos for an event in Times Square.

So will all these efforts work? It depends. One marketer worried that the campaign was too "underground" and buyers would have a difficult time locating the brand, but brand awareness has increased among the target market, and the Scion has experienced good sales in California. Even more, Scion hopes all its efforts to create value will translate into a long-term affinity for Toyota and strong brand loyalty when it comes time for these young owners to purchase higher-end vehicles.

Case Questions

1. Did Scion make a wise decision to avoid traditional media channels during the Scion campaign? Why or why not?

2. The Scion was built specifically to generate brand loyalty among novice car buyers. Will this long-term strategy work for Scion? Why or why not?

3. In what ways did the Scion create value for the target market?

18

Advertising and Sales Promotions

O ver the years, Altoids has used nontraditional advertising to help grow its market share in the breath mint category. Promoting a successful underground brand is a tricky prospect for marketers because traditional methods, such as mass media, can quickly kill its appeal. Leo Burnett, the advertising agency in charge of the Altoids campaign, also faced the problem of a very limited marketing budget. The solution: An extremely targeted campaign focused on those types of customers who were responsible for the company's Seattle success. Radio and television advertising would not work—too traditional and too expensive. Instead, Leo Burnett chose a mix of out-of-home media, such as billboards, ads on buses, and posters in bus stops. Out-of-home advertising offered the key advantage of reaching people on the move who didn't spend much time watching TV or listening to the radio.[1]

The graphics were simple and direct, featuring a picture of the tin can in which the mints are packaged and the tag line "the curiously strong mint." Sometimes

Hilary (left) and Haylie (right) Duff promote Ice Breakers Liquid Ice by friendly bickering, "Is it Liquid? Or is it Ice?"

487

simplicity begets elegance, and this simple campaign exceeded all expectations, achieving success in terms of both customers' ability to recall the brand and growth in sales volume.

As the U.S. breath freshener market continues to grow steadily, other candy companies also have been looking for a piece of the market. In 2004, Hershey introduced its Ice Breakers Liquid Ice and chose celebrities to promote it. Famous sisters, Hilary and Haylie Duff, publicly ponder "Is it Liquid? Or is it Ice?" and pleasantly bicker about who is right. Viewers can log onto www.liquidorice.com and cast their vote to side with one sister or the other, which enters them into a contest to win a trip to meet the Duff sisters, among other prizes, including supplies of Ice Breakers Liquid Ice.

Even without a lifetime supply, anyone can find Liquid Ice on convenience store shelves. It has captured a 14.5 percent market share and shows no sign of slowing growth. Clearly, Hershey's has garnered considerable consumer attention with its creative advertising campaign and is steadily chipping away at the leadership position Altoids enjoys, largely because of its own clever advertising.[2]

■ ■ ■

Advertising is a paid form of communication, delivered through media from an identifiable source, designed to persuade the receiver to take some action, now or in the future.[3] This definition provides some important distinctions between advertising and other forms of promotion, which we discussed in the previous chapter. First, unlike public relations, advertising is not free; someone has paid, with money, trade, or other means, to get the message shown. Second, advertising must be carried by some medium—television, radio, print, the Web, T-shirts, sidewalks, and so on. Third, legally, the source of the message must be known or knowable. Fourth, advertising represents a persuasive form of communication, designed to get the consumer to take some action. That desired action can range from "Don't drink and drive" to "Buy a new Mercedes."

Some activities that are called advertising really are not, such as word-of-mouth advertising. Even political advertising technically is not advertising because it is not for commercial purposes and thus is not regulated in the same manner as true advertising.

Advertising encompasses an enormous industry and clearly is the most visible form of marketing communications—so much so that many people think of marketing and advertising as synonymous. Global advertising expenditures are projected to exceed $600 billion, with half that amount being spent in the United States alone. It is not just a perception that advertising is everywhere; it *is* everywhere.[4]

Yet how many of the advertisements you were exposed to yesterday do you remember today? Probably not more than three or four. As you learned in Chapter 5, perception is a highly selective process. Consumers simply screen out messages that are not relevant to them. When you notice an advertisement, you may not react to it; even if you react to it, you may not remember it later. Say you remember seeing it—you still may not remember the brand or sponsor of the advertisement,

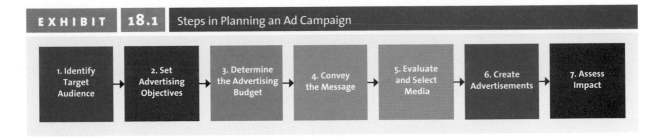

EXHIBIT | 18.1 | Steps in Planning an Ad Campaign

| 1. Identify Target Audience | 2. Set Advertising Objectives | 3. Determine the Advertising Budget | 4. Convey the Message | 5. Evaluate and Select Media | 6. Create Advertisements | 7. Assess Impact |

or, worse yet (from the advertiser's point of view), you may remember it as an advertisement for another product.[5]

To get you to remember their ad and the brand, advertisers must first get your attention. As we discussed in Chapter 17, the increasing number of communication channels and changes in consumers' media usage have made the job of advertisers far more difficult.[6] As our opening example demonstrated, advertisers are attempting to use creativity and a mix of media that offer better opportunities to reach their target markets.

As a consumer, you are exposed only to the end product—the finished advertisement. But many actions must take place before you actually get to see an ad. In this chapter, we begin by examining what it takes to plan a successful advertising campaign, from identifying a target audience to creating the actual ad and assessing performance. We conclude with a discussion of the regulatory and ethical issues in advertising, then move on to examine sales promotions and their use.

Designing a successful advertising program requires much planning; Exhibit 18.1 shows some of the key steps in the planning process, each of which helps ensure that the intended message reaches the right audience and has the desired effect. Now let's examine each of these steps.

1. Identify Target Audience

The success of an advertising program depends on how well the advertiser can identify its target audience. Firms conduct research to identify their target audience, then use the information they gain to set the tone for the advertising program and help them select the media they will use to deliver the message to that audience.

During this research, firms must keep in mind that their target audience may or may not be the same as current users of the product. Think about jewelry. Research shows that in a typical year, some 43 percent of the U.S. adult population—more than 85 million people—purchase jewelry. Although women have a significantly higher purchase incidence (48 percent) than men (36 percent), men spend significantly more money on their jewelry purchases than do women. Perhaps it is no surprise that the majority of men's jewelry purchases are gifts.[7]

Some advertising messages also may be directed at portions of audiences who are not part of the marketer's target

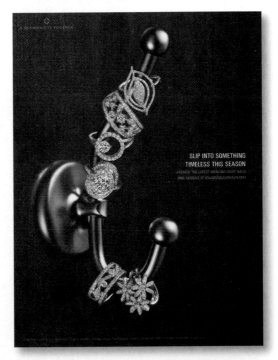

Who is the target audience for this ad, men or women?

market but who participate in the purchase process. Chrysler, for instance, runs ads for its minivans during Saturday morning children's viewing hours. These ads are designed to build brand awareness on the part of the children, who, Chrysler hopes, will influence their parents' minivan choices.[8]

2. Set Advertising Objectives

Advertising campaign objectives are derived from the overall objectives of the marketing program and clarify the specific goals that the ads are designed to accomplish. Generally, these objectives appear in the **advertising plan,** a subsection of the firm's overall marketing plan that explicitly outlines the objectives of the advertising campaign, how the campaign might accomplish those objectives, and how the firm can determine whether the campaign was successful.[9] An advertising plan is crucial because it will later serve as the yardstick against which advertising success or failure is measured.

Generally, when advertising to consumers, the objective is a **pull strategy** in which the goal is to get consumers to *pull* the product into the supply chain by demanding it. **Push strategies** also exist and are designed to increase demand by focusing on wholesalers, distributors, or salespeople. These campaigns attempt to motivate the seller to highlight the product, rather than the products of competitors, and thereby push the product onto consumers. In this chapter, we will focus on pull strategies. Push strategies are examined in Chapters 15, 16, and 19.

All advertising campaigns aim to achieve certain objectives: to inform, persuade, and remind customers. Another way of looking at advertising objectives is to examine an ad's focus. Is the ad designed to stimulate demand for a particular product or service, or more broadly for the institution in general? Also, ads can be used to stimulate demand for a product category or an entire industry, or for a specific brand, firm, or item. First we look at the broad overall objectives of inform, persuade, and remind. Then we examine advertising objectives based on the focus of the ad: product versus institutional and primary versus selective.

This ad informs consumers about "what's in" at T.J.Maxx.

Informative Advertising

Informative advertising communicates to create and build brand awareness, with the ultimate goal of moving the consumer through the buying cycle to a purchase. Such advertising helps determine some important early stages of a product's life cycle (PLC; see Chapter 11), particularly when consumers have little information about the specific product or type of product. Retailers often use informative advertising to tell their customers about an upcoming sales event or the arrival of new merchandise, as in this recent advertisement designed to inform consumers that T.J. Maxx has new merchandise available.

Persuasive Advertising

When a product has gained a certain level of brand awareness, firms use **persuasive advertising** to motivate consumers to take action. Persuasive advertising generally occurs in the growth and early maturity stages of the PLC,

Cover Girl's persuasive ads attempt to motivate consumers to take action: try the product, switch brands, or continue to buy the product.

when competition is most intense, and attempts to accelerate the market's acceptance of the product. In later stages of the PLC, persuasive advertising may be used to reposition an established brand by persuading consumers to change their existing perceptions of the advertised product. Firms, like Cover Girl in the ad above, often use persuasive advertising to convince consumers to take action—switch brands,[10] try a new product, or even continue to buy the advertised product.

Reminder Advertising

Finally, **reminder advertising** is communication used to remind or prompt repurchases, especially for products that have gained market acceptance and are in the maturity stage of their life cycle. For instance, have you ever gone to a restaurant with a group of friends and ordered a Coke when you really wanted iced tea? In this case, the product has achieved **top-of-the-mind awareness**, or a prominent place in people's memories that triggers a response without them having to put any thought into it. Just the sight of a reminder ad, like a Coca-Cola logo on the menu, may be enough to stimulate the desired response.

Focus of Advertisements

The ad campaign's objectives determine the specific ad's focus. To illustrate consider the two dichotomies depicted in Exhibit 18.2. The first dichotomy is between **product-focused advertisements**, which focus on informing, persuading, or reminding consumers about a specific product or service, and **institutional advertisements**, which inform, persuade, and remind consumers about issues related to places, politics, an industry, or a particular corporation. The second dichotomy

This umbrella reminds consumers to order a Coke.

EXHIBIT 18.2	Types of Advertising	
	Product Focused	**Institutional**
Primary Demand	Diet Coke generates demand for all diet sodas 	Got Milk? generates demand for the entire fluid milk category
Selective Demand	Diet Coke generates demand for Coca-Cola's diet soda 	Ronald McDonald Children's Charities generates demand for McDonald's Inc.

distinguishes those ads designed to generate demand for the product category or an entire industry (**primary demand**) from those designed to generate demand for a specific brand, firm, or item (**selective demand**).

Perhaps the best-known primary demand advertising campaign is the long-running institutional campaign, "Got Milk?" to encourage milk consumption by appealing to consumers' needs to affiliate with the milk-moustached celebrities shown in the ads.[11] A recent incarnation of the Got Milk? campaign, titled "Bones," also focuses on the beneficial properties of milk for building strong bones. This new focus represents a switch to a more informative appeal, combined with a mild emotional fear appeal in its assertion that failing to drink milk can lead to medical problems.

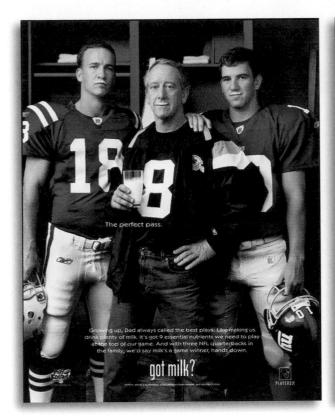

The perfect pass.

Growing up, Dad always called the best plays. Like making us drink plenty of milk. It's got 9 essential nutrients we need to play at the top of our game. And with three NFL quarterbacks in the family, we'd say milk's a game winner, hands down.

got milk?

Over the past 30 years, forearm fractures in young people have increased an alarming 42%. got milk?

One of the best-known campaigns for generating primary demand is the "Got Milk?" campaign (left). The latest incarnation of the campaign, titled "Bones" (right) has a more informative appeal, combined with a mild emotional fear appeal.

A special class of primary demand advertising is **public service advertising (PSA),** which focuses on public welfare and generally is sponsored by nonprofit institutions, civic groups, religious organizations, trade associations, or political groups.[12] PSAs represent a form of **social marketing,** which is the application of marketing principles to a social issue to bring about attitudinal and behavioral change among the general public or a specific population segment.[13] Because PSAs are a special class of advertising, under Federal Communication Commission (FCC) rules, broadcasters must devote a specific amount of free airtime to them. Some of the most successful PSA campaigns include wildfire prevention (Smokey the Bear), crime protection (McGruff, the Crime Dog), and seat belt usage (crash test dummies Vince and Larry).[14]

Because they often are designed by top advertising agencies for nonprofit clients, PSAs usually are quite creative and stylistically appealing. For example, what is your reaction to the TRUTH public service antismoking campaign summarized in Ethical Dilemma 18.1?

To illustrate how a brand moves from generating primary demand in the introductory stage of its PLC to generating **selective demand** during the growth and maturity stages, consider Pfizer's brand Rogaine. When it first appeared on the market, Rogaine was considered quite innovative and required a doctor's prescription. No other products existed to tackle the problem of "male pattern baldness." Pfizer's early ad campaigns were designed to inform consumers and generate demand for the product category. But as the category began to grow and mature, competitive treatments entered the market, especially once the product no longer required a prescription. As the market grew, Pfizer realized that both men and women experienced

Ethical Dilemma 18.1 The TRUTH Takes Hold

Just as is the case for other social marketing issues, getting young people to either stop smoking or never start offers a difficult challenge. Accomplishing attitudinal and/or behavioral changes with regard to an addictive product may be the toughest challenge of all for advertisers. Yet such changes were exactly the goals the American Legacy Foundation had in mind when it set out to "de-market" cigarettes to teenagers and children in 1999.

The foundation came into being as part of the historic tobacco settlement between various states' Attorneys General and the tobacco industry. One clause of the settlement demanded that $300 million per year be set aside for a Public Education Fund. And part of this Public Education Fund was devoted to "raising generations that would be smoke free."

The first step was to get young people's attention—never an easy task. The American Legacy Foundation decided to use fear appeals and shock ads to deliver the message. TRUTH provides "a hard-hitting media campaign that uses edgy television, radio and print ads featuring youth-led activism against tobacco companies ... confronting the tobacco industry with smoking-related death statistics or exposing the companies' marketing tactics."[15] Among the most vivid ads are those that depict body bags piled up in front of Philip Morris headquarters, gasping rats to dramatize that cigarettes include an ingredient in rat poison, and a dog walker offering to sell dog urine to tobacco companies because cigarettes contain urea.[16]

But how far is too far? Is this "in-your-face" style effective? Do advertisers need to go to these extremes to deliver their messages? Research findings generally have been mixed, but overall the campaign seems very effective in preventing nonsmokers from starting to smoke.[17] However, for youth that already smoke, other research has shown that the campaign has had the opposite effect: Instead of convincing them to quit smoking, the campaign has reinforced their commitment to the addictive act.

If you smoke, would this ad make you stop? If you don't smoke, would this ad influence you to refrain from starting?

thinning hair; to market effectively to both groups, it had to design different campaigns. The appeal used for men is much more emotional, that for women much more informational. Even the color schemes and graphics on the packages are vastly different. The advertiser's ability to understand the needs of the target market thus is crucial, because it helps the firm determine which type of advertising and appeal to use.

Regardless of whether the advertising campaign's objective is to inform, persuade, or remind; to focus on a particular product or the institution in general; or to stimulate primary versus selective demand, each campaign's objectives must be specific and measurable. For a brand awareness campaign, for example, the objective might be to increase brand awareness among the target market by 50 percent within six months. Another campaign's goal may be to persuade 10 percent of a competitor's customers to switch to the advertised brand. Once the advertising campaign's objectives are set, the firm sets the advertising budget.

Here's how to Take A Bite Out Of Crime online...

- Keep your name, address, phone number, school name, and any adult's credit card number to yourself.

- Don't agree to meet someone you met online without discussing it first with your parents.

- Stay out of chat rooms unless your mom or dad says it's okay.

- Tell your folks or another trusted adult if you see anything online that makes you uncomfortable. Save the info so an adult can report details to the Cyber Tipline (800-843-5678 or www.cybertipline.com).

- Don't open e-mails that are from people you don't know. Delete them. And don't click on links to sites that you don't recognize.

For more tips on Internet safety, visit www.mcgruff.org

3. Determine the Advertising Budget

The various budgeting methods for marketing communication (Chapter 17) also apply to budgeting for advertising. First, firms must consider the role that advertising plays in their attempt to meet their overall promotional objectives. Second, advertising expenditures vary over the course of the PLC. Third, the nature of the market and the product influence the size of advertising budgets.

Advertising for the Scion was less than 14 percent of the total promotional budget because Toyota used so many kinds of nontraditional media to get the attention of its young target customers (see the case at the end of Chapter 17). For other products or services, the advertising portion of the total promotional budget may be as high as 95 percent. It all depends on the objectives of the overall marketing communications campaign.

The nature of the market also determines the amount of money spent on advertising. For instance, less money is spent on advertising in B2B (business-to-business) marketing contexts than in B2C (business-to-consumer) markets. Personal selling, as we discuss in Chapter 19, likely is more important in B2B markets.

Public service advertising, like McGruff the Crime Dog, focuses on public welfare and generally is sponsored by nonprofit institutions, civic groups, religious organizations, trade associations, or political groups.

4. Convey the Message

In this step, marketers determine what they want to convey about the product or service. First, the firm determines the key message it wants to communicate to the target audience. Second, the firm decides what appeal would most effectively convey the message. We present these decisions sequentially, but in reality, they must be considered simultaneously.

The Message

The message provides the target audience with reasons to respond in the desired way. A logical starting point for deciding on the advertising message is to tout the key benefits of the product or service. The message should communicate its

Is Black and Decker doing a good job of selling a solution?

problem-solving ability clearly and in a compelling fashion. In this context, advertisers must remember that products and services solve problems, whether real or perceived. That is, people are not looking for 1/4-inch drill bits; they are looking for 1/4-inch holes.[18] Because there are many ways to make a 1/4-inch hole, a firm like Black and Decker must convey to consumers that its drill bit is the best way to get that hole.

Another common strategy differentiates a product by establishing its unique benefits. This distinction forms the basis for the **unique selling proposition (USP),** which is often the common theme or slogan in an advertising campaign. Briefly, a good USP communicates the unique attributes of the product and thereby becomes a snapshot of the entire campaign. Some of the most famous USPs include the following:

> Ford....Built Tough
>
> Nokia....Connecting People
>
> United....It's time to fly

The selling proposition communicated by the advertising must be not only *unique* to the brand but also *meaningful* to the consumer; it furthermore must be *sustainable* over time, even with repetition.

The unique selling proposition (USP) establishes a product or firm's unique benefits in an advertising campaign. Ford's USP is, "Built Tough" (left). Nokia uses, "Connecting People" (middle). United's USP is, "It's time to fly" (right).

The Appeal

Advertisers also use different appeals to portray their product or service. We discuss two categories: informational and emotional.

Informational Appeals   **Informational appeals** help consumers make purchase decisions by offering factual information and strong arguments built around relevant issues that encourage consumers to evaluate the brand favorably on the basis of the key benefits it provides.[19] Kimberley Clark, for example, relies heavily

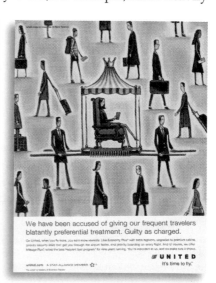

on informational appeals to sell Kleenex Anti-Viral tissues. Note the copy used on the company's Web site:

> Only KLEENEX® Anti-Viral* Tissue has a moisture-activated middle layer that is scientifically proven to kill cold and flu viruses.* When moisture from a runny nose, cough or sneeze comes in contact with KLEENEX® Anti-Viral* Tissue's special middle layer, cold and flu viruses are trapped and killed.*[20]

This appeal is perfectly suited to this type of product. The source of its competitive advantage is a tangible feature of the product. And by stressing the superior benefits of this product over regular facial tissue, the advertising copy directly delivers an informational persuasive message.[21]

Emotional Appeals An **emotional appeal** aims to satisfy consumers' emotional desires rather than their utilitarian needs. The key to a successful emotional appeal is the use of emotion to create a bond between the consumer and the brand. The emotions most often invoked in advertising include fear, safety, humor, happiness, love, comfort, and nostalgia.

Let's look again at Kimberley Clark's Kleenex line; it uses a completely different and emotional appeal for its regular facial tissue. Facial tissues can be closely tied to emotional moments that create the need to wipe away tears of joy or sorrow, and Kleenex attempts to reinforce this emotional trigger by sponsoring the TNT Tearjerker Movie.

Unlike the Anti-Viral campaign, this campaign relies on the implied need for Kleenex during dramatic films. Tangible product features, no longer the persuasive mechanism used to deliver the selling message as they are in informational appeals, do not even appear in the emotional appeal. There are many different types of appeals ranging from sex appeal (e.g., Tag Body Spray), need for affiliation, need for guidance (e.g., Betty Crocker), and attention (e.g., cosmetics).[22]

5. Evaluate and Select Media

The content of an advertisement is tied closely to the characteristics of the media that firms select to carry the message, and vice versa. **Media planning** refers to the process of evaluating and selecting the **media mix**—the combination of the media used and the frequency of advertising in each medium—that

Dressed to kill.

This ad for KLEENEX® Anti-Viral* Tissue provides an informational appeal *that helps consumers make purchase decisions based on factual information and strong favorable arguments.*

Kleenex sponsors the TNT Tearjerker Movie that features dramatic films that are renowned for the misty eyes, furtive nose-blowing, and downright weepiness that they inspire in their audiences.

will deliver a clear, consistent, compelling message to the intended audience.[23] For example, Target may determine that a heavy dose of television, radio, print, and billboards is appropriate for the holiday selling season between Thanksgiving and the end of the year.

Because the **media buy**, the actual purchase of airtime or print pages, is generally the largest expense in the advertising budget, marketers must make their decisions carefully. Television advertising is by far the most expensive. Total U.S. advertising expenditures per medium have remained roughly constant for some time: television 24 percent, direct mail 20 percent, newspapers 20 percent, radio 8 percent, yellow pages 6 percent, magazines 5 percent, and the Internet 2 percent. Other media, such as out-of-home advertising (e.g., billboards, bus wraps, posters) account for the remainder.[24] To characterize these various types of media, we again use a dichotomy: mass and niche media.

Mass and Niche Media

Mass media channels include national newspapers, magazines, radio, and television and are ideal for reaching large numbers of anonymous audience members. **Niche media** channels are more focused and generally used to reach narrower segments, often with unique demographic characteristics or interests. Cable television, direct mail, and specialty magazines such as *Skateboarder* or *Cosmo Girl* all provide examples of niche media. In some cases, niche media offer advertisers the opportunity to change and even personalize their messages, which is generally not an option with mass media. For example, magazine advertisers can print response cards with the name of the subscriber already on the card or change advertisements to reflect local differences, such as climate or preferences.

Choosing the Right Medium

For each class of media, each alternative has specific characteristics that make it suitable for meeting specific objectives (see Exhibit 18.3). For example, consumers use different media for different purposes, to which advertisers should match their messages. Television is used primarily for escapism and entertainment, so most television advertising relies on a mix of visual and auditory techniques. When Apple teamed up with the Irish rock band U2 to create an iPod special edition, it relied heavily on television advertising to introduce the product, which enabled Apple to create powerful visual images that matched the powerful soundtrack of U2's song "Vertigo" in a memorable ad without providing any detail about the advertised product or even informing viewers what an iPod was.

Communication media also vary in their ability to reach the desired audience. For instance, radio is a good medium for products such as grocery purchases or fast food because many consumers decide what to purchase either on the way to the store or while in the store. Because many people listen to the radio in their cars, it becomes a highly effective means to reach consumers at a crucial point in their decision process. As we discussed in Chapter 17, each medium also varies in its reach and frequency. Advertisers can determine how effective their media mix has been in reaching their target audi-

When Apple teamed up with Irish rock band U2 to create an iPod special edition, it relied heavily on television advertising because of its strong visual and auditory effects.

EXHIBIT 18.3	Types of Media Available for Advertising	
MEDIUM	**ADVANTAGES**	**DISADVANTAGES**
Television	• Has wide reach. • Incorporates sound and video.	• Has high cost. • Has cluttered airways. • Has more potential spillover.
Radio	• Is relatively inexpensive. • Can be selectively targeted. • Has wide reach.	• No video limits presentation. • Consumers give less focused attention than TV. • Exposure periods are short.
Magazines	• Is very targeted. • Subscribers pass along to others.	• Is relatively inflexible. • Has long lead times.
Newspapers	• Is flexible. • Is timely. • Can localize.	• Can be expensive in some markets. • Involves potential loss of control over placement. • Advertisements have short life span.
Internet	• Can be linked to detailed content. • Is highly flexible and interactive. • Allows for specific targeting.	• Costs not easily comparable to other media. • Is becoming cluttered. • Blocking software prohibits delivery.
Outdoors	• Is relatively inexpensive. • Offers opportunities for repeat exposure. • Is flexible.	• Is not easily targeted. • Has placement problems in some markets. • Exposure time is very short.
Direct Mail	• Is highly targeted. • Is flexible. • Allows for personalization.	• Is relatively expensive. • Is a cluttered environment. • Is often considered "junk mail."

Ikea uses a pulsing strategy when they set their advertising schedule. They advertise throughout the year, but have more advertising directed at the back-to-school market in August.

ence by calculating the total GRP (reach × frequency) of the advertising schedule, which we discuss next.

Determining the Advertising Schedule

Another important decision for the media planner is the **advertising schedule**, which specifies the timing and duration of advertising. There are three types of schedules:[25]

■ A **continuous** schedule runs steadily throughout the year and therefore is suited to products and services that are consumed continually at relatively steady rates and that require a steady level of persuasive and/or reminder advertising. For example, Procter & Gamble advertises its Tide brand of laundry detergent continuously.

■ **Flighting** refers to an advertising schedule implemented in spurts, with periods of heavy advertising followed by periods of no advertising. This pattern generally functions for products whose demand fluctuates, such

BACK TO SCHOOL SURVIVAL GUIDE
FROM YOUR ROOM AT HOME, TO THE DORM, TO OFF-CAMPUS LIVING!

$12.99

IKEA
www.IKEA-usa.com

as tennis racquets, which manufacturers may advertise heavily in the months leading up to and during the summer.

- **Pulsing** combines the continuous and flighting schedules by maintaining a base level of advertising but increasing advertising intensity during certain periods. For example, furniture retailer, Ikea, advertises throughout the year but boosts its advertising expenditures to promote school supplies in August.

6. Create Advertisements

After the advertiser has decided on the message, type of ad, and appeal, its attention must shift to the actual creation of the advertisement. During this step, the message and appeal are translated creatively into words, pictures, colors, and/or music. Often, the execution style for the ad will dictate the type of medium used to deliver the message. For example, in one ad campaign, crash tests demonstrating the safety of Toyota cars rely on the visual impact of the crash, softened by children who egg the tester to "Do it again, Bob." This style of execution only works on television. Therefore, it is common for advertisers to make decisions about their message and appeal, the appropriate medium, and the best execution concurrently.

Furthermore, advertisers often employ a combination of media to deliver a message. In such cases, they must maintain consistency across the execution styles so that the different executions deliver a consistent and compelling message to the target audience.

Although creativity plays a major role in the execution stage, advertisers must remain careful not to let their creativity overshadow the message. Whatever the execution style, the advertisement must be able to attract the audience's attention, provide a reason for the audience to spend its time viewing the advertisement, and accomplish what it set out to do. In the end, the execution style must match the medium and objectives.

Why is this gorilla smiling? Because the kangaroos have arrived at the Buenos Aires Zoo. This Clio winning ad delivers a compelling visual, a call to action (visit the zoo), and the advertiser's identification.

THE KANGAROOS HAVE ARRIVED. ZOO

Print advertising can be especially difficult because it is a static medium: no sound, no motion, only one dimension. The advertiser must convey its message using compelling visuals and limited text. The ad above is an example of a very effective print ad, so effective that it won a CLIO, the top advertising award.[26]

From the start, this compelling ad makes viewers wonder why the gorilla is smiling, and the answer, that "The kangaroos have arrived," is likely to prompt amused awareness that a new exhibit has opened. To ensure that viewers know who is advertising and how to answer the ad's call to action (i.e., visit the zoo), it also includes the zoo name and logo. In other ads, the advertiser might include a Web addess or telephone number to enable the target audience to answer different calls to action. For the Buenos Aires Zoo though, this ad delivers all the necessary elements: a compelling visual, a call to action, and the advertiser's identification.

For radio and television, some important execution elements include identifying the appropriate talent (actors or singers) to deliver the message and choosing the correct music and visuals. In 1974, when Jell-O brand was introducing its pudding line, it looked for a spokesperson viewed as credible, trustworthy, and likeable; it found Bill Cosby.[27] For more than 30 years, Cosby has been the voice and image of the Jell-O brand because he possesses all the features Jell-O was looking for, along with a voice and image that are immediately recognizable. Cosby has been featured in more than 70 television, 50 radio, and innumerable print advertisements for the pudding. This continuing relationship has made Cosby the longest-running active spokesperson for any brand.

7. Assess Impact

The effectiveness of an advertising campaign must be assessed before, during, and after the campaign has run. **Pretesting** refers to assessments performed before an ad campaign is implemented to ensure that the various elements are working in an integrated fashion and doing what they are intended to do.[28] **Tracking** includes monitoring key indicators, such as daily or weekly sales volume, while the advertisement is running to shed light on any problems with the message or the medium. **Posttesting** is the evaluation of the campaign's impact after it is has been implemented. At this last stage, advertisers assess the sales and/or communication impact of the advertisement or campaign.

Measuring sales impact can be especially challenging because of the many influences other than advertising on consumers' choices, purchase behavior, and attitudes. These influences include the level of competitors' advertising, economic conditions in the target market, sociocultural changes, and even the weather, all of which can influence consumer purchasing behavior. Advertisers must try to identify these influences and isolate those of the particular advertising campaign.

For frequently purchased consumer goods in the maturity stage of the PLC, such as soda, sales volume offers a good indicator of advertising effectiveness. Because their sales are relatively stable, and if we assume that the other elements of the marketing mix and the environment have not changed, we can attribute changes in sales volume to changes in advertising.

For other types of goods in other stages of the PLC, sales data offer but one of the many indicators that marketers need to examine to determine advertising effectiveness. For instance, in high growth markets, sales growth alone can be misleading because the market as a whole is growing. In such a situation, marketers measure sales relative to those of competitors to determine their relative market share. Firms find creative ways to identify advertising effectiveness; for example, digital cable allows them to present a specific advertisement to certain neighbor-hoods and then track sales by local or regional retailers.

Some product categories experience so many influences that it is almost impossible to identify advertising's contribution to any individual consumer's choice to purchase a particular product, especially for addictive products such as cigarettes and alcohol or those with potentially negative health consequences, such as fast food or high-sugar breakfast cereals. The EU is even facing demand for a ban on fast-food ads and other forms of food advertising to children. Although many people firmly believe that advertising for these products contributes significantly to obesity in children, academic research has not been able to show a causal relationship. Other factors, such as parental and peer influence, tend to reflect a higher causality relationship than does advertising.[29]

Regulatory and Ethical Issues in Advertising

In the United States, the regulation of advertising involves a complex mix of formal laws and informal restrictions designed to protect consumers from deceptive practices. Many federal and state laws, as well as a wide range of self-regulatory agencies and agreements, affect advertising (Exhibit 18.4). The primary federal agencies that regulate advertising activities are the Federal Trade Commission (FTC), Federal Communications Commission (FCC), and Food and Drug Administration (FDA). In addition to these agencies, others, such as the Bureau of Alcohol, Tobacco and Firearms and the U.S. Postal Service, regulate advertising to some degree.

The FTC is the primary enforcement agency for most mass media advertising. Occasionally, the FTC and FCC join together to investigate and enforce regulations on particular advertising practices. One special class of products is dietary supplements, many of which are classified as food products and therefore do not fall under the FDA's strict standards for drug advertising. Thus, companies can make unsubstantiated claims about them if they offer an accompanying disclosure statement, such as "This statement has not been evaluated by the FDA" or "This product is not intended to diagnose, treat, cure, or prevent any disease."[30] The FTC currently is conducting an investigation into whether claims made in many of these advertisements are actually deceptive. For now, it remains the responsibility of individual consumers to evaluate them.

EXHIBIT 18.4	Federal Agencies That Regulate Advertising	
Federal Agency	**General Purpose**	**Specific Jurisdiction**
Federal Trade Commission (FTC) (established 1914)	Enforces federal consumer protection laws.	Enforces truth in advertising laws; defines deceptive and unfair advertising practices.
Federal Communications Commission (FCC) (1934)	Regulates interstate and international communications by radio, television, wire, satellite, and cable.	Enforces restrictions on broadcasting material that promotes lotteries (with some exceptions); cigarettes, little cigars, or smokeless tobacco products; or that perpetuates a fraud. Also enforces laws that prohibit or limit obscene, indecent, or profane language.
Food and Drug Administration (1930)	Regulates food, dietary supplements, drugs, cosmetics, medical devices (including radiation-emitting devices such as cell phones), biologics (biological issues), and blood products.	Regulates package labeling and inserts, definition of terms such as "light" and "organic," and required disclosure statements (warning labels, dosage requirements, etc.).

Many product categories fall under self-regulatory restrictions or guidelines. For example, advertising to children is regulated primarily through self-regulatory mechanisms designed by the National Association of Broadcasters and the Better Business Bureau's Children's Advertising Review Unit. The only formal regulation of children's advertising appears in the Children's Television Act of 1990, which limits the amount of advertising broadcast during children's viewing hours.[31]

Recently, to make matters even more complicated for advertisers, state Attorneys General's offices have begun to inquire into various advertising practices and assert their authority to regulate advertising in their states. The EU also has increased its regulation of advertising for EU member nations. Many of these state and European regulations are more restrictive than existing federal or self-regulatory requirements.

Another difference between advertising regulations in the United States and the EU pertains to **puffery,** the legal exaggeration of praise, stopping just short of deception, lavished on a product.[32] In the United States, consumers are viewed as rational and capable of evaluating advertising claims. Does a certain sneaker brand really make you run faster and jump higher? Does Papa John's pizza really have "better ingredients" that make "better pizza"? In the EU, however, puffery is considered deception. For instance, Kraft had no problem advertising its orange-flavored drink Tang surrounded by oranges in the United States. But in Germany, the ad was declared deceptive because there are no oranges in Tang. Advertisers must understand these differences to keep from violating EU advertising laws.

Is this billboard ad an example of puffery or deception?

Sales Promotion

Advertising rarely provides the only means to communicate with target customers. As we discussed in Chapter 17, a natural link appears between advertising and sales promotion. **Sales promotions** are special incentives or excitement-building programs that encourage consumers to purchase a particular product or service, typically used in conjunction with other advertising or personal selling programs. Many sales promotions, like free samples or point-of-purchase (POP) displays, attempt to build short-term sales, whereas others, like loyalty programs, contests, and sweepstakes, have become integral components of firms' long-term customer relationship management (CRM) programs, which they use to build customer loyalty. In this section, we examine the various tools firms use for their sales promotions and how those tools complement the advertiser's efforts to achieve its strategic objectives.

We present the tools used in sales promotions, along with their advantages and disadvantages, in Exhibit 18.5 and discuss them next. Then, we examine some ways in which integrated marketing communication (IMC) programs make use of sales promotions.

The tools of any sales promotion can be focused on either channel members, such as wholesalers or retailers, or end-user consumers. Just as we delineated for advertising, when sales promotions are targeted at channel members, the marketer is employing a push strategy; when it targets consumers themselves, it is using a pull strategy. Some sales promotion tools can be used with either a push

This sales promotion deal for Payless ShoeSource is a short-term price promotion that encourages consumers to buy a second pair of shoes at one half off.

or pull strategy. We now consider each of the tools and how they are used.

Types of Sales Promotion

Coupons   A **coupon** is a certificate with a stated price reduction for a specific item or percentage of a purchase. More than 300 billion coupons are distributed every year in the United States, yet only about 2 percent of them are ever redeemed.[33] However, these redemption rates vary dramatically depending on how consumers obtain the coupon. Coupons carried in newspapers, magazines, in-store displays, and direct mail have very low redemption rates of only 1 to 2 percent, whereas those downloaded from the Internet experience a 56 percent redemption rate. The reason for this dramatic difference is that consumers seek out online coupons for specific items or stores, whereas many people who have no interest in purchasing the product receive traditional coupons.

Deals   A **deal** refers generally to a type of short-term price reduction that can take several forms, such as a "featured price," a price lower than the regular price; a "buy one, get one free" offer; or a certain percentage "more free" offer contained in larger packaging. Another form of a deal involves a special financing arrangement, such as reduced percentage interest rates or extended repayment terms. Deals encourage trial because they lower the risk for consumers by reducing the cost of the good, but they can also alter perceptions of value.

Premiums   A **premium** offers an item for free or at a bargain price to reward some type of behavior, such as buying, sampling, or testing. These rewards build goodwill among consumers, who often perceive high value in them. Premiums can be distributed in a variety of ways: They can be included in the product packaging, such as the toys inside cereal boxes; placed visibly on the package, such as a coupon for free milk on a box of Cheerios; handed out in the store; or delivered in the mail, such as the free perfume offers Victoria's Secret mails to customers.

Furthermore, premiums can be very effective if they are consistent with the brand's message and image and highly desirable to the target market. Finding a premium that meets these criteria at a reasonable cost can be serious challenge. At Burger King for instance, the average order cost is $5, while the average premium the fast-food giant distributes costs the company less than 50 cents.

Burger King offers premiums like this beetle-shaped ruler in conjunction with movie releases like the "Ant Bully." Premiums are either free or at a bargain price, and encourage buying, sampling, or testing.

Contests   A **contest** refers to a brand-sponsored competition that requires some form of skill or effort. The effort required by these contests often keeps participation lower than that for other forms of promotion. For instance, for more than 40 years, Pillsbury has awarded money and prizes to its bake-off grand prize winner. From all those who

E X H I B I T	18.5	Kinds of Sales Promotion

Kinds of Sales Promotion

PROMOTION	ADVANTAGES	DISADVANTAGES
Coupons	• Stimulates demand. • Allows for direct tracing of sales.	• Has low redemption rates. • Has high cost.
Deals	• Encourages trial. • Reduces consumer risk.	• May reduce perception of value.
Premiums	• Builds goodwill. • Increases perception of value.	• Consumers buy for premium not product. • Has to be carefully managed.
Contests	• Increases consumer involvement. • Generates excitement.	• Requires creativity. • Must be monitored.
Sweepstakes	• Encourages present consumers to consume more.	• Sales often decline after.
Samples	• Encourages trial. • Offers direct involvement.	• Has high cost to the firm.
Loyalty Programs	• Creates loyalty. • Encourages repurchase.	• Has high cost to the firm.
POP Displays	• Provides high visibility. • Encourages brand trial.	• Is difficult to get a good location in the store. • Can be costly to the firm.
Rebates	• Stimulates demand. • Increase value perception.	• Is easily copied by competitors. • May just advance future sales.
Product Placement	• Displays products nontraditionally. • Demonstrates product uses.	• Firm often has little control over display. • Product can be overshadowed.

submit recipes, 100 finalists are chosen and compete against one another; a panel of experts chooses the ultimate winner. The company also uses cobranding to encourage other brands, such as Splenda and Receta Rice, to sponsor the runner-up prizes for specific categories.[34] To be effective, contests must be advertised and enjoy high levels of retailer or dealer support.

Sweepstakes   A form of sales promotion that offers prizes based on a chance drawing of entrants' names, sweepstakes do not require the entrant to complete a task other than buy a ticket or fill out a form. Often the key benefit of sweepstakes is that they encourage current consumers to consume more if the sweepstakes form appears inside the packaging or with the product. Many states, however, specify that no purchase can be required to enter sweepstakes.

Samples   Sampling offers potential customers the opportunity to try a product or service before they make a buying decision. Distributing samples is one of the most costly sales promotion tools but also one of the most effective. As we describe in Adding Value 18.1, one of the key purposes of a recent Meow Mix promotion was to distribute samples of its new wet cat food to consumers who might then be motivated to purchase subsequently. As with many sampling offers, Meow Mix offered a coupon along with its samples.

Adding Value 18.1

The Cat's Meow

The Meow Mix Company had planned to keep its Fifth Avenue storefront in New York City open for only a week, but the traffic and media attention were so great that it quickly decided to add a second week.[41] The pop-up restaurant, named "the Meow Mix Café," welcomed cats and their owners in for a unique culinary experience for cats. The idea was to use the café to introduce consumers to a new "wet" food line.

Meow Mix, the top dry cat food brand, hoped to transition to wet food through a campaign that generated both publicity and brand trials. The café idea accomplished both beautifully. Cat owners brought their cats to what the Meow Mix team termed an "ESPN Zone for cats," with lots of interactive games, fun, and food. The café's rousing success garnered it 100 million press mentions and enabled the company to distribute 14,000 sample pouches of cat food. A side benefit of the campaign was the calls from potential franchisees wanting information about how to open their own Meow Mix cafés. In total, the firm estimated that its $150,000 investment would yield about $50 million in incremental sales the following year—not a bad return.

The Meow Mix Café in New York City was a temporary pop-up restaurant designed to promote Meow Mix cat food. Pop-up retail stores are set in temporary locations to generate excitement about a brand or product.

POP displays are merchandise displays located at the point of purchase, such as at the check-out counter in a grocery store.

Loyalty Programs   As part of a sales promotion program, **loyalty programs** are specifically designed to retain customers by offering premiums or other incentives to customers that make multiple purchases over time. Such sales promotions are growing increasingly popular and often tied to long-term CRM systems.

Point-of-Purchase Displays   **Point-of-purchase (POP) displays** are merchandise displays located at the point of purchase, such as at the checkout counter in a grocery store. Marketers spend almost as much on POP materials as they do on consumer magazine advertising, but the key to a successful POP is to make the display "pop out" in a crowded store. In addition, manufacturers must encourage retailers to feature and use the POP displays to maximize their investments.

Rebates   Rebates refer to a particular type of price reduction. Many products, such as cell phones, now offer significant mail-in rebates that may lower the price of the phone to $0 or perhaps less than $0. Firms offer such generous rebates because the likelihood that consumers will actually apply for the rebate is low, even though consumers indicate that rebate offers are a factor in their purchase decisions. The firms thus garner considerable value from rebates because they attract consumers with a minimal risk that the firm will have to pay off all the rebates offered.

Recently, heavy rebate users such as Best Buy have begun scaling back their programs.[35] Like any promotional tool, too much of a good thing can be a problem. Best Buy found that consumers were becoming increasingly annoyed by having to mail in the rebate forms and wait to receive their money. Many were requesting that the rebate be given at the time of purchase and wondering why this immediate promotion was not possible. In addition, a growing number of lawsuits claim rebate checks were never sent to consumers and that rebate offers contain overly detailed clauses that cause consumers to have to submit and resubmit their claims.[36]

Product Placement   When marketers use **product placement**, they include their product in nontraditional situations, such as in a scene in a movie or television program. The first visible movie product placement was Hershey's Reese's Pieces in the film *ET*. The product actually became part of the storyline, offered the candy high levels of visibility, and resulted in a large increase in sales.[37]

Although Hershey's did not pay to place Reese's Pieces in *ET*, other firms have been more than willing to shell out for product placements. For example, Exxon paid $300,000 to have its name appear in *Days of Thunder*, Pampers paid $50,000 to

How much do you think Coca-Cola had to pay American Idol to get this product placement?

be featured in *Three Men and a Baby*, and Cuervo Gold spent $150,000 for placement in *Tequila Sunrise*.[38] Especially because consumers who use digital video recorders report that they skip televised commercials 72.3 percent of the time, product placement is becoming increasingly important. Moreover, research shows that consumers recall product placements relatively well.[39]

Using Sales Promotion Tools

Marketers must be careful in their use of promotions, especially those that focus on lowering prices. Depending on the item, consumers may stock up when items are offered at a lower price, which simply shifts sales from the future to now and thereby leads to short-run benefits at the expense of long-term sales stability. For instance, using sales promotions like coupons to stimulate sales of household cleaning supplies may cause consumers to stockpile the products and decrease demand for those products in the future. But a similar promotion used with a perishable product like Dannon yogurt should increase its demand at the expense of competitors like Yoplait.

The tools connected to sales promotions are as varied as the imaginations of the marketers who devise them, and new forms are constantly popping up. For example, pop-up stores, like the Meow Mix Café in New York City pictured in Adding Value 18.1 on page 506, exist only for a limited time and generally focus on a new product or a limited group of products offered by a retailer, manufacturer, or service provider. These temporary storefronts give consumers a chance to inter-act with the brand and build brand awareness, but they are not designed primarily to sell the product. Instead, consumers who have visited the pop-up, the company hopes, will follow up with a visit to either another retailer that carries the products or the company's Web site.[40]

Retailers tend not to mind manufacturers' pop-up stores because most are de-signed to drive traffic to the retailers through give-aways of coupons and samples. Because pop-ups are short lived, they don't pose any long-term competition to retailers.

Many firms are also realizing the value of cross-promoting, when two or more firms join together to reach a specific target market. To achieve a successful cross-promotion, the two products must appeal to the same target market and together create value for consumers. Burger King, for instance recently ran a three-firm cross promotion: Motts Strawberry-Flavored Applesauce, designed to attract health-conscious parents; Star Wars memorabilia, designed to attract collectors and fans of the movie; and BK King of the Courts 3-on-3 College Basketball Tour-nament, designed to attract college students and fans of college basketball. Each of these cross-promotions targets a different market and attempts to create value in a slightly different way for Burger King consumers. However, the ultimate, overall goal for Burger King is to generate increased sales and greater brand loyalty.

The goal of any sales promotion is to create value for both the consumers and the firm. By understanding the needs of its customers, as well as how best to entice them to purchase or consume a particular product or service, a firm can develop promo-tional messages and events that are of interest to and achieve the desired response from those customers. Traditionally, the role of sales promotion has been to gener-ate short-term results, whereas the goal of advertising was to generate long-term results. As this chapter demonstrates, though, both sales promotion and advertising can generate both long- and short-term effects. The effective combination of both types of activities leads to impressive results for the firm and the consumers.

Summing Up

1. **How do firms plan advertising campaigns?**

   Firms (1) identify their target market; (2) set adver-tising objectives; (3) set the advertising budget; (4) depict their product or service; (5) evaluate and select the media; (6) create the ad; and (7) assess the impact of the ad.

2. **Why do firms advertise?**

   When firms are advertising to consumers, they are using a pull strategy; when advertising to supply chain members to induce them to carry and sell products, they are using a push strategy. All adver-tising campaigns are designed to either inform, persuade, or remind customers. Ads can also be used to stimulate demand for a particular category or industry, or for a specific brand, firm, or item. Finally, ad campaigns are used to stimulate either primary or selective demand.

3. **What appeals do advertisers use to get customers' attention?**

Advertising appeals are either informational or emotional. Informational appeals influence purchase decisions with factual information and strong arguments built around relevant key benefits that encourage consumers to evaluate the brand favorably. Emotional appeals indicate how the product satisfies emotional desires rather than utilitarian needs.

4. **How do firms determine which media to use?**

Firms can use mass media channels like newspapers or television to reach large numbers of anonymous audience members. Niche media, such as cable television, direct mail, and specialty magazines, are generally used to reach narrower segments with unique demographic characteristics or interests. When choosing the media, firms must match their objectives to the media. Also, certain media are better at reaching a particular target audience than others.

5. **What legal and ethical issues are of concern to advertisers?**

Advertising is regulated by a plethora of federal and state agencies. The most important federal agencies are the FTC, which protects consumers against general deceptive advertising; the FCC, which has jurisdiction over radio, television, wire, satellite, and cable and covers issues regarding the use of tobacco products and objectionable language; and the FDA, which regulates food, dietary supplements, drugs, cosmetics, and medical devices.

6. **How do sales promotions supplement a firm's IMC strategy?**

Sales promotions are special incentives or excitement-building programs that encourage purchase and include coupons, rebates, contests, free samples, and POP displays. They either push sales through the channel, as is the case with contests directed toward retail salespeople, or pull sales through the channel, as coupons and rebates do. Sales promotions usually occur in conjunction with other elements of a firm's IMC strategy, such as price promotions or loyalty programs.

Key Terms

- advertising, 488
- advertising plan, 490
- advertising schedule, 499
- contest, 504
- continuous advertising schedule, 499
- coupon, 504
- cross-promoting, 508
- deal, 504
- emotional appeal, 497
- flighting advertising schedule, 499
- informational appeal, 496
- informative advertising, 490
- institutional advertisements, 491
- loyalty program, 506
- mass media, 498
- media buy, 498
- media mix, 497
- media planning, 497
- niche media, 498
- persuasive advertising, 490
- point-of-purchase (POP) display, 506
- pop-up stores, 508
- posttesting, 501
- premium, 504
- pretesting, 501
- primary demand advertising, 492
- product placement, 507
- product-focused advertisements, 491
- public service advertising (PSA), 493
- puffery, 503
- pull strategy, 490
- pulsing advertising schedule, 500
- push strategy, 490
- rebate, 507
- reminder advertising, 491
- sales promotion, 503
- sampling, 505
- selective demand, 493
- selective demand advertising, 492
- social marketing, 493
- sweepstakes, 505
- top-of-the-mind awareness, 491
- tracking, 501
- unique selling proposition (USP), 496

Marketing Applications

1. Choose one of the ads featured in this book and identify its page number. What are the objectives of this ad? Does the ad have more than one objective? Explain your answer.

2. Using the same ad, explain whether it is using an informational or emotional appeal.

3. Microsoft spends millions of dollars each year on advertising for many different purposes. Using the 2 × 2 matrix in Exhibit 18.2, provide an example of how it might design a campaign for each type of ad.

4. Name three current advertising slogans you believe are particularly effective for developing a unique selling proposition.

5. Bernard's, a local furniture company, target markets college students with apartments and households of young people purchasing their first furniture items. If you worked for Bernard's, what type of media would you use for your advertising campaign? Justify your answer.

6. Should Bernard's use continuous, pulsing, or flighting for its advertising schedule? Why?

7. Suppose Lexus is introducing a new line of light trucks and has already created the advertising campaign. How would you assess the effectiveness of the campaign?

8. Suppose now that Lexus is planning a sales promotion campaign to augment its advertising campaign for the new line of light trucks. Which push and pull sales promotion tools do you believe would be most effective? Why?

9. Choose an ad that you believe unreasonably overstates what the product or service can do. (If you can't think of a real ad, make one up.) Explain whether the ad is actually deceptive or just puffery. How would your answer change if you lived in France?

10. You are invited to your six-year-old niece's birthday party and bring her the new superhero doll being advertised on television. She's thrilled when she unwraps the gift but is in tears a short time later because her new doll is broken. She explains that on TV, the doll flies and does karate kicks, but when she tried to play with the doll this way, it broke. You decide to call the manufacturer, and a representative tells you he is sorry your niece is so upset but that the ad clearly states the doll does not fly. The next time you see the televised ad, you notice very small print at the bottom that states the doll does not fly. You decide to write a letter to the FTC about this practice. What information should you include in your letter?

Toolkit

MAKE AN ADVERTISEMENT

Suppose you have been hired to develop a new ad for a product or service to help target the college student market. These ads will appear in student college newspapers around the world. Please use the toolkit provided at www.mhhe.com/grewal-levy to develop the ad.

Net Savvy

1. Go to the Web site for the Children's Advertising Review Unit (CARU), one of the major self-regulatory bodies for children's advertising, at www.caru.org. Click on the About Us tab and examine the history and activities of CARU. How does this form of regulation complement the more formal regulation of federal and state agencies? Now look under the News and Publications tab. Choose one of the press releases and discuss what action CARU took against the identified company or group. What was the main issue in the case?

2. A comprehensive source for all things advertising is a Web site run by the University of Texas at Austin's College of Communication: Ad World. It is the home of thousands of advertising-related links. Go to http://advertising.utexas.edu/world/index.asp and explore the site. Explain which you consider the most important tab. Find the tab labeled "job hunting" and click on some of the resources listed. What qualifications do you have to have to get a job in advertising? How important are internships to landing an advertising position?

Chapter Case Study

ADVERTISING DOLE'S FRUIT BOWLS[42]

Never a company to rest on its pineapples, in 1999 Dole stepped out of its traditional canned pineapple product category and introduced the Fruit Bowl. Using clever advertising, the company then successfully repositioned the product for a different target market in 2002.

Dole Food Company has been selling pineapples since 1851 and today is the world's largest producer and marketer of fresh fruit, fresh vegetables, fresh-cut flowers, and a growing line of packaged foods. Dole does business in more than 90 countries and employs 36,000 full-time employees, as well as 23,000 full-time seasonal (or temporary) employees worldwide.

Until the mid-1990s, Dole's main focus was canned pineapple, which it advertised primarily as an ingredient in recipes. But the market had begun to change. Consumers were spending less time on meal preparation and preferred convenience foods. So Dole developed a product that met the demand for convenience foods with Fruit Bowls: 4 ounces of bite-sized pieces of pineapple, mixed tropical fruits, and peaches. Because this product was designed to be consumed as a snack, not as an ingredient, it required a departure from Dole's traditional recipe-oriented advertising strategy.

Although it initially imagined its target market to be parents of children, Dole's research revealed that almost 54 percent of Fruit Bowls' sales came from households *without* kids—specifically, professional women on the go. As a result, in 2002, Dole introduced several new products, including larger, seven-ounce Fruit Bowls, Fruit 'N Gel Bowls, and reduced-sugar Fruit 'N Gel Bowls. The initial advertising campaign for Fruit Bowls had targeted women but only as moms/family caretakers, not as health-conscious, working women pressed for time.

For the new products, the advertising agency Dailey and Associates of Los Angeles targeted working women, aged 25 to 54 years. With the message that "Dole Fruit Bowls are fun to eat, healthy, and great on the go," the common thread of the multimedia campaign was the tag line: "Dole. Life is Sweet." By the end of 2003, volume growth at Dole also was sweet as customers continued to choose Dole's healthy snack over more traditional ones. By understanding the needs of consumers, modifying the product to meet those needs, and using advertising to convey the benefits of the product to different consumer segments, Dole was able to create a very successful product.

Which markets is Dole targeting with this ad?

Case Questions

1. Should Dole continue to go after different target markets with new ad campaigns? Why or why not?

2. What type of appeal is Dole using in the campaign "Dole. Life is Sweet"? What other appeals might it use? How would it do so?

3. In what ways did Dole create value for its target markets and itself?

19

Personal Selling and Sales Management

Despite modest beginnings, Marty Rodriguez has become a superstar in the world of real estate.[1] She grew up in a two-bedroom house in El Monte, California with her parents and 10 siblings. Her parents taught them that with hard work and good grades they would never have to settle for anything less than the best. Rodriguez took her parents' advice and worked two jobs as she took real estate courses at Rio Hondo College. In her first year as an agent, she and her partner sold $1 million. Her compassionate nature and perseverance was perfect for real estate sales.

During the real estate market collapse in the late 80s, many agents cut back on costs, but not Marty. Instead, she hired more people. By 1991, she was the first woman at Century 21 to earn over $1 million in gross closed commissions. That year also marked the start of three consecutive World Sales Champion titles, a feat no one else has accomplished. She received the same title again in 1997, one year after opening her own Century 21 Marty Rodriguez office. Despite these accomplishments, Marty Rodriguez doesn't sit on her laurels. She loves to sell houses, so that is what she does. She leaves the business end of the job to three of her children who work in her office.

Marty Rodriquez, Century 21's "All Time Sales Agent."

With all the success and opportunities Marty Rodriguez has received, she believes in giving back to her community. She and her team support local programs, for example, by serving on a committee to develop a sports activity center at her former high school. As a Hispanic she is proud that she is able to represent the culture, but does not feel confined by it. She is a member of the National Association of Hispanic Real Estate Professionals and hopes to be a role model not only for Hispanics, but for the real estate industry as a whole. With international recognition as Century 21's "All Time Sales Agent," this shouldn't be too hard.

■ ■ ■

Just like advertising, which we discussed in the last chapter, personal selling is so important in integrated marketing communications that it deserves its own chapter. Almost everyone is engaged in some form of selling. On a personal level, you sell your ideas or opinions to your friends, family, employers, and professors. Even if you have no interest in personal selling as a career, a strong grounding in the topic will help you in numerous career choices. Consider, for instance, Harry Turk, a very successful labor attorney. He worked his way through college selling alpaca sweaters to fraternities across the country. Although he loved his part-time job, Harry decided to become solely an attorney. When asked whether he misses selling, he said, "I use my selling skills every day. I have to sell new clients on the idea that I'm the best attorney for the job. I have to sell my partners on my legal point of view. I even use selling skills when I'm talking to a judge or jury." In this chapter though, we take a straightforward business perspective on selling.

The Scope and Nature of Personal Selling

Many salespeople now can rely on virtual offices, which enable them to communicate via the Internet with colleagues and customers.

Personal selling is the two-way flow of communication between a buyer or buyers and a seller that is designed to influence the buyer's purchase decision. Personal selling can take place in various situations: face-to-face, via video teleconferencing, on the telephone, or over the Internet. Approximately 13.5 million people are employed in sales positions in the United States,[2] including those involved in business-to-business (B2B) transactions—like manufacturers' representatives selling to retailers or other businesses—and those completing business-to-consumer (B2C) transactions, such as retail salespeople, real estate agents, and insurance agents. Salespeople are referred to in many ways: sales representatives or reps, account executives, agents. And as Harry Turk found, most professions rely on personal selling to some degree.

Salespeople don't always get the best coverage in popular media. In Arthur Miller's play *Death of a Salesman*, the main character, Willie Loman, leads a pathetic existence and suffers from the loneliness inherent in being a traveling salesman.[3] The characters in David Mamet's play *Glengarry Glen Ross* (which was also made into a movie) portray salespeople as crude, ruthless, and of questionable character. Unfortunately, these pow-

Entrepreneurial Marketing 19.1

Some People Just Love to Sell[4]

Motivated by his love of sales, entrepreneur Peter Groop took his one-man show and turned it into a $300 million company. No stranger to successful selling, Groop joined Hewlett-Packard fresh out of college. He was so good that HP promoted him to a sales manager position by the time he was 25 years of age.

But his new position took him away from the job he loved: sales. So he left HP, and after a year as a stockbroker, he started his own company. Reconnecting with his old friends at HP, he made a deal to sell smaller items that the HP sales force tended to neglect, working on a commission from HP for 10 percent of sales. Thus Fusion Sales Partners was born.

Fusion Sales Partners is a pure sales company. All associates are paid on commission, which is a fixed percentage of their sales. They get no salary and are not reimbursed for their expenses. Groop signs off personally on all new hires, whom he chooses because they have the selling "it" factor and are hungry to perform. According to Groop, compensation based 100 percent on commission is the only way to identify top talent. Top sales reps receive roughly 30 percent of the profit generated, as well as bonuses. For instance, Theresa Bryan booked $32.6 million, generating a gross profit of $327,000. She took home $98,100, along with seven $1,500 bonuses. It really does pay to sell.

erful Pulitzer Prize–winning pieces of literature weigh heavily on our collective conscious and often overshadow the millions of hardworking professional salespeople who have fulfilling and rewarding careers and who add value to their firm and provide value for their customers.

Professional selling can be such a satisfying career for several reasons. First, many people love the lifestyle. Salespeople are typically out on their own. Although they occasionally work with their managers and other colleagues, salespeople are usually responsible for planning their own day. This flexibility trans-

Professional selling can be a very lucrative career and is very visible to management.

lates into an easier balance between work and family than many office-bound jobs can offer. Many salespeople now can rely on virtual offices, which enable them to communicate via the Internet with colleagues and customers. Because salespeople are evaluated primarily on the results they produce, as long as they meet and exceed their goals, they experience little day-to-day supervision.

Second, the variety of the job often attracts people to sales. Every day is different, bringing different clients and customers, often in a variety of places. Their issues and problems and the solutions to those problems all differ and require creativity.

Third, professional selling and sales management can be a very lucrative career. Sales is among the highest-paying careers for college graduates, and compensation often includes perks, such as the use of a company car and bonuses for high performance. A top performer can have a total compensation package of over

$150,000; even lower-level salespeople can make well over $50,000. Although the monetary compensation can be significant, the satisfaction of being involved in interesting, challenging, and creative work is rewarding in and of itself.

Fourth, because salespeople are the frontline emissaries for their firm, they are very visible to management. Furthermore, it is fairly straightforward for management to identify top performers, which means that those high-performing salespeople who aspire to management positions are in a good position to get promoted. Entrepreneurial Marketing 19.1 describes the life of a super salesperson and his company, Fusion Sales Partners.

Personal Selling and Marketing Strategy

Although personal selling is an essential part of many firms' integrated marketing communications strategy, it offers its own unique contribution to the four Ps. Because of the one-to-one nature of sales, a salesperson is in a unique position to customize a message for a specific buyer. As a result, a preplanned sales presentation or demonstration can be altered at any time as the need arises. For instance, in a personal selling situation, the salesperson can probe the buyer for his or her potential reservations about a product or service, educate the buyer when appropriate, and ask for the order at the appropriate time. Also, unlike other types of promotion, the sales presentation can be directed toward those customers with the highest potential. This highly directed approach to promotion is important because experts estimate that the average cost of a single B2B sales call is about $330.[5]

As we discussed in Chapter 15, building strong supply chain relationships is a critical success factor. Who in the organization is better equipped to manage this relationship than the salesperson, the frontline emissary for the firm? The most successful salespeople are those who build strong relationships with their customers. They don't view themselves as being successful if they make a particular sale or one transaction at a time. Instead, they take a long-term perspective. Thus, building on the strategic relationship concept introduced in Chapter 15, **relationship selling** is a sales philosophy and process that emphasizes a commitment to maintaining the relationship over the long term and investing in opportunities that are mutually beneficial to all parties. Relationship salespeople work with their customers to find mutually beneficial solutions to their wants and needs. An IBM sales team, for instance, may be working with your university to provide you with the computer support and security you need.

Salespeople input customer information into their PDAs to develop a customer database for CRM systems.

Research has shown that a positive customer–salesperson relationship contributes to trust, increased customer loyalty, and the intent to continue the relationship with the salesperson.[6] To help build strong relationships, many firms undertake active customer relationship management (CRM) programs that identify and focus on building loyalty with the firm's most valued customers. Because the sales force interacts directly with customers, its members are in the best position to help a firm accomplish its CRM objectives.

CRM programs have several components. There is a customer database or data warehouse. Whether the salesperson is working for a retail store or manages a selling team for an aerospace contractor, he or she can record transaction information, customer contact information, customer preferences, and market segment information about the customer. Once the data has been analyzed and CRM programs developed, salespeople can help implement the programs. For instance, bankers use a "high-touch approach" in which they frequently call on their best customers or contact them by phone. A salesperson can contact customers when there are new products or changes to existing product lines. He or she can probe customers about what they liked or disliked about their recent transactions with the firm. Or the purpose of the call can be purely social. If done properly, customers will feel special and important when a salesperson calls just to see how things are going.

The Value Added by Personal Selling

Why have salespeople in the supply chain? They are expensive, and as we discuss later in this chapter, they can be a challenge to manage. Some firms, like retailers, have made the decision not to use a sales force and become, for the most part, almost completely self-service. But those that use personal selling as part of their integrated marketing communications program do so because it adds value to their product or service mix—that is, personal selling is worth more than it costs. Personal selling adds value by educating and providing advice, saving the customer time, and making things easier for the customer.[7]

Salespeople Educate and Provide Advice

Imagine how difficult it would be to buy a new suit, a diamond engagement ring, or a plasma TV without the help of a salesperson. Similarly, UPS wouldn't dream of investing in a new fleet of airplanes without the benefit of Boeing's selling team. Sure, it could be done, but customers see the value in and are willing to pay indirectly for the education and advice salespeople provide. Retail salespeople can provide valuable information about how a garment fits, new fashions, or directions for operating products. Boeing's sales team can provide UPS with the technical aspects of the aircraft, as well as the economic justification for the purchase.

Five years ago, many observers thought that travel agents and other service providers would be replaced by more efficient Internet services, and the Internet has certainly changed the way many consumers make travel decisions. Thousands use sites like Expedia.com and Travelocity.com or visit airlines, Amtrak, hotels, and car rental firms online to make reservations directly. But when booking a complicated trip or cruise or planning to visit an exotic locale, or for those who don't feel comfortable buying online, travel agents add significant value. They can help with itineraries, give helpful tips, and even save the customer money.

Salespeople Save Time and Simplify Buying

Time is money! Customers perceive value in time and labor savings. In many grocery and drugstore chains, salespeople employed by the vendor supplying merchandise straighten stock, set up displays, assess inventory levels, and write orders. In some cases, such as bakeries or soft drink sales, salespeople and truck drivers even bring in the merchandise and stock the shelves. These are all tasks that retail employees would otherwise have to do.

Sometimes, however, turning over too many tasks to suppliers' salespeople can cause problems. If they take over the inventory management function, for instance, they may buy a suboptimal quantity of competitors' products. They might also place competitor products in disadvantageous shelf positions. Salespeople can help facilitate a buying situation, but they shouldn't take it over.

The Personal Selling Process

Although selling may appear a rather straightforward process, successful salespeople follow several steps. Depending on the sales situation and the buyer's readiness to purchase, the salesperson may not use every step, and the time required for each step will vary depending on the situation. For instance, if a customer goes into The Gap already prepared to purchase some chinos, the selling process will be fairly quick. But if IBM is attempting to sell personal computers for the first time to a university, the process may take several months. With this in mind, let's examine each step of the selling process (Exhibit 19.1).

Step 1: Generate and Qualify Leads

The first step in the selling process is to generate a list of potential customers (leads) and assess their potential (qualify). Salespeople who already have an established relationship with a customer will skip this step, and it is not used extensively in retail settings. In B2B situations, however, it is important to work continually to find new and potentially profitable customers.

Salespeople generate leads in a variety of ways.[8] They can discover potential leads by talking to their current customers and networking at events such as industry conferences or chamber of commerce meetings. The Internet has been a boon for generating leads. For instance, salespeople can gather information collected on the firm's Web site or Google a few key words and instantly generate enough potential leads to keep them busy for weeks. Trade shows also offer an excellent forum for finding leads. These major events are attended by buyers who choose to be exposed to products and services offered by potential suppliers in an industry.

| EXHIBIT | 19.1 | The Personal Selling Process |

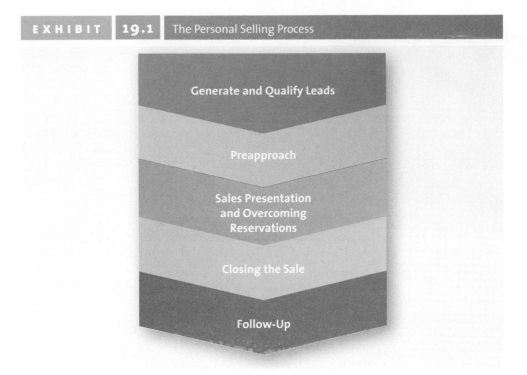

Generate and Qualify Leads

Preapproach

Sales Presentation and Overcoming Reservations

Closing the Sale

Follow-Up

For instance, the International Housewares Association hosts the International Home and Housewares show at McCormick Place in Chicago every March. About 15,000 U.S. buyers and more than 6,000 non-U.S. buyers attend to view products and services from over 2,100 exhibitors from 34 countries.[9]

Cold calls are a method of prospecting in which salespeople telephone or go to see potential customers without appointments. Telemarketing is similar to a cold call, but it always occurs over the telephone. Sometimes professional telemarketing firms, rather than the firm's salespeople, make such calls. However, cold calls and telemarketing have become less popular than they were in the past. First, the success rate is fairly low because the potential customer's need has not been established ahead of time. As a result, these methods can be very expensive. Second, both federal and state governments have begun to regulate the activities of telemarketers. Federal rules prohibit telemarketing to consumers whose names appear on the national Do-Not-Call list, which is maintained by the Federal Trade Commission. Even for those consumers whose names are not on the list, the rules prohibit calling before 8:00 a.m. or after 9:00 p.m. (in the consumer's time zone) or after the consumer has told the telemarketer not to call. Federal rules also prohibit unsolicited fax messages and unsolicited telephone calls, as well as e-mail messages to cell phones.

After salespeople generate leads, they must qualify those leads by determining whether it is worthwhile to pursue them and attempt to turn them into customers. In a retail setting, qualifying potential can be a very dangerous and potentially illegal practice. Retail salespeople should never "judge a book by its cover" and assume that a person in the store doesn't fit the store's image or cannot afford to purchase

A great place to generate leads is at a trade show.

Retail salespeople should never "judge a book by its cover" and assume that a person in the store doesn't fit the store's image or cannot afford to purchase there.

there. Imagine going to an upscale jewelry store to purchase an engagement ring, only to be snubbed because you are dressed in your everyday, casual school clothes. But in B2B settings, where the costs of preparing and making a presentation can be substantial, the seller must assess a lead's potential. Salespeople should consider, for instance, whether the potential customer's needs pertain to a product or a service. They should also assess whether the lead has the financial resources to pay for the product or service.

Step 2: Preapproach

The **preapproach** occurs prior to meeting the customer for the first time and extends the qualification of leads procedure described in Step 1. Although the salesperson has learned about the customer during the qualification stage, in this step, he or she must conduct additional research and develop plans for meeting with the customer. Suppose, for example, a management consulting firm wants to sell a bank a new system for finding checking account errors. The consulting firm's salesperson should first find out everything possible about the bank: How many checks does it process? What system is the bank using now? What are the benefits of the consultant's proposed system compared with the competition? The answers to these questions provide the basis for establishing value for the customer.

Having done the additional research, the salesperson establishes goals for meeting with the customer; it is important that he or she know ahead of time exactly what should be accomplished. For instance, the consulting firm's salesperson can't expect to get a commitment from the bank that it will buy on the first visit. But a demonstration of the system and a short presentation about how the system would benefit the customer would be appropriate. It is often a good idea to practice the presentation prior to the meeting using a technique known as **role playing,** in which the salesperson acts out a simulated buying situation while a colleague or manager acts as the buyer. Afterward, the practice sales presentation can be critiqued and adjustments can be made.

Step 3: Sales Presentation and Overcoming Reservations

These salespeople are role playing. The woman standing at the easel is acting out a simulated buying situation while her colleagues act as the buying group. Afterward they will critique her presentation.

The Presentation   Once all the background information has been obtained and the objectives for the meeting are set, the salesperson is ready for a person-to-person meeting. Let's continue with our bank example. During the first part of the meeting, the salesperson needs to get to know the customer, get his or her attention, and create interest in the presentation to follow. The beginning of the presentation may be the most important part of the entire selling process, because this is where the salesperson establishes exactly where the cus-

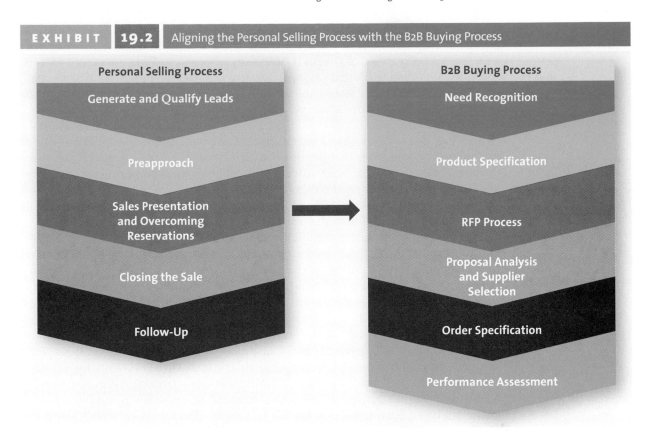

EXHIBIT | **19.2** | Aligning the Personal Selling Process with the B2B Buying Process

Personal Selling Process

Generate and Qualify Leads

Preapproach

Sales Presentation and Overcoming Reservations

Closing the Sale

Follow-Up

B2B Buying Process

Need Recognition

Product Specification

RFP Process

Proposal Analysis and Supplier Selection

Order Specification

Performance Assessment

tomer is in his or her buying process (Exhibit 19.2). (For a refresher on the B2B buying process, see Chapter 6.) Suppose, for instance, the bank is in the first stage of the buying process, need recognition. It would not be prudent for the salesperson to discuss the pros and cons of different potential suppliers because doing so would assume that the customer already had reached Stage 4, proposal analysis and customer selection. By asking a series of questions, however, the salesperson can assess the bank's need for the product or service and adapt or customize the presentation to match the customer's need and stage in the decision process.[10]

Asking questions is only half the battle; carefully listening to the answers is equally important. Some salespeople, particularly inexperienced ones, believe that to be in control, they must do all the talking. Yet it is impossible to really understand where the customer stands without listening carefully. What if the COO says, "It seems kind of expensive"? If the salesperson isn't listening carefully, he or she won't pick up on the subtle nuances of what the customer is really thinking. In this case, it probably means the COO doesn't see the value in the offering.

When the salesperson has gotten a good feel for where the customer stands, he or she can apply that knowledge to help the customer solve its problem or satisfy its need. The salesperson might begin by explaining the features or characteristics of the system that will reduce checking account errors. It may not be obvious, based solely on these features, however, that the system adds value beyond the bank's current practices. Using the answers to some of the questions the salesperson posed earlier in the meeting, he or she can clarify the product's advantages over current or past practices, as well as the overall benefits of adopting the new system. The salesperson might explain, for instance, that the bank can expect a 20 percent improvement in checking account errors and that, based on the size of the bank and number of checks it processes per year, this improvement would represent $2 million in annual savings. Because the system costs $150,000 per year and will take only three weeks to integrate into the current system, it will add significant and almost immediate value.

Handling Reservations   An integral part of the sales presentation is handling reservations or objections that the buyer might have about the product or service. Although reservations can arise during each stage of the selling process, they are very likely to occur during the sales presentation. Customers may raise reservations pertaining to a variety of issues, but they usually relate in some way to value, such as that the price is too high for the level of quality or service.

Good salespeople know the types of reservations buyers are likely to raise. They may know, for instance, that their service is slower than competitors' or that their selection is limited. Although not all reservations can be forestalled, effective salespeople can anticipate and handle some. For example, when the bank COO said the check service seemed expensive, the salesperson was ready with information about how quickly the investment would be recouped.

Similar to other aspects of the selling process, the best way to handle reservations is to relax and listen, then ask questions to clarify any reservations. For example, the salesperson could respond to the COO's reservation by asking, "How much do you think the bank is losing through checking account errors?" Her answer might open up a conversation about the positive trends in a cost/benefit analysis. Such questions are usually more effective than trying to prove the customer's reservation is not valid because the latter approach implies the salesperson isn't really listening and could lead to an argument. In an attempt to handle reservations and start the process of closing the sale, a salesperson may offer creative deals or incentives that may be unethical (see cartoon below).

Step 4: Closing the Sale

Closing the sale means obtaining a commitment from the customer to make a purchase. Without a successful close, the salesperson goes away empty handed, so many salespeople find this part of the sales process very stressful. Although losing a sale is never pleasant, salespeople who are involved in a relationship with their customers must view any particular sales presentation as part of the progression toward ultimately making the sale. An unsuccessful close on one day may just be a means of laying the groundwork for a successful close the next meeting.

Although we have presented the selling process in a series of steps, closing the sale rarely follows the other steps so neatly. However, good salespeople listen carefully to what potential customers say and pay attention to their body language. Reading these signals carefully can help salespeople achieve an early close. Suppose that our hypothetical bank, rather than being in the first step of the buying process, were in the final step of negotiation and selection. An astute salesperson will pick up on these signals and ask for the sale.

Step 5: Follow-Up

"It ain't over till it's over."
—Yogi Berra[11]

With relationship selling, it is never really over, even after the sale has been made. The attitudes customers develop after the sale become the basis for how they will purchase in the future. The follow-up therefore offers a prime opportunity for a salesperson to solidify the customer relationship through great service quality. Let's apply the five service quality dimensions we discussed in Chapter 12 to the follow-up:[12]

- **Reliability.** The salesperson and the supporting organization must deliver the right product or service on time.

- **Responsiveness.** The salesperson and support group must be ready to deal quickly with any issue, question, or problem that may arise.

- **Assurance.** Customers must be assured through adequate guarantees that their purchase will perform as expected.

- **Empathy.** The salesperson and support group must have a good understanding of the problems and issues faced by their customers. Otherwise, they cannot give them what they want.

- **Tangibles.** Because tangibles reflect the physical characteristics of the seller's business, such as its Web site, marketing communications, and delivery materials, their influence is more subtle than that of the other four service quality dimensions. That doesn't mean it is any less important. For instance, retail customers are generally more pleased with a purchase if it is carefully wrapped in nice paper instead of being haphazardly thrown into a crumpled plastic bag. The tangibles offer a signal that the product is of high quality, even though the packaging has nothing to do with the product's performance.

A post-sale follow-up letter, call, or e-mail, is the first step in initiating a new order and sustaining the relationship.

When customers' expectations are not met, they often complain—about deliveries, the billing amount or process, the product's performance, or after-sale services such as installation or training. Effectively handling complaints is critical to the future of the relationship. As we noted in Chapter 12, the best way to handle complaints is to listen to the customer, provide a fair solution to the problem, and resolve the problem quickly.

The best way to nip a postsale problem in the bud is to check with the customer right after he or she takes possession of the product or immediately after the service has been completed. This speed demonstrates responsiveness and empathy; it also shows the customer that the salesperson and the firm care about customer satisfaction. Finally, a postsale follow-up call, e-mail, or letter takes the salesperson back to the first step in the sales process for initiating a new order and sustaining the relationship.

Many technological advances help facilitate the selling process, as we find in the next section.

The Impact of Technology and the Internet on Personal Selling

Technology and the Internet have had significant impacts on the role of personal selling in recent years. Salespeople have instant access to their customers and their firm through cell phones, PDAs (personal digital assistants), and the Internet. They can make appointments, take orders, solve problems, and get information at any time and from almost any place.

Prior to the Internet's explosion, it was cumbersome to perform research on products, customers, or competitors. Salespeople would rely on a research staff for this information, and it could take weeks for the research to be completed and sent through the mail. Customer information, if it was available at all, was typically a manual system that individual salespeople kept in a notebook or on a series of cards. There were no customer data warehouses and no formal CRM systems. Today, salespeople have all this information at their fingertips, as long as they are connected to the Internet. They can easily access their company's customer database and surf the Web for product and competitive information at any time and virtually anywhere.

Technology has also made sales training programs more effective, easier, and, often, less expensive than in the past. Rather than incurring the time and expense of flying a group of salespeople to one location, companies can conduct distance learning and training through videoconferencing. Some firms also offer online training courses. Salespeople can view the material, which contains product information or selling techniques, and take tests on the information at a time convenient to them. Instead of the traditional, bulky, and sometimes overlooked bulletins and product catalogs, companies can distribute material effectively via e-mail.

Technology has changed the lives of salespeople and sales training. Companies can conduct distance learning and training through videoconferencing.

Because customers also have better access to information through these technological innovations, salespeople have gained time to participate in the more

creative and technical aspects of selling. Customers can check their order status and pricing or get product information from the selling firm's extranet. They can even place their own order electronically, if they so choose, without the aid of a salesperson. In some cases, because the selling job has become more streamlined as a result of such technological advances, firms have been able to trim back their sales force expenses without any simultaneous loss in productivity. To learn how technology has changed the way college textbooks are sold, for example, consider Adding Value 19.1.

Adding Value 19.1

Technology-Facilitated Textbook Selling

Have you ever considered how the textbook you are reading right now might have been sold with the aid of technology? Sam Hussey is a senior account manager for McGraw-Hill/Irwin, the publisher of this text, in Massachusetts. In his early years with the firm, he would go on campus with a briefcase full of books. He'd stop by various professors' offices, talk to them about possible book adoptions, and show them the various features of the books in his bag. He would communicate with the home office and his customers by phone, fax, or mail. If a professor needed a book in a hurry, Hussey would call the distribution center, and a person would take down all the information by hand—a time-consuming and potentially error-prone system. Although Hussey maintained all his customer information in a "little black book," McGraw-Hill/Irwin had no comprehensive customer database. The company did not know, for instance, which instructors were using which books. Without that information, it was impossible to implement an adequate CRM system.

Things are different for Hussey today. Because McGraw-Hill/Irwin now has an integrated CRM system, he knows exactly who is using which specific texts. He can plan his sales calls so that he knows whom he plans to see, what books they are currently using, and which books he plans to sell. Once in the professor's office, he can demonstrate—on his computer or the professor's—special features of the text, accompanying PowerPoint slides, or the book-related Internet content. If the professor needs a book, Hussey places the order over the Internet. Because McGraw-Hill/Irwin keeps

Sam Hussey, senior account manager at McGraw-Hill Irwin, has a very different job today than he did just a few years ago—all because of advances in technology.

most of its book contents in a digital database, Hussey can create custom course material for professors, including text, cases, and articles. He uses an electronic ordering system, linked to the publisher's custom publishing operation, to create a sample book that will be delivered to the professor in about a week. Once approved, the book can be printed and delivered to the local bookstore for purchase by students, just like you.

Ethical and Legal Issues in Personal Selling

While ethical and legal issues permeate all aspects of marketing, they are particularly important for personal selling. Unlike advertising and other communications with customers, which are planned and executed on a corporate level, personal selling involves a one-to-one, and often face-to-face, encounter with the customer. Thus, sellers' actions are not only highly visible to customers but also to other stakeholders, such as the communities in which they work.

Ethical and legal issues arise in three areas in personal selling. First, there is the relationship between the sales manager and the sales force. Second, in some situations, an inconsistency might exist between corporate policy and the salesperson's ethical comfort zone. Third, both ethical and legal issues can arise when the salesperson interacts with the customer.

The Sales Manager and the Sales Force

Like any manager, a sales manager must treat people fairly and equally in everything he or she does. With regard to the sales force, this fairness must include hiring, promotion, supervision, training, assigning duties and quotas, compensation and incentives, and firing.[13] Federal laws cover many of these issues. For instance, equal employment opportunity laws make it unlawful to discriminate against a person in either hiring or promotion because of race, religion, nationality, sex, or age.

The Sales Force and Corporate Policy

Sometimes salespeople face a conflict between what they believe represents ethical selling and what their company asks them to do to make a sale. Suppose an insurance agent, whose compensation is based on commission, which is a fixed percentage of their sales, sells a homeowner's policy to a family that has just moved to New Orleans, an area prone to flooding as a result of hurricanes. Even though the policy covers hurricane damage, it does not cover water damage from hur-

ricanes. If the salesperson discloses the inadequate coverage, the sale might be lost because additional flood insurance is very expensive. What should the salesperson do? Salespeople must live within their own ethical comfort zone. If this, or any other situation, is morally repugnant to the salesperson, he or she must question whether they want to be associated with the company.[14]

Salespeople also can be held accountable for illegal actions sanctioned by the employer. If the homeowner asks if the home is above the floodplain or whether water damage from flooding is covered by the policy, and it is company policy to intentionally mislead potential customers, both the salesperson and the insurance dealership could be susceptible to legal action.

Salespeople must live within their own ethical comfort zone. Should insurance salespeople disclose inadequate hurricane coverage and risk not making the sale?

The Salesperson and the Customer

Being the frontline emissaries for a firm, salespeople have a duty to be ethically and legally correct in all their dealings with their customers. Not only is it the right thing to do, it simply means good business. Long-term relationships can deteriorate quickly if customers believe that they have not been treated in an ethically proper manner. Unfortunately, salespeople sometimes get mixed signals from their managers or simply do not know when their behaviors might be considered unethical or illegal. Formal guidelines can help, but it is also important to integrate these guidelines into training programs in which salespeople can discuss various issues that arise in the field with their peers and managers. Most important, however, is for sales managers to lead by example. If managers are known to cut ethical corners, it shouldn't surprise them when their salespeople do the same. Ethical Dilemma 19.1 considers the ethical issues that pharmaceutical salespeople face.

Perhaps nowhere is ethical selling more hotly debated than in the pharmaceutical industry. Physicians have become accustomed to the perks offered by the pharmaceutical representatives who visit their office and restock their shelves with product samples, extras such as free tickets to Broadway musicals. It's a fine line between buying a prospect's time to demonstrate your wares and bribing him or her to prescribe your firm's drugs.

According to Pennsylvania-based Scott-Levin Consulting, promotional budgets for pharmaceuticals have reached nearly $14 billion, with roughly 56,000 people in the sales force. Incidentally, that's about one rep and $100,000 dollars for every 11 practicing physicians.

Pharmaceutical companies hand out samples liberally as a central part of their marketing program. The National Institute for Healthcare Management suggests the cost figure reaches about $7.2 billion in samples each year. Many patients benefit from these samples; however, most companies only give out samples of their high-priced products. The net result, according to a study by Washington University, becomes that many doctors dispense and prescribe drugs that are not their primary drug of choice.

At the end of the day, many ethical decisions rest on the shoulders of the independent sales representatives. Are they using tactics that promote the best healthcare options for the patients, or are they simply pushing their product? On a broader scale, are they inflating medication costs as a result of these selling methods so that, ultimately, the customer cannot afford the prescription anyway?

Are pharmaceutical salespeople promoting the best healthcare option for the patients, or are they simply pushing their product?

Managing the Sales Force

Like any business activity involving people, the sales force requires management. Sales management involves the planning, direction, and control of personal selling activities, including recruiting, selecting, training, motivating, compensating, and evaluating, as they apply to the sales force.[16]

Managing a sales force is a rewarding yet complicated undertaking. In this section, we examine how sales forces can be structured, some of the most important issues in recruiting and selecting salespeople, sales training issues, ways to compensate salespeople, and finally, how to supervise and evaluate salespeople.

Sales Force Structure

Imagine the daunting task of putting together a sales force from scratch. Will you hire your own salespeople, or should they be manufacturer's representatives? What will be each salesperson's primary duties: order takers, order getters, sales support? Finally, will they work together in teams? In this section, we examine each of these issues.

Large companies with established brands like Pepsi often use a company sales force instead of independent agents. Because the salespeople are company employees, the manufacturer has more control over what they do. Pepsi's salespeople, like this one in Mexico, deliver products, stack the shelves, and keep track of inventory.

Company Sales Force or Manufacturer's Representative

A **company sales force** is comprised of people who are employees of the selling company. **Independent agents**, also known as **manufacturer's representatives** or **"reps,"** are salespeople who sell a manufacturer's products on an extended contract basis but are not employees of the manufacturer. They are compensated by commissions and do not take ownership or physical possession of the merchandise.

Manufacturer's representatives are useful for smaller firms or firms expanding into new markets because such companies can achieve instant and extensive sales coverage without having to pay full-time personnel. Good sales representatives have many established contacts and can sell multiple products from noncompeting manufacturers during the same sales call. Also, the use of manufacturers' representatives facilitates flexibility; it is much easier to replace a rep than an employee and much easier to expand or contract coverage in a market with a sales rep than with a company sales force.

Company sales forces are more typically used for established product lines. Because the salespeople are company employees, the manufacturer has more control over what they do. If, for example, the manufacturer's strategy is to provide extensive customer service, the sales manager can specify exactly what actions a company sales force must take. In contrast, because manufacturer's representatives are paid on a commission basis, it is difficult to persuade them to take any action that doesn't directly lead to sales.

Salesperson Duties

Although the life of a professional salesperson is highly varied, salespeople generally play three important roles: order getting, order taking, and sales support.

Order Getting An **order getter** is a salesperson whose primary responsibilities are identifying potential customers and engaging those customers in discussions to attempt to make a sale. An order getter is also responsible for following up with the customer to ensure that the customer is satisfied and to build the relationship. In B2B settings, order getters are primarily involved in new buy and modified new buy situations (see Chapter 6). As a result, they require extensive sales and product knowledge training. The Coca-Cola salesperson who goes to Safeway's headquarters to sell a special promotion of Vanilla Coke is an order getter.

Order Taking An **order taker** is a salesperson whose primary responsibility is to process routine orders or reorders or rebuys for products. Colgate employs order takers around the globe like this one in India who go into stores and distribution centers that already carry Colgate products to check inventory, set up displays, write new orders, and make sure everything is going smoothly.

Sales Support **Sales support personnel** enhance and help with the overall selling effort. For example, if a CompUSA customer begins to experience computer problems, the Technology Assurance Program (TAP) purchased with the product will cover the cost of repair.[17]

Ordertakers process routine orders or reorders or rebuys for products.

Those employees who respond to the customer's technical questions and repair the computer serve to support the overall sales process.

Combination Duties Although some salespeople's primary function may be order getting, order taking, or sales support, others fill a combination of roles. For instance, a computer salesperson at Staples may spend an hour with a customer educating him or her about the pros and cons of various systems and then make the sale. The next customer might simply need a specific printer cartridge. A third customer might bring in a computer and seek advice about an operating system problem. The salesperson was first an order getter, next an order taker, and finally a sales support person.

Some firms use **selling teams** that combine sales specialists whose primary duties are order getting, order taking, or sales support but who work together to service important accounts. As companies become larger and products more complicated, it is nearly impossible for one person to perform all the necessary sales functions.

Recruiting and Selecting Salespeople

When the firm has determined how the sales force will be structured, it must find and hire salespeople. Although superficially this task may sound as easy as posting the job opening on the Internet or running an ad in a newspaper, it must be performed carefully because firms don't want to hire the wrong person—salespeople are very expensive to train.

The most important activity in the recruiting process is to determine exactly what the salesperson will be doing and what personal traits and abilities a person should have to do the job well. For instance, the Coca-Cola order getter who goes to Safeway to pitch a new product will typically need significant sales experience, coupled with great communication and analytical skills. Coke's order takers need to be reliable and able to get along with lots of different types of people in the stores, from managers to customers.

When recruiting salespeople, is it better to look for candidates with innate sales ability, or can a good training program make anyone a successful salesperson? In other words, are good salespeople born or are they made?[18] By a margin of seven to one in a survey of sales and marketing executives, respondents believed that training and supervision are more critical determinants of selling success than the salesperson's inherent personal characteristics.[19] Yet some of those same respondents noted that they knew "born salespeople" and that personal traits are important for successful sales careers. So, it appears that to be a successful salesperson, while it helps to have good training, the first requirement is to possess certain personal traits.

Good salespeople, particularly in difficult selling situations like in door-to-door sales, don't easily take no for an answer. They keep coming back until they get a yes.

What are those personal traits? Managers and sales experts have identified the following:[20]

- **Personality.** Good salespeople are friendly, sociable, and, in general, like being around people. Customers won't buy from someone they don't like.

- **Optimism.** Good salespeople tend to look at the bright side of things. Optimism also may help them be resilient—the third trait.

- **Resilience.** Good salespeople don't easily take no for an answer. They keep coming back until they get a yes.

- **Self-motivation.** As we have already mentioned, salespeople have lots of freedom to spend their days the way they believe will be most productive. But if the salespeople are not self-motivated to get the job done, it probably won't get done.

- **Empathy.** Empathy is one of the five dimensions of service quality discussed previously in this chapter and in Chapter 12. Good salespeople must care about their customers, their issues, and their problems.

Sales Training

Even people who possess all these personal traits need training. All salespeople benefit from training about selling and negotiation techniques, product and service knowledge, technologies used in the selling process, time and territory management, and company policies and procedures.

Firms use varied delivery methods to train their salespeople, depending on the topic of the training, what type of salesperson is being trained, and the cost versus the value of the training. For instance, an on-the-job training program is excellent for communicating selling and negotiation skills because managers can observe the sales trainees in real selling situations and provide instant feedback. They can also engage in role-playing exercises, in which the salesperson acts out a simulated buying situation and the manager critiques the salesperson's performance.

A much less expensive, but for some purposes equally valuable, training method is the Internet. Online training programs have revolutionized the way training happens in many firms. Firms can provide new product and service knowledge, spread the word about changes in company policies and procedures, and share selling tips in a user-friendly environment that salespeople can access anytime and anywhere. Distance learning sales training programs through teleconferencing enable a group of salespeople to participate with their instructor or manager in a virtual classroom. And testing can occur online as well. Online sales training may never replace the one-on-one interaction of on-the-job training for advanced selling skills, but it is quite effective and efficient for many other aspects of the sales training task.

Wyeth Pharmaceuticals develops, manufacturers, and markets products for the treatment of health issues such as cardiovascular disease, central nervous system disabilities, and vaccinations.[21] Wyeth trains its 700 to 1,000 new recruits per year through a combination of online lessons, manuals, and one-on-one training. As a result, the district manager has the ability and flexibility to train salespeople and emerge with a productive employee in a matter of days.

Motivating and Compensating Salespeople

An important goal for any effective sales manager is to get to know his or her salespeople and determine what motivates them to be effective. Some salespeople prize their freedom and like to be left alone, whereas others want attention and are more productive when they receive accolades for a job well done. Still others are motivated primarily by monetary compensation. Great sales managers determine how best to motivate each of their salespeople according to what is most important to each individual. Although sales managers can emphasize different motivating factors, except in the smallest companies, the methods used to compensate salespeople must be fairly standardized and can be divided into two categories: financial and nonfinancial.

Financial Rewards Salespeople's compensation usually has several components. Most salespeople receive at least part of their compensation as a **salary**, a fixed sum of money paid at regular intervals. Another common financial incentive is a commission, which, as we've already mentioned, is money paid as a percentage of the sales volume or profitability. A **bonus** is a payment made at management's discretion when the salesperson attains certain goals; bonuses usually are given only periodically, such as at the end of the year. A **sales contest** is a short-term incentive designed to elicit a specific response from the sales force. Prizes might be cash or other types of financial incentives. For instance, Volkswagen may give a free trip to Germany for the salesperson who sells the most high-end Phaetons.

The bulk of any compensation package is made up of salary, commission, or a combination of the two. The advantage of a salary plan is that salespeople know exactly what they will be paid, and sales managers therefore have more control over their salespeople. For instance, salaried salespeople can be directed to spend a certain percentage of their time handling customer service issues. Using a commission system, however, salespeople have only one objective—make the sale! Thus, a commission system provides the most incentive for the sales force to sell.

With more than 14 percent of the market, the electronics giant Best Buy has overcome many obstacles to beat its competition. Much of Best Buy's success follows the company's customer-focused strategy that employs a noncommissioned sales force. The move, which prompted industry scorn and alienated several vendors, turned out to serve the company well in the long run and has revolutionized an industry once characterized by the "hard sell."[22]

Mary Kay recognizes success with unusually large rewards that have both symbolic and high material value—pink Cadillacs!

Nonfinancial Rewards As we have noted, good salespeople are self-motivated. They want to do a good job and make the sale because it makes them feel good. But this good feeling also can be accentuated by recognition from peers and management. For instance, the internal monthly magazine at the cosmetics firm Mary Kay Inc. provides an outlet for not only selling advice but also companywide recognition of individual salespeople's accomplishments.[23]

Nonfinancial rewards should have high symbolic value, as plaques, pens, or rings do. Free trips or days off are also effective rewards. More important than what the reward is, however, is the way it is operationalized. For instance, an award should be given at a sales meeting and publicized in the company newsletter. It should also be done in good taste, because if the award is perceived as tacky, no one will take it seriously.[24] Mary Kay recognizes salespeople's success with unusually large rewards that have both high symbolic and high material value. About 94,000 Independent Beauty Consultants and Sales Directors have earned the use of a famous pink Cadillac.

Evaluating Salespeople

Salespeople's evaluation process must be tied to their reward structure. If salespeople do well, they should receive their just rewards, in the same way that, if you do well on your exams and assignments in a class, you should earn a good grade. However, salespeople should only be evaluated and rewarded for those activities and outcomes that fall under their control. For instance, if Federated Department Stores makes a unilateral decision to put Diesel jeans in all its stores after a negotiation with Diesel's corporate headquarters in Italy, the Diesel sales representatives responsible for individual Federated stores should not receive credit for making the sale, nor should they get all the windfall commission that will ensue from the added sales.

Considering this guiding principle—evaluate and reward salespeople for what they do and not for what they don't do—how should sales managers evaluate their salespeople? The answer is never easy because measures must be tied to performance, and there are many ways to measure performance in a complex job like selling. For example, evaluating performance on the basis of monthly sales alone fails to consider how profitable the sales were, whether any progress was made to build new business that will be realized sometime in the future, or the level of customer service the salesperson provided. Because the sales job is multifaceted with many contributing success factors, sales managers should use multiple measures.[25]

Evaluation measures are either *objective* or *subjective.* Sales, profits, and the number of orders represent examples of objective measures. Although each is somewhat useful to managers, such measures do not provide an adequate perspective for a thorough evaluation because there is no means of comparison with other salespeople. For instance, suppose salesperson A generated $1 million last year, but salesperson B generated $1.5 million. Should salesperson B automatically receive a significantly higher evaluation? Now consider that salesperson B's territory has twice as much potential as salesperson A's. Knowing this, we might suppose that salesperson A has actually done a better job. For this reason, firms use ratios like profit per customer, orders per call, sales per hour, or expenses compared to sales as their objective measures.

Whereas objective measures are quantitative, subjective measures seek to assess salespeople's behavior: what they do and how well they do it. By their very nature, subjective measures reflect one person's opinion about another's performance. Thus, subjective evaluations can be biased and should be used cautiously and only in conjunction with multiple objective measures.

Personal selling is an integral component of some firms' integrated marketing communications strategy. Although it doesn't make sense for all firms, it is widely used in B2B markets, as well as in B2C markets in which the price of the merchandise is relatively high and customers need some one-to-one assistance before they can buy. Due to the relatively high expense of maintaining a personal selling force, it is important that salespeople be adequately trained, motivated, and compensated.

Summing Up

1. How does personal selling add value?

Although the cost of an average B2B sales call is expensive (about $330), many firms believe they couldn't do business without their sales force. Customers can buy many products and services without the help of a salesperson, but in many other cases, it is worth the extra cost built into the price of a product to be educated about the product or get valuable advice. Salespeople can also simplify the buying process and therefore save the customer time and hassle.

2. What is the personal selling process?

Although we discuss selling in terms of steps, it truly represents a process, and the time spent in each step varies according to the situation. In the first step, the salesperson generates a list of viable customers. During the second step, the preapproach, the salesperson gathers information about the customer and prepares for the presentation. The third step, the sales presentation, consists of a personal meeting between the salesperson and the customer. Through discussion and by asking questions, the salesperson learns where the customer is in its buying process and tailors the discussion around what the firm's product or service can do to meet that customer's needs. During the fourth step, the close, the salesperson asks for the order. Finally, during the follow-up, the salesperson and support staff solidifies the long-term relationship by making sure the customer is satisfied with the purchase and addressing any complaints. The follow-up therefore sets the stage for the next purchase.

3. How do technology and the Internet affect personal selling?

Technology in general and the Internet in particular have caused fundamental changes in the lives of professional salespeople. The ability to be in constant contact with customers and the home office enables salespeople to instantly make appointments; answer questions; and get customer, product, and shipping information. Technology has also streamlined the sales training process.

4. What are the key functions of a sales manager?

The first task of a sales manager, assuming a firm is starting a sales force from scratch, is to determine whether to use a company sales force or manufacturer's representatives. Then sales managers must then determine what the primary selling responsibilities will be—order getter, order taker, or sales support. The sales manager recruits and selects salespeople, but because there are all sorts of sales jobs, he or she must determine what it takes to be successful and then go after people with those attributes. In the next step, training, firms can choose between on-the-job and online training. Sales managers are also responsible for motivating and compensating salespeople. Most salespeople appreciate a balance of financial and nonfinancial rewards for doing a good job. Finally, sales managers are responsible for evaluating their salespeople. Normally, salespeople should be evaluated on a combination of objective measures, such as sales per hour, and subjective measures, such as how friendly they appear to customers.

Key Terms

- bonus, 531
- closing the sale, 522
- cold calls, 519
- commission, 526
- company sales force, 528
- independent agents, 528
- leads, 518
- manufacturer's representative, 528

- order getter, 528
- order taker, 528
- personal selling, 514
- preapproach, 520
- qualify, 518
- relationship selling, 516
- reps, 528
- role playing, 520

- salary, 531
- sales contest, 531
- sales management, 527
- sales support personnel, 528
- selling teams, 529
- telemarketing, 519
- trade shows, 518

Marketing Applications

1. How has your perception of what it would be like to have a career in sales changed since you read this chapter?

2. "Salespeople just make products cost more." Agree or disagree with this statement and discuss why you've taken that position.

3. Choose an industry or a specific company that you would like to work for as a salesperson. How would you generate and qualify leads?

4. Why is it important for salespeople to be good listeners? To be good at asking questions?

5. Suppose you are a sales manager at a large electronics store like Best Buy. What can you do to ensure that your customers are satisfied with the service they have received?

6. Imagine that a time machine has transported you back to 1957. How was a day in the life of an office furniture salesperson different in 1957 than it is in 2007?

7. What are some of the potentially ethically troubling and illegal situations facing professional salespeople, and how should they deal with them?

8. Why would Gillette use a company sales force, while a small independent manufacturer of organic shaving cream uses manufacturer's representatives?

9. Similar to a sales manager and a salesperson, your instructors evaluate your performance to assign you a grade. Choose one of your classes and analyze the advantages and disadvantages of the objective and subjective bases used to evaluate your performance.

10. A customer raises the following reservations. How do you respond?

    a. "I really like all the things this copier does, but I don't think it's going to be very reliable. With all those features, something's got to go wrong."

    b. "Your price for this printer is higher than the price I saw advertised on the Internet."

11. Imagine that you have just been hired by a construction supply company as a salesperson. You are asked what you think would be a "fair" compensation package for you. Using the information from the chapter, make a list of all the elements that should be included in your compensation package. What changes, if any, should be made over time?

12. You have taken a summer job in the windows and doors department of a large home improvement store. During sales training, you learn about the products, how to best address customers' needs, why the lifetime value of the customer concept is so important to a store like this, and how to sell the customer the best product to fit their needs regardless of price point. One day your manager informs you that you are to recommend Smith Windows to every window customer. Smith Windows are more expensive and don't really provide superior benefit except in limited circumstances. The manager is insistent that you recommend Smith. Not knowing what else to do, you recommend Smith Windows to customers who would have been better served by lower cost windows. The manager rewards you with a sales award. Later the manager tells you that he received an all-expenses-paid cruise for his family from Smith Windows. What, if anything, should you do with this information?

Net Savvy

1. There are many codes of conduct in the selling profession. The Direct Selling Association publishes one example. Go to www.dsa.org and click on the tab for the Code of Ethics. What type of conduct does the DSA address in the code? How is the code enforced? Do you feel this code is adequate to control the behavior of people engaged in direct selling? Why or why not?

2. To learn more about careers in sales, go to www.bls.gov, the Web site for the Bureau of Labor Statistics. This site contains a wealth of information about careers in all fields. Find the link to the Occupational Outlook Handbook. Bring up the handbook and then click on "Sales" in the right-hand column. Choose any of the sales fields listed, and explore that career field. What experience is necessary to be hired for that job? What is the median salary? What do earners in the highest 10 percent of performance earn? Is job growth anticipated in that field?

Chapter Case Study

TEL-SOFT SOLUTIONS: MAKING THE SALE[26]

When Vicki Cambridge reached her office, she had a message from Mike Smith, the regional sales manager, to meet him in his office regarding the ABC Telecom order. Vicki Cambridge is a senior sales associate for Tel-Soft Solutions Inc., a firm that markets software designed for telecommunications companies. The ABC Telecom order represents a multimillion dollar contract for Tel-Soft and would help ABC Telecom boost its productivity levels and revenue for the region. To prepare for the meeting, Vicki reviews her sales call report notes on the ABC Telecom account.

Tel-Soft Solutions

Tel-Soft provides software solutions to large telecommunications firms and has an established track record for delivering an exceptional standard of quality and high levels of customer service. This excellent reputation allows Tel-Soft to charge a substantial premium, ranging from 10 to 20 percent above the market leader.

The telecommunications software services market has been dominated for two decades by this market leader. Tel-Soft holds the second position in the marketplace, with a considerably lower but growing market share. Only one other competitor, an aggressive, small, low-price player, holds a significant market share; this provider has made inroads into the market in the past several years through its aggressive sales tactics.

Tel-Soft has just built a new facility and hired 50 new software programmers. Therefore, the company must generate new business to meet its higher financial goals; even more important in the short-run, it must keep the new programmers working on interesting projects to retain them.

ABC Telecom

ABC Telecom is a division of a major U.S.-based telecommunications firm that provides voice, data, fax, Internet, and videoconferencing services. Its purchasing department negotiates contracts for software services and coordinates the interface among a variety of members from different departments. The business environment for telephone services has become highly competitive in recent years, leading to tight budgets and higher levels of scrutiny of the value added by vendors. Competition is fierce, as large numbers of end-user customers are considering new phone providers, which results in considerably lower revenues.

ABC Telecom has been consistently buying software development services from the market leader since 1991 and is generally satisfied with its service. A recent change in corporate leadership, however, has increased concerns about its overreliance on one vendor for a particular service. Also, because of the difficult economic climate, the company is concerned about the cost of software services and whether it is necessary to provide such a high service level.

Vicki's Call Report

A call report is like a diary of sales calls made to a particular client. The notes in Vicki's ABC Telecom file pertaining to the current negotiations began on June 4:

> **June 4** I contacted Bethany O'Meara, Chief Purchasing Officer at ABC Telecom, to introduce myself to her and get a sense of what their future software needs might be. She told me that the slowed business climate had caused ABC Telecom to institute a program for increased efficiency in operations and that they would be looking to negotiate a new contract for software solutions. She gave me some insights into the technological aspects of their needs.

> **June 18** Met with Jon Aaronson, Head of R&D, to explain our productivity-enhancing solutions. Went into considerable depth explaining how Tel-Soft could service their needs and learned what they were looking for in a provider. I went over some specific product

specification issues, but Jon did not seem impressed. But he did ask for a price and told me that the final decision rested with Brad Alexander, the Chief Financial Officer.

July 2   Presented to Bethany O'Meara and Jon Aaronson. They first asked about the price. I gave them a quote of $3.3 million. They suggested that other services were much cheaper. I explained that our price reflected the latest technology and that the price differential was an investment that could pay for itself several times over through faster communication speeds. I also emphasized our reputation for high-quality customer service. While the presentation appeared to meet their software needs, they did not seem impressed with the overall value. I also sent a copy of the presentation in report form to Brad Alexander and attempted to get an appointment to see him.

July 9   Contacted Jon Aaronson by phone. He told me that we were in contention with three other firms and the debate was heated. He stated that the other firms were also touting their state-of-the-art technology. Discussed a lower price of $3.1 million. Also encouraged him to visit Tel-Soft headquarters to meet with the product manager who oversaw the product development efforts and would manage the implementation of the product. He wasn't interested in making the two-day trip even though it would spotlight our core competencies.

July 15   Received a conference call from Brad Alexander and Jon Aaronson to discuss the price. Brad said

What are the key points Vicki should make in her presentation?

the price was still too high and that he could not depreciate that amount over the life of the software and meet target levels of efficiency. He wanted a final quote by August 6.

The Final Pitch

Vicki prepared for her meeting with Mike by going over her notes and market data about the competitors. Mike's voicemail indicated that they would be meeting to put together their best possible proposal.

Questions

Help Vicki prepare her sales presentation.

1.   Who should be at the presentation?
2.   How should Vicki start the meeting?
3.   What are the key points she should make in her presentation?
4.   What reservations should she expect? How should she handle them?

glossary

administered vertical marketing system A *supply chain* system in which there is no common ownership and no contractual relationships, but the dominant channel member controls the channel relationship.

advanced shipping notice An electronic document that the supplier sends the retailer in advance of a shipment to tell the retailer exactly what to expect in the shipment.

advertising A paid form of communication from an identifiable source, delivered through a communication channel, and designed to persuade the receiver to take some action, now or in the future.

advertising allowance Tactic of offering a price reduction to channel members if they agree to feature the manufacturer's product in their advertising and promotional efforts.

advertising plan A section of the firm's overall marketing plan that explicitly outlines the objectives of the advertising campaign, how the campaign might accomplish those objectives, and how the firm can determine whether the campaign was successful.

advertising schedule The specification of the timing and duration of advertising.

affective component A component of *attitude* that reflects what a person feels about the issue at hand—his or her like or dislike of something.

AIDA model A common model of the series of mental stages through which consumers move as a result of marketing communications: *Awareness* leads to *Interests*, which lead to *Desire*, which leads to *Action*.

alpha testing An attempt by the firm to determine whether a product will perform according to its design and whether it satisfies the need for which it was intended; occurs in the firm's research and development (R&D) department.

attitude A person's enduring evaluation of his or her feelings about and behavioral tendencies toward an object or idea; consists of three components: *cognitive, affective,* and *behavioral.*

autocratic buying center A buying center in which one person makes the decision alone, though there may be multiple participants.

B2B (business-to-business) The process of selling merchandise or services from one business to another.

B2C (business-to-consumers) The process in which businesses sell to consumers.

Baby Boomers Generational cohort of people born after World War II, between 1946 and 1964.

bait and switch A deceptive practice of luring customers into the store with a very low advertised price on an item (the bait), only to aggressively pressure them into purchasing a higher-priced model (the switch) by disparaging the low-priced item, comparing it unfavorably with the higher-priced model, or professing an inadequate supply of the lower-priced item.

behavioral component A component of *attitude* that comprises the actions a person takes with regard to the issue at hand.

benefit segmentation The grouping of consumers on the basis of the benefits they derive from products or services.

beta testing Having potential consumers examine a product prototype in a real-use setting to determine its functionality, performance, potential problems, and other issues specific to its use.

big-box food retailer Comes in three types: supercenter, hypermarket, and warehouse club; larger than *conventional supermarket;* carries both food and nonfood items.

blog (weblog or Web log) A Web page that contains periodic posts; corporate blogs are new form of marketing communications.

bonus A payment made at management's discretion when the salesperson attains certain goals; usually given only periodically, such as at the end of the year.

boycott A group's refusal to deal commercially with some organization to protest against its policies.

brand The name, term, design, symbol, or any other features that identify one seller's good or service as distinct from those of other sellers.

brand association The mental links that consumers make between a brand and its key product attributes; can involve a logo, slogan, or famous personality.

brand awareness Measures how many consumers in a market are familiar with the brand and what it stands for; created through repeated exposures of the various brand elements (brand name, logo, symbol, character, packaging, or slogan) in the firm's communications to consumers.

brand dilution Occurs when a brand extension adversely affects consumer perceptions about the attributes the core brand is believed to hold.

brand equity The set of assets and liabilities linked to a brand that add to or subtract from the value provided by the product or service.

brand extension The use of the same brand name for new products being introduced to the same or new markets.

brand licensing A contractual arrangement between firms, whereby one firm allows another to use its brand name, logo, symbols, or characters in exchange for a negotiated fee.

brand loyalty Occurs when a consumer buys the same brand's product or service repeatedly over time rather than buying from multiple suppliers within the same category.

brand personality Refers to a set of human characteristics associated with a brand, which has symbolic or self-expressive meanings for consumers.

brand repositioning (rebranding) A strategy in which marketers change a brand's focus to target new markets or realign the brand's core emphasis with changing market preferences.

break-even analysis Technique used to examine the relationships among cost, price, revenue, and profit over different levels of production and sales to determine the *break-even point.*

break-even point The point at which the number of units sold generates just enough revenue to equal the total costs; at this point, profits are zero.

breakthroughs See *pioneers*.

bricks-and-mortar retailer A traditional, physical store.

business ethics Refers to a branch of ethical study that examines ethical rules and principles within a commercial context, the various moral or ethical problems that might arise in a business setting, and any special duties or obligations that apply to persons engaged in commerce.

business-to-business (B2B) marketing The process of buying and selling goods or services to be used in the production of other goods and services, for consumption by the buying organization, or for resale by wholesalers and retailers.

buyer The buying center participant who handles the paperwork of the actual purchase.

buying center The group of people typically responsible for the buying decisions in large organizations.

C2C (consumer-to-consumer) The process in which consumers sell to other consumers.

cash discount Tactic of offering a reduction in the invoice cost if the buyer pays the invoice prior to the end of the discount period.

category depth The number of stock keeping units (SKUs) within a category.

category killer A specialist that offers an extensive assortment in a particular category, so overwhelming the category that other retailers have difficulty competing.

category specialist A retailer that offers a narrow variety but a deep assortment of merchandise.

cause-related marketing Commercial activity in which businesses and charities form a partnership to market an image, a product, or a service for their mutual benefit; a type of promotional campaign.

checking The process of going through the goods upon receipt to ensure they arrived undamaged and that the merchandise ordered was the merchandise received.

click-through tracking A way to measure how many times users click on banner advertising on Web sites.

closing the sale Obtaining a commitment from the customer to make a purchase.

cobranding The practice of marketing two or more brands together, on the same package or promotion.

cognitive component A component of *attitude* that reflects what a person believes to be true.

cold calls A method of prospecting in which salespeople telephone or go to see potential customers without appointments.

collaboration, planning, forecasting, and replenishment (CPFR) An inventory management system that uses an electronic data interchange (EDI) through which a retailer sends sales information to a manufacturer.

commercial speech A message with an economic motivation, that is, to promote a product or service, to persuade someone to purchase, and so on.

commission Compensation or financial incentive for salespeople based on a fixed percentage of their sales.

communication channel The medium—print, broadcast, the Internet—that carries the message.

communication gap A type of *service gap;* refers to the difference between the actual service provided to customers and the service that the firm's promotion program promises.

company sales force Comprised of people who are employees of the selling company and are engaged in the selling process.

compensatory decision rule At work when the consumer is evaluating alternatives and trades off one characteristic against another, such that good characteristics compensate for bad ones.

competitive intelligence (CI) Used by firms to collect and synthesize information about their position with respect to their rivals; enables companies to anticipate market developments rather than merely react to them.

competitive parity A firm's strategy of setting prices that are similar to those of major competitors.

competitor orientation A company objective based on the premise that the firm should measure itself primarily against its competition.

competitor-based pricing A strategy that involves pricing below, at, or above competitors' offerings.

competitor-based pricing method An approach that attempts to reflect how the firm wants consumers to interpret its products relative to the competitors' offerings; for example, setting a price close to a competitor's price signals to consumers that the product is similar, whereas setting the price much higher signals greater features, better quality, or some other valued benefit.

complementary products Products whose demand curves are positively related, such that they rise or fall together; a percentage increase in demand for one results in a percentage increase in demand for the other.

concentrated segmentation strategy A marketing strategy of selecting a single, primary target market and focusing all energies on providing a product to fit that market's needs.

concept testing The process in which a concept statement that describes a product or a service is presented to potential buyers or users to obtain their reactions.

concepts Brief written descriptions of a product or service; its technology, working principles, and forms; and what customer needs it would satisfy.

conclusive research Provides the information needed to confirm preliminary insights, which managers can use to pursue appropriate courses of action.

consensus buying center A buying center in which all members of the team must reach a collective agreement that they can support a particular purchase.

consultative buying center A buying center in which one person makes the decision but he or she solicits input from others before doing so.

consumer decision rules The set of criteria that consumers use consciously or subconsciously to quickly and efficiently select from among several alternatives.

contest A brand-sponsored competition that requires some form of skill or effort.

continuous advertising schedule Runs steadily throughout the year and therefore is suited to products and services that are consumed continually at relatively steady rates and that require a steady level of persuasive or reminder advertising.

contractual vertical marketing system A system in which independent firms at different levels of the supply chain join together through contracts to obtain economies of scale and coordination and to reduce conflict.

contribution per unit Equals the price less the variable cost per unit. Variable used to determine the break-even point in units.

control phase The part of the strategic marketing planning process when managers evaluate the performance of the marketing strategy and take any necessary corrective actions.

convenience goods/services Those for which the consumer is not willing to spend any effort to evaluate prior to purchase.

convenience store Type of retailer that provides a limited number of items at a convenient location in small store with speedy checkout.

conventional supermarket Type of retailer that offers groceries, meat, and produce with limited sales of nonfood items, such as health and beauty aids and general merchandise, in a self-service format.

corporate brand (family brand) The use of a firm's own corporate name to brand all of its product lines and products.

corporate social responsibility Refers to the voluntary actions taken by a company to address the ethical, social, and environmental impacts of its business operations and the concerns of its stakeholders.

corporate vertical marketing system A system in which the parent company has complete control and can dictate the priorities and objectives of the supply chain; it may own facilities such as manufacturing plants, warehouse facilities, retail outlets, and design studios.

cost of ownership method A value-based method for setting prices that determines the total cost of owning the product over its useful life.

cost-based pricing A pricing strategy that involves first determining the costs of producing or providing a product and then adding a fixed amount above that total to arrive at the selling price.

cost-based pricing method An approach that determines the final price to charge by starting with the cost, without recognizing the role that consumers or competitors' prices play in the marketplace.

countertrade Trade between two countries where goods are traded for other goods and not for hard currency.

country culture Entails easy-to-spot visible nuances that are particular to a country, such as dress, symbols, ceremonies, language, colors, and food preferences, and more subtle aspects, which are trickier to identify.

coupon Provides a stated discount to consumers on the final selling price of a specific item; the retailer handles the discount.

cross-docking distribution center A distribution center to which vendors ship merchandise prepackaged and ready for sale. So the merchandise goes to a staging area rather than into storage. When all the merchandise going to a particular store has arrived in the staging area, it is loaded onto a truck, and away it goes. Thus, merchandise goes from the receiving dock to the shipping dock—cross dock.

cross-price elasticity The percentage change in demand for product A that occurs in response to a percentage change in price of product B; see *complementary products*.

cross-promoting Efforts of two or more firms joining together to reach a specific target market.

cross-shopping The pattern of buying both premium and low-priced merchandise or patronizing both expensive, status-oriented retailers and price-oriented retailers.

cultural imperialism The belief that one's own culture is superior to that of other nations; can take the form of an active, formal policy or a more subtle general attitude.

culture The set of values, guiding beliefs, understandings, and ways of doing things shared by members of a society; exists on two levels: visible artifacts (e.g., behavior, dress, symbols, physical settings, ceremonies) and underlying values (thought processes, beliefs, and assumptions).

cumulative quantity discount Pricing tactic that offers a discount based on the amount purchased over a specified period and usually involves several transactions; encourages resellers to maintain their current supplier because the cost to switch must include the loss of the discount.

customer excellence Involves a focus on retaining loyal customers and excellent customer service.

customer oriented pricing Pricing orientation that explicitly invokes the concept of customer value and setting prices to match consumer expectations.

customer relationship management (CRM) A business philosophy and set of strategies, programs, and systems that focus on identifying and building loyalty among the firm's most valued customers.

customer service Specifically refers to human or mechanical activities firms undertake to help satisfy their customers' needs and wants.

data mining The use of a variety of statistical analysis tools to uncover previously unknown patterns in the data stored in databases or relationships among variables.

data warehouses Large computer files that store millions and even billions of pieces of individual data.

deal A type of short-term price reduction that can take several forms, such as a "featured price," a price lower than the regular price; a "buy one, get one free" offer; or a certain percentage "more free" offer contained in larger packaging; can involve a special financing arrangement, such as reduced percentage interest rates or extended repayment terms.

deceptive advertising A representation, omission, act, or practice in an advertisement that is likely to mislead consumers acting reasonably under the circumstances.

decider The buying center participant who ultimately determines any part of or the entire buying decision—whether to buy, what to buy, how to buy, or where to buy.

decision heuristics Mental shortcuts that help consumers narrow down choices; examples include price, brand, and product presentation.

decline stage Stage of the product life cycle when sales decline and the product eventually exits the market.

decoding The process by which the receiver interprets the sender's message.

delivery gap A type of *service gap;* the difference between the firm's service standards and the actual service it provides to customers.

demand curve Shows how many units of a product or service consumers will demand during a specific period at different prices.

democratic buying center A buying center in which the majority rules in making decisions.

demographic segmentation The grouping of consumers according to easily measured, objective characteristics such as age, gender, income, and education.

demographics Information about the characteristics of human populations and segments, especially those used to identify consumer markets such as age, gender, income, and education.

department store A retailer that carries many different types of merchandise (broad variety) and lots of items within each type (deep assortment); offers some customer services; and is organized into separate departments to display its merchandise.

derived demand The linkage between consumers' demand for a company's output and its purchase of necessary inputs to manufacture or assemble that particular output.

determinant attributes Product or service features that are important to the buyer and on which competing brands or stores are perceived to differ.

differentiated marketing strategy A strategy through which a firm targets several market segments with a different offering for each.

diffusion of innovation The process by which the use of an innovation, whether a product or a service, spreads throughout a market group over time and over various categories of adopters.

direct investment When a firm maintains 100 percent ownership of its plants, operation facilities, and offices in a foreign country, often through the formation of wholly owned subsidiaries.

direct marketing Sales and promotional techniques that deliver promotional materials individually to potential customers.

discount store A type of retailer that offers a broad variety of merchandise, limited service, and low prices.

dispatcher The person who coordinates deliveries to distribution centers.

distribution center A facility for the receipt, storage, and redistribution of goods to company stores or customers; may be operated by retailers, manufacturers, or distribution specialists.

distribution intensity The number of supply chain members to use at each level of the supply chain.

distributive fairness Pertains to a customer's perception of the benefits he or she received compared with the costs (inconvenience or loss) that resulted from a service failure.

diversification strategy A growth strategy whereby a firm introduces a new product or service to a market segment that it does not currently serve.

drugstore A specialty store that concentrates on health and personal grooming merchandise, though pharmaceuticals may represent more than 60 percent of its sales.

dumping The practice of selling a good in a foreign market at a price that is lower than its domestic price or below its cost.

duty See *tariff.*

early adopters The second group of consumers in the diffusion of innovation model, after *innovators,* to use a product or service innovation; generally don't like to take as much risk as innovators but instead wait and purchase the product after careful review.

early majority A group of consumers in the diffusion of innovation model that represents approximately 34 percent of the population; members don't like to take much risk and therefore tend to wait until bugs are worked out of a particular product or service; few new products and services can be profitable until this large group buys them.

economic situation Macroeconomic factor that affects the way consumers buy merchandise and spend money, both in a marketer's home country and abroad; see *inflation, foreign currency fluctuations,* and *interest rates.*

elastic Refers to a market for a product or service that is price sensitive; that is, relatively small changes in price will generate fairly large changes in the quantity demanded.

electronic data interchange (EDI) The computer-to-computer exchange of business documents from a retailer to a vendor and back.

emotional appeal Aims to satisfy consumers' emotional desires rather than their utilitarian needs.

empowerment In context of service delivery, means allowing employees to make decisions about how service is provided to customers.

encoding The process of converting the sender's ideas into a message, which could be verbal, visual, or both.

English auction Goods and services are simply sold to the highest bidder.

environmental concerns Include, but are not limited to, the excessive use of natural resources and energy, refuse from manufacturing processes, excess trash created by consumer goods packages, and hard-to-dispose-of products like tires, cell phones, and computer monitors.

ethical climate The set of values within a marketing firm, or in the marketing division of any firm, that guide decision making and behavior.

evaluative criteria Consist of a set of salient, or important, attributes about a particular product.

event sponsorship Popular PR tool; occurs when corporations support various activities (financially or otherwise), usually in the cultural or sports and entertainment sectors.

everyday low pricing (EDLP) A strategy companies use to emphasize the continuity of their retail prices at a level somewhere between the regular, nonsale price and the deep-discount sale prices their competitors may offer.

evoked set Comprises the alternative brands or stores that the consumer states he or she would consider when making a purchase decision.

exchange The trade of things of value between the buyer and the seller so that each is better off as a result.

exchange control Refers to the regulation of a country's currency *exchange rate.*

exchange rate The measure of how much one currency is worth in relation to another.

exclusive geographic territories Territories granted to one or very few retail customers by a manufacturer using an exclusive distribution strategy; no other customers can sell a particular brand in these territories.

experience curve effect Refers to the drop in unit cost as the accumulated volume sold increases; as sales continue to grow, the costs continue to drop, allowing even further reductions in the price.

experimental research A type of quantitative research that systematically manipulates one or more variables to determine which variable has a causal effect on another variable.

exploratory research Attempts to begin to understand the phenomenon of interest; also provides initial information when the problem lacks any clear definition.

exporting Producing goods in one country and selling them in another.

extended problem solving A purchase decision process during which the consumer devotes considerable time and effort to analyzing alternatives; often occurs when the consumer perceives that the purchase decision entails a lot of risk.

external locus of control Refers to when consumers believe that fate or other external factors control all outcomes.

external reference price A higher price to which the consumer can compare the selling price to evaluate the purchase.

external search for information Occurs when the buyer seeks information outside his or her personal knowledge base to help make the buying decision.

extranet A collaborative network that uses Internet technology to link businesses with their suppliers, customers, or other businesses.

extreme value retailer A general merchandise discount store found in lower-income urban or rural areas.

feedback loop Allows the receiver to communicate with the sender and thereby informs the sender whether the message was received and decoded properly.

financial risk Risk associated with a monetary outlay; includes the initial cost of the purchase, as well as the costs of using the item or service.

first movers Product pioneers that are the first to create a market or product category, making them readily recognizable to consumers and thus establishing a commanding and early market share lead.

fixed costs Those costs that remain essentially at the same level, regardless of any changes in the volume of production.

flighting advertising schedule An advertising schedule implemented in spurts, with periods of heavy advertising followed by periods of no advertising.

floor-ready merchandise Merchandise that is ready to be placed on the selling floor immediately.

focus group interview A research technique in which a small group of persons (usually 8 to 12) comes together for an intensive discussion about a particular topic, with the conversation guided by a trained moderator using an unstructured method of inquiry.

foreign currency fluctuations Changes in the value of a country's currency relative to the currency of another country; can influence consumer spending.

franchisee See *franchising*.

franchising A contractual agreement between a *franchisor* and a *franchisee* that allows the franchisee to operate a business using a name and format developed and supported by the franchisor.

franchisor See *franchising*.

frequency Measure of how often the audience is exposed to a communication within a specified period of time.

functional needs Pertain to the performance of a product or service.

gatekeeper The buying center participant who controls information or access to decision makers and influencers.

General Agreement on Tariffs and Trade (GATT) Organization established to lower trade barriers, such as high tariffs on imported goods and restrictions on the number and types of imported products that inhibited the free flow of goods across borders.

general merchandise retailer May be a *discount store, specialty store, category specialist, department store, drugstore, off-price retailer*, or *extreme value retailer*; may sell through multiple channels, such as the Internet and catalogs.

Generation X Generational cohort of people born between 1965 and 1976.

Generation Y Generational cohort of people born between 1977 and 1995; biggest cohort since the original postwar baby boom.

generational cohort A group of people of the same generation—typically have similar purchase behaviors because they have shared experiences and are in the same stage of life.

generic A product sold without a brand name, typically in commodities markets.

geodemographic segmentation The grouping of consumers on the basis of a combination of geographic, demographic, and lifestyle characteristics.

geographic segmentation The grouping of consumers on the basis of where they live.

global labor issues Includes concerns about working conditions and wages paid to factory workers in developing countries.

globalization Refers to the processes by which goods, services, capital, people, information, and ideas flow across national borders.

globalization of production Also known as *offshoring*; refers to manufacturers' procurement of goods and services from around the globe to take advantage of national differences in the cost and quality of various factors of production (e.g., labor, energy, land, capital).

goods Items that can be physically touched.

gray market Employs irregular but not necessarily illegal methods; generally, it legally circumvents authorized channels of distribution to sell goods at prices lower than those intended by the manufacturer.

green marketing Involves a strategic effort by firms to supply customers with environmentally friendly merchandise.

gross domestic product (GDP) Defined as the market value of the goods and services produced by a country in a year; the most widely used standardized measure of output.

gross national income (GNI) Consists of GDP plus the net income earned from investments abroad (minus any payments made to nonresidents who contribute to the domestic economy).

gross rating points (GRP) Measure used for various media advertising—print, radio, or television; *GRP = reach × frequency*.

growth stage Stage of the product life cycle when the product gains acceptance, demand and sales increase, and competitors emerge in the product category.

habitual decision making A purchase decision process in which consumers engage with little conscious effort.

high/low pricing A *pricing* strategy that relies on the promotion of sales, during which prices are temporarily reduced to encourage purchases.

horizontal price fixing Occurs when competitors that produce and sell competing products collude, or work together, to control prices, effectively taking price out of the decision process for consumers.

human development index (HDI) A composite measure of three indicators of the quality of life in different countries: life expectancy at birth, educational attainment, and whether the average incomes are sufficient to meet the basic needs of life in that country.

ideal point The position at which a particular market segment's ideal product would lie on a *perceptual map*.

ideas Intellectual concepts—thoughts, opinions, and philosophies.

implementation phase The part of the strategic marketing planning process when marketing managers (1) identify and evaluate different opportunities by engaging in segmentation, targeting, and positioning (see *STP*) and (2) implement the marketing mix using the four Ps.

improvement value Represents an estimate of how much more (or less) consumers are willing to pay for a product relative to other comparable products.

impulse buying A buying decision made by customers on the spot when they see the merchandise.

income effect Refers to the change in the quantity of a product demanded by consumers due to a change in their income.

independent (conventional) supply chain A loose coalition of several independently owned and operated supply chain members—a manufacturer, a wholesaler, and a retailer—each attempt to satisfy their own objectives and maximize their own profits, often at the expense of the other members.

independent agents Salespeople who sell a manufacturer's products on an extended contract basis but are not employees of the manufacturer; also known as *manufacturer's representatives* or *reps*.

in-depth interview An exploratory research technique in which trained researchers ask questions, listen to and record the answers, and then pose additional questions to clarify or expand on a particular issue.

individual brands The use of individual brand names for each of a firm's products.

inelastic Refers to a market for a product or service that is price insensitive; that is, relatively small changes in price will not generate large changes in the quantity demanded.

inflation Refers to the persistent increase in the prices of goods and services.

influencer The buying center participant whose views influence other members of the buying center in making the final decision.

informational appeal Used in a promotion to help consumers make purchase decisions by offering factual information and strong arguments built around relevant issues that encourage them to evaluate the brand favorably on the basis of the key benefits it provides.

informative advertising Communication used to create and build brand awareness, with the ultimate goal of moving the consumer through the buying cycle to a purchase.

infrastructure The basic facilities, services, and installations needed for a community or society to function, such as transportation and communications systems, water and power lines, and public institutions like schools, post offices, and prisons.

initiator The buying center participant who first suggests buying the particular product or service.

innovation The process by which ideas are transformed into new products and services that will help firms grow.

innovators Those buyers who want to be the first to have the new product or service.

inseparable A characteristic of a service: it is produced and consumed at the same time; that is, service and consumption are inseparable.

institutional advertisements Used to inform, persuade, and remind consumers about issues related to places, politics, an industry, or a particular corporation.

intangible A characteristic of a service; it cannot be touched, tasted, or seen like a pure product can.

integrated marketing communications (IMC) Represents the promotion dimension of the four Ps; encompasses a variety of communication disciplines—general advertising, personal selling, sales promotion, public relations, direct marketing, and electronic media—in combination to provide clarity, consistency, and maximum communicative impact.

intensive distribution A strategy designed to get products into as many outlets as possible.

interest rates These represent the cost of borrowing money.

internal locus of control Refers to when consumers believe they have some control over the outcomes of their actions, in which case they generally engage in more search activities.

internal reference price Price information stored in the consumer's memory that the person uses to assess a current price offering—perhaps the last price he or she paid or what he or she expects to pay.

internal search for information Occurs when the buyer examines his or her own memory and knowledge about the product or service, gathered through past experiences.

International Monetary Fund (IMF) Established with the original General Agreement on Tariffs and Trade (GATT); primary purpose is to promote international monetary cooperation and facilitate the expansion and growth of international trade.

intranet A secure communication system contained within one company, such as between the firm's buyers and distribution centers.

introduction stage Stage of the product life cycle when innovators start buying the product.

joint venture Formed when a firm entering a new market pools its resources with those of a local firm to form a new company in which ownership, control, and profits are shared.

just-in-time (JIT) inventory systems Inventory management systems designed to deliver less merchandise on a more frequent basis than traditional inventory systems; the firm gets the merchandise "just in time" for it to be used in the manufacture of another product, in the case of parts or components, or for sale when the customer wants it, in the case of consumer goods; also known as *quick response (QR) systems* in retailing.

knowledge gap A type of *service gap*; reflects the difference between customers' expectations and the firm's perception of those expectations.

laggards Consumers who like to avoid change and rely on traditional products until they are no longer available.

lagged effect A delayed response to a marketing communication campaign.

late majority The last group of buyers to enter a new product market; when they do, the product has achieved its full market potential.

lead time The amount of time between the recognition that an order needs to be placed and the arrival of the needed merchandise at the seller's store, ready for sale.

lead users Innovative product users who modify existing products according to their own ideas to suit their specific needs.

leader pricing Consumer pricing tactic that attempts to build store traffic by aggressively pricing and advertising a regularly purchased item, often priced at or just above the store's cost.

leads A list of potential customers.

learning Refers to a change in a person's thought process or behavior that arises from experience and takes place throughout the consumer decision process.

lifestyles A component of *psychographics*; refers to the way a person lives his or her life to achieve goals.

limited problem solving Occurs during a purchase decision that calls for, at most, a moderate amount of effort and time.

logistics management The integration of two or more activities for the purpose of planning, implementing, and controlling the efficient flow of raw materials, in-process inventory, and finished goods from the point of origin to the point of consumption.

loss leader pricing Loss leader pricing takes the tactic of *leader pricing* one step further by lowering the price below the store's cost.

loyalty program Specifically designed to retain customers by offering premiums or other incentives to customers who make multiple purchases over time.

loyalty segmentation Strategy of investing in loyalty initiatives to retain the firm's most profitable customers.

macroenvironmental factors Aspects of the external environment that affect a company's business, such as the culture, demographics, social issues, technological advances, economic situation, and political/regulatory environment.

manufacturer brands (national brands) Brands owned and managed by the manufacturer.

manufacturer's representative See *independent agents*.

markdowns Reductions retailers take on the initial selling price of the product or service.

market development strategy A growth strategy that employs the existing marketing offering to reach new market segments, whether domestic or international.

market growth rate The annual rate of growth of the specific market in which the product competes.

market penetration strategy A growth strategy that employs the existing marketing mix and focuses the firm's efforts on existing customers.

market penetration pricing strategy A pricing strategy of setting the initial price low for the introduction of the new product or service, with the objective of building sales, market share, and profits quickly.

market positioning Involves the process of defining the marketing mix variables so that target customers have a clear, distinctive, desirable understanding of what the product does or represents in comparison with competing products.

market segment A group of consumers who respond similarly to a firm's marketing efforts.

market segmentation The process of dividing the market into groups of customers with different needs, wants, or characteristics—who therefore might appreciate products or services geared especially for them.

marketing An organizational function and a set of processes for creating, *capturing*, communicating, and delivering value to customers and for managing customer relationships in ways that benefit the organization and its stakeholders.

marketing channel The set of institutions that transfer the ownership of and move goods from the point of production to the point of consumption; consists of all the institutions and marketing activities in the marketing process.

marketing ethics Refers to those ethical problems that are specific to the domain of marketing.

marketing information system (MkIS) A set of procedures and methods that apply to the regular, planned collection, analysis, and presentation of information that then may be used in marketing decisions.

marketing mix (four Ps) Product, price, place, and promotion—the controllable set of activities that a firm uses to respond to the wants of its target markets.

marketing plan A written document composed of an analysis of the current marketing situation, opportunities and threats for the firm, marketing objectives and strategy specified in terms of the four Ps, action programs, and projected or pro forma income (and other financial) statements.

marketing research A set of techniques and principles for systematically collecting, recording, analyzing, and interpreting data that can aid decision makers involved in marketing goods, services, or ideas.

mass customization The practice of interacting on a one-to-one basis with many people to create custom-made products or services; providing one-to-one marketing to the masses.

mass media Channels that are ideal for reaching large numbers of anonymous audience members; include national newspapers, magazines, radio, and television.

maturity stage Stage of the product life cycle when industry sales reach their peak, so firms try to rejuvenate their products by adding new features or repositioning them.

media buy The actual purchase of airtime or print pages.

media mix The combination of the media used and the frequency of advertising in each medium.

media planning The process of evaluating and selecting the *media mix* that will deliver a clear, consistent, compelling message to the intended audience.

micromarketing An extreme form of segmentation that tailors a product or service to suit an individual customer's wants or needs; also called *one-to-one marketing*.

mission statement A broad description of a firm's objectives and the scope of activities it plans to undertake; attempts to answer two main questions: What type of business is it? What does it need to do to accomplish its goals and objectives?

modified rebuy Refers to when the buyer has purchased a similar product in the past but has decided to change some specifications, such as the desired price, quality level, customer service level, options, or so forth.

monopolistic competition Occurs when there are many firms that sell closely related but not homogeneous products; these products may be viewed as substitutes but are not perfect substitutes.

motive A need or want that is strong enough to cause the person to seek satisfaction.

multichannel retailers Retailers that sell merchandise in more than one retail channel (e.g., store, catalog, and Internet).

need recognition The beginning of the consumer decision process; occurs when consumers recognize they have an unsatisfied need and want to go from their actual, needy state to a different, desired state.

negative word of mouth Occurs when consumers spread negative information about a product, service, or store to others.

new buy In a B2B setting, a purchase of a good or service for the first time; the buying decision is likely to be quite involved because the buyer or the buying organization does not have any experience with the item.

niche media Channels that are focused and generally used to reach narrow segments, often with unique demographic characteristics or interests.

noise Any interference that stems from competing messages, a lack of clarity in the message, or a flaw in the medium; a problem for all communication channels.

noncommercial speech A message that does not have an economic motivation and therefore is fully protected under the First Amendment.

noncompensatory decision rule At work when consumers choose a product or service on the basis of a subset of its characteristics, regardless of the values of its other attributes.

noncumulative quantity discount Pricing tactic that offers a discount based on only the amount purchased in a single order; provides the buyer with an incentive to purchase more merchandise immediately.

North American Industry Classification System (NAICS) codes U.S. Bureau of Census classification scheme that categorizes all firms into a hierarchical set of six-digit codes.

objective-and-task method An IMC budgeting method that determines the cost required to undertake specific tasks to accomplish communication objectives; process entails setting objectives, choosing media, and determining costs.

observation An exploratory research method that entails examining purchase and consumption behaviors through personal or video camera scrutiny.

odd prices Prices that end in odd numbers, usually 9, such as $3.99.

off-price retailer A type of retailer that offers an inconsistent assortment of merchandise at relatively low prices.

offshoring See *globalization of production*.

oligopolistic competition Occurs when only a few firms dominate a market.

one-to-one marketing See *micromarketing*.

online couponing A promotional Web technique in which consumers print a coupon directly from a site and then redeem the coupon in a store.

online referring A promotional Web technique in which consumers fill out an interest or order form and are referred to an offline dealer or firm that offers the product or service of interest.

operational excellence Involves a firm's focus on efficient operations and excellent supply chain management.

order getter A salesperson whose primary responsibilities are identifying potential customers and engaging those customers in discussions to attempt to make a sale.

order taker A salesperson whose primary responsibility is to process routine orders or reorders or rebuys for products.

organizational culture Reflects the set of values, traditions, and customs that guide an firm's employees' behavior.

panel research A type of quantitative research that involves collecting information from a group of consumers (the panel) over time; data collected may be from a survey or a record of purchases.

perceived value The relationship between a product or service's benefits and its cost.

perception The process by which people select, organize, and interpret information to form a meaningful picture of the world.

perceptual map Displays, in two or more dimensions, the position of products or brands in the consumer's mind.

performance risk Involves the perceived danger inherent in a poorly performing product or service.

perishability A characteristic of a service: it cannot be stored for use in the future.

personal needs Relate to ways people satisfy their inner desires.

personal selling The two-way flow of communication between a buyer and a seller that is designed to influence the buyer's purchase decision.

persuasive advertising Communication used to motivate consumers to take action.

physiological needs Those relating to the basic biological necessities of life: food, drink, rest, and shelter.

pioneers New product introductions that establish a completely new market or radically change both the rules of competition and consumer preferences in a market; also called *breakthroughs*.

planning phase The part of the strategic marketing planning process when marketing executives, in conjunction with other top managers, (1) define the mission or vision of the business and (2) evaluate the situation by assessing how various players, both in and outside the organization, affect the firm's potential for success.

point-of-purchase (POP) display A merchandise display located at the point of purchase, such as at the checkout counter in a grocery store.

political/regulatory environment Comprises political parties, government organizations, and legislation and laws.

pop-up stores Temporary storefronts that exist for only a limited time and generally focus on a new product or a limited group of products offered by a retailer, manufacturer, or service provider; give consumers a chance to interact with the brand and build brand awareness, but are not designed primarily to sell the product.

postpurchase dissonance The psychologically uncomfortable state produced by an inconsistency between beliefs and behaviors that in turn evokes a motivation to reduce the dissonance; buyers' remorse.

posttesting The evaluation of an IMC campaign's impact after it is has been implemented.

preapproach In the personal selling process, occurs prior to meeting the customer for the first time and extends the qualification of leads procedure; in this step, the salesperson conducts additional research and develops plans for meeting with the customer.

predatory pricing A firm's practice of setting a very low price for one or more of its products with the intent to drive its competition out of business; illegal under both the Sherman Act and the Federal Trade Commission Act.

premarket test Conducted before a product or service is brought to market to determine how many customers will try and then continue to use it.

premium An item offered for free or at a bargain price to reward some type of behavior, such as buying, sampling, or testing.

premium pricing A competitor-based pricing method by which the firm deliberately prices a product above the prices set for competing products to capture those consumers who always shop for the best or for whom price does not matter.

prestige products or services Those that consumers purchase for status rather than functionality.

pretesting Assessments performed before an ad campaign; is implemented to ensure that the various elements are working in an integrated fashion and doing what they are intended to do.

price The overall sacrifice a consumer is willing to make—money, time, energy—to acquire a specific product or service.

price bundling Consumer pricing tactic of selling more than one product for a single, lower price than what the items would cost sold separately; can be used to sell slow-moving items, to encourage customers to stock up so they won't purchase competing brands, to encourage trial of a new product, or to provide an incentive to purchase a less desirable product or service to obtain a more desirable one in the same bundle.

price discrimination The practice of selling the same product to different resellers (wholesalers, distributors, or retailers) or to the ultimate consumer at different prices; some, but not all, forms of price discrimination are illegal.

price elasticity of demand Measures how changes in a price affect the quantity of the product demanded; specifically, the ratio of the percentage change in quantity demanded to the percentage change in price.

price fixing The practice of colluding with other firms to control prices.

price lining Consumer market pricing tactic of establishing a price floor and a price ceiling for an entire line of similar products and then setting a few other price points in between to represent distinct differences in quality.

price skimming A strategy of selling a new product or service at a high price that *innovators* and *early adopters* are willing to pay in order to obtain it; after the high-price market segment becomes saturated and sales begin to slow down, the firm generally lowers the price to capture (or skim) the next most price sensitive segment.

price war Occurs when two or more firms compete primarily by lowering their prices.

pricing tactics Short-term methods, in contrast to long-term pricing strategies, used to focus on company objectives, costs, customers, competition, or channel members; can be responses to competitive threats (e.g., lowering price temporarily to meet a competitor's price reduction) or broadly accepted methods of calculating a final price for the customer that is short term in nature.

primary data Data collected to address specific research needs.

primary demand advertising Ads designed to generate demand for the product category or an entire industry.

primary package The packaging the consumer uses, such as the toothpaste tube, from which he or she typically seeks convenience in terms of storage, use, and consumption.

private exchange Occurs when a specific firm, either buyer or seller, invites others to join to participate in online information exchanges and transactions; can help streamline procurement or distribution processes.

private-label brands Brands developed and marketed by a retailer and available only from that retailer; also called *store brands.*

procedural fairness Refers to the customer's perception of the fairness of the process used to resolve complaints about service.

product Anything that is of value to a consumer and can be offered through a voluntary marketing exchange.

product assortment The complete set of all products offered by a firm; also called the *product mix.*

product category An assortment of items that the customer sees as reasonable substitutes for one another.

product design See *product development.*

product development Also called *product design;* entails a process of balancing various engineering, manufacturing, marketing, and economic considerations to develop a product's form and features or a service's features.

product development strategy A growth strategy that offers a new product or service to a firm's current target market.

product excellence Involves a focus on achieving high-quality products; effective branding and positioning is key.

product life cycle Defines the stages that new products move through as they enter, get established in, and ultimately leave the marketplace and thereby offers marketers a starting point for their strategy planning.

product line A group of products that consumers may use together or perceive as similar in some way.

product line breadth The number of product lines, or variety, offered by the firm.

product line depth The number of categories within a product line.

product lines Groups of associated items, such as those that consumers use together or think of as part of a group of similar products.

product mix See *product assortment.*

product placement Inclusion of a product in nontraditional situations, such as in a scene in a movie or television program.

product-focused advertisements Used to inform, persuade, or remind consumers about a specific product or service.

profit orientation A company objective that can be implemented by focusing on *target profit pricing, maximizing profits,* or *target return pricing.*

projective technique A type of qualitative research in which subjects are provided a scenario and asked to express their thoughts and feelings about it.

prototype The first physical form or service description of a new product, still in rough or tentative form, that has the same properties as a new product but is produced through different manufacturing processes, sometimes even crafted individually.

PSSP hierarchy of needs Argues that when lower-level, more basic needs (physiological and safety) are fulfilled, people turn to satisfying their higher-level human needs (social and personal); see *physiological, safety, social,* and *personal needs.*

psychographics Used in segmentation; delves into how consumers describe themselves; allows people to describe themselves using those characteristics that help them choose how they occupy their time (behavior) and what underlying psychological reasons determine those choices.

psychological needs Pertain to the personal gratification consumers associate with a product or service.

psychological risk Associated with the way people will feel if the product or service does not convey the right image.

public relations The organizational function that manages the firm's communications to achieve a variety of objectives, including building and maintaining a positive image, handling or heading off unfavorable stories or events, and maintaining positive relationships with the media.

public service advertising (PSA) Advertising that focuses on public welfare and generally is sponsored by nonprofit institutions, civic groups, religious organizations, trade associations, or political groups; a form of *social marketing.*

puffery The legal exaggeration of praise, stopping just short of deception, lavished on a product.

pull strategy Designed to get consumers to pull the product into the supply chain by demanding it.

pulsing advertising schedule Combines the continuous and flighting schedules by maintaining a base level of advertising but increasing advertising intensity during certain periods.

purchasing power parity (PPP) A theory that states that if the exchange rates of two countries are in equilibrium, a product purchased in one will cost the same in the other, expressed in the same currency.

pure competition Occurs when different companies sell commodity products that consumers perceive as substitutable; price usually is set according to the laws of supply and demand.

push strategy Designed to increase demand by motivating sellers—wholesalers, distributors, or salespeople—to highlight the product, rather than the products of competitors, and thereby push the product onto consumers.

qualify The process of assessing the potential of sales leads.

quantity discount Pricing tactic of offering a reduced price according to the amount purchased; the more the buyer purchases, the higher the discount and, of course, the greater the value.

questionnaire A form that features a set of questions designed to gather information from respondents and thereby accomplish the researchers' objectives; questions can be either unstructured or structured.

quick response An inventory management system used in retailing; merchandise is received just in time for sale when the customer wants it; see *just-in-time (JIT) systems.*

quota Designates the maximum quantity of a product that may be brought into a country during a specified time period.

radio frequency identification (RFID) tags Tiny computer chips that automatically transmit to a special scanner all the information about a container's contents or individual products.

reach Measure of consumers' exposure to marketing communications; the percentage of the target population exposed to a specific marketing communication, such as an advertisement, at least once.

rebate A consumer discount in which a portion of the purchase price is returned to the buyer in cash; the manufacturer, not the retailer, issues the refund.

receiver The person who reads, hears, or sees and processes the information contained in the message or advertisement.

receiving The process of recording the receipt of merchandise as it arrives at a distribution center or store.

reference group One or more persons whom an individual uses as a basis for comparison regarding beliefs, feelings, and behaviors.

reference price The price against which buyers compare the actual selling price of the product and that facilitates their evaluation process.

relational orientation A method of building a relationship with customers based on the philosophy that buyers and sellers should develop a long-term relationship.

relationship selling A sales philosophy and process that emphasizes a commitment to maintaining the relationship over the long term and investing in opportunities that are mutually beneficial to all parties.

relative market share A measure of the product's strength in a particular market, defined as the sales of the focal product divided by the sales achieved by the largest firm in the industry.

reminder advertising Communication used to remind consumers of a product or to prompt repurchases, especially for products that have gained market acceptance and are in the maturity stage of their life cycle.

reps See *independent agents*.

request for proposals (RFP) A process through which buying organizations invite alternative suppliers to bid on supplying their required components.

resellers Marketing intermediaries that resell manufactured products without significantly altering their form.

retailing The set of business activities that add value to products and services sold to consumers for their personal or family use; includes products bought at stores, through catalogs, and over the Internet, as well as services like fast-food restaurants, airlines, and hotels.

retrieval set Includes those brands or stores that the consumer can readily bring forth from memory.

reverse auction The buyer provides specifications to a group of sellers, who then bid down the price until the buyer accepts a specific bid.

reverse engineering Involves taking apart a competitor's product, analyzing it, and creating an improved product that does not infringe on the competitor's patents, if any exist.

ritual consumption Refers to a pattern of behaviors tied to life events that affect what and how people consume.

role playing A good technique for practicing the sales presentation prior to meeting with a customer; the salesperson acts out a simulated buying situation while a colleague or manager acts as the buyer.

rule-of-thumb methods Budgeting methods that bases the IMC budget on either the firm's share of the market in relation to competition, a fixed percentage of forecasted sales, or what is left after other operating costs and forecasted sales have been budgeted.

safety needs One of the needs in the PSSP hierarchy of needs; pertain to protection and physical well-being.

salary Compensation in the form of a fixed sum of money paid at regular intervals.

sales contest A short-term incentive designed to elicit a specific response from the sales force.

sales management Involves the planning, direction, and control of personal selling activities, including recruiting, selecting, training, motivating, compensating, and evaluating, as they apply to the sales force.

sales orientation A company objective based on the belief that increasing sales will help the firm more than will increasing profits.

sales promotions Special incentives or excitement-building programs that encourage the purchase of a product or service, such as coupons, rebates, contests, free samples, and point-of-purchase displays.

sales support personnel Employees who enhance and help with a firm's overall selling effort, such as by responding to the customer's technical questions or facilitating repairs.

sampling Offers potential customers the opportunity to try a product or service before they make a buying decision.

scanner research A type of quantitative research that uses data obtained from scanner readings of UPC codes at checkout counters.

scenario planning A process that integrates macroenvironmental information in an attempt to understand the potential outcomes of different applications of a firm's marketing mix; enables a firm to predict, monitor, and adapt to the ever-changing future.

seasonal discount Pricing tactic of offering an additional reduction as an incentive to retailers to order merchandise in advance of the normal buying season.

secondary data Pieces of information that have already been collected from other sources and usually are readily available.

secondary package The wrapper or exterior carton that contains the primary package and provides the UPC label used by retail scanners; can contain additional product information that may not be available on the primary package.

selective demand Demand for a specific brand.

selective demand advertising Ads designed to generate demand for a specific brand, firm, or item.

selective distribution Lies between the intensive and exclusive distribution strategies; uses a few selected customers in a territory.

self-concept The image a person has of him- or herself; a component of *psychographics*.

self-values Goals for life, not just the goals one wants to accomplish in a day; a component of *psychographics* that refers to overriding desires that drive how a person lives his or her life.

selling teams Combinations of sales specialists whose primary duties are order getting, order taking, or sales support but who work together to service important accounts.

sender The firm from which an IMC message originates; the sender must be clearly identified to the intended audience.

Seniors America's fastest-growing generational cohort; people aged 55 to 64 years.

service Any intangible offering that involves a deed, performance, or effort that cannot be physically possessed.

service Intangible customer benefits that are produced by people or machines and cannot be separated from the producer.

service gap Results when a service fails to meet the expectations that customers have about how it should be delivered.

service quality Customers' perceptions of how well a service meets or exceeds their expectations.

share of wallet The percentage of the customer's purchases made from a particular retailer.

shopping goods/services Those for which consumers will spend time comparing alternatives, such as apparel, fragrances, and appliances.

situation analysis Second step in a marketing plan; uses of a SWOT analysis that assesses both the internal environment with regard to its **S**trengths and **W**eaknesses and the external environment in terms of its **O**pportunities and **T**hreats.

situational factors Factor affecting the consumer decision process; those that are specific to the situation that may override, or at least influence, psychological and social issues.

size discount The most common implementation of a quantity discount at the consumer level; the larger the quantity bought, the less the cost per unit (e.g., per ounce).

slotting allowances Fees firms pay to retailers simply to get new products into stores or to gain more or better shelf space for their products.

social marketing The application of marketing principles to a social issue to bring about attitudinal and behavioral change among the general public or a specific population segment.

social needs One of the needs in the PSSP hierarchy of needs; relate to one's interactions with others.

specialty goods/services Products or services toward which the customer shows a strong preference and for which he or she will expend considerable effort to search for the best suppliers.

specialty store A type of retailer that concentrates on a limited number of complementary merchandise categories in a relatively small store.

standards gap A type of *service gap*; pertains to the difference between the firm's perceptions of customers' expectations and the service standards it sets.

status quo pricing A competitor-oriented strategy in which a firm changes prices only to meet those of competition.

stealth marketing A strategy to attract consumers using promotional tactics that deliver a sales message in unconventional ways, often without the target audience knowing that the message even has a selling intent.

stock keeping units (SKUs) Individual items within each product category; the smallest unit available for inventory control.

store brands See *private-label brands*.

STP The processes of segmentation, targeting, and positioning that firms use to identify and evaluate opportunities for increasing sales and profits.

straight rebuy Refers to when the buyer or buying organization simply buys additional units of products that had previously been purchased.

strategic alliance A collaborative relationship between independent firms, though the partnering firms do not create an equity partnership; that is, they do not invest in one another.

strategic business unit (SBU) A division of the firm itself that can be managed and operated somewhat independently from other divisions and may have a different mission or objectives.

strategic marketing planning process A set of steps a marketer goes through to develop a strategic marketing plan.

strategic relationship (partnering relationship) A supply chain relationship that the members are committed to maintaining long term, investing in opportunities that are mutually beneficial; requires mutual trust, open communication, common goals, and credible commitments.

structured questions Closed-ended questions for which a discrete set of response alternatives, or specific answers, is provided for respondents to evaluate.

substitute products Products for which changes in demand are negatively related; that is, a percentage increase in the quantity demanded for product A results in a percentage decrease in the quantity demanded for product B.

substitution effect Refers to consumers' ability to substitute other products for the focal brand, thus increasing the price elasticity of demand for the focal brand.

supply chain The group of firms that make and deliver a given set of goods and services.

supply chain conflict (channel conflict) Results when supply chain members are not in agreement about their goals, roles, or rewards.

supply chain management Refers to a set of approaches and techniques firms employ to efficiently and effectively integrate their suppliers, manufacturers, warehouses, stores, and transportation intermediaries into a seamless value chain in which merchandise is produced and distributed in the right quantities, to the right locations, and at the right time, as well as to minimize systemwide costs while satisfying the service levels their customers require.

survey A systematic means of collecting information from people that generally uses a *questionnaire*.

sustainable competitive advantage Something the firm can persistently do better than its competitors.

sweepstakes A form of sales promotion that offers prizes based on a chance drawing of entrants' names.

syndicated data Data available for a fee from commercial research firms such as Information Resources Inc. (IRI), National Purchase Diary Panel, and ACNielsen.

target marketing/targeting The process of evaluating the attractiveness of various segments and then deciding which to pursue as a market.

target profit pricing A pricing strategy implemented by firms when they have a particular profit goal as their over-riding concern; uses price to stimulate a certain level of sales at a certain profit per unit.

target return pricing A pricing strategy implemented by firms less concerned with the absolute level of profits and more interested in the rate at which their profits are generated relative to their investments; designed to produce a specific return on investment, usually expressed as a percentage of sales.

tariff A tax levied on a good imported into a country; also called a *duty*.

technological advances Macroenvironmental factor that has greatly contributed to the improvement of the value of both products and services in the past few decades.

telemarketing A method of prospecting in which sales-people telephone potential customers.

test marketing Introduces a new product or service to a limited geographical area (usually a few cities) prior to a national launch.

ticketing and marking Creating price and identification labels and placing them on the merchandise.

top-of-the-mind awareness A prominent place in people's memories that triggers a response without them having to put any thought into it.

total cost The sum of the *variable* and *fixed costs*.

tracking Includes monitoring key indicators, such as daily or weekly sales volume, while the advertisement is running to shed light on any problems with the message or the medium.

trade agreements Intergovernmental agreements designed to manage and promote trade activities for specific regions.

trade area The geographical area that contains the potential customers of a particular retailer or shopping center.

trade deficit Results when a country imports more goods than it exports.

trade shows Major events attended by buyers who choose to be exposed to products and services offered by potential suppliers in an industry.

trade surplus Results when a country exports more goods than it imports.

trading bloc Consists of those countries that have signed a particular trade agreement.

traditional distribution center A warehouse in which merchandise is unloaded from trucks and placed on racks or shelves for storage.

transactional orientation Regards the buyer-seller relationship as a series of individual transactions, so anything that happened before or after the transaction is of little importance.

transmitter An agent or intermediary with which the sender works to develop the marketing communications; for example, a firm's creative department or an advertising agency.

Tweens Generational cohort of people born between 1996 and 2000; not quite teenagers, but not young children either: in beTWEEN.

undifferentiated segmentation strategy (mass marketing) A marketing strategy a firm can use if the product or service is perceived to provide the same benefits to everyone, with no need to develop separate strategies for different groups.

uniform delivered pricing The shipper charges one rate, no matter where the buyer is located.

unique selling proposition (USP) A strategy of differentiating a product by communicating its unique attributes; often becomes the common theme or slogan in the entire advertising campaign.

universal product code (UPC) The black-and-white bar code found on most merchandise.

universal set Includes all possible choices for a product category.

unstructured questions Open-ended questions that allow respondents to answer in their own words.

user The person who consumes or uses the product or service purchased by the buying center.

value Reflects the relationship of benefits to costs, or what the consumer *gets* for what he or she *gives*.

Value and Lifestyle Survey (VALS2) A psychographic tool developed by SRI Consulting Business Intelligence; classifies consumers into eight segments: innovators, thinkers, believers, achievers, strivers, experiencers, makers, or survivors.

value-based pricing A pricing strategy that involves first determining the perceived value of the product from the customer's point of view and then pricing accordingly.

value-based pricing method An approach that focuses on the overall value of the product offering as perceived by consumers, who determine value by comparing the benefits they expect the product to deliver with the sacrifice they will need to make to acquire the product.

variability A characteristic of a service: its quality may vary because it is provided by humans.

variable costs Those costs, primarily labor and materials, that vary with production volume.

vertical marketing system A supply chain in which the members act as a unified system; there are three types: *administrated*, *contractual*, and *corporate*.

vertical price fixing Occurs when parties at different levels of the same marketing channel (e.g., manufacturers and retailers) collude to control the prices passed on to consumers.

viral marketing A marketing phenomenon that encourages people to pass along a marketing message to other potential consumers.

voice-of-customer (VOC) program An ongoing marketing research system that collects customer inputs and integrates them into managerial decisions.

Web tracking software Used to assess how much time viewers spend on particular Web pages and the number of pages they view.

wholesalers Those firms engaged in buying, taking title to, often storing, and physically handling goods in large quantities, then reselling the goods (usually in smaller quantities) to retailers or industrial or business users.

World Bank Group A development bank that provides loans, policy advice, technical assistance, and knowledge-sharing services to low- and middle-income countries in an attempt to reduce poverty in the developing world.

World Trade Organization (WTO) Replaced the GATT in 1994; differs from the GATT in that the WTO is an established institution based in Geneva, Switzerland, instead of simply an agreement; represents the only international organization that deals with the global rules of trade among nations.

zone of tolerance The area between customers' expectations regarding their desired service and the minimum level of acceptable service—that is, the difference between what the customer really wants and what he or she will accept before going elsewhere.

zone pricing The shipper sets different prices depending on a geographical division of the delivery areas.

Chapter 1

1. Paul R. La Monica, "Google Sets $2.7 Billion IPO," *CNN Money*, April 30, 2004; AOL, http://www.aim.com (accessed October 25, 2004); Google, http://www.google.com (accessed October 25, 2005); "The Future of Amazon.com," *Forrester* (Forrester Research), September 2003; Carrie A. Johnson, Charles P. Wilson, and Sharyn Leaver, "Amazon Edges Out eBay in Shopping Experience Satisfaction," *Forrester* (Forrester Research), October 4, 2004; Charlene Li, Paul Sonderegger, and Sheiler Baxter, "Where Google Is Headed," *Forrester* (Forrester Research), February 23, 2004; Charles S. Golvin, Chris Charron, Charles Q. Strohm, and Ayanna Lonian, "IM Adoption—Far from in Lockstep—Marches On," *Forrester* (Forrester Research), September 30, 2003.

2. The American Marketing Association, http://www.marketingpower.com/content4620.php (accessed April 12, 2005). Word in italics was added by the authors. More discussion on marketing is provided by Stephen L. Vargo and Robert F. Lusch, "Evolving to a New Dominant Logic for Marketing," *Journal of Marketing* 68 (January 2004), pp. 1–17; and George S. Day, John Deighton, Das Narayandas, Evert Gummesson, Shelby D. Hunt, C.K. Prahalad, Roland T. Rust, and Steven M. Shugan, "Invited Commentaries on 'Evolving to a New Dominant Logic for Marketing,'" *Journal of Marketing* 68 (January 2004), pp. 18–27. Also see W. Stephen Brown, Frederick E. Webster Jr., Jan-Benedict E.M. Steenkamp, William L. Wilkie, Jagdish N. Sheth, Rajendra S. Sisodia, Roger A. Kerin, Deborah J. MacInnis, Leigh McAlister, Jagmohan S. Raju, Ronald J. Bauerly, Don T. Johnson, Mandeep Singh, and Richard Staelin, "Marketing Renaissance: Opportunities and Imperatives for Improving Marketing Thought, Practice, and Infrastructure," *Journal of Marketing*, 69, no. 4 (2005), pp. 1–25.

3. The idea of the four Ps was conceptualized by E. Jerome McCarthy, *Basic Marketing: A Managerial Approach* (Homewood, IL: Richard D. Irwin, 1960). Also see Walter van Watershoot and Christophe Van den Bulte, "The 4P Classification of the Marketing Mix Revisited," *Journal of Marketing* 56 (October 1992), pp. 83–93.

4. Statistics taken from Beverage Marketing Corporation, a New York-based research and consulting firm, http://www.bottledwaterweb.com (accessed June 12, 2006).

5. http://www.entrepreneurialexchange.org/bee.php?c=86 (accessed August 4, 2005); Naomi Aoki, "Reebok Goes Hollywood to Refashion Its Marketing," *Boston Globe*, October 3, 2004; www.reebok.com (accessed May 25, 2006); Greg Lindsay, "The Rebirth of Cool: Reebok Has Given Up on Trying to Beat Nike at the Hard-Core Sports Game, Instead, It Wants to Become the Shoe Brand for Hip-Hoppers, Hipsters, and Other Fashion-Forward Urbanites," *Business 2.0*, 5, no. 8 (September 2004), p. 108; and Joseph Pereira and Stephanie King, "Phat News: Rappers Choose Reebok Shoes," *The Wall Street Journal*, November 14, 2003, p. B.1.

6. Based on David Simchi-Levi, Philip Kaminsky, and Edith Simchi-Levi, *Designing and Managing the Supply Chain: Concepts, Strategies and Case Studies*, 2d ed. (New York: McGraw-Hill Irwin, 2003); and Michael Levy and Barton A. Weitz, *Retailing Management*, 6th ed. (New York: McGraw-Hill Irwin, 2007).

7. Web sites such as http://www.whymilk.com/ and http://www.milkdelivers.org/campaign/index.cfm provide examples of this popular campaign.

8. George S. Day, "Aligning the Organization with the Market," *Marketing Science Institute* 5, no. 3 (2005), pp. 3–20.

9. Dhruv Grewal, Kent B. Monroe, and R. Krishnan, "The Effects of Price Comparison Advertising on Buyers' Perceptions of Acquisition Value and Transaction Value," *Journal of Marketing* 62 (April 1998), pp. 46–60; Kent B. Monroe, *Pricing: Making Profitable Decisions*, 3d ed. (New York: McGraw-Hill, 2004).

10. Peter G. Wray, "Loyalty as Art," August 2002, http://www.pgw.co.uk/artaug02.html, accessed 6/7/04.

11. http://www.cm4p.com/art003.html, accessed 8/7/05.

12. http://www.cm4p.com/art003.html, accessed 8/7/05.

13. Shelley Emling, "Low-Cost Flying No Longer Just a U.S. Sensation," *Atlanta Journal*, December 26, 2003, p. F1.

14. In 2005, the *Journal of Marketing* ran a special section entirely devoted to relationship marketing. The section included these articles: William Boulding, Richard Staelin, Michael Ehret, and Wesley J. Johnston, "A Customer Relationship Management Roadmap: What Is Known, Potential Pitfalls, and Where to Go," *Journal of Marketing* 69, no. 4 (2005), pp. 155–66; Jacquelyn S. Thomas and Ursula Y. Sullivan, (2005), "Managing Marketing Communications with Multichannel Customers," *Journal of Marketing* 69, no 4 (2005), pp. 239–51; Lynette Ryals, "Making Customer Relationship Management Work: The Measurement and Profitable Management of Customer Relationships," *Journal of Marketing* 69, no. 4 (2005), pp. 252–261; and Martha Rogers (2005), "Customer Strategy: Observations from the Trenches," *Journal of Marketing* 69 no. 4 (2005), pp. 262–3.

15. Rajendra K. Srivastava, Tasadduq A. Shervani, and Liam Fahey, "Marketing, Business Processes, and Shareholder Value: An Embedded View of Marketing Activities and the Discipline of Marketing," *Journal of Marketing* 63, special issue (1999), pp. 168–79; R. Venkatesan and V. Kumar, "A Customer Lifetime Value Framework for Customer Selections and Resource Allocation Strategy," *Journal of Marketing* 68, no. 4 (October 2004), pp. 106–25; V. Kumar, G. Ramani and T. Bohling, "Customer Lifetime Value Approaches and Best Practice Applications," *Journal of Interactive Marketing* 18, no. 3 (Summer 2004), pp. 60–72; and J. Thomas, W. Reinartz, and V. Kumar, "Getting the Most Out of All Your Customers," *Harvard Business Review* (July–August 2004), pp. 116–23.

16. Hennes & Mauritz AB, http://www.hm.com (accessed October 4, 2005).

17. Zara, http://www.zara.com (accessed October 4, 2004).

18. Ahold, http://www.ahold.com (accessed October 4, 2004).

19. Jason Singer and Martin Fackler, "In Japan, Adding Beer, Wine to Latte List," *The Wall Street Journal* (July 15, 2003), p. B1; and Sharon Pian Chan, "Cornering Japan: Starbucks, Tully's Do Battle in Famously Fickle Market," *Seattle Times*, August 22, 2002, p. A1.

20. Royal Ford, "Automobila: Toyota Makes Emotional Appeal with Zippy New Line," *Boston Globe,* March 13, 2003, p. E1; Zachary Rodgers, "Toyota Bows Web/Mobile Gaming Campaign for Scion," *Clickz*, July 8, 2004, http://www.clickz.com; April 12, 2006 "Forehead Advertising Goes Mainstream with Toyota," *Adrants* (April 8, 2004). http://www.adrants.com; and Jason Stein, "Scion National Launch Gets Offbeat Support," *Automotive News* 78, no. 6104 (2004), p. 18.

21. "UPS Delivers Expanded Services to Small and Medium Businesses," http://www.pressroom.ups.com/pressreleases/current/0,1088,4384,00.html (accessed January 7, 2006).

22. Kellogg's NA Co., http://www.kelloggs.com/kelloggco/corporate_citizenship/index.html (accessed October 4, 2005).

23. http://www.colgate.com/app/Colgate/US/Corp/LivingOurValues/CoreValues.cvsp (accessed May 16, 2005).

24. Ben & Jerry's Homemade Holdings, Inc., http://www.benjerry.com/our_company/our_mission/ (accessed August 4, 2006).

25. Calvert, "Corporate Responsibility and Investor Confidence Survey," November 18, 2003, http://www.harrisinteractive.com. Also see The Trustees of Boston College, "The State of Corporate Citizenship in the United States: 2003," July 2003.

26. http://dictionary.reference.com/search?q=Entrepreneurship (accessed May 16, 2005).

27. Pixar, http://www.pixar.com/ (accessed April 11, 2005).

28. http://www.macworld.com/news/2006/01/24/disneypixar/index.php (accessed January 27, 2006).

29. Harpo Productions, Inc., http://www2.oprah.com/about/press/about_press_bio.jhtml (accessed April 11, 2005).

30. This case was written by Jeanne L. Munger in conjunction with the textbook authors Dhruv Grewal and Michael Levy for class discussion rather than to illustrate either effective or ineffective marketing practice. Jeanne Munger is an Associate Professor at the University of Southern Maine.

31. http://investor.ebay.com/downloads/sund_metrics.pdf; http://investor.ebay.com/downloads/sund_revenue.pdf (accessed August 17, 2006).

Chapter 2

1. Disney, http://www.wdisneyw.co.uk/palmickey.html (accessed October 14, 2004); Disney, "Mickey Mouse," http://disney.go.com/vault/archives/characterstandard/mickey/mickey.html; Disney, Fact Book and Annual Report, http://disney.go.com/corporate/investors (2003); Debra D'Agostino, "Walt Disney World Resorts and CRM Strategy," *eWeek.com*, December 1, 2003.

2. Donald Lehman and Russell Winer, *Analysis for Marketing Planning*, 5th ed. (Burr Ridge, IL: McGraw-Hill/Irwin, 2001); David Aaker, *Strategic Market Management*, 6th ed. (New York: John Wiley, 2001).

3. http://www.marketingpower.com/live/mg-dictionary.php?SearchFor=marketing+plan&Searched=1, (accessed August 31, 2006).

4. Andrew Campbell, "Mission Statements," *Long Range Planning* 30 (1997), pp. 931–33.

5. Alfred Rappaport, *Creating Shareholder Value: The New Standard for Business Performance* (New York: Wiley, 1988); Robert C. Higgins and Roger A. Kerin, "Managing the Growth-Financial Policy Nexus in Marketing," *Journal of Marketing* 59, no. 3 (1983), pp. 19–47; and Roger Kerin, Vijay Mahajan, and P. Rajan Varadarajan, *Contemporary Perspectives on Strategic Market Planning* (Boston: Allyn & Bacon, 1991), Chapter 6.

6. Coca-Cola, http://www2.coca-cola.com/ourcompany/mission_vision_values.htm (accessed September 2, 2006).

7. Cynthia Montgomery, "Creating Corporate Advantage," *Harvard Business Review* 76 (May–June 1998), pp. 71–80; Shelby Hunt and Robert Morgan, "The Comparative Advantage Theory of Competition," *Journal of Marketing* 59, no. 2 (1995), pp. 1–15; Kathleen Conner and C.K. Prahalad, "A Resource-Based Theory of the Firm: Knowledge versus Opportunism," *Organizational Science* 7 (September–October 1996), pp. 477–501; David Collins and Cynthia Montgomery, "Competing on Resources: Strategy for the 1990s," *Harvard Business Review* 73 (July–August 1995), pp. 118–28; William Werther and Jeffrey Kerr, "The Shifting Sands of Competitive Advantage," *Business Horizons* 38 (May–June 1995) pp. 11–17; "10 Quick Wins to Turn Your Supply Chain into a Competitive Advantage," http://marketindustry.about.com/library/bl/bl_ksa0112.htm?terms=competitive+advantage January (2002); "Multi-Channel Integration: The New Market Battleground," Market Forward Inc. http://www.pwcris.com/ March (2001).

8. Max Ward, VP of Information Technology, Staples Inc. Presentation at Babson College, 2005.

9. Mavis Scanlon, "Cox Spins a Web of Marketing Success," *Cable World* 15, no. 29 (2003), p. 32.

10. Ned Desmond, "Google's Next Runaway Success: Adwords Select Kicks in a Network Effect for Online Advertising," *Business 2.0*, November 2002.

11. http://www.daimlerchrysler.com (accessed August 31, 2006).

12. Natalie Mizik and Robert Jacobson, "How Brand Attributes Drive Financial Performance," *Marketing Science Institute* 5, no. 3 (2005), pp. 21–40.

13. Roger Kerin, Vijay Mahajan, and P. Rajan Varadarajan, *Contemporary Perspectives on Strategic Market Planning* (Boston: Allyn & Bacon, 1991), Chapter 6. See also Susan Mudambi, "A Topology of Strategic Choice in Marketing," *International Journal of Market & Distribution Management* (1994), pp. 22–25.

14. *PR Newswire*, "Clicks Closer to True Convergence with Redesign of hsn.com; Electronic Retailing Giant's New Web Site Will Cater to Both Multi-Channel Shoppers and First-Time Customers," November 3, 2003.

15. John M. Higgins, "NBC: In the Money," January 26, 2006, www.broadcastingcable.com; Jason Flynn, "Advice from the Trenches: How to Increase Upsell Revenue," *CRM Magazine*, February 2003, www.dcrm.infotoday.com (accessed August 31, 2006).

16. Elisabeth Rosenthal, "Buicks, Starbucks and Fried Chicken. Still China?" *The New York Times*, February 25, 2002, p. A4.

17. *PR Newswire*, "Time Inc. to Launch ALL YOU: Women's Magazine Will Be Sold Initially in Wal-Mart Stores Beginning Sept '04," March 29, 2004.

18. This Ethical Dilemma was prepared by Professor Ross Petty, Babson College. For references to the various Microsoft antitrust lawsuits, see http://jurist.law.pitt.edu/microsof.htm (accessed August 31, 2006).

19. FedEx, "FedEx Completes Acquisition of Kinko's; Strategic Move Allows FedEx to Capitalize on Key Business Trends," Press Release, http://www.fedex.com, February 12, 2004; "FedEx Expanding Business by Buying Kinko's," *Light & Medium Truck* 17, no. 1 (2004), p. 6; "FedEx Completes Kinko's Buy," *Journal of Commerce Online Edition*, February 12, 2004, p. 1, http://www.fedex.com (accessed August 31, 2006).

20. Speakers Platform, http://www.speaking.com/speakers/paulorfalea.html (accessed April 11, 2005).

21. Michael Treacy and Fred Wiersema, *The Disciplines of Market Leaders* (Reading, MA: Addison Wesley, 1995).

22. Gerrard Macintosh and Lawrence Lockshin, "Market Relationships and Store Loyalty: A Multi-Level Perspective," *International Journal of Research in Marketing* 14 (1997), pp. 487–97.

23. R. Venkatesan and V. Kumar, "A Customer Lifetime Value Framework for Customer Selections and Resource Allocation Strategy," *Journal of Marketing* 68, no. 4 (October 2004), pp. 106–25. V. Kumar, G. Ramani, and T. Bohling, "Customer Lifetime Value Approaches and Best Practice Applications," *Journal of Interactive Marketing*, 18, no. 3 (Summer 2004), pp. 60–72. J. Thomas, W. Reinartz, and V. Kumar (2004), "Getting the Most Out of All Your Customers," *Harvard Business Review* (July–August 2004), pp. 116–23.

24. Frederick Reichheld and W. Earl Sasser, Jr., "Zero Defections: Quality Comes to Services," *HBR OnPoint*, Harvard Business Review publication. September 1, 1990.

25. Frederick Reichheld and W. Earl Sasser, Jr., "Zero Defections: Quality Comes to Services," *HBR OnPoint*, Harvard Business Review publication. September 1, 1990.

26. Jo Marney. "Bringing Consumers Back for More." *Marketing Magazine* 33 (September 10, 2001); Niren Sirohi, Edward McLaughlin, and Dick Wittink, "A Model of Consumer Perceptions and Store Loyalty Intentions for a Supermarket Marketer," *Journal of Marketing* 74, no. 3 (1998), pp. 223–47.

27. Mary Jo Bitner, "Self Service Technologies: What Do Customers Expect?" *Marketing Management*, Spring 2001, pp. 10–34; Mary Jo Bitner, Stephen W. Brown, and Matthew L. Meuter, "Technology Infusion in Service Encounters," *Journal of Academy of Marketing Science* 28, no. 1 (2000), pp. 138–49; Matthew L. Meuter, Amy L. Ostrom, Robert I. Roundtree, and Mary Jo Bitner, "Self-Service Technologies: Understanding Customer Satisfaction with Technology-Based Service Encounters," *Journal of Marketing* 64, no. 3 (2000), pp. 50–64; A. Parasuraman and Dhruv Grewal, "The Impact of Technology on the Quality-Value-Loyalty Chain: A Research Agenda," *Journal of the Academy of Marketing Science* 28, no. 1 (2000), pp. 168–74.

28. Virgin Atlantic, http://www.virgin-atlantic.com/our_story_history.view.do; "Virgin Atlantic Airways Continues to Adhere to its Objective of Supplying Travelers in All Classes with the Best Travel Quality at the Lowest Cost Possible," *Travel Agent* 290, no. 12 (1998), p. 34ff; "Virgin Atlantic's Customer-Service Packages Include a Drive-Through Check-in Service and an Improved Frequent-Flier Program," *Air Transport World* 34, no. 5 (1997).

29. S.A. Shaw and J. Gibbs, "Procurement Strategies of Small Marketers Faced with Uncertainty: An Analysis of Channel Choice and Behavior," *International Review of Market, Distribution and Consumer Research* 9, no. 1 (1999), pp. 61–75.

30. *BusinessWeek*, "The Top 100 Brands," http://www.businessweek.com/pdfs/2003/0331_globalbrands.pdf (accessed August 29, 2006).

31. Lexus, http://www.lexus.com/about/history/index_1997_1983.html (accessed June 15, 2005).

32. "The Kellogg Way," *Businessline*, Chennai, India, March 20, 2003, p. 1.

33. William Werther and Jeffrey Kerr, "The Shifting Sands of Competitive Advantage," *Business Horizons* 38 (May–June 1995), pp. 11–17.

34. This case was written by Jeanne L. Munger in conjunction with Dhruv Grewal and Michael Levy for a class discussion rather than to illustrate an effective or ineffective marketing practice. Jeanne Munger is an associate professor at the University of Southern Maine.

35. National Medal of Technology, listing of year 2000 winners, http://www.thetech.org (accessed August 27, 2006).

36. David Armstrong and Jerry Guidera, "Rolling Along: Lobbying Campaign Could Determine Fate of a Hyped Scooter," *The Wall Street Journal*, March 1, 2002, p. A.1.

37. John Heilemann, "Reinventing the Wheel," *Time*, December 10, 2001, pp. 76–82.

38. Heilemann, "Reinventing the Wheel."

39. *PR Newswire*, "Brookstone to Become First and Only Nationwide Retail Store and Mainstream Catalog Partner to Sell Segway™ HT," October 29, 2003.

40. Segway, *Segway Newsletter* 2 (2002), http://www.segway.com/connect/newsletters/general_002.html (accessed September 1, 2006).

41. Heilemann, "Reinventing the Wheel."

42. This discussion is adapted from Roger A. Kerin, Eric N. Berkowitz, Steven W. Hartley, and William Rudelius, *Marketing*, 7th ed. (Burr Ridge, Il: McGraw-Hill/Irwin, 2003), p. 39.

Chapter 3

1. http://www.jnj.com/our_company/our_credo/index.htm (accessed September 1, 2006).

2. http://www.tylenol.com, press release, "McNeil Consumer and Specialty Pharmaceuticals Announces a Nationwide Recall of Children's Tylenol Meltaways-80 mg, Children's Tylenols Softchews-80mg, and Jr. Tylenol Meltaways-106mg," (accessed September 1, 2006).

3. Theodore Levitt, *Marketing Imagination* (Detroit, MI: The Free Press, 1983).

4. http://en.wikipedia.org/wiki/Business_ethics (accessed August 30, 2006).

5. William L. Wilkie and Elizabeth S. Moore, "Marketing's Contributions to Society," *Journal of Marketing* 63 (Special Issue, 1999), pp. 198–219.

6. http://www.gallup.com (accessed September 1, 2006).

7. http://www.ethics.org/nbes2003/2003nbes_summary.html (accessed August 3, 2005).

8. http://www.cmomagazine.com/info/release/090104_ethics.html (accessed September 1, 2006).

9. http://www.bsr.org (accessed September 1, 2006).

10. "Business Ethics: Corporate Social Responsibility Report," *Business Ethics*, Spring 2004, http://www.business-ethics.com/100best.htm (accessed September 1, 2006).

11. http://www.comminit.com/experiences/pdskdv62003/experiences-1423.html (accessed August 30, 2006).

12. http://www2.coca-cola.com/citizenship/africa_program.html (accessed August 30, 2006).

13. Malhotra, Naresh K. and Gina L. Miller (1998), "An Integrated Model for Ethical Decisions in Marketing Research," *Journal of Business Ethics*, 17 (February), 263–280; A. Parasuraman, Dhruv Grewal and R. Krishnan (2007), *Marketing Research*, 2nd Edition, Boston, MA: Houghton Mifflin Company, pp. 44–49; J. R. Sparks and S. D. Hunt (1998), "Marketing Researcher Ethical Sensitivity: Conceptualization, Measurement, and Exploratory Investigation," *Journal of Marketing*, April, 92–109; Kimmel, Allan J. and N. Craig Smith (2001), "Deception in Marketing Research: Ethical, Methodological and Disciplinary Implications," *Psychology & Marketing*, 18 (7) 663; Ralph W Giacobbe and Madhav N Segal (2000), "A Comparative Analysis of Ethical Perceptions in Marketing Research: U.S.A. vs. Canada," *Journal of Business Ethics*, 27 (October), 229–246.

14. http://www.marketingpower.com/content435.php (accessed August 3, 2005).

15. http://www.generalmills.com/corporate/index.aspx (accessed August 29, 2006).

16. This question is based on deontological theory, an ethical theory concerned with duties and rights. Deontological ethical theories are based on the existence of a universal principle—such as respect for others, honesty, fairness, or justice—that forms the basis for determining what is right. See Kate McKone-Sweet, Donna Greenberg, and Lydia Moland, "Approaches to Ethical Decision Making," *Babson College Case Development Center*, 2003.

17. This question is based on the theory of act utilitarianism, which requires that a person act so that his or her actions result in more good than harm to his or her society. In essence, act utilitarianism involves a cost/benefit analysis in which the decision maker accounts for all the possible costs and benefits and arrives at the solution that is optimal for the greatest number of interested parties. In other words, the best decision is the one by which everyone benefits without incurring loss. See Kate McKone-Sweet, Donna Greenberg, and Lydia Moland, "Approaches to Ethical Decision Making," *Babson College Case Development Center*, 2003.

18. This question is based on the theory of rule utilitarianism, which requires that a person act in such a way that the rule on which his or her action is based produces more benefit than harm. For example, the rule "I will do whatever it takes to get ahead" may not always produce the most benefit if getting ahead requires that the person ignore the consequences of his or her actions to others; in this case, the rule is immoral. See Kate McKone-Sweet, Donna Greenberg, and Lydia Moland, "Approaches to Ethical Decision Making," *Babson College Case Development Center*, 2003.

19. This question is based on the theory of personal virtue, which requires a person to act only in such a way that cultivates character traits that enable that person to live peacefully with him- or herself and with others. According to theories promoted by Aristotle, individuals should develop the virtues of honesty, bravery, generosity, and justice for others. See Kate McKone-Sweet, Donna Greenberg, and Lydia Moland, "Approaches to Ethical Decision Making," *Babson College Case Development Center*, 2003.

20. http://www.newstarget.com/007572.html (accessed August 29, 2006).

21. http://www.caru.org/news/2005/sparkle.pdf (accessed August 30, 2006).

22. http://www.scu.edu/ethics/publications/iie/v7n2/fetzer.html (accessed August 26, 2006).

23. http://www.scu.edu/ethics/publications/iie/v7n2/fetzer.html.

24. Elizabeth Butler, "Six Flags New Orleans Rides Out Crisis after Deadly Park Incident," New Orleans City Business, July 28, 2003, p. 1.

25. http://www.drj.com/bookstore/drj502a.htm (accessed August 30, 2006).

26. http://edbrenegar.typepad.com/leading_questions/2005/05/real_life_leade.html (accessed August 30, 2006).

27. Carolyn Hotchkiss, "Business Ethics: One Slide Cases," Babson College, Wellesley, MA, 2004.

28. http://www.usatoday.com/news/nation/2004-03-23-tshirts_x.htm (accessed August 25, 2006).

29. http://www.marketingpower.com/live/mg-dictionary.php?SearchFor=direct+marketing&Searched=1 (accessed August 5, 2005).

30. This case was written by Catharine Curran-Kelly (University of Massachusetts at Dartmouth) in conjunction with the textbook authors (Dhruv Grewal and Michael Levy) for the basis of class discussion rather than to illustrate either effective or ineffective marketing practice.

Chapter 4

1. Ryan McCormick, "Weight Loss Companies Vie for Business of 190 Million Overweight Americans," Dolan Media Newswires, *Long Island Business News*, January 9, 2004; "Up-and-Coming Markets: From Children to 'Tweens' to Adults to Baby Boomers, Nutraceuticals Producers Are Staring at a World of Opportunity, Especially in the Areas of Weight Loss, Diabetes and Heart Health," *Nutraceuticals World* 6, no. 10, p. 32; Franchise Zone, http://www.entrepreneur.com/franzone/details/0,5885,12-12---282265-,00.html (accessed April 17, 2005); Darden Restaurants, http://www.Seasons52.com, press release; and Elaine Walker, "Restaurants Putting Health on the Menu," *Miami Herald*, September 29, 2003; Elizabeth Lee, "Menus: Chain Restaurants Catering to Latest Diet Crazes," *Atlanta Journal*, February 2, 2004, www.ajc.com; www.curves.com (accessed September 6, 2006).

2. Peter F. Drucker, *The Essential Drucker* (New York: Harper Collins, 2001).

3. Michael Tchong, *Trendscape* (2004), www.trendsetters.com.

4. Matt Fish, "Silicon Belly: The Value of Competitive Intelligence," November 10, 2003, http://lexis-nexis.com (accessed September 6, 2006).

5. Justin Pope, "When Rivals Get Each Other's Secret Products, It's No Surprise," September 15, 2003, Associated Press, http://lexis-nexis.com (accessed September 5, 2006).

6. Steven Gray, "Gillette in a Lather over Schick's Challenge for $1.7 Billion Razor Market," *Seattle Times*, January 14, 2004.

7. Jack Neff, "Gillette, Schick Fight with Free Razors," *Advertising Age* 74, no. 48, p. 8.

8. Justin Pope, "Schick Says Judge Ruled in Its Favor in Gillette Patent Case," http://www.SFGate.com; Pope, "When Rivals Get Each Other's Secret Products"; Gillette Company, "The Gillette Company Files Suit against Energizer Holdings, Inc., Charges Violation of Gillette Mach3 Patent by Schick Quattro," August 12, 2003, http://www.Gillette.com (accessed September 5, 2006).

9. Andrew Caffey, "Gillette Wins Legal Fight with Schick," *Knight Ridder Tribune Business News*, April 30, 2005.

10. Abelson, Jean, "For Fusion, Gillette Plans a Super Bowl Blitz," *Knight Ridder Tribune Business News*, January 27, 2006, p.1.

11. Valerie Reitman, "Toyota Motor Shows Its Mettle after Fire Destroys Parts Plant," *The Wall Street Journal*, May 8, 1997.

12. Michael Solomon, *Consumer Behavior: Buying, Having and Being* (Upper Saddle River, NJ: Prentice Hall, 2006).

13. John Feto, "Name Games," *American Demographics*, February 15, 2003.

14. "Orthodox," *American Demographics*, May 2004, p. 35.

15. Allison Stein Wellner, "The Next 25 Years," *American Demographics*, April 24–27, 2003.

16. Social Welfare Research Institute, "Good Tidings for a New Year: The $41 Trillion Transfer of Wealth Is Still Valid," http://www.bc.edu/research/swri/meta-elements/ssi/wcvol3.html.

17. Kristin Davis, "Oldies but Goodies; Marketers, Take Note: Baby boomers Have Lots of Money to Spend," *U.S. News & World Report*, Washington edition, March 14, 2005, p. 45.

18. http://www.calreinvest.org/PredatoryLending/Top10PredatoryPractices7.2.html Accessed 8/7/05

19. Michael Weiss, "Chasing Youth," *American Demographics*, October 2002, pp. 35–41.

20. "Trends in Pampering," *American Demographics*, November 2002, p. 16.

21. James Tenser, "Ageless Aging of Boom-X," *Advertising Age*, January 2, 2006, 77 (1), pp. 18–19; Tabitha Armstrong, "GenX Family Values," *The Lane Report,* January 1, 2005, p. 41.

22. Pamela Paul, "Getting Inside Gen Y," *American Demographics* 23, no. 9.

23. Noah Rubin Brier, "Move Over Prime-Time!" *American Demographics*, July/August 2004, pp. 14–20; John Hoeffel, "The Next Baby Boom" *American Demographics*, October 1995, pp. 22–31.

24. J.K. Wall, "Tweens Get Retailers into Parents' Wallets," *Knight Ridder Tribune Business News*, September 12, 2003, p. 1. Research attributed to WonderGroup in Cincinnati.

25. Mindy F. Ji and James U. McNeal, "How Chinese Children's Commercials Differ from Those of the United States," *Journal of Advertising* 30, no. 3 (Fall 2001), pp. 79–91.

26. The term "Speeders" was coined by Cynthia Cohen, President, Strategic Mindshare.

27. U.S. Bureau of the Census, http://www.census.gov/hhes/www/income.html (accessed September 3, 2006).

28. Hammacher Schlemmer, http://www.Hammacher.com, online catalog.

29. U.S. Bureau of the Census, http://www.census.gov/population/www/socdemo/educ-attn.html.

30. BillSaver University, "Household Spending Facts and Figures," http://www.billsaver.com/household.html (accessed September 3, 2006).

31. Bethany Clough, "Home-Improvement Store Empower Female Customers with Do-It-Herself Tools," *Knight Ridder Tribune Business Service*, March 20, 2005, p. 1; Fara Warner, "Yes, Women Spend (And Saw and Sand)," *The New York Times*, February 29, 2004, p. C1.

32. Pallavi Gogoi, "I Am Woman, Hear Me Shop," *BusinessWeek*, February 14, 2005, p. 23.

33. Rebecca Gardyn and John Fetto, "Race, Ethnicity and the Way We Shop," *American Demographics*, February 2003, pp. 30–33; Alison Stein Wellner, "Diversity in America," *American Demographics*, November 2002; Alison Stein Wellner, "Hispanics: The Growing Force," *American Demographics*, November 2002, S8–S10.

34. William H. Frey, "Zooming in on Diversity," *American Demographics*, July/August 2004, pp. 24–32.

35. Gardyn and Fetto, "Race, Ethnicity."

36. Gardyn and Fetto, "Race, Ethnicity."

37. "Surging Hispanic Market Draws Interest at Retail," *Discount Store News*, October 26, 1998, p. 112. Wellner, "Hispanics: The Growing Force."

38. This section draws heavily from Jacquelyn A. Ottman, *Green Marketing: Opportunity for Innovation* (Chicago: NTC Publishing, 1997), also available online at http://www.greenmarketing.com.

39. Anita Roddick, "Nothing Like a Dame," *Time European*, October 2, 2004, www.time.com (accessed May 11, 2005); Megan Jones, "A New Way of Doing Business with Anita Roddick," www.shareintl.org (accessed May 11, 2005); http://www.anitaroddick.com/aboutanita.php (accessed May 10, 2005); The Body Shop International, http://www.thebodyshopinternational.com/web/tbsgl/about_people.jsp#anita (accessed May 10, 2005); and The Body Shop International, http://www.the-bodyshopinternational.com/epages/wizard/images/CLIENT81114671995601_lg.pdf (accessed September 1, 2006).

40. Caleb Silver, "LexisNexis Acknowledges More ID Theft," *CNNMoney.com*, April 12, 2005, http://money.cnn.com; "LexisNexis Security Breach," April 13, 2005, WCBS radio broadcast.

41. *Sales and Marketing Management,* "Do Not Call Is Constitutional," http://www.salesandmarketing.com/smm/headlines/article_display.jsp?vnu_content_id=2093460; AARP, http://www.aarp.org/research/press/presscurrentnews/Articles/a2004-02-18-donot-call.html; Direct Marketing Association, "Appellate Court Rules on Do Not Call List," http://www.the-dma.org/cgi/dispnewsstand?article=1858; "Do-Not-Call Registry Faces Tougher Challenge: Second Judge Blocks List, Citing Free Speech Concerns," www.cnn.com, September 26, 2003; Federal Trade Commission, "Compliance with Do Not Call Registry Exceptional," http://www.ftc.gov/opa/2004/02/dncstats0204.htm (accessed September 6, 2006).

42. *Sales and Marketing Management,* "Do Not Call Is Constitutional," http://www.salesandmarketing.com/smm/headlines/article_display.jsp?vnu_content_id=2093460 (accessed September 6, 2006).

43. Martin Peers, "Buddy, Can You Spare Some Time?" *The Wall Street Journal*, January 26, 2004, B1, B3. Statistics from Harris Interactive.

44. Peers, "Buddy."

45. YourDictionary.com, http://www.yourdictionary.com (accessed September 5, 2006).

46. The scenario planning process presented here was adapted from that used first by Royal Dutch/Shell in the early 1970s and follows the steps set forth by consultants at Bain & Co.,http://www.bain.com/bainweb/consulting_expertise/capabilities_detail.asp?capID=50. See also Michael D. Watkins and Max H. Bazerman, "Predictable Surprises: The Disasters You Should Have Seen Coming," *Harvard Business Review*, March 2003, pp. 5–12.

47. "How Corporations Learn from Scenarios," *Strategy & Leadership* 31, no. 2, p. 5; Liam Fahey and Robert M. Randall, *Learning from the Future Competitive: Foresight Scenarios* (Hoboken, NJ: Wiley, 1998).

48. David B. Yofee, "Wal-Mart, 2005," *Harvard Business School*, April 14, 2005; "Is Wal-Mart Food for America?" *The Asian Wall Street Journal*, December 6, 2005, p. 1; www.census.gov; "Wal-Mart Saves Working Families," *PR Newswire*, November 4, 2005; Lauren Weber, "The Debate Intensifies: Is the Corporate Giant Good for Our Communities?" *Newsday*, November 21, 2005.

49. Parija Bhatnagar, "Wal-Mart's Hot on India, No. 1 Retailer Sings Nation's Praises to Analysts; Calls Market a 'Huge Organic Growth Opportunity,'" http://money.cnn.com/2005/06/06/news/fortune500/walmart_india/, 2005.

50. This case was written by Jeanne L. Munger and Jacquelyn Ottman in conjunction with the textbook authors (Dhruv Grewal and Michael Levy) for use in a class discussion rather than to illustrate either effective or ineffective marketing practices. It builds on a case written and published by Jacquelyn Ottman in her book *Green Marketing: Opportunity for Innovation.* Jeanne Munger is an associate professor at the University of Southern Maine. Jacquelyn Ottman is the president of J. Ottman Consulting, Inc., a New York-based marketing consulting firm that specializes in helping businesses derive competitive advantage from eco-innovation and green marketing. She is the author of *Green Marketing: Opportunity for Innovation.*

51. Stonyfield Farms, http://www.stonyfield.com, press release.

Chapter 5

1. Kim S. Nash, "Netflix: Box-Office Star; DVD Renter Netflix Uses Customer-Tracking Software and Elbow Grease to Keep the Crowds Coming," *eWeek.com*, January 16, 2004; Steve Ditlea, "Netflix Effect," *Adweek Magazine's Technology Marketing* 22, no. 10 (November 2002), pp. 24–29; Paul Sweeting, "Blockbuster Likely to Have Huge Hangover; Dividend May Cost Chain at Least $1 Billion," *Video Business*, February 16, 2004.

2. Dhruv Grewal, Gopalkrishnan R. Iyer, R. Krishnan, and Arun Sharma, "The Internet and the Price-Value-Loyalty Chain," *Journal of Business Research*, 56 (May 2003), p. 391.

3. R. Puri, "Measuring and Modifying Consumer Impulsiveness: A Cost-Benefit Accessibility Framework," *Journal of Consumer Psychology* 5 (1996), pp. 87–113.

4. Pamela Sebastian, "'Aspirational Wants' Form the Basis of a Modern Retailing Strategy," *The Wall Street Journal*, October 15, 1998, p. A1; Barry Babin, William Darden, and Mitch Griffin, "Work and/or Fun: Measuring Hedonic and Utilitarian Shopping Value," *Journal of Consumer Research* 20 (March 1994), pp. 644–56.

5. "Prince Charming: Some 30 Years after His First Design, Manolo Blahnik Is Sitting Pretty atop Footwear's Highest Throne," *FN (Footwear News),* December 8, 2003.

6. Harley-Davidson, http://www.harley-davidson.com/CO/HIS/en/history.asp?locale=en_US&bmLocale=en_US (accessed April 21, 2005); Harley-Davidson, "Harley Owners Group," http://www.harley-davidson.com/ex/hog/template.asp?locale=en_US&bmLocale=en_US&fnc=miss&loc=join (accessed April 21, 2005); "Technological Breakthrough in the Top 100 Brands: Joanna Doonar Identifies that Technology Brands Are the Interbrand Survey's Three Highest Climbers," *Brand Strategy*, 10 (August 2003); Jeff Morris, "Easy Rider," *Operations & Fulfillment*, November 1, 2002.

7. http://www.google.com/corporate/history.html (accessed September 3, 2006).

8. Ran Hock, "A New Era of Search Engines: Not Just Web Pages Anymore," *Online Magazine* 26, no. 5 (September 2002), pp. 20–27.

9. http://www.google.com/corporate/index.html (accessed September 3, 2006).

10. The term *determinance* was first coined by James Myers and Mark Alpert nearly three decades ago. http://www.sawtoothsoftware.com/productforms/ssolutions/ss12.shtml (accessed September 4, 2006).

11. http://www.sawtoothsoftware.com/productforms/sso-lutions/ss12.shtml (accessed September 4, 2006).

12. Jim Oliver, "Finding Decision Rules with Genetic Algorithms, http://www.umsanet.edu.bo/docentes/gchoque/MAT420L07.htm (accessed June 2004).

13. Paul S. Richardson, Alan S. Dick, and Arun K. Jain, "Extrinsic and Intrinsic Cue Effects on Perceptions of Store Brand Quality," *Journal of Marketing* 58 (October 1994), pp. 28–36; Rajneesh Suri and Kent B. Monroe, "The Effects of Time Constraints on Consumers' Judgments of Prices and Products," *Journal of Consumer Research* 30 (June 2003), pp. 92–104.

14. Merrie Brucks, Valerie A. Zeithaml, and Gillian Naylor, "Price and Brand Name as Indicators of Quality Dimensions for Consumer Durables," *Journal of the Academy of Marketing Science* 28, no. 3 (2000), pp. 359–74; Niraj Dawar and Philip Parker, "Marketing Universals: Consumers' Use of Brand Name, Price, Physical Appearance, and Retailer Reputation as Signals of Product Quality," *Journal of Marketing* 58 (April 1994), pp. 81–95; William B. Dodds, Kent B. Monroe, and Dhruv Grewal, "Effects of Price, Brand, and Store Information on Buyers' Product Evaluations," *Journal of Marketing Research* 28 (August 1991), pp. 307–19.

15. Mary Jo Bitner, "Servicescapes: The Impact of Physical Surroundings on Customers and Employees," *Journal of Marketing* 56 (April 1992), pp. 57–71; Dhruv Grewal and Julie Baker, "Do Retail Store Environmental Factors Affect Consumers' Price Acceptability? An Empirical Examination," *International Journal of Research in Marketing* 11 (1994), pp. 107–15; Eric R. Spangenberg, Ayn E. Crowley, and Pamela W. Henderson, "Improving the Store Environment: Do Olfactory Cues Affect Evaluations and Behaviors?" *Journal of Marketing* 60 (April 1996), pp. 67–80; Kirk L. Wakefield and Jeffrey G. Blodgett, "Customer Response to Intangible and Tangible Service Factors," *Psychology and Marketing* 16 (January 1999), pp. 51–68.

16. http://www.expedia.com/daily/service/about.asp?rfrr=-1087 (accessed September 4, 2006).

17. Youngme Moon and John A. Quelch, "Starbucks: Delivering Customer Service," *Harvard Business Review*, July 31, 2003.

18. http://www.forbes.com/home/2002/08/21/0821hatesites.html (accessed September 3, 2006); Charles Wolrich, "The Best Corporate Complaint Sites," *Forbes.com*, August 21, 2002; Leslie Jaye Goff, "[Your company name here]sucks.com: When an Angry Consumer Slams Your Organization Online, You Want to Slam Back," www.computerworld.com/printhtis/1998/0,4814,31861,00.

html; John Simmons, "Stop Moaning about Gripe Sites and Log On," *Fortune*, April 2, 2001, p. 181.

19. A.H. Maslow, *Motivation and Personality* (New York: Harper & Row, 1970).

20. William D. Perreault, Jr., and E. Jerome McCarthy, *Basic Marketing: A Global-Managerial Approach*, 15th ed. (Burr Ridge Il.: Irwin/McGraw-Hill, 2005), p. 159.

21. Michael Levy and Barton A. Weitz, *Retailing Management*, 6th ed. (Burr Ridge IL: Irwin/Mc-Graw-Hill, 2007), Chapter 4.

22. Margaret Magnarelli, "Big Spenders," *Parents*, March 2004.

23. Sandra Yin, "Kids; Hot Spots," *American Demographics*, December 1, 2003; Peter Francese, "Trend Ticker: Trouble in Store," *American Demographics*, December 1, 2003.

24. The concept of atmospherics was introduced by Philip Kotler, "Atmosphere as a Marketing Tool," *Journal of Retailing* 49 (Winter 1973), pp. 48–64.

25. http://www.zipcar.com/about/ (accessed September 4, 2006); "Growth Is on the Way," *European Rubber Journal*, 184, no. 4 (April 2002), p. 20 (1); Steven Rosenberg, "The Art of Parking: It Works for Candy, so Why Not for Cars? A Boston Architect Proposes a Pez-Like Dispenser to Solve the City's Parking Woes," *The Boston Globe*, March 21, 2004; Brad Grimes, "Leave the Driving to Zipcar; With the Help of the Internet and Wireless Technology, Car Sharing Revs up in Urban Areas," *PC Magazine*, February 17, 2004; http://www.myrtlebeachonline.com/mld/sun-news/news/local/7668955.htm; http://www.wjla.com/news/stories/0304/133051.html.

26. Anna S. Mattila and Jochen Wirtz, "Congruency of Scent and Music as a Driver of In-Store Evaluations and Behavior," *Journal of Retailing* 77, no. 2 (Summer 2001), pp. 273–89; Teresa A. Summers and Paulette R. Hebert, "Shedding Some Light on Store Atmospherics; Influence of Illumination on Consumer Behavior," *Journal of Business Research* 54, no. 2 (November 2001), pp. 145–50; for a review of this research, see Joseph A. Bellizzi and Robert E. Hite, "Environmental Color, Consumer Feelings, and Purchase Likelihood," *Psychology and Marketing* 9, no. 5 (September–October 1992), pp. 347–63; J. Duncan Herrington and Louis Capella, "Effects of Music in Service Environments: A Field Study," *Journal of Services Marketing* 10, no. 2 (1996), pp. 26–41; Richard F. Yalch and Eric R. Spangenberg, "The Effects of Music in a Retail Setting on Real and Perceived Shopping Times," *Journal of Business Research* 49, no. 2 (August 2000), pp. 139–48; Michael Hui, Laurette Dube, and Jean-Charles Chebat, "The Impact of Music on Consumer's Reactions to Waiting for Services," *Journal of Retailing* 73, no. 1 (1997), pp. 87–104; and Julie Baker, Dhruv Grewal, and Michael Levy, "An Experimental Approach to Making Retail Store Environmental Decisions," *Journal of Retailing* 68 (Winter 1992), pp. 445–60; Maxine Wilkie, "Scent of a Market," *American Demographics* (August 1995), pp. 40–49; Spangenberg, Crowley, Henderson, "Improving the Store Environment: Do Olfactory Cues Affect Evaluations and Behaviors?"; Paula Fitzgerald Bone and Pam Scholder Ellen, "Scents in the Marketplace: Explaining a Fraction of Olfaction," *Journal of Retailing* 75, no. 2 (Summer 1999), pp. 243–63.

27. Julie Baker, Dhruv Grewal, Michael Levy, and Glenn Voss, "Wait Expectations, Store Atmosphere and Store Patronage Intentions," *Journal of Retailing* 79, no. 4 (2003), pp. 259–68.

28. This case was written by Jeanne L. Munger in conjunction with Dhruv Grewal and Michael Levy for the basis of class discussion rather than to illustrate either effective or ineffective marketing practices. Jeanne Munger is an associate professor at the University of Southern Maine.

29. This background information is based on Micheline Maynard, "Get Smart," *Fortune (Europe)*, April 30, 2001, p. 48; Philip Siekman, "The Smart Car is Looking More So," *Fortune*, April 15, 2002, p. 310H.

30. Judy Feldman, "Price Points," *Money*, October 2001, pp. 146–47.

31. Feldman, "Price Points."

32. Jean Halliday, "Mercedes Mimics Mini by Using Offbeat Tactics," *Automotive News*, January 5, 2004, p. 16B.

Chapter 6

1. Ajay K. Kohli and Bernard J. Jaworski, "Market Orientation: The Construct, Research Propositions, and Managerial Implications," *Journal of Marketing* 54, no. 2 (April 1990), pp. 1–13; John C. Narver and Stanly F. Slater, "The Effect of Market Orientation on Business Profitability," *Journal of Marketing* 54, no. 4 (October 1990), pp. 20–33; Arun Sharma, R. Krishnan, and Dhruv Grewal, "Value Creation in Markets: A Critical Area of Focus for Business-to-Business Markets," *Industrial Marketing Management* 30, no. 4 (2001), pp. 391–402.

2. www.att.com.

3. E. Webster Frederick, Jr., "Understanding the Relationships among Brands, Consumers and Resellers," *Journal of the Academy of Marketing Science* 28, no. 1 (Winter 2000), pp. 17–24.

4. Paul Bray, "The Challenge Facing Distributors," *Computer Reseller News*, October 11, 2000.

5. Gary Baker, et al., "An Exchanging Advantage: Supply Chain Innovation in the New Economy," *Arthur Andersen: The White Paper Series*, No. 2 (Autumn 2000), Automotive Industry.

6. Adam Feuerstein, "Private Net Markets Are Taking Off," *Upside Today-The Tech Insider* 24, no. 4, (August 2000), electronically accessed.

7. Brian Chapman and Chip W. Hardt, "Purchasing Lessons for Schools," *The McKinsey Quarterly*, no. 4 (2003), electronically accessed.

8. "Federal Domestic Spending Tops $2 Trillion in 2003, Census Bureau Reports," http://www.census.gov/Press-Release/www/releases/archives/governments/002939.html, (accessed September 5, 2006).

9. Department of Defense, "Fiscal 2005 Department of Defense Budget Release," www.defenselink.com, February 2, 2004.

10. Navi Radjou with Laurie M. Orlov and Nicole Belanger, "The Defense Contractors' Supply Chain Imperative," *Forrester Research*, August 15, 2003, which provides sizing from December 2002 Forrester Report "SCM Processes Replace Apps: 2003–2008."

11. www.census.gov/epcd/www/naics.html.

12. http://www.census.gov/epcd/naics02/N2SIC51.HTM.

13. http://www.census.gov/epcd/naics02/SICN02E.HTM#S48.

14. This illustration, which exemplifies how Toyota works with its suppliers, is based on Jeffrey K. Liker and Thomas Y. Choi, "Building Deep Supplier Relationships," *Harvard Business Review*, December 2004, pp. 104–14.

15. Toyotasupplier.com (accessed September 6, 2006).

16. Toyotasupplier.com (accessed September 6, 2006).

17. http://www.marketingpower.com/live/mg-dictionary-view435.php. These definitions are provided by www.marketingpower.com (the American Marketing Association's Web site). We have bolded our key terms.

18. http://www.pulsus.com/clin-pha/08_02/lexc_ed.htm (accessed September 6, 2006).

19. http://www.goer.state.ny.us/train/onlinelearning/FTMS/500s1.html.

20. Erika Morphy, "Volkswagen Takes on Covisint in the B2B Auction Arena," *CRM Daily*, July 13, 2001; "The Purchasing Department of Volkswagen," presentation, http://www.volkswagen-ir.de/download/InvPres_01/20010518VWSanzENG.pdf (accessed May 16, 2005); Martin Hofmann, Emily-Sue Sloane, and Elena Malykhina, "VW Revs its B2B Engine," *Optimize*, March 2004, pp. 22–26; "FAQ," http://www.vwgroupsupply.com/; "Volkswagen Expands B2B Platform: Volkswagen Has Expanded its Business-to-Business Platform to Allow Suppliers to Easily Manage their Financial Dealings with the Company via the Internet," *Computer World* 9, no. 7 (November 2002).

21. Susan Kuchinskas, "Data-Based Dell," *Adweek Magazine's Technology Marketing* 23, no. 6 (September 2003), p. 20.

22. Barton A. Weitz, Stephen B. Castleberry, and John F. Tanner, *Selling Building Partnerships*, 5th ed. (Burr Ridge, IL: McGraw Hill Irwin, 2003), p. 93.

23. http://www1.us.dell.com/content/topics/global.aspx/power/en/ps1q03cs_douglas?c=us&l=en&s=corp (accessed February 20, 2006). "The Douglas County School System upgraded and increased its inventory of computer systems while reducing the systems' total cost of ownership."

24. http://www.dell4hied.com/resource_detail.php?ri=520&zp=3&si=34 (accessed Febraury 20, 2006). "Streaming Video keeps MBA Students in the Loop and Up to Date."

25. http://www.dell4k12.com/tpl_case_study.php?ri=425&si=1 (accessed March 4, 2005).

26. Daniel G. Jacobs, "Anatomy of a Supply Chain," *Transportation & Distribution* 44, no. 6 (June 2003), p. 60; F. Andrews, "Dell, It Turns Out, Has a Better Idea than Ford," *The New York Times*, January 26, 2000, p. C12.

27. K.C. Laudon and C.G. Traver, *E-Commerce: Business, Technology, Society*, 2d ed. (Boston, MA: Pearson, 2004).

28. K.C. Laudon and C.G. Traver, *E-Commerce: Business, Technology, Society*, 2d ed. (Boston, MA: Pearson, 2004).

29. Sandy Jap, "An Exploratory Study of the Introduction of Online Reverse Auctions," *Journal of Marketing* 67, no. 3, (July 2003), electronically accessed; R. Tassabehji, W. A. Taylor, R. Beach, A. Wood, "Reverse E-auctions and Supplier-Buyer Relationships: an Exploratory Study," *International Journal of Operations and Production Management,* 26, no. 2, (2006), pp. 1–19; Sandy Jap, Going Going, Gone," *Harvard Business Review,* 78, no. 6, electronically accessed; "Reverse Auctions Gain Momentum as Cost Tool-Chipmakers Grudgingly Join in Online Bids," *Spencer Chin,* March 3, 2003, p. 1.

30. This case was written by Jeanne L. Munger in conjunction with the textbook authors (Dhruv Grewal and Michael Levy) for the basis of class discussion rather than to illustrate either effective or ineffective marketing practices. Jeanne Munger is an associate professor at the University of Southern Maine.

31. Weyerhaeuser, www.weyerhaeuser.com.

32. 2004 Housing Facts, Figures and Trends, National Association of Home Builders.

33. Ibid.

34. Barry A. Rappaport and Tamara A. Cole, *1997 Economic Census—Construction Sector Special Study, Housing Starts Statistics: A Profile of the Homebuilding Industry* (July 2000).

Chapter 7

1. "Who's Getting It Right? American Brands in the Middle Kingdom," *Time* 164, no. 17 (October 25, 2004), p. A14; "Cracking China," www.chiefexecutive.net 199 (June 2004); Normandy Madden and Jack Neff, "P&G Adapts Attitude towards Local Markets," *Advertising Age* (Midwest region edition) 75, no. 8 (February 23, 2004), p. 28; http://www.pg.com.eg/history4.cfm.

2. Pierre-Richard Agenor, *Does Globalization Hurt the Poor?* (Washington, DC: World Bank, 2002); "Globalization: Threat or Opportunity," International Monetary Fund, http://www.imf.org/external/np/exr/ib/2000/041200.htm#II (accessed on September 18, 2006).

3. Charles W.L. Hill, *Global Business Today*, 3rd edition (New York: Irwin McGraw-Hill, 2004).

4. David Rosenbaum, "Next stop, New Delhi; The strategic debate over offshoring is over," *CIO* 19, no. 8, (February 1, 2006) p.1.

5. Rachel Kronrad, "Outsourcing Backlash Brewing," CBS News, 2004, http://www.cbsnews.com/stories/2004/01/19/national/main594119.shtml (accessed August 28, 2005).

6. http://www.pbs.org/wgbh/commandingheights/hi/people/pe_name.html.

7. http://www.econ.iastate.edu/classes/econ355/choi/wtoroots.htm.

8. http://www.wto.org/english/thewto_e/whatis_e/tif_e/org6_e.htm.

9. http://web.worldbank.org/WBSITE/EXTERNAL/EXTABOUTUS/0,,pagePK:50004410~piPK:36602~theSitePK:29708,00.html.

10. For a full description of criticisms of the IMF, see http://www.imf.org/external/np/exr/ccrit/eng/cri.htm; for a list of criticisms of the World Bank, see http://www.art-sci.wustl.edu/~nairobi/wbissues.html (accessed August 28, 2005).

11. Social Science Research Council, http://www.ssrc.org/sept11/essays/teaching_resource/tr_globalization.htm (accessed September 2, 2005).

12. http://www.acdi-cida.gc.ca/CIDAWEB/webcountry.nsf/VLUDocEn/Cameroon-Factsataglance#def.

13. http://en.wikipedia.org/wiki/Purchasing_power_parity (accessed September 19, 2005); O'Sullivan-Sheffrin, *Macroeconomics: Principles and Tools activeBook*, 3rd edition: (Upper Saddle River: Prentice Hall, 2002).

14. http://hdr.undp.org/reports/global/2001/en/. Nobel Prize–winning economist Amartya Sen has proposed that developing countries should also be measured according to the capabilities and opportunities that people within that particular country possess.

15. http://www.tdctrade.com/econforum/tdc/tdc050101.htm

16. "Rural India, Have a Coke," http://www.businessweek.com/magazine/content/02_21/b3784134.htm

17. David L. Scott, *Wall Street Words: An A to Z Guide to Investment Terms for Today's Investor* (Boston: Houghton Mifflin, 2003).

18. "Trade War Looms Over Steel Dispute," March 6, 2002, http://news.bbc.co.uk/1/hi/business/1856760.stm (accessed September 11, 2006).

19. http://economics.about.com/library/glossary/bldef-dumping.htm (accessed September 11, 2006); Scott, *Wall Street Words.*

20. http://www.bloomberg.com/apps/news?pid=10000103&sid=ajtpC2UYVKwk&refer=us.

21. http://en.wikipedia.org/wiki/Exchange_rate.

22. "Half of Europeans Distrust American Companies," 2004 http://www.gmi-mr.com/gmipoll/press_room_wppk_pr_12272004.phtml (accessed September 11, 2006).

23. "Philippines Implement Countertrade Program for Vietnamese Rice," *Asia Pulse Pte Limited,* April 27, 2005.

24. http://ucatlas.ucsc.edu/trade/subtheme_trade_blocs.php (accessed March 5, 2005).

25. http://www.unescap.org/tid/mtg/postcancun_rterta.pps#1.

26. http://www.answers.com/main/ntquery?method=4&dsid=2222&dekey=European+Union&gwp=8&curtab=2222_1.

27. http://www.fas.usda.gov/itp/CAFTA/cafta.html (accessed September 10, 2006).

28. Training Management Corporation (TMC), *Doing Business Internationally: The Cross Cultural Challenges, Seminar and Coursebook* (Princeton, NJ: Trade Management Corporation, 1992).

29. Geert Hofstede, "Management Scientists Are Human," *Management Science* 40 (January 1994), pp. 4–13; Geert Hofstede and Michael H. Bond, "The Confucius Connection from Cultural Roots to Economic Growth," *Organizational Dynamics* 16 (Spring 1988), pp. 4–21; Masaaki Kotabe and Kristiaan Helsen, *Global Marketing Management* (Hoboken, NJ: John Wiley & Sons, 2004).

30. http://www.geert-hofstede.com/ (accessed September 10, 2006).

31. Donghoon Kim, Yigang Pan, and Heung Soo Park, "High versus Low Context Culture: A Comparison of Chinese, Korean and American Cultures," *Psychology and Marketing* 15, no. 6 (1998), pp. 507–21.

32. Angela Andal-Ancion and George Yip, "Smarter Ways to Do Business with the Competition," *European Business Forum* (Spring 2005), pp. 32–37.

33. "Joint Venture with Ting Hsin Brings Tesco to China," *MMR[o]* 11, no. 11 (July 26, 2004), p. 13.

34. http://www.cyber-ark.com/networkvaultnews/pr_20031110.asp.

35. Bruce D. Keillor, Michael D'Amico, and Veronica Horton, "Global Consumer Tendencies," *Psychology and Marketing* 18, no. 1 (2001), pp. 1–20.

36. http://www.consumerpsychologist.com/food_marketing.htm.

37. http://ro.unctad.org/infocomm/anglais/orange/market.htm; http://www.tropicana.com/index.asp?ID=27.

38. Charles W.L. Hill, *Global Business Today*, 3rd edition (New York: Irwin McGraw-Hill, 2004).

39. Charles W.L. Hill, *Global Business Today*, 3rd edition (New York: Irwin McGraw-Hill, 2004).

40. Glenn Collins, "Going Global Involves More Than Many US Companies Think," *The New York Times*, January 2, 1997, p. C10.

41. http://www.pringles.it/.

42. Kelly Santana, "MTV Goes to Asia: Entertainment Giant Woos and Wows Audiences with Combination of Foreign and Local Talent," *Yale Global Online*, 2003, http://yaleglobal.yale.edu/display.article?id=2211.

43. Mary Anne Raymond, John F. Tanner Jr., and Jonghoon Kim, "Cost Complexity of Pricing Decisions for Exporters in Developing and Emerging Markets," *Journal of International Marketing* 9, no. 3 (2001), pp. 19–40.

44. Terry Clark, Masaaki Kotabe, and Dan Rajaratnam, "Exchange Rate Pass-Through and International Pricing Strategy: A Conceptual Framework and Research Propositions," *Journal of International Business Studies* 30, no. 2 (1999), pp. 249–68.

45. http://www.literacyonline.org/explorer/compare.iphtml?ID1=78&ID2=79&ID3=27&ID4=12&ID5=127.

46. http://www.aeforum.org/latest.nsf.

47. http://www.brandchannel.com/features_effect.asp?pf_id=274.

48. Charles W.L. Hill, *Global Business Today*, 3d edition (New York: Irwin McGraw-Hill, 2004).

49. George Hager, "Bush Plays Free-Trade Game," *USA Today*, May 2, 2002.

50. Paul Meller, "The W.T.O. Said to Weigh In on Product Names," *The New York Times*, November 18, 2004, p. 1; Mark Jarvis, "Which Bud's for You?" *BrandChannel*, January 5, 2004 http://www.brandchannel.com/start1.asp?fa_id=191(accessed on September 5, 2005); Paul Byrne, "Austrian Court Rules in Favor of Anheuser Busch," *PR Newswire*, December 31, 2004.

51. BBC News "Disposable Planet," http://news.bbc.co.uk/hi/english/static/in_depth/world/2002/disposable_planet/waste/statsbank.stm (accessed on September 5, 2005).

52. Alladi Venkatesh, "Postmodernism Perspective for Macromarketing: An Inquiry into the Global Information and Sign Economy," *Journal of Macromarketing* 19, no. 12 (1999), p. 153 –169.

53. Michael R. Czinkota and Ilkka A. Ronkainen, "An International Marketing Manifesto," *Journal of International Marketing* 11, no. 1 (2003), pp. 13–27.

54. http://www.nike.com/nikebiz/nikebiz.jhtml?page=25&cat=businessmodel.

55. http://users.aber.ac.uk/pjm04/linguisticimperialism.html#culturalimperialism.

56. Farnaz Fassihi, "As Authorities Frown, Valentine's Day Finds Place in Iran's Heart; Young and in Love Embrace Forbidden Holiday; A Rush on Red Roses," *The Wall Street Journal*, February 12, 2004, p. A.1

57. Thomas Friedman, *The Lexus and The Olive Tree: Understanding Globalization* (New York: Anchor, 2000).

58. www.ikea.com.

59. Youngme Moon, "IKEA Invades America," *Harvard Business School Publications*, #9-504-094 (2004).

60. James Schofield, "Ikea Wows the Russians," February 22, 2002, http://news.bbc.co.uk/1/hi/business/1836004.stm.

Chapter 8

1. "The U.S. Market for Hair Care Products," *Packaged Facts*, February 2005.

2. Amy Merrick, "Christopher & Banks Shuns Trends in Fashion, Targets Mothers in 40s," *The Wall Street Journal*, May 9, 2003, wsj.com.

3. B. Joseph Pine, *Mass Customization: The New Frontier in Business Competition* (Cambridge, MA: Harvard Business School Publishing, 1999); James H. Gilmore and B. Joseph Pine, eds., *Markets of One: Creating Customer-Unique Value through Mass Customization* (Cambridge, MA: Harvard Business School Publishing, 2000).

4. Deborah Kong, "Grocers Feeding Hispanic Tastes," *Chicago Tribune,* July 7, 2003, Chicago Tribune.com.

5. Melanie Shortman, "Gender Wars," *American Demographics*, April 2002, p. 22.

6. Jagdish Sheth, Banwari Mittal, and Bruce I. Newman, *Customer Behavior: Consumer Behavior and Beyond* (Fort Worth, TX: The Dryden Press, 1999).

7. Tamara Mangleburg, M. Joseph Sirgy, Dhruv Grewal, Danny Axsom, Maria Hatzios, C. B. Claiborne, and Trina Bogle, "The Moderating Effect of Prior Experience in Consumers' Use of User-Image Based versus Utilitarian Cues in Brand Attitude," *Journal of Business & Psychology* 13 (Fall 1998), pp. 101–13; M. Joseph Sirgy et al., "Direct versus Indirect Measures of Self-Image Congruence," *Journal of the Academy of Marketing Science* 25, no. 3 (1997), pp. 229–41.

8. Sheth, Mittal, and Newman, *Customer Behavior.*

9. http://www.chsinternational.com/index.asp (accessed September 21, 2005).

10. VALS1, the original lifestyle survey, assessed general values and lifestyles. The VALS survey focuses more on values and lifestyles related to consumer behavior and thus has more commercial applications. Another lifestyle segmentation system is Yankelovich's Monitor Mindbase, yankelovich.com.

11. Michael D. Lam, "Psychographic Demonstration: Segmentation Studies Prepare to Prove Their Worth," *Pharmaceutical Executive*, January 2004.

12. Michael J. Weiss, *The Clustered World* (Boston: Little, Brown, 2000).

13. Stowe Shoemaker and Robert Lewis, "Customer Loyalty: The Future of Hospitality Marketing," *Hospitality Management* 18 (1999), p. 349.

14. V. Kumar and Denish Shah, "Building and Sustaining Profitable Customer Loyalty for the 21st Century," *Journal of Retailing* 80, no. 4 (2004), p. 317–330.

15. http://www.united.com/page/article/0,6722,1171,00.html (accessed September 12, 2006).

16. Pete Jacques, "Aspirational Segmentation," *LIMRA's MarketFacts Quarterly* 22 (Spring 2003), p. 2[0].

17. Cannon Consulting, "Growth Specialty Retail Opportunity Retailer Profile: Talbots," February 2005, available at http://www.naa.org/horizon/specialty_retail/256,1,Growth Specialty Retail Opportunity.

18. G.R. Iyer, A.D. Miyazaki, D. Grewal, and M. Giordano, "Linking Web-Based Segmentation to Pricing Tactics," *Journal of Product & Brand Management* 11, no. 5, (2002), pp. 288–302; B. Jaworski and K. Jocz, "Rediscovering the Consumer," *Marketing Management*, September/October 2002, pp. 22–27; L. Rosencrance, "Customers Balk at Variable DVD Pricing," *Computer World*, September 11, 2000, p. 4; M. Stephanek, "None of Your Business: Customer Data Were Once Gold to E-Commerce. Now, Companies are Paying a Price for Privacy Jitters," *BusinessWeek*, June 26, 2000, p. 78; D. Wessel, "How Technology Tailors Price Tags," *The Wall Street Journal*, June 23, 2001, p. A1.

19. http://www.aa.com/content/AAdvantage/program Details/eliteStatus/main.jhtml (accessed March 3, 2005).

20. http://www.microsoft.com/info/cookies.htm (accessed September 30, 2005).

21. Dhruv Grewal, "Marketing Is All about Creating Value: 8 Key Rules," in *Inside the Mind of Textbook Marketing* (Boston, MA: Aspatore Inc., 2003), 79–96.

22. James L. Heskett, W. Earl Sasser Jr., and Leonard A. Schlesinger, *The Service Profit Chain: How Leading Companies Link Profit and Growth to Loyalty, Satisfaction, and Value* (New York: Simon & Schuster Adult Publishing Group, 1997); Christopher D. Ittner and David F. Larcker, "Are Nonfinancial Measures Leading Indicators of Financial Performance? An Analysis of Customer Satisfaction," *Journal of Accounting Research* 35 (Supplement 1998), pp. 1–35; Thomas O. Jones and E. Earl Sasser Jr., "Why Satisfied Customers Defect," *Harvard Business Review*, November/December 1995, pp. 88–99; A. Parasuraman and Dhruv Grewal, "The Impact of Technology on the Quality-Value-Loyalty Chain: A Research Agenda," *Journal of the Academy of Marketing Science* 28, no. 1 (2000), pp. 168–74; Frederick F. Reichheld, "Loyalty-Based Management," *Harvard Business Review* 2 (March/April 1993), pp. 64–73; Frederick F. Reichheld, "Loyalty and the Renaissance of Marketing," *Marketing Management* 2, no. 4 (1994), pp. 10–21; Frederick F. Reichheld and Phil Schefter, "E-Loyalty," *Harvard Business Review*, July/August 2000, pp. 105–13; Anthony J. Rucci, Richard T. Quinn, and Steven P. Kirn, "The Employee-Customer-Profit Chain at Sears," *Harvard Business Review*, January/February 1998, pp. 83–97; Roland T. Rust, Valarie Zeithaml, and Katherine N. Lemon, *Driving Customer Equity* (New York: The Free Press, 2000); Russell S. Winer, "A Framework for Customer Relationship Management," *California Management Review* 43, no. 4 (2001), pp. 89–105; Valarie Zeithaml, Roland T. Rust, and Katherine N. Lemon, "The Customer Pyramid: Creating and Serving Profitable Customers," *California Management Review* 43, no. 4 (2001), pp. 118–42.

23. Datamonitor: Hallmark Cards, Inc., May, 2005. "Greeting Cards Facts and Figures", *Souvenirs, Gifts & Novelties*," May, 2005.

24. http://www.cspinet.org/liquidcandy/index.html (accessed September 12, 2006).

25. Jack Neff, "Value Positioning Becomes a Priority," *Advertising Age* 75, no. 8 (2004), p. 24.

26. Jean Halliday, "Maloney Wants Volvo Viewed as Both Safe and Luxurious," *Advertising Age* 75, no. 12 (2004), p. 22.

27. http://www.nutraingredients-usa.com/news/news-ng.asp?id=22520-cadbury-bu; http://www.dpsu.com/nr_nantucket_040105.html; http://www.juiceguys.com/faq.php?category=5 (accessed September 12, 2006).

28. Bob Ingram, "Squeeze Play," *Progressive Grocer* 85 (2) February 1, 2006, Datamonitor: Juices, December, 2005.

29. http://www.mypyramid.gov (accessed September 5, 2006).

30. Ingram, "Squeeze Play."

31. Mary Connelly, "Chrysler Dealers' Pitch: Made by Mercedes; Salespeople Likely to Tout Shared Parts," *Automotive News*, January 19, 2004.

32. This case was written by Jeanne L. Munger and Julie Rusch in conjunction with the textbook authors (Dhruv Grewal and Michael Levy) for the basis of class discussion rather than to illustrate either effective or ineffective marketing practices. Jeanne Munger is an associate professor at the University of Southern Maine.

33. http://www.sodexhousa.com (accessed September 5, 2006).

34. Developed from material taken from "Case Study—Sodexho Marriott Services," Claritas brochure, *Analytical Services*, available at http://www.clusterbigip1.claritas.com/claritas/pdf/analyticalbrochure.pdf; "Generations Restaurant Gets a Face Lift," *Indiana State University News & Events*, August 13, 2001, available at http://www.indstate.edu/news/archive/2001/aug/generations.html (accessed September 10, 2006).

Chapter 9

1. Gary Loveman, "Diamonds in the Data Mine," *Harvard Business Review* 81, no. 5 (May 2003), pp. 109–13; http://www.harrahs.com[0] (accessed September 20, 2006).

2. Hoffman, Thomas, "Harrah's Bets on LoyaltyProgram in Caesars Deal," *computerworld.com*. June 27, 2005 (accessed February 22, 2006).

3. A. Parasuraman, Dhruv Grewal, and R. Krishnan, *Marketing Research* (Boston, MA: Houghton Mifflin, 2004), p. 9.

4. http://www.marketingpower.com/live/content19312.php (accessed September 20, 2006).

5. Holly Bailey, "Where the Voters Are," *Newsweek* 143, no. 13 (March 29, 2004), p. 67.

6. "Loews Cineplex Boosts Sales by 17 Percent Using Siebel eBusiness Applications," press release, http://www.siebel.com/news-events/press_releases/2003/030805_loews.shtm (accessed September 18, 2006).

7. Bruno, Joe B. "Credit Card Hacking Could Affect Millions," June 2005, http://abcnews.go.com/Business/wireStory?id=861020 (accessed October 12, 2005).

8. http://www.copia.com/tcpa/ (accessed September 16, 2006).

9. Lona M. Farr, "Whose Files Are They Anyway? Privacy Issues for the Fundraising Profession," *International Journal of Nonprofit and Voluntary Sector Marketing* 7, no. 4 (November 2002), p. 361.

10. http://www.whirlpool.com/home.jsp (accessed November 12, 2004); Parasuraman, Grewal, and Krishnan, *Marketing Research*; Greg Steinmetz and Carl Quintanilla, "Whirlpool Expected Easy Going in Europe, and It Got a Big Shock," *The Wall Street Journal*, April 10, 1998, pp. A1, A6.

11. Erhard K. Valentin, "Commentary: Marketing Research Pitfalls in Product Development," *Journal of Product & Brand Management* 3, no. 4-6 (1994), pp. 66–69.

12. http://www.marketingpower.com/live/content19312.php (accessed July 16, 2005); http://www.infores.com/public/us/default.htm (accessed July 16, 2005); "Sophisticated Data Gives Insights into What's Shaping the H&BA Market," *Chain Drug Review* 26, no. 11 (June 21, 2004), p. 211; "Are You Season-Savvy? Celebrate the Opportunity to Manage Seasonal Candy Sales More Strategically," *Confectioner* 89, no. 3 (April 2004), p. 38.

13. Dan B. Wood, "At the DNC, It's a Blog-Eat-Blog World," *Christian Science Monitor*, July 28, 2004, p. 10; http://www.cogsci.princeton.edu/cgi-bin/webwn[0] (accessed July 17, 2005); http://radio.weblogs.com/0001011/categories/scobleizer/ (accessed July 17, 2005); Jena McGregor, "It's a Blog World After All," *Fast Company* 81 (April 2004), p. 84.

14. http://radio.weblogs.com/0001011/categories/scobleizer/ (accessed September 20, 2006).

15. Linda Tischler, "Every Move You Make," *FastCompany* 81 (April 2004), p. 73; "Miller Launches Beer in Fridge Pack Cans," August 2004, http://www.foodproductiondaily.com; Richard Elliot and Nick Janket-Elliot, "Using Ethnography in Strategic Consumer Research," *Qualitative Market Research* 6, no. 4 (2003), p. 215. www.envirosell.com/case_studies.html# (accessed September 20, 2006).

16. Keith McDevitt, "Driving the Message Home. Why Lexus Chose Newspapers to Convey the Meaning of Luxury for the Launch of the ES 300 and Position the Car as a Personal Oasis of Tranquility and Freedom," *Marketing Magazine* 107, no. 5 (February 4, 2002), p. 14.

17. Allison Fass, "Collective Opinion," Forbes.com November 11, 2005, accessed electronically.

18. Stanley E. Griffis, Thomas J. Goldsby, and Martha Cooper, "Web-Based and Mail Surveys: A Comparison of Response, Data and Cost," *Journal of Business Logistics* 24, no. 2 (2003), pp. 237–59; Chris Gautreau, "Getting the Answers," *The Greater Baton Rouge Business Report* 22, no. 29 (September 28, 2004), p. 17; Alf Nucifora, "Weaving Web Surveys That Work," *njbiz* 15, no. 46 (November 11, 2002), p. 28.

19. This example was based on information taken from Coinstar's Web site (http://www.coinstar) and a case study about Coinstar, available on the SPSS Inc. company Web site (http://www.spss.com) (accessed September 18, 2006).

20. For a more thorough discussion of effective written reports, see Parasuraman, Grewal, and Krishnan, *Marketing Research*, Ch. 16.

21. Jennifer Alsever, "Electronic Stores Discover Women Marketing Survey Spurs New Tactics," *Denver Post*, February 16, 2004, p. C1.

22. This case was written by Jeanne L. Munger and Julie Rusch in conjunction with the textbook authors (Dhruv Grewal and Michael Levy) for the basis of class discussion rather than to illustrate either effective or ineffective marketing practice. Jeanne Munger is an associate professor at the University of Southern Maine.

23. Women are involved in purchasing their own apparel as well as that for boyfriends, husbands, and children.

24. "Nike Chases Women," *Marketing Magazine* 107, no. 32 (August 12, 2002), p. 22.

25. Fara Warner, "Nike's Women's Movement," *Fast Company* 61 (August 2002), pp. 70–75.

26. Kellee "Sparky" Harris, "Research Commissioned by Nike Helped it Reach Women Online," *Sporting Goods Business* 34, no. 8 (June 11, 2001), p. 12.

Chapter 10

1. http://www.diesel.com/contact_diesel/html/company.html[0], accessed August 5, 2005; Lars Brandle, "Warner International Gets Fuel with Diesel," *Billboard* 116, no. 12 (March 20, 2004), p. 5; "The Driving Force behind Diesel," *BusinessWeek Online*, January 20, 2003[0], www.businessweek.com; "Diesel-Casual Innovative Designerware that Sells," *imagesfashion.com* 4, no. 6 (July 2003).

2. American Marketing Association, *Dictionary of Marketing Terms* (Chicago, IL: American Marketing Association, 2004), available at http://www.marketingpower.com/live/mg-dictionary-view329.php?

3. "All Colgate Toothpastes," http://www.colgate.com (accessed September 16, 2006).

4. William P. Putsis Jr. and Barry L. Bayus, "An Empirical Analysis of Firms' Product Line Decisions," *Journal of Marketing Research* 38, no. 1 (February 2001), pp. 110–18.

5. Bruce G.S. Hardie and Leonard M. Lodish, "Perspectives: The Logic of Product-Line Extensions," *Harvard Business Review*, November–December 1994, p. 54.

6. John A. Quelch and David Kenny, "Extend Profits, Not Product Lines," *Harvard Business Review*, September–October 1994, pp. 153–60.

7. Rekha Balu, "Heinz to Trim Its Work Force as Much as 9%," *The Wall Street Journal*, February 18, 1999 (ProQuest Document ID 39039688).

8. Jim Mateja, "Chicago Tribune New Cars Column," *Knight Ridder Tribune Business News*, July 13, 2003 (ProQuest Document ID: 357908581).

9. "J&J to Buy Skin-Care Business," *The Wall Street Journal*, December 18, 1998, p. 1.

10. http://scjohnson.com/products/ (accessed September 20, 2006).

11. Sally Beatty, "Levi Strauss Sells Low-Cost Jeans to Target in Bid to Increase Sales," *The Wall Street Journal*, December 4, 2003, p. B10.

12. Ibid.; Louis Lee, "Jean Therapy, $23 a Pop," *BusinessWeek*, June 28, 2004, pp. 91, 93.

13. "Fitting In: In Bow to Retailers' New Clout, Levi Strauss Makes Alterations," *The Wall Street Journal*, June 17, 2004, pp. A1, A15.

14. Ernest Beck, "Unilever to Cut 25,000 Jobs, Close Factories—Consumer-Goods Company to Focus on Core Brands in Restructuring Asian," *The Wall Street Journal*, February 23, 2000, p. 2.

15. http://www.bankofamerica.com/newsroom/press/press.cfm?PressID=press.20040824.04.htm (accessed September 20, 2006).

16. http://www.bankofamerica.com/deposits/checksave/index.cfm?template=check_overview&statecheck=MA (accessed September 14, 2006).

17. Kevin Lane Keller, *Strategic Brand Management: Building, Measuring, and Managing Brand Equity*, 2d ed. (Upper Saddle River, NJ: Prentice Hall, 2003).

18. This discussion on the advantages of strong brands is adapted from Keller, *Strategic Brand Management*, pp. 104–12; Elizabeth S. Moore, William L. Wilkie, and Richard J. Lutz, "Passing the Torch: Intergenerational Influences as a Source of Brand Equity," *Journal of Marketing* 66, no. 2 (April 2002), p. 17.

19. Angela Y. Lee and Aparna A. Labroo, "The Effect of Conceptual and Perceptual Fluency on Brand Evaluation," *Journal of Marketing Research* 41, no. 2 (May 2004), pp. 151–65.

20. http://www.interbrand.com/best_brands_2004.asp (accessed September 14, 2006). The net present value of the earnings over the next 12 months is used to calculate the value.

21. David A. Aaker, *Managing Brand Equity*, New York: Free Press, 1991.

22. Polo Ralph Lauren Corporate Report 2004, available at http://media.corporate-ir.net/media_files/NYS/RL/reports/04ar/PRL2004AR.pdf (accessed September 16, 2006).

23. David A. Aaker, "Measuring Brand Equity Across Products and Markets," *California Management Review* 38 (Spring 1996), pp. 102–20.

24. Keller, *Strategic Brand Management*.

25. Jennifer L. Aaker, "Dimensions of Brand Personality," *Journal of Marketing Research* 34, no. 3 (August 1997), pp. 347–56.

26. Kevin Lane Keller, "Conceptualizing, Measuring, and Managing Customer-Based Brand Equity," *Journal of Marketing* 57, no. 1 (January 1993), pp. 1–22.

27. Dave Larson, "Building a Brand's Personality from the Customer Up," *Direct Marketing*, October 2002, pp. 17–21.

28. http://www.marketingpower.com/live/mg-dictionary.php?SearchFor=brand+loyalty&Searched=1 (accessed September 17, 2006).

29. James H. McAlexander, John W. Schouten, and Harold F. Koenig, "Building Brand Community," *Journal of Marketing* 66, no. 1 (January 2002), pp. 38–54.

30. Christine Bittar, "Big Brands: Stronger than Dirt," *BrandWeek*, June 23, 2003, pp. S52–53.

31. "President's Choice Continues Brisk Pace," *Frozen Food Age*, March 1998, pp. 17–18.

32. Laura Liebeck, "Private Label Goes Premium," *Discount Store News*, November 4, 1996, p. F38; "New Private-Label Alternatives Bring Changes to Supercenters, Clubs," *DSN Retailing Today*, February 5, 2001, p. 66.

33. Mathew Boyle, "Brand Killers," *Fortune*, August 11, 2003, p. 89ff.

34. Michael Levy and Barton A. Weitz, *Retailing Management*, 6th ed. (New York: McGraw-Hill/Irwin, 2007).

35. http://www.pg.com.

36. For recent research on brand extensions, see Subramanian Balachander and Sanjoy Ghose, "Reciprocal Spillover Effects: A Strategic Benefit of Brand Extensions," *Journal of Marketing* 67, no. 1 (January 2003), pp. 4–13; Kalpesh Kaushik Desai and Kevin Lane Keller, "The Effects of Ingredient Branding Strategies on Host Brand Extendibility," *Journal of Marketing* 66, no. 1 (January 2002), pp. 73–93; Tom Meyvis and Chris Janiszewski, "When Are Broader Brands Stronger Brands? An Accessibility Perspective on the Success of Brand Extensions," *Journal of Consumer Research* 31, no. 2 (September 2004), pp. 346–57.

37. David Aaker, "Brand Extensions: The Good, the Bad, and the Ugly," *Sloan Management Review*, 31 (Summer 1990), pp. 47–56.

38. http://www.braun.com.

39. http://www.dell.com.

40. http://www.fritolay.com/consumer.html.

41. Vanitha Swaminathan, Richard J. Fox, and Srinivas K. Reddy, "The Impact of Brand Extension Introduction on Choice," *Journal of Marketing* 65, no. 3 (October 2001), pp. 1–15.

42. Jennifer Aaker, Susan Fournier, and S. Adam Brasel, "When Good Brands Do Bad," *Journal of Consumer Research* 31, no. 1 (June 2004), pp. 1–16.

43. Barbara Loken and Deborah Roedder John, "Diluting Brand Beliefs: When Do Brand Extensions Have a Negative Impact?" *Journal of Marketing* 57, no. 3 (July 1993), pp. 71–84.

44. Aaker, "Brand Extensions," pp. 47–56.

45. David A. Aaker and Kevin Lane Keller, "Consumer Evaluations of Brand Extensions," *Journal of Marketing* 54, no. 1 (January 1990), pp. 27–41.

46. Susan M. Broniarczyk and Joseph W. Alba, "The Importance of the Brand in Brand Extension," *Journal of Marketing Research* 31, no. 2 (May 1994), pp. 214–28.

47. http://www.ritzcarlton.com/corporate/about_us/history.asp (accessed September 16, 2006).

48. Hoover's Company Information, *Hoover's Online*, 2004; Melissa Master, "Overreaching," *Across the Board*, March/April 2001, pp. 20–26; David Taylor, *Brand Stretch: Why 1 in 2 Extensions Fail and How to Beat the Odds* (New York: John Wiley & Sons, 2004); Melanie Wells, "Red Baron," *Forbes*, July 3, 2000, p. 150.

49. http://www.hoovers.com/virgin-group/—ID__41676—/free-co-factsheet.xhtml, accessed August 30, 2005.

50. Kate Fitzgerald, "A New Addition to Cobranding's Menu," *Credit Card Management*, 16 (November 2003), pp. 40–44.

51. This section is based on Akshay R. Rao and Robert W. Ruekert, "Brand Alliances as Signals of Product Quality," *Sloan Management Review*, 36 (Fall 1994), pp. 87–97.

52. "FedEx Expands Alliance with Kinko's," *Journal of Commerce*, August 11, 2000, p. WP.

53. "FedEx and Kinko's to Deliver Increased Threat," *DSN Retailing Today*, May 17, 2004, p. 17.

54. T. Kippenberger, "Co-Branding as a Competitive Weapon," *Strategic Direction* 18 (October), pp. 31–33.

55. Tom Blacket and Bob Boad, eds., *Co-Branding: The Science of Alliance* (London: Macmillan Press, 1999).

56. David A. Aaker, *Brand Portfolio Strategy* (New York: The Free Press, 2004).

57. Keller, *Strategic Brand Management*.

58. Doug Desjardins, "LIMA Foresees Huge 2nd Half for Entertainment Properties," *DSN Retailing Today*, June 21, 2004, pp. 6, 37.

59. Keller, *Strategic Brand Management*.

60. http://www.lacoste.com/usa/.

61. Dwight Oestricher, "Marvel: Powerhouse Potential? Other Heroes Spawned by Spider-Man Creator Could Pay Off," *The Wall Street Journal*, May 8, 2002, p. B9 ff.

62. Anna Wilde Mathews, "Lord of the Things-Separate Companies Hold Rights to the Products From 'Rings' Books, Films," *The Wall Street Journal*, December 17, 2001, p. B1ff.

63. Stephen Brown, Robert V. Kozinets, and John F. Sherry Jr., "Teaching Old Brands New Tricks: Retro Branding and the Revival of Brand Meaning," *Journal of Marketing* 67, no. 2 (July 2003), p. 19.

64. Chuck Salter, "Whirlpool Finds Its Cool," *Fast Company* 95 (June 2005), p. 73.

65. Karen Benezra, "Youth Will Be Sold," *Brandweek*, July 14, 1997, pp. 28–30.

66. Christine Bittar, "Cosmetic Changes beyond Skin Deep," *Brandweek*, May 17, 2000, pp. 20, 22.

67. Lisa Granatstein, "Back to Cool," *Mediaweek*, June 21, 2004, pp. 25–26.

68. Bethany McLean, "Gallo Moves Its Wine Upmarket," *Strategic Direction*, February 2001, pp. 12–13.

69. Ibid.

70. Brian Wansink, "Making Old Brands New," *American Demographics*, December 1997, pp. 53–58.

71. Wansink, "Making Old Brands New."

72. Sandy Parlin, "Secondary Packaging Adds Value," *Beverage Industry*, February 2004, p. 48.

73. Parlin, "Secondary Packaging."

74. William Makely, "Being the Beauty, Being the Brand," *Global Cosmetic Industry*, January 2004, pp. 28–30.

75. "Packages: Tracing an Evolution," *Packaging Digest*, December 2003, pp. 37–42.

76. U.S. Department of Agriculture, Food Safety and Inspection Service, "Nutrition Labeling of Ground or Chopped Meat and Poultry Products and Single-Ingredient Products," *Federal Register* 66 (2001), pp. 4969–99; John C. Kozup, Elizabeth H. Creyer, and Scot Burton, "Making Healthful Food Choices: The Influence of Health Claims and Nutrition Information on Consumers' Evaluations of Packaged Food Products and Restaurant Menu Items," *Journal of Marketing* 67, no. 2 (April 2003), pp. 19–35.

77. "Danone Expands Goodies Low-Fat Line of Desserts," *Marketing*, February 12, 2004, p. 4; http://www.landwriter.co.uk/landwriter/premium/TemplateParser.asp?aId=3778&page=FreeTemplate, accessed August 30, 2005.

78. "MarketLooks: Ready Meals & Side Dishes," PackagedFacts, May 2004, http://www.packagedfacts.com; Deborah Ball, Sarah Ellison, Janet Adamy, and Geoffrey A. Fowler, "Recipes without Borders?" *The Wall Street Journal*, August 18, 2004, *wsj.com*.

79. This case was written by Jeanne L. Munger and Julie Rusch in conjunction with the textbook authors Dhruv Grewal and Michael Levy for the basis of class discussion rather than to illustrate either effective or ineffective marketing practices. Jeanne Munger is an associate professor at the University of Southern Maine.

80. http://www.bandaid.com/brand_story.shtml; http://www.bandaid.com/new_products.shtml; Christine Bittar, "J&J Stuck on Expanding BAND-AID® Franchise," *Brandweek*, March 3, 2003, p. 4; Richard Gutwillig, "Billion-Dollar Bandages," *Supermarket Business*, August 15, 2000, p. 58; "United States Top 10 First Aid Tape/Bandages/Gauze Brands Ranked by Dollar Sales and Unit Volume for 2003," *Chain Drug Review*, June 21, 2004, p. 238; Andrea M. Grossman, "Personal and Beauty Care: News Bites," *Drug Store News*, January 11, 1999, p. 61; "O-T-C Health Care: United States Over-the-Counter Heath Care Product Sales in Dollars and Percent Change for 2003," *Chain Drug Review*, May 24, 2004, p. 32.

81. Christine Bittar, "J&J Stuck on Expanding Band-Aid Franchise," *Brandweek* 44, no. 9 (March 3, 2003), p. 4.

Chapter 11

1. IDEO, http://www.ideo.com (accessed September 18, 2006); Tom Kelley (with Jonathan Littman), *The Art of Innovation: Lessons in Creativity from IDEO, America's Leading Design*

Firm (New York: Doubleday/Currency Books, 2001); Bruce Nussbaum, "The Power of Design," *BusinessWeek*, May 17, 2004, p. 86ff; Brad Stone, "Reinventing Everyday Life," *Newsweek*, October 27, 2003, p. 90ff.

2. http://www.dove.com.

3. Koen Pauwels, Jorge Silva-Risso, Shuba Srinivasan, and Dominique M. Hanssens, "New Products, Sales Promotions, and Firm Value: The Case of the Automobile Industry," *Journal of Marketing* 68, no. 4 (October 2004), p. 142.

4. A number of articles on variety seeking are available. For example, see Andrea Morales, Barbara E. Kahn, Cynthia Huffman, Leigh McAlister, and Susan M. Bronizrszyk, "Perceptions of Assortment Variety: The Effects of Congruency between Consumer's Internal and Retailer's External Organization," *Journal of Retailing* 81 (2) (2005), pp. 159–69.

5. Kalpesh Kaushik Desai and Kevin Lane Keller, "The Effects of Ingredient Branding Strategies on Host Brand Extendibility," *Journal of Marketing* 66, no. 1 (January 2002), pp. 73–93.

6. Rajesh K. Chandy, Jaideep C. Prabhu, and Kersi D. Antia, "What Will the Future Bring? Dominance, Technology Expectations, and Radical Innovation," *Journal of Marketing* 67, no. 3 (July 2003), pp. 1–18; Harald J. van Heerde, Carl F. Mela, and Puneet Manchanda, "The Dynamic Effect of Innovation on Market Structure," *Journal of Marketing Research* 41, no. 2 (May 2004), pp. 166–83.

7. Clayton M. Christensen and Michael E. Raynor, *The Innovator's Solution*. Boston, MA: Harvard Business School Press, 2003.

8. Philip Kotler, *Marketing Management*, 11th ed. (Upper Saddle River, NJ: Prentice-Hall, 2003), pp. 330–31. Kotler's work was based on the following research: William T. Robinson and Claes Fornell, "Sources of Market Pioneer Advantages in Consumer Goods Industries," *Journal of Marketing Research* 22, no. 3 (August 1985), pp. 305–17; Glen L. Urban, T. Carter, S. Gaskin, and Z. Mucha, "Market Share Rewards to Pioneering Brands: An Empirical Analysis and Strategic Implications," *Management Science* 32 (June 1986), pp. 645–59; and G.S. Carpenter and Kent Nakamoto, "Consumer Preference Formation and Pioneering Advantage," *Journal of Marketing Research* 26, no. 3 (August 1989), pp. 285–98.

9. Raji Srinivasan, Gary L. Lilien, and Arvind Rangaswamy, "First in, First out? The Effects of Network Externalities on Pioneer Survival," *Journal of Marketing* 68, no. 1 (January 2004), p. 41.

10. Cyndee Miller, "Little Relief Seen for New Product Failure Rate," *Marketing News*, June 21, 1993, pp. 1, 10; *BusinessWeek*, "Flops," August 16, 1993, p. 76ff.; Lori Dahm, "Secrets of Success: The Strategies Driving New Product Development at Kraft," *Stagnito's New Products Magazine* 2 (January 2002), p. 18ff.

11. http://www.marketingpower.com (accessed September 18, 2006).

12. http://www.quickmba.com (accessed September 16, 2006).

13. Subin Im and John P. Workman Jr., "Market Orientation, Creativity, and New Product Performance in High-Technology Firms," *Journal of Marketing* 68, no. 2 (April 2004), p. 114.

14. Mike Clendenin, "Taiwan Unfurls DVD Spec," *Electronic Engineering Times*, May 23, 2005, p. 26.

15. Standard & Poor's, *Industry Surveys: Healthcare: Pharmaceuticals*, June 24, 2004.

16. Glen L. Urban and John R. Hauser, "'Listening In' to Find and Explore New Combinations of Customer Needs," *Journal of Marketing* 68, no. 2 (April 2004), p. 72; Steve Hoeffler, "Measuring Preferences for Really New Products," *Journal of Marketing Research* 40, no. 4 (November 2003), pp. 406–20.

17. Glen L. Urban and John R. Hauser, *Design and Marketing of New Products*, 2nd ed. (Upper Saddle River, NJ: Prentice Hall, 1993), pp. 120–21.

18. Dahm, "Secrets of Success."

19. http://www.betterproductdesign.net/tools/user/lead-user.htm (accessed November 12, 2004); Eric von Hippel, "Successful Industrial Products from Consumers' Ideas," *Journal of Marketing* 42, no. 1 (January 1978), pp. 39–49; Eric von Hippel, "Lead Users: A Source of Novel Product Concepts," *Management Science* 32 (1986), pp. 791–805; Eric von Hippel, *The Sources of Innovation* (New York: Oxford University Press, 1988); Glen L. Urban and Eric von Hippel, "Lead User Analysis for the Development of Industrial Products," *Management Science* 34 (May 1988), pp. 569–82.

20. Karl T. Ulrich and Steven D. Eppinger, *Product Design and Development*, 2nd ed. (Boston, MA: Irwin-McGraw-Hill, 2000).

21. http://www.marketingpower.com (accessed September 18, 2006).

22. Ulrich and Eppinger, *Product Design and Development*, p. 166.

23. Ely Dahan and V. Srinivasan, "The Predictive Power of Internet-Based Product Concept Testing Using Visual Depiction and Animation," *Journal of Product Innovation Management* 17 (2000), pp. 99–109.

24. http://www.marketingpower.com (accessed September 18, 2006).

25. Ulrich and Eppinger, *Product Design and Development*.

26. Tonya Vinas, "P&G Seeks Alternatives to Animal Tests," *Industry Week* 253, no. 7 (July 2004), p. 60; "EU to Ban Animal Tested Cosmetics," www.cnn.com (accessed March 31, 2006); www.leapingbunny.org; Gary Anthes, "P&G Uses Data Mining to Cut Animal Testing," www.computerworld.com. December 06, 1999.

27. Ulrich and Eppinger, *Product Design and Development*, pp. 212–13; Henry Dreyfuss, *Designing for People* (New York: Paragraphic Books, 1967).

28. Paschalina (Lilia) Ziamou and S. Ratneshwar, "Innovations in Product Functionality: When and Why are Explicit Comparisons Effective?" *Journal of Marketing* 67, no. 2 (April 2003), pp. 49–61.

29. http://www2.acnielsen.com/products/crs_bases2.shtml (accessed September 20, 2006).

30. Philip Kotler, *Marketing Management*, 11th ed. (Upper Saddle River, NJ: Prentice-Hall, 2003).

31. Patricia Sellers, "P&G: Teaching an Old Dog New Tricks," *Fortune*, May 31, 2004, pp. 166–80.

32. Dahm, "Secrets of Success"; Bob Condor, "Coca-Cola Introduces Smaller Soft Drink Cans in Chicago Area," *Knight Ridder Tribune Business News*, November 3, 2002 (ProQuest Document ID: 230366931).

33. http://www.infores.com/public/us/analytics/product-portfolio/bscannewprodtest.htm, accessed April 2, 2006.

34. Productscan Online, which maintains a database of all new products launched each year, named these five new products as the top innovations from more than 30,000 U.S. and Canadian product introductions; NACS Online, "Productscan Online Pinpoints What's New and Notable," http://www.nacsonline.com/NACS/News/Daily_News_Archives/December2003/nd1223034.htm (accessed September 19, 2006).

35. Product Development Management Association, *The PDMA Handbook of New Product Development*, 2nd ed., Kenneth K. Kahn, ed. (New York: John Wiley & Sons, 2004).

36. Ashwin W. Joshi and Sanjay Sharma, "Customer Knowledge Development: Antecedents and Impact on New Product Success," *Journal of Marketing* 68, no. 4 (October 2004), p. 47.

37. Yuhong Wu, Sridhar Balasubramanian, and Vijay Mahajan, "When Is a Preannounced New Product Likely to Be Delayed?" *Journal of Marketing* 68, no. 2 (April 2004), p. 101.

38. http://www.pdma.org/ (accessed September 15, 2006).

39. Theodore Levitt, *Marketing Imagination* (New York: The Free Press, 1986).

40. Donald R. Lehmann and Russell S. Winer, *Analysis for Marketing Planning*, 6th ed. (Boston: McGraw-Hill/Irwin, 2004).

41. Urban and Hauser, *Design and Marketing*.

42. Thomas K. Arnold, "VHS Is on Its Way to Becoming a Modern-Day Dinosaur," *Video Store Magazine*, October 6–October 12, 2002, p. 20; Erik Gruenwedel, "MPAA: Rising DVD Penetration at VHS Expense," *Video Store Magazine*, March 28–April 3, 2004, p. 44.

43. Geoffrey Colvin, "Admit It: You, too, Are Paris Hilton," *Fortune*, December 29, 2003, p. 57.

44. Scott Kirsner, "Can TiVo Go Prime Time?" *Fast Company*, August 2000, p. 82; *The Economist*, "Business: A Farewell to Ads? Advertising and Television," April 17, 2004, p. 70; *Technology Review*, "Technology: How TiVo Works," May 2004, pp. 80–81; Mark Basch, "Digital Video Recorder to Change How People View TV," *Knight Ridder Tribune Business News*, June 30, 2004.

45. Miriam Jordan and Jonathan Karp, "Machines for the Masses; Whirlpool Aims Cheap Washer at Brazil, India and China; Making Due with Slower Spin," *The Wall Street Journal*, December 9, 2003, p. A19.

46. Om Malik, "The New Land of Opportunity," *Business 2.0*, July 2004, pp. 72–79.

47. Claire Briney, "Wiping Up the Market," *Global Cosmetic Industry* 172, no. 4 (April 2004), pp. 40–43.

48. Kara Swisher, "Home Economics: The Hypoallergenic Car; Wave of Cleaning Products Caters to Finicky Drivers; Premoistened Auto Wipes," *The Wall Street Journal* (eastern edition), May 6, 2004, p. D.1.

49. http://www.toiletwand.com (accessed September 20, 2006).

50. http://www.dfj.com/nanocar/ (accessed September 20, 2006).

51. Niccolo d'Aquino, "Rome: Walking on Air," *Europe*, March 1997, p. 40; Mercedes M. Cardona, "Italian Shoemaker Moving into U.S.," *Advertising Age*, April 24, 2000, p. 20; *The Economist*, "Business: The Ferrari of Footwear; Italian Shoes," March 13, 2003, p. 81; Maureen Kline, "Blessed Relief for Sweaty Feet: Ventilated Shoes from Geox are Winning Fans-And Raking in Profits," *BusinessWeek*, March 22, 2004, p. 28ff.

52. Roy Bragg, "LP Vinyl Records Are Making a Comeback in Audiophile Circles," *Knight Ridder Tribune Business News*, January 3, 2004 (ProQuest Document ID: 521358371); Susan Adams, "You, the Record Mogul," *Forbes*, October 27, 2003, p. 256ff.

53. Kevin J. Clancy and Peter C. Krieg, "Product Life Cycle: A Dangerous Idea," *Brandweek*, March 1, 2004, p. 26; Nariman K. Dhalla and Sonia Yuseph, "Forget the Product Life-Cycle Concept," *Harvard Business Review* (January–February 1976), p. 102ff.

54. Peter Golder and Gerard Tellis, "Cascades, Diffusion, and Turning Points in the Product Life Cycle," MSI Report No. 03-120, 2003.

55. Jay Bolling, "DTC: A Strategy for Every Stage," *Pharmaceutical Executive*, November 2003, pp. 110–17.

56. This case was written by Susan White Newell and Jeanne L. Munger in conjunction with the textbook authors Dhruv Grewal and Michael Levy for the basis of class discussion rather than to illustrate either effective or ineffective marketing practice. Jeanne Munger is an associate professor at the University of Southern Maine.

57. "Apple unveils video iPod," AppleInsider October 12, 2005; www.appleinsider.com/article.php?id=1315 (accessed September 20, 2006); "Video iPod Shocks Affiliates, Spawns New TV Industry," www.adrants.com/2005/10video-ipod-shocks-affiliates-spawns-new.php (accessed October 17, 2006); Kenhi Hall, "Sony's iPod Assault Is No Threat to Apple," *Business Week*, March 13, 2006. p. 53; David Pogue, "Almost iPod, but in the End a Samsung," *The New York Times*, March 9, 2006, www.nytimes.com (accessed September 20, 2006); David Becker, "It's All about the iPod," *CNET Networks*, www.news.com, April 18, 2005. Scott VanCamp, "They March to His Rhythm," *Brandweek* 45, no. 36 (October 11, 2004), Special Section, pp. M36–40; Beth Snyder Bulik, "The iPod Economy," *Advertising Age* 75, no. 42 (October 18, 2004), pp. 1–2.

Chapter 12

1. "Teaching the Tenets of Tea," *The Gourmet Retailer* 24, no. 10 (October 2003), p. 48; Joseph Rosenbloom, "Peet's Coffee and Tea: Competing against Starbucks," *Inc.*, June 1, 2002, p. NA; David Goll, "Peet's Expands Push into Supermarkets," *East Bay Business Times*, August 29, 2003, p. 7.

2. Leonard L. Berry and A. Parasuraman, *Marketing Services: Competing through Quality* (New York: The Free Press, 1991), p. 5.

3. http://www.bea.doc.gov/bea/newsrel/gdp_indy_high-lights.pdf (accessed September 10, 2005).

4. Valarie A. Zeithaml, A. Parasuraman, and Leonard L. Berry, *Delivering Quality Service: Balancing Customer Perceptions and Expectations* (New York: The Free Press, 1990).

5. Alison Overhold, "Listening to Starbucks," *Fast Company* 84 (July 2004), pp. 50–57.

6. "Developing a Deeper Understanding of Post-Purchase Perceived Risk and Repeat Purchase Behavioral Intentions in a Service Setting," (with M. Levy, Jerry Gotlieb and Gopal Iyer), 2006, Unpublished Working Paper, Babson College; Mary Jo Bitner, Stephen W. Brown, and Matthew L. Mueter "Technology Infusion in Service Encounters," *Journal of the Academy of Marketing Science*, 28 (1) (2000), pp. 138–49; Jerry Gotlieb, Dhruv Grewal, Michael Levy, and Joan Lindsey-Mullikin, "An Examination of Moderators of the Effects of Customers' Evaluation of Employee Courtesy on Attitude toward the Service Firm," *Journal of Applied Social Psychology* 34 (April 2004), pp. 825–47.

7. Choice Hotels, "Special Guest Policies," 2004, http://www7.choicehotels.com/ires/en-US/html/GuestPolicies?sid=hPTj.2R6oelpGw.7 (accessed September 10, 2006).

8. http://www.clubmed.com (accessed September 20, 2006).

9. Jeff Bennett, "Technology Trends: More Shoppers Find Self-Checkout Easy; Major Retailers Turn to Automation for Customers," *Detroit Free Press Business*, March 1, 2003, http://www.freep.com/money/business/scan1_20030301.htm (accessed November 10, 2004); http://www.ncr.com/products/pdf/hardware/fastlane_capa-bilities.pdf (accessed November 11, 2004); Matt Pillar, "Self-Checkout: Self-Serving or Customer Centric?" *Integrated Solutions for Retailers*, July 2004, http://ism-retail.com/articles/2004_07/040710.htm (accessed November 10, 2004).

10. The discussion of the Gap Model and its implications draws heavily from Michael Levy and Barton A. Weitz, *Retailing Management*, 6th ed. (Burr Ridge, IL: Irwin/McGraw-Hill, 2007) and also is based on Deon Nel and Leyland Pitt, "Service Quality in a Retail Environment: Closing the Gaps," *Journal of General Management* 18 (Spring 1993), pp. 37–57; Zeithaml, Parasuraman, and Berry, *Delivering Quality Customer Service*; Valerie Zeithaml, Leonard Berry, and A. Parasuraman, "Communication and Control Processes in the Delivery of Service Quality," *Journal of Marketing* 52, no. 2 (April 1988), pp. 35–48.

11. Kenneth Clow, David Kurtz, John Ozment, and Beng Soo Ong, "The Antecedents of Consumer Expectations of Services: An Empirical Study across Four Industries," *The Journal of Services Marketing* 11 (May–June 1997), pp. 230–48; Ann Marie Thompson and Peter Kaminski, "Psychographic and Lifestyle Antecedents of Service Quality Expectations," *Journal of Services Marketing* 7 (1993), pp. 53–61.

12. Zeithaml, Berry, and Parasuraman, *Delivering Quality Customer Service*.

13. John Adams, "BofA's 'Customer Voice' Sounds off in ePayments," *Direct Access* 17, no. 5 (May 2004), p. 37.

14. Leonard Berry and A. Parasuraman, "Listening to the Customer—The Concept of a Service-Quality Information System," *Sloan Management Review* 38, no. 3 (1997), pp. 65–77; A. Parasuraman and Dhruv Grewal, "Serving Customers and Consumers Effectively in the 21st Century," working paper (1998), University of Miami, Coral Gables, FL.

15. Teena Lyons, "Complain to Me—If You Can," *Knight Ridder Tribune News*, December 4, 2005, p. 1.

16. Press Release "Famed Restaurateur & Entrepreneur Phil Romano Partners with Compass Group," September 26, 2003, www.cgnad.com; Scott Hume, "Phil Romano," January 13, 2006, www.hospitalitymagazine.com (accessed September 18, 2006); Nancy Nichols, "Romano's Revenge," *D Magazine*, December 1, 2004.

17. http://www.nwa.com/plan/index.html (accessed September 20, 2006).

18. Cheryl Dahle, "Four Tires, Free Beef," *Fast Company* 74 (September 2003), p. 36.

19. Jim Poisant, *Creating and Sustaining a Superior Customer Service Organization: A Book about Taking Care of the People Who Take Care of the Customers* (Westport, CT: Quorum Books, 2002); "People-Focused HR Policies Seen as Vital to Customer Service Improvement," *Store*, January 2001, p. 60; Michael Brady and J. Joseph Cronin, "Customer Orientation: Effects on Customer Service Perceptions and Outcome Behaviors," *Journal of Service Research*, February 2001, pp. 241–51; Michael Hartline, James Maxham III, and Daryl McKee, "Corridors of Influence in the Dissemination of Customer-Oriented Strategy to Customer Contact Service Employees," *Journal of Marketing* 64, no. 2 (April 2000), pp. 25–41.

20. Conrad Lashley, *Empowerment: HR Strategies for Service Excellence* (Boston: Butterworth/Heinemann, 2001).

21. "Future Success Powered by Employees," *DSN Retailing Today*, January 2006. 44 (23A) pp. 22–24.

22. Leonard L. Berry, *Discovering the Soul of Service: The Nine Drivers of Sustainable Business Success* (New York: The Free Press, 1999); Bob Nelson, "These Workers Can't Contain Their Excitement," *ABA Bank Marketing* 35, no. 7 (September 2003), p. 14.

23. Alicia Grandey and Analea Brauburger, "The Emotion Regulation behind the Customer Service Smile," in *Emotions in the Workplace: Understanding the Structure and Role of Emotions in Organizational Behavior*, eds. R. Lord, R. Klimoski, and R. Kanfer (San Francisco: Jossey-Bass, 2002); Mara Adelman and Aaron Ahuvia, "Social Support in the Service Sector: The Antecedents, Processes, and Consequences of Social Support in an Introductory Service," *Journal of Business Research* 32 (March 1995), pp. 273–82.

24. Colin Armistead and Julia Kiely, "Creating Strategies for Managing Evolving Customer Service," *Managing Service Quality* 13, no. 2 (2003), pp. 64–171; http://www.robertspector.com/NordWay_extract.html (accessed September 20, 2006).

25. "Marriott Deploys NCR Self-Service Kiosks; Global Hotel Chain Pilots Check-In, Check-Out Solution From World's Leading Self-Service Technology Provider" *TMC Net*, June 3, 2004, http://www.tmcnet.com/usubmit/2004/jun/1045424.htm (accessed September 20, 2006).

26. Barton Goldenburg, "Customer Self-Service: Are you Ready?" *CRM Magazine*, May, 2004, http://www.destinationcrm.com/articles/default.asp?ArticleID=4011 (accessed September 20, 2006).

27. Rhett H. Walker, Margaret Craig-Lees, Robert Hecker, and Heather Francis, "Technology-Enabled Service Delivery: An Investigation of Reasons Affecting Customer Adoption and Rejection," *International Journal of Service Industry Management* 13, no. 1 (2002), pp. 91–107; Mary Jo Bitner, Steven W. Brown, and Matthew L. Meuter, "Technology Infusion in Service Encounters," *Journal of the Academy of Marketing Science* 28, no. 1 (2000), pp. 138–49; Stephen W. Brown, "Service Recovery through IT," *Marketing Management* 6 (Fall 1997), pp. 25–27; P.A. Dabholkar, "Technology-Based Service Delivery: A Classification Scheme for Developing Marketing Strategies," in *Advances in Services Marketing and Management*, Vol. 3, eds. T.A. Swartz, Deborah E. Bowen, and Stephen W. Brown (Greenwich, CT: JAI Press, 1994), pp. 241–71.

28. Armistead and Kiely, "Creating Strategies"; A. Parasuraman, "Technology Readiness Index—A Multiple-Item Scale to Measure Readiness to Embrace New Technologies," *Journal of Service Research* 2, no. 4 (2000), pp. 307–20; C. Voss, "Developing an e-Service Strategy," *Business Strategy* 11, no. 1 (2000), pp. 21–33; J. Walsh and S. Godfrey, "The Internet: A New Era in Customer Service," *European Management Journal* 18, no. 1 (2000), pp. 85–92.

29. "Everyone's Internet = Poor Service & False Advertising," www.complaints.com. June 11, 2000 (accessed September 20, 2006).

30. Subimal Chatterjee, Susan A. Slotnick, and Matthew J. Sobel, "Delivery Guarantees and the Interdependence of Marketing and Operations," *Production and Operations Management* 11, no. 3 (Fall 2002), pp. 393–411; Piyush Kumar, Manohar Kalawani, and Makbool Dada, "The Impact of Waiting Time Guarantees on Customers' Waiting Experiences," *Marketing Science* 16, no. 4 (1999), pp. 676–785.

31. K. Douglas Hoffman, Scott W. Kelley, and H.M. Rotalsky, "Tracking Service Failures and Employee Recovery Efforts," *Journal of Services Marketing* 9, no. 2 (1995), pp. 49–61; Scott W. Kelley and Mark A. Davis, "Antecedents to Customer Expectations for Service Recovery," *Journal of the Academy of Marketing Science* 22 (Winter 1994), pp. 52–61; Terrence J. Levesque and Gordon H.G. McDougall, "Service Problems and Recovery Strategies: An Experiment," *Canadian Journal of Administrative Sciences* 17, no. 1 (2000), pp. 20–37; James G. Maxham III and Richard G. Netemeyer, "A Longitudinal Study of Complaining Customers' Evaluations of Multiple Service Failures and Recovery Efforts," *Journal of Marketing* 66, no. 3 (October 2002), pp. 57–71; Amy K. Smith, Ruth N. Bolton, and Janet Wagner, "A Model of Customer Satisfaction with Service Encounters Involving Failure and Recovery," *Journal of Marketing Research* 36, no. 3 (August 1999), pp. 356–72; Scott R. Swanson and Scott W. Kelley, "Attributions and Outcomes of the Service Recovery Process," *Journal of Marketing Theory and Practice* 9 (Fall 2001), pp. 50–65; Stephen S. Tax and Stephen W. Brown, "Recovering and Learning from Service Failure," *Sloan Management Review* 40, no. 1 (1998), pp. 75–88; Stephen S. Tax, Stephen W. Brown, and Murali Chandrashekaran, "Consumer Evaluations of Service Complaint Experiences: Implications for Relationship Marketing," *Journal of Marketing* 62, no. 2 (April 1998), pp. 60–76; Scott Widmier and Donald W. Jackson Jr., "Examining the Effects of Service Failure, Customer Compensation, and Fault on Customer Satisfaction with Salespeople," *Journal of Marketing Theory and Practice* 10 (Winter 2002), pp. 63–74; Valarie A. Zeithaml and Mary Jo Bitner, *Services Marketing: Integrating Customer Focus across the Firm* (New York: McGraw-Hill, 2003).

32. James Maxham III, "Service Recovery's Influence on Consumer Satisfaction, Positive Word-of-Mouth, and Purchase Intentions," *Journal of Business Research* (October 2001), pp. 11–24; Michael McCollough, Leonard Berry, and Manjit Yadav, "An Empirical Investigation of Customer Satisfaction after Service Failure and Recovery," *Journal of Service Research* (November 2000), pp. 121–37.

33. "Correcting Store Blunders Seen as Key Customer Service Opportunity," *Stores*, January 2001, pp. 60–64; Stephen W. Brown, "Practicing Best-in-Class Service Recovery: Forward-Thinking Firms Leverage Service Recovery to Increase Loyalty and Profits," *Marketing Management*, Summer 2000, pp. 8–10; Tax, Brown, and Chandrashekaran, "Customer Evaluations"; Amy Smith and Ruth Bolton, "An Experimental Investigation of Customer Reactions to Service Failures and Recovery Encounters: Paradox or Peril?" *Journal of Service Research* 1 (August 1998), pp. 23–36; Cynthia Webster and D. S. Sundaram, "Service Consumption Criticality in Failure Recovery," *Journal of Business Research* 41 (February 1998), pp. 153–59.

34. Ko de Ruyter and Martin Wetsel, "The Impact of Perceived Listening Behavior in Voice-to-Voice Service Encounters," *Journal of Service Research* (February 2000), pp. 276–84.

35. Hooman Estelami, "Competitive and Procedural Determinants of Delight and Disappointment in Consumer Complaint Outcomes," *Journal of Service Research* (February 2000), pp. 285–300.

36. Michael Tsiros, Anne Roggeveen, and Dhruv Grewal (2006), "Compensation as a Service Recovery Strategy: When Does It Work?" Unpublished Working Paper, Babson College. Amy K. Smith, Ruth N. Bolton, and Janet Wagner, "A Model of Customer Satisfaction with Service Encounters Involving Failure and Recovery," *Journal of Marketing Research* 36 (August 1999), pp. 356–72. Scott R. Swanson and Scott W. Kelley, "Attributions and Outcomes of the Service Recovery Process," *Journal of Marketing: Theory and Practice* 9 (Fall 2001), pp. 50–65.

37. David Carter and Darren Rovell, "It's a Homerun: Customer Service Greatness in the Minor Leagues," *Financial Times*, June 27, 2003.

38. Stephen S. Tax and Stephen W. Brown, "Recovering and Learning from Service Failure," *Sloan Management Review* 40, no. 1 (Fall 1998), pp. 75–89.

39. USAA, "USAA to Reduce Auto Insurance Rates by Average of 7 Percent," press release, June 18, 2004, http://www.usaa.com (accessed September 20, 2006).

40. L. Biff Motley, "Dealing with Unsatisfied Customers," *ABA Bank Marketing* 35, no. 10 (December 2003), p. 45.

41. This case was written by Morgan Wolters in conjunction with the textbook authors (Dhruv Grewal and Michael Levy) for the basis of class discussion rather than to illustrate either effective or ineffective marketing practice.

42. Mary Ellen Burris, "New PA Service Center," http://www.wegmans.com (accessed September 19, 2005); Mary Ellen Burns, "ACHOOOO...," http://www.wegmans.com (accessed September 19, 2005); "The Wegmans Way," *Fortune* 151, no. 2 (January 24, 2005), pp. 62–64, 66, 68; Mary Glynn, "Wegmans Plans to Rebuild a Depew Store," *Knight Ridder Tribune Business News*, June 8, 2005, p. 1.

Chapter 13

1. Michael Arndt, "Giving Fast Food a Run for Its Money," *BusinessWeek*, April 17, 2006, pp. 62, 64; "Panera Adds Natural Chicken," *Restaurant Business* 104 (10) (June 15, 2005) p. 51.

2. Kent B. Monroe, *Pricing: Making Profitable Decisions*, 3rd ed. (New York: McGraw-Hill, 2003); Dhruv Grewal, Kent B. Monroe, and R. Krishnan, "The Effects of Price Comparison Advertising on Buyers' Perceptions of Acquisition Value and Transaction Value," *Journal of Marketing* 62 (April 1998), pp. 46–60.

3. "American Shoppers Economize, Show Greater Interest in Nutrition and Awareness of Food Safety Issues, According to Trends in the United States: Consumer Attitudes and the Supermarket 2003," http://www.fmi.org/media/mediatext.cfm?id=534 (accessed December 10, 2005): A key finding was that, low price third most important feature in selecting a supermarket and viewed important by 83%; see also "The New Value Equation," *Supermarket News* 50 (June 10, 2002), p. 12.

4. Anthony Miyazaki, Dhruv Grewal, and Ronnie Goodstein, "The Effects of Multiple Extrinsic Cues on Quality Perceptions: A Matter of Consistency," *Journal of Consumer Research* 32 (June 2005), pp. 146–53; William B. Dodds, Kent B. Monroe, and Dhruv Grewal, "The Effects of Price, Brand, and Store Information on Buyers' Product Evaluations," *Journal of Marketing Research* 28 (August 1991), pp. 307–19.

5. Robert J. Dolan, "Note on Marketing Strategy," *Harvard Business School* (November 2000), pp. 1–17; Dhruv Grewal and Larry D. Compeau, "Pricing and Public Policy: An Overview and a Research Agenda," *Journal of Public Policy & Marketing* 18 (Spring 1999), pp. 3–11.

5. Monroe, *Pricing: Making Profitable Decisions*.

6. Tony Bacon and Paul Day, *The Fender Book: A Complete History of Fender Electric Guitars*, 2nd ed. (London: Balafon Books, 1998); http://www.fender.com (accessed September 20, 2006); http://www.mrgearhead.com/squierfaq/historyfaqSQ.html (accessed September 20, 2006).

7. JetBlue Airways Corporation 10K, "Factsheet," December 31, 2004, http://www.jetblue.com/learnmore/factsheet.html (accessed November 30, 2005).

8. http://www.jetblue.com/learnmore/timeline.html (accessed September 20, 2006).

9. Monroe, *Pricing: Making Profitable Decisions*.

10. http://www.marketingpower.com/mg-dictionary-view669.php? (accessed September 19, 2006).

11. http://www.marketingpower.com/mg-dictionary-view669.php? (accessed September 20, 2006).

12. Joan Lindsey-Mullikin and Dhruv Grewal, "Market Price Variation: The Availability of Internet Market Information," *Journal of the Academy of Marketing Science*, 2006.

13. Ruth N. Bolton and Venkatesh Shankar, "An Empirically Derived Taxonomy of Retailer Pricing and Promotion Strategies," *Journal of Retailing* 79, no. 4 (2003), pp. 213–24; Rajiv Lal and Ram Rao, "Supermarket Competition: The Case of Every Day Low Pricing," *Marketing Science* 16, no. 1 (1997), pp. 60–80.

14. A. R. Rao, M. E. Bergen, and S. Davis, "How to Fight a Price War," *Harvard Business Review* 78 (March–April 2000), pp. 107–16.

15. Rao, Bergen, and Davis, "How to Fight a Price War."

16. Brian M. Campbell, "The Wright Amendment Consumer Penalty," The Campbell-Hill Aviation Group, Inc., June 7, 2005, http://www.setlovefree.com/consumer_penalty.html; Eric Torbenson, "Flights to Missouri not Full: Southwest, American Ticket Sales Are Test Case for Wright Repeal," *Knight Ridder Tribune News,* February 17, 2006, p. 1.

17. *Merriam-Webster's Dictionary of Law*, 1996.

18. "Fujitsu Institutes New Warranty Policy For Plasmavision® Monitors," May 15, 2002, http://www.plasmavision.com/buying_online.htm[o] (accessed January 25, 2005).

19. Joseph P. Bailey, "Electronic Commerce: Prices and Consumer Issues for Three Products: Books, Compact Discs, and Software," *Organization for Economic Cooperation and Development, OECD, GD* 98 (1998), p. 4; J. Yannis Bakos, "Reducing Buyer Search Costs: Implications for Electronic Marketplaces," *Management Science* 43, no. 12 (1997), pp. 1676–92; Erik Brynjolfsson and Michael D. Smith, "Frictionless Commerce? A Comparison of Internet and Conventional Retailers," *Management Science* 46, no. 4 (2000), pp. 563–85; Rajiv Lal and Miklos Sarvary, "When and How Is the Internet Likely to Decrease Price Competition?" *Marketing Science* 18, no. 4 (1999), pp. 485–503; Xing Pan, Brian T. Ratchford, and Venkatesh Shankar, "Can Price Dispersion in Online Markets be Explained by Differences in E-Tailer Service Quality?" *Journal of the Academy of Marketing Science* 30, no. 4 (2002), pp. 433–45; Michael D. Smith, "The Impact of Shopbots on Electronic Markets," *Journal of the Academy of Marketing Sciences* 30, no. 4 (2002), pp. 446–54; Michael D. Smith and Erik Brynjolfsson, "Consumer Decision-Making at an Internet Shopbot: Brand Still Matters," *The Journal of Industrial Economics* 49 (December 2001), pp. 541–58; Fang-Fang Tang and Xiaolin Xing, "Will the Growth of Multi-Channel Retailing Diminish the Pricing Efficiency of the Web?" *Journal of Retailing* 77, no. 3 (2001), pp. 319–33; Florian Zettlemeyer, "Expanding to the Internet: Pricing and Communications Strategies When Firms Compete on Multiple Channels," *Journal of Marketing Research* 37 (August 2000), pp. 292–308; Dhruv Grewal, Gopalkrishnan R. Iyer, R. Krishnan, and Arun Sharma, "The Internet and the Price-Value-Loyalty Chain," *Journal of Business Research* 56 (May 2003), pp. 391–98; Gopalkrishnan R. Iyer, Anthony D. Miyazaki, Dhruv Grewal, and Maria Giordano, "Linking Web-Based Segmentation to Pricing Tactics," *Journal of Product & Brand Management* 11, no. 4/5 (2002), pp. 288–302.

20. This case was written by Larry D. Compeau in conjunction with the textbook authors (Dhruv Grewal and Michael Levy) for the basis of class discussion rather than to illustrate either effective or ineffective marketing practice.

Chapter 14

1. http://www.dlp.com/ (accessed September 26, 2006); http://www.business2.com/b2/web/articles/0,17863,1019460,00.html?promoid=yahoo (accessed September 20, 2006); http://www.embedded.com/showArticle.jhtml?articleID=35300003 (accessed September 20, 2005); http://www.pcmag.com/article2/0,1759,1433482,00.asp (accessed September 20, 2005); http://www.amkor.com/news/pressreleases/ShowPR.cfm?ID=222 (accessed September 30, 2005).

2. Thomas T. Nagle and Reed K. Holden, *The Strategy and Tactics of Pricing*, 3rd ed. (Upper Saddle River, NJ: Pearson, 2002).

3. Dhruv Grewal and Jeanne Munger, "Carpet Pro Solutions," case study (2005), unpublished case study, Babson College.

4. Lisa E. Bolton, Luk Warlop, and Joseph W. Alba, "Consumer Perceptions of Price (Un)Fairness," *Journal of Consumer Research* 29 (March 2003), pp. 474–91; Margaret C. Campbell, "Perceptions of Price Unfairness: Antecedents and Consequences," *Journal of Marketing Research* 36 (May 1999), pp. 187–99; Peter R. Darke and Darren W. Dahl, "Fairness and Discounts: The Subjective Value of a Bargain," *Journal of Consumer Psychology* 13, no. 3 (2003), pp. 328–38; Sarah Maxwell, "What Makes a Price Increase Seem 'Fair'?" *Pricing Strategy & Practice* 3, no. 4 (1995), pp. 21–27.

5. Paige Lauren Deiner, "Discount Showdown: Dollar Stores Winning Out over Big-Box Cousins with Customer Service, Convenient Locations," *Knight Ridder Tribune Business News*, March 11, 2006, p. 1.; Cecile B. Corral, "Perdue Tuning Up Dollar General," *Home Textiles Today*, 27, no. 18 (January 30, 2006), p. 6.; Debbie Howell, "Dollar General's Cal Turner Sr. Dead at 85," *DSN Retailing Today* 39, no. 23 (December 11, 2000), pp. 6–7. "Extreme Value Store Shopper," *DSN Retailing Today*, January 5, 2004, p. 4.

6. A. Biswas, E.J. Wilson, and J.W. Licata, "Reference Pricing Studies in Marketing: A Synthesis of Research Results," *Journal of Business Research* 27, no. 3 (1993), pp. 239–56; A. Biswas, "The Moderating Role of Brand Familiarity in Reference Price Perceptions," *Journal of Business Research* 25 (1992), pp. 251–62; A. Biswas and E. Blair, "Contextual Effects of Reference Prices in Retail Advertisements," *Journal of Marketing* 55 (1991), pp. 1–12; Larry D. Compeau and Dhruv Grewal, "Comparative Price Advertising: An Integrative Review," *Journal of Public Policy & Marketing* 17 (Fall 1998), pp. 257–73; Rajesh Chandrashekaran and Dhruv Grewal, "Assimilation of Advertised Reference Prices: The Moderating Role of Involvement," *Journal of Retailing* 79, no. 1 (2003), pp. 53–62; David M. Hardesty and William O. Bearden, "Consumer Evaluations of Different Promotion Types and Price Presentations: The Moderating Role of Promotional Benefit Level," *Journal of Retailing* 79, no. 1 (2003), pp. 17–25.

7. Dhruv Grewal, Kent B. Monroe, and R. Krishnan, "The Effects of Price Comparison Advertising on Buyers' Perceptions of Acquisition Value and Transaction Value," *Journal of Marketing* 62 (April 1998), pp. 46–60.

8. Noreen M. Klein and Janet E. Oglethorpe, "Reference Points in Consumer Decision Making," in *Advances in Consumer Research*, Vol. 14, eds. Melanie Wallendorf and Paul Anderson (Provo, UT: Association for Consumer Research, 1987), pp. 183–87.

9. J.E. Urbany, W.O. Bearden, and D.C. Weilbaker, "The Effect of Plausible and Exaggerated Reference Prices on Consumer Perceptions and Price Search," *Journal of Consumer Research* 15 (1988), pp. 95–110.

10. Michael Levy and Barton A. Weitz, *Retailing Management*, 6th ed. (Burr Ridge, IL: Irwin/McGraw-Hill, 2007).

11. Robert Schindler, "The 99 Price Ending as a Signal of a Low-Price Appeal," *Journal of Retailing* 82, no. 1 (2006).

12. Schindler, "The 99 Price Ending."

13. Merrie Brucks, Valerie A. Zeithaml, and Gillian Naylor, "Price and Brand Name as Indicators of Quality Dimensions for Consumer Durables," *Journal of the Academy of Marketing Science* 28, no. 3 (2000), pp. 359–74; William B. Dodds, Kent B. Monroe, and Dhruv Grewal, "Effects of Price, Brand, and Store Information on Buyers' Product Evaluations," *Journal of Marketing Research* 28 (August 1991), pp. 307–19.

14. Brucks, Zeithaml, and Naylor, "Price and Brand Name as Indicators"; Niraj Dawar and Philip Parker, "Marketing Universals: Consumers' Use of Brand Name, Price, Physical Appearance, and Retailer Reputation as Signals of Product Quality," *Journal of Marketing* 58 (April 1994), pp. 81–95; Dodds, Monroe, and Grewal, "Effects of Price, Brand, and Store Information"; Paul S. Richardson, Alan S. Dick, and Arun K. Jain, "Extrinsic and Intrinsic Cue Effects on Perceptions of Store Brand Quality," *Journal of Marketing* 58 (October 1994), pp. 28–36; Anthony Miyazaki, Dhruv Grewal, and Ronnie Goodstein, "The Effect of Multiple Extrinsic Cues on Quality Perceptions: A Matter of Consistency," *Journal of Consumer Research* 32 (June 2005), pp. 146–153.

15. Marion Hume, "If You've Got It, Flaunt It," *Time*, 25, no. 12 (March 28, 2005), p. 63.; "Karl Lagerfeld: Fashion Designer, France," *BusinessWeek* Online, www.businessweek.com, May 30, 2005 (accessed September 1, 2006).

16. This section draws from Levy and Weitz, *Retailing Management*.

17. Sha Yang and Priya Raghubir, "Can Bottles Speak Volumes? The Effect of Package Shape on How Much to Buy," *Journal of Retailing* 81, no. 4 (2005), pp. 269–281.

18. "Merger and Acquisition Activity Impacts Coupon Promotion Volume, Study Finds," *The Food Institute Report*, March 5, 2001, p. 4.

19. Compeau and Grewal, "Comparative Price Advertising"; Larry D. Compeau, Dhruv Grewal, and Diana S. Grewal, "Adjudicating Claims of Deceptive Advertised Reference Prices: The Use of Empirical Evidence," *Journal of Public Policy & Marketing* 14 (Fall 1994), pp. 52–62; Dhruv Grewal and Larry D. Compeau, "Comparative Price Advertising: Informative or Deceptive?" *Journal of Public Policy & Marketing* 11 (Spring 1992), pp. 52–62; Larry Compeau,

Joan Lindsey-Mullikin, Dhruv Grewal, and Ross Petty, "An Analysis of Consumers' Interpretations of the Semantic Phrases Found in Comparative Price Advertisements," *Journal of Consumer Affairs* 38 (Summer 2004), pp. 178–87.

20. Joanna Grossman, "The End of Ladies Night in New Jersey," *Find Law's Legal Commentary*, 2004, http://writ.news.findlaw.com/grossman/20040615.html (accessed November 29, 2005); Joyce Howard Price, "Ladies Night Ruled Discriminatory," *The Washington Times*, 2004, http://washingtontimes.com/national/20040602-111843-2685r.htm (accessed November 29, 2005).

21. http://www.usatoday.com/life/music/news/2002-09-30-cd-settlement_x.htm (accessed September 30, 2006).

22. http://www.cnn.com/US/9711/04/scotus.antitrust/ (accessed September 20, 2006).

23. http://www.plasmavision.com; *Stereophile Guide to Home Theater*, http://www.guidetohometheater.com (accessed September 20, 2006). This case was written by Larry D. Compeau in conjunction with the textbook authors (Dhruv Grewal and Michael Levy) for the basis of class discussion rather than to illustrate either effective or ineffective marketing practice.

24. *Stereophile Guide to Home Theater* 3, no. 1 (Spring 1997), pp. 26–45.

25. *Stereophile Guide to Home Theater* 4 (September 1998), p. 91.

26. *Stereophile Guide to Home Theater* 6 (July/August 2000), p. 75.

Chapter 15

1. http://www.zara.com/v04/eng/home.php (accessed September 20, 2006); Pankaj Ghemawat and Jose Luis Nueno, "Zara: Fast Fashion," Harvard Business School Case Number 9-703-497 (April 1, 2003); http://www.inditex.com/english/home.htm (accessed July 20, 2006); Guillermo D'Andrea and David Arnold, "Zara," Harvard Business School Case Number 9-503-050 (March 12, 2003); http://www.gapinc.com/financmedia/financmedia.htm (accessed March 13, 2005); http://www.hm.com/us/start/start/index.jsp# (accessed June 4, 2005); http://www.benetton.com/press/ (accessed September 3, 2006); Stephen Tierney, "New Look's Supply Chain Obsession," *Frontline Solutions* 12, no. 6 (October 2003), pp. 24–25.; David Bovet and Joseph Martha, "E-Business and Logistics Unlocking the Rusty Supply Chain," *Logistics Quarterly* 6, no. 4 (Winter 2000), pp. 1–3; Jane M. Folpe, "Zara Has a Made-to-Order Plan for Success," *Fortune* 142, no. 5 (September 2000), pp. 80–82; Carlta Vitzthum, "Just-in-Time Fashion: Spanish Retailer Zara Makes Low-Cost Lines in Weeks by Running Its Own Show," *The Wall Street Journal* (Eastern Edition), May 18, 2001, p. B1.

2. Based on David Simchi-Levi, Philip Kaminsky, and Edith Simchi-Levi, *Designing and Managing the Supply Chain: Concepts, Strategies and Case Studies*, 2d ed. (New York: McGraw-Hill Irwin, 2003); Michael Levy and Barton A. Weitz, *Retailing Management*, 5th ed. (New York: McGraw-Hill Irwin, 2004).

3. http://www.marketingpower.com/live/mg-dictionary.

4. http://www.marketingpower.com/live/mg-dictionary. Definition from the Council of Logistics Management.

5. Navi Radjou, Henry H. Harteveldt, and Colin Teubner, "Airlines: Fix Your MRO Supply Chains to Save Big," *Forrester*, February 4, 2004 (including footnotes 2–5).

6. http://www.marketingpower.com/live/mg-dictionary.

7. "The Idol Life: Michael Dell," http://www.entrepreneur.com/article/0,4621,295495-2,00.html. (accessed September 5, 2006).

8. Steven Burke, "Michael Dell," *CRN*, December 15, 2003; Daniel G. Jacobs, "Anatomy of a Supply Chain," *Transportation and Distribution* 44, no. 6 (June 2003); "What Michael Dell Knows That You Don't," *Fortune Small Business* 12, no. 5 (June 2000), p. 18.

9. Sharyn Leaver, Joshua Walker, and Tamara Mendelsohn, "Hasbro Drives Supply Chain Efficiency with BPM," *Forester Research*, July 22, 2003.

10. Paul Briggs, "Putting the Supply Chain in Perspective [Collaborative Planning, Forecasting & Replenishment]" *Canadian Transportation Logistics* 103, no. 4 (April 2000), p. 16.

11. Case Study, "Nabisco Inc. and Wegmans Food Markets," available at http://www.cpfr.org/cpfr_pdf/08_4_1_Nabisco_And_Wegman_Pilot.pdf.

12. This section draws from Levy and Weitz, *Retailing Management*, Chapter 10.

13. Dan Berthiaume, "Wear Aware," *Chain Store Age, Retail Technology Quarterly*, May 2005, pp. 24A–26A; Alex Niemeyer, Minsok Pak, and Sanjay Ramaswamy, "Smart Tags for Your Supply Chain," *McKinsey Quarterly*, no. 4, 2003, p. 6–10; "Supermarkets Turn to Electronic Price Tags, Self-Service Checkout," *The Orange County Register*, September 9, 2003 (accessed from LexisNexis); Lamont Wood, "Retail's Biggest RFID Project," *Chain Store Age*, October 2004 p. 11A; "RFID Chips Are a Gamble that Business Can't Resist," *Marketing Week*, October 2004, p. 23.

14. Larry Kellam, "P&G Rethinks Supply Chain," *Optimize*, October 2003, p. 35.

15. Laurie Sullivan, "Road Work in China," *InformationWeek* (August 30, 2003), pp. 30–35.

16. Thomas W. Gruen, Daniel S. Corsten, and Sundar Bharadwaj, "Retail out of Stocks: A Worldwide Examination of Extent, Causes, and Consumer Responses," unpublished working paper, May 7, 2002; Nirmalya Kumar, "The Power of Trust in Manufacturer-Retailer Relationships," *Harvard Business Review*, November–December 1996, pp. 92–106; Mark E. Parry and Yoshinobu Sato, "Procter & Gamble: The Wal-Mart Partnership," University of Virginia case #M-0452 (1996).

17. http://www.marketingpower.com/live/mg-dictionary.

18. David J. Kaufmann, "The Big Bang: How Franchising Became an Economic Powerhouse the World Over," *Entrepreneur Magazine*, January 2004, attributed to International Franchise Association (IFA).

19. http://entrepreneur.com/franzone/listings/about/1,5841,1601,00.html?RankId=F5 (accessed April 17, 2006).

20. Ghemawat and Nueno, "ZARA: Fast Fashion."

21. Erin Anderson and Anne Coughlan, "Structure, Governance, and Relationship Management," in *Handbook of Marketing*, eds. B. Weitz and R. Wensley (London: Sage, 2002).

22. Laurie Sullivan, "Best Buy Puts a Spin on RFID," *CommDesign*, October 17, 2005, available at http://www.commsdesign.com/showArticle.jhtml?articleID=172301609 (accessed September 20, 2006); "Security System to Balance Privacy and Supply Chain," *RFID Update*, August 12, 2005, available at www.rfidupdate.com/articles/index.php?id=932 (accessed October 20, 2005); Miyako Ochkubo, Koutarou Suzuki, and Shingo Kinoshita, "RFID Privacy Issues and Technical Challenges," *Communications of the ACM* 48, no. 9 (September 2005), pp. 66–71.

23. Erin Anderson and Barton Weitz, "The Use of Pledges to Build and Sustain Commitment in Distribution Channels," *Journal of Marketing Research* 29 (February 1992), pp. 18–34.

24. This case was written by Jeanne L. Munger in conjunction with the textbook authors (Dhruv Grewal and Michael Levy) for the basis of class discussion rather than to illustrate either effective or ineffective marketing practice. Jeanne Munger is an associate professor at the University of Southern Maine.

25. Mellissa S. Monroe, "Wal-Mart Is Rewriting Rules, Dominating World's Supply Chain," *Knight Ridder Tribune Business News*, November 10, 2003, p. 1.

26. Richard J. Schonberger, "The Right Stuff, Revisited," *MSI* 21, no. 9 (September 2003), p. 26.

27. Staff, "Logisticstoday's 10 Best Supply Chains," *Logisticstoday*, December 2003, p. 20.

Chapter 16

1. Jeff Caplan, "Obscure Logos Could Be All the Rage," *Fort Worth-Star Telegram*, 2004, http://proquest.umi.com (accessed July 7, 2004); "Retail's Recipe for Hip," *Chain Store Age* 79 (2003), pp. 42–44, http://global.factive.com (accessed July 7, 2004); Amy Tsao, "Urban Outfitters Is Dressed to Party," *BusinessWeek Online*, 2004, http://web.lexis-nexis.com (accessed September 20, 2006).

2. http://www.stores.org/pdf/GlobalRetail4.pdf.

3. These statistics exclude motor vehicle and parts dealers and food services. *Retail Industry Indicators* (August 2004), Washington, DC; National Retail Foundation, http://www.census.gov/mrts/www/data/html/nsal05.html, p. 7.

4. Includes North American industrial codes 441-448 and 451-454. U.S. Census Bureau, "2002 Economic Census: Table 1. Advance Summary Statistics for the United States 2002 NAICS Basis," March 24, 2004, http://www.census.gov/econ/census02/advance/TABLE1.HTM; Lisa Wilson, "Retail Industry Study," *SBTDC* (January 2001), http://www.sbtdc.org/pdf/retail.pdf.

5. www.factfinder.census.gov (accessed September 26, 2006).

6. For descriptions of the Wheel of Retailing theory, see Stanley Hollander, "The Wheel of Retailing: What Makes Skilled Managers Succumb to the 'Prosper, Mature, and Decay' Pattern?" *Marketing Management*, Summer 1996, pp. 63–65; Stephen Brown, "Postmodernism, the Wheel of Retailing, and Will to Power," *The International Review of Retail, Distribution, and Consumer Research*, July 1995, pp. 387–412; Arieh Goldman, "Institutional Change in Retailing: An Updated Wheel of Retailing," in *Foundations of Marketing Channels*, eds. A. Woodside, J. Sims, D. Lewison, and I. Wilkenson (Austin, TX: Lone Star, 1978), pp. 193–201. For a description of the Accordion Theory, see Stanley C. Hollander, "Notes on the Retail Accordion," *Journal of Retailing* 42 (Summer 1966), pp. 20–40, 54. For a description of the Dialectic Process theory, see Thomas J. Maronick and Bruce J. Walker, "The Dialectic Evolution of Retailing," in *Proceedings: Southern Marketing Association*, ed. Barnett Greenberg (Atlanta: Georgia State University, 1974), p. 147. For descriptions of Natural Selection theory, see A.C.R. Dreesmann, "Patterns of Evolution in Retailing," *Journal of Retailing* (Spring 1968), pp. 81–96; Murray Forester, "Darwinian Theory of Retailing," *Chain Store Age*, August 1995, p. 8. A summary of these theories can be found in Michael Levy and Barton A. Weitz, *Retailing Management*, 6th ed. (Burr Ridge, IL: Irwin/McGraw-Hill, 2007).

7. Michael Levy, Dhruv Grewal, Robert A. Peterson, and Bob Connolly, "The Concept of the Big Middle," *Journal of Retailing* 81, no. 2 (2005), pp. 83–88.

8. Michael Treacy and Fred Wiersema, *The Disciplines of Market Leaders* (Reading, MA: Addison Wesley, 1995).

9. Robert J. Frank, Elizabeth A. Mihas, Laxman Narasimhan, and Stacey Rauch, "Competing in a Value-Driven World," McKinsey & Company Report, February 2003.

10. Aaron Bernstein, "A Major Swipe at Sweatshops," *BusinessWeek*, May 23, 2005, p. 98; "The Gap (clothing retailer)," http://www.wikipedia.org, (accessed September 24, 2006); "Landmark Workers' Rights Lawsuit Settled," February 16, 2003, http://www.cleanclothes.org (accessed September 20, 2006); Don Tapscott, "Time of Transparency," *Intelligent Enterprise* 7, no. 10 (June 12, 2004), pp. 12–24; "Workers Sue Wal-Mart over Sweatshop Conditions," September 13, 2005, http://www.nosweat.org.uk//article.php?sid=1390 (accessed October 21, 2005); "Disney in China: Making Children's Books at the Nord Race Factories," National Labor Committee, August 2005, http://www.nlcnet.org (accessed September 26, 2006).

11. http://www.sa-intl.org (accessed September 26, 2006).

12. Julie Baker, A. Parasuraman, Dhruv Grewal, and Glenn Voss, "The Influence of Multiple Store Environment Cues on Perceived Merchandise Value and Patronage Intentions," *Journal of Marketing*, 66 (April 2001), pp. 120–41; Eric R. Spangenberg, Ayn E. Crowley, and Pamela W. Henderson, "Improving the Store Environment: Do Olfactory Cues Affect Evaluations and Behaviors?" *Journal of Marketing* 60 (April 1996), pp. 67–80; Michael K. Hui and John E.G. Bateson, "Perceived Control and the Effects of Crowding and Consumer Choice on the Service Experience," *Journal of Consumer Research* 18 (September 1991), pp. 174–84.

13. Leonard Berry, Kathleen Seiders, and Dhruv Grewal, "Understanding Service Convenience," *Journal of Marketing* 66 (July 2002), pp. 1–17.

14. This section draws from Dhruv Grewal, Gopalkrishnan R. Iyer, and Michael Levy, "Internet Retailing: Enablers, Limiters, and Market Consequences," *Journal of Business Research* 57 (2004), pp. 703–13.

15. John M. de Figueiredo, "Finding Sustainable Profitability in Electronic Commerce," *Sloan Management Review* 41 (Spring 2000), pp. 41–52.

16. "Amazon Services and the Bombay Company Announce E-Commerce Alliance," 2003, http://phx.corporate-ir.net (accessed October 4, 2005); "Jeff Bezos," 2003, http://www.wordiq.com/definition/jeff_bezos (accessed September 14, 2006); "Jeffrey P. Bezos," 2000, http://www.ie.metu.edu (accessed September 4, 2005).

17. http://www.senzatempo.com/ (accessed September 30, 2006).

18. Grewal, Iyer, and Levy, "Internet Retailing."

19. Delroy Alexander, "Grocers, Drugstores Mixing It Up in Food Fight," *Chicago Tribune*, March 14, 2004 (accessed from LexisNexis).

20. Dan Nephin, "Sheetz Success Starting to Take Off," *Pittsburgh Post Gazette*, February 17, 2004 (accessed from LexisNexis).

21. Tracy Mullin, "Reinventing Supermarkets," *Chain Store Age* 81, no. 7 (2005).

22. Mark Hamstra, "Whole Foods Sees Benefits From Wal-Mart's Incursion," *SN: Supermarket News* 54, no. 20 (2006).

23. Julia Boorstin and Eugenia Levenson, "Here's Mr. Macy," *Fortune*, November 16, 2005.

24. Faye Brookman, "Brooks Jumps to 4th in Drugstore Ranks," *WWD* 187, no. 74, (April 9, 2004), p. 9; "Industry: Drug Stores," http://www.finance.yahoo.com (accessed September 4, 2006).

25. "An Industry That's Regaining Its Fighting Trim," *Chain Drug Review*, June 7, 2004, p. 20.

26. Thomas Lee, "Supervalu's Extreme Grocery Discounter Is Star Performer," *Minneapolis Star Tribune*, April 16, 2004 (online access); Brent Shavely, "Save-A-Lot Expansion Targets Underserved Detroiters," *Crain's Detroit Business* 20, no. 42 (October 18, 2004), p. 33; Teresa F. Lindeman, "Limited Assortment Grocery Stores Battle Supermarkets in Pennsylvania," *Knight Ridder Tribune Business News*, October 17, 2004, p. 1.

27. Tim Craig, "The Closeout Secret Is Out," *DSN Retailing Today* 42, no. 11 (June 9, 2003), p. 11.

28. David P. Schulz, "Triversity Top 100 Retailers: The Nation's Biggest Retail Companies," http://www.stores.org, 2001 (accessed September 5, 2006).

29. This case was written by Jeanne L. Munger (University of Southern Maine) in conjunction with the textbook authors Dhruv Grewal and Michael Levy for the basis of class discussion rather than to illustrate either effective or ineffective marketing practice. The authors thank Max Ward, Vice President of Technology at Staples, who provided valuable input for the development of this case. They also acknowledge that parts of the case are based on information provided by W. Caleb McCann (in collaboration with J.P. Jeannet, Dhruv Grewal, and Martha Lanning), "Staples," in *Fulfillment in E-Business*, ed. Petra Schuber, Ralf Wolfle, and Walter Dettling (Germany: Hanser, 2001) pp. 239–52 (in German).

30. http://www.bizjournals.com/boston/stories/2004/03/01/daily53.html (accessed September 20, 2006).

Chapter 17

1. Ann M. Mack, "Driving Through the Clutter: Volvo's Car Marketing," *BrandWeek*, November 27, 2000, pp. IQ34–37; Jim Nail, "Integrated Marketing Best Practices," Forrester Research Wholeview Tech Strategy Research Brief Series, April 1, 2003[0]; Donald I. Hammonds, "Toyota Scion a Hit at only $12,400," *Pittsburgh Post-Gazette*, Wednesday, June 16, 2004, http://www.post-gazette.com/pg/04168/332359.stm (accessed September 20, 2006).

2. T. Duncan and C. Caywood, "The Concept, Process, and Evolution of Integrated Marketing Communication," in *Integrated Communication: Synergy of Persuasive Voices*, eds. E. Thorson and J. Moore (Mahwah, NJ: Lawrence Erlbaum Associates, 1996); http://jimc.medill.northwestern.edu/2000/pettegrew.htm.

3. Deborah J. MacInnis and Bernard J. Jaworski, "Information Processing from Advertisements: Toward an Integrative Framework," *Journal of Marketing* 53, no. 4 (October 1989), pp. 1–23.

4. Deborah J. MacInnis, Christine Moorman, and Bernard J. Jaworski, "Enhancing and Measuring Consumers' Motivation, Opportunity," *Journal of Marketing* 55, no. 4 (October 1991), pp. 32–554. Joan Meyers-Levy, "Elaborating on Elaboration: The Distinction between Relational and Item-Specific Elaboration," *Journal of Consumer Research* 18 (December 1991), pp. 358–67.

5. E.K. Strong, *The Psychology of Selling* (New York: McGraw Hill, 1925).

6. John Philip Jones, "What Makes Advertising Work?," *The Economic Times*, July 24, 2002.

7. http://www.legamedia.net/lx/result/match/0591dfc9787c111b1b24dde6d61e43c5/index.php.

8. http://www.mediafinder.com (accessed September 4, 2006).

9. http://www.oxygen.com/basics/founders.aspx (accessed September 5, 2006); http://www.oxygen.com/press (accessed September 6, 2006); Nadine Heintz, "Thinking Inside the Box," *Inc.* 26, no. 7 (July, 2004), pp. 90–95; Jon Lafayette, "Oxygen Turns to Its Stars," *TelevisionWeek*, 24, no. 9, (February 28, 2005), pp. 3–4.

10. Jef I. Richards and Catharine M. Curran, "Oracles on Advertising: Searching for a Definition," *Journal of Advertising* 31, no. 2 (2002), p. 63.

11. http://www.onlinewbc.gov/docs/starting/glossary.html#d (accessed October 11, 2004).

12. Don Peppers, Martha Rogers, and Bob Dorf, "Is Your Company Ready for One-to-One Marketing?" *Harvard Business Review* 77, no. 1 (1999), pp. 151–61; http://www.managingchange.com/guestcon/highimp.htm (accessed September 26, 2006).

13. Carl Obermiller and Eric R. Spangenberg, "On the Origin and Distinctness of Skepticism toward Advertising," *Marketing Letters* 11, no. 4 (2000), p. 311.

14. http://www.yoplait.com/breastcancer_lids.aspx (accessed September 22, 2006).

15. Jackie Huba, "A Just Cause Creating Emotional Connections with Customers," 2003, http://www.inc.com/articles/2003/05/25537.html.

16. http://www.yoplait.com/breastcancer_lids.aspx (accessed October 25, 2004).

17. http://www.coneinc.com/Pages/buzz3.html (accessed October 22, 2004).

18. "iUpload Takes Datamations First Blogging Win," February 28, 2006, www.itmanagement.eartweb.com, (accessed April 19, 2006); Nicole Ziegler Dizon, "Corporations Enter into World of Blogs," *San Francisco Gate*, June 6, 2006, www.sfgate.com (accessed September 26, 2006); Mark Berger, "Annie's Homegrown: 'Bernie's Blog' Case Study," www.backbonemedia.com (accessed September 26, 2006); "Corporate Blogging Survey" www.backbonemedia.com (accessed September 26, 2006).

19. "iUpload Takes Datamations First Blogging Win," February 28, 2006, www.itmanagement.eartweb.com, (accessed April 19, 2006); Dizon, "Corporations Enter into World of Blogs"; Mark Berger, "Annie's Homegrown: 'Bernie's Blog' Case Study," www.backbonemedia.com (accessed September 24, 2006); "Corporate Blogging Survey" www.backbonemedia.com (accessed September 24, 2006).

20. http://www.consideryourselfwarned.com (accessed September 20, 2006); http://www.childrennow.org/newsroom/news-04/cam-ra-05-03-04.cfm (accessed October 11, 2004).

21. Michael Singer, "Microsoft, SINA Send SMS Message to China," 2004, http://internetnews.com/ent-news/article.php/1585181 (accessed September 25, 2006).

22. This section draws from Michael Levy and Barton A. Weitz, *Retailing Management*, 6th ed. (Burr Ridge, IL: McGraw-Hill/Irwin, 2007).

23. http://www.riger.com/know_base/media/understanding.html (accessed November 15, 2004).

24. http://www.cdc.gov/tobacco/overview/chron96.htm (accessed September 26, 2006).

25. In general, commercial speech is defined as a communication that proposes a commercial transaction, such as a specific offer to buy or sell a product (e.g., Virginia Pharmacy sells prescription drugs). Speech that does not specifically propose a commercial transaction may still be considered commercial speech. Factors to consider (*Bolger* v. *Youngs Drug Products*) include (1) appearance in an advertisement, (2) reference to a specific product, (3) reference to a product generically when the speaker has strong market position, and (4) the economic motivation of speaker. However, the mere fact that a speech is made for an economic motive does not make it commercial speech (*New York Times* v. *Sullivan*). Speech may be "commercial" even if it includes references that "link the product to a current public debate." http://www.kylewood.com/firstamendment/commercial.htm.

26. Roger Parloff, "Talk Ain't Cheap: First Amendment Ruling against Nike," *Marketing Magazine*, September 9, 2002; Roberto Ceniceros, "Suit over Nike Public Statements Upheld," *Business Insurance*, May 12, 2002; Eugene Volokh, "Nike and the Free Speech Knot," *The Wall Street Journal*, June 30, 2003, p. A16; Anonymous, "Supreme Court Won't Hear Nike Speech Case," *The Quill* 91, no. 6 (2003), p. 6; Russell Mokhiber, "Nike's Come from Behind Win," *Multinational Monitor* 24, no. 10 (2003), p. 7.

27. http://www.cnn.com/2004/TECH/internet/04/26/godsend.controversy.reut/ (accessed September 5, 2005).

28. Richard Kielbowicz and Linda Lawson, "Unmasking Hidden Commercials in Broadcasting: Origins of the Sponsorship Identification Regulations 1927–1963," 2004, http://www.law.indiana.edu/fclj/pubs/v56/no2/Kielbowicz%20Finals%20round%20IV.pdf (accessed September 4, 2005). More case/settlement details in IM.

29. http://www.onpoint-marketing.com/stealth-marketing.htm (accessed September 20, 2006).

30. Rob Walker, "The Hidden (in Plain Sight) Persuaders," *The New York Times*, December 5, 2004, p. 69.

31. http://www.marketingterms.com/dictionary/viral_marketing/ (accessed September 26, 2006).

32. K. Onah Ha, "It's a Neopet World: Popular Site for Kids Stirs Controversy," *San Jose Mercury News*, September 14, 2004.

33. Christopher Reynolds, "Game Over," *American Demographics* 26, no. 1 (2004), pp. 35–39.

34. This case was written by Catherine Curran-Kelley in conjunction with the textbook authors (Dhruv Grewal and Michael Levy) for the basis of class discussion rather than to illustrate either effective or ineffective marketing practice. Catherine Curran-Kelley is an assistant professor at the University of Massachusetts at Dartmouth.

35. Jonathan Fahey, "For the Discriminating Body-Piercer," *Forbes* 171, no. 10 (2003), p. 136.

36. Jean Halliday, "Toyota Goes Guerilla to Roll Scion," *Advertising Age* 74, no. 32 (2003), p. 4.

37. Halliday, "Toyota Goes Guerilla," p. 17.

Chapter 18

1. Lamar Outdoor Advertising, "Altoids Curiously Strong Mints," case study, http://www.lamaroutdoor.com/main/whylamar/CaseStudies/Altoids.cfm (accessed September 26, 2005).

2. Julie Jargon, "Wrigley's New Mints Are Curiously Weak," *Chicago Business*, January 7, 2006, www.chicagobusiness.com/cgi-bin/news.pl?id=19051 (accessed September 26, 2006); "Press Release: Ice Breakers Liquid Ice Causes First-Ever Disagreement between Superstars Hilary and Haylie Duff," February 18, 2005, www.hersheyfoods.com (accessed September 26, 2006).

3. Jef I. Richards and Catherine M. Curran, "Oracles on 'Advertising': Searching for a Definition," *Journal of Advertising* 31, no. 2 (Summer 2002), pp. 63–77.

4. http://www.brandweek.com/bw/news/financial/article_display.jsp?vnu_content_id=1001615315 (accessed September 26, 2006); "Global Ad Spending Expected To Grow 6%," *Brandweek*, December 06, 2005.

5. Raymond R. Burke and Thomas K. Srull, "Competitive Interference and Consumer Memory for Advertising," *Journal of Consumer Research* 15 (June 1988), pp. 55–68; Kevin Lane Keller, "Memory Factors in Advertising: The Effect of Advertising Retrieval Cues on Brand Evaluation," *Journal of Consumer Research* 14 (December 1987), pp. 316–33; Kevin Lane Keller, "Memory and Evaluation Effects

in Competitive Advertising Environments," *Journal of Consumer Research* 17 (March 1991), pp. 463–77; Robert J. Kent and Chris T. Allen, "Competitive Interference Effects in Consumer Memory for Advertising: The Role of Brand Familiarity," *Journal of Marketing* 58, no. 3 (July 1994), pp. 97–106.

6. Anthony Bianco, "The Vanishing Mass Market," *BusinessWeek*, July 12, 2004, pp. 61–68.

7. http://retailindustry.about.com/library/bl/q2/bl_um041701.htm (accessed September 26, 2006).

8. http://www.inastrol.com/Articles/990601.htm (accessed September 26, 2006).

9. http://advertising.utexas.edu/research/terms/index.asp#O (accessed September 26, 2006).

10. Matthew Shum, "Does Advertising Overcome Brand Loyalty? Evidence from the Breakfast Cereal Market," *Journal of Economics and Management Strategy* 13, no. 2 (2004), pp. 77–85.

11. http://www.gotmilk.com/fun/decade/year_1993.html (accessed September 26, 2006).

12. http://advertising.utexas.edu/research/terms/index.asp#P (accessed November 15, 2004).

13. http://www.grantstream.com/glossary.htm (accessed September 26, 2006).

14. http://www.adcouncil.org/research/adweek_report/ (accessed November 15, 2004).

15. http://www.apha.org/journal/nation/truthcover0504.htm (accessed September 26, 2006).

16. Alina Tugend, "Cigarette Makers Take Anti-Smoking Ads Personally," *The New York Times*, October 27, 2002, Business section.

17. http://www.aef.com/06/news/data/2003/2239 (accessed October 15, 2004).

18. Theodore Leavitt, *The Marketing Imagination* (New York: The Free Press, 1986).

19. George E. Belch and Michael A. Belch, *Advertising and Promotion: An Integrated Marketing Communications Perspective*, 7th ed. (New York: McGraw-Hill/Irwin, 2007).

20. http://www.kleenex.com/us/av/index.asp (accessed September 26, 2006).

21. Bret A.S. Martin, Bodo Lang, and Stephanie Wong, "Conclusion, Explicitness in Advertising: The Moderating Role of Need for Cognition and Argument Quality on Persuasion," *Journal of Advertising* 32, no. 4 (2004), pp. 57–65.

22. Michael Petracca and Madeleine Sorapure, eds., *Common Culture: Reading and Writing about American Popular Culture* (Upper Saddle River, NJ: Prentice Hall, 1998).

23. http://wps.prenhall.com/ca_ph_ebert_busess_3/0,6518,224378-,00.html.

24. http://www.admedia.org/ (accessed September 26, 2006).

25. William F. Arens, *Contemporary Advertising*, 8th ed. (New York: McGraw Hill, 2003).

26. http://adsoftheworld.com/media/print/buenos_aires_zoo_ape.

27. http://www.kraftfoods.com/jello/main.aspx?s=&m=jlo_news_jun04.

28. Dean M. Krugman, Leonard N. Reid, S. Watson Dunn, and Arnold M. Barban, *Advertising: Its Role in Modern Marketing* (New York: The Dryden Press, 1994), pp. 221–26.

29. Stanford L. Grossbart and Lawrence A. Crosby, "Understanding Bases of Parental Concern and Reaction to Children's Food Advertising," *Journal of Marketing* 48, no. 3 (1984), pp. 79–93; Brian M. Young, "Does Food Advertising Influence Children's Food Choices? A Critical Review of Some of the Recent Literature," *International Journal of Advertising* 22, no. 4 (2003), p. 441.

30. http://ods.od.nih.gov/factsheets/DietarySupplements.asp (accessed September 26, 2006).

31. Catharine M. Curran and Jef I. Richards, "The Regulation of Children's Advertising in the US," *The International Journal of Advertising and Marketing to Children* 2, no. 2 (2000).

32. http://advertising.utexas.edu/research/terms/index.asp#O (accessed September 26, 2006).

33. This section draws from Tom Duncan, *Principles of Advertising and IMC*, 2nd ed. (Burr Ridge, IL: Irwin/McGraw-Hill, 2005).

34. http://www.pillsbury.com/bakeoff/index.asp (accessed September 25, 2006).

35. http://www.msnbc.msn.com/id/7357071/ (accessed September 26, 2006).

36. http://www.engadget.com/entry/1234000103038638/ (accessed September 26, 2006).

37. http://www.itvx.com/SpecialReport.asp (accessed September 26, 2006).

38. http://www.snopes.com/business/market/mandms.asp (accessed September 26, 2006).

39. http://www.itvx.com/SpecialReport.asp (accessed September 26, 2006).

40. Betsy Spethmann, "For a Limited Time Only," *Promo: Ideas, Connections and Brand*, 2004, http://promomagazine.com/mag/marketing_limited_time/.

41. http://www.meowmix.com/newsevents/meowcafe.asp (accessed September 26, 2006).

42. This case is based on material from Stephanie Thompson, "Dole Pumps Fun into Fruit in $20M Effort," *Brandweek*, March 29, 1999; http:// www.dole.com/; Stuart Aizenberg, "Dole Introduces Fruit Bowls and EZ-O Fruit Snacks," *Automatic Merchandiser*, September 1, 2001; Daily & Associates, "Dole Fruit Bowls 2002 Franchise Advertising Strategy"; Betta Gallego, Dole Food Company, "Presentation to the Association of National Advertisers" (ANA), April 21, 2004; "'Good-For-You' Snacks Poised to Transform Snack Market; Nutritional Snacks Outperform More Traditional Products Over 5-Year Period," *PR Newswire*, June 22, 2004. This case was written by Catherine Curran-Kelley in conjunction with the textbook authors (Dhruv Grewal and Michael Levy) for the basis of class discussion rather than to illustrate either effective or ineffective marketing practice. Catherine Curran-Kelley is an assistant professor at the University of Massachusetts at Dartmouth.

Chapter 19

1. "Marty Rodriguez," www.c21martyrodriguez.com (accessed September 26, 2006); Michelle Hofman, "Minority Companies Make a Difference," *Realtor Magazine Online*, July 1, 2003, www.realtor.org (accessed September 26, 2006).

2. U.S. Department of Labor, "Occupational Employment and Wages: Sales and Related Occupations," May 2004.

3. This section draws from Mark W. Johnston and Greg W. Marshall, *Relationship Selling and Sales Management* (Burr Ridge, IL: Irwin/McGraw-Hill, 2004).

4. John Anderson, "The Ultimate Sales Force," *Inc.*, June 2004, http://www.inc.com/magazine/20040601/sales_ultimate.html (accessed September 26, 2006); Kate Milani, "Renegades Rule in Outsourced Sales," *Baltimore Business Journal* 22, no. 16 (September 3, 2004), http://www.bizjournals.com/baltimore/stories/2004/09/06/smallb1.html?page=1 (accessed September 24, 2006); Eilene Zimmerman, "How I Got Here," *Sales and Marketing Management* 155, no. 11 (November 2003), p. 64; http://www.fusionsalespartners.com/; [o] Kimberly L. McCall, "Straight to the Outsource: Feeling the Crunch? Then It May Be Time to Look Outside Your Company for Help," *Entrepreneur*, September 2003, http://www.findarticles.com/p/articles/mi_moDTI/is_9_31/ai_107524477 (accessed September 25, 2006).

5. Reed Research Group, "Evaluating the Cost of Sales Calls," *Corporate Advertising Research Reports (CARR)*, http://www.cahnerscarr.com (accessed October 26, 2004).

6. Michael Beverland, "Contextual Influences and the Adoption and Practice of Relationship Selling in a Business-to-Business Setting: An Exploratory Study," *Journal of Personal Selling and Sales Management*, Summer 2001, p. 207.

7. Bill Stinnett, *Think Like Your Customer*, 1st ed. (Burr Ridge, IL: McGraw-Hill, 2004).

8. Johnston and Marshall, *Relationship Selling and Sales Management*.

9. http://www.housewares.org/ihshow/ (accessed September 25, 2006).

10. Barton A. Weitz, Harish Sujan, and Mita Sujan, "Knowledge, Motivation, and Adaptive Behavior: A Framework for Improving Selling Effectiveness," *Journal of Marketing*, October 1986, pp. 174–91.

11. http://www.quotedb.com/quotes/1303 (accessed September 20, 2006).

12. Mark W. Johnston and Greg W. Marshall, *Churchill/Ford/Walker's Sales Force Management*, 7th ed. (Burr Ridge, IL: McGraw-Hill/Irwin, 2002).

13. Johnston and Marshall, *Churchill/Ford/Walker's Sales Force Management*.

14. "Ethical Breach," *Sales & Marketing Management*, July 2004.

15. Erin Stout, "Doctoring Sales," *Salesandmarketing.com*, May 2001; "Pushing Pills; Pharmaceuticals," *The Economist* 366, no. 8311 (February 15, 2003), p. 65; R. Stephen Parker and Charles E. Pettijohn, "Ethical Considerations in the Use of Direct-to-Consumer Advertising and Pharmaceutical Promotions: The Impact on Pharmaceutical Sales and Physicians," *Journal of Business Ethics* 48, no. 3 (December 2, 2003), p. 279; "Pharmaceutical Sales Ethics: New Reforms or Business As Usual?" press release, July 23, 2004, http://www.medzilla.com/press72304.html (accessed September 26, 2006); Kate Moore and Jahi Harvey, "Drug Companies Push Pills to Doctors ," *MorningJournal.com*, August 7, 2002.

16. http://www.marketingpower.com/live/mg-dictionary.

17. http://www.compusa.com, Technology Services (accessed September 15, 2006).

18. Johnston and Marshall, *Relationship Selling and Sales Management*, pp. 375–6; Johnston and Marshall, *Churchill/Ford/Walker's Sales Force Management*.

19. Rene Y. Darmon, "Where Do the Best Sales Force Profit Producers Come From?" *Journal of Personal Selling and Sales Management* 13, no. 3 (1993), pp. 17–29.

20. Julie Chang, "Born to Sell?" *Sales and Marketing Management*, July 2003, p. 36.

21. http://www.sumtotalsystems.com (accessed September 4, 2006).

22. Laura Heller, "Cutting Commissions Is the Key That Turns Merchandise—and Turns on the Fun," *DSN Retailing Today* 42 (September 8, 2003), p. 17.

23. "Mary Kay: Where's the Money," http://www.marykay.com (accessed September 5, 2006); http://www.Marykay.com/lsoulier; "Mary Kay Museum," www.addisontexas.net (accessed September 5, 2006).

24. Johnston and Marshall, *Relationship Selling* p. 368; Bill Kelley, "Recognition Reaps Rewards," *Sales and Marketing Management*, June 1986, p. 104 [reprinted from Thomas R. Wotruba, John S. Macfie, and Jerome A. Collem, "Effective Sales Force Recognition Programs," in *Industrial Marketing Management* 20, pp. 9–15].

25. For a discussion of common measures used to evaluate salespeople, see Johnston and Marshall, *Churchill/Ford/Walker's Sales Force Management*, p. 482.

26. This hypothetical case was developed by Jeanne Munger (University of Southern Maine) in conjunction with the textbook authors (Dhruv Grewal and Michael Levy) as a basis for class discussion rather than to illustrate either effective or ineffective marketing practice.

credits

Chapter 1

Photos/ads: p. 5, ©2006 Google; p. 6, ©AOL LLC.; p. 6, [eBay Mark] is a trademark of eBay Inc.; p. 7, AP Photo/Keystone, Walter Bieri; p. 9, Photo by ChinaFotopress/Getty Images; p. 10, Shooting Star; p. 11, Photo by Thos Robinson/Getty Images; p. 12, ©Michael Hruby; p. 12, Copyright © H&H Bagels 2006; p. 13, ©Henry Diltz/CORBIS; p. 15, Courtesy National Fluid Milk Processor Promotion Board; Agency: Lowe Worldwide, Inc.; p. 16, H. Armstrong Roberts/Retrofile/Getty Images; p. 16, Jamie Grill/Iconica/Getty Images; p. 16, ©Royalty-Free/Corbis; p. 16, Claran Griffin/Stockbyte Platinum/Getty Images; p.16, © Royalty-Free/Corbis; p. 18, Andrew Ward/Life File/Getty Images; p. 20, Courtesy Zara International, Inc.; p. 20, Courtesy easyJet; p. 21, Courtesy H&M, Hennes & Mauritz L.P.; p. 21, Courtesy of Nestle S.A.; p. 21, Courtesy of Honda North America, Inc.; p. 21, Courtesy SWATCH LTP, www.swatch.com; p. 23, McGraw-Hill Companies, Inc./Gary He, photographer; p. 23, Courtesy Scion, Toyota Motor Sales, U.S.A., Inc.; p. 26, Shooting Star; p. 26, Photo by Thomas Cooper/Getty Images; p. 29, These Materials have been reproduced with the permission of eBay, Inc. COPYRIGHT © 2006 EBAY INC. ALL RIGHTS RESERVED.

Exhibits: Exhibit 1.10, http://www.benjerry.com/our_company/our_mission/index.cfm.

Chapter 2

Photos/ads: p. 31, Photo by Pascal Le Segrtain/Getty Images; p. 34, Used with permission. © Mothers Against Drunk Drivers 2005; p. 35, ©Michael Hruby; p. 36, ©Michael Hruby; p. 37, The McGraw-Hill companies, Inc./Andrew Resek, photographer; p. 39, Courtesy SIRIUS Satellite Radio; p. 40, Photo courtesy Staples, Inc.; p. 42, Courtesy DaimlerChrysler Corporation; p. 44, Frederic J. Brown/AFP/Getty Images; p. 45, ©Michael Hruby; p. 46, Courtesy Orfalea Family Foundation; p. 48, Roger Tully/Stone/Getty Images; p. 49, Courtesy Crispin Porter & Bogusky/Miami; p. 50, Courtesy Team One Advertising; p. 51, Courtesy of Southwest Airline; p. 54, The McGraw-Hill Companies, Inc./Jill Braaten, photographer.

Chapter 3

Photos/ads: p. 60, Courtesy McNeil Pharmeceuticals; p. 62, Dynamic Graphics/JupiterImages; p. 63, AP Photo/Pat Sullivan; p. 65, © Dennis MacDonald/Photo Edit; p. 67, Ryan McVay/Getty Images; p. 67, Courtesy The Coca-Cola Company; p. 72, Royalty-Free CORBIS; p. 74, cMichael Hruby; p. 75, Courtesy Brown-Forman Wines; p. 76, ©Digital Vision; p.77, AP Photo/Mario Lopez; p. 83, Dynamic Graphics/JupiterImages.

Exhibits/boxes: Exhibit 3.1, Gallup Poll, "Attitudes about the Ethical Standards of Various Professions". Used by permission; Exhibit 3.2, "American Marketing Association's Code of Ethics, Ethical Norms and Values for Marketers" (www.marketing-power.com). Reprinted by permission of The American Marketing Association; Exhibit 3.6, Adapted by permission of the author from Kate McKone-Sweet, Danna Greenberg, and Lydia Moland, "Approaches to Ethical Decision Making," Babson College Case Development Center, 2003; Adding Value 3.2, Elizabeth Butler, "Six Flags New Orleans Rides Out Crisis after Deadly Park Incident," New Orleans City Business, July 28, 2003, p. 1. Used by permission; Exhibit 3.8, Tom Morris, The Art of Achievement: Mastering the 7Cs of Success in Business and in Life, Fine Communications, 2003. Used by permission.

Chapter 4

Photos/ads: p.86, Courtesy Curves International, Inc.; p.89, Courtesy The Gillette Company; p.89, Courtesy Energizer Holdings, Inc.; p.90, AP Photo/Al Behrman; p.92, Jack Hollingsworth/Getty Images; p.94, Photo by Ed Taylor/Taxi/Getty Images; p.95, Photo by Brian Bahr/Getty Images; p.95, ©Chuck Savage/CORBIS; p.96, BananaStock/JupiterImages; p.97, Courtesy of Hammacher Schleemmer, www.hammacher.com; p.97, AP Photo/Ed Betz; p.98, ©Brent Jones; p.99, Comstock/PictureQuest; p.100, ©2006 Oldemarak, LLC. Reprinted with permission. The Wendy's name, design and logo are registered trademarks of Oldemark, Llc and are licensed to Wendy's International, Inc.; p.101, Courtesy Ford Motor Company; p.103, Photo by CBS Photo Archive/Getty Images; p.104, AP Photo/Ric Feld; p.105, Kaz Chiba/Getty Images; p.109, Photo by Tim Boyle/Getty Images; p.111, Sebastian D'Souza/AFP/Getty Images; p.114, Courtesy Stonyfield Farm; p.115, Courtesy Stonyfield Farm.

Exhibits: Exhibit 4.5, "Gen Y and the future of mall retailing," American Demographics, December 2002 24. (11) p.J1. Used by permission of Crain Communications; Exhibit 4.8, Reprinted by permission of Jon T. Kilpinen, Department of Geography and Meterology, Valparaiso University; Exhibit 4.14, Reprinted with permission of Thomas Holmes.

Chapter 5

Photos/ads: p.118, Reproduced by permission of Netflix, Inc., Copyright © 2006 Netflix, Inc. All rights reserved; p. 121, Copyright edmonds.com., Inc.; p.121, AP Photo/Jennifer Graylock; p.122, AP Photo/Ann Johansson; p.125, ©M. Hruby; p.126, Andrew Wakeford/Getty Images; p.126, ©M. Hruby; p.127, ©M. Hruby; p.129, Courtesy Expedia, Inc.; p.131, Photo by Warner Bros./Getty Images; p.135, The McGraw-Hill Companies, Inc./Andrew Resek, photographer; p.136, Copyright ©Ron Kimball/Ron Kimball Stock – All rights reserved; p.138, Thinkstock/JupiterImages; p.140, Coutesy Zipcar; p.140, Courtesy Outback Steakhouse; Photographer: Tim Healy/people; Photographer: Terry Zelen/Interior; p.141, Courtesy Albertson's, Inc.; p.144, Courtesy smart GmbH; p.145, Courtesy smart GmbH.

Chapter 6

Photos/ads: p.150, Photo by Paul McConnell/Getty Images; p.151, Courtesy AT&T, Inc.; p.153, Royalty-Free/CORBIS; p.153, Janis Christie/Getty Images; p.153, Nick Koudis/Getty Images; p.156, Copyright ©Ron Kimball/Ron Kimball Stock – All rights reserved; p.157, ©Toyota Motor Engineering & Manufacturing North America; p.158, ©Worth Canoy/Icon SMI/Corbis; p. 162, ©Custom Medical Stock Photo; p.164, AP Photo/Fabian Bimmer; p.166, Dynamicgrapics/Jupiterimages; p.167, AP Photo/Harry Cabluck; p.171, Courtesy Weyerhaeuser Company.

Chapter 7

Photos/ads: p. 176, ©The Procter & Gamble Company. Used by permission; p. 178, STR/AFP/Getty Images; p. 179, AP Photo/J. Scott Applewhite; p. 184, ©Royalty-Free/Corbis; p. 185, ©John Van Hasselt/CORBIS SYGMA; p. 185, AP Photo/Greg Baker; p. 187, Photo by Tim Boyle/Getty Images; p. 187, ©Gail Mooney/CORBIS; p. 187, Stephen Alvarez/National Geographic/Getty Images; p.188, AP Photo/Bullit Marquez; p. 189, ©Digital Vision/Getty Images; p. 192, John Rowley/Digital Vision/Getty Images; p. 194, Courtesy YUM! Brands, Inc.; p. 194, Courtesy Starbuck's Corporation; p. 194, Courtesy Yum! Brands, Inc.; p. 194, Courtesy Star Alliance; p. 195, Courtesy Tesco PLC; p. 196, ©M. Hruby; p. 197, Courtesy Honda de Mexico S.A. de C.V.; p. 197, Courtesy American Honda Motor Co., Inc; p. 199, Hoang Dinh Nam/AFP/Getty Images; p. 200, AP Photo/Michele Limina; p. 201, ©Digital Vision; p. 202, Digital Vision/Getty Images; p. 206, ©Antoine Gyori/Corbis.

Exhibits: Exhibit 7.1, www.epi.org/issueguides/offshoring/figure12.gif. Used by permission of Economic Policy Institute; Exhibit 7.4, © 2006 The Economist Newspaper Ltd. All rights reserved. Reprinted with permission. Further reproduction prohibited. www.economist.com; Exhibit 7.5, www.nationmaster.com/red/graph/eco_ hum_dev_ind-economy-human-development-index&int=-1&b_map=1#; Exhibit 7.6, www.prb.org/Content/NavigationMenu/ PRB/Educators/Human_Population/ Population_Growth/Population_Growth. htm. Used by permission of Population Reference Bureau; Exhibit 7.10 Data from Geert Hofstede, Culture's Consequences, 2nd edition (Thousand Oaks, Sage 2001), copyright © Geert Hofstede, reproduced with permission.

Chapter 8

Photos/ads: p. 230, Courtesy L'Oreal USA, Inc.; p. 213, CourtesyAu Bon Pain; p. 213, Courtesy Reebok International, Ltd; p. 214, Courtesy Lands' End; p. 216 *both*, Courtesy The Gillette Company; p. 216, *See above*; p. 217, ©Benetton Group SPA; Photo by: Oliviero Toscani; p. 220, Ryan McVay/Getty Images; p. 220, Ryan McVay/Getty Images; p. 221, Stockbyte/Punchstock Images; p. 221, Getty Images; p. 221, Ryan McVay/Getty Images; p. 222, Ed Taylor/Taxi/Getty Images; p. 225, ©Jerry Arcieri/Corbis; p. 225, The McGraw-Hill Companies, Inc./Andrew Resek, photographer; p. 226, ©Ron Kimball; p. 228, Courtesy Carhartt, Inc.; p. 228, Courtesy Shooting Star; p. 230, Courtesy Volvo Cars of North America, LLC; p. 232, Courtesy Cadbury Schweppes Americas Beverages; p. 234, Courtesy DaimlerChrysler; p. 238, Courtesy Sodexho.

Exhibits/boxes: Exhibit 8.4, Source: SRI Consulting Business intelligence, www.sricbi.com/VALS/; Adding Value 8.1, Reprinted with permission from Pharmaceutical Executive, Vol. 24, No. 1, 2004, pp. 78-82. Pharmaceutical Executive is a copyrighted publication of Advanstar Communications Inc. All rights reserved; Adding Value 8.2, Reprinted by permission of LIMRA, a financial services research and consulting organization.

Chapter 9

Photos/ads: p. 242, AP Photo/Jose F. Moreno; p. 242, ©Bill Aron/PhotoEdit, Inc.; p. 243, ©James Leynse/Corbis; p. 244, The McGraw-Hill Companies, Inc./John Flournoy, Photographer; p. 245, Courtesy Whirlpool Corporation; p. 247, ©Royalty-Free/Corbis; p. 249, Courtesy Information Resources, Inc.; p. 250, ©Spencer Grant/PhotoEdit, Inc.; p. 251, ©Robert Scoble/ Microsoft Corporataion; p. 253, ©Photodisc; p. 253, The McGraw-Hill Companies, Inc./ John Flournoy, Photographer; p. 254, Photo courtesy Staples, Inc.; p. 255, ©2006 The LEGO Group; p. 257, The McGraw-Hill Companies, Inc./John Flournoy, Photographer; p. 259, Courtesy Coinstar, Inc.; p. 262, Digital Vision/ Getty Images; p. 265, ©Frank Rumpenhorst/ dpa/Corbis.

Exhibits: Exhibit 9.7, Parasuraman, A., Dhruv Grewal and R. Krishnan, Marketing Research, Second Edition. Copyright © 2007 by Houghton Mifflin Company. Adapted with permission.

Chapter 10

Photos/ads: p. 270, Courtesy KesselsKramer/ The Netherlands; p. 271 all, Courtesy Colgate-Palmolive Company; p. 273, PORSCHE, CAYENNE, the Porsche Crest are registered trademarks and the distinctive shapes of Porsche automobiles are trademarks of Dr. Ing. h.c.F. Porsche AG. Used with permission of Porsche Cars North America, Inc. All rights reserved. Do not copy without the permission of Porsche Cars North America, Inc.; p. 276, ©American Honda Motor Co., Inc.; p. 278, ©M. Hruby.; p. 280, Courtesy Regis Corporation; p. 281, Copyright State Farm Mutual Automobile Insurance Company 2005. Used by permission; p. 282, Photo courtesy My Young Auntie/New York; p. 283, ©M. Hruby; p. 284, Courtesy General Electric Company; p. 285, ©2006 Kellogg North America Company; p. 286, ©M. Hruby; p. 287, Photo by Stephane L'hostis/Getty Images; p. 289 both, LaCoste S.A; p. 290, Courtesy Whirlpool Corporation; p. 292, ©M. Hruby; p. 292, ©M. Hruby; p. 296 ©M. Hruby.

Exhibits/boxes: Exhibit 10.1, Colgate Product Assortment, www.colgate.com; Exhibit 10.2, Kevin Lane Keller, Strategic Brand Management, 2nd ed. Prentice Hall, 2003. Used by permission; Adding Value 10.1, FAST COMPANY by LINDA TISCHLER. Copyright 2006 by MANSUETO VENTURES LLC. Reproduced with permission of MANSUETO VENTURES LLC in the format Textbook via Copyright Clearance Center; Exhibit 10.4, "The World's 10 Most Valuable Brands," The Business Week/ Interbrand Annual Ranking of the 2006 Best Global Brands. Used by permission; C10.1 Band-Aid product inventions, Band-Aid.com

Chapter 11

Photos/ads: p. 300, ©Michael Newman/ Photo Edit; p. 300, Courtesy Tivo, Inc.; p. 300, Courtesy Polaroid Corporation; p. 300, ©The Procter & Gamble Company. Used by permission; p. 301, ©M. Hruby; p. 302 all, ©The Arbor Strategy Group, Inc.; p. 304, Photo by Paul Thomas/Photodisc Green/Getty Images; p. 306, ©Michael Newman/PhotoEdit, Inc.; p. 309, Photo by Dave Hogan/Getty Images; p. 310, Ryan McVay/Getty Images; p. 313, The McGraw-Hill Companies, Inc.; p. 314, ©2006 Kellogg North America Company; p. 314, ©M. Hruby; p. 314, Courtesy The Coca-Cola Company; p. 314, ©M. Hruby; p. 314, ©The Arbor Strategy Group, Inc.; p. 317, Photo by: Ryan McVay/Photodisc Blue/Getty Images;

p. 317, Comstock Images/Alamy; p. 318, ©M. Hruby; p. 320 Courtesy GEOX S.p.A; p. 324, The McGraw-Hill Companies, Inc./Lars A. Niki, photographer.

Chapter 12

Photos/ads: p. 328, Courtesy Weber Shandwick; p. 329, Dynamic Graphics/Jupiter Images; p. 329, ©Jose Fuste Raga/CORBIS; p. 329, The McGraw-Hill Companies, Inc./ Andrew Resek, photographer; p. 329, John A. Rizzo/Getty Images; p. 329, ©Charles Bowman/Alamy; p. 329, ©Photodisc; p. 329, Brand X Pictures/Getty Images; p. 330, Photo by David McNew/Getty Images; p. 331, Dynamic Graphics/Jupiter Images; p. 332, Courtesy Enterprise Rent-A-Car; p. 333, Courtesy NCR Corporation; p. 333, Courtesy Geek Housecalls, Inc.; p. 334, Courtesy Club Med; p. 335, ©Buddy Mays/CORBIS; p. 336, ©Dan Holmberg/CORBIS; p. 340, Courtesy Pooch Palace; p. 342, ©Royalty-Free/CORBIS; p. 344, Courtesy Container Store; p. 347, ©Royalty-Free/Corbis; p. 349, ©Michael Newman/PhotoEdit, Inc.; p. 352, Courtesy Wegmans Food Markets, Inc.

Chapter 13

Photos/ads: p. 356, Courtesy Panera Bread Company; p. 357, Courtesy IKEA; p. 360, Courtesy Ryanair Holdings plc; p. 361, Courtesy Saturn Corporation; p. 361 *both*, Courtesy Paradigm Electronics, Inc.; p. 362, Courtesy Fender Musical Instruments Corporation; p. 364, ©Dennis MacDonald/ PhotoEdit, Inc.; p. 364, ©Bill Aron/PhotoEdit, Inc.; p. 365, Photo provided by JetBlue; p. 367, Courtesy Mercedes Benz USA, Inc.; p. 367, ©David Young-Wolff/PhotoEdit, Inc.; p. 371, Allan Danahar/Digital Vision/Getty Images; p. 371, Inti St Clair/Photodisc Red/Getty Images; p. 374, Courtesy Columbian Coffee Federation, Inc.; p. 375, ©FUJITSU 2000-2006; p. 376, Courtesy Hennes & Mauritz L.P.; p. 376, AP Photo/Richard Vogel.

Chapter 14

Photos/ads: p. 383, Digital Vision/PunchStock; p. 385, Courtesy Ferrari S.p.A.; p. 386, Courtesy Motorola, Inc.; p. 388, AP Photo/William Thomas Cain; p. 389, Courtesy Family Dollar Stores; p. 390, Courtesy Sears, Roebuck and Co.; p. 391, Courtesy Wal-Mart Stores, Inc.; p. 391, ©Jeff Greenberg/PhotoEdit; p. 393, Photo by Kurt Vinion/Getty Images; p. 395, Photo by Sean Gallup/Getty Images; p. 395, Photo by Lucien Capehart Photography/Getty Images; p. 398, ©M. Hruby; p. 399, ©M. Hruby; p. 400, ©M. Hruby; p. 401, ©Jeff Greenberg/ PhotoEdit, Inc.; p. 402, ©Tom Prettyman/ PhotoEdit; p. 403, © Royalty-Free/Corbis.

Chapter 15

Photos/ads: p. 410 *both*, Courtesy Zara International, Inc.; p. 413, ©Thinkstock/Alamy/Getty Images; p. 417, ©Gianni Giansanti/Sygma/Corbis; p. 417, ©Ray Stubblebine/Reuters/Corbis; p. 419, David Buffington/Getty Images; p. 420, Courtesy ADT Security Services, Inc.; p. 420, Photodisc Red/Getty Images; p. 421 *both*, ©2006 NIKE; p. 422, ©James Leynse/Corbis; p. 424, Courtesy The Stanley Works; p. 426, ©Jeff Greenberg/PhotoEdit; p. 426, ©Susan Van Etten/PhotoEdit; p. 427, ©Tessuto E Colore srl; p. 430, ©2006 Cole Haan.

Chapter 16

Photos/ads: p. 440 *both*, Courtesy Urban Outfitters, Inc.; p. 441, ©M. Hruby; p. 443, Courtesy The Men's Warehouse, Inc.; p. 443, Photo by Getty Images for Teen Vogue; p. 444, Courtesy Macy's East; p. 446, Courtesy Bass Pro Shops; p. 447, Courtesy J.C. Penney; p. 448, Courtesy Walgreen Co.; p. 449, AP Photo/Andy Rogers; p. 450, Courtesy Senzatempo; p. 450, Photo by Tim Boyle/Getty Images; p. 450 *both*, Courtesy J. Crew; p. 454, AP Photo/Ric Feld; p. 456, Courtesy Save-A-Lot Food Stores, Inc.

Chapter 17

Photos/ads: p. 464, Courtesy Volvo Cars of North America; Courtesy The Home Depot, Inc.; p. 468, ©M. Hruby; p. 468 *both*, ©2006 Kellogg North America Company; p. 471, Photo by: Evan Agostini/Liaison Agency/Getty Images; p. 473, Courtesy Palm, Inc.; p. 474, ©General Mills; p. 475, Courtesy Rollerblade USA Corp.; p. 476, ©Annie's Homegrown; p. 476, ©Tag Fragrance Co.; p. 479, Courtesy Barnes & Noble, Inc.; p. 481, Photo by Frazer Harrison/Getty Images; p. 484, Courtesy Scion, Toyota Motor Sales, U.S.A., Inc.; p. 485 Courtesy Scion, Toyota Motor Sales, U.S.A., Inc.

Chapter 18

Photos/ads: p. 487, Photo by Peter Kramer/Getty Images; p. 489, Courtesy The Diamond Trading Company; Agency: J. Walter Thompson U.S.A., Inc.; p. 490, ©TJX Companies, Inc.; p. 491, ©The Procter & Gamble Company. Used by permission; p. 491, AP Photo/Eugene Hoshiko; p. 492, Courtesy The Coca-Cola Company; p. 492, Courtesy National Fluid Milk Processor Promotion Board; Agency: Lowe Worldwide, Inc.; p. 492, Courtesy The Coca-Cola Company; p. 492, Courtesy McDonald's USA, LLC; p. 493, Courtesy National Fluid Milk Processor Promotion Board; Agency: Lowe Worldwide, Inc.; p. 493, California Milk Processor Board; Agency: Goodby, Silverstein & Partners; p. 494, Courtesy American Legacy Foundation; p. 495, Courtesy National Citizens Crime Prevention; p. 496, Courtesy The Black & Decker Corporation; p. 496, Courtesy Ford Motor Company; p. 496, ©2006 Nokia; p. 496, Courtesy UAL Corporation; p. 497 *both*, ©Kimberly-Clark Corporation; p. 498, Photo by Tim Mosenfelder/Getty Images; p. 499, Courtesy IKEA; p. 500, Courtesy Del Campo/Nazca Saatchi & Saatchi/Buenos Aires; p. 503, ©Bill Aron/PhotoEdit, Inc.; p. 504, Courtesy Payless Shoe Source, Inc.; p. 506 *both*, Courtesy The Meow Mix Company; p. 506 ©Michael Newman/PhotoEdit; p. 507, AP Photo/Paul Sakuma; p. 510, Courtesy Dole Food Company, Inc.

Chapter 19

Photos/ads: p. 513, Courtesy Marty Rodriguez; p. 514, ©Royalty-Free/Corbis; p. 515, Thinkstock/JupiterImages; p. 516, ©Royalty-Free/Corbis; p. 518, ©2006 Expedia, Inc. All rights reserved; p. 519, ©Royalty-Free/Corbis; p. 520, Photo by Evan Agostini/Getty Images; p. 521, ©Susan Van Etten/PhotoEdit, Inc.; p. 523, ©Susan Van Etten/PhotoEdit, Inc.; p. 524, Ryan McVay/Getty Images; p. 525, Courtesy Sam Hussey; p. 526, AP Photo/Charlie Riedel; p. 527, ©Custom Medical Stock Photo; p. 528, Courtesy Pepsico; p. 528 ©Mark Tuschman/CORBIS; p. 530, ©Royalty-Free/Corbis; p. 531, Courtesy Mary Kay, Inc.; p. 536 Dynamic Graphics/JupiterImages.

name index

company index

subject index